CLYMER™

POWERBOAT

MAINTENANCE MANUAL

The World's Finest Publisher of Mechanical How-To Manuals

INTERTEC PUBLISHING

P.O. Box 12901, Overland Park, Kansas 66282-2901

FIRST EDITION
First Printing March, 1996

Printed in U.S.A.

ISBN: 0-89287-654-9

Library of Congress: 95-75758

Technical illustrations by Michael St. Clair.

The publisher would like to credit the following companies for providing additional technical illustrations and photographs:

- *Hunter Engineering*
  11250 Hunter Dr.
  Bridgeton, MO 63044
- *Century Manufacturing/Solar*
  9235 Penn Ave. South
  Minneapolis, MN 55431
- *Star Brite*
  4041 S. W. 47 Ave.
  Fort Lauderdale, FL 33314
- *Lowrance Electronics*
  12000 E. Skelly Drive
  Tulsa, OK 74128

INTERTEC BOOKS

President and CEO Raymond E. Maloney
General Manager Randy Stephens

The following books and guides are published by Intertec Publishing.

CLYMER SHOP MANUALS
Boat Motors and Drives
Motorcycles and ATVs
Snowmobiles
Personal Watercraft

ABOS/INTERTEC BLUE BOOKS AND TRADE-IN GUIDES
Recreational Vehicles
Outdoor Power Equipment
Agricultural Tractors
Lawn and Garden Tractors
Motorcycles and ATVs
Snowmobiles and Personal Watercraft
Boats and Motors

AIRCRAFT BLUEBOOK-PRICE DIGEST
Airplanes
Helicopters

AC-U-KWIK DIRECTORIES
The Corporate Pilot's Airport/FBO Directory
International Manager's Edition
Jet Book

I&T SHOP SERVICE MANUALS
Tractors

INTERTEC SERVICE MANUALS
Snowmobiles
Outdoor Power Equipment
Personal Watercraft
Gasoline and Diesel Engines
Recreational Vehicles
Boat Motors and Drives
Motorcycles
Lawn and Garden Tractors

Contents

Chapter Five
Stern Drive and Inboard Engines 73

Chapter Six
Stern Drive and Inboard Drive Units 117

Chapter Seven
Electrical System 159

Chapter Eight
Marine Electronics 185

Chapter Nine
Galley 204

Chapter Ten
Fresh Water Systems 241

Chapter Eleven
Heads 256

Chapter Twelve
Trailers and Towing 303

Index 331

Chapter One

General Information

All boats suffer gradual deterioration from a number of causes. Marine growths cling to the hull, reducing performance or damaging the structure. Corrosive atmospheric conditions etch any exposed metal. Galvanic corrosion eats away underwater metal that is not adequately protected. Parts of the boat work against each other in normal use, eventually wearing them down to the point of failure.

To keep your boat serviceable and safe, you must spot deterioration before it becomes serious, identify the cause, and prevent further damage by repairing or replacing damaged parts.

Every boat needs maintenance—some more than others. Everyone is convinced that wooden boats require a lot of maintenance. In the early days of fiberglass, prospective owners were led to believe the new material was virtually "maintenance free." Some actually believed it for a short time, but soon discovered that fiberglass boats, like every boat ever made, require maintenance. In fact, surveys have shown that fiberglass boats require as much attention as a comparable wooden boat.

Many maintenance jobs are too complex for the average owner. Troubleshooting and repairing most electronic gear is strictly for professionals. In fact, only federally licensed technicians can legally work on radiotelephone equipment. Repairs involving structural parts are, likewise, best left to professionals. Jobs such as replacing hull timbers or patching a large hole in fiberglass require special equipment and skills.

MANUAL ORGANIZATION

This book describes maintenance procedures well within the capabilities of anyone intelligent and dexterous enough to operate a boat. More complex jobs should be entrusted to a reputable boatyard. Also, there are some jobs which the owner could do, but which a boatyard can do far more easily and even less expensively.

Chapter Two describes common boat maintenance tools. Many will be familiar to you if you have worked on an automobile or made minor repairs around the house. Others are specialized for marine maintenance.

Chapter Three describes maintenance required to keep the hull and deck surfaces sound and attractive. Complete instructions for painting and refinishing your boat permit you to get professional results with little or no previous experience. All you need is patience and a willingness to see the job through.

Chapters Four, Five and Six describe routine maintenance of engines and final drive units. This information permits you to minimize deterioration and get maximum performance from the power unit. Clymer Shop Manuals provide detailed information for most power units. Major repairs, however, should probably be referred to a qualified mechanic.

Chapter Seven covers electrical systems found aboard powerboats and includes troubleshooting and repair procedures.

Chapter Eight includes maintenance and repair of most popular appliances found in the galley. Coverage of stoves include alcohol, kerosene, and LPG/LNG systems.

Chapters Nine and Ten discuss fresh water systems and heads in common use. A knowledge of how these systems work aids immeasurably in troubleshooting them when they don't work.

Chapter Eleven describes most marine electronics systems used aboard small boats. Nearly all maintenance of these units must be performed by a qualified technician. However, some things can be done by the owner.

Chapter Twelve provides all the information necessary to keep your trailer and tow vehicle in good condition. A poorly maintained trailer is a menace to your boat, your tow vehicle and your life.

NOTES, CAUTIONS AND WARNINGS

The terms NOTE, CAUTION and WARNING have specific meanings in this manual. A NOTE provides additional information to make a step or procedure easier or clearer. Disregarding a NOTE could cause inconvenience, but would not cause damage or personal injury.

A CAUTION emphasizes areas where equipment damage could result. Disregarding a CAUTION could cause permanent mechanical damage; however, personal injury is unlikely.

A WARNING emphasizes areas where personal injury or even death could result from negligence. Mechanical damage may also occur. WARNINGS *are to be taken seriously.* In some cases, serious injury or death has resulted from disregarding similar warnings.

TORQUE SPECIFICATIONS

Torque specifications throughout this manual are given in foot-pounds (ft.-lb.) and Newton meters (N•m). Newton meters are being adopted in place of meter-kilograms in accordance with the International Modernized Metric System. Existing torque wrenches calibrated in meter-kilograms can be used by performing a simple conversion: move the decimal point one place to the right. For example, 4.7 mkg = 47 N•m. This conversion is accurate enough for mechanics' use even though the exact mathematical conversion is 3.5 mkg = 34.3 N•m.

MAINTENANCE SCHEDULE

The frequency of most maintenance tasks depends on the number of hours of use. Some jobs, though, should be done seasonally regardless of the amount of use. **Table 1** summarizes maintenance tasks that are usually required.

LAY UP/WINTER STORAGE

It is very important to store a boat properly. Many components can be permanently damaged by disuse or freezing temperatures. **Table 2** summarizes which components require attention. Refer to the appropriate chapter for layup and recommissioning procedures for specific systems.

Table 1 MAINTENANCE

Maintenance task	Chapter
Auxiliary power generator	Six
Batteries	Four, Five, Six
Electronic equipment	Eight
Galley equipment	Nine
Head	Nine
Hull	Three
Bottom paint	
Topsides/deck finish	
Clean and wax	
Outboard/inboard and stern drive engines	Four, Five
Potable water system	Ten
Trailer	Twelve
Hitch	
Lights	
Wheels/tires	

Table 2 LAY-UP SUMMARY

Item	Preparation
Exterior hull and deck surfaces	Clean and touch-up, see Chapter Three
Outboard motor	See Chapter Four
Inboard/stern drive engine	See Chapter Five
Batteries and electrical	See Chapter Seven
Galley	See Chapter Nine
Water system	Fill system with nontoxic antifreeze as described in Chapter Ten
Head	See Chapter Eleven
Electronic equipment	Remove if theft is possible
Trailer	Clean and touch-up paint. Protect tires as described in Chapter Twelve

Chapter Two

Tools, Fasteners and Safety Equipment

Having the right tools on hand when needed can make maintenance chores safer and much more enjoyable. Good tools do the job neater and faster than improvised or poor quality tools.

This chapter describes various hand tools required to perform virtually any repair job aboard your boat. Each tool is described and recommendations as to proper size are made for those not familiar with hand tools.

A lasting repair requires the use of proper fasteners. The type, size, and material of each fastener used on your boat must be deliberately chosen. The sections on fasteners and corrosion make selection simple.

Besides using the right tools for a job, you should use the right safety equipment. Boat repairs involve exposure to a number of potential hazards. These hazards include exposure to high level noise and flying debris from power equipment and exposure to harmful and even toxic chemicals found in solvents and paints, particularly antifouling paints. It is possible to work safely in this environment if common sense and the right personal protection gear is used. This chapter provides help in selecting this important equipment.

GENERAL TOOLS

A number of tools are required to maintain a boat in top condition. You may already have some around for other work such as home and car repairs. There are also tools made especially for marine equipment, and you may have to purchase them. In any case, a wide variety of quality tools will make repairs more effective and convenient.

Top quality tools are essential, and also more economical. Poor grade tools are made of inferior materials and are thick, heavy and clumsy to use. Their rough finish makes them difficult to clean and they usually don't stand up long.

Quality tools are made of alloy steel and are heat treated for greater strength. They are lighter and better balanced than inferior ones. Their surface finish is smooth, making them a pleasure to work with and easy to clean. The initial cost of quality tools may be relatively high, but longer life and ease of use make them less expensive in the long run.

Some tools are forged from bronze, especially for marine use. They are rustproof, spark resistant, non-magnetic, and impervious to corrosive saltwater and battery acid. Spark proof tools like these are used with safety in explosive atmospheres like ordinance depots, chemical plants, and marine engine rooms.

It is aggravating to search and search for a certain tool in the middle of a repair, only to find it covered with grime. Keep your tools in a tool box. Keep related or similar tools stored together. After using a tool, wipe off dirt and grease with a clean cloth and replace it in its correct place.

Screwdrivers

The screwdriver is a very basic tool, but many people don't use it properly and do more damage than repair. The slot on a screw has definite dimensions and shape. A screwdriver must be selected to conform to that shape. A small screwdriver in a large screw slot will twist the screwdriver out of shape and damage the slot. A large screwdriver on a small slot will also damage the slot. In addition, since the sides of the screw slot are parallel, the sides of the screwdriver near the tip must be parallel. If the tip sides are tapered, the screwdriver wedges itself out of the slot; this makes the screw difficult to remove and may damage the slot.

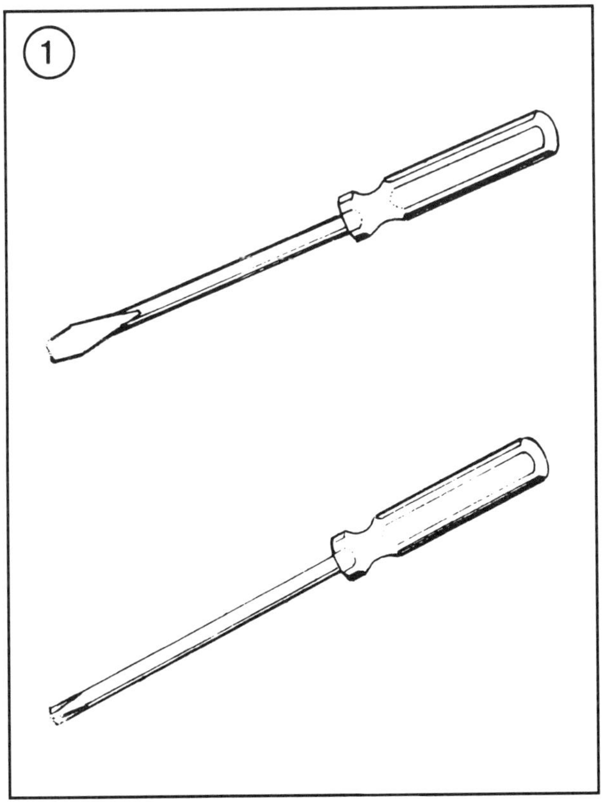

Two basic types of screwdrivers are required: a common screwdriver and a Phillips screwdriver. Both types are illustrated in **Figure 1**.

Screwdrivers are available in sets which often include an assortment of common and Phillips blades. If you purchase individual screwdrivers, as a minimum obtain:

a. Common screwdriver, 5/16 × 6 in. blade.
b. Common screwdriver, 3/8 × 12 in. blade.
c. Phillips screwdriver, size 2, 6 in. blade.

Use screwdrivers only for driving screws. Never use a screwdriver for prying or chiseling. In addition, never use a common screwdriver to remove a Phillips or Allen head screw; you can damage the head so that even the proper tool will not remove the screw.

Keep screwdrivers in proper condition and they will last longer and perform better. Always keep the tip in good condition. **Figure 2** shows how to grind the tip to proper shape if it is damaged. Note the parallel sides at the tip.

Pliers

Pliers come in a wide range of types and sizes. They are useful for cutting, bending and crimping. They should never be used to cut hardened objects or to turn nuts or bolts. **Figure 3** shows several pliers useful aboard boats.

Each type of pliers has a specialized function. Combination or slip-joint pliers are general purpose pliers and are used mainly for holding and bending. Needlenose pliers are used to grasp or bend small objects, or objects in a difficult to reach area. Arc-joint pliers (sometimes called channel-lock pliers) can be adjusted to hold various sizes of objects while the jaws remain parallel to grip round objects such as pipe or tubing. Locking pliers (sometimes called vise-grip pliers) are used as pliers or to grip oblects very tightly. Although there are many more types of specialized pliers, the ones described here are the most common.

2

Correct way to grind blade

Correct taper and size

Taper too steep

Box-end and Open-end Wrenches

Box-end wrenches and open-end wrenches are available in sets or separately in a variety of

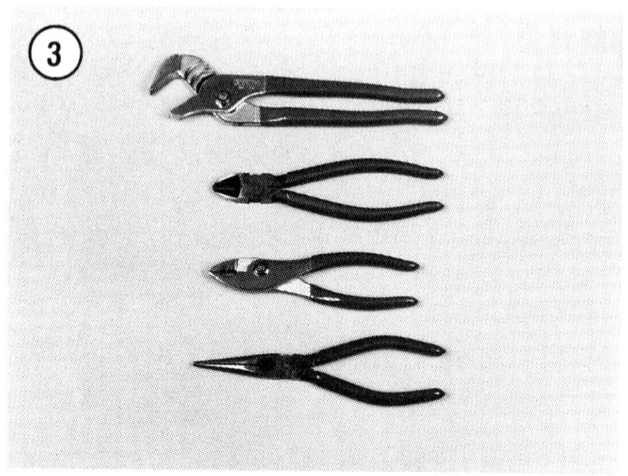

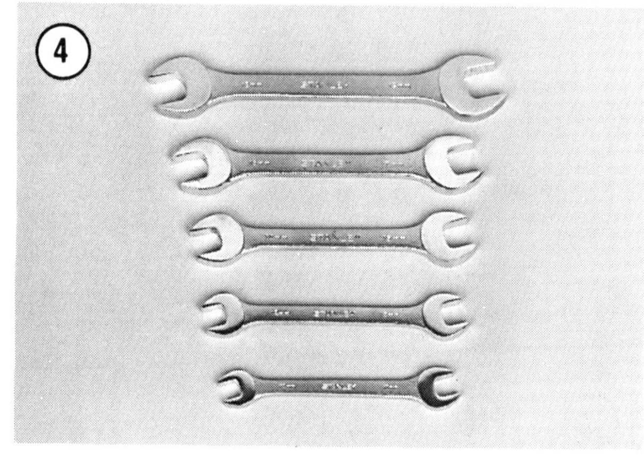

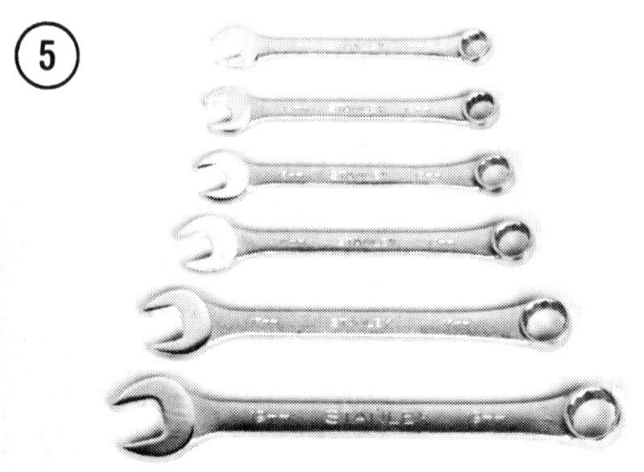

sizes. See **Figure 4** and **Figure 5**. The size stamped near the end refers to the distance between 2 parallel flats on a hex head nut or bolt.

European and Asian engines and equipment use metric hardware; English and American engines use U.S. standard (inch) hardware. Separate wrench sizes are made for metric use and for U.S. standard use.

Box-end wrenches are usually superior to open-end wrenches. Open-end wrenches grip a nut on only 2 flats. Unless it fits well, it may slip and round off the points on the nut. The box-end wrench grips all 6 flats. Both 6-point and 12-point openings on box-end wrenches are available. The 6-point gives superior holding power; the 12-point allows a shorter swinging radius when working in a confined area.

Combination wrenches which are open on one end and boxed on the other are also available. Both ends are the same size.

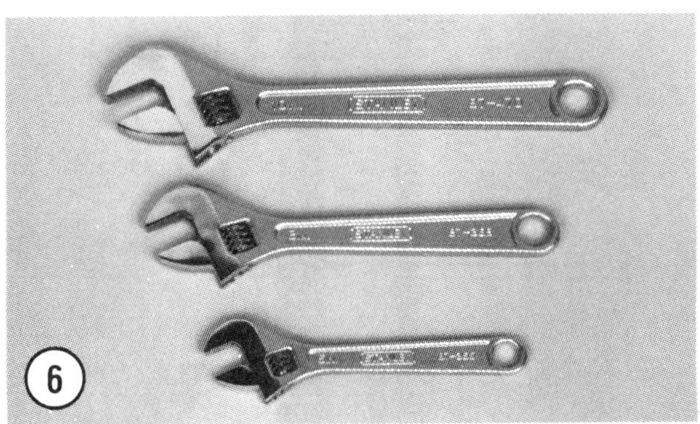

6

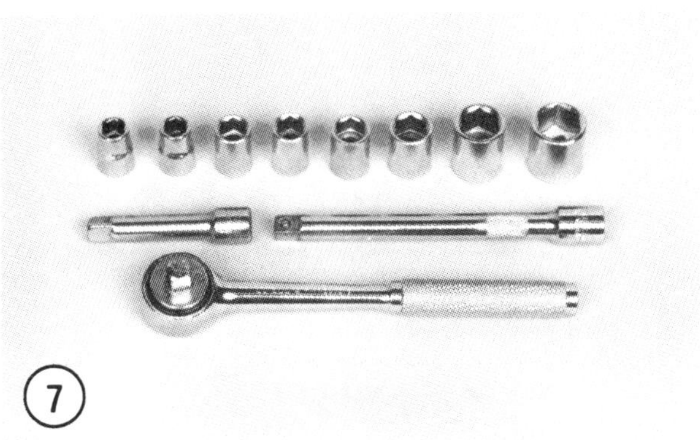

7

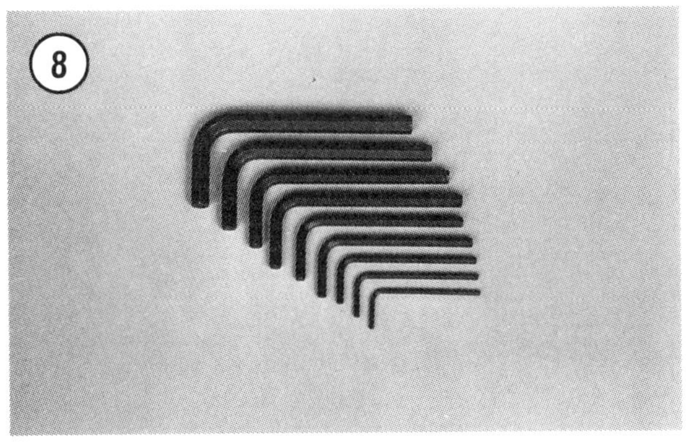

8

Adjustable (Crescent) Wrenches

An adjustable wrench (also called a crescent wrench) can be adjusted to fit nearly any nut or bolt head. See **Figure 6**. However, it can loosen or slip, causing damage to the nut. Use only when other wrenches are not available.

Adjustable wrenches come in sizes ranging from 4 in. to 18 in. overall. A 6 in. or 8 in. size is recommended as an all-purpose wrench.

Socket Wrenches

This type wrench is undoubtedly the fastest, safest, and most convenient to use, especially when working in a cramped engine compartment. See **Figure 7**. Sockets which attach to a ratchet handle are available with 6-point or 12-point openings and 1/4, 3/8, 1/2, and 3/4 in. drives. The drive size indicates the size of the square drive hole which mates with the ratchet handle. Sockets are available in metric and inch sizes.

Allen Wrenches

These hex-shaped wrenches fit similar shaped recesses in the top of Allen-head screws and bolts. See **Figure 8**. Allen-head screws are most common on engines, but may turn up on almost any marine hardware.

Clamps

Clamps come in a variety of sizes and shapes. Selection depends on the job at hand. They are essential for holding things while being glued or screwed together. They are also handy for emergency repairs, making good temporary fasteners.

Figure 9 shows some of the many types available. From top to bottom, they are:

a. Pipe clamp.

b. Handscrew.

c. C-clamp (sometimes called a G-clamp).

Hammer and Mallets

Hammers are designed for specialized purposes, though many people use one hammer universally. Two hammer types are most useful for boat maintenance:

a. Claw hammer

b. Ball-peen hammer

The claw hammer is mainly for carpentry work. One end is for driving nails, the other (claw) for pulling nails. The ball-peen hammer (**Figure 10**) is used for metal work. The ball end can be used to shape contours in thin sheet metal.

Mallets also come in a variety of types. The hammer heads are usually made of relatively soft material such as:

a. Wood.

b. Rubber.

c. Plastic (hard).

d. Lead.

Their most important use in boat maintenance is for freeing stuck parts. Where a steel hammer could cause permanent damage to stuck fasteners or cast parts, a mallet will apply good striking force without marring the part.

Drills

Drilling can be accomplished with several tools, depending on the material to be drilled. Most common are:

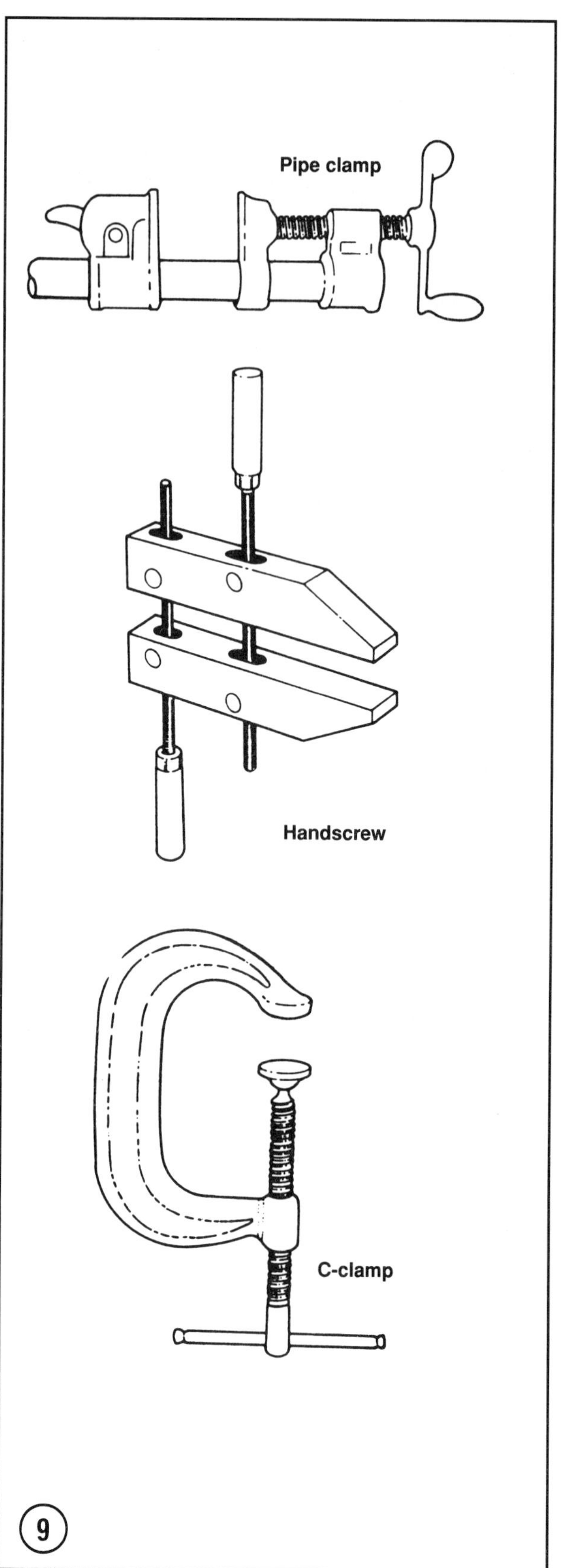

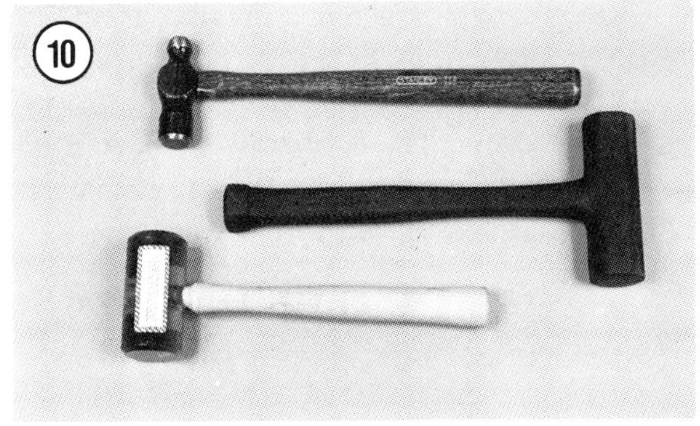

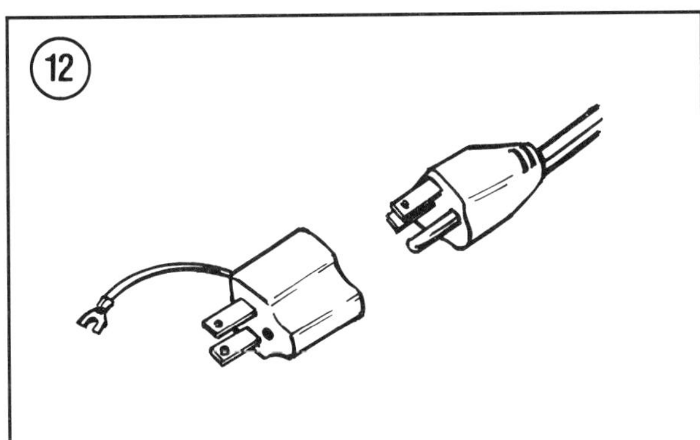

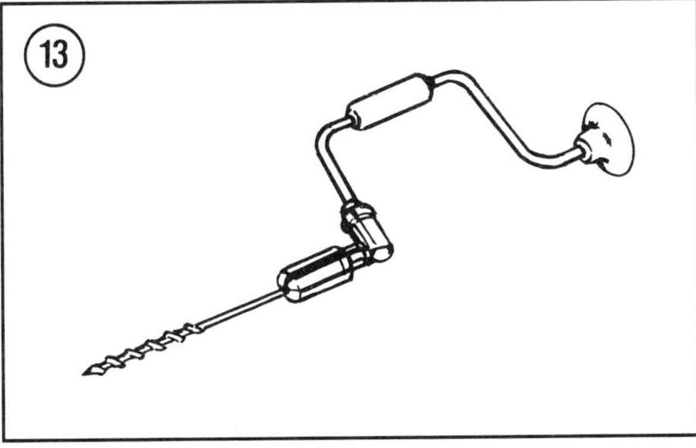

a. Hand drill.

b. Electric drill.

Hand drills are very useful aboard boats since they do not require electric power. See **Figure 11**. When used with the proper bit, they can be used to drill any wood and many soft metals such as copper, aluminum and some iron.

An electric drill is more efficient since it is faster and more powerful than a hand drill. However, there are some disadvantages. Most require a source of AC voltage which is not available on most boats when underway. AC isn't always available at dockside, either. Furthermore, AC is potentially very dangerous. The drill must have a 3-prong plug and must be plugged into a 3-prong grounded socket. There are two important precautions to heed with any electric tool.

WARNING
*Do not use an adapter like the one shown in **Figure 12** to connect a 3-prong plug to a 2-prong socket. Fatal shock is extremely likely. If you drop the tool overboard while it is connected, stand clear of the connecting cord. Shut off the power to the socket at the main switch before trying to recover the tool. Chances are the circuit breaker or fuse will blow immediately, but don't take any chances.*

When using an electric drill, apply gentle but firm pressure. Too light pressure will permit the bit to wander away from the area to be drilled. Too heavy pressure will stall the drill or cause excessive heat which can damage the bit and the material being drilled. Hold the drill firmly and do not let it waver back and forth; this enlarges the hole.

A brace is used when drilling large holes. See **Figure 13**. Naturally, a brace is a type of hand drill. Select the proper bit as described in the next section.

Twist Drill Bits

Twist drills shown in **Figure 14** are commonly used for metal and wood work. In order to work properly, a drill bit must be sharpened properly for the material to be drilled. The drill bit must also be turned at or near an optimum speed, determined by the bit size and material to be drilled.

A drill bit must be properly shaped and sharpened to work efficiently to produce the desired hole size. The following should be kept in mind:

a. Cutting edges must be sharp and equal in length.
b. The included angle made by the cutting edges is normally about 120°. Regrind as shown in **Figure 15** for harder or softer materials.
c. Clearance must be provided behind cutting edges so the edge can bite into the material. This angle is normally 12°. See **Figure 15**.

Several inexpensive fixtures which attach to an electric drill are available to regrind and sharpen drill bits.

Auger Bits

Auger bits are used for boring large holes in wood with a common brace. See **Figure 16**. Never use them in an electric drill.

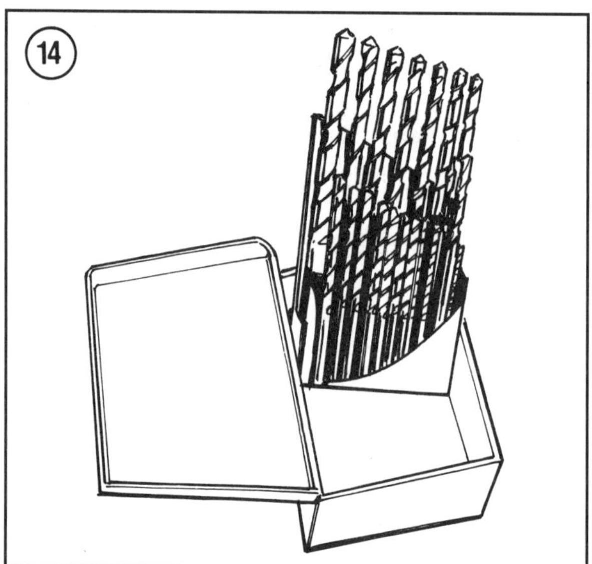

Usually they are available in sizes from 1/4-1/2 in. (in 1/16 in. increments). The single twist auger is a very rigid, strong tool, capable of very powerful boring. The double twist auger is not as strong as a single twist auger, but produces a very smooth hole; it is strong enough for most cabinet work.

Hole Saws

Hole saws are used when very large holes must be bored in wood, fiberglass or thin, soft metal such as aluminum. Two types are most common. The type shown in **Figure 17** may be

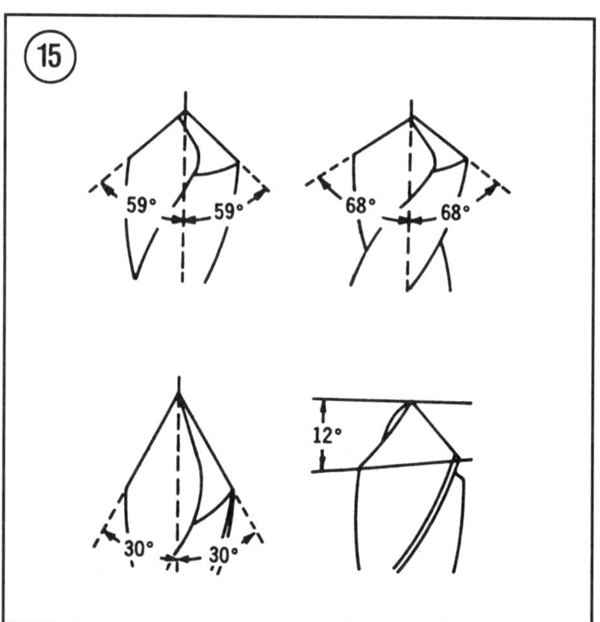

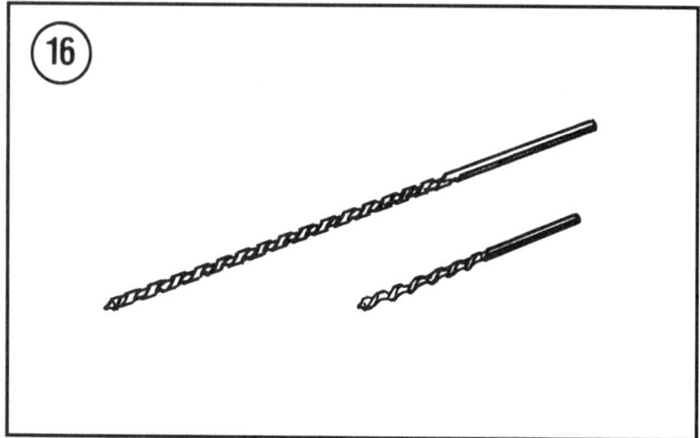

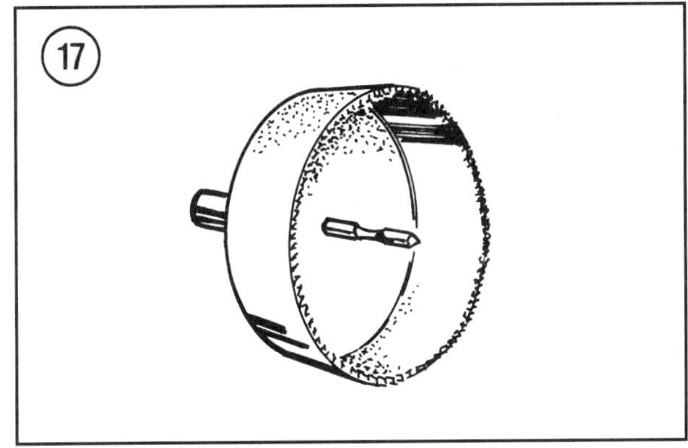

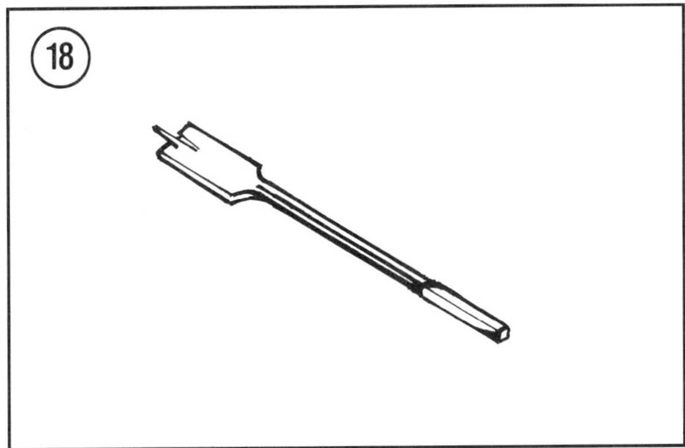

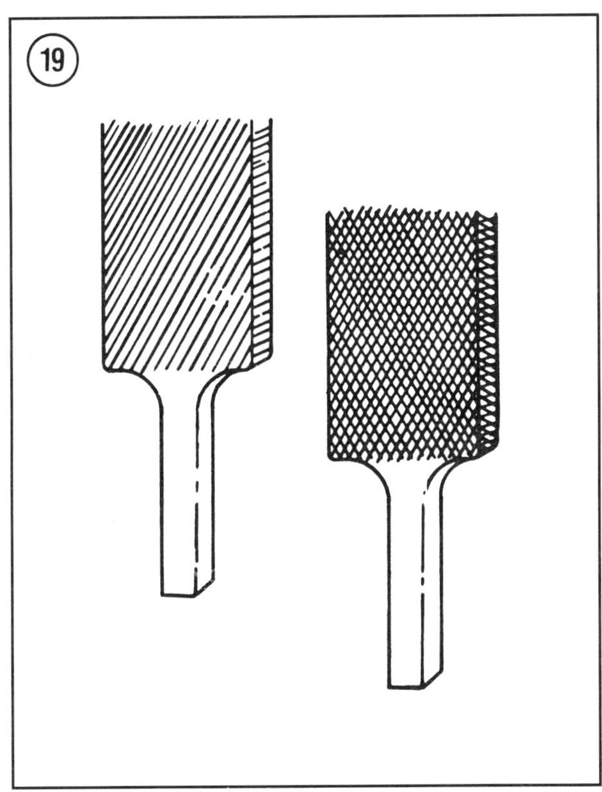

used for wood or thin metal. It consists of a mandrel saw, and pilot drill. To use it, mount the desired diameter saw in the mandrel. Install the combination in an electric drill. Place the pilot drill in the center of the new hole location. Keep the drill absolutely vertical and cut the hole.

Another type of hole saw is shown in **Figure 18**. Actually, it is more like a specialized bit. It can only be used for wood and soft materials like plastic. Use this saw exactly as you would a bit in an electric drill.

Files

An assortment of files can make certain shaping and smoothing jobs fast and easy. They come in such a wide variety of types, shapes and sizes that nearly any shaping or smoothing job can be accomplished.

Files may be square, triangular, round, half round, flat and many other specialized shapes. **Table 1** lists common shapes and their intended use.

It is also important to choose a file with the proper teeth. Files can be single cut or double cut. See **Figure 19**. Single cut files have parallel teeth set about 65° to the center line of the file. They are intended for smoothing and finishing. Double cut files have crisscrossing teeth. The resulting diamond teeth cut very fast and are intended for rough work and heavy shaping jobs.

File teeth arc also graded as to fineness and size. Files with rough, large teeth are called bastard files; files with relatively smooth teeth are called smooth files.

A rasp is a file with large teeth which tear the material rather than cut it. They are used on wood and other soft materials such as plastic, lead and aluminum. They cut rough, but very rapidly.

Hand Sanders

For many applications, particularly when sanding compound or rounded shapes, sandpaper is used without a block. But when large, relatively flat expanses are sanded, a good block permits more uniform pressure without as much strain.

A small, smooth piece of scrap wood can be used as a block. Simply wrap the sandpaper around it as shown in **Figure 20**.

Commercial sanding blocks are available also. See **Figure 21**. They grip the sandpaper firmly and often have soft padding under the paper. Usually they are easier to hold and less tiring than a simple wooden block.

Power Sanders

Several power sanders are available. Most common for boat work are:

a. Disc sander.

b. Vibrating sander.

c. Belt sander.

A disc sander can be a special power tool made only for sanding (**Figure 22**) or it may be an attachment which can be chucked into an electric drill (**Figure 23**). In either case, an abrasive disc mounts over a hard rubber or foam plastic base.

Disc sanders are useful for paint removal or coarse sanding of wood which will be finished later with finer methods. Circular scoring is unavoidable and can be quite severe if you are careless. With care, scoring can be removed with an orbital sander or heavy hand sanding.

Vibrating sanders (see **Figure 24**) are used for finish work. Attachments are made to convert power drills to vibrating sanders, but they are not very good. Invest in a good quality vibrating sander as it is an often-used tool that will last for years. Some vibrating sanders can be set to produce an orbital motion or a back-and-forth motion. Standard size sandpaper or abrasive sheets can be cut with scissors to fit the sander.

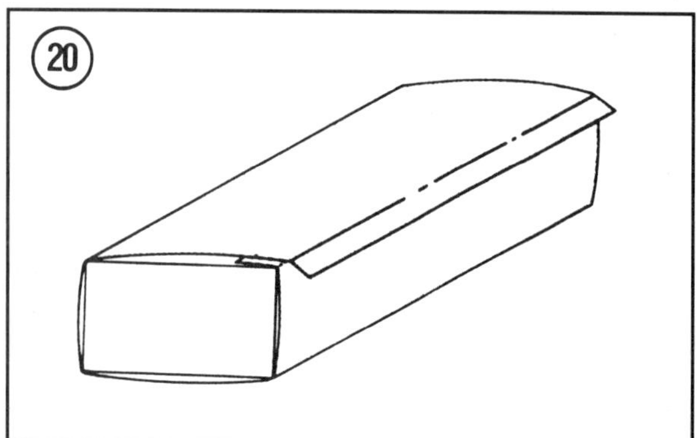

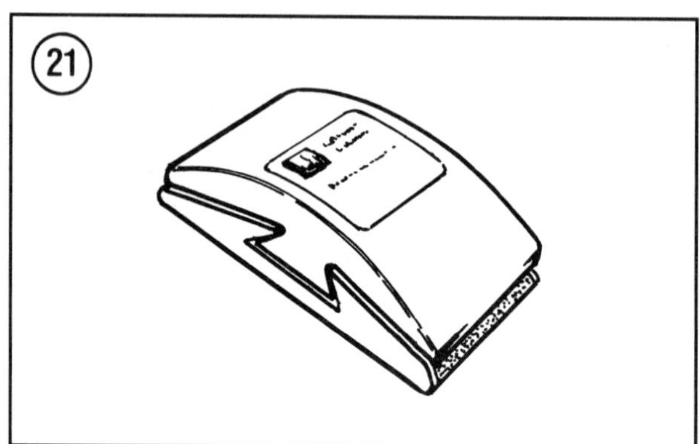

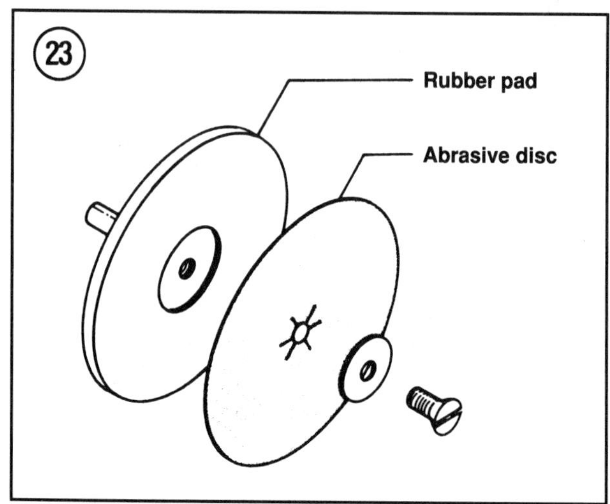

Belt sanders (see **Figure 25**) are used for very large expanses where heavy cutting is necessary. Special belts designed for the sander must be used. This sander must be held firmly and flatly or the belt edges can severely score the surfaces.

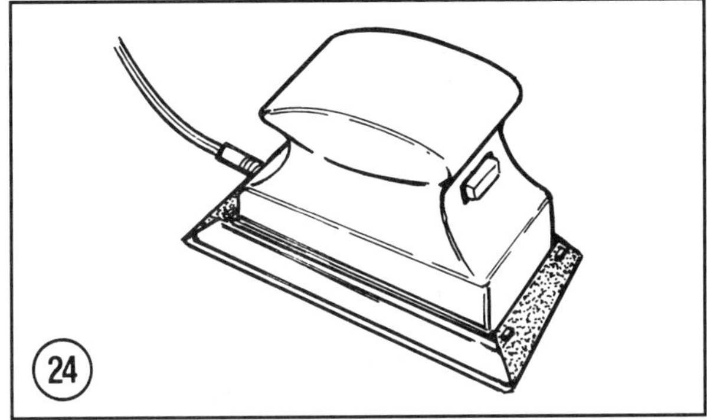

24

25

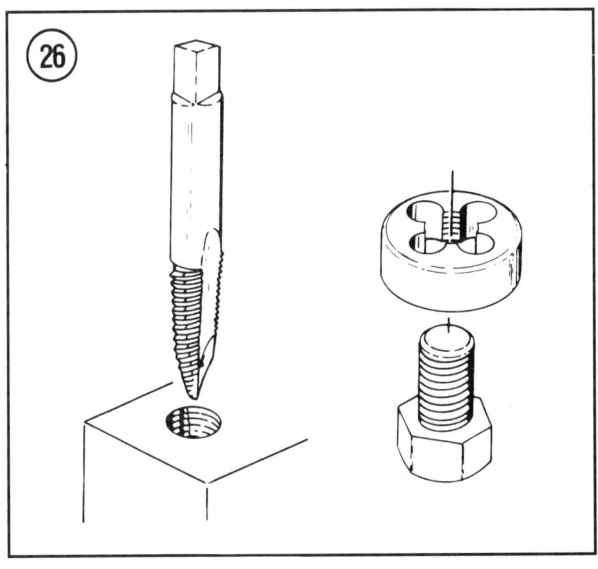

26

Use it for rough sanding large areas, then finish with an orbital sander or hand sanding.

All of these sanders, plus very heavy duty industrial sanders, are available from rental centers for a modest fee. Because small, good quality disc and vibrating sanders are relatively inexpensive and so often used, it is well worth purchasing them. However, if you have a lot of rough sanding to do at one time, it will be more economical to rent a belt or industrial duty disc sander.

MECHANIC'S TIPS

Removing Frozen Nuts and Screws

When a fastener rusts or corrodes and cannot be removed, several methods may be used to loosen it. First apply penetrating oil such as Liquid Wrench (available at any hardware store). Apply it liberally. Rap the fastener several times with a small hammer; don't hit it hard enough to cause damage.

For frozen screws, apply oil as described, then insert a screwdriver in the slot and rap the top of the screwdriver with a mallet. This loosens the rust so the screw can be removed in the normal way. If the screw head is too damaged to use a screwdriver, grip the head with locking pliers and twist the screw out.

For a frozen bolt or nut, apply penetrating oil, then tap it with a mallet. Twist off with the proper size wrench. If the points are rounded off, grip it with locking pliers as described for screws.

Stripped Threads

Occasionally, threads are stripped through carelessness or impact damage. Often the threads can be cleaned up by running a tap (for internal threads on nuts) or die (for external threads on bolts) through the threads. See **Figure 26**.

Broken Screw or Bolt

When the head breaks off a screw or bolt, several methods are available for removing the remaining portion.

If a large portion of the remainder projects out, try gripping it with locking pliers. If the projecting portion is too small, try filing it to fit a wrench or cut a slot in it to fit a screwdriver. See **Figure 27**.

If the head breaks off flush, try using a screw extractor. To do this, center punch the exact

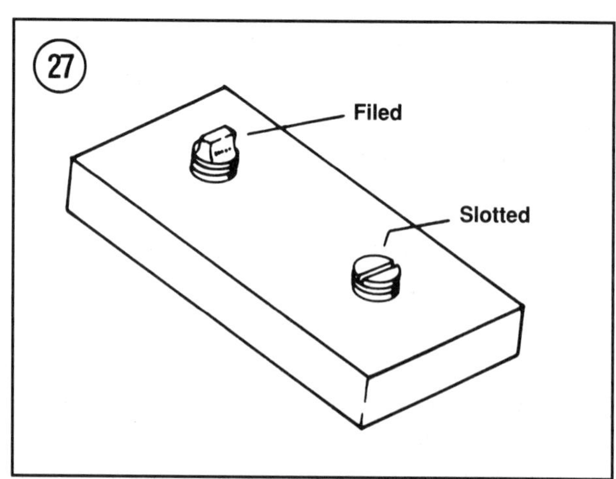

28

REMOVING BROKEN SCREWS AND BOLTS

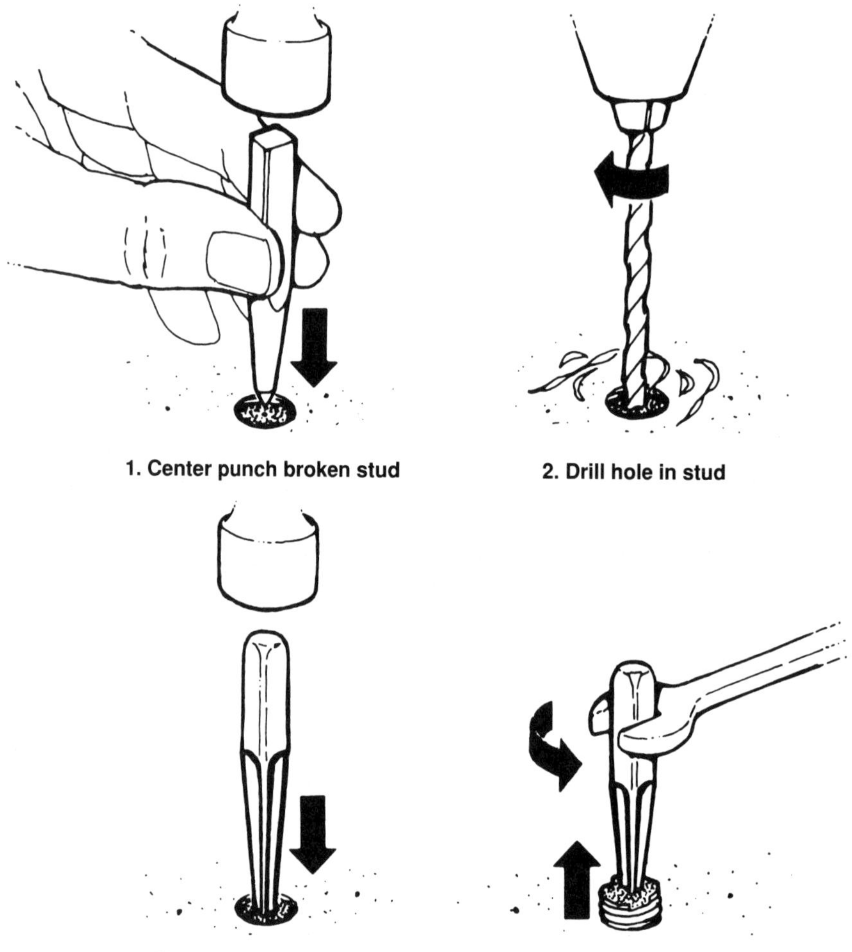

1. Center punch broken stud

2. Drill hole in stud

3. Tap in screw extractor

4. Remove broken stud

center of the remaining portion of the screw or bolt. Drill a small hole into the screw and tap the extractor into the hole. Back the screw out with a wrench on the extractor. See **Figure 28.**

TOOLS FOR PAINTING AND REFINISHING

Nearly anyone with care, patience and the proper tools can produce a professional-looking paint job. This section helps you choose the tools you will need and explains their use.

Paint Brushes

You must have good quality brushes to do a professional job. Poor quality brushes lose bristles and do not spread the finish smoothly. Brushes may have natural animal bristles or nylon filaments. A good brush has bristles which taper slightly from the butt to the tip.

Brushes are shaped for a number of specialized purposes. The following are most useful for boat use.

a. 4 in. wall brush—bottom painting.

b. 3 in. wall brush—topsides, decks, etc.

c. 1 in. oval sash brush—small areas, close quarters.

d. Badger bristle brush with full chisel point—applying varnish.

If a brush is to be stored or used for a different type of paint, the brush must be cleaned thoroughly. First wipe the brush on newspaper to remove excess paint. Soak and clean the brush in a solvent or thinner as recommended on the paint label.

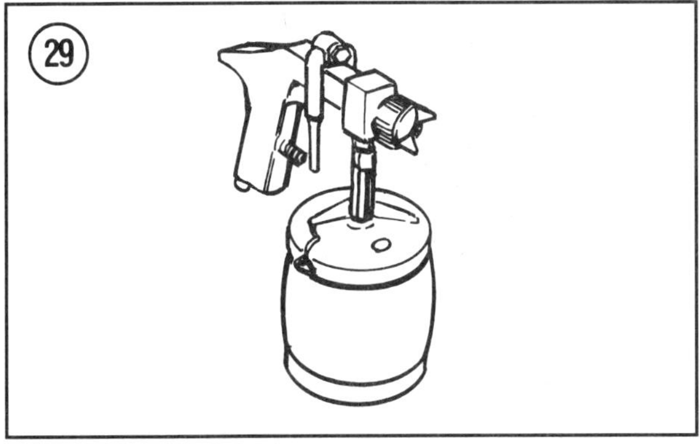

29

CAUTION

Do not slap the brush on a board or other surface to shake out the liquid. This damages the bristles.

Use turpentine or mineral spirits to clean or thin oil paint or enamel. Use denatured alcohol for shellac products. Other special materials such as epoxy resin and vinyl resin require special solvents; read the manufacturer's label.

After cleaning with solvent, wash the brush thoroughly in soapy water. Wrap the clean brush in several thicknesses of newspaper and lay it flat for storage. Do not stand the brush on end.

Hardened paint is difficult (or impossible) to remove from a brush. Several brush cleaning liquids on the market may soften the paint so that it can be removed. A painter's comb or wire brush may also help. It is a tedious, messy job which can be avoided by proper cleaning in the first place.

Spray Equipment

Spray painting usually does a quicker and better job than brushing, particularly on relatively large areas.

Most suitable spray systems consist of a spray gun with a refillable paint container, compressor and connecting hose. See **Figure 29**. Compressors vary in size from very small portable ones to large fixed ones. They may be driven by an electric motor, gasoline or diesel engine.

Finding the proper spraying technique is a matter of practice and experience. The type of paint and surface to be painted determine:

a. How much thinner to add (see paint label).

b. How fast to move gun.

c. How close to surface.

d. Proper nozzle tip.

Practice on an old board to be sure the gun is properly adjusted and the paint sufficiently thinned.

After each use, empty the paint container and refill with a small quantity of thinner compatible with the paint type. Flush the gun out with the thinner several times. Disassemble the nozzle and container and clean all parts thoroughly with the thinner. Allow parts to dry before reassembly.

WARNING
Never spray antifouling paints containing toxins. The fine particles are easily inhaled by you and anyone nearby.

Paint Rollers

Paint rollers (**Figure 30**) are much faster than brushes for large flat areas. Different rollers are recommended for relatively flat paint such as metallic bottom paint, and glossy surface paint. Rollers will not work in close where the surface turns sharply such as between the doghouse and deck, nor will a roller work well around fittings. In these cases, work as close as possible then tie in the gaps with a small brush.

Rollers can be cleaned and reused. However, they soak up a great deal of paint and are very messy to clean. Fortunately, they are relatively inexpensive and can be discarded after use. The roll holders are worth cleaning in a suitable solvent.

Paint Bucket

Professional painters always use a paint bucket. Disposable paper ones are very inexpensive. Pour paint from the can into a bucket so that the level is about 2-3 in. from the bottom. This keeps paint off the ferrule and handle if you dunk the brush in too far. A paint bucket also keeps the outside of the paint can free of messy drips caused by wiping the brush on the edge.

Paint Cup

A paint cup holds small quantities of paint or varnish conveniently and contains a wire to wipe your brush on. Buy a cup about the size of a large coffee mug at a department store. Epoxy or solder a large stiff wire across the cup as shown in **Figure 31**.

If the cup does not have a handle, you can hold it securely as shown in **Figure 32**. Each time you dip your brush, wipe it gently on the wire. This removes excess paint or varnish, which runs down into the cup instead of down the outside.

Tack Rag

A tack rag is necessary to remove all traces of dust, grit and sanding particles from a surface just before painting. No ordinary cloth or painter's duster can clean the surface as well, and

30

31

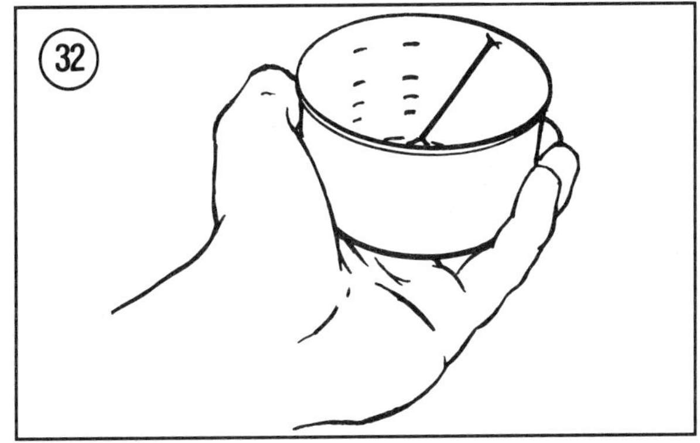

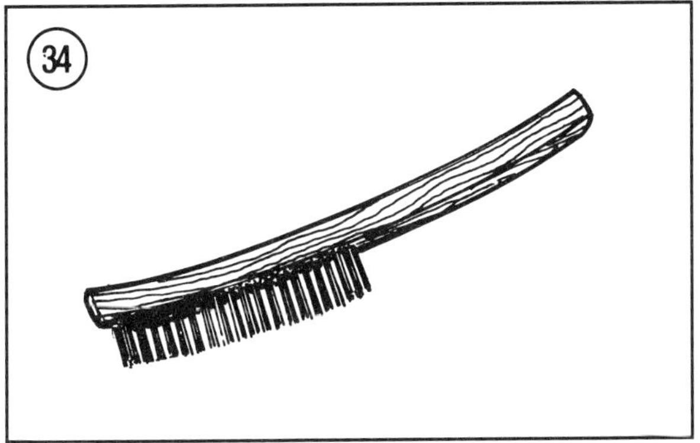

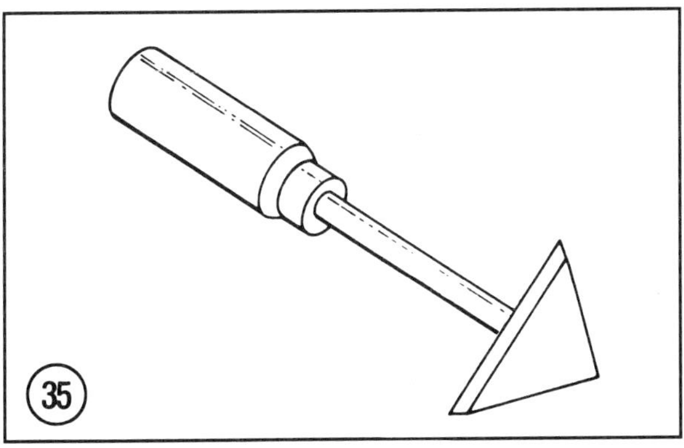

no professional finisher would do a job without using one.

Several manufacturers sell tack rags. Any marine chandlery or hardware store should have them. If you wish, you can make your own.

1. Soak a yard square piece of cheesecloth, linen or cotton cloth in warm water.
2. Wring it out and pour on a small amount of turpentine.
3. Wring it out again and spread it over cardboard or newspaper.
4. Pour a trickle of spar varnish over the whole surface of the cloth. Don't overdo it—about a tablespoon is fine.
5. Wring the cloth out tightly and spread it out again.
6. Hang the cloth to dry for 30-45 minutes before use.

To use, fold the cloth into a square slightly larger than your hand. Lightly wipe the surface to be painted with the cloth. When finished shake the rag out, roll it up, and store it in a tightly sealed jar. If the rag dries out, add a little water, turpentine and varnish to restore it. Discard it when it becomes excessively dirty.

Wire Brushes

Wire brushes are invaluable for removing rust, scale or loose paint. Brushes come in many sizes and shapes. The most useful are the block type (**Figure 33**) and narrow ones with a handle (**Figure 34**).

Scrapers

Scrapers can be very handy for removing old paint or varnish. **Figure 35** shows a common type of scraper. Keep the scraper sharp with a fine-tooth flat file. Don't change the angle of the cutting edge. Round off the corners to help prevent gouging the underlying material.

Abrasive Papers (Sandpaper)

Sanding is a very important part of refinishing, whether done to remove the old finishes or to smooth between new finishes. Choosing the right sandpaper and sanding method is vital to a professional-looking job.

A very large number of papers are available, but only a few are of interest here. The abrasive material can be garnet, aluminum oxide or silicon carbide.

Four grades are required for most jobs.

a. Coarse—designated 1 (50).

b. Medium—designated 1/0 (80).

c. Fine—designated 3/0 (120).

d. Very fine—designated 5/0 (180) or 6/0 (220).

Sandpaper on a paper base must be used dry. Others with a synthetic base and marked "wet or dry" or "waterproof" can be used either wet or dry. Wet sanding enameled or varnished surfaces produces a very fine finish. Soak the sandpaper in water before using and keep it wet while in use. Wipe the sanded surface with a wet cloth or sponge, then wipe with a dry lint-free cloth.

Bronze Wool

Bronze wool comes in many grades from coarse to very fine. Use it as you would sandpaper to remove old finishes.

CAUTION
Do not use steel wool for marine work. Steel wool leaves small shreds of steel imbedded in the surface which rust and discolor the final finish. Use only bronze wool.

Torches

A blow torch or propane torch can be useful for removing large areas of paint. The heat from the torch softens the paint so that it can be scraped away easily. Do not use on sections of hull near the fuel tank(s).

WARNING
Be sure to keep a fire extinguisher nearby when using a torch. When you set the torch down, make sure the flame is not directed toward anything that could burn.

CORROSION

Metals in marine use are subjected to relatively corrosive conditions. Corroding metals either wear away or change chemically—usually for the worse. An understanding of how corrosion occurs can help you select fasteners and fittings of the right metal to minimize damage from corrosion.

There are two main corrosive processes in a marine environment:

a. Atmospheric.

b. Galvanic.

Of the two, galvanic corrosion can occur faster and more destructively than atmospheric, but it is far less understood by many.

Atmospheric corrosion occurs because corrosive elements such as oxygen, carbon dioxide, sulfur compounds and chlorine compounds are present in the air. When they come in contact with a wet metal surface on a boat, they etch or corrode the metal.

Galvanic corrosion is a simple process, but many boat owners don't really understand it. It is actually the same electrical process that occurs in an automotive (lead-acid) battery.

Every metal has a specific electrical potential; some higher, some lower. The galvanic series shown in **Table 2** is simply a ranking of metals from those of highest potential to those of lowest potential. Various names are used to describe metals with the highest potential such as least noble, active and anodic. Metals of lower potential are said to be noble, passive and cathodic.

When 2 metals are put together in the presence of an electrolyte (water), an electrical current flows from the most anodic to the most cathodic metal. The most anodic metal corrodes, while the most cathodic metal is actually protected. This is precisely what happens in a lead-acid battery—which are nothing more than 2 metals (lead and zinc) immersed in an electrolyte (sulfuric acid and water). The same "battery" is formed when a stainless steel fastener is used on an aluminum hull soaked by a saltwater electrolyte. An electric current flows from the aluminum hull to the stainless steel fastener.

The magnitude of the electric current and therefore, the degree of corrosion, depends on several factors.

a. Distance between metals in the galvanic series.
b. Strength of electrolyte.
c. Relative sizes of the 2 metals.

The difference of potential between 2 metals close together in the galvanic series will be small. The current flow generated will be small and corrosion will be light. The farther apart the metals are in the series, the larger the difference of potential and the heavier the corrosion.

Electrolyte strength also affects corrosion. Fresh water is a relatively poor electrolyte. Corrosion will be lighter than that occurring between the same 2 metals in saltwater, an excellent electrolyte.

The relative size of the 2 different metals affects the amount of corrosion. Corrosion can be quite high when bronze and steel are together in an electrolyte such as saltwater. Suppose small steel fasteners are used to join bronze parts and the assembly is submerged in saltwater. The steel fasteners will rapidly corrode and the parts can separate. Now suppose small bronze fasteners are used to join steel plates. Corrosion of the steel will be quite small, even negligible, around the bronze fasteners. In fact, the bronze fasteners will receive cathodic protection. For this reason, fasteners should be selected that are equal or lower in potential in the galvanic series than the metal being joined.

Always keep in mind that antifouling bottom paints often contain metallic substances. The particular element involved can react with the hull or nearby fittings up or down the galvanic scale (**Table 2**) as the case may be. Severe damage can be done by carelessly using the wrong type of bottom paint!

Preventing Atmospheric Corrosion

There are some precautions that may be taken to prevent atmospheric corrosion. First, select materials with high resistance to the corrosive atmosphere. Materials such as monel, stainless steel and bronze are good examples. Next, keep salt from accumulating on the metal. A hose-down after each trip will help considerably.

Preventing Galvanic Corrosion

There are a number of rules to follow when selecting materials to prevent galvanic corrosion.

1. Whenever possible, join metal parts with fasteners made of the same material.
2. Separate dissimilar metals with an insulating (dielectric) material such as paint, phenolic, bakelite or plastic.
3. Make certain the smallest material is the most cathodic.

Galvanic corrosion can be used to protect parts. Magnesium, zinc and aluminum are most anodic. When connected to any other metal, they become the anode. Therefore, they corrode, sacrificially saving the other metal part.

FASTENER MATERIALS

Boat fasteners are subjected to high stress and corrosive conditions. Therefore, they must be carefully chosen. Most fasteners are metal, but in each case, the right metal must be selected if they are to last in a corrosive environment.

Many materials are suitable for marine use. Several are discussed in detail in the following sections. In general, boat builders prefer these materials in the following order.

a. Monel.
b. T316 stainless steel.
c. Silicon bronze.
d. 18-8 stainless steel.
e. Chrome-plated brass.
f. Naval bronze.
g. Brass.
h. Aluminum.

Bronze and Brass

Bronze and brass are very common materials for marine hardware because of their resistance to rust. Both materials are alloys of copper, tin and zinc; only the proportions change. Bronze has little or no zinc, while brass has little or no tin. Of the two, bronze alloys are the most important. Three bronze alloys are commonly used:

a. Phosphor bronze.
b. Naval bronze.
c. Silicon bronze.

Phosphor bronze is composed of copper, tin and a small amount of phosphorus. Naval bronze is essentially brass (copper-zinc) to which a small quantity of antimony has been added. Silicon bronze is a general name applied to several copper-silicon alloys. All have good corrosion resistant properties; silicon bronze has the highest strength.

Brass is occasionally used in marine work. However, saltwater causes brass to become brittle and deteriorate. Brass should not be used where stress is likely.

Copper

Copper is very soft and easily worked. Except as an alloy (bronze, brass), its marine use is limited primarily to copper sheathe the bottoms of wooden hulls and as nails for small planked boats.

Monel

Monel, an alloy of about 2/3 nickel and 1/3 copper, is probably the best material available for marine fasteners. It has excellent strength and is extremely corrosion resistant. It is also comparatively expensive. Practically any common marine fastener is available in monel. Monel is usually nonmagnetic. However, under some cold-working manufacturing processes, it can develop some magnetic properties.

Stainless Steel

Stainless steel has become increasingly more common as a marine fastener material. Stainless steel alloy 18-8 is usually stronger and more resistant to corrosion than naval bronze. Even more corrosion resistant is T316 stainless steel, formed by adding 2-3% molybdenum to 18-8 stainless steel.

Titanium

Some fasteners made of titanium are available. This exotic and very expensive metal has excellent corrosion resistance to saltwater. Most important, though, it has a very high strength-to-

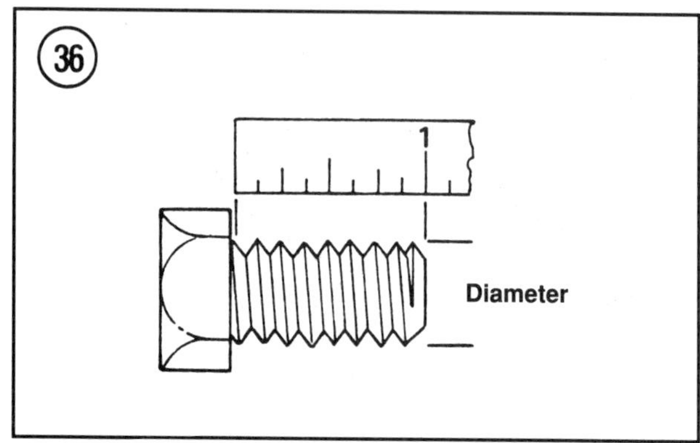

weight ratio, making it useful for spars and hardware on racing boats.

Aluminum

Aluminum fasteners are used almost exclusively for joining aluminum parts such as riveting aluminum hulls. They are also used to join aluminum parts to wood. Aluminum is far too high (anodic) in the galvanic series, compared to other common marine materials, to be used without careful attention to protecting it from galvanic corrosion.

FASTENER TYPES

To better understand and select basic hand tools, a knowledge of various fasteners is important. This knowledge will also aid in selecting replacements when fasteners are damaged or corroded beyond use.

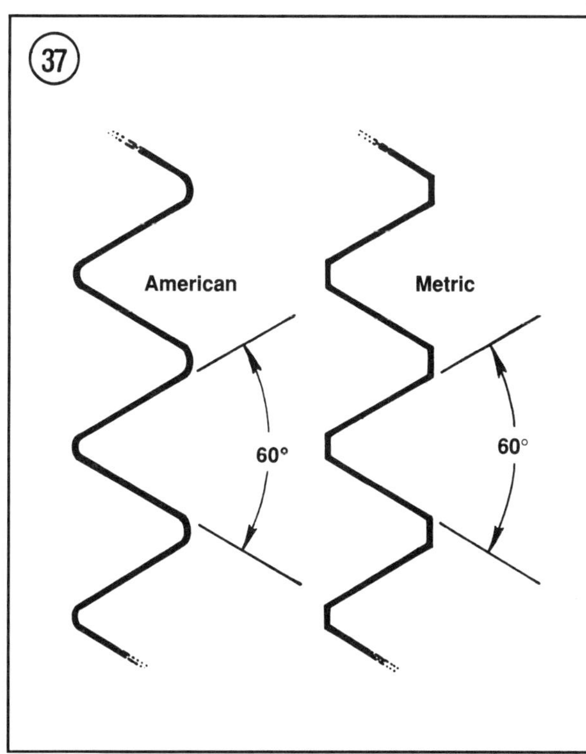

Threads

Nuts, bolts and screws are manufactured in a wide range of thread patterns. To join a nut and bolt, the diameter of the bolt and the diameter of the hole in the nut must be the same. It is equally important that the threads on both be properly matched.

The best way to ensure that the threads on 2 fasteners are compatible is to turn the nut on the bolt with fingers only. If much force is required, check the thread condition on both fasteners. If thread condition is good, but the fasteners jam, the threads are not compatible. Take the fasteners to a hardware store or chandlery for proper mates.

Four important specifications describe every thread:

a. Diameter.

b. Threads per inch.

c. Thread pattern.

d. Thread direction.

Figure 36 shows the first two specifications. Thread pattern is more subtle. Italian and British standards exist, but the most commonly used by marine equipment manufacturers are American standard and metric standard. The threads are cut differently as shown in **Figure 37**.

Most threads are cut so that the fastener must be turned clockwise to tighten it. These are called right-hand threads. Some fasteners have left-hand threads; they must be turned counterclockwise to be tightened. Left-hand threads are used in locations where the normal rotation of the equipment would tend to loosen a right-hand threaded fastener.

Machine Screws

There are many different types of machine screws. **Figure 38** shows a number of screw heads requiring different types of turning tools. Heads are also designed to protrude above the fastened material (round) or to be slightly recessed into the fastened material (flat).

When replacing a damaged screw, take it to a hardware store or chandlery. Match the head type, diameter and threads exactly. In addition, match the type of metal used. For example, if the old screw is bronze, the new one must also be bronze to resist corrosion and rust.

Bolts

Commonly called bolts, the technical name for these fasteners is cap screws. They are normally specified by diameter, threads-per-inch (tpi), and length. For example, 1/4-20 × 1 specifies a bolt of 1/4 in. diameter with 20 tpi and 1 in. long. The measurement across two flats on the head indicates the proper wrench size to be used.

When replacing damaged bolts, follow same advice given above for machine screws.

Wood Screws

Wood screws are similar in construction to tapping screws. Wood screws usually have a shallower thread and greater pitch (fewer threads/inch) than tapping screws, however. As discussed below, tapping screws are replacing wood screws in many applications.

Figure 39 shows the parts of a wood screw. When choosing a wood screw, 3 factors should be considered. First, the thickness of the material dictates the length of the screw. The kind of material and strength of the joint required determine the diameter of the screw. Finally, the surface finish appearance determines the screw head type.

Wood screws are normally specified by shank diameter and length. Shank diameters are not in inches; they are coded from No. O (about 1/16

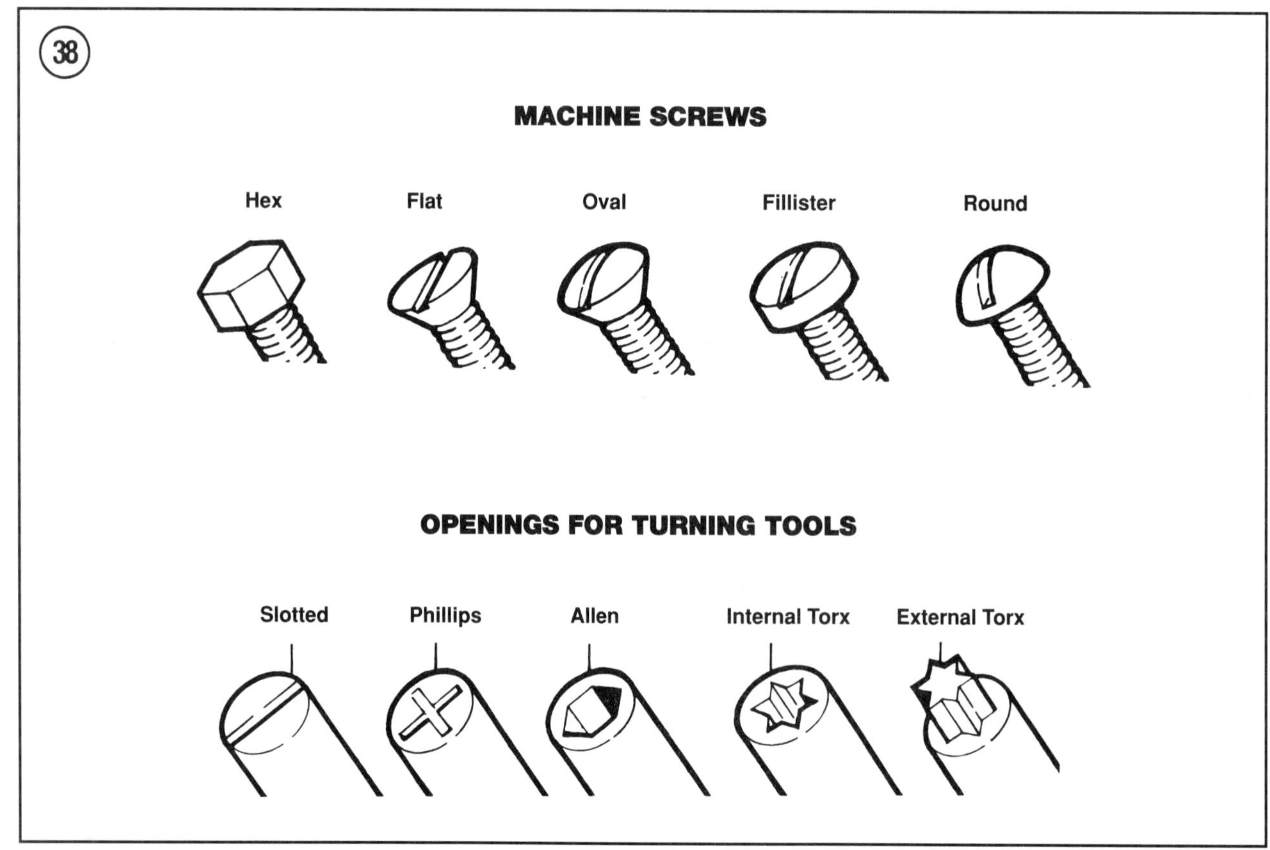

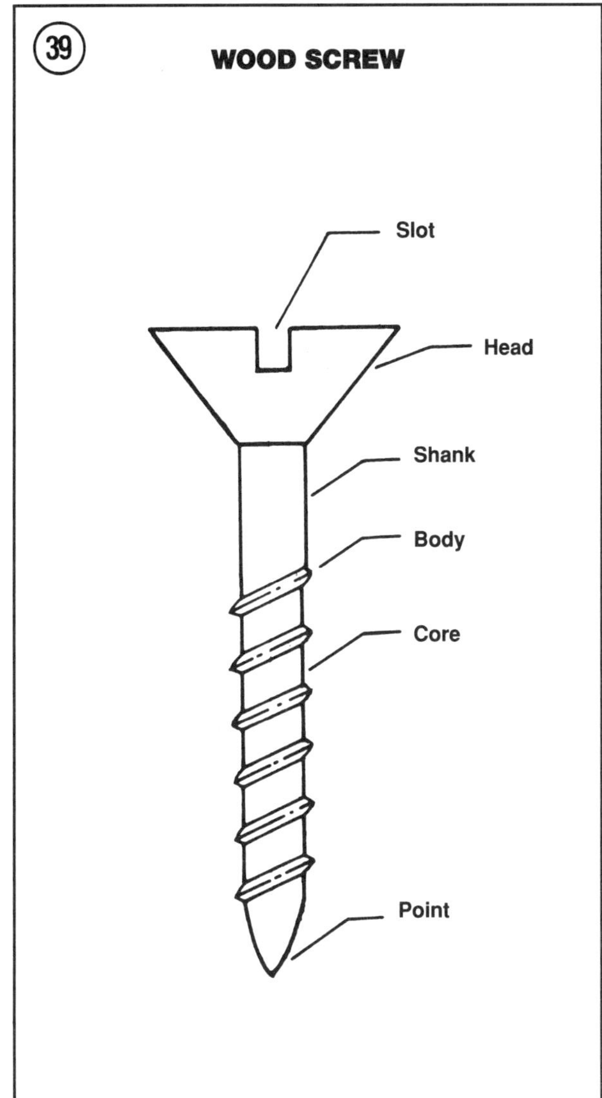

in.) to No. 30 (about 1/2 in.). A No. 10-3/4 wood screw has a No. 10 shank and a 3/4 in. length.

Sheet Metal (Tapping) Screws

Popularly called sheet metal screws, they are technically tapping screws. See **Figure 40**. They form threads in the materials they join. Their popular name derives from their use in joining light sheet metal. However, in nearly every place a wood screw is used, a tapping screw is superior. Tapping screws are usually stronger and easier to drive than wood screws.

Self-tapping screw sizes are specified in the same way as wood screws.

Nuts

Nuts are manufactured in a variety of types and sizes. Most nuts are hexagonal (six-sided) and fit on bolts, screws, and studs with the same diameter and threads-per-inch.

Figure 41 shows several commonly used nuts. The common nut is normally used with a lockwasher. The self-locking nut has a nylon insert which prevents it from loosening and does not require a locknut. To indicate the size of a nut, manufacturers specify the diameter of the opening and the threads-per-inch (tpi). For ex-

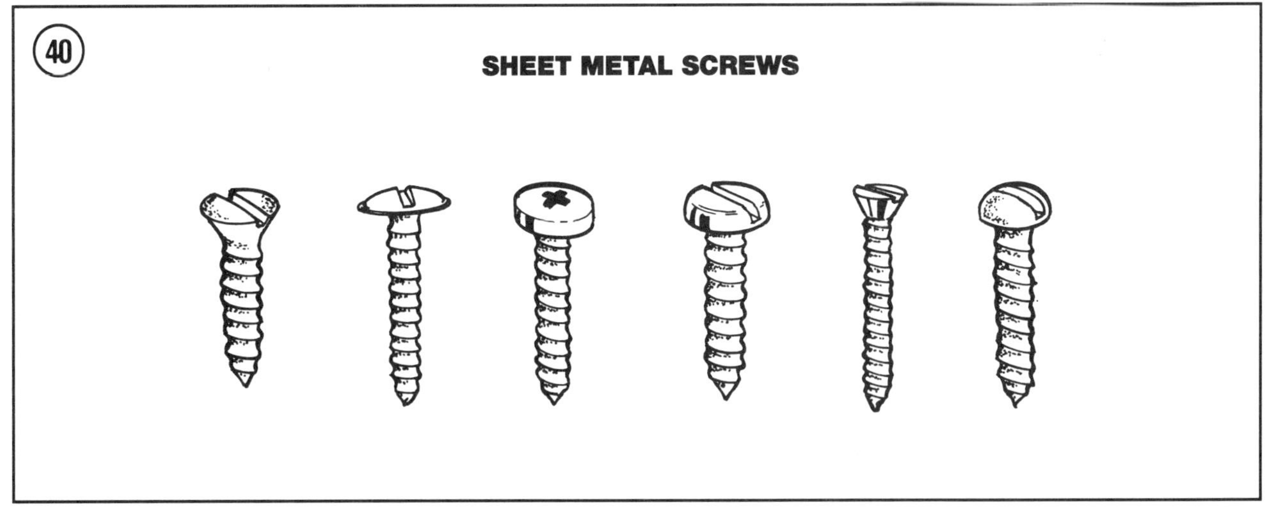

ample, 1/4-20 indicates a 1/4 in. opening and 20 tpi. In addition, the measurement across 2 flats on the nut indicates the proper wrench size to be used.

A wing nut (**Figure 41**) is designed for fast removal by hand without special tools.

When replacing a damaged nut, take it to a hardware store or chandlery. Match the type, diameter, and threads exactly. In addition, match the type of metal used.

Washers

There are two major types of washers—flat washers and lockwashers. Flat washers are simple discs with a hole to fit a screw or bolt. Lockwashers are designed to prevent a fastener from working loose due to vibration, expansion and contraction. **Figure 42** shows several washers. Note that flat washers are often used between a lockwasher and a fastener to act as a smooth bearing surface. This permits the fastener to be turned easily with a tool.

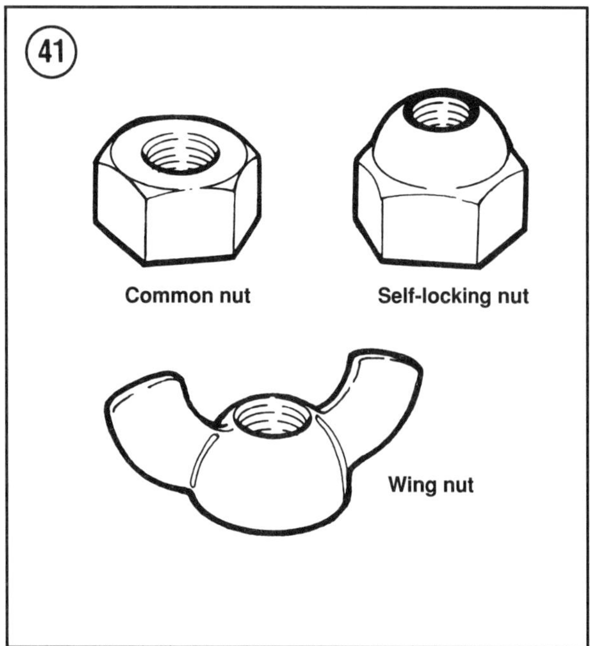

Cotter Pins

Cotter pins (**Figure 43**) are used to secure special kinds of fasteners. The threaded stud must have a hole in it; the nut or nut lock piece has projections that the cotter pin fits between. This type of nut is called a "castellated nut." Cotter pins should not be reused after removal.

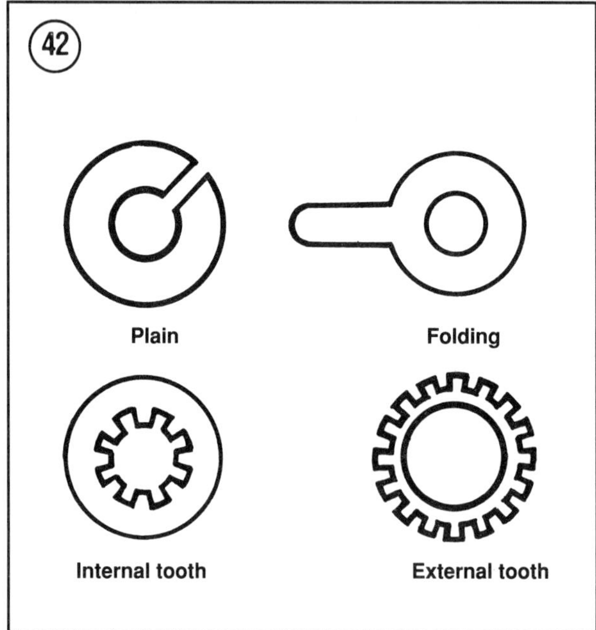

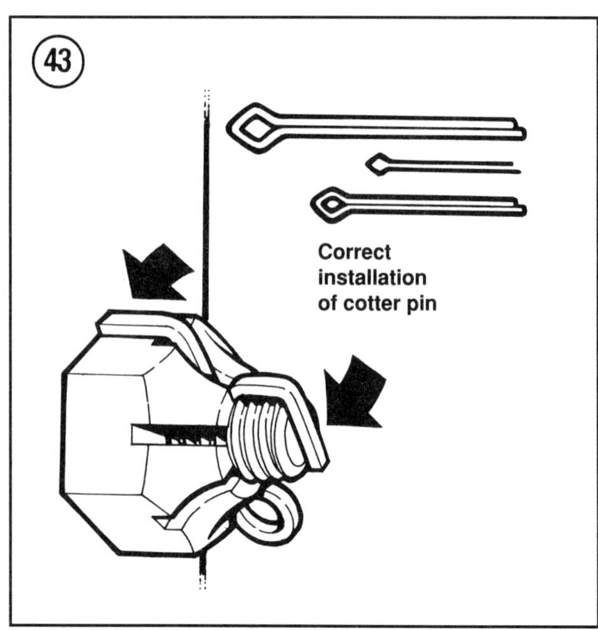

Snap Rings

Snap rings can be of an internal or external design. They are used to retain items on shafts (external type) or within tubes or housings (internal type). Snap rings can be reused if they are not distorted during removal. In some applications, snap rings of varying thickness can be selected to control the end play of shafts or assemblies.

Threaded Nails

Several threaded nail designs are available. **Figure 44** shows several representative types.

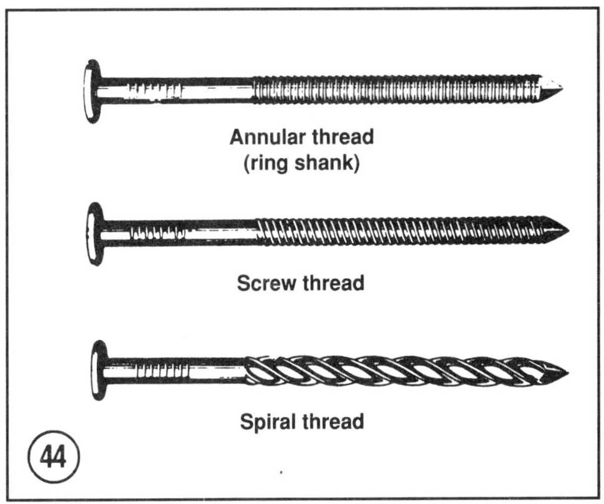

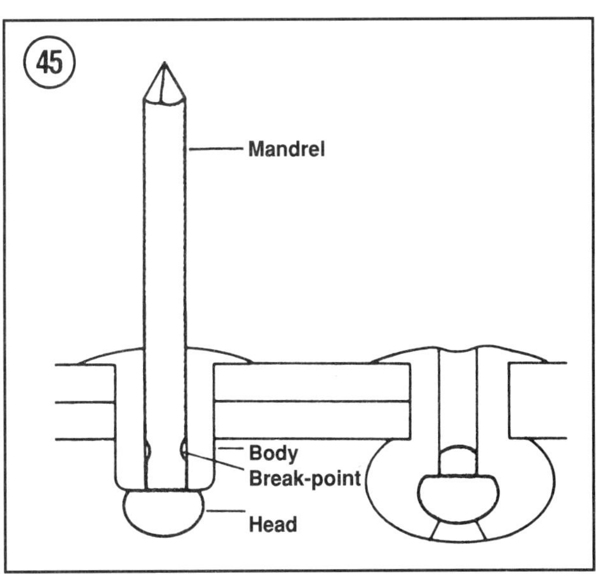

These nails are available in monel, 18-8 and T316 stainless steel, silicon bronze, 80-20 brass, commercial bronze and copper.

Advantages of threaded nails are numerous. They are less costly than screws, but stronger and easier to drive. They have superior resistance to backing out. In fact, it is impossible to remove one without damaging the wood.

An assortment of these nails should be stowed aboard for emergency repairs.

Rivets

Most rivets require special, expensive equipment to set and are of little use to boat owners. There is one exception. Aluminum pop rivets (**Figure 45**) can be installed with a very inexpensive handgun.

Many repairs can be made aboard boats with pop rivets. However, keep in mind that aluminum is not very successful as a fastening material except when joining aluminum parts. Aluminum is too anodic in the galvanic series and corrodes rapidly when in contact with nearly any other marine material.

SAFETY EQUIPMENT

Boat maintenance, particularly refinishing and hull repairs, involve tools and materials that could present a hazard if precautions are not taken.

a. Eye protection.
b. Hearing protection.
c. Gloves.
d. Respirators.

Eye Protection

Selecting appropriate eye protection is an important task. Boat mainenance carries a number of risks to eyes. The most obvious is injury from flying objects or particles. Grinding, cutting and impacts of many materials produce flying particles that can damage your eyes. For these hazards, ordinary safety glasses offer adequate protection. See **Figure 46**.

Ordinary prescription glasses do not provide adequate protection. If they have glass lenses, they do not offer sufficient impact resistance. They also don't provide side protection, though side guards can sometimes be added which offer some protection.

Safety lenses are usually made from polycarbonate material—the same material used to make shatter-proof prescription lenses. You should clean safety glasses with the same care that you would prescription glasses to prevent scratching them.

Unfortunately, some materials cannot be removed from safety lenses with ordinary lens cleaning materials. For example, overspray from spray painting. Many solvents will attack the polycarbonate lenses.

Goggles are meant to protect your eyes from a number of different hazards including impacts, splashes, harmful gases and even sparks. See **Figure 47**. Goggles intended primarily for protection against flying objects have small ventilation holes around the periphery. This permits some air flow through the goggles which makes them more comfortable to wear and minimizes lens fogging.

A face shield provides protection to your eyes in addition to safety glasses or goggles. See **Figure 48**. It also provides protection for your face. A face shield should not be worn alone. It is only to be worn in addition to other eye protection. Face shields, like other eye protection are made from polycarbonate materials.

For protection while welding, more specialized equipment necessary. One of the main hazards from welding is from ultraviolet and infrared radiation. This requires specially coated lenses to reduce the radiation to safe levels. The other major hazard is, of course, burns from

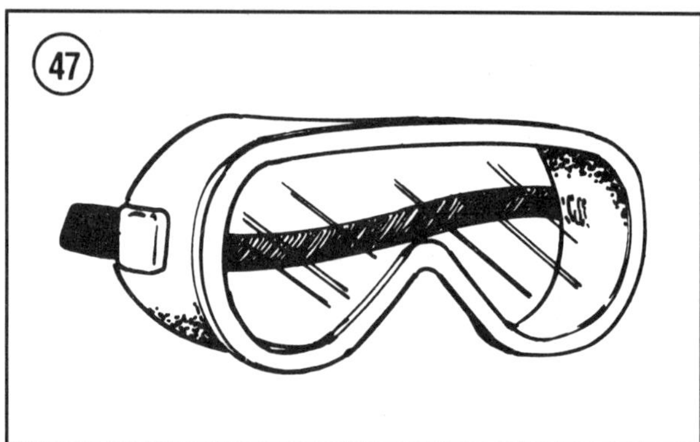

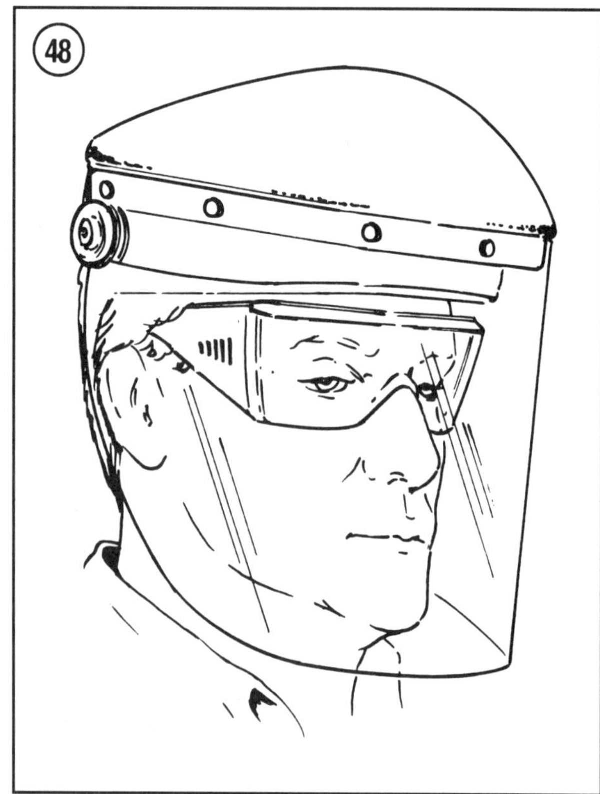

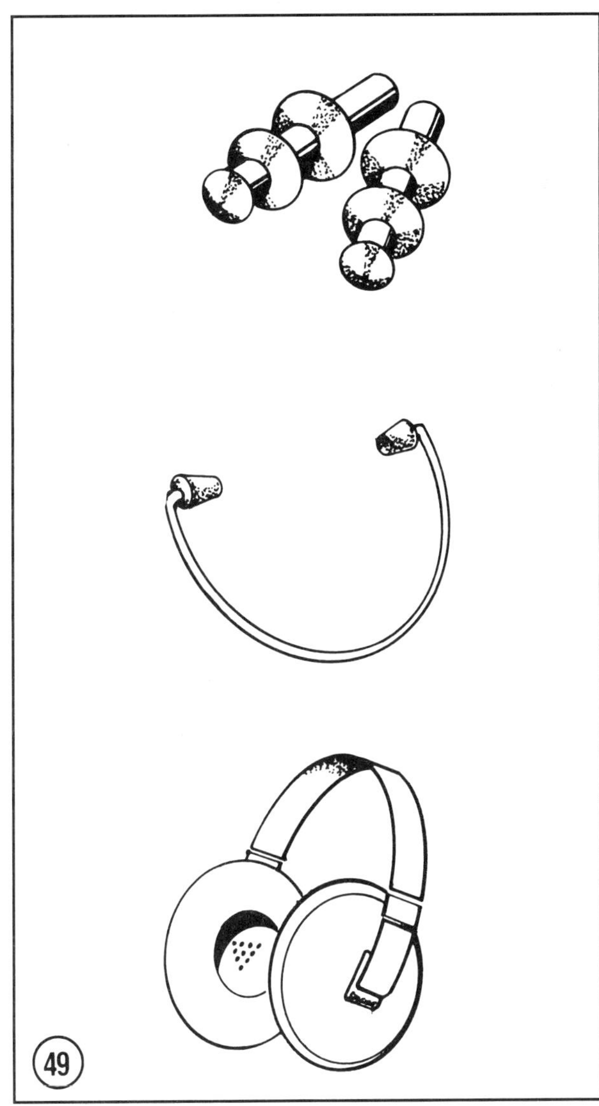
49

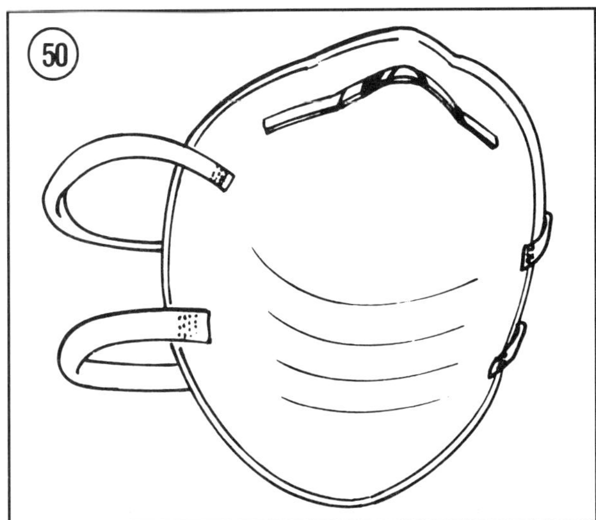
50

spattering metal. In most cases, a welder's eye shield will prevent burns of this type.

Hearing Protection

Noise generated by some power tools, particularly sanders and grinders, and noise from hammering may cause hearing impairment. Some people are more susceptible than others. The safest course is to wear ear protection when using these tools.

There are three major types of hearing protection equipment, earplugs, hearing bands and ear muffs. See **Figure 49**. In many cases, the selection of one type is a matter of preference. However, there are some differences in the range and degree of protection afforded by each type.

Respiratory Protection

There are at least a dozen different types of respirators from simple dust or particulate masks to self-contained breathing apparatus. Choosing the right respirator is a matter of finding one that allows you to work safely and comfortably.

Be watchful for danger signs as you work with a respirator. Leave the work area immediately if you experience any of the following:

a. Difficulty breathing.
b. Dizziness or other distress.
c. Irritation of eyes, nose or skin.
d. Smell or taste the contaminants.
e. Damage to the respirator.

Incidentally, those with beards or other facial hair between the sealing flange of the respirator and their face should not wear tight fitting respirators. Facial hair prevents a safe seal and leakage may cause exposure to the hazardous contaminants the respirator was designed to protect against.

Dust-Mist Respirators

Dust-mist respirators are designed to provide minimal protection against inhalation of dusts, fumes and mists. See **Figure 50**. The level of protection depends on the design of the mask. Not all dust-mist respirators offer the same protection.

Nontoxic particle masks are intended for protection against nuisance levels of nonhazardous dusts and powders, such as produced when sanding.

WARNING
Do not use this type of mask where toxic dusts or mists are present, such as when sanding toxic antifouling coatings or during spray painting.

Dust-mist respirators are one-piece devices intended for disposal after one or more uses. Half-mask respirators are also available with replaceable dust-mist cartridges. These may be more comfortable, offer better filtering and lower breathing resistance than one-piece devices.

Air Purifying Respirators

Air purifying respirators have replaceable cartridges or canisters designed to protect against specific contaminants. See **Figure 51**. Some cartridges simply filter out or trap airborne contaminants with mechanical filters. These are effective against dusts, mists and fumes from metals such as found in antifouling paints. This kind of filter actually becomes more effective with use as the trapped particles serve to trap other particles. At some point, though, the filter becomes too clogged, and should be replaced if breathing becomes uncomfortable.

Gloves and Aprons

Gloves are designed to protect against a number of different kinds of exposures. Most work gloves are simply designed to protect against cuts and abrasions from routine tasks. They also provide a better grip in some situations.

Gloves may also be necessary to protect your hands against chemicals, particularly solvents, thinners, paints, adhesives and other potentially harmful liquids. Gloves for this purpose range from simple latex "surgical" gloves to heavy duty corrosion resistance gloves. Of course, latex gloves are easily damaged and should not be used where there is a risk of rupturing the thin material. Gloves should be selected to be compatible with the materials contained in boat repair materials that you will be handling.

Table 1 TYPES OF FILES

Types	Cross-section	Use
Square		Enlarging rectangular holes or slots
Triangular (3-cornered)		Forming square corners in rectangular holes
Round (rat-tail)		Enlarging or shaping round or oblong holes
Half round		Shaping flat or round surfaces; general purpose
Knife edge		Shaping corners of irregular holes
Flat		General purpose, flat shaping

Table 2 GALVANIC SERIES

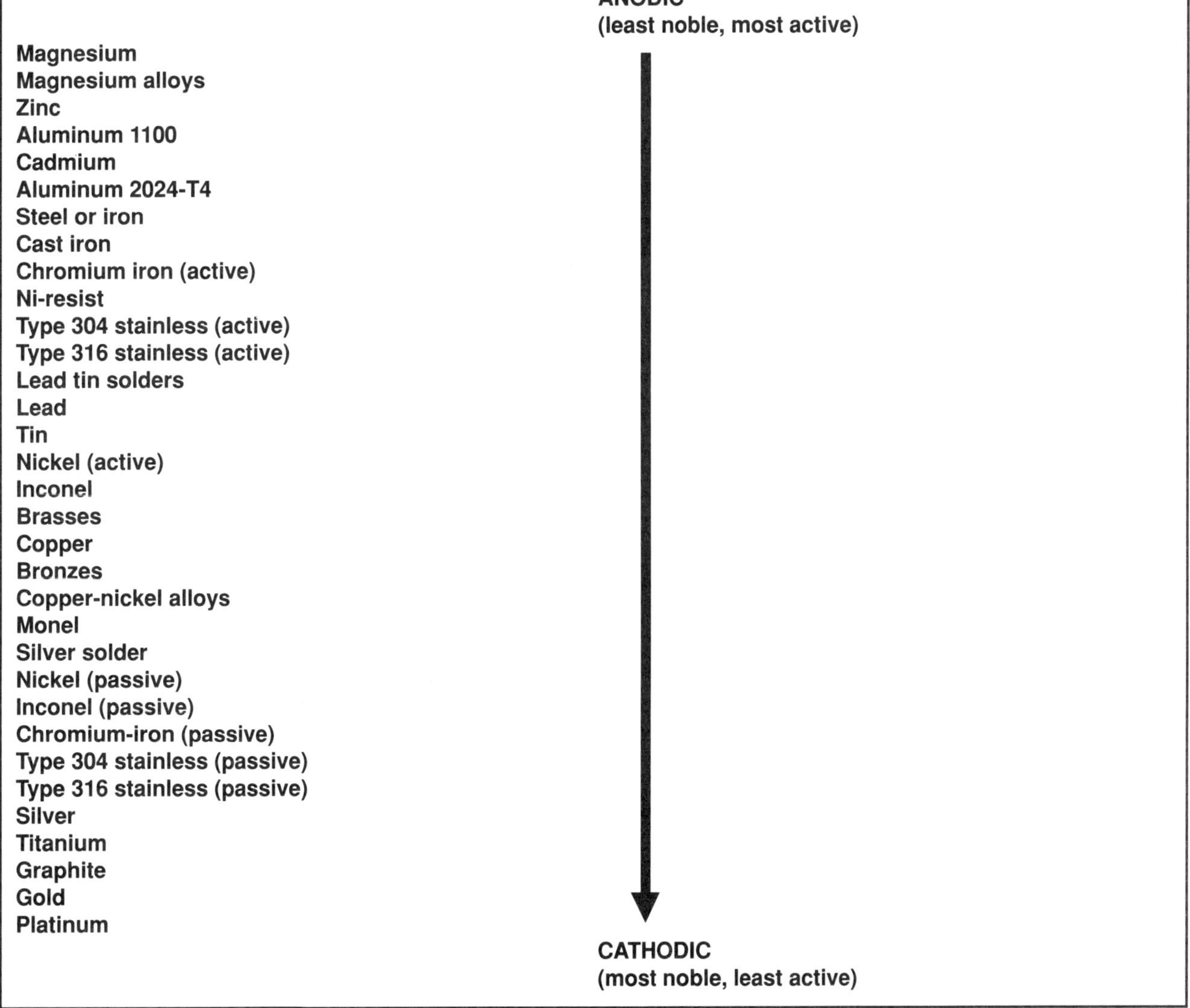

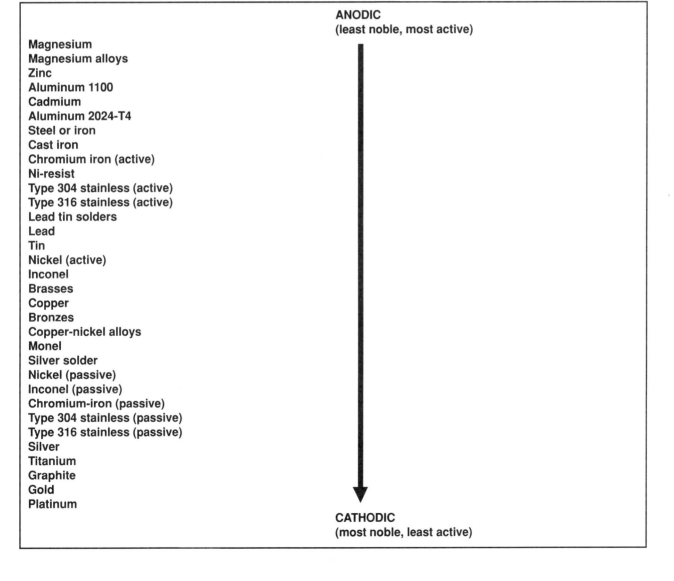

ANODIC
(least noble, most active)

Magnesium
Magnesium alloys
Zinc
Aluminum 1100
Cadmium
Aluminum 2024-T4
Steel or iron
Cast iron
Chromium iron (active)
Ni-resist
Type 304 stainless (active)
Type 316 stainless (active)
Lead tin solders
Lead
Tin
Nickel (active)
Inconel
Brasses
Copper
Bronzes
Copper-nickel alloys
Monel
Silver solder
Nickel (passive)
Inconel (passive)
Chromium-iron (passive)
Type 304 stainless (passive)
Type 316 stainless (passive)
Silver
Titanium
Graphite
Gold
Platinum

CATHODIC
(most noble, least active)

Chapter Three

Hull Maintenance and Refinishing

There is no such thing as a maintenance-free boat. All boats, whether wood, metal or fiberglass, require periodic attention to keep them sound and looking good.

When a boat finish is new, simple cleaning and minor touch ups will keep the finish looking good for quite some time. Eventually, though, any exterior finish, including fiberglass gelcoat, will deteriorate to a point where painting will become necessary.

This chapter describes procedures for keeping your boat in good condition. When refinishing becomes necessary, these procedures and paint recommendations will enable you to do a professional looking job.

SYNTHETIC PAINT SYSTEMS

Most common marine synthetic paints are:

a. Alkyd.

b. Silicone alkyd.

c. Epoxy.

d. Polyurethane.

e. Vinyl.

Each has characteristics which make it particularly suited for certain applications. Characteristics of each are described in the following sections.

Coating manufacturers are careful to design a complete family of materials to work with a particular coating to ensure compatibility. Not only are you selecting a particular coating, but you are selecting at least a primer and thinner that are compatible. Avoid mixing products from different manufacturers unless both manufacturers agree that they are compatible, or you have other experience to draw on. Mistakes can be costly and in some cases disastrous.

Alkyd Resin

Alkyd resin is a synthetic paint with good durability, gloss and color retention. In addition, alkyd finishes are oil and fume resistant. Alkyd resin is suitable for deck and topsides of wood, metal or fiberglass boats. It should not be used as a bottom finish. Alkyd resin is a traditional coating that is still preferred by many boat owners, but it can be more difficult to apply than the newer polyurethane coatings.

Silicone Alkyd Resin

When alkyd resin is fortified with silicone, it has even greater color and gloss retention ability than unmodified alkyd resin, but is still considered to be difficult to apply. The addition of silicone also improves moisture resistance and surface hardness. Silicone alkyd resin is a suitable topside and deck finish, but should not be used as a bottom finish.

Epoxy Resin

Epoxy resin combines excellent hardness, abrasion resistance, chemical resistance and adhesion, as well as long life. Epoxy resin may be used as a deck and topside finish and also makes an excellent bottom finish for trailerable or beachable boats which are subjected to abrasion, but do not require antifouling protection.

Epoxy resin can be applied to wood, metal or fiberglass. Bare wood or metal must be primed first. Use a primer specified on the manufacturer's label to be certain it is compatible; if not, epoxy may not bond properly. Bare fiberglass can be primed or not. If it is not primed, the epoxy resin will form a chemical as well as mechanical bond with the fiberglass resin.

Epoxy resin can be applied directly over most existing finishes provided the old finish has been on at least 6 months. If in doubt, paint a small test area first.

To insure a good bond, the original finish must be sanded smooth. Epoxy resin will not adhere to vinyl, styrene or antifouling paints; remove these finishes completely first. Epoxy resin cannot be used over rubber, neoprene (synthetic rubber) or vinyl fabrics.

Epoxy paints are normally 2-part systems. The "A" curing agent must be mixed with the "B" pigmented resin exactly as described by the manufacturer. After mixing, the paint has a pot life of 24-48 hours; that is, it must be used in that period or it will harden in the container. Unmixed, epoxy has a nearly unlimited shelf life.

Epoxy paint flows and levels very well. It can be brushed. rolled or sprayed on. Use natural bristle brushes as the resin can attack synthetic bristles such as nylon. If you spray it on, thin it as directed by the manufacturer.

CAUTION

Use a thinner recommended by the manufacturer.

Epoxy paints are sensitive to temperature and humidity when being applied. The temperature should be above 70° F and the humidity below 90%. Most epoxy will cure tack-free in a few hours under these conditions. Curing is faster with higher temperatures. Below 70° F, curing can be very slow. Infrared lights can be used to speed curing. Full curing may take several days.

Polyurethane Paint

Polyurethane paints produce a durable, high gloss finish. Polyurethanes dry by reaction between ingredients and absorption of moisture. In fact, the higher the relative humidity, the faster polyurethane dries tack-free. In addition, the paint has a very long pot life.

Polyurethanes are as good as epoxy at resisting chemical attack. Polyurethane is better than epoxy at resisting abrasion and wear. Many polyurethanes contain ultraviolet screening chemicals to minimize sun deterioration.

Polyurethanes are available in one-part and two-part formulations. Two-part formulations include a base and reactor that allow some control of the curing process for the professional, but they require more attention to detail than one-part formulations. In most cases, do-it-yourselfers will appreciate one-part polyurethane products which require no mixing and are easy to apply.

Antifouling Paints

The traditional method of discouraging barnacles, algae and other aquatic growths from attaching to the bottom of the boat has been to apply some sort of biocide. Wooden ships used copper sheathing for centuries to solve the problem. Later, coatings were formulated that included toxic chemicals such as arsenic, mercury and copper compounds—all toxic to life.

Some formulations use man-made organic chemicals such as tri-butyl-tin-fluoride (TBTF) or tri-butyl-tin-oxide (TBTO) suspended in poly-vinyl-chloride (PVC). The finish is hard and slick for maximum boat speed. Since these are organic toxicants, they do not corrode steel and aluminum as much as copper compounds do. Also, since TBTO and TBTF are colorless, the paint may be tinted any color desired.

The whole point of chemical biocides is to kill marine life. Unfortunately, this effect is not limited to aquatic life that attaches itself to your boat. With thousands of boats leaching out toxic chemicals in every marina, the water becomes toxic over a wide area. Fish, shellfish and marine mammals are poisoned and some of these poisons find their way into our own food supplies. The U.S. Environmental Protection Agency stepped in to regulate antifouling coatings and their application. Many state environmental protection agencies have also developed laws and regulations dealing with antifouling coatings.

Cuprous oxide is still widely used as an antifouling coating ingredient. In most cases, any product you buy over the counter will use this chemical. TBTO, on the other hand, is highly regulated. It may only be applied by someone who is EPA-certified for this job. Furthermore, its use is limited to aluminum hulls, hulls over 82 feet in length and outboard motor or lower drive units.

Most antifouling paints must remain in the water to work effectively. If the boat is hauled for any length of time, the paint breaks down and is no longer effective. The boat must be recoated after winter storage or any lengthy period out of water. However, there are some copper compound antifouling paints that can withstand long periods out of water. Interlux MICRON CSC is typical of these coatings. Antifouling protection is activated when the boat is in the water. When it is hauled the paint becomes dormant and does not deteriorate as rapidly as conventional antifouling coatings.

Incidentally, there is a new class of "foul release" systems that do not use toxic biocides. Interlux Veridian 2000 is an example. The idea behind Veridian 2000 is to produce a finish so smooth and slippery that marine organisms cannot get a grip on the surface in the first place. An added bonus is that underway, water does not "grip" the hull making the boat more slippery and faster. The drawbacks limit this product to the most dedicated. It must be applied at a Veridian 2000 Application Center with high pressure airless spray equipment and it is very expensive. There are no plans to offer it as a do-it-yourself product.

Seymour of Sycamore also has a "foul release" coating called Hard Coat. This material is intended to be wiped on over the existing gel coat. The product comes in a package containing 13 ounces, enough for a typical 20 foot boat from the waterline down. It provides a slick barrier that protects the boat's finish and releases marine organisms.

Estimating Bottom Paint Coverage

With some bottom coatings costing several hundred dollars a gallon, it is important to be able to estimate the number of gallons required beforehand. The following simple formula calculates the number of gallons required for one coat of bottom paint:

$$0.85 \times \left[\frac{\text{LOA} \times \text{Beam}}{\text{Coverage}}\right] = \text{gallons per single coat}$$

where,

LOA = Boat's length overall in feet.
Beam = Boat's width at the widest point in feet
Coverage = Number of square feet of coverage per gallon listed on the manufacturer's label.

Varnishes

Varnishes may be:

a. Alkyd resin.
b. Phenolic resin.
c. Polyurethane resin.

Major characteristics of these finishes were described earlier. This section covers special considerations when choosing one of these resins as a clear varnish for brightwork.

Unmodified alkyd resin produces a very pale clear finish. It will not stain or yellow with age as phenolic resin will. Alkyd resin also has superior gloss retention and durability. However, alkyd resin does not have the fullness and lustrous depth of other varnishes. This resin is used where its pale color and non-yellowing characteristics are important such as over blonde or bleached mahogany.

Phenolic resin yields a rich fullness and deep luster to brightwork. This resin darkens and yellows on drying. It has excellent durability and may have ultraviolet screening chemicals in it to minimize sun deterioration. Phenolic resin dries moderately hard and has fair chemical resistance. Phenolic resin is chosen mainly for its durability and appearance.

Polyurethane resin is the best choice for most brightwork. Polyurethane is paler than phenolic resin and shows less age discoloration. When dry, it is unexcelled for hardness and resistance to abrasion. It is also highly resistant to chemical contaminants. Unlike other varnishes, polyurethane can be applied in heavy coats under hot summer sun; other varnishes would wrinkle badly. Polyurethane is the most durable varnish available. It is used wherever a hard, durable, glossy finish is desired. Its abrasion resistance makes it the best choice for decks and cockpits.

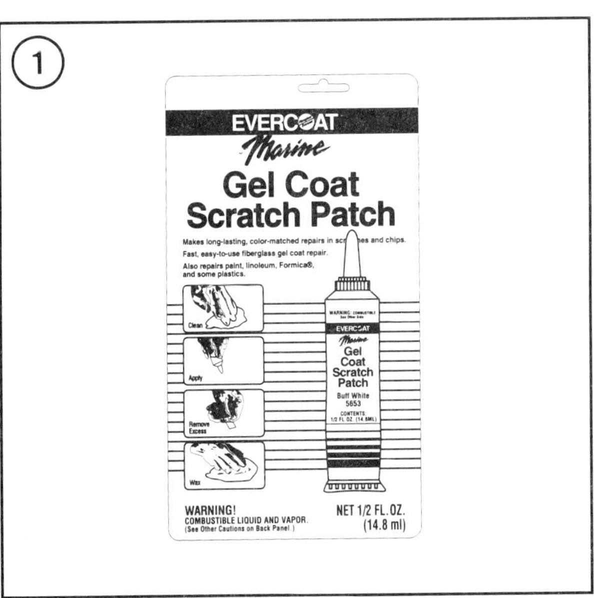

Gelcoat Repair Kits

Major gelcoat repairs are better left to professionals, but there are a number of products on the market for smaller do-it-yourself gelcoat repairs. More traditional methods of gelcoat repair are described later.

If the damage is very minor, a hairline crack or a scratch, you can use something like Evercoat's Gel Coat Scratch Patch. See **Figure 1**. This material comes in a limited number of colors, but does not require a catalyst. You simply clean the area to be repaired, squeeze the stuff in, wipe off the excess and let it dry. Once it sets up you can wax it—no sanding is required. Clear Gel Coat Scratch Patch is ideal for small scratches in metal flake finishes.

Most gelcoat repair kits consist of a plastic filler with a catalyst. See **Figure 2**. Some are available in premixed "factory" colors for many boats. If your boat is reasonably new and on the list, premixed colors might work out. If your boat is not on the list or suffers from weathering, you might as well just buy a neutral color filler, usually white, and match it using coloring agents available from the same manufacturer. Evercoat makes a Gel Coat Repair Kit which includes a small amount of polyester resin gel, hardener and several different coloring agents to match almost anything. Apply as directed. No sanding is required.

If you have a larger area to patch, both Spectrum and Fibre-Glass Evercoat make neutral color plastic fillers in quart and gallon sizes which can be tinted using their own coloring agents. See **Figure 3**. These and others are available at most marine chandleries.

Thinners, Reducers, and Solvents

Thinners, reducers and solvents are formulated to work only with a specific paint system. Before adding these chemicals to any paint or marine compound, read the labels carefully to be sure they are compatible.

There are several classes of thinners, reducers and solvents.

a. Epoxy.
b. Vinyl.
c. General paint.
d. Marine compound reducer.
e. Fungicidal compound thinner.

Wood Preservatives

Wood is susceptible to decay caused by mold, fungi and other microscopic plants. These organisms feed on wood and proliferate when moisture and temperature conditions are right. Though called "wet rot" or "dry rot," the 2 are essentially the same. There is really no such thing as "dry rot"—these organisms need moisture.

Some measures can be taken to minimize rot (described later), but fungicides are the only really effective way to combat decay.

Most fungicides contain either pentachlorophenol, or copper napthanate dispersed in a penetrating petroleum solvent. Copper fungicides are green. They can be painted over, although the green may bleed through the first coat. Pentachlorophenol fungicides are usually clear. They are useful for brightwork which will later be varnished.

2

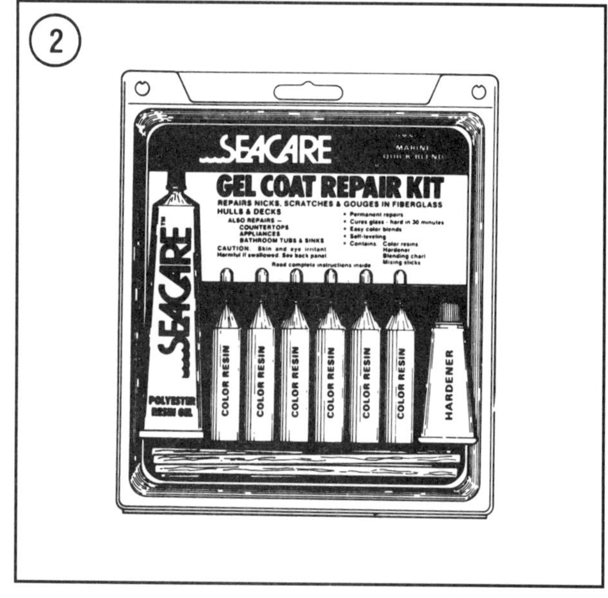

3

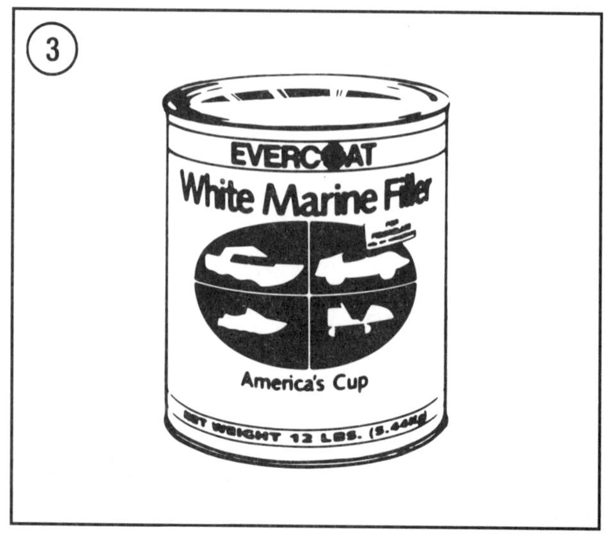

Mixing Paint

Most complaints that a paint doesn't cover or dries to different shades stem from improper mixing. Here is the best way.

1. Pour off the top 1/3 of the paint into another clean can.
2. Stir the remaining paint with a wide paddle.

NOTE

If there is any hard settled material on the bottom, break it up and blend it in completely.

3. Continue stirring and gradually add paint that was poured off.
4. When paint is uniform, pour it back and forth between the 2 containers.
5. Stir frequently during use.

MAINTAINING WOOD

Wood has been the traditional hull material for thousands of years. Its strength, durability, workability and beauty are hard to beat even with modern materials. But wooden boats have suffered recently in the marketplace. Modern materials are believed to be nearly maintenance free, while wood is believed to be a maintenance headache. This is simply not true. Some boatyard operators have estimated that a wooden boat requires only about 30% more maintenance than a fiberglass boat.

This section describes a comprehensive inspection procedure which should be done every 2-3 months. In addition, there are instructions for caulking and painting wooden hulls and topsides.

Cleaning

As often as necessary, wash the boat with water and mild detergent. Use a sponge or bristle brush to scrub off dirt. Rinse thoroughly with fresh water.

Wood Rot

A large variety of fungal organisms feed on wood. They break down the cellular structure of the wood by eating the cellulose. As structural parts deteriorate, fastenings no longer hold and serious and irreversible damage occurs.

Rot occurs where fresh water accumulates and stands for some time. Saltwater inhibits fungus and does not cause fungicidal rot. Fresh water usually comes from condensation, rain water or leakage from the fresh water system.

Good ventilation and a dry environment are the best ways to prevent rot. There should be some circulation through the entire hull, including hanging lockers and heads with doors. Weather permitting, open all hatches, ports and cowl ventilators to promote circulation. Keep a light bulb or special damp-chaser heating element on at all times when the boat is dockside to keep air as dry as possible. Fungi cannot survive in a dry, well-ventilated hull.

While adequate ventilation is a good preventive, it is not fool-proof. Every 2-3 months, you should thoroughly inspect the entire hull for signs of rot. Use a flashlight to inspect hard-to-reach areas. Test suspected areas with a pick to make sure that the wood is firm and not punky or soft. Tap wood with a hammer; rotted wood has a dull sound compared to solid wood.

If you find any rot, ascertain the reason. Look for leaks where rain water could enter or condensation collect. Correct the problem immediately.

Infected wood should be treated when found. If damage is not extensive, carefully cut away rot with a knife or sharp chisel. Saturate exposed good wood with fungicidal wood preservative. If damage is extensive, the affected wood member should be replaced.

Inspection

Wooden boats are susceptible to structural damage caused by a wide variety of marine plant and animal life. Every 2-3 months, the entire boat should be inspected to determine what damage, if any, these organisms have caused.

1. When the boat is hauled, go over the entire exterior very thoroughly. Check planking to be sure fastenings are sound and holding. Corroding fastenings may bleed rust around the fastened area. In addition, rust accumulation may push out the wooden plug (bung) covering the fastener so that it protrudes slightly from the planking. If this occurs, the fastener must be replaced or a new fastener installed alongside the old.
2. Inspect all caulked seams for signs of leakage. Recaulk if necessary.
3. Inspect the backbone assembly where possible. Check particularly all joints between individual sections of the assembly; the fastenings can work loose.
4. Check all floor timbers for rot and looseness.
5. Make sure all limber holes in the bilge are clean and unobstructed. If plugged with debris, rot-inducing water can accumulate in the bilge.
6. Inspect any internal ballast. Internal pigs accumulate a tremendous amount of dirt and grime which promotes fungi growth. If really filthy, remove internal ballast and clean bilge thoroughly. Iron pigs should be sandblasted and dipped in epoxy paint before reinstalling them.

Recaulking

1. Clean out old brittle caulking compound with a scraper.
2. Wire brush the seams to remove remaining compound particles.

3A. If the old cotton is clean, tight and not rotten, leave it in place and go to Step 8.

3B. If the old cotton is unsatisfactory, remove it. Make a tool from a piece of large stiff wire to hook the cotton and pull it out.

4. Wire brush the seams to clean them out.
5. Make up ropes from strands of caulking cotton. To do this, lay out 2 strands of cotton and roll them tightly together between your hands. Wind the resulting rope into a ball. Make up similar ropes with 3 or more strands to fit the wider seams.
6. Select a cotton rope that will fill the seam about 1/3 when tightly compacted with a caulking iron. Use a single strand for very narrow seams.
7. Pound the cotton tightly into the seam with a caulking iron and light mallet blows. Do not force the cotton completely through hull.
8. Fill the seams with elastomeric sealant. Use a putty knife or caulking gun. Make sure no bubbles are trapped.

NOTE

Make sure the sealant you choose can be painted over. Polysulfide sealants can be painted, but not all silicone sealants can. Read the manufacturer's label; if it does not specifically state that it can be painted over, don't use it.

9. When cured, cut the sealant flush with the planking with a single edge razor blade.

Painting Wooden Hulls

Though wood is durable and strong, it must be properly maintained to retain these qualities. A well-painted surface is absolutely essential to protect the wood from weathering. In addition, fungicidal preservatives are available to minimize rot due to living organisms. The following sections describe methods and materials necessary to keep your wood in top condition.

Surface Preparation (Bare Wood)

Bare bottom-sides are prepared as follows.

1. Sand to remove surface irregularities.

2A. If antifouling paint will be used, no primers, sealers, undercoats or preservatives should be used on the bottom.

2B. If enamel or racing bronze will be used, apply a wood sealer and let dry overnight.
3. Lightly sand the sealer to remove grain fibers that may have raised.

Bare topsides require a slightly different treatment.
1. Sand the entire surface to remove surface irregularities.
2. Apply a clear wood sealer and let it dry overnight.
3. Lightly sand the sealer to remove grain fibers that may have raised.
4. Apply 1 or 2 coats of undercoat. Let each coat dry overnight and sand lightly between coats with 220 grit paper.
5. After drying overnight, sand the final undercoat with 220 grit paper.

Surface Preparation (Previously Painted)

Previously painted surfaces require little preparation if the old paint is in good condition and free of blisters, peeling or "alligatoring."
1. Wash it thoroughly with TSP (tri sodium phosphate) to remove all grease and salt. Rinse with fresh water.
2. Scrape off all marine growth.
3. Sand with 120-220 grit paper.

Bottom Painting (Antifouling Protection)

Antifouling protection is particularly important on wooden hulls. While metal and fiberglass hulls become slow and unsightly from marine growth, wooden hulls will actually sustain structural damage. The different types of antifouling paint are described earlier in this chapter.

New coats of antifouling paint can be applied over old coats in many cases, but check with the manufacturer of the new paint first. There may be no need to remove old coats if they are not cracked or peeling. Clean the bottom thoroughly, sand with medium grit sandpaper and apply 2 new coats.

CAUTION
The new paint must be the same as, or compatible with, the old coats. If you are not sure, remove all old coats.

Painting an uncoated, bare bottom is easy. Do not use primers, undercoats or preservatives which will prevent the antifouling paint from penetrating the wood. Also, do not use any thinner unless the label clearly states to do so. Apply 2-3 coats to bare wood with a brush or roller. Read the label on the can to determine the proper drying time between coats and drying time (if any) before launching.

Bottom Painting (Hard Enamel)

Many small boats and some one-design racing boats are in the water only when underway. Most of the time, they are on a trailer. These boats do not require antifouling protection. Instead, they need a hard scratch resistant surface which will not be damaged during launching and recovery.

Several special bottom coatings are manufactured. Most are based on polyurethane or epoxy. Follow the directions on maker's label.

CAUTION
Topside enamels are not recommended for underwater use.

Some of these products, such as epoxy racing bronze, must be applied over bare wood. Most others require that the bare wood be sealed first. Use the sealer recommended on the paint label.

Topside Painting

A high-quality, topside finish is possible only when the surface has been carefully prepared. This is described thoroughly in an earlier section.

Nearly any quality deck or topside paint can be applied to wood. Characteristics of different paint systems are described fully at the beginning of this chapter.

Polyurethane and epoxy finishes may be too slippery for decks where sure footing is essential. Add a small amount of non-skid agent to the paint before application. Either coat the entire deck with this specially prepared paint or mask off selected areas for treatment.

MAINTAINING ALUMINUM

Aluminum alloy is becoming increasingly popular as a boat building material. Formerly restricted to small dinghies and runabouts, aluminum alloy is used increasingly for larger sailboats and power cruisers. Aluminum alloys are also popular for engine parts, drive units, spars and deck fittings.

Though noted for great strength and durability, aluminum must be protected from corrosive saltwater. A number of methods are possible. Anodizing and anodizing processes alter the chemical structure of the surface aluminum to make it more resistant to corrosion. This works satisfactorily against atmospheric corrosion, but not against direct salt spray which pits the surface with white deposits. The best protection for aluminum alloys is a quality marine finish. The finest finish of all is epoxy or polyurethane over an already anodized surface.

This section describes maintenance and painting procedures for all aluminum surfaces in hulls, decks, and fittings.

Cleaning and Preventive Maintenance

As often as necessary, wash the boat with water and mild detergent. Use a sponge or bristle brush to scrub dirt off. Rinse thoroughly with fresh water.

Inspect the surface for cracks. Repair cracks in sheet aluminum as described later. Touch up any surface damage to the paint finish.

Painting Aluminum

Aluminum should be painted for maximum protection. The surface must be carefully prepared or the paint will not adhere well. Follow the procedures in the next sections exactly to obtain the best results.

Antifouling coatings which use cuprous oxide cannot be used over aluminum boats. The copper in the paint and the aluminum cause electrolysis which will seriously corrode the aluminum hull. Special antifouling paints are formulated for use on aluminum hulls and other components such as outboard motors and lower drive units. Those which contain TBTO cannot be applied by a do-it-yourself boat owner. They must be applied by someone who is EPA-certified to do so.

Some manufacturers specify using ordinary metallic antifouling paints on the bottom of an aluminum hull. This is possible if several thick barrier coats protect the metal from the antifouling paint. However, it is a questionable practice. Every time the hull is scratched, the barrier coats are removed and no longer protect the scratched area. To prevent damage, the hull must be hauled several times a season for touch-ups.

Repairing Dents and Scratches

Aluminum boats are susceptible to scratches and dents above and below the waterline. Small dents in sheet aluminum can be knocked out with

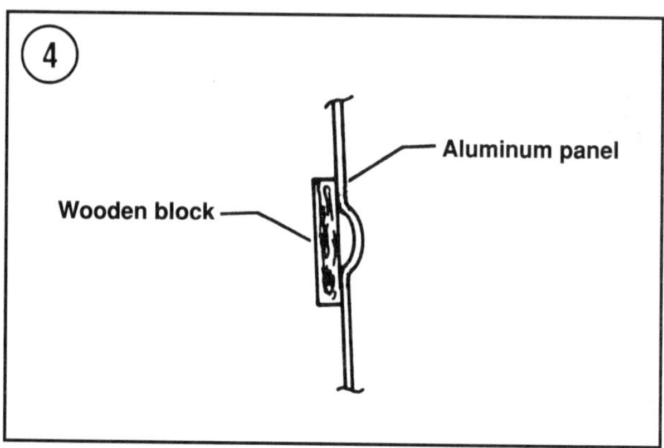

a block of wood and a rubber mallet. Place the block behind the surface as shown in **Figure 4**. Hammer around the edges of the dent, gradually working toward the center. If both sides of the dent are not accessible, filling with epoxy putty is the only answer.

Several epoxy putties are on the market. Typical are Regatta Epoxydur Fairing Compound or Dolfinite Eputty. These products can be trowelled on and sanded or filed after hardening. When the surface is smooth, paint over it as you would aluminum.

Some epoxy putty can be applied over aluminum after washing with a compatible solvent. Others should be applied after the wash primer. Read the manufacturer's label.

Patching Aluminum

Aluminum is simple to patch if the damage is not too extensive. Very small holes can be filled with epoxy putty. Putty a scrap of aluminum behind the hole to keep the putty in place. See **Figure 5**. Fill in the hole and sand flush when cured. Small holes can also be patched by drilling or reaming the hole so that it is round and inserting an appropriate size rivet. Larger holes require a more elaborate patch.

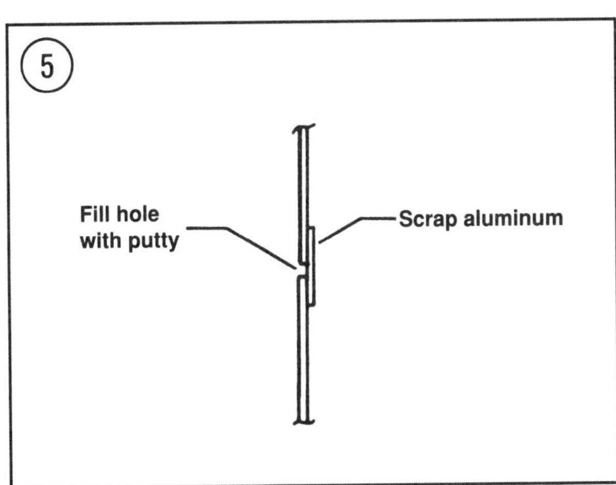

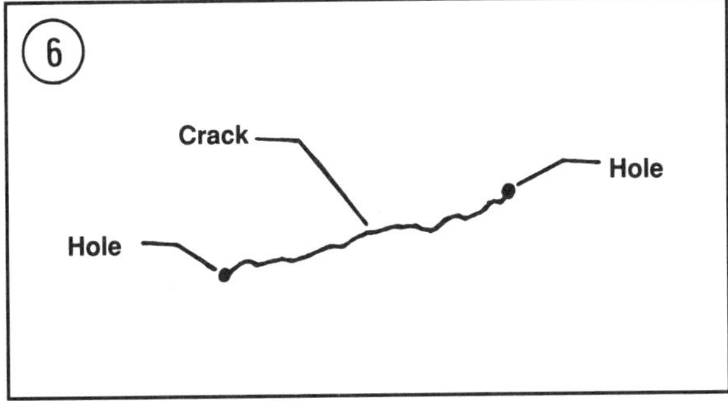

1. Cut a patch from scrap aluminum slightly larger than the damaged area.
2. Shape it to any hull curves by holding it in place and hammering it to fit using a rubber mallet.
3. File the edges of the hole so that no burrs or raised areas prevent a flush fit.
4. Drill stopping holes at the ends of cracks to prevent them from spreading. See **Figure 6**.
5. Place the patch in position, preferably on the inside of the hull.
6. Drill rivet holes every 1/2-3/4 in. around the patch and through the hull.
7. Spread caulking compound such as silicone sealant around the edges of patch.
8. Rivet the patch to the hull.
9. If the patch is on the inside, fill in exposed edges of the hull with epoxy putty and fair in with the surrounding hull.

Surface Preparation and Painting (Bare Metal)

1. Wash the surface thoroughly with clean solvent or brush cleaner to remove grease and oil.
2. Sand lightly with medium grit emery cloth or 100 grit paper to roughen surface.

NOTE
If sand blasting equipment is available, use 80 mesh white silica sand.

3. Clean the surface with a clean rag or tack cloth.

CAUTION
Do not wipe with thinner, solvent or gasoline.

4. Apply one coat of "wash primer." Do not try to cover the metal completely.
5. Apply 2 coats of anti-corrosive zinc chromate primer to the topsides and 4 coats to the bottom-sides.
6. Apply 1-2 finish coats. On bottom-sides, use a high quality polyurethane coating. If antifouling protection is required, make sure the bottom paint is compatible with aluminum. See *Painting Aluminum*. Above the water-line, use any quality topside paint.

Surface Preparation and Painting (Painted Surface)

If old paint is firm, not peeling and otherwise in good condition, little preparation is required.
1. Wash the surface thoroughly with TSP (tri sodium phosphate) to remove grease and salt. Rinse with fresh water.
2. Scrape off all marine growth.
3. Sand with 120-220 grit paper.
4. Apply 1-2 finish coats. On bottom-sides, use a high quality polyurethane coating. If antifouling protection is required, make sure the bottom paint is compatible with aluminum. See *Painting Aluminum*. Above the water-line, use any quality topside paint.

MAINTAINING STEEL

Steel is the boat building material most vulnerable to corrosion. Besides vulnerability to electro-chemical corrosion (galvanic), it is more susceptible to the corrosive effects of salt air. Therefore, considerable thought should go into painting a steel hull.

Most manufacturers have developed products especially for steel. It is wise to select a manufacturer, then use those products throughout the procedure.

This section describes maintenance and painting procedures for all steel surfaces above and below the waterline.

Cleaning and Preventive Maintenance

Steel requires more diligent regular maintenance than any other boat building material. Though very strong, it depends on a well-prepared and well-maintained surface coat for durability; bare steel cannot survive in a marine environment.

As often as necessary, wash the boat with water and mild detergent. Use a sponge or bristle brush to scrub dirt off. Rinse thoroughly with fresh water.

Rust stains cannot be removed by washing. If rust has seeped through the paint, but the surface paint is unbroken, try rubbing compound or wet sanding; touch up with spray paint if necessary. If the paint surface is broken or cracked and rust is bleeding, the rust and surrounding flaky paint must be chipped away to clean the bare metal. When repainting the area, follow the procedure for priming and painting covered below.

Surface Preparation

New steel must be carefully prepared even if not rusted. During the rolling process, sheet steel forms a fine mill-scale which can flake off later. Naturally, any protective coating flakes off with it. Before painting any new steel surface, sandblast the entire hull. Incidentally, weathering will produce the same effect, although it takes a lot longer.

Sandblasting is also necessary to remove rust and paint on previously coated steel. After sandblasting, remove remaining small areas of rust with a heavy wire brush. If you are very ambitious, you can chip flaking rust away with a chipping hammer, then wire brush any remaining rust.

Priming and Painting

Steel should be acid-etched, primed with several coats (usually 4) of anti-corrosive primer, then coated with at least 2 finish coats.

Different paint systems require different application procedures too numerous to outline here. The general procedure recommended by most manufacturers is outlined under *Priming and Painting Aluminum.*

On topsides and decks, any quality deck or topside paint is suitable for steel. Refer to the discussion of synthetic paints for characteristics of each type.

If antifouling protection is required, select the product carefully. Cuprous oxide paints can be used if a good barrier coat is applied first, according to the manufacturer's instructions.

MAINTAINING FIBERGLASS

Fiberglass is the most widely used boat building material today. Most boats are molded polyester or epoxy compound reinforced with fiberglass. The polyester resin in contact with the mold usually contains pigment and becomes the smooth outer surface gelcoat. A mold release agent applied to the mold prevents the gelcoat from sticking. When the mold is removed, some mold release remains imbedded in the gelcoat.

Fiberglass has traditionally been difficult to paint. In most cases, the mold release is the culprit. Designed to prevent adhesion to the mold, it has the same effect on paint.

Another problem is the gelcoat itself. The gelcoat polyester may vary widely, both chemically and physically, among different boat builders. A paint system which works well on one boat may fail on another. When painting a fiberglass boat, always use a paint system designed specifically for fiberglass and follow the manufacturer's directions explicitly.

One problem with older fiberglass boats that seems to have reached almost epidemic proportions is gelcoat blistering. Boats from the 60's that were typically hand layed fiberglass do not seem to have this problem. Boats from the 70's seem to be particularly prone and even brand new boats can develop this problems. There are a number of different reasons for blistering, but usually they are caused because gelcoat is not completely impervious to water. Some water permeates the gelcoat and finds its way into air pockets or areas where laminate adhesion is poor. Some boatyards think this can lead to structural failure if not taken care of. Talk it over with your favorite boatyard. If you have any doubts, don't hesitate to get a second opinion. It can cost thousands of dollars to do the job right.

A few blisters may be sanded down to bare fiberglass, allowed to dry out and refinished. If there are many blisters caused by this kind of problem, the best solution is to strip the hull to bare fiberglass and refinish it. In fact, it may be necessary to grind away the outside matte layer to permanently fix the problem.

Blisters may also be caused by incompatibility problems between the primer and other coatings or between successive layers of coatings. This kind of problem does not lead to structural problems and can be fixed by removing the offending coatings and recoating the hull. You may get away with treating each blister if there are just a few, but if there are too many, you face a losing battle.

Cleaning and Preventive Maintenance

Though fiberglass hulls require less maintenance than hulls of other materials, they are not indestructible. Ultraviolet rays from the sun and abrasion at dockside cause minor cosmetic damage which can detract from the boat's overall appearance.

Maintaining a fiberglass boat finish is similar to maintaining an automobile finish. As often as necessary, wash the boat thoroughly with water and detergent. Use a sponge for loose dirt and a soft-bristle brush for more stubborn areas. Rinse off with fresh water and dry with a clean damp chamois or turkish toweling.

Stains can be difficult to remove. Oil, grease and tar can be removed with kerosene or paint thinner. As soon as stain is gone, wash the area with detergent and water; do not leave solvent of any kind on gelcoat for any length of time.

Stains from food or drink are particularly persistent if the surface has not been well waxed. Several liquid fiberglass cleaners are on the market and may work on these stains. You may also try a household cleanser with bleach: but go easy, as most are fairly abrasive.

NOTE
Many boat owners swear by Bon Ami household cleaner. It is non-abrasive and much less expensive than most cleaners specifically formulated for boats.

When the boat is clean and dry, apply a good coat of wax. Automotive waxes are commonly used, but they are not satisfactory. They are formulated for acrylic or alkyd auto finishes. Fiberglass gelcoat is more porous and more likely to fade. Special fiberglass waxes are available which fill in the pores to give the surface a hard, high-gloss finish. In addition. they contain chemicals to screen out harmful ultraviolet rays.

WARNING
Never wax upper surfaces of decks where sure footing is necessary. Waxed gelcoat is dangerously slippery, wet or dry.

If the gelcoat surface is faded and dull, some measures are possible to restore the original gloss. First try rubbing the surface out with fiberglass paste cleaner. These cleaners are far less abrasive than automotive rubbing compounds, which may remove too much gelcoat.

In stubborn cases, the harsher automotive rubbing compound may be necessary. Try it in an inconspicuous area first. This harsh treatment may make things worse.

For really poor finishes, try wet-sanding lightly with 800 grit paper. This method takes off considerable gelcoat, so be careful not to sand through to bare fiberglass. The finished surface will be fairly thin. Keep it waxed, because you will not be able to rub it out again. If the resulting surface is not satisfactory, paint it as described elsewhere in this chapter.

Removing Gelcoat Scratches

If scratches are not too deep, they can be sanded out using the following procedure. To repair deep scratches, refer to next procedure, *Repairing Gelcoat Damage*.

Be careful when sanding gelcoat. Some applications are not very thick and you may cut through. If this happens, you will have to spray a gelcoat finish over the area. See *Spraying Gelcoat*.

1. Wipe the scratched area with acetone. Saturate the cloth so that all loose material is removed.

WARNING
Acetone must be used carefully. It is very flammable. It also has a number of adverse health effects. Wear eye protection

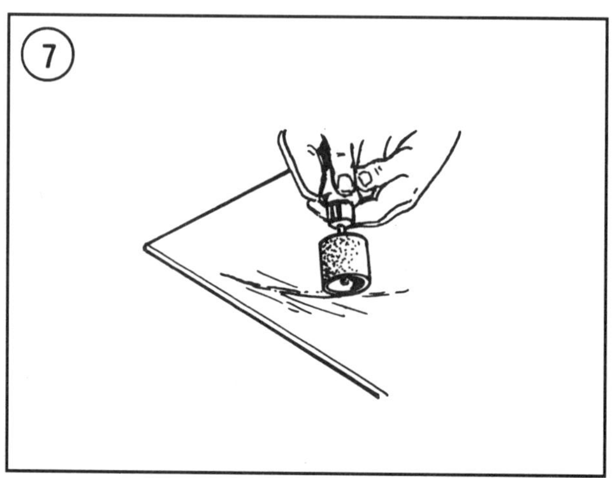

and latex gloves. Use only in a well-ventilated area.

2. Block-sand the scratch with 220 grit paper to remove it.
3. Wipe the area with a water-saturated cloth.
4. Wet-sand the area with 400 grit paper.
5. Wet-sand the area with 600 grit paper.
6. Buff the patched area with rubbing compound to restore gloss.

Repairing Gelcoat Damage

No matter how careful you are, sooner or later the gelcoat will suffer a scratch, nick, or gouge. Trailerable boats seem to get more than their share. Fortunately, gelcoat repairs are not too difficult if you follow the procedure below or use one of the commercially available repair kits described earlier.

1. Clean the damaged area thoroughly with acetone.

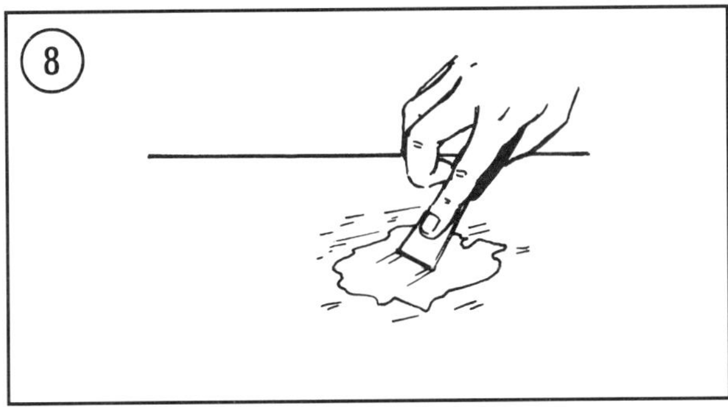

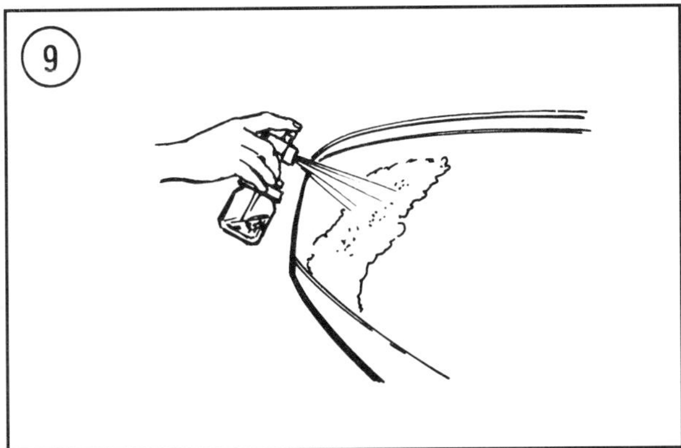

WARNING

Acetone must be used carefully. It is very flammable. It also has a number of adverse health effects. Wear eye protection and latex gloves. Use only in a well-ventilated area.

2. Form a V-groove along the scratch with a burr or sanding sleeve in a power drill. See **Figure 7.**
3. Remove flaky edges and feather edges back beyond the damaged area. Use 100-220 grit paper.
4. Clean the area with a dry cloth to remove all dust.

CAUTION

Do not touch the repair area with your hands.

5. Mix matching gelcoat with Cab-o-Sil (a fiberglass filler) to produce a smooth thick putty. Mix until all lumps and air bubbles are removed.
6. Add catalyst according to the manufacturer's instructions. Mix thoroughly or there may be small uncured spots in the patched area.
7. Pack the prepared gelcoat into the scratch with a putty knife. See **Figure 8**. Force it in tightly to avoid air bubbles. Build up the damaged area about 1/16 in. above surface to allow for shrinkage.
8. Spray the repaired area with polyvinyl alcohol (PVA) to prevent entry of air. See **Figure 9**. If PVA is not available, cover the patched area with cellophane. Squeeze the cellophane down with a single edge razor blade.
9. When the putty has cured, remove the cellophane or PVA (wash off with water).
10. Block-sand the patch with 220 grit paper.
11. If there are pinholes in the patch, fill them with gelcoat and cover again with cellophane or PVA. When cured, remove the cellophane or PVA and sand again with 220 grit paper.
12. Wet-sand the patched area with 400 grit paper.
13. Wet-sand with 600 grit paper.

14. Buff the patched area with rubbing compound to restore gloss.

Repairing Blisters

There are many causes of hull blisters. Before deciding on a course of action, try to determine why the hull has blistered. Is it a simple problem of incompatibility between coats in the bottom finish or is it a problem with water reaching the fiberglass laminates? If the problem is incompatibility between coats, you may be able to sand away the finish to remove the blisters, then recoat the area. If blistering from this cause is extensive, you should strip the bottom coats from the hull and reapply them from scratch as described under *Painting Fiberglass*.

Blisters caused by water permeating the gelcoat can be more serious. If there are only a few blisters, you may get away with grinding the area down to the dry laminate. Normally, this just means grinding away the thin gelcoat and maybe the matte layer underneath. You will have to build this area back up again with epoxy resin and refinish with a compatible bottom coating.

If the blistering from this cause is extensive, you will have to remove the gelcoat and as much of the matte layer as necessary to ensure a dry clean surface. Unless you have a very small boat, this is a big job. You can save about half the money over a complete professional job by having the professionals sandblast the hull for you, then you can refinish it yourself. In any event you are probably looking at several thousand dollars. After sandblasting, have the pro's check the hull with a moisture meter to ensure a laminate moisture content of 1% or less.

Once the hull is clean and dry, you will have to build the hull surface back up with an epoxy barrier or sealer coat. You will probably have to roll on 5-10 coats to do this. Use an epoxy barrier coat from the same manufacturer as the bottom paint you plan to use to ensure compatibility. Follow the manufacturer's instructions for applying the barrier coat and the final coats.

Spraying Gelcoat

Gelcoat may be sprayed on small areas to hide repairs. Use any good quality spray gun, following this procedure.

1. Remove all scratches in the surface by wet-sanding with 400, then 600 grit paper.
2. Mask the area to be sprayed. Leave at least 2 inches around the area. If you spray right up to or over the tape, a thick lap line will form and be difficult to remove.
3. Cover all areas which will be exposed to any overspray.
4. Clean the area to be sprayed with acetone.
5. Thin the prepared gelcoat about 25% with acetone to obtain a good, sprayable consistency.

CAUTION
Do not thin more than 50% or the finish will be dull.

6. Add catalyst to the gelcoat. Use the exact amount recommended by manufacturer. Mix thoroughly to prevent uneven cure.
7. Spray on about 10-15 mils of gelcoat. This is equivalent to about 2-3 passes with the gun.
8. Spray a very thin film of polyvinyl alcohol (PVA) over the gelcoat immediately. This seals off air and speeds curing. It also protects from dust.
9. Remove masking tape.
10. When gelcoat has cured, wet-sand with 400 grit paper to remove all traces of "orange-peel" and lap lines caused by tape.
11. Wet-sand with 600 grit paper.
12. Buff the area with fiberglass rubbing compound to restore gloss.

Painting Fiberglass

The original gelcoat finish should last for many years if properly cleaned and waxed. But in time, most finishes will begin to chalk and fade. Dark colors such as black, red and dark blue deteriorate the fastest. If the problem is just fading, rubbing and buffing may restore the finish. However, if the finish is uneven and mottled looking, it must be repainted.

Choice of paint for fiberglass is important. Some boat owners use acrylic and alkyd paints on fiberglass, but these tend to be soft and some don't adhere well. Epoxy and polyurethane finishes are the best choice for fiberglass. They provide excellent adhesion, resistance to chalking and good color retention.

Surface Preparation (Unpainted Gelcoat)

1. Scrub the surface thoroughly with detergent and water.
2. Wash the hull thoroughly with fiberglass solvent wash to remove mold release or other waxes from the surface.

CAUTION

Use plenty of clean rags, discarding them often, as wax builds up on them. Otherwise, you will just spread the wax around. Wipe downward only.

3. Wash the boat again with detergent and water.
4. Sand the entire surface to be painted with medium grade production paper (80-120 grit). Sand until the surface has a matte finish with no gloss at all.
5. Above the waterline, sand surfaces to be painted with 240-320 grit paper to remove any scratches. This is not necessary below the waterline where antifouling paint will be used.
6. Wipe off sanding dust with a clean, solvent-dampened rag.
7. Fill deep scratches and gouges with a special fiberglass filler. Read the label to be sure it is formulated for fiberglass. Mix and apply as directed on the label.
8. Sand filled spots flush with the surrounding area with 320 grit paper; finish with 600 grit paper.

Surface Preparation (Painted Surface)

1. Scrub the surface thoroughly with detergent and water.

WARNING

Wear goggles when scrubbing metallic antifouling paints; some of these are extremely caustic and can cause permanent eye damage.

2A. If old paint is not peeling or cracked, sand the surface to be repainted with medium grit paper (80- 120 grit). Remove all gloss. Be careful when sanding sharp edges or corners or you may cut through the old paint and gelcoat.

WARNING

Wear an air purifying respirator (See ***Air Purifying Respirators*** *for recommendations) while sanding any antifouling paint. Dust from copper, mercury, TBTO and TBTF is very toxic.*

2B. If the old paint is in poor condition, remove it down to the original gelcoat.

NOTE

Use a power sander if possible. If this is too slow try one of the chemical paint removers on the market. Test it on a small inconspicuous area first to make sure it won t damage the gelcoat. Even if it doesn't damage the test area don't leave it on the surface any longer than necessary.

3. Wash the boat again with detergent and water.
4. Sand the entire surface to be painted with medium grade production paper (80-120 grit). Sand until the surface has a matte finish with no gloss at all.
5. Above waterline, sand surfaces to be painted with 240-320 grit paper to remove any scratches. This is not necessary below the waterline where antifouling paint will be used.
6. Wipe off sanding dust with clean solvent-dampened rag.

7. Fill deep scratches and gouges with a special fiberglass filler. Read the label to be sure it is formulated for fiberglass. Mix and apply as directed on label.
8. Sand filled spots flush with surrounding area with 320 grit paper; finish with 600 grit paper.

Bottom Painting (Antifouling Protection)

When fiberglass was first introduced, manufacturers touted the complete freedom from maintenance with the material. Unfortunately, no one told the barnacles and other marine growth found in most waters. In many cases, fiberglass gives them a firmer foot-hold. Unlike wood, fiberglass will not be structurally damaged, but growth will slow the boat and it is very unsightly.

In many cases, antifouling paint can be applied over bare gelcoat, if the surface is carefully prepared as described earlier. However, this is not always effective.

Priming the bare gelcoat with a special non-sanding fiberglass primer will provide for better adhesion. Follow the manufacturer's directions exactly. Usually the primer must dry 2 hours, but not more than 8-12, depending on manufacturer. After priming, coat the bottom with 2 coats of antifouling bottom paint.

CAUTION
Alcohol-solvent paints are not compatible with fiberglass primer.

Stir the paint frequently during application to ensure even toxicant dispersion. Let each coat dry the recommended time before applying the next. Also let the final coat dry as recommended before launching the boat.

If painting over a previously painted bottom, priming may not be necessary, but check with the manufacturer of the new coating first. As long as the old paint is in good condition, prepare the surface as described earlier and apply 2 coats of antifouling paint. The new paint must be compatible with the old. See earlier section describing compatibility of different paint systems.

Bottom Painting (Non Antifouling)

If antifouling protection is not required, coat the bottom with a racing bronze, polyurethane or epoxy enamel formulated for underwater use. Many topside enamels are not suitable for use underwater.

The procedure is the same as for antifouling painting. In most cases, a primer is not necessary. However, many manufacturers recommend a white undercoat to increase adhesion and hide surface blemishes that would produce an uneven gloss. White undercoat is specially formulated for this purpose. It dries harder than the finish coat, which prevents "checking." Checking occurs when a hard finish is applied over a softer surface.

Topsides

Usually more care is necessary on topsides finishing because it shows more. Prepare the surface as described in an earlier section. Coat with polyurethane or epoxy topside enamel.

Priming is usually not necessary; follow the manufacturer's recommendation. However, if surface blemishes have been filled or glazed, a coat of white undercoat will even out the surface tone, producing a more uniform final finish.

Polyurethane and epoxy produce very slick finishes which may be too slippery for decks. Add a small amount of non-skid agent such as Woolsey Non-Skid Agent or Regatta Non-Skid Dry Granules to the paint before application. Either coat the entire deck with this specially prepared paint or mask off selected areas for treatment.

Chapter Four

Outboard Motors

Modern outboard motors are smooth, reliable sources of power. Unfortunately, most boat owners neglect their outboard just as long as it continues to run. When the motor won't start, outboard motors in general are blamed. Like any engine, an outboard thrives on use. An occasional running and regular preventive maintenance will pay for itself with a dependable engine that lasts a long time.

The basics of maintaining an outboard are the same as for any engine.

1. Run the engine periodically. Even a few minutes every week (except during lay-up) will keep things lubricated.
2. Perform regular scheduled maintenance.
3. Fix minor troubles immediately before they become major ones.

SHOP MANUAL

A shop manual for the model and year of your outboard motor is essential. While this chapter gives you general service information that is common to most outboards, you will need a shop manual for more specific information. Clymer Shop Manuals cover everything from simple adjustments to complete overhaul and are available for most outboard motors.

FOUR-STROKE FUNDAMENTALS

A 4-stroke engine requires 2 crankshaft revolutions (4 strokes of the piston) to complete a cycle. **Figure 1** explains the operation of a gasoline 4-stroke engine.

TWO-STROKE FUNDAMENTALS

A 2-stroke engine requires only one crankshaft revolution (2 strokes of the piston) to complete a cycle. **Figure 2** explains the operation of a gasoline 2-stroke engine.

(1)

4-STROKE GASOLINE OPERATING PRINCIPLES

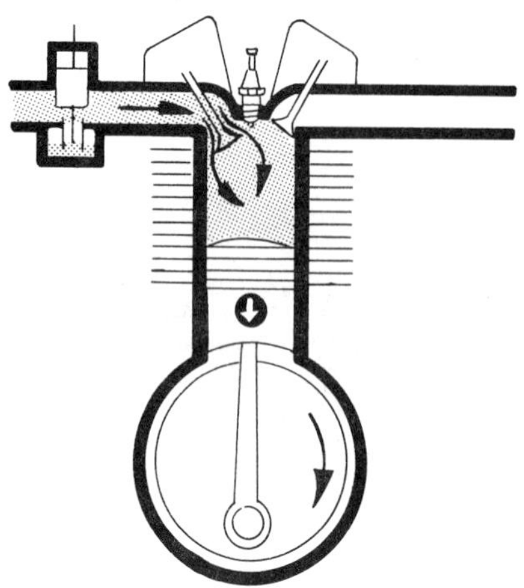

As the piston travels downward, the exhaust valve is closed and the intake valve opens, allowing the new air-fuel mixture from the carburetor to be drawn into the cylinder. When the piston reaches the bottom of its travel (BDC), the intake valve closes and remains closed for the next 1 1/2 revolutions of the crankshaft.

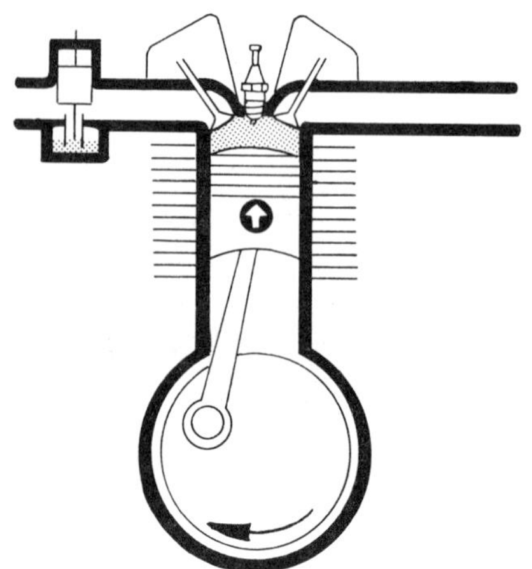

While the crankshaft continues to rotate, the piston moves upward, compressing the air-fuel mixture.

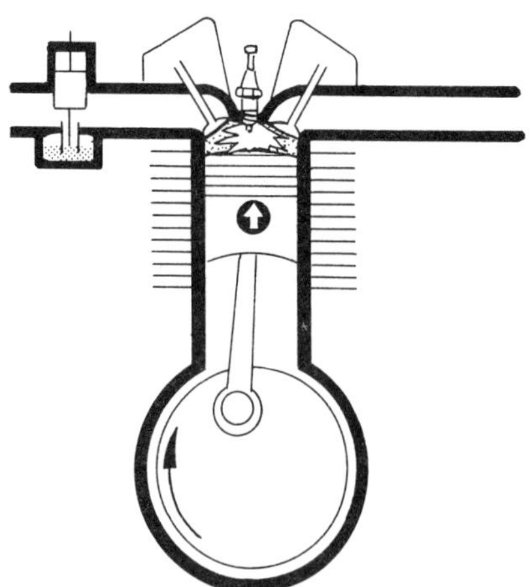

As the piston almost reaches the top of its travel, the spark plug fires, igniting the compressed air-fuel mixture. The piston continues to top dead center (TDC) and is pushed downward by the expanding gases.

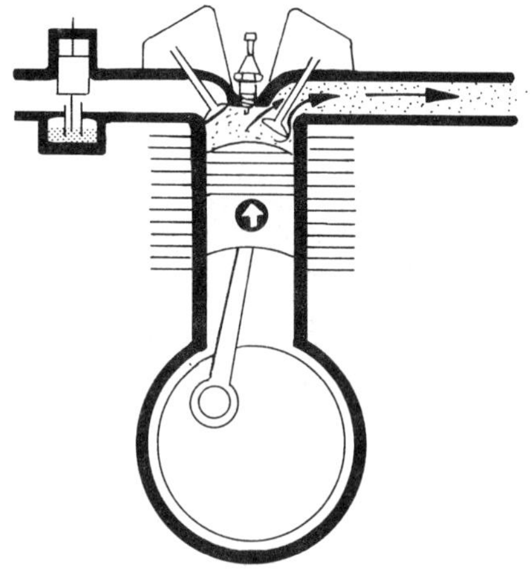

When the piston almost reaches BDC, the exhaust valve opens and remains open until the piston is near TDC. The upward travel of the piston forces the exhaust gases out of the cylinder. After the piston has reached TDC, the exhaust valve closes and the cycle starts all over again.

(2)

2-STROKE OPERATING PRINCIPLES

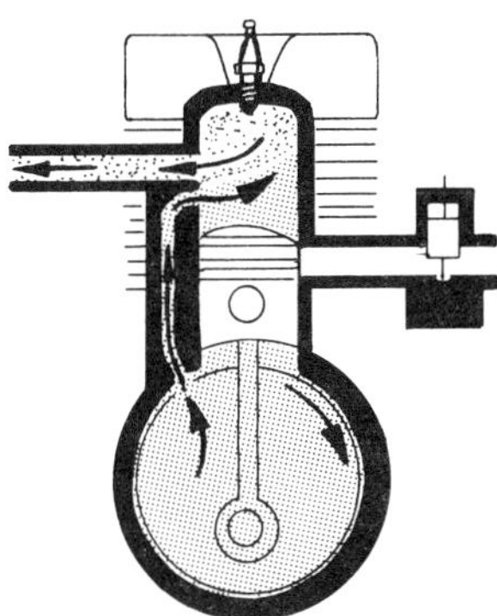

As the piston travels downward, it uncovers the exhaust port (A) allowing the exhaust gases to leave the cylinder. A fresh air-fuel charge, which has been compressed slightly in the crankcase, enters the cylinder through the transfer port (B). Since this charge engers under pressure, it also helps to push out the xhaust gases.

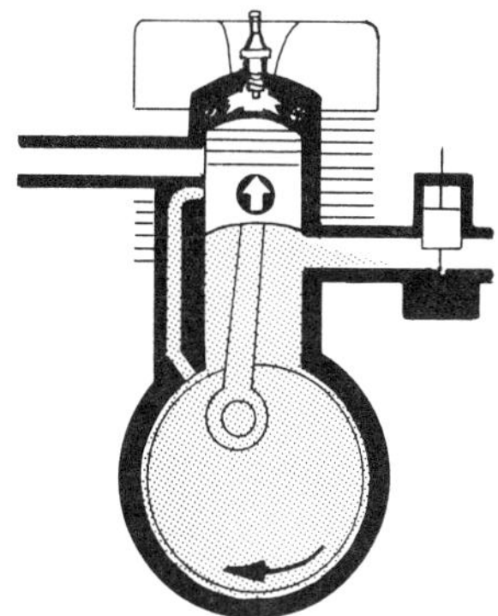

While the crankshaft continues to rotate, the piston moves upward, covering the transfer (B) and exhaust (A) ports. The piston compresses the new air-fuel mixture and creates a low-pressure area in the crankcase at the same time. As the piston continues to travel, it uncovers the intake port (C). A fresh air-uel charge from the carburetor (D) is drawn into the crankcase through the intake port.

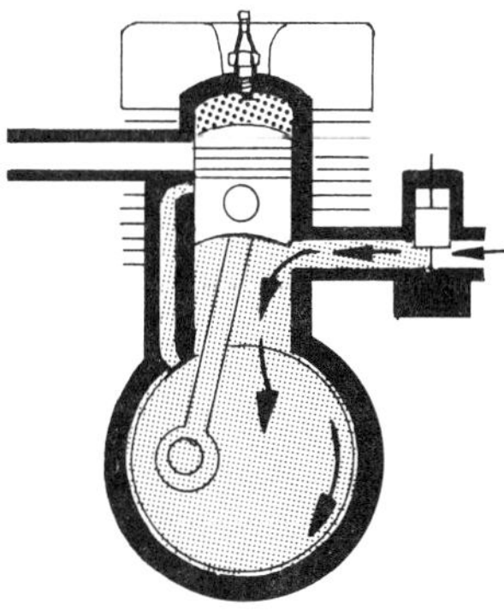

As the piston almost reaches the top of its travel, the spark plug fires, igniting the compressed air-fuel mixture. The piston continues to top dead center (TDC) and is pushed downward by the expanding gases.

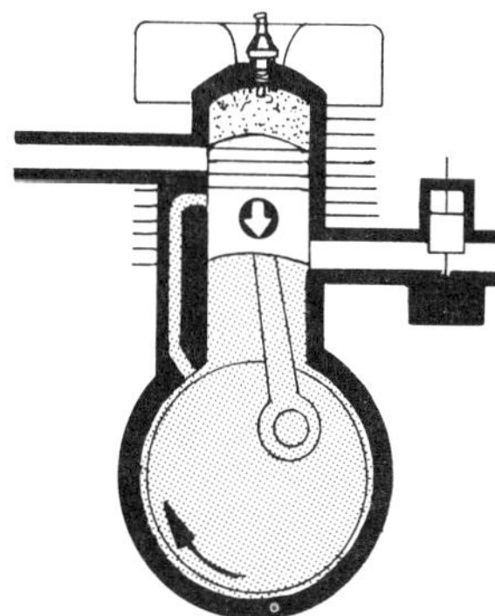

As the piston travels down, the exhaust gases leave the cylinder and the complete cycle starts all over again.

DAILY CARE

Your outboard requires a certain minimum amount of care every time you use it. Besides using the correct fuel/oil mixture and flushing the cooling system after use (if recommended by the manufacturer), you should inspect the motor before each use.

Inspection

Outboards may sit idle for quite some time between uses. Unless you make a point of inspecting the motor, deterioration can get serious before you notice it. When starting the motor, follow this simple routine.

1. Remove the cover.
2. Check the condition of the starter rope, if so equipped. These fray and deteriorate.
3. Check spark plug wires. Make sure they are securely connected and in good condition.
4. Check all fuel lines. Make certain they are securely clamped and in good condition. A loose or leaky fuel line is a serious fire hazard.
5. Install the cover.
6. Start the motor and make sure that water emerges from the cooling system "tell-tale" port.

PROPER FUEL SELECTION

Use regular or premium unleaded gasoline with a *minimum* pump octane rating of 67 on 2-30 hp or 87 on all other models. For optimum performance and maximum engine life, gasoline with an octane rating of 89 or higher is recommended. Premium grade gasoline produced by a national brand refinery is specifically recommended for high performance outboard motors. Premium grade gasoline (91-93 octane) contains a high concentration of detergent and dispersant additives that prevent carbon deposits on pistons and rings.

Be careful where you buy gasoline. The quality of pump gasoline can vary considerably even at the same service station or fuel dock. One problem is that gasoline does not store well. Some of the ingredients are very volatile and evaporate or decompose in time. Another problem is condensate which will sink to the bottom of the bulk storage tank, but frequently gets sucked up with the fuel. To make matters worse, refineries change the characteristics at different times of the year to make sure that road vehicles run well. If you use pump gas, make sure that you buy at a major brand outlet with high traffic. This will ensure fairly fresh fuel each time you buy.

Sour Fuel

Gasoline should not be stored for more than 60 days. Gasoline forms gum and varnish deposits as it ages. Such fuel will cause starting problems, carburetor plugging and poor performance. Several fuel additives are available which can prevent gum and varnish formation during storage or periods of non-use.

Premix fuel used for 2-stroke motors does not store as well as gasoline without oil. You should only mix enough fuel for immediate use. Always use fresh gasoline when preparing premix fuel.

Alcohol Extended Gasoline

There are other potential problems with pump gasoline in certain areas of the country. New federal clean air laws have forced refiners to offer oxygenated fuels in many urban areas during certain times of the year, usually the cooler months. The oxygen added to the fuel is in the form of alcohol (to form so-called gasohol) or methyl tertiary butyl ether (MTBE). If in doubt about the fuel, ask the gasoline supplier or local government agencies charged with enforcing clean air standards in your area.

Alcohol may also be added to gasoline as an octane booster, although this fact may not be advertised.

Most outboards should run as well on this fuel as the non-oxygenated fuel as long as the fuel does not contain more than 10% ethanol alcohol or 5% methanol alcohol with 5% co-solvents, and meets the minimum octane requirements for your motor. However, oxygenated fuels may run a little leaner and require rejetting the carb(s) one jet size richer.

CAUTION
Do not use gasoline containing more than 10% ethanol or 5% methanol regardless of octane rating.

PROPER ENGINE OIL SELECTION (4-STROKES)

Oil for 4-stroke engines is graded by the American Petroleum Institute (API) and the Society of Automotive Engineers (SAE) in several categories. Oil containers display these ratings on the top or label (**Figure 3**).

API oil grade is indicated by letters, oils for gasoline engines are identified by an "S" and oils for diesel engines are identified by a "C." Most modern gasoline engines require SF or SG graded oil. Automotive and marine diesel engines use CC or CD graded oil.

Viscosity is an indication of the oil's thickness, or resistance to flow. The SAE uses numbers to indicate viscosity; thin oils have low numbers and thick oils have high numbers. A "W" after the number indicates that the viscosity testing was done at low temperature to simulate cold weather operation. Engine oils fall into the 5W-20W to 20-50 range.

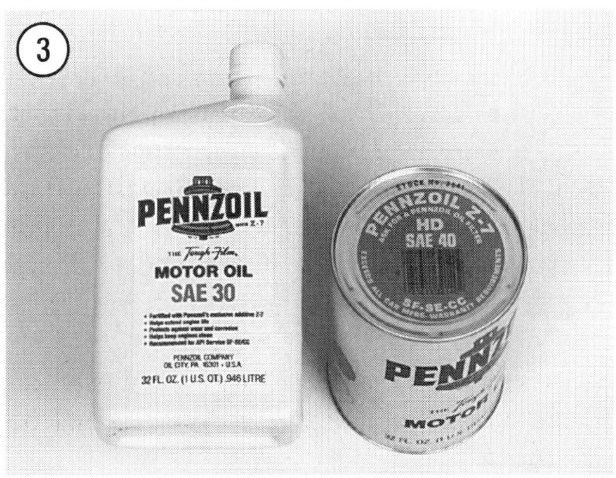

Single grade oils generally become more viscous (thicker) at low temperatures and less viscous (thinner) at high temperatures. Multi-grade oils (for example, 10W-40) are specially formulated to maintain a constant viscosity throughout a wide range of temperatures.

PROPER ENGINE OIL SELECTION (2-STROKES)

Two-stroke engines are lubricated by mixing oil with the fuel. The internal components of the engine are lubricated as the fuel/oil mixture passes through the crankcase and cylinders.

Besides choosing the right gasoline, you must also select the correct oil for your outboard motor. Outboard motor manufacturers specifically recommend using oil that is certified as TCW-3 by the National Marine Manufacturer's Association (NMMA). If a 2-stroke oil is so certified, it will be indicated on the oil container. See **Figure 4**.

To qualify for NMMA certification, an oil must pass a series of rigorous tests. These tests include lubricity, general performace, tendencies to promote preignition, rust prevention, fluidity and filterability.

Most outboard manufacturers have their own private label oil. While it is not absolutely necessary to use the manufacturer's oil, doing so is recommended and ensures that the oil meets all required certifications and standards for your particular outboard motor. If you do not use the manufacturer's oil, be sure to use a good quality oil certified NMMA TCW-3.

Another consideration is the type of oil used as a base. Two-stroke oils may be petroleum based (refined from natural crude oil) or synthetic (man-made). Most oils available today are petroleum based, and they are certainly cheaper than synthetics. However, synthetics can be carefully designed to be very clean burning while maintaining the high film strength needed for modern high performance outboard motors.

CAUTION
Do not, under any circumstances, use multigrade or other high detergent automotive oil or oil containing metallic additives. Such oil is harmful to 2-stroke engines, and may result in piston scoring, bearing failure or other engine damage.

It is never a good idea to mix different oil brands or types. Different types may react with each other and separate out. If you are going to experiment with different oils, start with an empty oil reservoir or with fresh gasoline for premixing.

PREMIXING FUEL (2-STROKES)

The correct ratio of fuel to oil is very important with a 2-stroke motor. The oil in the fuel lubricates the internal engine parts. If there is too much oil, spark plugs foul easily, carbon accumulation is rapid, and the engine runs too hot. If there is not enough oil, engine wear is excessive. On some outboards, particularly smaller models, the oil is mixed directly with the fuel in precise proportions. Always use the ratio established by the engine manufacturer.

Some common ratios are 50: 1, 40: 1 and 25:1. For example, 50:1 means 50 parts gasoline to 1 part oil. A 6 gallon tank, which is 48 pints of fuel, requires approximately 1 pint of oil. Special measuring cups which permit measuring exact amount of oil required for any ratio and any fuel quantity are on the market. If you can't find one at your local outboard dealer or marine chandlery, try a motorcycle dealer.

It is important to mix the oil with the gasoline in a certain way. Never pour the oil into an empty tank. The best way is to fill the tank about 1/4 full, then add all the oil. Install the filler cap and shake the tank well to dissolve the oil. Then add the remaining fuel and shake the tank again. If you are mixing fuel for a motor with an integral tank, mix the fuel in a separate one gallon can first, then pour the mixture into the tank.

WARNING
Gasoline is an extreme fire hazard. Never use gasoline near heat, sparks or flame. Do not smoke while mixing fuel.

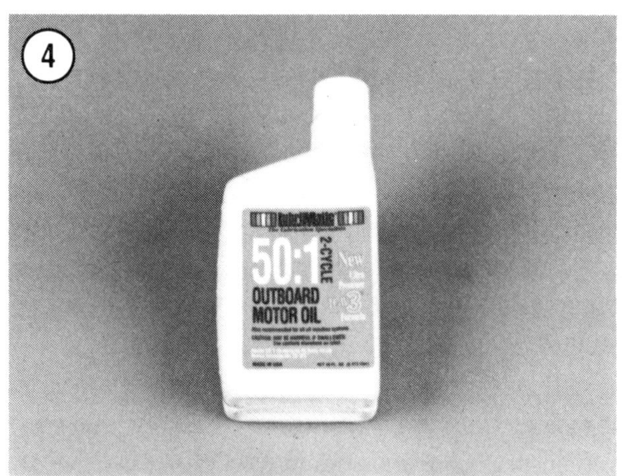

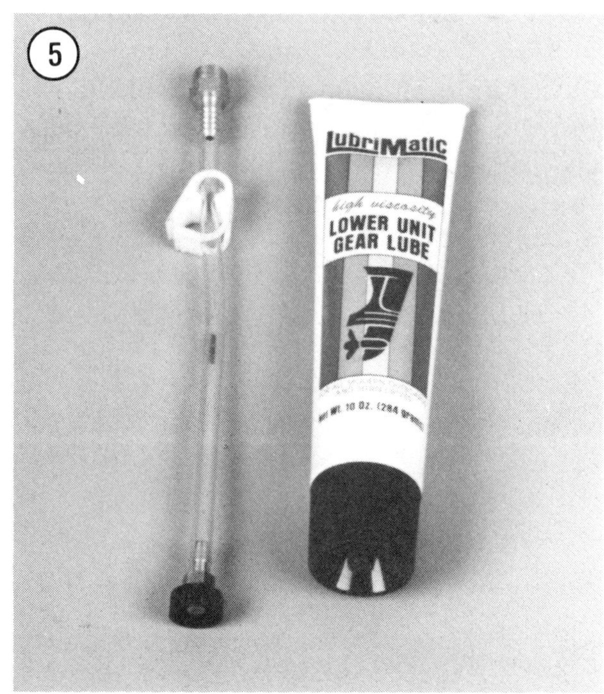

CONSISTENT PREMIXING

The carburetor idle adjustment is sensitive to fuel mixture variations which result from the use of different oils and gasolines or from inaccurate measuring and mixing. This could result in readjustment of the idle needle to compensate for variations in the fuel/oil mixture. To prevent the necessity for constant readjustment of the carburetor from one batch of fuel to the next, always be consistent. Prepare each batch of fuel exactly the same as the previous one.

Premixed fuel sold at some marinas is not recommended for use. The quality and consistency of premixed fuel can vary greatly. The possibility of engine damage resulting from using an incorrect fuel mixture far outweighs the convenience offered by premixed fuel. This is especially true if the marina uses alcohol or other additives in its gasoline.

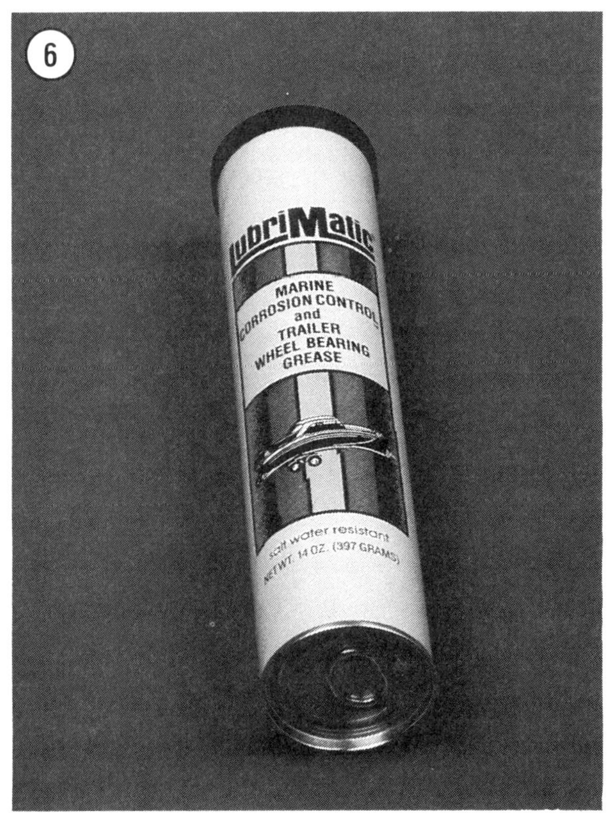

OIL INJECTION SYSTEM (2-STROKES)

Some owners object to the mess of dealing with premix so outboard manufacturers offer oil injection on some models, usually the larger ones. Oil is kept in a small onboard tank and blended with the fuel on demand. This may be added in some constant fuel/oil ratio or the outboard may be equipped to provide a variable ratio. The fuel tank in any oil injection outboard system contains ordinary fuel without oil. Not only does this eliminate the mess of premix, it allows more precise control of the amount of oil injected.

OTHER LUBRICANTS

Gear Oil

Gear lubricants are assigned SAE viscosity numbers under the same system as 4-stroke engine oil. Gear lubricant falls into the SAE 70-250 range (**Figure 5**). Some gear lubricants are multigrade; for example, SAE 85W-90 is a common grade of gear lubricant.

Three types of marine gear lubricant are generally available: SAE 90 hypoid gear lubricant is designed for older manual-shift units; Type C gear lubricant contains additives designed for electric shift mechanisms; High viscosity gear lubricant is a heavier oil designed to withstand the shock loading of high-performance engines or units subjected to severe duty use. Always use a gear lubricant of the type specified by the unit's manufacturer.

Grease

The National Lubricating Grease Institute (NLGI) grades greases by number according to the consistency of the grease. These ratings range from No. 000 to No. 6, with No. 6 being the most solid. A typical multipurpose grease is NLGI No. 2 (**Figure 6**). For specific applications, equipment manufacturers may require grease with an additive such as molybdenum disulfide (MOS2).

ENGINE FLUSHING

Manufacturers differ in their recommendations to flush an outboard motor. The best advice is to flush the engine after each use, particularly in saltwater or very silty water. Special flushing attachments to connect a garden hose to the motor are available. Here is a general procedure that should work for almost any outboard motor.

1. Attach a flushing device according to its manufacturer's instructions.
2. Connect a garden hose between a water tap and the flushing device. See **Figure 7**.
3. Open the water tap partially. Do not use full pressure.
4. Shift into NEUTRAL, then start the engine. Keep the engine at idle speed.
5. Adjust the water flow so that there is a slight loss of water around the rubber cups of the flushing device.
6. Check the engine to make sure that water is emerging from the "tell-tale" nozzle. If not, stop the engine immediately and determine the cause of the problem.

CAUTION
Flush the engine for at least 5 minutes after use in saltwater.

7. Flush the engine until the discharged water is clear. Stop the engine.
8. Close the water tap and remove the flushing device from the gearcase.

SHEAR PIN REPLACEMENT

On small outboard motors, the output shaft couples to the propeller with a shear pin. A large nut secured with a cotter pin keeps the propeller on the shaft. If the propeller hits an obstruction, the shear pin breaks, preventing any damage to the engine or propeller. When the shear pin breaks, the engine still runs, but the propeller cannot spin until the pin is replaced.

To replace a shear pin:

1. Straighten the ends of the cotter pin and remove it. See **Figure 8**, typical.
2. Unscrew the hub nut.

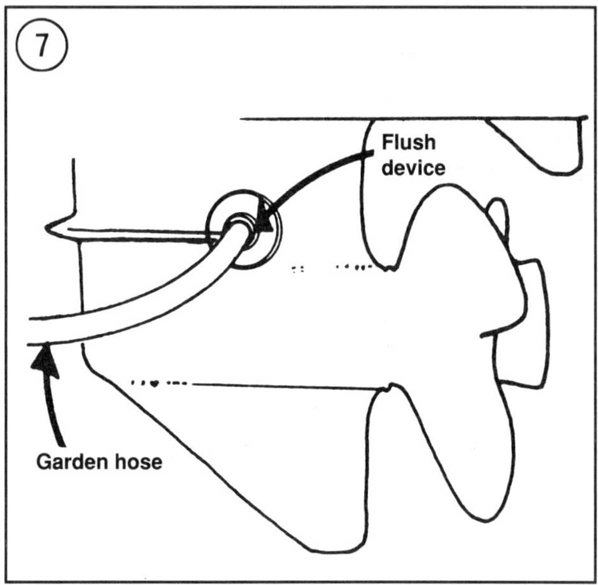

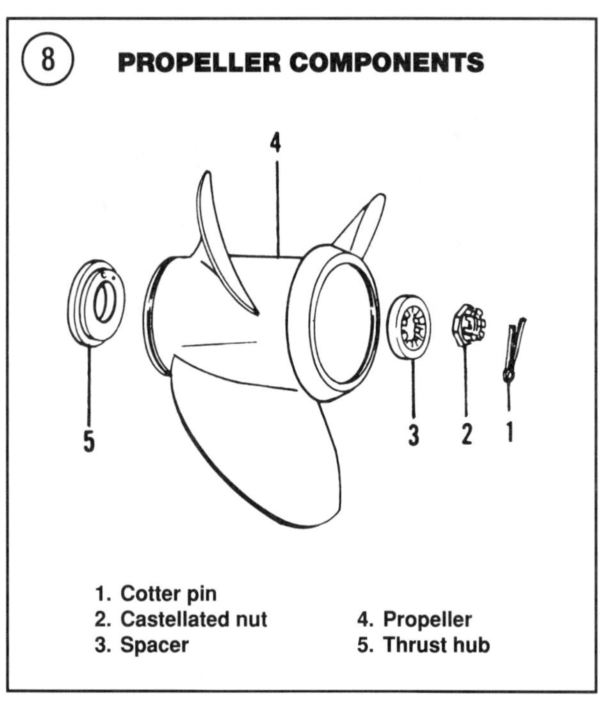

3. Pull off the propeller.
4. Remove broken halves of the shear pin.
5. Install a new shear pin in the shaft. See **Figure 9**.

CAUTION
Do not substitute anything else for the shear pin. Use a shear pin made specifically for the purpose. Substitutes may be too strong and not shear properly, causing expensive engine damage.

6. Install propeller.
7. Install hub nut finger-tight.
8. Loosen the nut as necessary to align shaft holes with nut and install cotter pin. Bend ends of pin over to secure it.

CAUTION
Do not tighten nut to align holes. Overtightening may prevent the shear pin from breaking when necessary to protect the engine.

9 **PROPELLER COMPONENTS**

1. Cotter pin
2. Propeller
3. Shear pin

LUBRICATION

Changing Drive Unit Oil

Oil in the drive unit must be changed at least every 100 hours of operation. Most models have a screw-in drain plug at the bottom of the unit. On some, there is a separate filler hole, though others use the drain as a filler hole. See the owner's manual or shop manual for your engine for details.

Use the special lubricant recommended by the manufacturer. Don't make any substitutes.

CAUTION
Do not use regular automotive gear lube in the lower drive unit. Its expansion and foam characteristics are not suitable for marine use.

Linkages and Cables

Throttle and choke linkage to the carburetor, and gear shift linkage and steering cables (if equipped), must be lubricated every 100 hours. Follow the manufacturer's recommendation for lubricants.

CAUTION
Lubricant substitutions are risky even for general lubrication. Some excellent quality white greases on the market are fine for automotive and general use, but get gummy in a salt environment.

ANTICORROSION MAINTENANCE

1. Flush the cooling system with freshwater as described under *Engine Flushing* in this chapter after each use in saltwater. Wash the exterior with freshwater.
2. Dry the exterior of the motor and apply primer over any paint nicks and scratches. Do

4

not use antifouling paints containing mercury or copper. Do not paint sacrificial anodes or the trim tab.

3. Check sacrificial anodes and replace any that are less than 2/3 their original size. To test for proper anode installation, proceed as follows:
   a. Calibrate an ohmmeter on the R x 1000 or high-ohm scale.
   b. Connect one ohmmeter lead to a good engine ground and the remaining lead to the anode. If necessary, clean a spot on the anode and the engine to ensure a good contact. The resistance should be very low.
   c. If the resistance is high, remove the anode and thoroughly clean the mounting surfaces of the anode, the motor and the threads of the mounting screws.
   d. Reinstall the anode and retest as previously described. If the resistance is still high between the anode and motor, replace the anode.

4. Check for corrosion between the gearcase housing and propeller shaft bearing housing. If allowed to accumulate it can eventually split the housing and destroy the lower unit assembly. If the motor is used in saltwater, remove the propeller and bearing housing at least once per year for inspection. See the appropriate shop manual for details.

TUNE-UP

A tune-up consists of a series of inspections, adjustments and parts replacement to compensate for normal wear and deterioration of outboard motor components. Regular tune-up is important to maintain sufficient power, performance and economy. Most manufacturers recommend a tune-up every 6 months or 50 hours of operation, whichever comes first. In limited use, the engine should be tuned at least once per year.

Since proper outboard motor operation depends on a number of interrelated system functions, a tune-up consisting of only one or two corrections will seldom give satisfactory results. For best results, a thorough and systematic procedure of analysis and correction is necessary.

Prior to performing a tune-up, flush the outboard motor as described in this chapter to check for satisfactory water pump operation.

The tune-up process recommended by most manufacturers includes the following:

a. Compression test.
b. Spark plug service.
c. Lower unit and water pump check.
d. Fuel system service.
e. Remove carbon deposits from combustion chamber(s).
f. Ignition system service.
g. Battery, starter motor and solenoid check, if so equipped.
h. Inspect wiring harness.
i. Engine synchronization and adjustment.
j. On-the-water performance test.

Any time the fuel or ignition systems are adjusted or require parts replacement, the engine timing, synchronization and linkage adjustment *must* be checked. The procedures vary considerably from model to model. Refer to the appropriate shop manual for details. Perform the synchronization and linkage adjustment procedure *before* running the performance test.

Compression Test

An accurate compression test gives an indication of the condition of the basic working parts of the engine. It is also an important first step in any tune-up, as a motor with low or uneven compression between cylinders cannot be satisfactorily tuned. Any compression problem discovered during the test must be corrected before continuing with the tune-up procedure.

1. Start the engine and warm to normal operating temperature.
2. Remove all spark plugs as described in this chapter.

3. Connect a compression tester to the top spark plug hole according to its manufacturer's instructions. See **Figure 10**.
4. Make sure the throttle is in the wide-open position, then crank the engine through at least 4 compression strokes. Record the gauge reading.
5. Repeat Step 3 and Step 4 on each remaining cylinder.

While minimum cylinder compression should not be less than 100 psi (689 kPa), the actual readings are not as important as the differences in readings between cylinders when interpreting the results. A variation of more than 15 psi (103.4 kPa) indicates a problem with the lower reading cylinder, such as defective head gasket, worn or sticking piston rings and/or scored pistons or cylinder walls. On V4 and V6 cross flow motors, compare compression readings from cylinders on the same bank, not cylinders on opposite banks.

If unequal or low compression is noted, pour a tablespoon of engine oil into the suspect cylinder and repeat Steps 3 and 4. If this raises the compression by 10 psi (69 kPa) or more, the piston rings are worn and should be replaced.

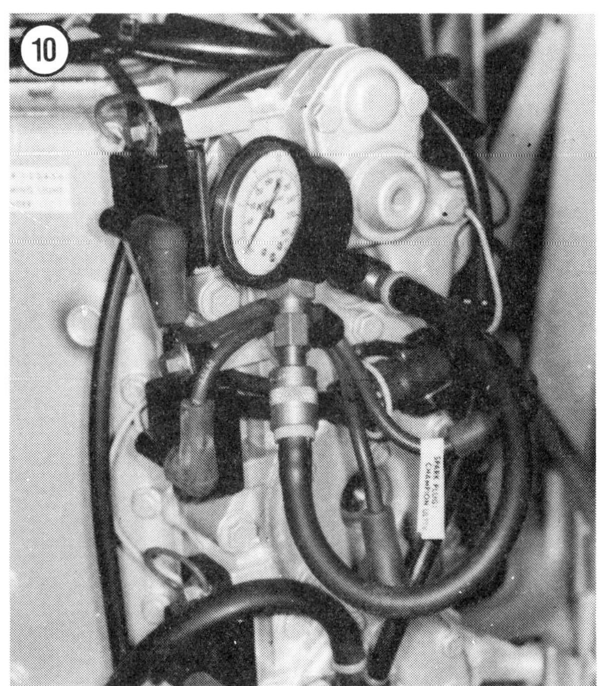
10

If evidence of overheating is noted (discolored or scorched paint), but the compression test is normal, check the cylinder(s) visually through the transfer ports for possible scoring. A cylinder can be slightly scored and still deliver a relatively good compression reading. In such a case, it is also good practice to recheck the water pump and cooling system for possible causes of overheating.

If the outboard runs normally and the compression test is acceptable, continue the tune-up procedure.

4

Spark Plug Selection

Use the spark plug type and heat range recommended by the manufacturer under most running conditions. Some recommend spark plugs with conventional electrodes, while others recommend surface gap spark plugs if the outboard motor is subjected to sustained high-speed operation.

Under severe operating conditions, the recommended spark plug may foul or overheat. In such cases, check the ignition and carburetion systems to be sure they are operating correctly. If no defect is found, replace the spark plug with one of a hotter or colder heat range as required.

CAUTION
Some models, particularly larger ones, use suppression spark plugs. Using non-suppression spark plugs will result in erratic ignition system operation, and may interfere with electronic equipment used aboard.

Spark Plug Removal

1. Blow any foreign material from around the spark plugs using compressed air.

CAUTION
When the spark plugs are removed, dirt surrounding the base of the plugs can fall into the cylinder, causing serious engine damage.

2. Disconnect the spark plug wires by twisting the wire boot back and forth while pulling outward. Pulling on the wire instead of the boot will cause internal damage to the wire.
3. Remove the spark plugs using an appropriate size spark plug wrench or socket. Arrange the plugs in the order removed, so you know which cylinder they were removed from.
4. Examine each spark plug. See **Figure 11** for a conventional spark plug and **Figure 12** for a surface gap plug. Compare plug condition with **Figure 13** (conventional) or **Figure 14** (surface gap). Spark plug condition can be an indicator of engine condition and warn of developing trouble.
5. Check the make and heat range of each spark plug. All should be of the same make and heat range.
6. Discard the plugs. Although they could be cleaned and reused if in good condition, the best tune-up results will be obtained by installing new spark plugs.

Spark Plug Gapping (Conventional)

New spark plugs should be carefully gapped to ensure reliable, consistent plug operation. Use a special spark plug tool with a wire gauge to measure electrode gap. **Figure 15** shows a common spark plug gapping tool.

1. If necessary, install the spark plug's gasket onto the plug. On some brands of plugs, the terminal end (**Figure 16**) must also be screwed onto the plug.
2. Measure the plug gap. If the gap is correct, you will feel a slight drag as you pull the wire through. If you don't feel any drag, or if you cannot put the wire gauge, bend the side electrode with the gapping tool (**Figure 17**) to change the gap as necessary. Remeasure the gap after adjusting.

CAUTION
Never close the electrode gap by tapping the plug on a solid surface. Doing so can damage the plug internally. Always use the gapping tool to open or close the gap.

Spark Plug Installation

Improper installation is a common cause of poor spark plug performance in outboard motors. The gasket on the plug must be fully compressed against a clean plug seat to provide an effective seal against combustion gases, but also to provide effective heat transfer to cool the plug.

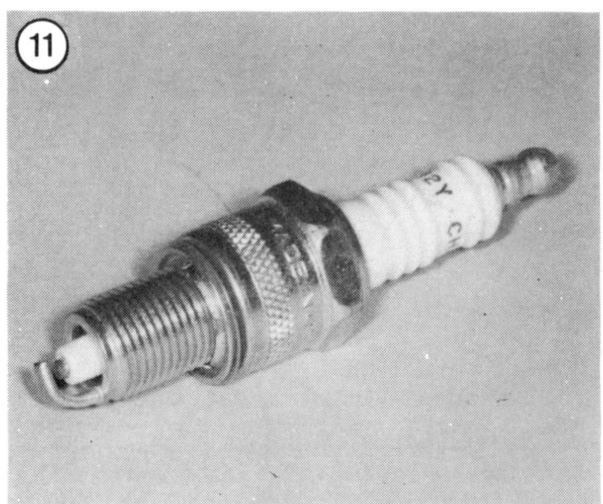
11

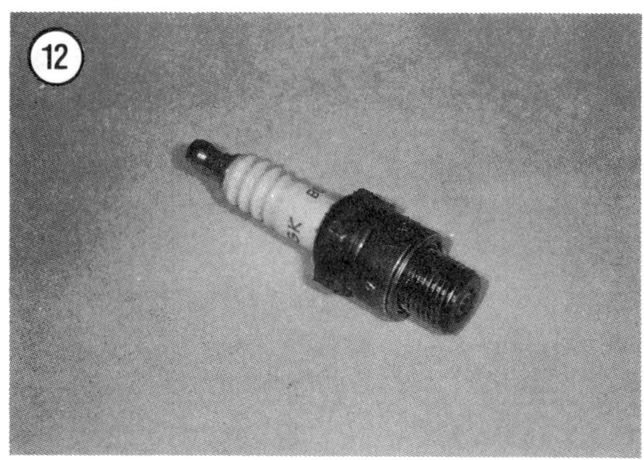
12

(13)

SPARK PLUG ANALYSIS (CONVENTIONAL GAP SPARK PLUGS)

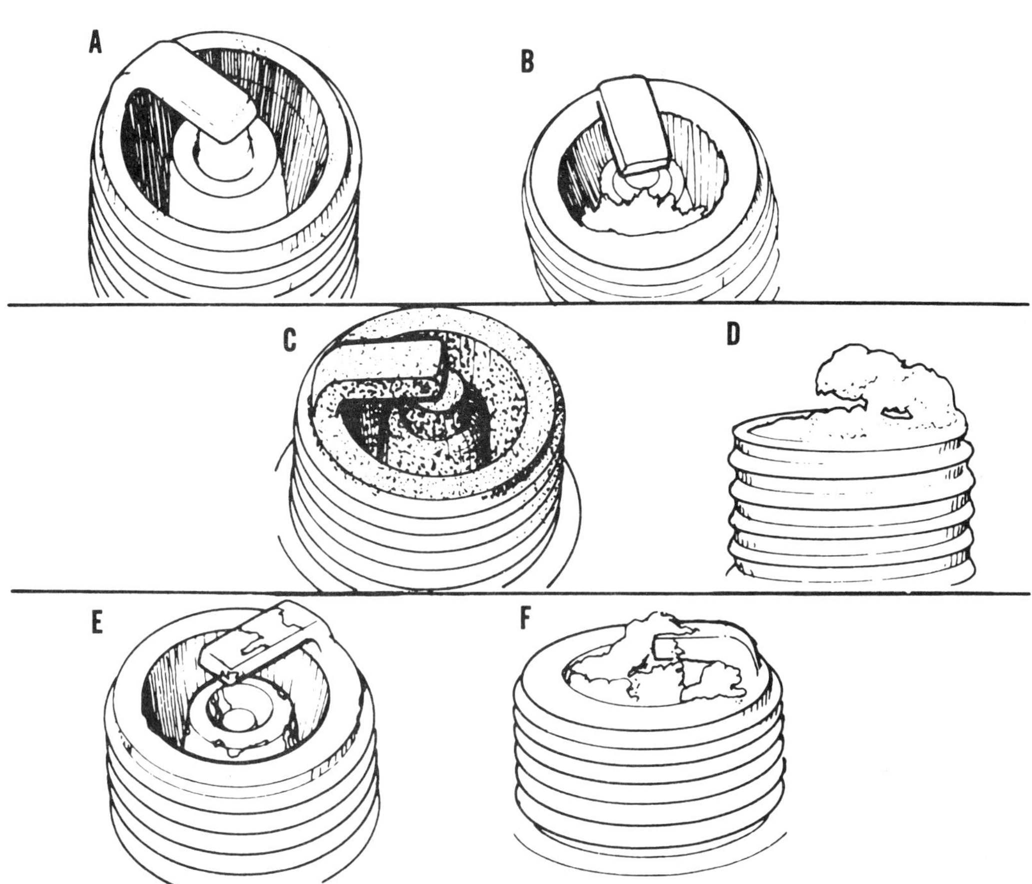

A. Normal—Light tan to gray color of insulator indicates correct heat range. Few deposits are present and the electrodes are not burned.

B. Core bridging—These defects are caused by excessive combustion chamber deposits striking and adhering to the firing end of the plug. In this case, they wedge or fuse between the electrode and core nose. They originate from the piston and cylinder head surfaces. Deposits are formed by one or more of the following:
   a. Excessive carbon in cylinder.
   b. Use of non-recommended oils.
   c. Immediate high-speed operation after prolonged trolling.
   d. Improper fuel-oil ratio.

C. Wet fouling—Damp or wet, black carbon coating over entire firing end of plug. Forms sludge in some engines. Caused by one or more of the following:
   a. Spark plug heat range too cold.
   b. Prolonged trolling.
   c. Low-speed carburetor adjustment too rich.
   d. Improper fuel-oil ratio.
   e. Induction manifold bleed-off passage obstructed.
   f. Worn or defective breaker points.

D. Gap bridging—Similar to core bridging, except the combustion particles are wedged or fused between the electrodes. Causes are the same.

E. Overheating—Badly worn electrodes and premature gap wear are indicative of this problem, along with a gray or white "blistered" appearance on the insulator. Caused by one or more of the following:
   a. Spark plug heat range too hot.
   b. Incorrect propeller usage, causing engine to lug.
   c. Worn or defective water pump.
   d. Restricted water intake or restriction somewhere in the cooling system.

F. Ash deposits or lead fouling—Ash deposits are light brown to white in color and result from use of fuel or oil additives. Lead fouling produces a yellowish brown discoloration and can be avoided by using unleaded fuels.

4

SURFACE GAP SPARK PLUG ANALYSIS

A

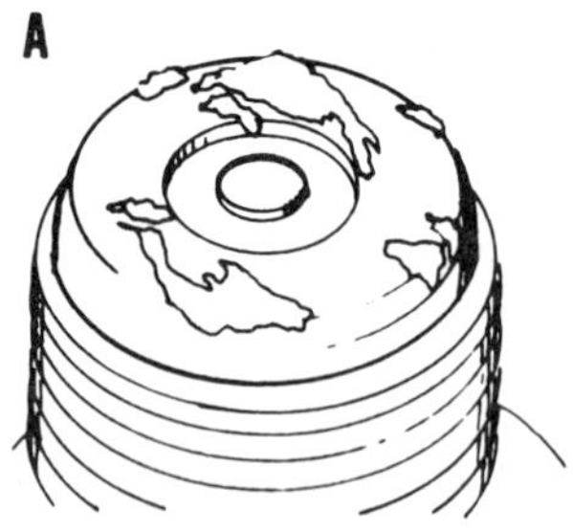

B

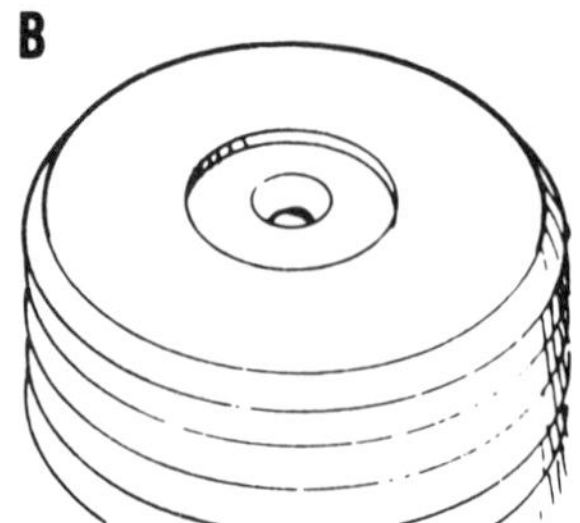

C

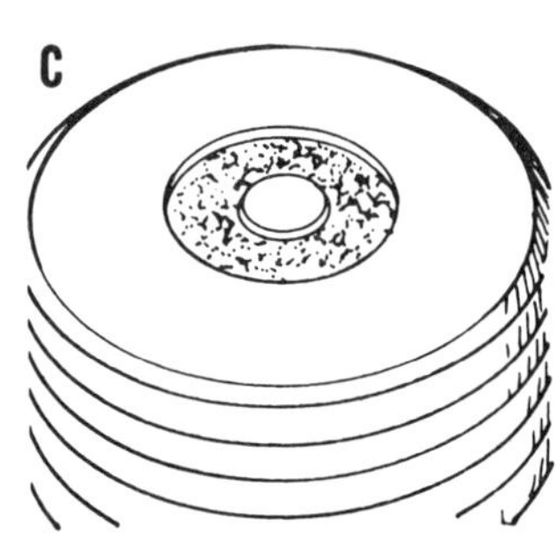

D

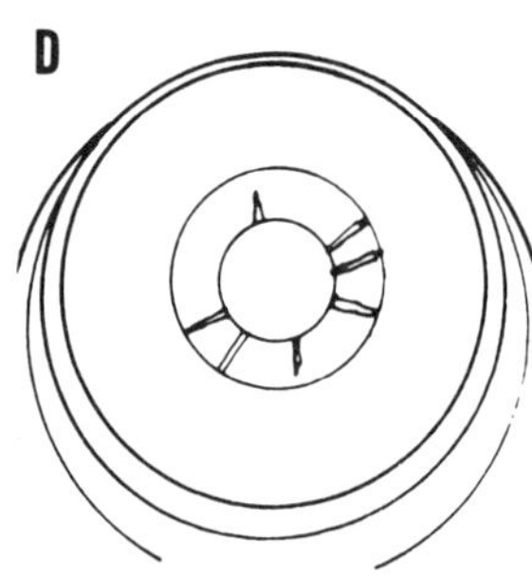

E

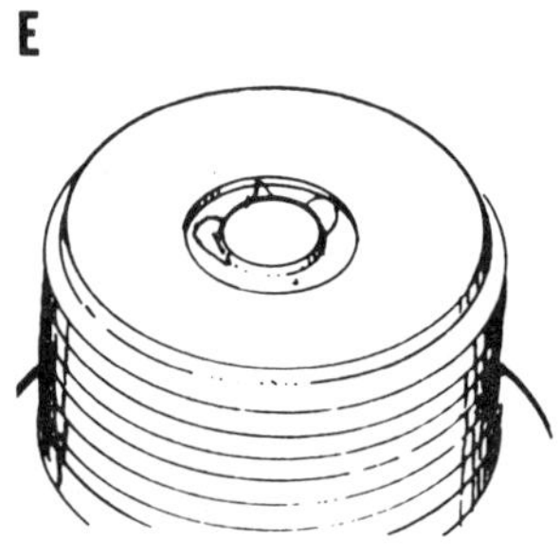

F

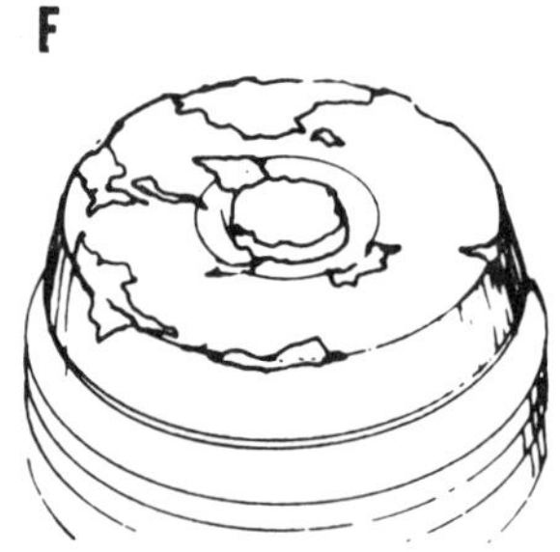

A. Normal—Light tan or gray colored deposits indicate that the engine/ignition system condition is good. Electrode wear indicates normal spark rotation.

B. Worn out—Excessive electrode wear can cause hard starting or a misfire during acceleration.

C. Cold fouled—Wet oil-fuel deposits are caused by "drowning" the plug with raw fuel mix during cranking, overrich carburetion or an improper fuel-oil ratio. Weak ignition will also contribute to this condition.

D. Carbon tracking—Electrically conductive deposits on the firing end provide a low-resistance path for the voltage. Carbon tracks form and can cause misfires.

E. Concentrated arc—Multi-colored appearance is normal. It is caused by electricity consistently following the same firing path. Arc path changes with deposit conductivity and gap erosion.

F. Aluminum throw-off—Caused by preignition. This is not a plug problem but the result of engine damage. Check engine to determine cause and extent of damage.

1. Inspect the spark plug threads in the cylinder head and clean with a thread chaser if necessary. See **Figure 18.** Thoroughly clean the spark plug seating area in the cylinder head prior to installing new plugs.

2. Screw each spark plug into the cylinder head by hand, until seated. If force is necessary to turn the plug, it may be cross threaded. Remove the plug and try again.

3. Tighten the plugs using a suitable torque wrench to 17-20 ft.-lb. (23-27 N.m). If a torque wrench is not available, seat the plug finger-tight, then tighten an additional 1/4 turn with the appropriate size wrench.

4. Inspect each spark plug wire before reconnecting it. If insulation is damaged or deteriorated, install a new wire. Push the wire onto the plug. Make sure the wire terminal is fully seated on the plug.

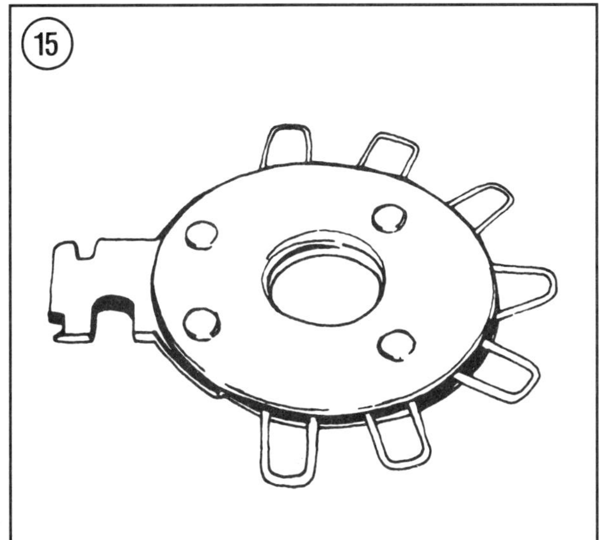

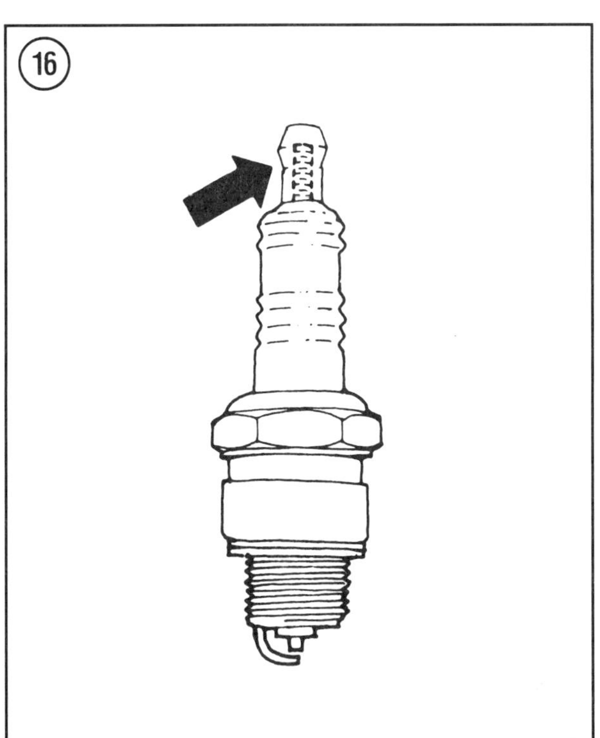

Lower Unit and Water Pump

A faulty water pump or one that performs poorly can result in extensive engine damage from overheating. Therefore, it is good practice to replace the pump impeller, seals and gaskets once per year or any time the lower unit is

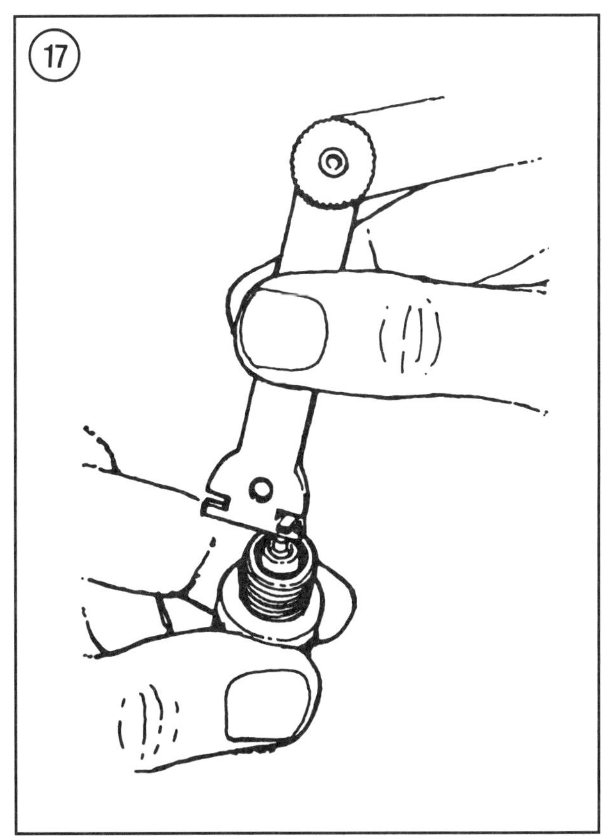

removed for service. See the appropriate shop manual for the procedure.

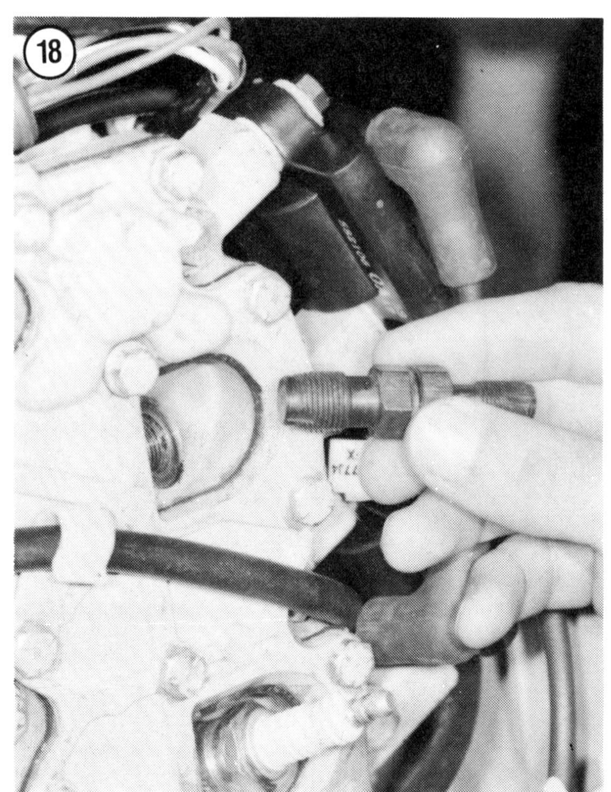

Fuel Lines

1. Inspect all fuel hoses and lines for kinks, leaks, deterioration or other damage.
2. Disconnect the fuel lines and blow out with compressed air to dislodge any contamination or foreign material.
3. Coat fuel line fittings sparingly with a light gasket sealing compound then reconnect the lines.

Fuel Filter

Most outboards have a disposable, inline fuel filter (**Figure 19**) to remove minor debris from the fuel. Replace the filter once per year or sooner if contaminated fuel is encountered. In addition, some models equipped with a fuel pump have a filter screen in the pump under the pump cover (**Figure 20**).

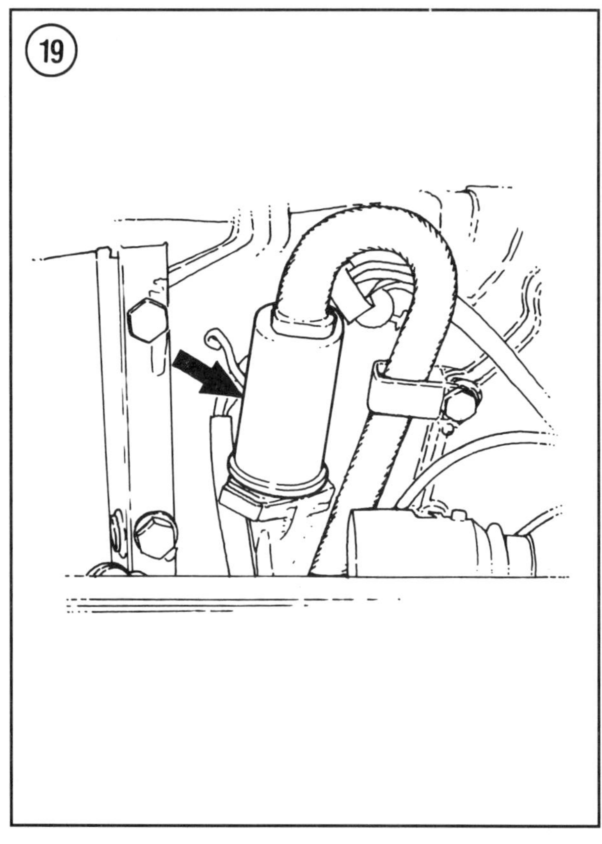

On models equipped with an integral fuel tank, a filter screen may be installed on the fuel shut-off valve (**Figure 21**) attached to the fuel tank. The filter should be removed and cleaned once per year, or sooner if contaminated fuel is en-countered.

Ignition Service

Small motors usually have breaker points and a condenser which should be replaced during the tune-up procedure. Refer to the shop manual for your model.

Larger motors often have electronic ignitions which do not require any kind of periodic parts replacement, but may need adjustment. Refer to the shop manual for your model.

Internal Wiring Harness Check

1. Check the wiring harness for frayed or chafed insulation. Repair as necessary.
2. Check for loose connections between the wires and terminal ends.
3. Check the harness connector for bent electrical pins.

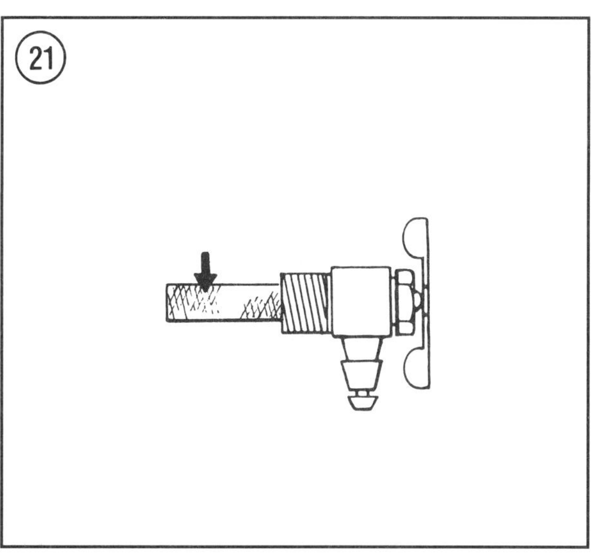

4. Check the harness connector for corrosion. Clean as necessary.

Removing Combustion Chamber Carbon

All engines suffer somewhat from carbon accumulation on the piston crowns and combustion chambers. Carbon deposits caused by oil in the fuel makes accumulation more rapid in 2-stroke engines.

Carbon deposits effectively raise the compression ratio and make the engine more prone to knock and ping with the normal grade of gasoline. In addition, carbon particles may glow from combustion and preignite the incoming fuel/air mixture before the spark plug can; preignition can cause considerable engine damage.

Every 200 hours or so, the cylinder head must be removed and all carbon deposits cleaned away. This is a job for your dealer unless you have the proper skills and a shop manual for your particular engine.

Several fuel additives are available to reduce formation of carbon in combustion chambers and exhaust system. These should be used regularly to prevent buildup.

Performance Test

The boat should be performance tested with an average load and with the motor tilted at an angle that will allow the boat to ride on an even keel. If equipped with an adjustable trim tab, it should be properly adjusted to allow the boat to steer in either direction with equal ease.

Check the engine rpm at wide-open throttle. If not within the maximum rpm range specified for your motor, check the propeller pitch. A propeller with excessive pitch will not allow the engine to reach the correct operating range; a propeller with insufficient pitch will allow the engine to overspeed.

For optimum results, adjust the idle mixture and idle speed with the outboard running at idle speed in forward gear, with the correct propeller installed and boat movement unrestrained.

High-Elevation Modification

If the outboard motor is used primarily at high-altitude, the carburetor should be rejetted to lean the fuel mixture due to the reduction in air density.

The propeller used must allow the motor to run within the recommended speed range. The correct propeller should place full throttle speed in the middle of the recommended operating range. Changing the propeller for operation at high altitude will recover only that engine power lost by not operating within the proper rpm range.

Always rejet and prop the outboard for the lowest elevation at which the boat will be operated to prevent the possibility of power head damage from an excessively lean mixture. If the boat is to be used at both high and low elevations, you should have 2 sets of jets, and 2 propellers.

TROUBLESHOOTING

Nearly all modern outboards, if properly maintained, start very easily and run reliably. If the motor doesn't start quickly, especially if it has in the past, don't wear yourself out pulling and pulling on the starter cord. Find out what the problem is and fix it. The following are symptoms and the most likely cause of trouble.

1. Motor won't start.
   a. Check fuel in tank.
   b. Make sure that fuel line is properly connected to engine and remote tank.
   c. Prime carburetor again.
   d. Not enough choke. Pull choke out all the way. Make sure choke is functioning properly.
   e. Flooded engine. Usually strong smell of gas around engine. Push choke off, disconnect fuel line or shut off fuel petcock and crank until flooding is eliminated.
2. Motor won't idle.
   a. Dirty or defective spark plug(s). Remove and clean or replace.
   b. Carburetor adjustment. Adjust low speed adjustment until idle is correct.
   c. Wrong fuel/oil mixture.
3. Motor won't deliver sufficient power.
   a. Restriction in fuel line. Make sure fuel line is not kinked or blocked by dirt.
   b. Ignition system requires tune-up.
   c. Cylinder heads require decarbonizing.
4 Steam coming from exhaust outlets (engine overheating) .
   a. Water inlet blocked or restricted.
   b. Water pump defective.
5. Excessive vibration.
   a. Broken or bent propeller.
   b. One or more cylinders not firing (except single cylinder engines).
   c. Loose flywheel.
   d. Internal damage.
6. Starter motor won't crank.
   a. Battery low or dead.

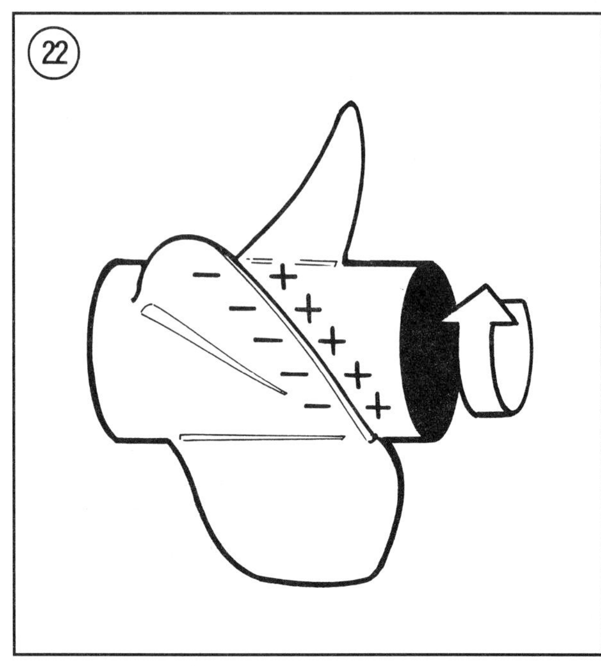

b. Corroded or broken wires to starter or solenoid.

c. Defective starter solenoid.

PROPELLERS

The propeller is the final link between the boat's drive system and the water. A perfectly maintained engine and hull are useless if the propeller is the wrong type or has been allowed to deteriorate. Although propeller selection for a specific situation is beyond the scope of this book, the following information on propeller construction and design will allow you to discuss the subject intelligently with your marine dealer.

How a Propeller Works

As the curved blades of a propeller rotate through the water, a high-pressure area is created on one side of the blade and a low-pressure area exists on the other side of the blade (**Figure 22**). The propeller moves toward the low-pressure area, carrying the boat with it.

Figure 23 identifies important features of a propeller which are designed to make different propellers suitable for different jobs.

The blade tip is the point on the blade farthest from the center of the propeller hub. The blade tip separates the leading edge from the trailing edge.

The leading edge is the edge of the blade nearest to the boat. During normal rotation, this is the area of the blade that first cuts through the water.

The trailing edge is the edge of the blade farthest from the boat.

The blade face is the surface of the blade that faces away from the boat. During normal rotation, high pressure exists on this side of the blade.

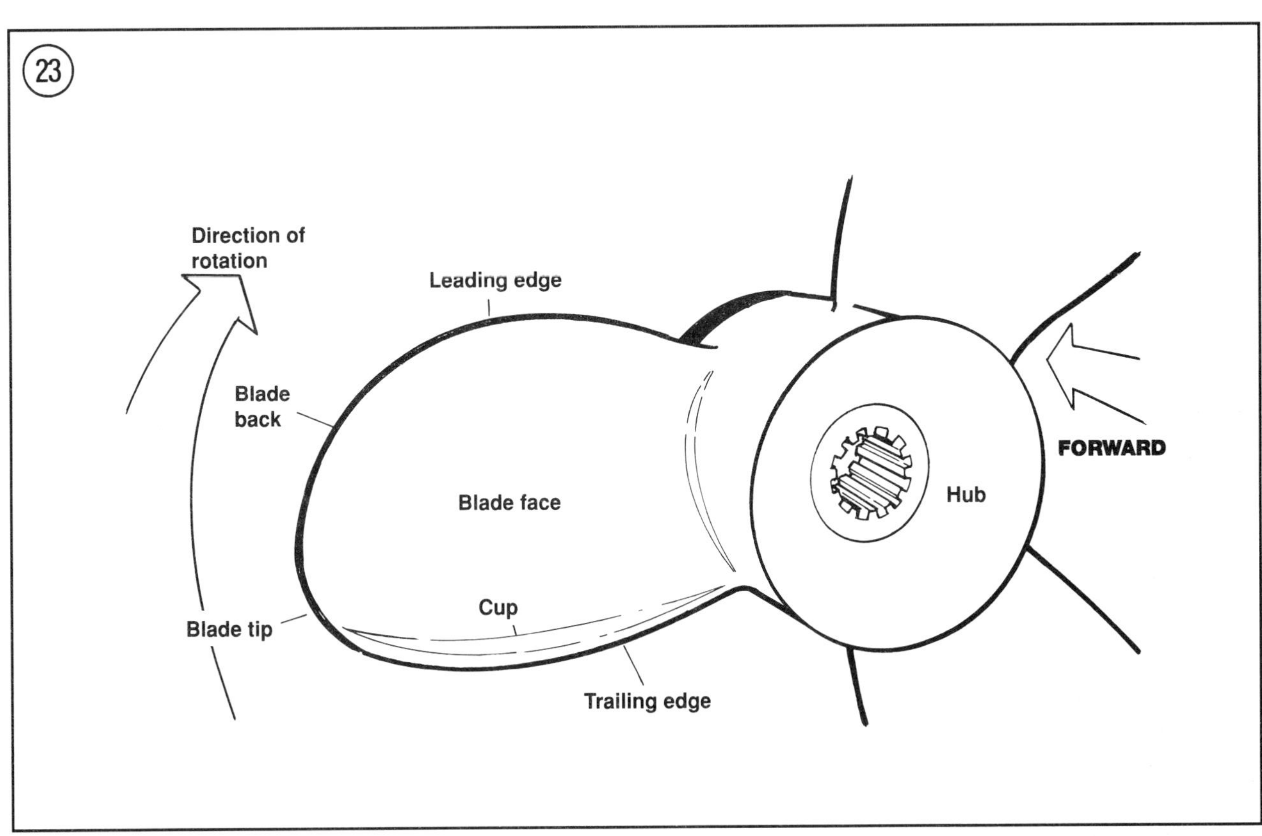

The blade back is the surface of the blade that faces toward the boat. During normal rotation, low pressure exists on this side of the blade.

The cup is a small curve or lip on the trailing edge of the blade.

The hub is the central portion of the propeller. It connects the blades to the propeller shaft (part of the boat's drive system). On some drive systems, engine exhaust is routed through the hub; in this case, the hub is made up of an outer and an inner portion, connected by ribs.

A diffuser ring is used on through-hub exhaust models to prevent exhaust gases from entering the blade area.

Diameter

Propeller diameter is the distance from the center of the hub to the blade tip, multiplied by 2. That is, it is the diameter of the circle formed by the blade tips during propeller rotation (**Figure 24**).

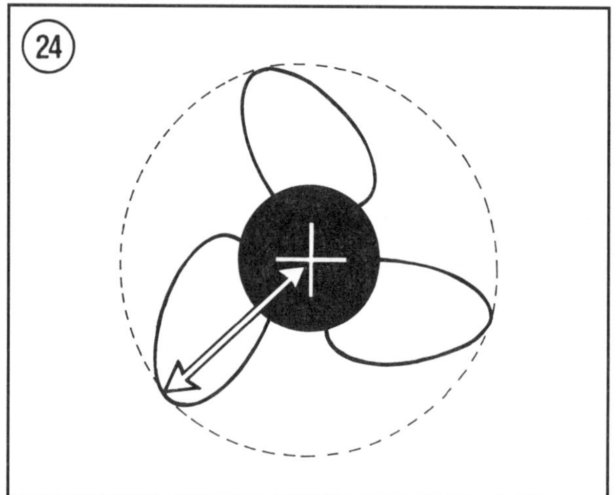

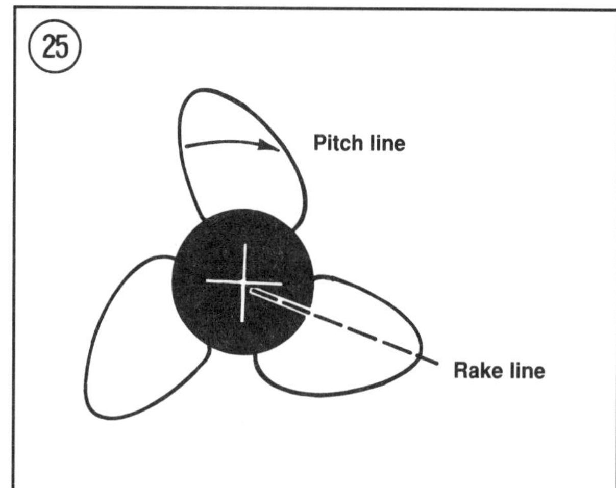

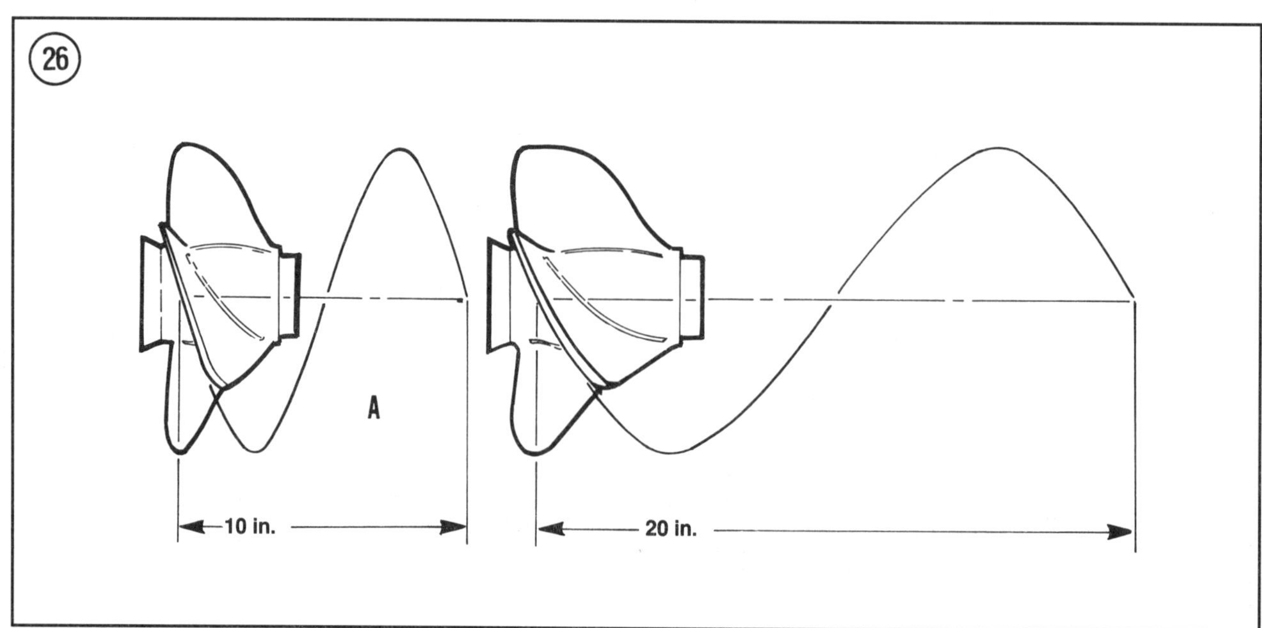

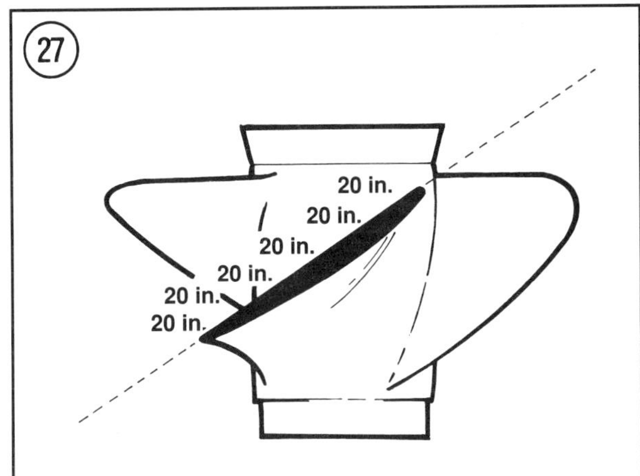

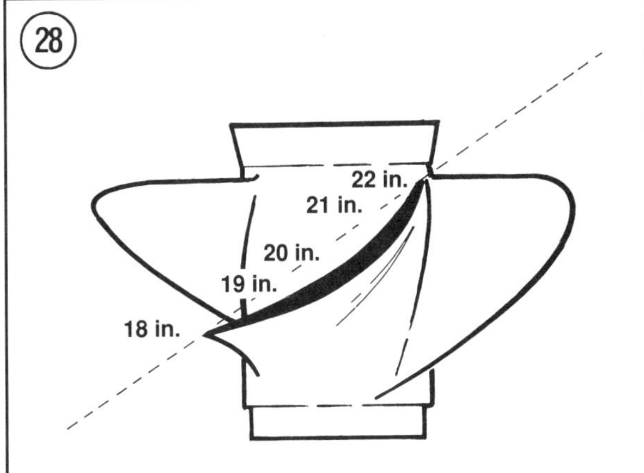

Pitch and rake

Propeller pitch and rake describe the placement of the blade in relation to the hub (**Figure 25**).

Pitch is expressed by the theoretical distance that the propeller would travel in one revolution. In A, **Figure 26**, the propeller would travel 10 inches in one revolution. In B, **Figure 26**, the propeller would travel 20 inches in one revolution. This distance is only theoretical; during actual operation, the propeller achieves about 80% of its rated travel due to propeller slippage.

Propeller blades can be constructed with constant pitch (**Figure 27**) or progressive pitch (**Figure 28**). Progressive pitch starts low at the leading edge and increases toward the trailing edge. The propeller pitch specification is the average of the pitch across the entire blade.

Blade rake is specified in degrees and is measured along a line from the center of the hub to the blade tip. A blade that is perpendicular to the hub (A, **Figure 29**) has 0 degrees of rake. A blade that is angled from perpendicular (B, **Figure 29**) has a rake expressed by its difference from per-

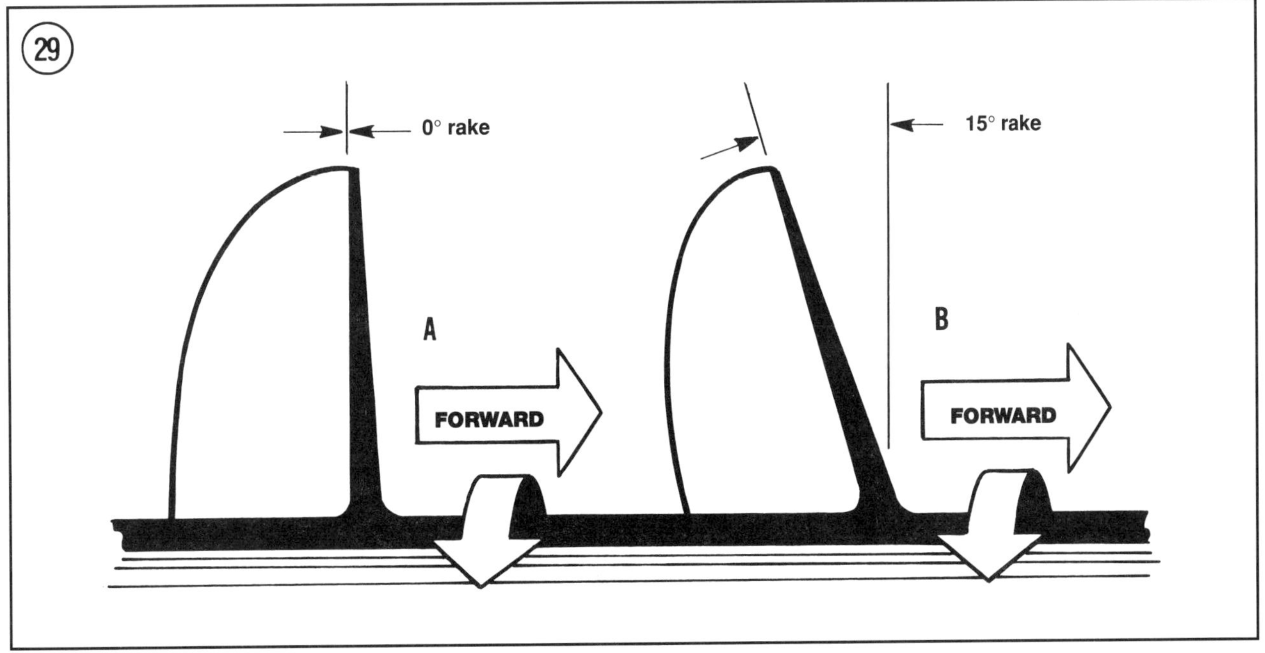

pendicular. Most propellers have rakes ranging from 0-20°.

Blade thickness

Blade thickness is not uniform at all points along the blade. For efficiency, blades should be as thin as possible at all points while retaining enough strength to move the boat. Blades tend to be thicker where they meet the hub and thinner at the blade tip **(Figure 30)**. This is to support the heavier loads at the hub section of the blade. This thickness is dependent on the strength of the material used.

When cut along a line from the leading edge to the trailing edge in the central portion of the blade **(Figure 31)**, the propeller blade resembles an airplane wing. The blade face, where high pressure exists during normal rotation, is almost flat. The blade back, where low pressure exists during normal rotation, is curved, with the thinnest portions at the edges and the thickest portion at the center.

Propellers that run only partially submerged, as in racing applications, may have a wedge-shaped cross-section **(Figure 32)**. The leading edge is very thin; the blade thickness increases toward the trailing edge, where it is the thickest. If a propeller such as this is run totally submerged, it is very inefficient.

Number of blades

The number of blades used on a propeller is a compromise between efficiency and vibration. A one-blade propeller would be the most efficient, but it would also create high levels of vibration. As blades are added, efficiency decreases, but so do vibration levels. Most propellers have three blades, representing the most practical trade-off between efficiency and vibration.

Material

Propeller materials are chosen for strength, corrosion resistance and economy. Stainless

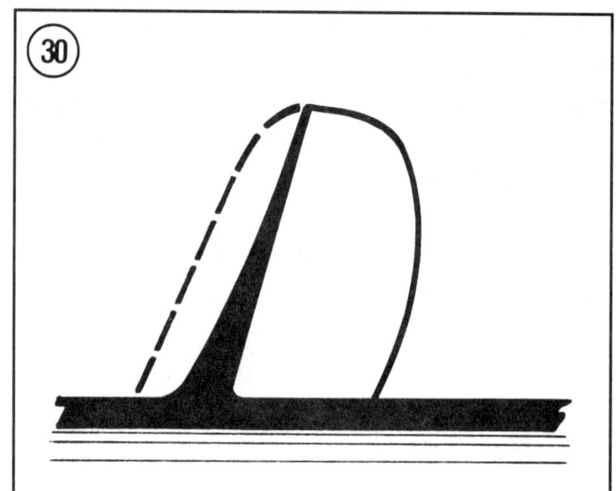

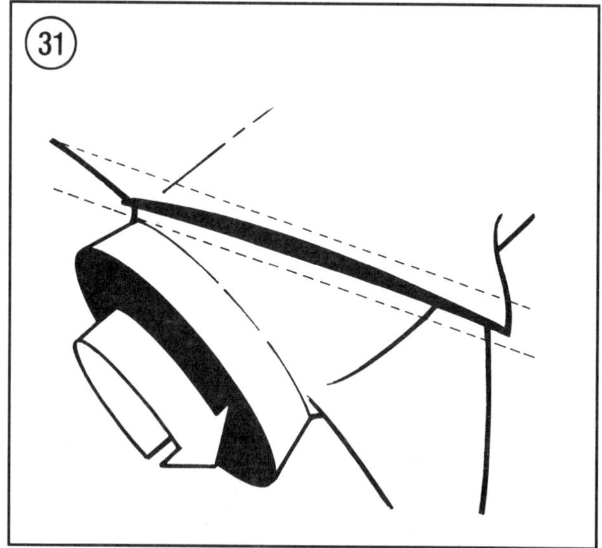

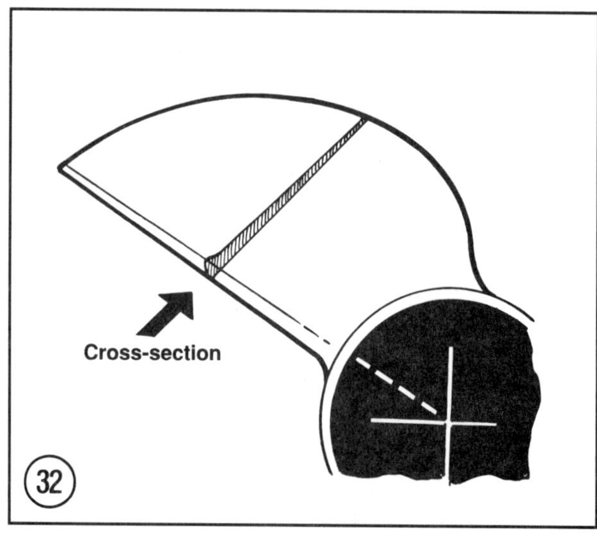

steel, aluminum and bronze are the most commonly used materials. Bronze is quite strong but rather expensive. Stainless steel is more common than bronze because of its combination of strength and lower cost. Aluminum alloys are the least expensive but usually lack the strength of steel. Plastic propellers may be used in some low horsepower applications. Plastic propellers also make an excellent onboard spare.

Direction of rotation

Propellers are made for both right-hand and left-hand rotation although right-hand is the most commonly used. When seen from behind the boat in forward motion, a right-hand propeller turns clockwise and a left-hand propeller turns counterclockwise. Off the boat, you can tell the difference by observing the angle of the blades (**Figure 33**). A right-hand propeller's blades slant from the upper left to the lower right; a left-hand propeller's blades are the opposite.

Cavitation and Ventilation

Cavitation and ventilation are *not* interchangeable terms; they refer to two distinct problems encountered during propeller operation.

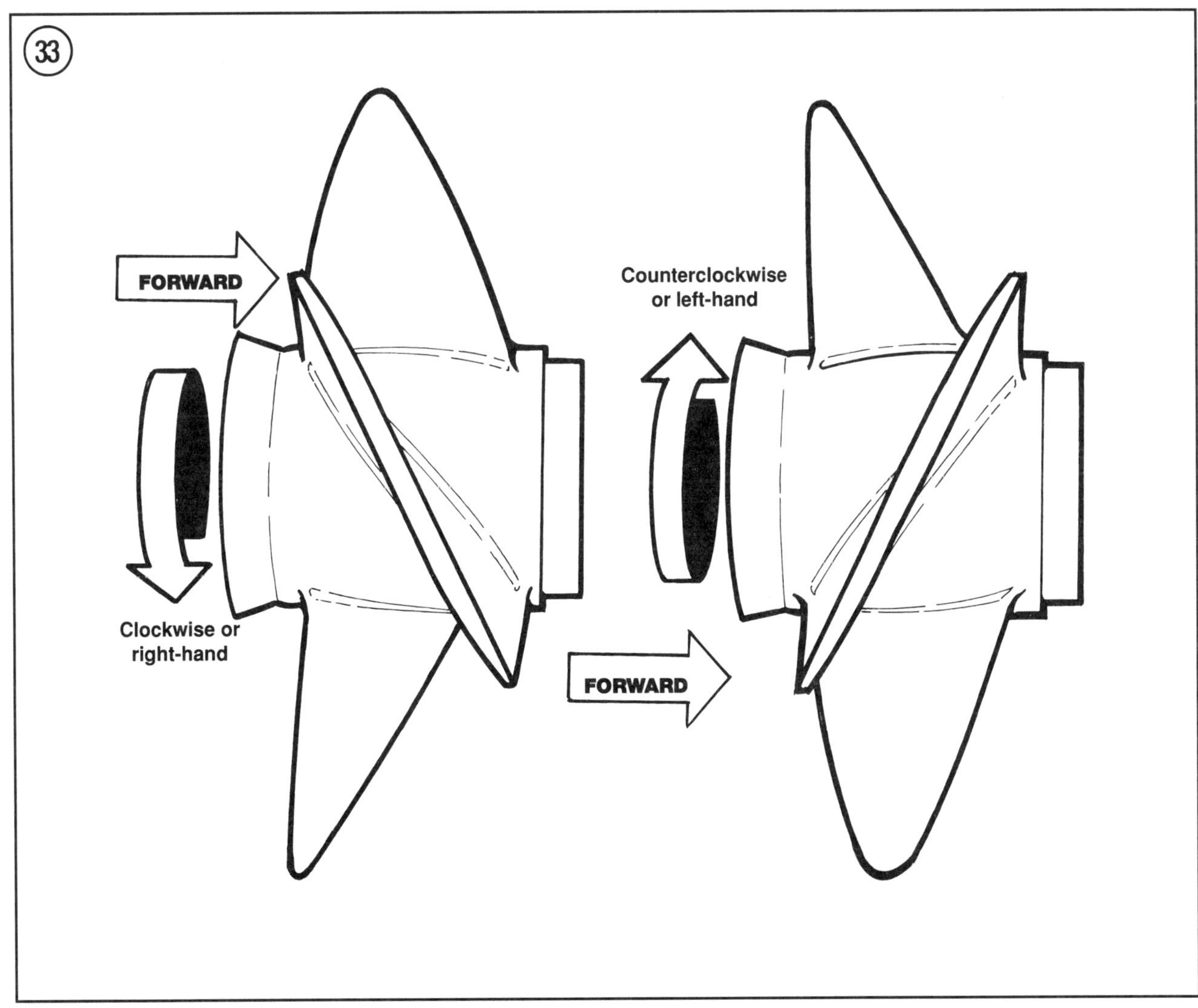

To understand cavitation, you must first understand the relationship between pressure and the boiling point of water. At sea level, water will boil at 212° F. As pressure increases, such as within an engine's closed cooling system, the boiling point of water increases—it will boil at some temperature higher than 212° F. The opposite is also true. As pressure decreases, water will boil at a temperature lower than 212° F. If pressure drops low enough, water will boil at typical ambient temperatures of 50-60° F.

We have said that, during normal propeller operation, low-pressure exists on the blade back. Normally, the pressure does not drop low enough for boiling to occur. However, poor blade design or selection, or blade damage can cause an unusual pressure drop on a small area of the blade (**Figure 34**). Boiling can occur in this small area. As the water boils, air bubbles form. As the boiling water passes to a higher pressure area of the blade, the boiling stops and the bubbles collapse. The collapsing bubbles release enough energy to erode the surface of the blade.

This entire process of pressure drop, boiling and bubble collapse is called "cavitation." The damage caused by the collapsing bubbles is called a "cavitation burn." It is important to remember that cavitation is caused by a decrease in pressure, *not* an increase in temperature.

Ventilation is not as complex a process as cavitation. Ventilation refers to air entering the blade area, either from above the surface of the water or from a through-hub exhaust system. As the blades meet the air, the propeller momentarily over-revs, losing most of its thrust. An added complication is that as the propeller over-revs, pressure on the blade back decreases and massive cavitation can occur.

Most outboards have a plate above the propeller area designed to keep surface air from entering the blade area (**Figure 35**). This plate is correctly called an "antiventilation plate," although you will often *see* it called an "anticavitation plate." Through hub exhaust systems also have specially designed hubs to keep exhaust gases from entering the blade area.

ACCIDENTAL IMMERSION

Immersion in water, fresh or salt, can mean the end for an outboard motor. Water finds its way into the motor where it can corrode precision parts beyond repair.

Obviously, the best protection against accidental immersion is prevention. A small chain

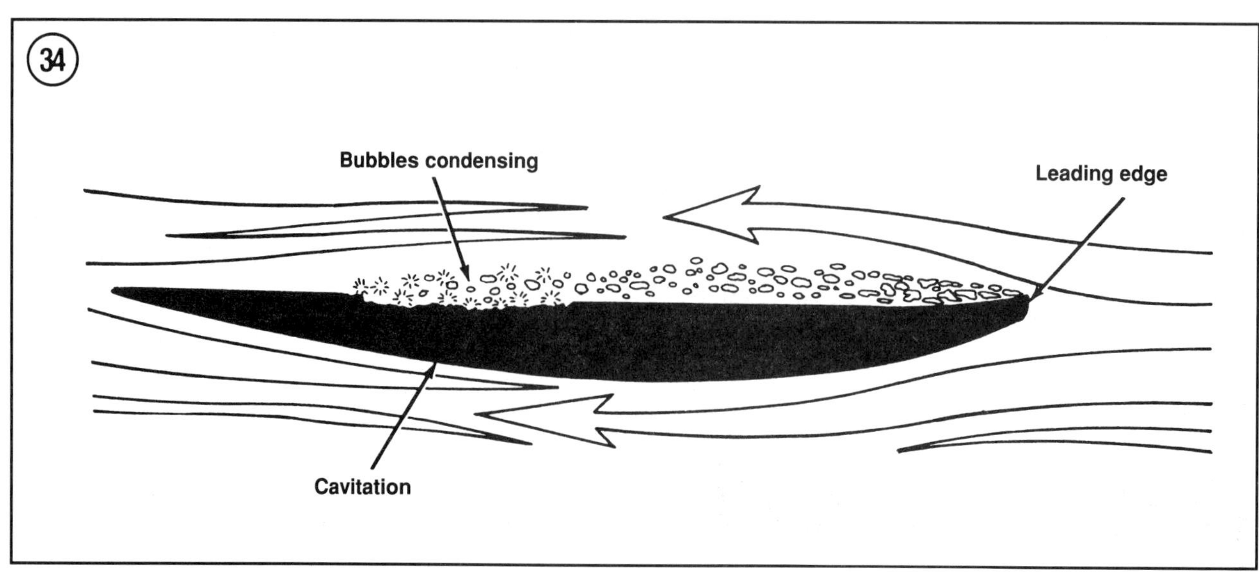

secured to the transom and a strong area of the outboard will prevent immersion and loss should the clamps loosen or the mounting bracket break.

If the motor was not running when submerged, chances of recovering the engine without damage are fairly good. However, if the motor was running, damage can be extensive. Most serious is the possibility that sand and dirt were drawn into the engine before it stopped.

CAUTION
If there is any sign that dirt or sand could have entered motor, do not use the procedure below or rotate the flywheel. Rinse off the motor with fresh water and take it to a repair shop within 3 hours. If this is not possible, resubmerge the motor in fresh water and take it in as soon as possible.

1. Rinse the motor with fresh water.
2. Disconnect the spark plug leads and remove the plugs.
3. Hold motor horizontally with the spark plug holes facing down. Rotate the flywheel with the starter cord 25 to 30 times to work out water.

CAUTION
If there is any binding when rotating the flywheel, go to Step 8 and do not attempt to start the motor. Most likely a connecting rod is bent. Have the motor serviced immediately.

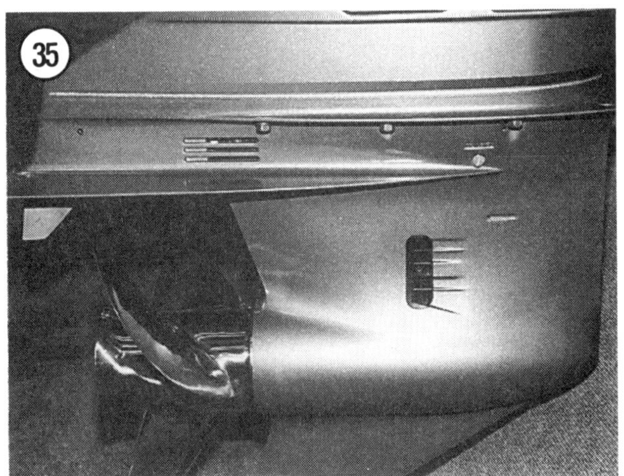

4. Remove the carburetor and clean it with solvent. Alcohol or kerosene used for the galley stove work well and are relatively safe.

WARNING
Gasoline may be the only solvent on board at the time. If you must use it, keep a fire extinguisher nearby, do not allow smoking or open flames, and be careful not to strike metal parts together.

5. Install the carburetor and spark plugs. If you use old plug gaskets, tighten the plugs 1/4 turn after finger-tight.
6. Start the motor in the normal manner. Run it for 1/2 hour or more.
7. If the motor fails to start, remove the spark plugs and look for water between the electrodes. Blow them dry, then reinstall the plugs and try to start the motor again.
8. If all attempts to start the motor fail, or the fly-wheel binds when turned, take the motor to a repair shop within 3 hours after recovery. If you cannot do this, resubmerge the motor in fresh water to avoid exposure to the atmosphere. Take it to a repair shop as soon as possible thereafter.

LAY-UP AND STORAGE

The major consideration during preparation for storage is to protect the outboard motor from rust, corrosion and dirt or other contamination.

1. Drain the fuel tank.
2. Run the motor until all fuel in the carburetor is used.
3. Flush the cooling system with fresh water, even if the manufacturer states flushing is unnecessary.

NOTE
Several adapters are on the market to fit a garden hose to the engine for flushing. If none is available, force water under pressure into the water intake. As an alternative, run the engine briefly at low speed in a fresh water test tank.

4

4. Remove the spark plug(s). Squirt about 1/2 tea-spoon of oil directly into the spark plug hole(s). Rotate the flywheel one revolution.
5. Place a drop of clean engine oil on the spark plug threads. Install the plugs and tighten finger-tight. Then, tighten the plugs 1/2 turn with a spark plug wrench. Do not overtighten.
6. Change the drive unit oil regardless of time since last changed. Use the oil recommended by the manufacturer.
7. Clean the entire engine with solvent. Remove large grease and dirt deposits with a bristle brush soaked in solvent. Remove all lubricant from moving parts such as shift linkage, throttle linkage, and so forth.
8. Lubricate all moving parts with water-resistant white grease.
9. Spray the entire engine with a light protective coat of WD-40 or silicone spray.
10. Store the motor upright in a clean dry place. A protective cover will keep out dust and dirt.
11. Service the battery as follows:
   a. Disconnect the battery cables from the battery, first the negative then the positive cable.
   b. Remove all grease, corrosion or other contamination from the battery surface.
   c. Check the electrolyte level in each cell and fill with distilled water as necessary. The electrolyte level in each cell should not be higher than 3/16 in. (4.8 mm) above the perforated baffles.
   d. Lubricate the terminal bolts with grease or petroleum jelly.

CAUTION
A discharged battery can be damaged by freezing.

   e. With the battery in a fully-charged condition (specific gravity at 1.260-1.275), store in a dry location where the temperature will not drop below freezing.
   f. Recharge the battery every 45 days or whenever the specific gravity drops below 1.230. Before charging, cover the plates with distilled water, but not more than 3/16 in. (4.8 mm) above the battery baffles. The charge rate should not exceed 6 amps. Discontinue charging when the specific gravity reaches 1.260 at 80° F (27° C).
   g. Before returning the battery to service, remove the excess grease from the terminals, leaving a small amount.

RECOMMISSIONING

Recommissioning an outboard does not require any special consideration, if the motor was layed-up properly. Install the battery on electric start models. Make sure the battery is fully charged. Fill the fuel tank with the proper fuel/oil mixture and start the engine in the normal manner. There may be some tendency for the plugs to foul from the oil squirted in during lay-up preparation. If the engine is difficult to start or runs roughly. remove the plugs and clean them in solvent. When dry, check and adjust the electrode gap and install them.

Chapter Five

Stern Drive and Inboard Engines

Marine engines thrive on use. Running the engine circulates oil throughout the engine, preventing buildup of sludge and corrosion. Cooling water also circulates to all parts of the system. An idle engine is subject to all kinds of corrosion and trouble.

Besides running the engine, you should have an on-going schedule of preventive maintenance. Engines are subject to tremendous stresses and wear from high pressure and friction. Regular maintenance insures that your engine will give good performance, dependability, and safety throughout its normal life. Neglect leads to premature failure, usually when you need the engine most.

SHOP MANUAL

A shop manual for the model and year of your engine and drive unit are essential. While this chapter can give you general service information that is common to most installations, you will need a shop manual for more specific information. Clymer Shop Manuals cover everything from the simplest adjustments to complete overhaul and are available for most engines and drive units.

BASIC ENGINE SYSTEMS

Diesel and gasoline powered engines are alike in more ways than they are different. Gasoline engines use a carburetor to atomize a fuel with air. The mixture is compressed by the pistons and ignited by a carefully timed spark to produce combustion. Diesel engines use a mechanical fuel injection system to inject carefully timed and metered amounts of fuel to each cylinder. The pistons compress the fuel/air mixture. Heat generated by the tremendous compression pressure ignites the mixture rather than having a spark do it. In all other respects, gasoline and diesel engines are virtually identical.

The following sections describe major systems in both types of engines. A knowledge of how each system works will help troubleshooting should trouble develop.

Diesel Fuel Systems

The fuel system for all diesel engines in marine use are similar. **Figure 1** shows a typical system consisting of the fuel tank, fuel filters, fuel lift pump, fuel injection pump and injectors. The fuel lift pump, mechanically driven by the engine, draws fuel from the fuel tank. All diesel engines should have a primary fuel filter between the fuel tank and the fuel lift pump, though many are delivered from the factory without one.

The primary filter removes water, dirt and debris from the fuel. The primary filter may have a see-through glass or plastic bowl so that water contamination is visible. There may also be a petcock for draining off a sample of fuel to check for contamination.

The fuel lift pump delivers fuel through a secondary fuel filter to the fuel injection pump. The secondary fuel filter removes very small particles of dirt, debris and water from the fuel. The fuel injection pump, in turn, delivers precisely timed and metered quantities of fuel to the injectors at each cylinder. Overflow (return) lines are provided from the secondary fuel filter (some models), the fuel injection pump and the injectors back to the fuel tank.

Cleanliness is vital to the proper operation of the fuel system. The fuel injection components are made to precise tolerances and even the smallest particle of dirt or trace of water in the system will destroy the fuel system efficiency or stop the engine completely. The overwhelming majority of diesel engine problems can be traced to contaminated fuel.

Diesel fuel may be contaminated by dirt, water or even bacteria. The primary and secondary filters do a good job of filtering out most of these, especially when they are changed frequently. There are a number of additives for diesel fuel that are also worthwhile. A biocide may be added to the fuel tank to discourage growth of bacteria in the fuel. Other additives are available to absorb water in the fuel tank so that it can be safely

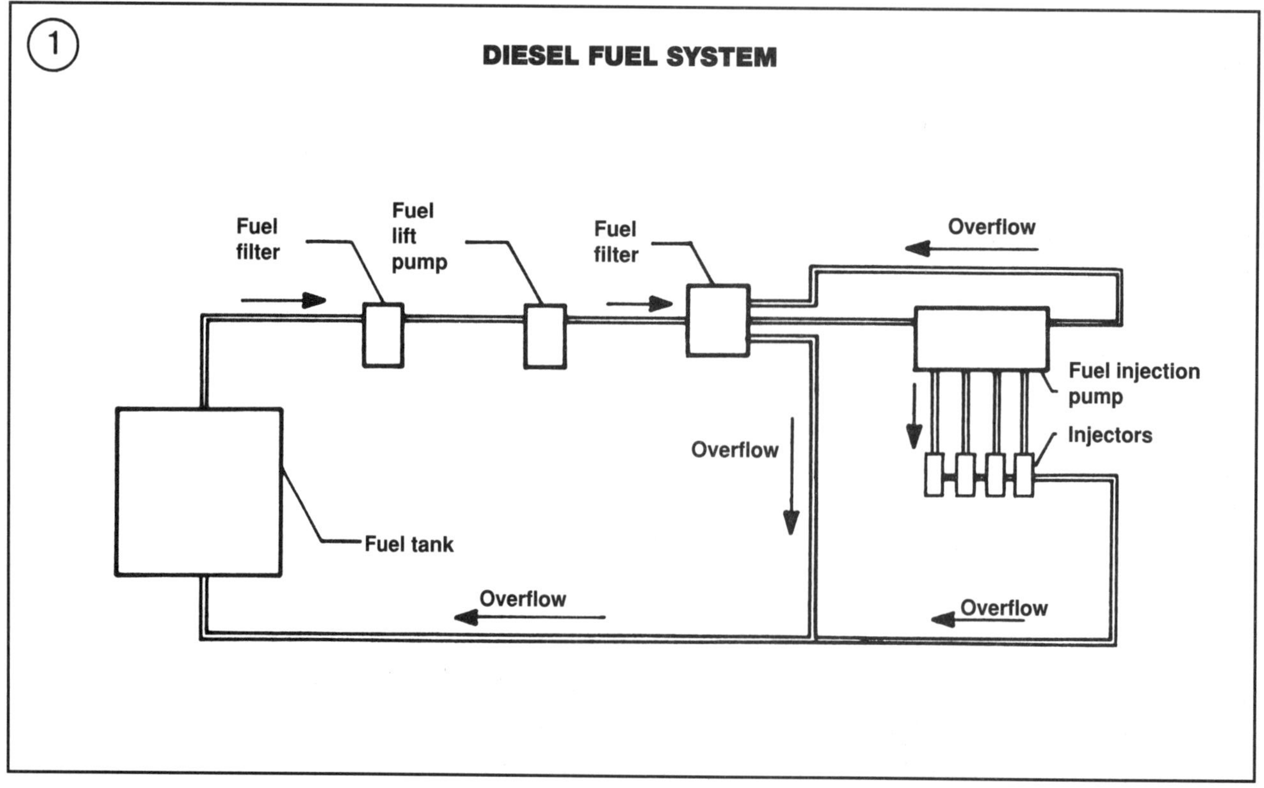

burned in the engine with the fuel. Make sure the additive you select does not contain alcohol which may attack seals in the fuel system. Safe products are available at any marine chandlery or marine engine dealer.

Gasoline Fuel System

Gasoline fuel systems are similar to diesel fuel systems, but they are usually simpler. See **Figure 2**. A mechanical fuel pump on the engine draws fuel from the tank. The tank has a filler pipe and a vent which permits air to enter the tank as fuel leaves. Some installations have a fuel filter/water separator between the tank and the fuel pump; if not, you can easily add one. The fuel pump delivers fuel to the carburetor, which atomizes it and delivers it to the cylinders via the intake manifold.

Engine Cooling Systems

Engine cooling systems are either open circuit or closed circuit. With open circuit cooling, water from outside the boat is used. A seawater pump on the engine block draws water from outside the hull through a seacock and feeds the water into the exhaust manifold water jacket. From the exhaust manifold, this "raw water" flows into the front of the cylinder block where it circulates around the cylinders and through the cylinder head water jackets. Finally, the water discharges into the exhaust stream and out of the boat.

On some installations, water passes from the exhaust manifold water jacket through an oil cooler before entering the cylinder block.

Coolant temperature is controlled by a thermostat to a maximum of approximately 120° F(49° C). A pressure relief valve releases excessive water pressure when the thermostat is closed.

The only advantage of open circuit or direct cooling is lower initial cost of the installation. Engine temperatures normally remain around 90-100° F (32-38° C), and in no event, should be permitted to go above 120° F (49° C). To prevent scale buildup in the water passages, engines should work with a coolant temperature of 150-180° F(65-82° C). Lower than normal coolant temperature causes considerably heavier engine wear with direct raw water cooling, and increased oil sludge formation. In addition, a cold engine is noisier than one running at the correct temperature.

Closed circuit cooling, also called fresh water cooling, consists of a closed circuit of fresh water circulating through the engine block and a heat exchanger. The fresh water, in turn, is cooled by an open circuit raw water system flowing through the heat exchanger.

A typical system is shown in **Figure 3**. A water pump on the engine block draws coolant from the heat exchanger into the exhaust manifold water jacket. From the manifold, the coolant enters the cylinder block, circulates around the cylinders and through the cylinder head water jackets. Finally, the coolant discharges from the cylinder head back to the heat exchanger for cooling.

Water from outside the hull is used to cool the fresh water coolant as it passes through the heat exchanger. A raw water pump mounted on the engine block or inside the stern drive unit draws outside water into the heat exchanger. Water from the heat exchanger flows to the exhaust outlet and is discharged overboard. In some cases, the raw water discharge is used for water injection into the exhaust silencing system.

A thermostat is mounted at the cylinder head outlet connection to maintain coolant at the correct operating temperature. On pressurized systems, coolant temperatures should be about 190° F (88° C). On unpressurized systems, best coolant temperature is about 170° F (77° C).

2
GASOLINE FUEL SYSTEM
Vent
Filler
Intake manifold
Carburetor
Fuel tank
Fuel filter and water separator
Fuel pump

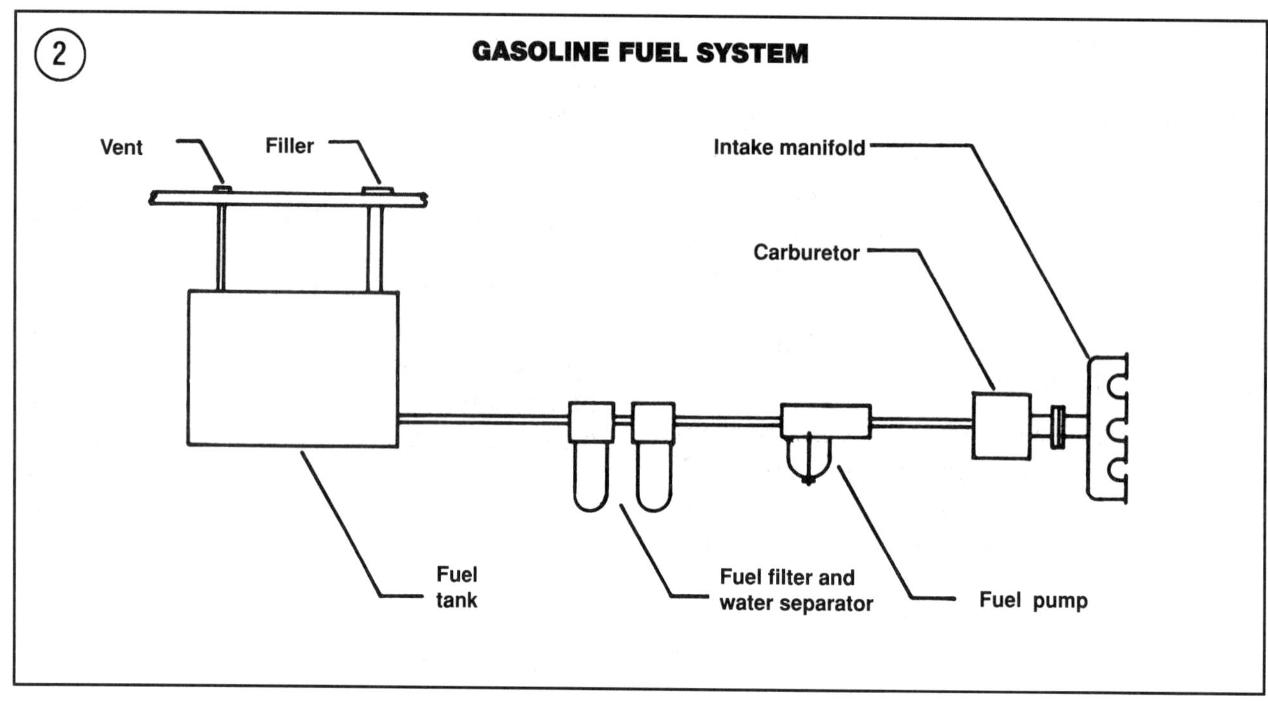

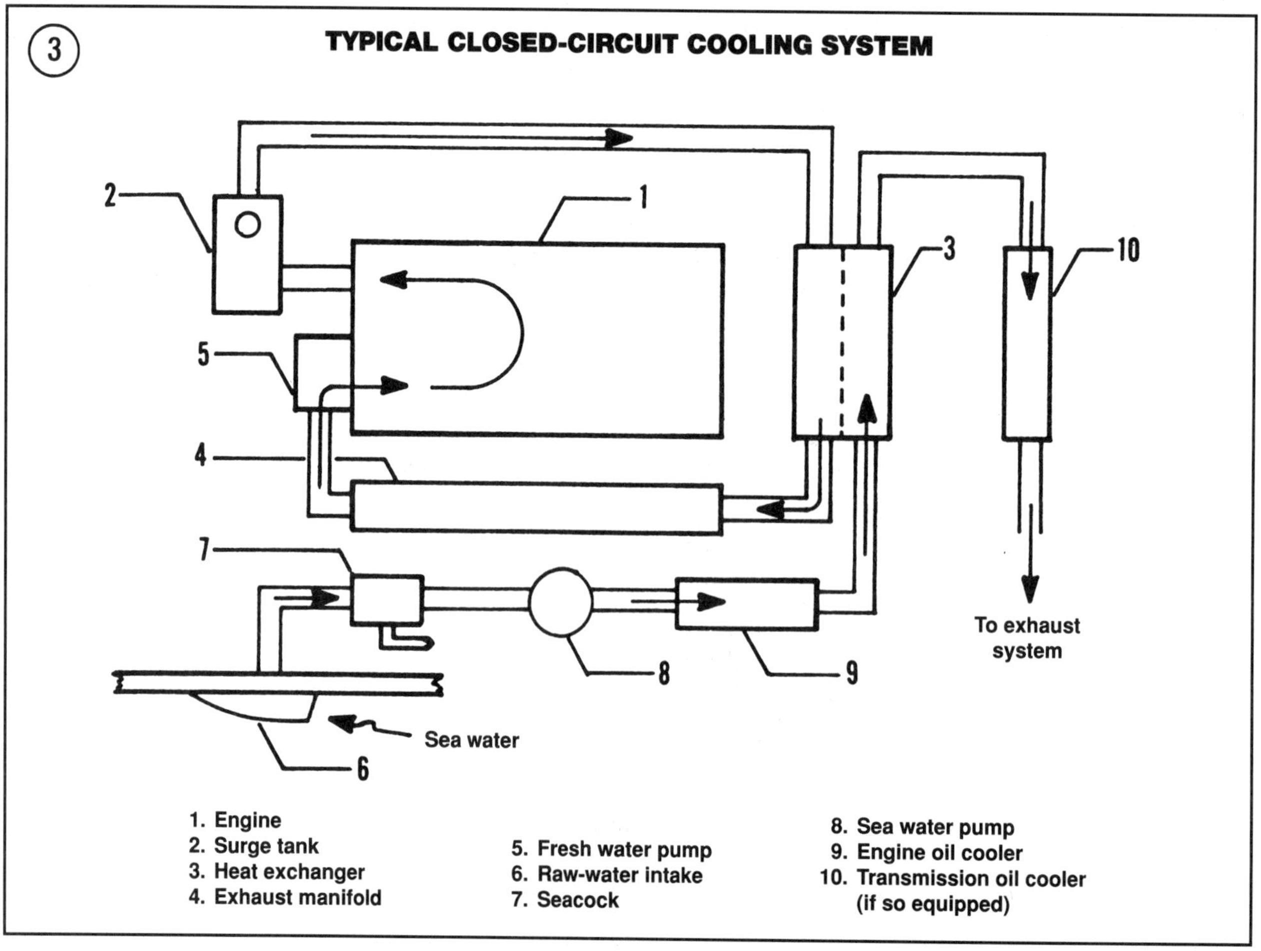

3
TYPICAL CLOSED-CIRCUIT COOLING SYSTEM
1
2
3
4
5
6
7
8
9
10
Sea water
To exhaust system
1. Engine
2. Surge tank
3. Heat exchanger
4. Exhaust manifold
5. Fresh water pump
6. Raw-water intake
7. Seacock
8. Sea water pump
9. Engine oil cooler
10. Transmission oil cooler (if so equipped)

Exhaust System

Exhaust systems are classified as dry exhaust and wet exhaust. The dry type, shown in **Figure 4** (typical), is not very common. Exhaust gases heat the pipe. This not only radiates a lot of heat in the engine room, but also presents a serious fire hazard. The end which passes through the hull must be carefully insulated. In addition, this type exhaust is relatively noisy.

The wet exhaust system overcomes the problems inherent in dry systems. See **Figure 5**, typical. The exhaust-carrying inner pipe is enveloped by a water-carrying outer hose. Under normal running conditions, the outer hose stays cool enough to touch. Exhaust fumes from the jacketed line enter a muffler where they mix directly with the water from the jacket. This further cools the gases and silences exhaust noise. Gases and water exit from muffler through a common line.

The exhaust system requires no periodic maintenance other than inspection for exhaust and water leaks, damage or corrosion. Every time you start the engine, check the exhaust outlet to be sure water is exiting. If not, shut the engine down and determine the cause.

FUEL REQUIREMENTS (GASOLINE)

Use regular or premium unleaded gasoline with a *minimum* pump octane rating of 87. For optimum performance and maximum engine life, gasoline with an octane rating of 89 or higher is recommended. Premium grade gasoline produced by a national brand refinery is specifically recommended for high performance engines. Premium grade gasoline (91-93 octane) contains a high concentration of detergent and dispersant additives that prevent carbon deposits on pistons and rings. If your engine is highly modified for performance, even higher octane gasoline, such as 102 octane aviation gas, may be required. However, it does no good to run a higher octane than the engine requires.

Be careful where you buy gasoline. The quality of pump gasoline can vary considerably even

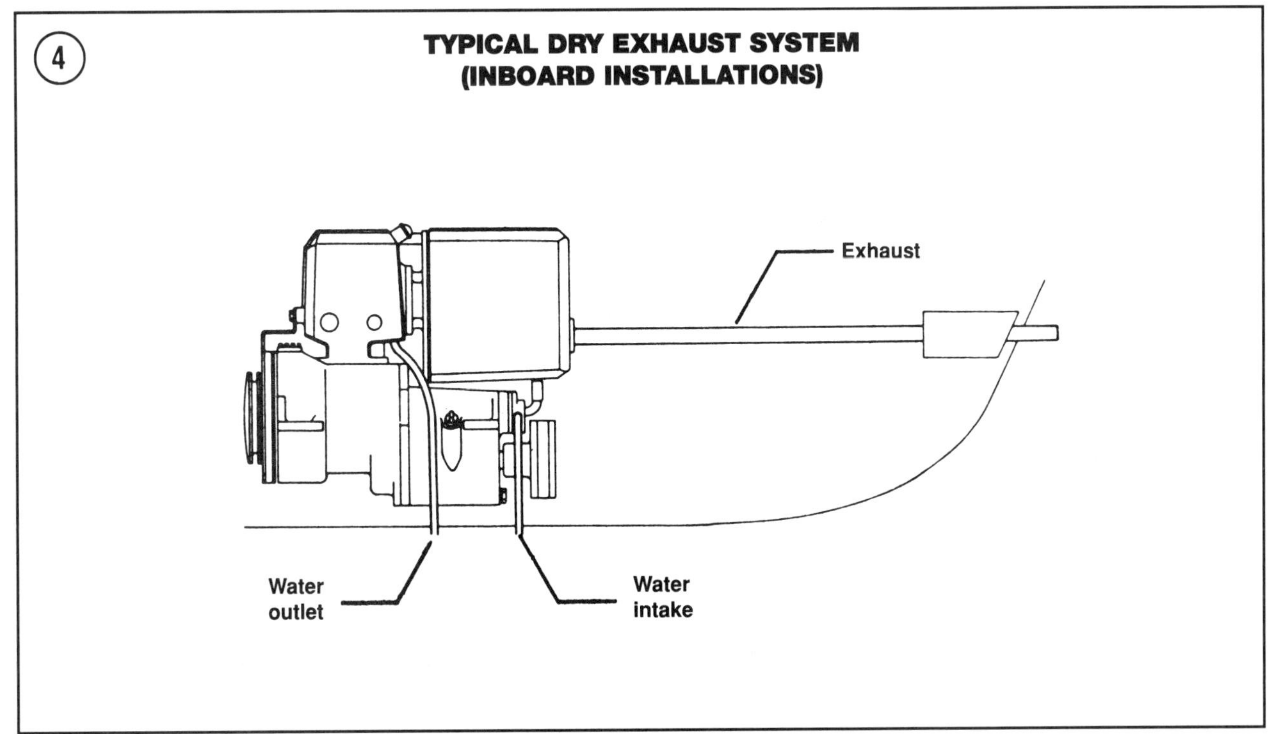

at the same service station or fuel dock. One problem is that gasoline does not store well. Some of the ingredients are very volatile and evaporate or decompose in time. Another problem is condensate which sinks to the bottom of the bulk storage tank, and frequently gets sucked up with the fuel. To make matters worse, refineries change the characteristics at different times of the year to make sure that road vehicles run well. If you use pump gas, make sure that you buy at a major brand station with high traffic. This will ensure fairly consistent and fresh fuel each time you buy.

Sour Fuel

Gasoline should not be stored for more than 60 days. Gasoline forms gum and varnish deposits as it ages. Such fuel will cause starting problems, carburetor plugging and poor performance. Several fuel additives are available which can prevent gum and varnish formation during storage or periods of non-use.

Alcohol Extended Gasoline

There are other potential problems with pump gas in certain areas of the country. New federal clean air laws have forced refiners to offer oxygenated fuels in many urban areas during certain times of the year, usually the cooler months. The oxygen added to the fuel is in the form of alcohol (to form so-called gasohol) or methyl tertiary butyl ether (MTBE). If in doubt about the fuel, ask the gasoline supplier or local government agencies charged with enforcing clean air standards in your area.

Alcohol may also be added to gasoline as an octane booster, although this fact may not be advertised.

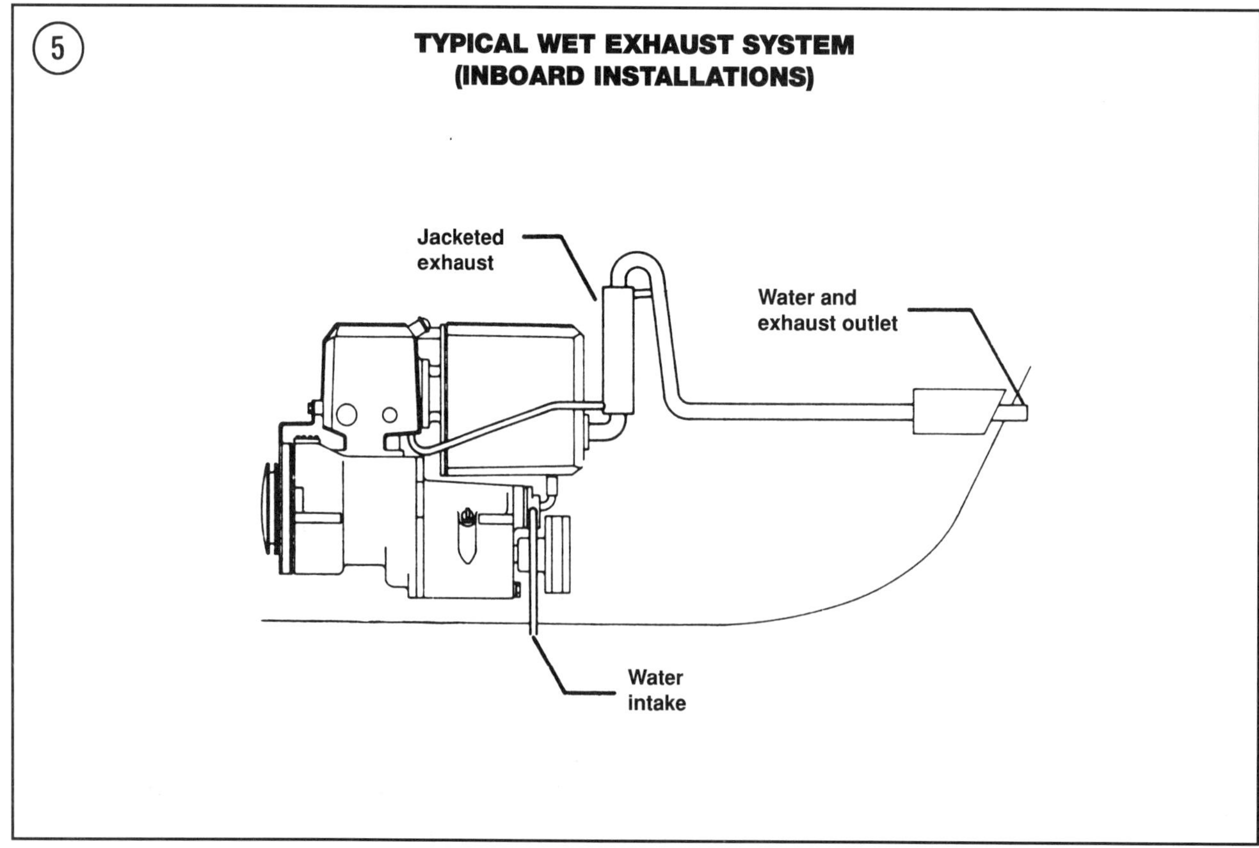

Most engines should run as well on this fuel as the non-oxygenated fuel as long as the fuel does not contain more than 10% ethanol alcohol or 5% methanol alcohol with 5% co-solvents, and meets the minimum octane requirements for your motor. However, oxygenated fuels may run a little leaner and require carburetor adjustment.

CAUTION
Do not use gasoline containing more than 10 percent ethanol or 5 percent methanol regardless of octane rating.

Fuel Requirements (Diesel)

Use only No. 2 diesel fuel when the ambient temperature is above 20° F. Use only winterized No. 2 diesel or No. 1 diesel fuel when the temperature is below 20° F. Never use any other diesel fuels or fuel additives.

CAUTION
Never use diesel fuel which has been stored in a galvanized container. The zinc in the metal plating will be dissolved by the fuel and can cause serious damage if it gets into the injection pump or nozzles.

WARNING
Never use ether or similar starting fluids in the diesel engine. The glow plugs may ignite the fluid and cause serious engine damage or personal injury.

PROPER ENGINE OIL SELECTION

Oil for 4-stroke engines is graded by the American Petroleum Institute (API) and the Society of Automotive Engineers (SAE) in several categories. Oil containers display these ratings on the top or label (**Figure 6**).

API oil grade is indicated by letters, oils for gasoline engines are identified by an "S" and oils for diesel engines are identified by a "C." Most modern gasoline engines require SF or SG graded oil. Automotive and marine diesel engines use CC or CD graded oil.

Viscosity is an indication of the oil's thickness, or resistance to flow. The SAE uses numbers to indicate viscosity; thin oils have low numbers and thick oils have high numbers. A "W" after the number indicates that the viscosity testing was done at low temperature to simulate cold weather operation. Engine oils fall into the 5W-20W to 20-50 range.

Single grade oils generally become more viscous (thicker) at low temperatures and less viscous (thinner) at high temperatures. Multi-grade oils (for example, 10W-40) are specially formulated to maintain a *constant* viscosity throughout a wide range of temperatures.

Gear Oil

Gear lubricants are assigned SAE viscosity numbers under the same system as 4-stroke engine oil. Gear lubricant falls into the SAE 72-250 range (**Figure 7**). Some gear lubricants are multi-grade; for example, SAE 85W-90.

Three types of marine gear lubricant are generally available: SAE 90 hypoid gear lubricant is designed for older manual-shift units; Type C gear lubricant contains additives designed for electric shift mechanisms; High viscosity gear lubricant is a heavier oil designed to withstand the shock loading of high-performance engines or units subjected to severe duty use. Always use a gear lubricant of the type specified by the unit's manufacturer.

Grease

Greases are graded by the National Lubricating Grease Institute (NLGI). Greases are graded by number according to the consistency of the grease; these ratings range from No. 000 to No. 6, with No. 6 being the most solid. A typical multipurpose grease is NLGI No. 2 (**Figure 8**). For specific applications, equipment manufacturers may require grease with an additive such as molybdenum disulfide (MbS2).

PRE-OPERATIONAL CHECKS

Before starting the engine for the first time each day, perform the following checks.

1. Remove engine compartment cover and check for the presence of raw gasoline fumes. If any gasoline fumes can be smelled, determine their source and correct the problem before proceeding.

WARNING
Always have a Coast Guard-approved fire extinguisher close at hand when working around the engine.

2. Check the engine oil level with the dipstick as described in this chapter. Add oil if the level is low.
3. Check the electrolyte level in each battery cell as described in this chapter. Add distilled water, if needed.
4. Check the power steering pump fluid level, if so equipped.
5. Check the condition of all drive belts. If a belt is in doubtful condition, replace it. Spare belts are difficult to obtain offshore.
6. Check all water hoses for leaks, loose connections and general condition. Repair or replace as necessary.
7. Visually check the fuel filter sediment bowl, if so equipped. Clean bowl and replace element if dirty.
8. Check the oil level in the stern drive unit as described in this chapter. Add lubricant if necessary.
9. Check the fluid level in the hydraulic trim system reservoir, if so equipped. Add fluid if necessary.
10. Check the bilge for excessive water. Drain or pump dry if water is present.
11. Check the propeller for nicks, dents, missing metal or other damage. Repair or replace if damaged.
12. Turn on the fuel tank valve(s).
13. Connect the battery cables to the battery (if disconnected).
14. Reinstall the engine compartment cover.

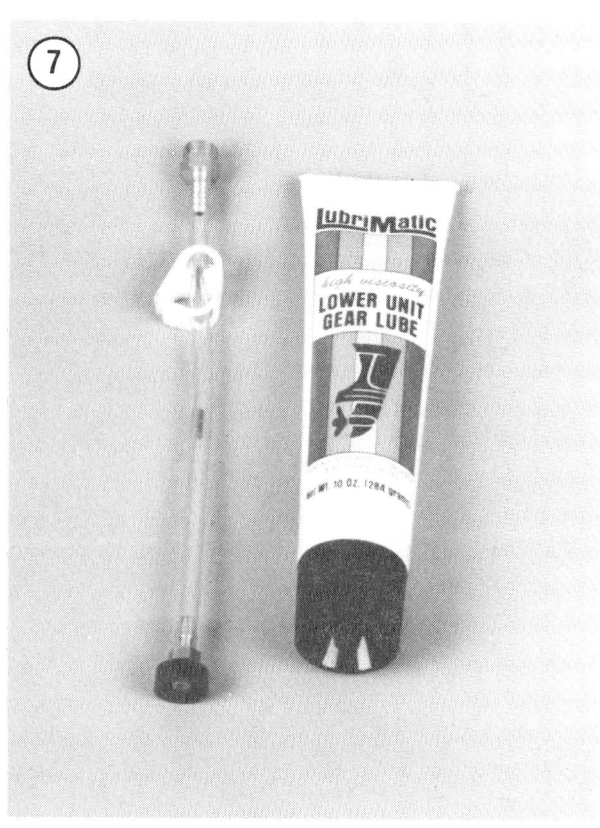

STARTING CHECK LIST

After performing the pre-operational checks, the following starting check list should be followed.

1. Operate the engine compartment blower for at least 5 minutes before starting the engine.

2. *Stern drive models:* Make sure that the stern drive unit is fully down or in operating position.

3. *Gasoline models:* If the engine is cold, prime it by operating the throttle one or two times. If equipped with a manual choke, set it to the closed position.

4. Make sure that the gearshift lever is in NEUTRAL.

WARNING
Always have a Coast Guard-approved fire extinguisher close at hand when starting the engine.

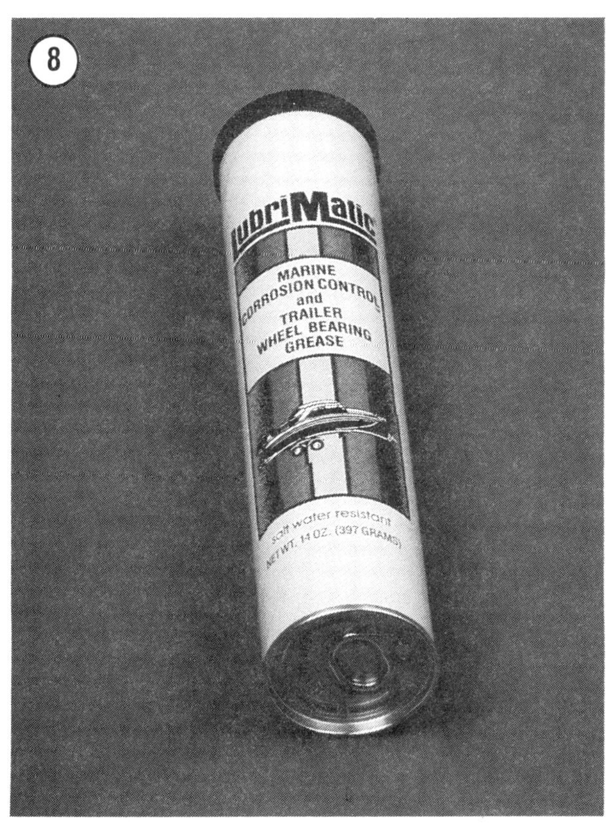

5. Start the engine and run at idle speed for a few minutes.

CAUTION
Prolonged operation of the engine with the gearshift lever in NEUTRAL can cause damage to gears in the stern drive unit due to improper circulation of lubricant.

6. Note the gauges and warning lights to make sure that the engine is not overheating, that proper oil pressure is present and that the battery is not discharging. If any of these conditions occur, shut the engine down at once. Determine the cause and correct the problem before proceeding. 5

POST-OPERATIONAL CHECKS

Perform the following maintenance after each use.

1. If the boat was used in salt or polluted water, flush the cooling system with fresh water as described in this chapter. This will minimize corrosion and buildup of deposits in the cooling system.
2. Disconnect the battery cables from the battery. You may want to remove the battery from the boat to prevent its theft.
3. Shut off the fuel tank valve(s).
4. Top off the fuel tank(s), if possible. This will minimize the possibility of moisture condensation in the tank(s).
5. If water is present in the bilge, either drain or pump dry.
6. Wash the interior and exterior surfaces of the boat with fresh water.

PERIODIC MAINTENANCE

Periodic maintenance is vitally important to keep your engine running at its peak and to minimize wear. Most maintenance is scheduled according to hours of use, but some items must be done at least once a season regardless of use.

Table 1 (gasoline) and **Table 2** (diesel) summarizes the maintenance normally required and the time interval recommended by most engine manufacturers.

Except for the method that fuel enters the cylinders, gasoline engines and diesel engines are very similar. Maintenance procedures in the following sections apply to both unless specified otherwise.

Generally, the following simple steps will keep your engine running dependably for many years.

1. Run the engine periodically, even a few minutes every week except during lay-up. This chapter includes special winter lay-up procedures.
2. Perform regular scheduled maintenance. This chapter includes procedures for many popular engines. If yours is not included, follow the owner's manual supplied with your engine.
3. Fix minor troubles immediately before they become major. You may be able to handle very simple jobs yourself. If you doubt your ability, let a professional do it.
4. Keep an accurate engine log. The log should include:
   a. Hours run.
   b. Oil pressure at normal rpm and operating temperature.
   c. Coolant temperature at normal rpm and operating temperature.

Routine Checks

The following simple checks should be performed prior to each trip.

1. Check engine oil level. Level should be between the 2 marks on the dipstick, but never below. Top up if necessary.
2. Check battery electrolyte level. Top up with distilled water.
3. Check coolant level.
4. Immediately after starting the engine, check oil pressure if gauge is installed.
5. Check the level in the fuel tank.
6. Check the ammeter or voltmeter for battery charging.
7. If the engine has an open cooling system, open the seacocks.
8. Check the general engine compartment or engine room condition. Particularly look for signs of coolant, fuel and engine oil leaks.
9. As soon as the engine starts, look for water at the exhaust outlet if engine has a heat exchanger cooling system. If water doesn't emerge, stop the engine immediately.

Checking Oil Level

All engines will consume a certain amount of oil as a lubricating and cooling agent. The rate of consumption is highest during a new engine's break-in period, but should stabilize after ap-

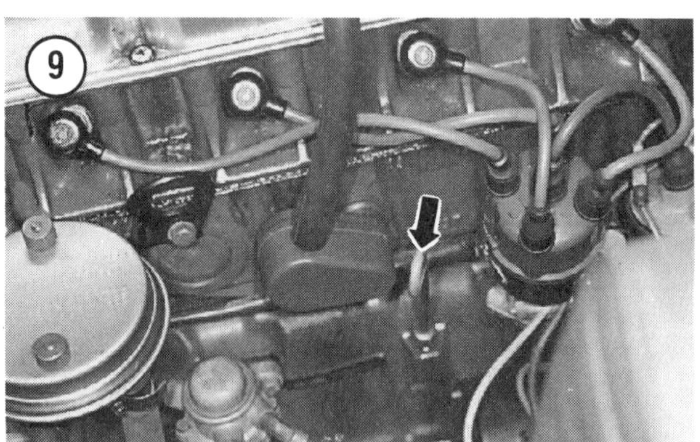

proximately 100 hours of operation. It is not unusual for a 4-cylinder engine to consume up to a quart of oil in 5-10 hours of wide-open throttle operation.

Check the oil level at least every 2 weeks during the boating season. If the boat is used more frequently, check the level each time the engine is shut down, allowing approximately 5 minutes for the oil in the upper end to drain back into the crankcase oil pan.

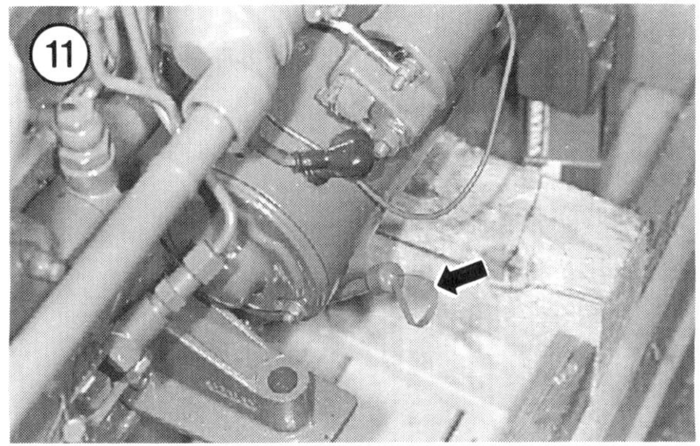

11

12

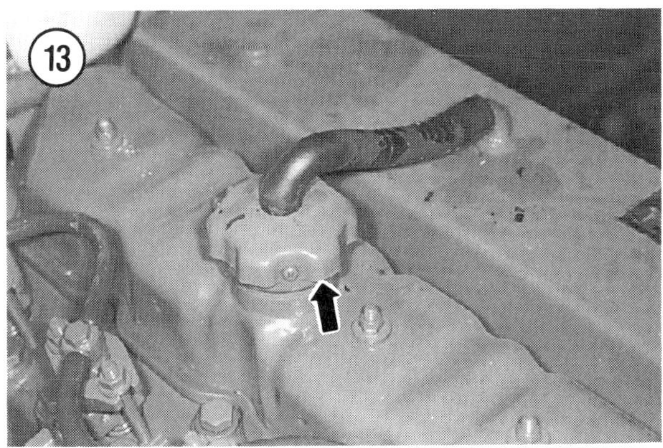

13

1. With the boat at rest in the water and the engine off, pull out the dipstick. See **Figure 9** (inline), **Figure 10** (V6 and V8) or **Figure 11** (diesel) for typical locations. Wipe it with a clean rag or paper towel, reinsert it and pull it out again. Observe the oil level on the dipstick.

NOTE
Some dipsticks have "ADD" and "FULL" lines. Others read "ADD 1 QT." and "OPERATING RANGE." In either case, keep the oil level above the "ADD" line.

2A. Gasoline engines—Top up to the "FULL" or "OPERATING RANGE" mark on the dipstick if necessary. On GM V6 and V8 models, use an oil carrying an API designation of SG and a viscosity rating of SAE 20W-50 or 15W-50. On all other models, use an oil carrying an API designation of at least SG and a viscosity rating of SAE 10W-30 or 10W-40. Remove the oil filler cap and add oil through the opening in the rocker arm cover. See **Figure 12**.

2B. Diesel engines—Top up to the "FULL" or "OPERATING RANGE" mark on the dipstick if necessary, using any good quality automotive diesel oil carrying an API designation of SG/CD. Use SAE 20W-30 for temperatures above 50° F or SAE 10W for temperatures below 50° F. Remove the oil filler cap (**Figure 13**) and add oil through the opening in the rocker arm cover.

Engine Oil and Filter Change

Most installations do not leave enough space to permit the use of the drain plug in the crankcase oil pan. For this reason, an oil drain suction pump is the most common device used to drain the oil from the crankcase. The pump has a long flexible hose which is inserted into the oil dipstick tube and fed into the crankcase. Several makes of pumps are available from marine supply dealers. Such pumps may be hand-operated, motorized or operated by an electric drill motor (**Figure 14**).

Used oil should be discharged into a sealable container for proper disposal. Plastic bleach and milk containers are excellent for this. The oil can be taken to a service station or other facility that offers collection or recycling of used oil.

NOTE
Do not dispose of oil in the trash. Never dump used oil overboard.

The installed angle of the engine affects the oil level in the crankcase. To assure that the oil is drained and replaced properly, perform the following procedure with the boat at rest in the water.

1. Start the engine and warm it to normal operating temperature, then shut it off.

NOTE
Warm oil drains more quickly and thoroughly than cold oil, taking more impurities with it.

2. Remove the dipstick, wipe it clean and place it out of the way.
3. Insert the oil drain pump hose into the oil dipstick tube as far as it will go.
4. Insert the other pump hose into a sealable container large enough to hold the oil from the crankcase. Most engine crankcases hold 4-6 qts. of oil.
5. Operate the pump until it has removed all of the oil possible from the crankcase. Remove pump hose from dipstick tube.
6. Place a drain pan or other suitable container under the filter to catch any oil spillage when the filter is removed. See **Figure 15**.
7. Unscrew the filter counterclockwise. Use the filter wrench if the filter is too tight or too hot to remove by hand.

WARNING
A small amount of oil may be spilled when the filter is removed. Hold a small

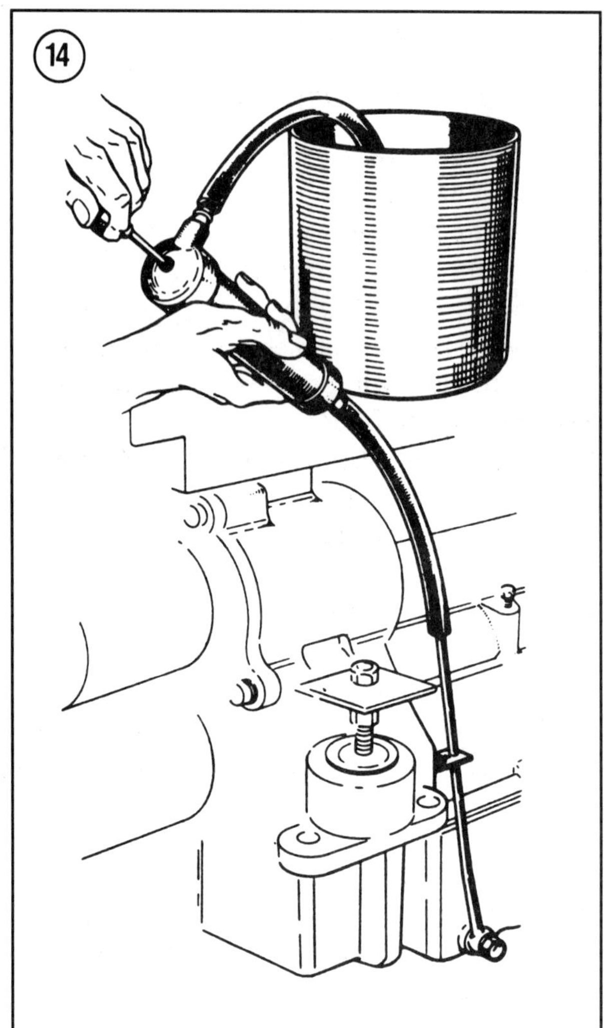

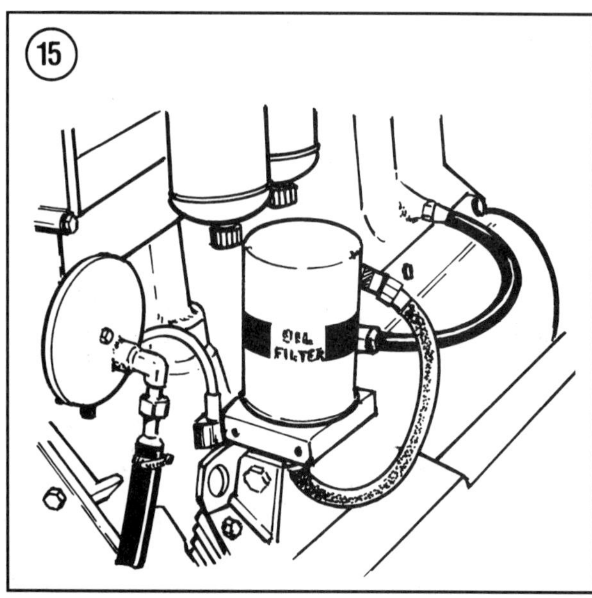

waste container under the element as it is unscrewed. Oil accumulation in the bilge is a serious fire hazard.

8. Wipe the gasket surface on the engine block clean with a paper towel.
9. Coat the neoprene gasket on the new filter with a thin coat of clean engine oil.
10. Screw the new filter onto the engine *by hand* until the gasket just touches the engine block. At this point, there will be a very slight resistance when turning the filter.
11. Tighten the filter another 1/2-3/4 turn *by hand.* If the filter wrench is used, the filter will probably be overtightened. This can damage the filter or cause an oil leak.
12. Remove the oil filler cap from the rocker arm cover.
13. Reinstall the dipstick in the dipstick tube.
14. Determine the crankcase capacity of your engine from the owner's manual. Pour the specified amount of oil into the rocker arm cover opening and install the oil filler cap. Wipe up any spills on the rocker arm cover with a clean cloth.
15. Start the engine and check immediately for oil pressure. Stop the engine if the oil pressure does not come up to normal within about 15-30 seconds.

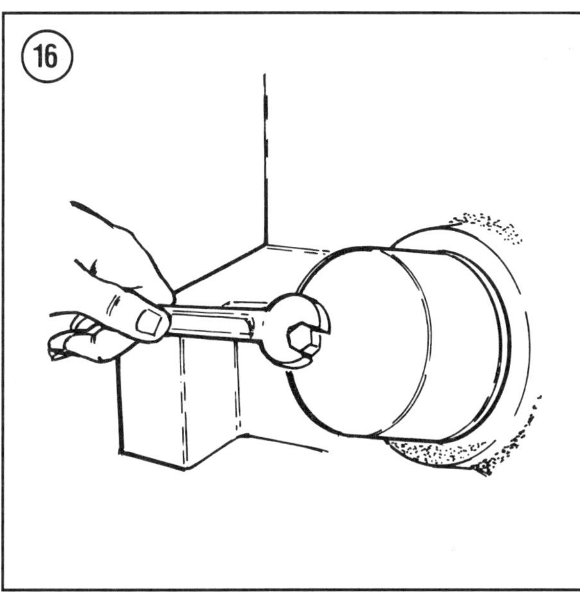

16. Check the area under and around the oil filter for leaks while the engine is running.
17. Let the engine idle for a few minutes, then shut the engine off.
18. Wait a few minutes for oil to return to the crankcase, then remove the dipstick. Wipe the dipstick clean with a paper towel and reinsert it in the dipstick tube. Remove the dipstick a second time and check the oil level. Add oil, if necessary, to bring the level up to the "FULL" or "OPERATING RANGE" mark, but do *not* overfill.

Engine Oil Filter Replacement (Spin-on Type)

Oil filters are usually the disposable spin-on type frequently found on automobiles and easily available through automotive suppliers. The filter is replaced at the same time as the engine oil. See *Engine Oil and Filter Change* procedure.

Engine Oil Filter Replacement (Cartridge Type)

Some engines, particularly those that are not based on automotive engines, use a cartridge type filter. The engine oil filter should be replaced every 150 hours or 3 months when the engine oil is changed. This should be done after the old oil is drained and before the new oil is poured in.

1. Unscrew the bolt on the filter cover. See **Figure 16.**
2. Remove filter cover and discard oil filter element. See **Figure 17**.
3. Clean inside of cover with solvent.
4. Replace rubber seal in casting.
5. Install new filter element and cover. Tighten the cover bolt just enough to achieve a leak-proof seal.
6. After new engine oil has been poured in, run the engine and check for oil leaks around the filter cover.

Gasoline Engine Fuel Filters

Gasoline inboard engine fuel systems may use one or more of the following fuel filters:

a. A fuel pump strainer (**Figure 18**).

b. A disposable canister filter (**Figure 19**).

c. A carburetor fuel inlet filter (**Figure 20**).

d. A water-separating fuel filter (**Figure 21**).

Replace each filter after 100 hours of operation or at least once a year. If operating conditions are severe, filters should be replaced more often.

NOTE

*In areas where only poor quality fuel is available or where moisture tends to condense in fuel tanks, it is advisable to install an inline fuel filter to remove moisture and other contaminants. See **Figure 22**. These are sold as accessory items by marine supply dealers.*

Fuel Pump Strainer Service

The fuel pump strainer may be located on the end of the fuel line threaded into the fuel pump (**Figure 18**) or under the pump cover (**Figure 23**). Clean the outside of the pump to remove any contamination, then remove the screw or pump cover. Clean or replace the strainer as required. Reinstall the screw or pump cover and make sure that the gasket seals properly.

Canister-Type Fuel Filter Replacement

This type of fuel filter looks like an oil filter (**Figure 19**) and is replaced using a procedure similar to that for oil filter replacement. Unscrew the filter canister from the filter adapter (using a filter wrench, if necessary) and discard. Wipe the neoprene gasket on the new filter with a thin film of clean engine oil and screw the filter onto the adapter until it is snug—do not overtighten. Start the engine and check for leaks.

Carburetor Fuel Inlet Filter Replacement

Refer to **Figure 20** for this procedure.

1. Place one wrench on the carburetor inlet nut (A, **Figure 20**). Place a second wrench on the fuel line connector nut (B, **Figure 20**). Hold the fuel inlet nut from moving and loosen the connector nut.
2. Disconnect the fuel line from the inlet nut fitting, then unscrew and remove the inlet nut.

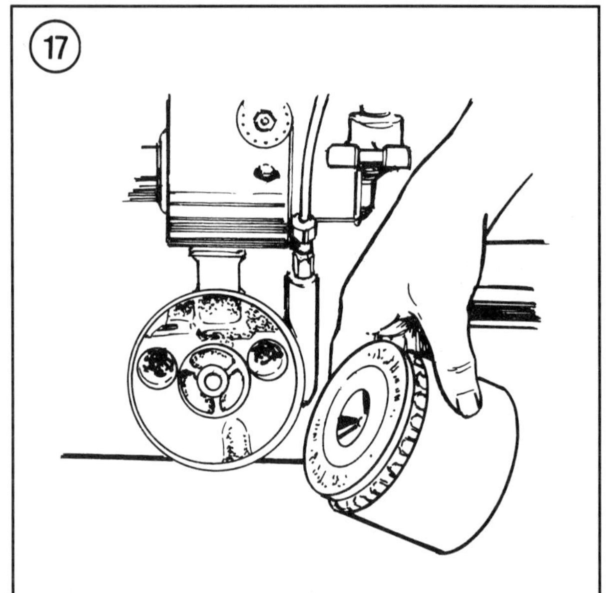

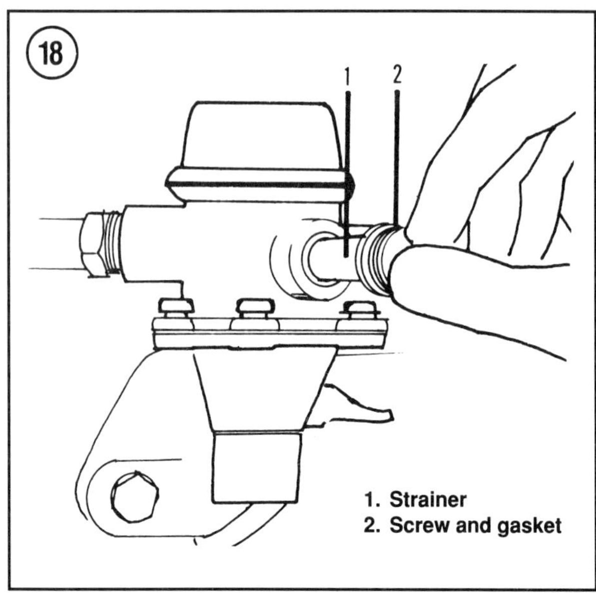

3. Remove the filter element and spring from the carburetor fuel inlet.
4. Remove and discard the inlet nut gasket.

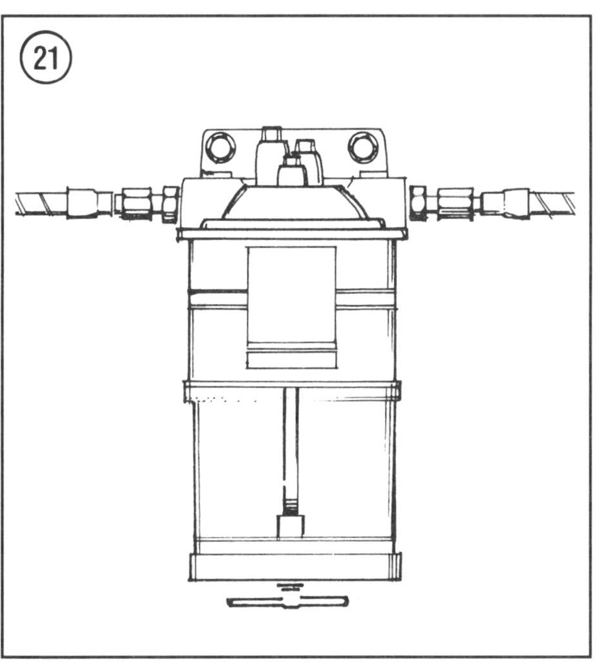

5. Installation is the reverse of removal. Make sure the end of the filter with a hole faces the inlet nut. Use a new gasket. Tighten the inlet nut and connector nut snugly.
6. Start the engine and check for leaks.

Water-Separating Fuel Filter Replacement

Refer to **Figure 21** for this procedure.
1. Check the transparent bowl to see if there is any water in the fuel. If water is present, open the petcock at the bottom of the filter and drain the water.
2. Clean all contamination from the filter housing.
3. Loosen the center bolt at the top of the adapter and remove the container and filter.
4. Remove the filter from the container and discard it.
5. Installation is the reverse of removal. Operate the fuel pump lever and prime the fuel system. Start the engine and check for leaks.

5

Inline Filter Replacement

Refer to **Figure 22** for this procedure.
1. Loosen each hose clamp screw.
2. Slide the clamp back on the hose.
3. Remove each hose from its filter fitting by twisting the hose off.
4. Position a new filter with the arrow indicating direction of flow pointing toward the carburetor.

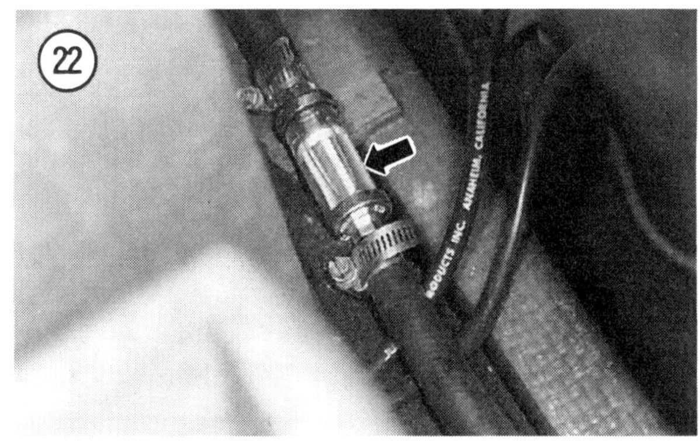

5. Reverse Steps 1-3. Start the engine and check for leaks.

Diesel Engines Fuel Filters

Diesel engine fuel systems may use one or more of the following fuel filters:

a. A fuel pump pre-filter **(Figure 24).**

b. A disposable canister filter (**Figure 25**).

c. A water-separating secondary fuel filter (**Figure 26**).

Replace each filter after 100 hours of operation or at least once a year. If operating conditions are severe, filters should be replaced more often. The fuel system should be bled as described under *Bleeding Diesel Fuel System* in this chapter to prevent hard starting after filter service.

Fuel Pump Pre-Filter Service

The fuel pump pre-filter is located under the fuel pump cover **(Figure 24**). Clean the outside of the fuel pump to remove contamination. Remove the pump cover and lift the pre-filter from the pump. Clean the filter in fresh diesel fuel and reinstall in the pump. Reinstall the pump cover and make sure that the gasket seals properly by priming the pump with the hand lever. Bleed the fuel system as described in this chapter.

Canister-Type Fuel Filter Replacement

This type of fuel filter looks like a long oil filter **(Figure 25**). To remove the filter, loosen the nut at the bottom of the canister. Unscrew the filter canister from the filter adapter and discard. Wipe the neoprene gasket on the new filter with a thin film of clean diesel oil. Fill the filter with clean diesel fuel, then screw the filter onto the adapter and tighten the nut at the bottom of the canister snugly. Bleed the fuel system as described in this chapter. Start the engine and check for leaks.

Water-Separating Fuel Filter Replacement

1. Check the transparent bowl to see if there is any water or other contamination in the fuel. If water is present, open the petcock at the bottom of the filter and drain the bowl.

2. Clean all contamination from the outside of the filter housing.

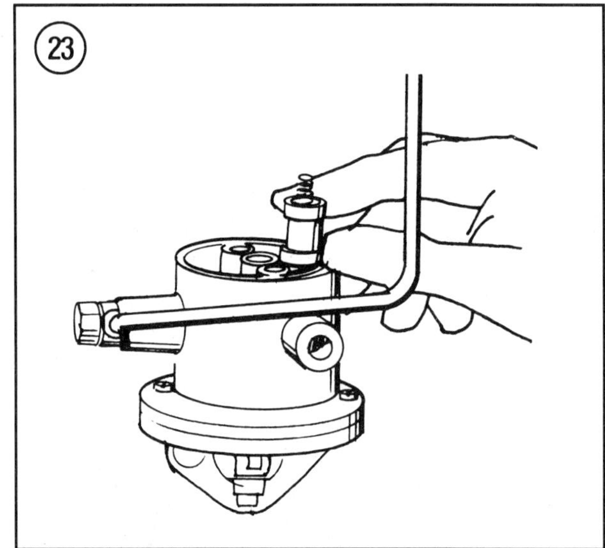

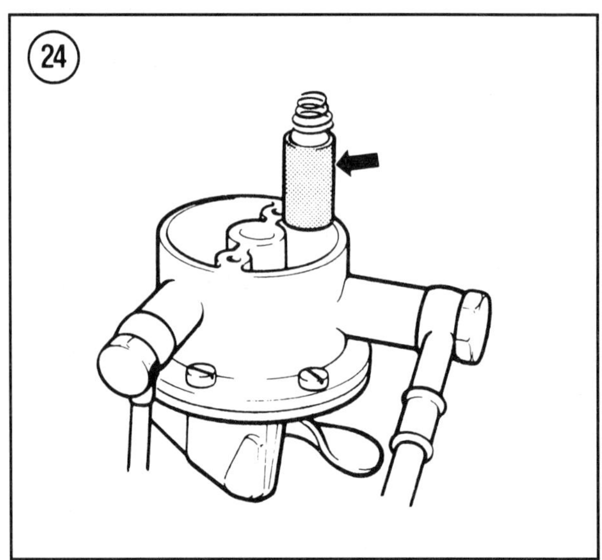

3. Loosen the center bolt on the housing cover and remove the container with the filter.

4. Remove the filter from the container and discard it.

5. Installation is the reverse of removal. Operate the fuel pump lever and bleed the fuel system as described in this chapter. Start the engine and check for leaks.

Carburetor Flame Arrestor

The flame arrestor serves as both an air filter and as a safety measure against backfiring. See **Figure 27**. Remove the flame arrestor at least once per season. Wash in solvent, then air dry thoroughly and reinstall.

WARNING
Do not use an automotive type air cleaner housing. The flame arrestor must be U.S. Coast Guard approved.

Drive Belt Condition and Tension

Drive belts operate the alternator, circulating pump and power steering pump (if so equipped) on all engines. See **Figure 28**.

5

Check drive belt condition at least once a year. Replace the belt(s) if it shows any signs of wear, cracking or other defects.

Drive belt tension should be checked periodically by the deflection method. Press downward firmly on the belt at a point midway between 2 pulleys (A, **Figure 28**). The belt should deflect about 3/8 in. (10 mm). If deflection is outside this range, adjust the belt tension as follows.

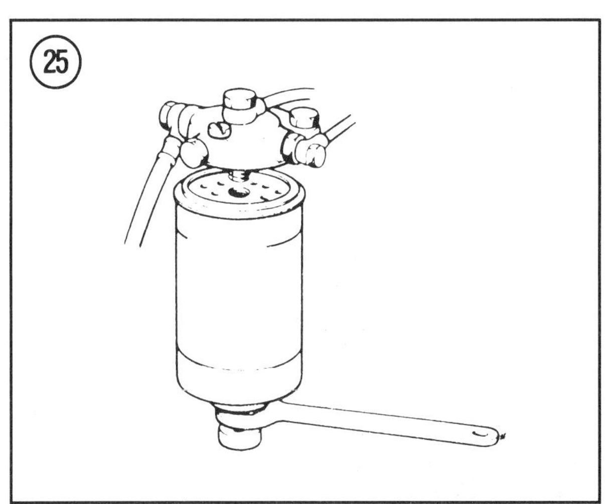

1. Loosen the alternator adjustment and pivot bolts. See B and C, **Figure 28**.
2. Move the alternator toward or away from the engine as required.

CAUTION
Do not pry directly on the alternator end frame to move the unit as this can cause internal damage. Insert a prying tool in the bracket adjustment slot and pry against the mounting ear.

3. Tighten the adjustment bolt (B, **Figure 28**), release pressure on the alternator, then tighten the pivot bolt (C, **Figure 28**.

Power Steering Pump

Some late-model engines may be equipped with a power steering pump and remote reservoir. Check fluid level periodically (**Figure 29**) and top up if necessary with a good quality power steering fluid.

Sea Water Strainer Service

Some engines are equipped with a sea water strainer housing. The plastic strainer inside should be removed, cleaned and reinstalled every 25 hours.

1. Remove the cover from the housing.
2. Lift the strainer screen from the housing. See **Figure 30**.
3. Remove any debris or contamination from the strainer screen. Replace the screen if its seal is damaged.
4. Rinse the screen thoroughly in fresh water.
5. Remove the rubber washer and sealing disc from the cover, if so equipped. Wipe the inside of the cover with water-resistant grease, then reinstall the sealing disc and washer.
6. Reverse Step 1 and Step 2 to reinstall the filter. Start the engine and check for leakage.

Closed Cooling System

Visually inspect the level and condition of coolant in the expansion tank (if so equipped) or remove the pressure cap on the thermostat housing and check the coolant level and condition in the housing.

The pressure cap should not be removed when the engine is warm or hot. If removing the cap is unavoidable, cover it with a thick rag or wear heavy leather gloves. Turn the cap slowly counterclockwise against the first stop (about 1/4 turn). Let all pressure (hot coolant and steam) escape. Then press the cap down and turn counterclockwise to remove.

WARNING
If the cap is removed too soon, scalding coolant will escape and could cause a serious burn.

Top up, if necessary, with a 50/50 mixture of ethylene glycol (or equivalent) and water. If the coolant looks rusty or dirty, flush the system as described in this chapter.

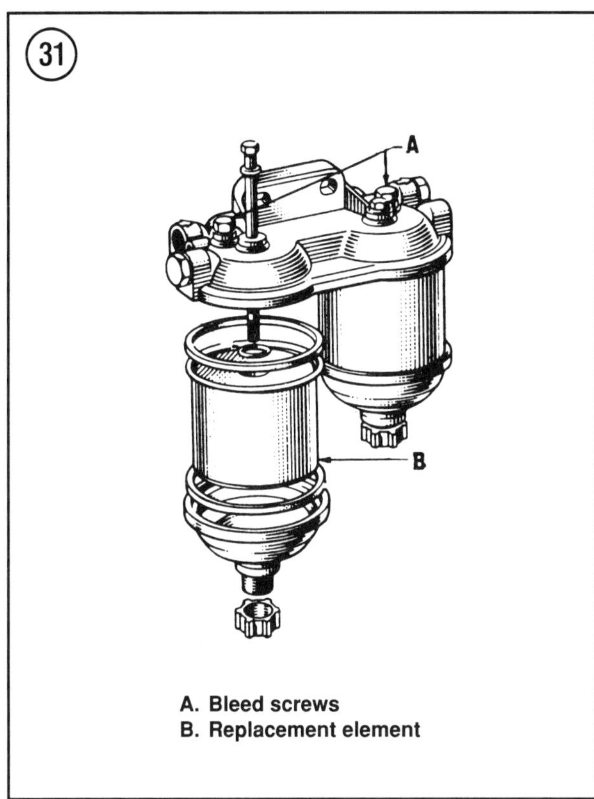

A. Bleed screws
B. Replacement element

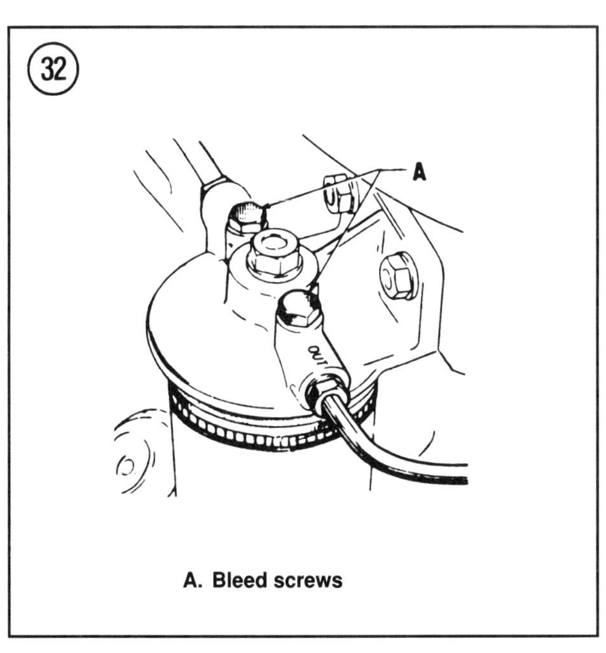

A. Bleed screws

Diesel Engine Air Filters

Replace the main air filter on diesel engines (if so equipped) every 200 hours.

Replace the crankcase ventilation air filter on diesel engines (if so equipped) every 200 hours or whenever oil starts to flow from the vent.

Bleeding Diesel Fuel System

Air can enter the fuel system as a result of running out of fuel, leaks in the system, or changing fuel filters or lines. Air in the system will cause difficult starting, erratic running or loss of power. The sections which follow describe the bleeding procedure for typical engines.

1. Make certain that there is sufficient fuel in the fuel tank and that the fuel shut-off valve is turned on.
2. Loosen the bleed screws on inlet side of fuel filter about 2 or 3 turns (**Figure 31** and **Figure 32**).
3. Operate the priming lever on the fuel lift pump (**see Figure 33**) until fuel completely free of air is expelled. Tighten the bleed screw.

CAUTION
Slight pressure with the wrench will seal all the bleed screws tightly. Do not use excessive pressure as the castings are soft and threads strip easily.

NOTE
If the fuel pump eccentric is on maximum lift, the pump priming lever will not operate. In this case, rotate the engine as necessary with the starter until the priming lever works.

4. Loosen the bleed screw on the outlet side of the filter and repeat Step 3.
5. Loosen the bleed screw on injection pump nearest to the inlet line and repeat Step 3.
6. Loosen the remaining bleed screw on the injection pump and repeat Step 3.

CAUTION
Operate engine for at least 10 minutes before leaving dockside to make sure that all the air has been purged from the system.

7. Loosen the union nut at the fuel injection pump inlet. See **Figure 34**, typical. Operate the priming lever on the fuel lift pump until escaping fuel is air-free, then retighten the union nut.

NOTE
This entire procedure must be performed until all signs of air bubbles have disappeared. This could take 4 or 5 minutes of hand priming.

8. Loosen the unions at the injector ends of the high pressure fuel pipes.
9. Open the throttle fully and ensure the stop control is in the "run" position.
10. Rotate the engine with the starter motor until air-free fuel flows from all fuel pipes. If the battery is fully charged, this operation should take 30-60 seconds.
11. Tighten the unions at the fuel pipes.
12. Run the engine and make sure it is running properly.

NOTE
After bleeding the system, if the engine runs satisfactorily for a few minutes, then stops, air must be trapped in the fuel injection pump and the entire bleeding procedure must be repeated.

GASOLINE ENGINE TUNE-UP

An engine tune-up is a series of mechanical adjustments made to get peak performance from the engine. A tune-up should be performed every 250-300 hours—sooner if the engine becomes hard to start, runs roughly at any power setting, or doesn't seem to have the same power. Running the engine when it needs a tune-up can lead to abnormal wear.

Due to the large number of different engines, it is impossible to provide specific tune-up instructions for each one. This information is contained in the owner's manual available from the manufacturer. Many owner's manuals, however, neglect to mention the order in which parts of the tune-up should be performed. The information in this section applies to all gasoline stern drive and inboard engines.

Since different systems in an engine interact to affect overall performance, tune-up must be accomplished in the following order.

a. Valve adjustment (if necessary).
b. Compression check.
c. Ignition system work.
d. Carburetor inspection and adjustment.

Marine vs. Automotive Parts

Since many marine engines are based on automotive engines, there is a temptation to use automotive parts. This is especially true since marine parts are more expensive than compara-

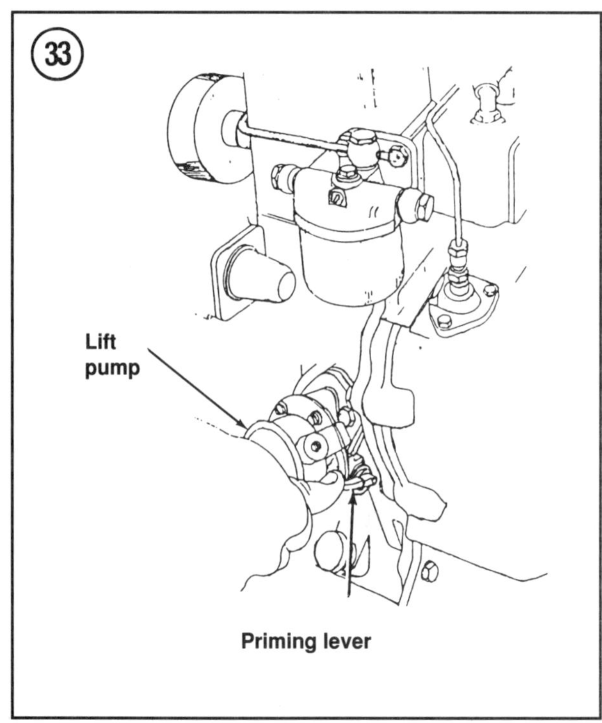

ble automotive parts (contact breaker points, distributors, carburetors, etc.). The reason is that marine parts are designed to operate in a more severe environments. For safety, automotive parts should not be substituted, even when the parts appear to be identical.

Valve Adjustment

This is a series of simple mechanical adjustments which establish a specified clearance between the valve stems and valve operating gear. If the clearance is too small, valves may be burned or distorted. Too much clearance results in excessive noise and valve train wear. In either case, engine power is reduced.

Most late-model V6 and V8 engines have hydraulic lifters which operate with zero lash or no clearance. Periodic valve adjustment is generally not required on models equipped with hydraulic lifters. Adjustment may be necessary, however if any valve train components are removed or replaced.

The shop manual for your particular engine provides a valve adjustment procedure. In addition, the following hints will help.

1. Determine from the shop manual whether valve clearance should be adjusted with the engine warm or cold. Warm means the engine is at normal operating temperature; run the engine at a fast idle until the temperature gauge registers in the normal operating range. If the shop manual specifies a cold engine, let the engine cool overnight and adjust valves the next day before running it.

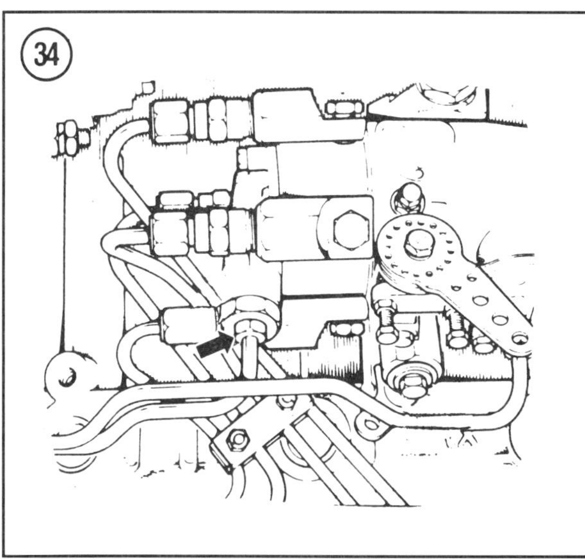

2. Remove the spark plugs. The engine crankshaft must be rotated by hand several times during adjustment. Removing the plugs makes rotation much easier.

3. Determine valve clearances from the shop manual. Often the clearances for exhaust valves and intake valves differ, for example, 0.010 in. clearance for exhaust valves and 0.008 in. for intake valves. This is measured with flat feeler gauges; make sure you have the proper sizes on hand.

COMPRESSION TEST (GASOLINE ENGINES)

Check the compression of each cylinder before attempting a tune-up. If more than a 20 lb. difference exists between the highest and lowest reading cylinders, the engine cannot be tuned to develop its maximum power.

1. If the boat is not in the water, install a flush-test device to provide water before operating engine.

2. Warm the engine to normal operating temperature, then shut it off.

3. Remove the flame arrestor and make sure that the choke and throttle valves are completely open.

4. Disconnect the coil high tension lead from the distributor cap tower (**Figure 35,** typical) and ground the lead.

5. Remove the spark plugs.

6. Connect the compression tester to the No. 1 cylinder (**Figure 36**) according to manufacturer's instructions (**Figure 37).**

7. Use a remote starter button or have an assistant crank the engine until there is no further rise in pressure.

8. Remove the compression tester and record the reading. Relieve the tester pressure valve.

9. Repeat Steps 6-8 for each cylinder.

When interpreting the results, actual readings are not as important as the difference between readings. All readings for Volvo OHC engines

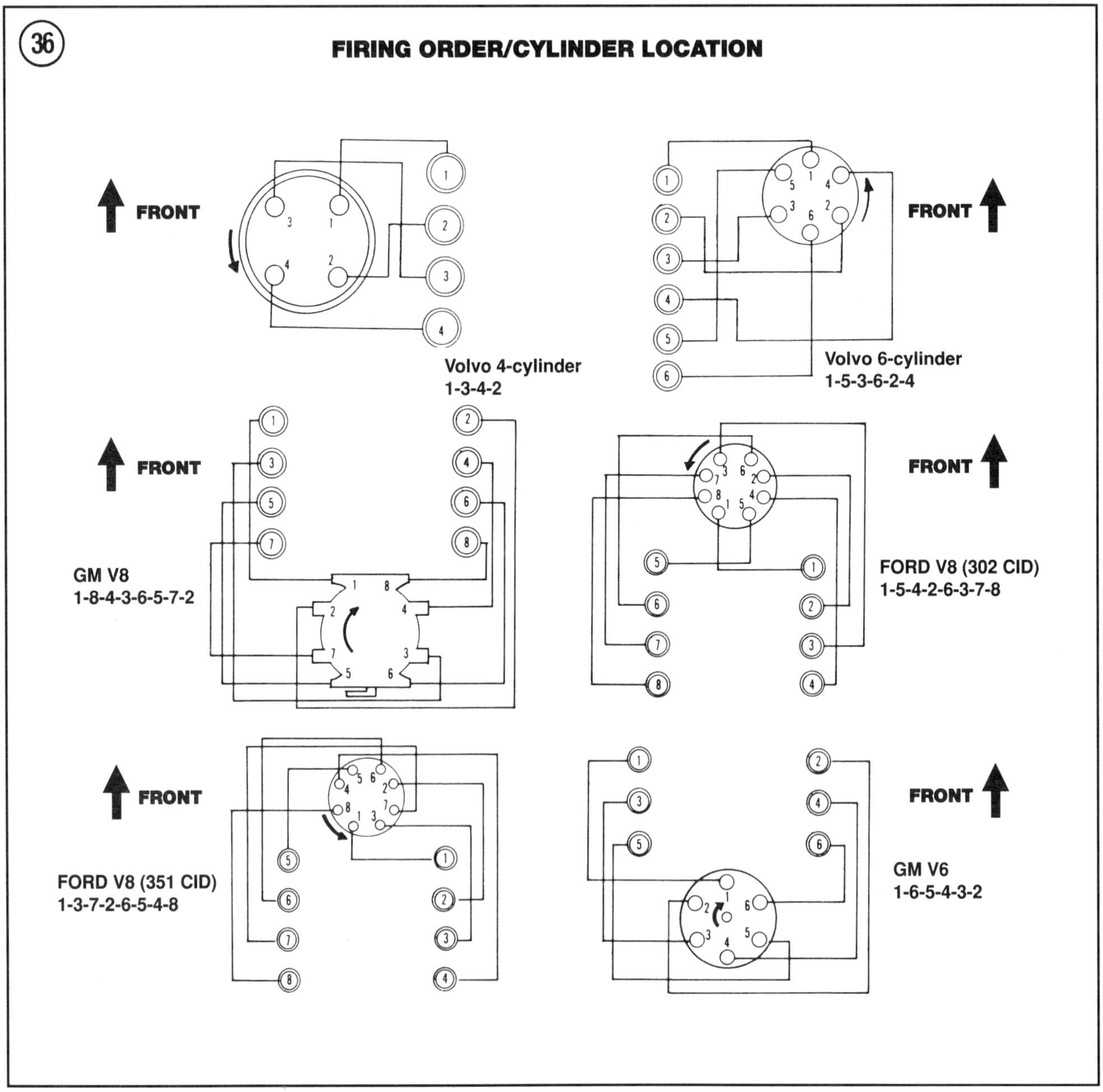

36

FIRING ORDER/CYLINDER LOCATION

FRONT

Volvo 4-cylinder
1-3-4-2

FRONT

Volvo 6-cylinder
1-5-3-6-2-4

FRONT

GM V8
1-8-4-3-6-5-7-2

FRONT

FORD V8 (302 CID)
1-5-4-2-6-3-7-8

FRONT

FORD V8 (351 CID)
1-3-7-2-6-5-4-8

FRONT

GM V6
1-6-5-4-3-2

should be approximately 140 psi; readings for Volvo pushrod engines should be approximately 170 psi. All GM engines should be approximately 142-156 psi. The lowest reading on Ford engines should be within 75 percent of the highest. Any variation between cylinders of less than 20% (GM) or 25% (Ford) is acceptable. Greater differences indicate that engine repair is required because of worn or broken rings, leaky or sticking valves or a combination of all.

If the compression test indicates a problem (excessive variation in readings), isolate the cause with a wet compression test. This is performed in the same way as the dry test, except that about 1 tablespoon of heavy engine oil (at least SAE 30) is poured down the spark plug hole before performing Steps 6-8. If the wet compression readings are much greater than the dry compression readings, the trouble is probably caused by worn or broken rings. If there is little difference between the wet and dry readings, the problem is probably due to leaky or sticking valves. If 2 adjacent cylinders read low on both tests, the head gasket may be leaking.

Use a vacuum gauge and compare the vacuum gauge and compression tester readings to isolate the problem more closely. **Figure 38** provides interpretation of vacuum gauge readings.

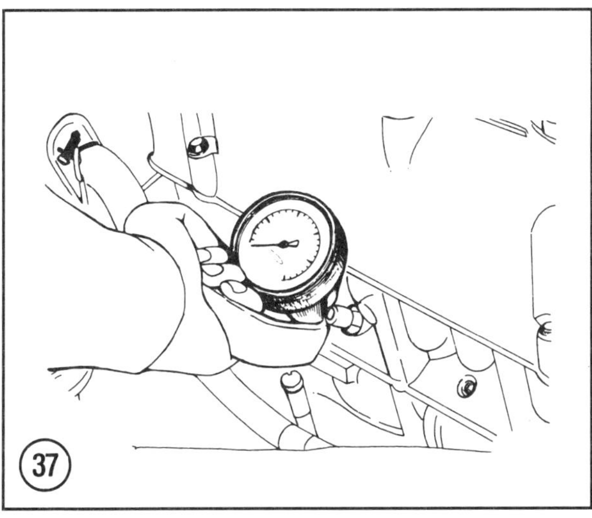

IGNITION SERVICE

This phase of the tune-up consists of:

a. Spark plug replacement.
b. Breaker point replacement and adjustment.
c. Distributor cap and rotor inspection.
d. Spark plug wire inspection.
e. Ignition timing adjustment.

The engines used in inboard or stern drive installations may use either a mechanical contact breaker point ignition system or an electronic ignition system. 5

WARNING
Most engine compartments are very cramped. Be careful not to get fingers, hair or clothing caught in moving engine parts. In addition, watch out for hot areas such as the exhaust manifold.

Spark Plug Removal

CAUTION
Whenever the spark plugs are removed, dirt from around them can fall into the spark plug holes. This can cause expensive engine damage.

1. Blow out any foreign matter from around the spark plugs with compressed air. Use a compressor if you have one or a can of inert gas available at photo stores.
2. Disconnect the spark plug wires by twisting the wire boot back and forth on the plug insulator while pulling upward (**Figure 39**). Pulling on the wire instead of the boot will damage the wire.
3. Remove the plugs with an appropriate size spark plug socket. Keep the plugs in order so you know which cylinder each came from. See **Figure 40**.
4. Examine each spark plug and compare its appearance to **Figure 41**. Electrode appearance is a good indication of performance in each cylinder and permits early recognition of developing trouble.

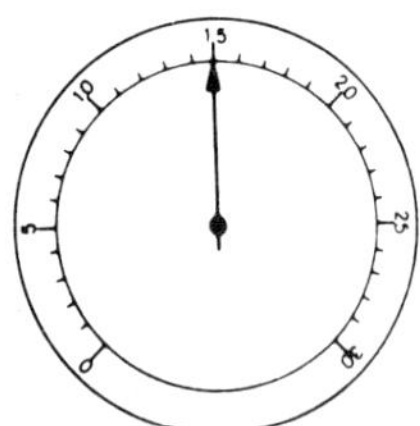

1. NORMAL READING
Reads 15 in. at idle.

2. LATE IGNITION TIMING
About 2 inches too low at idle.

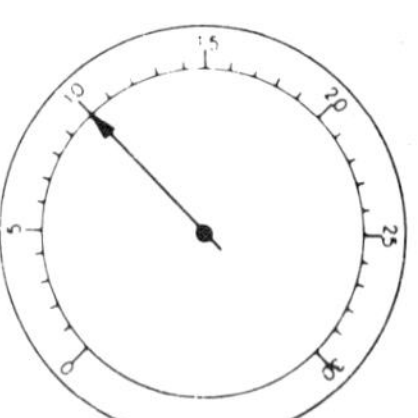

3. LATE VALVE TIMING
About 4 to 8 inches low at idle.

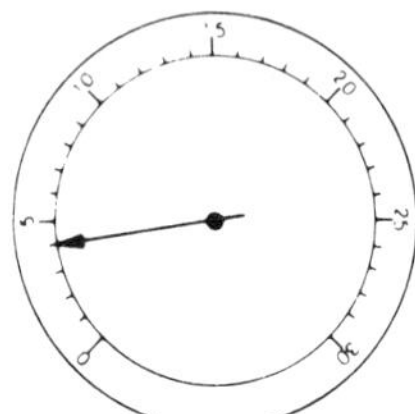

4. INTAKE LEAK
Low steady reading.

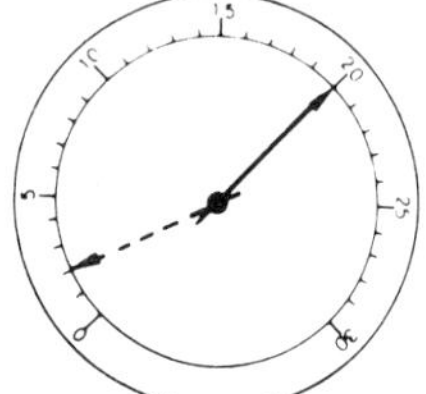

5. NORMAL READING
Drops to 2, then rises to 25 when accelerator is rapidly depressed and released.

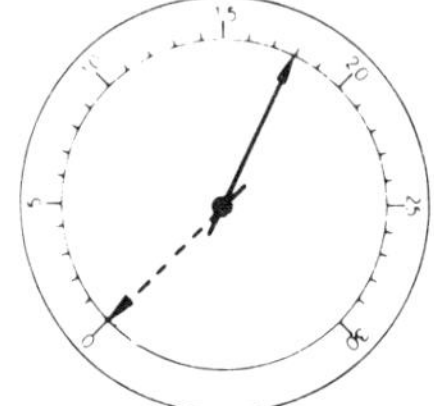

6. WORN RINGS, DILUTED OIL
Drops to 0, then rises to 18 when accelerator is rapidly depressed and released.

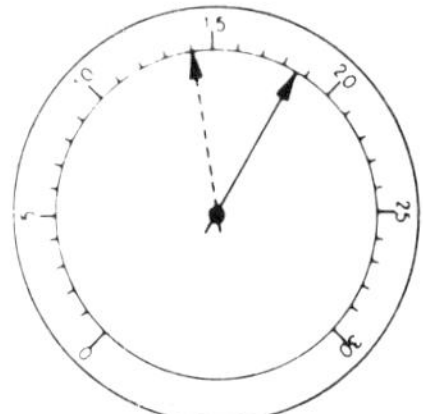

7. STICKING VALVE(S)
Normally steady. Intermittently flicks downward about 4 in.

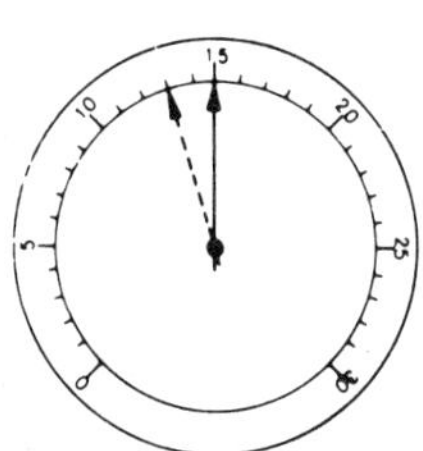

8. LEAKY VALVE
Regular drop about 2 inches.

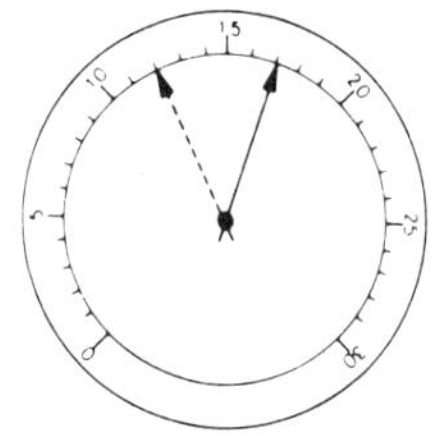

9. BURNED OR WARPED VALVE
Regular, evenly spaced down-scale flick about 4 in.

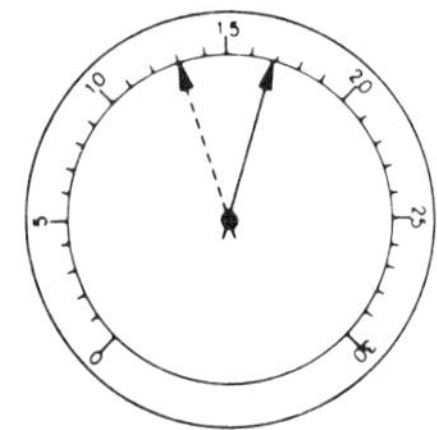

10. WORN VALVE GUIDES
Oscillates about 4 in.

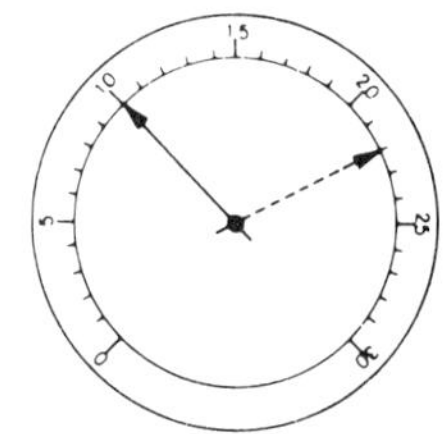

11. WEAK VALVE SPRINGS
Violent oscillation (about 10 in.) as rpm increases. Often steady at idle.

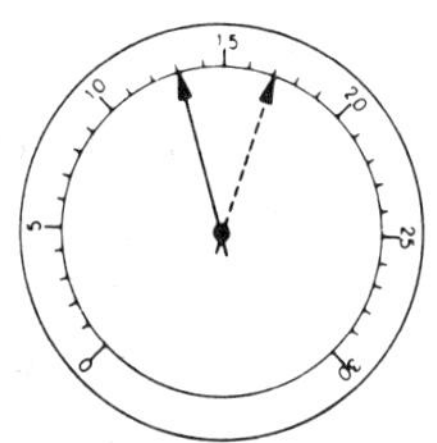

12. IMPROPER IDLE MIXTURE
Floats slowly between 13-17 in.

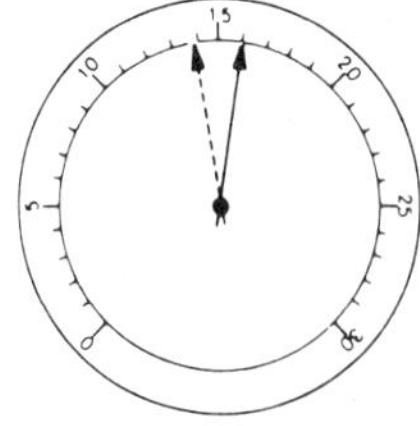

13. SMALL SPARK GAP or DEFECTIVE POINTS
Slight float between 14-16 in.

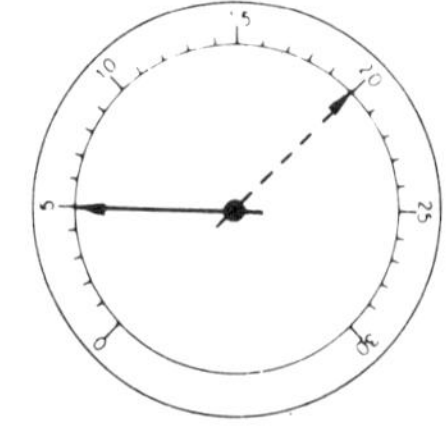

14. HEAD GASKET LEAK
Gauge floats between 5-19 in.

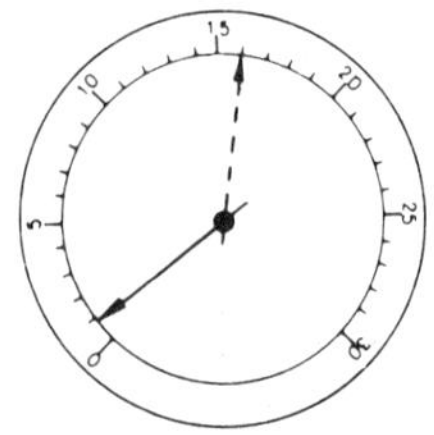

15. RESTRICTED EXHAUST SYSTEM
Normal when first started. Drops to 0 as rpm increases. May eventually rise to about 16.

5. Discard the plugs. Although they could be cleaned, regapped and reused if in good condition, they seldom last very long. New plugs are inexpensive and far more reliable.

Spark Plug Gapping and Installation

New plugs should be carefully gapped to ensure a reliable, consistent spark. Use a special spark plug tool with a wire gauge. See **Figure 42** for two common types.

1. Remove the plugs from the box. Tapered seat plugs do not use gaskets. Some plug brands may have small end terminals that must be screwed on before the plugs can be used.
2. Determine the correct gap setting from the engine owner's manual. Insert the appropriate size wire gauge between the electrodes. If the gap is correct, there will be a slight drag as the wire is pulled through. If there is no drag or if the wire will not pull through, bend the side electrode with the gapping tool **(Figure 43)** to change the gap. Recheck the gap with the wire gauge.

CAUTION
Never try to close the electrode gap by tapping the spark plug on a solid surface. This can damage the plug internally. Always use the special tool to open or close the gap.

3. Apply a drop of engine oil to the threads of each spark plug. Screw each plug in by hand until it seats. Very little effort is required. If force is necessary, the plug may be cross-threaded. Unscrew it and try again.
4. Tighten the spark plugs. If you have a torque wrench, tighten to 15-20 ft.-lb. (20-30 Nm). If not, tighten the plugs with your fingers, then tighten an additional 1/16 turn (tapered seat) or 1/4 turn (gasket-type) with the plug wrench.
5. Install the wires to their correct cylinder location.

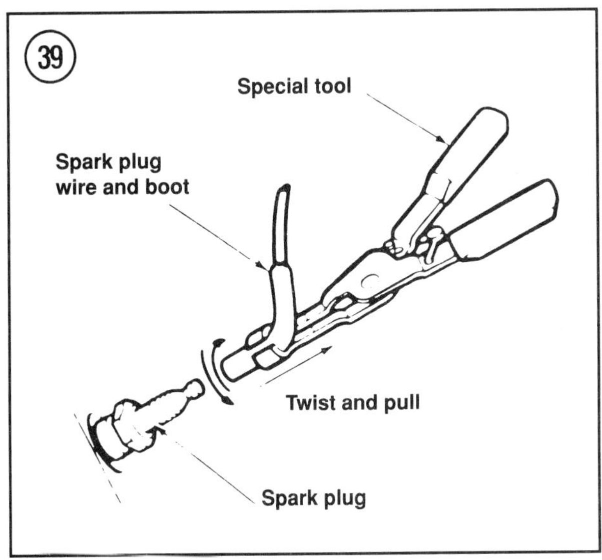

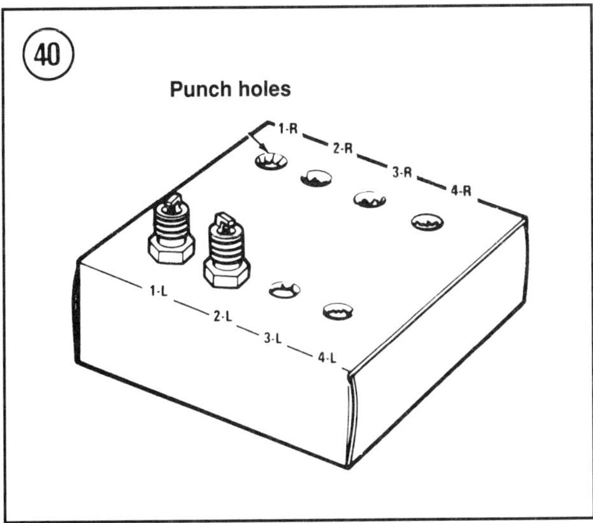

Spark Plug Wires

Spark plug wires, especially the noise suppresser type, deteriorate with age. Check each wire carefully for cracks in the insulation. If any wire is questionable, replace all of them. Every 2 years, replace them regardless of condition.

Some marine engine suppliers carry pre-cut wire kits. Simply replace old wires with the proper length wires from kit. If a kit is not available, or you wish to save some money, purchase the wire and end terminals from any automotive or marine engine parts supplier and cut them yourself. Take a sample of the existing wire to the supplier to be sure that you get the same kind. To avoid mistakes, remove one wire at a time, cut a new wire the same length, install the end terminals and install the new wire on engine.

Distributor Cap, Wires and Rotor

1. Wipe all ignition wires with a cloth slightly moistened in solvent. Carefully bend each wire and inspect insulation, cable nipple and spark plug boot for abrasions, cracks or deterioration. Clean any corroded terminals. Replace wires as required.

2. Unsnap or unscrew the distributor cap attachment devices as required and remove the cap. See **Figure 44**. Pull the cap straight up and off the distributor to prevent rotor blade damage.

3. Check the carbon button and electrodes inside the distributor cap for dirt, corrosion or arcing. See **Figure 45**. Check the cap for cracks and make sure the vent screen is clean and fits

SPARK PLUG ANALYSIS

A. Normal—Light tan to gray color of insulator indicates correct heat range. Few deposits are present and the electrodes are not burned.

B. Core bridging—These defects are caused by excessive combustion chamber deposits striking and adhering to the firing end of the plug. In this case, they wedge or fuse between the electrode and core nose. They originate from the piston and cylinder head surfaces. Deposits are formed by one or more of the following:
  a. Excessive carbon in cylinder.
  b. Immediate high-speed operation after prolonged trolling.

C. Wet fouling—Damp or wet, black carbon coating over entire firing end of plug. Forms sludge in some engines. Caused by one or more of the following:
  a. Spark plug heat range too cold.
  b. Prolonged trolling.
  c. Low speed carburetor adjustment too rich.
  d. Worn or defective breaker points.

D. Gap bridging—Similar to core bridging, except the combustion particles are wedged or fused between the electrodes. Causes are the same.

E. Overheating—Badly worn electrodes and premature gap wear are indicative of this problem, along with a gray or white "blistered" appearance on the insulator. Caused by one or more of the following:
  a. Spark plug heat range too hot.
  b. Incorrect propeller usage, causing engine to lug.
  c. Worn or defective water pump.
  d. Restricted water intake or restriction somewhere in the cooling system.

F. Ash deposits or lead fouling—Ash deposits are light brown to white in color and result from use of fuel or oil additives. Lead fouling produces a yellowish brown discoloration and can be avoided by using unleaded fuels.

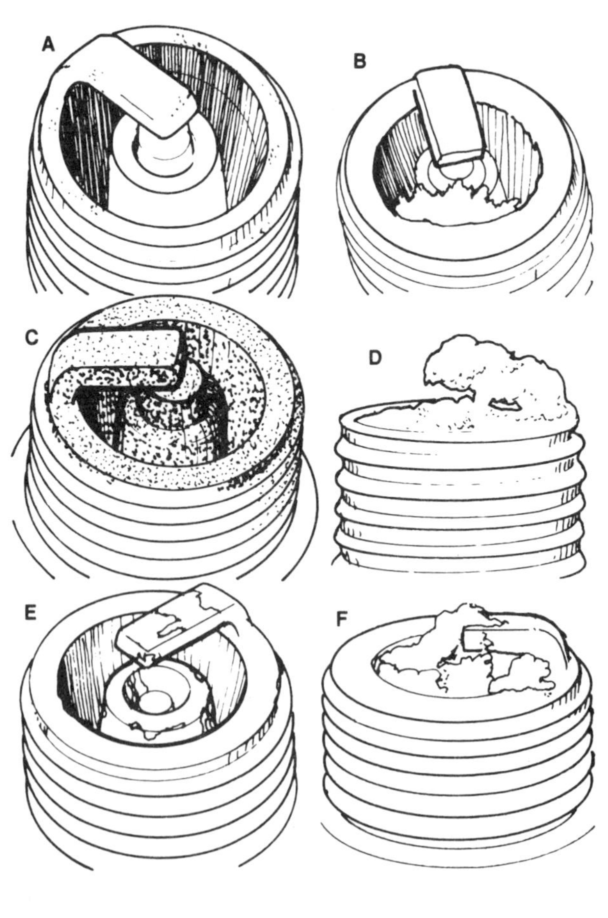

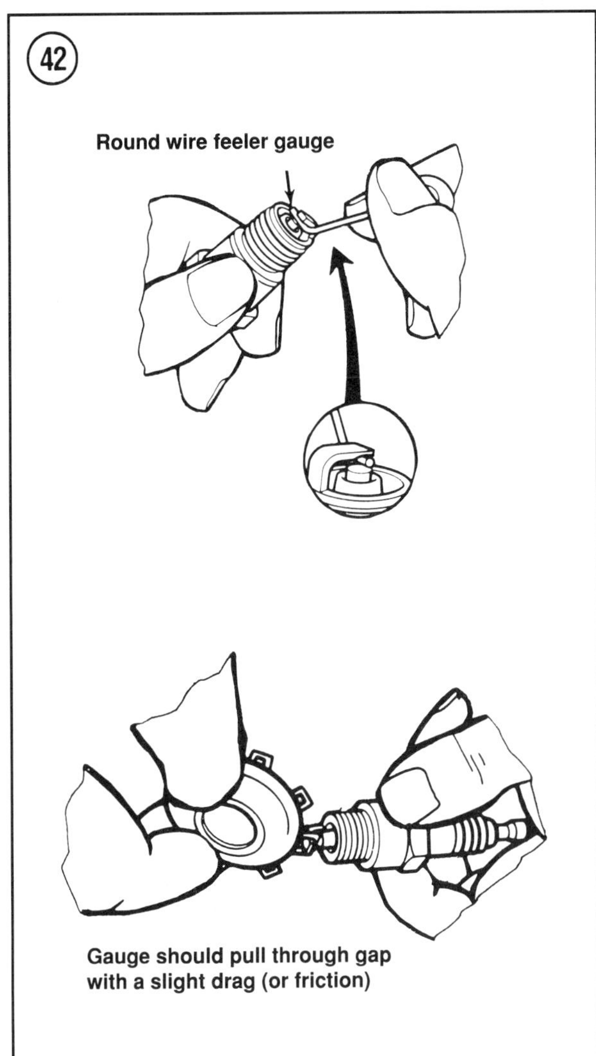

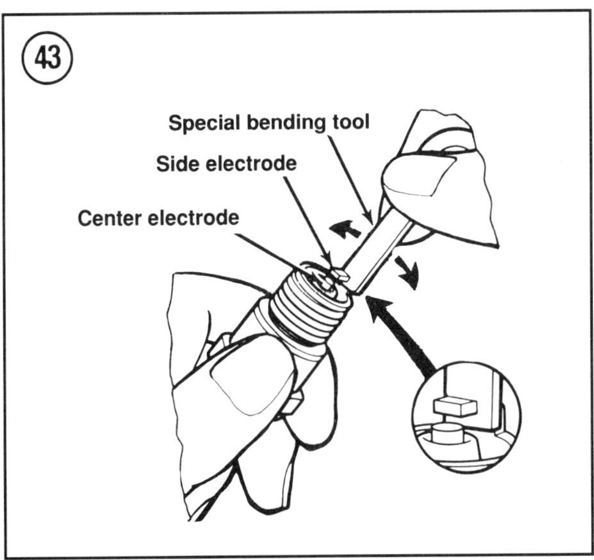

correctly. Replace the cap and rotor as a set if necessary.

4. Lift the rotor straight up and off the distributor shaft (**Figure 46**). Wipe the rotor with a clean, damp cloth. Check for burns, arcing, cracks and other defects. Replace the rotor and cap as a set if necessary.

5. Align the tang inside the rotor with the slot in the distributor shaft. Press the rotor onto the shaft until it is fully seated.

6. Grasp the rotor, twist it clockwise (GM and Volvo engines) or counterclockwise (Ford engines) and then release it. The rotor should return quickly to its original position when released. If not, the distributor advance mechanism requires service. This should be done by a dealer.

7. Install the distributor cap. Snap theclips in place or tighten the screws as required. See **Figure 44**.

Contact Breaker Point Replacement

The breaker points and condenser should be replaced during a tune-up. Copy the distributor number and use it to obtain the correct replacement parts. Set the dwell to the specifications in the engine owner's manual, then check ignition timing.

NOTE
Breaker point sets used in marine distributors have corrosion-resistant springs. Do not use automotive breaker points as a replacement. Use only NMMA marine-approved parts.

1. Remove distributor cap and rotor as described in this chapter.

2. Loosen the primary terminal nut and disconnect the primary lead. See **Figure 47**.

3. Unscrew the retaining screw(s) from the condenser and the breaker assembly. Observe the location of the ground wire so it may be installed in the same place, then remove the condenser and

breaker assembly from the distributor. See **Figure 48**.

NOTE
On distributors using a felt lubricating cam wick, install a new wick and proceed with Step 5.

4. Wipe the cam and breaker plate clean. See **Figure 49**. Lightly coat the cam with special distributor cam grease. Never use oil or common grease; they are likely to find their way onto the contact points.
5. Install the new contact breaker assembly and condenser in the distributor but do not tighten the locking screw. Make sure the ground lead, condenser lead and primary lead are installed exactly as they were before. Double check the connections and screw to ensure that they are tight.

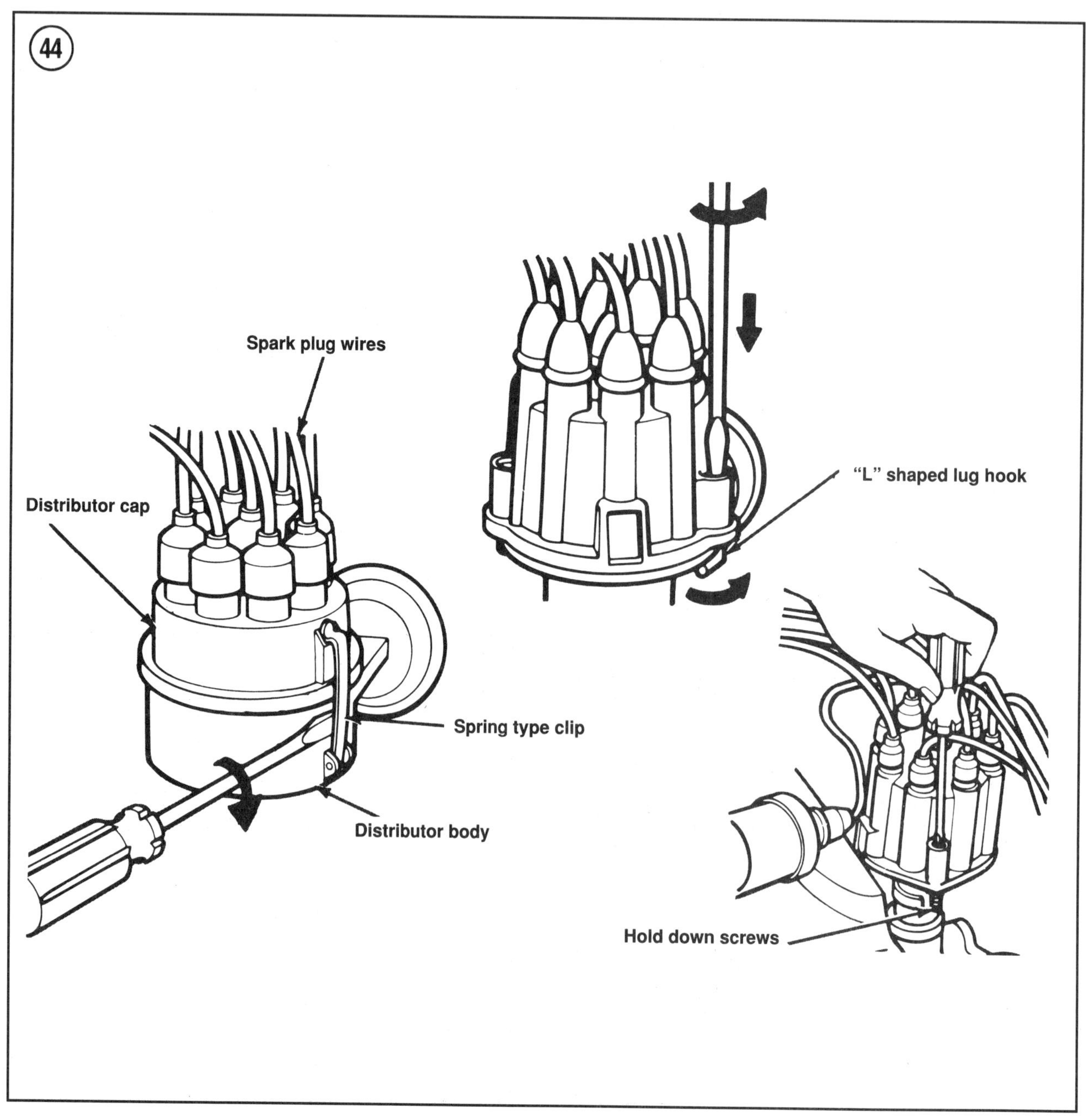

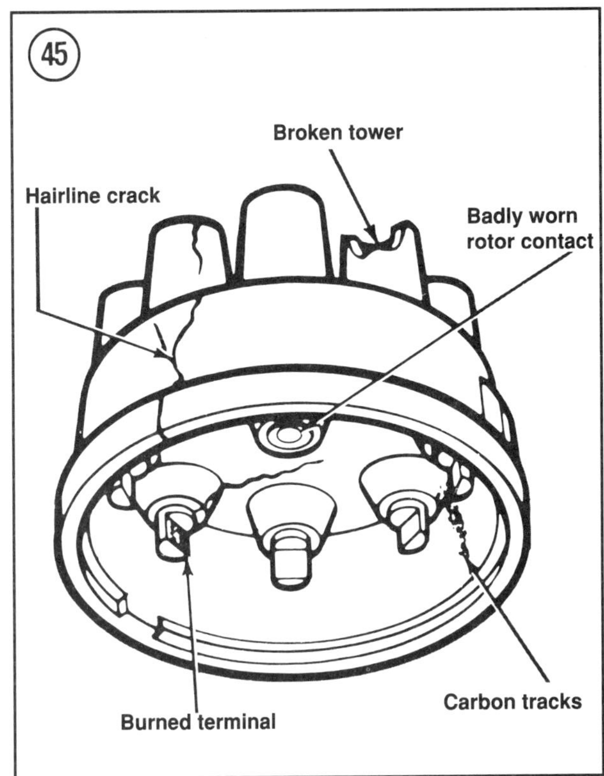

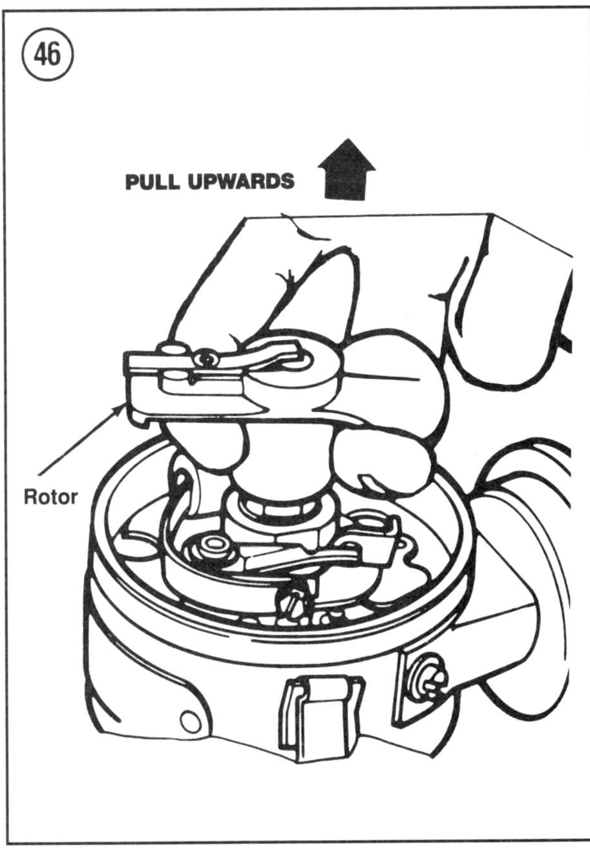

6. With the points closed, make certain the contact surfaces are properly aligned with each other **(Figure 50).** Make adjustments as required, bending the stationary arm of the points only. If reusing old points, they should not be realigned.

7. Check inside of distributor shaft. If a felt wick is installed, lubricate it with 1-3 drops of SAE 30 engine oil **(Figure 51)**.

8. Adjust breaker point gap as described in this chapter.

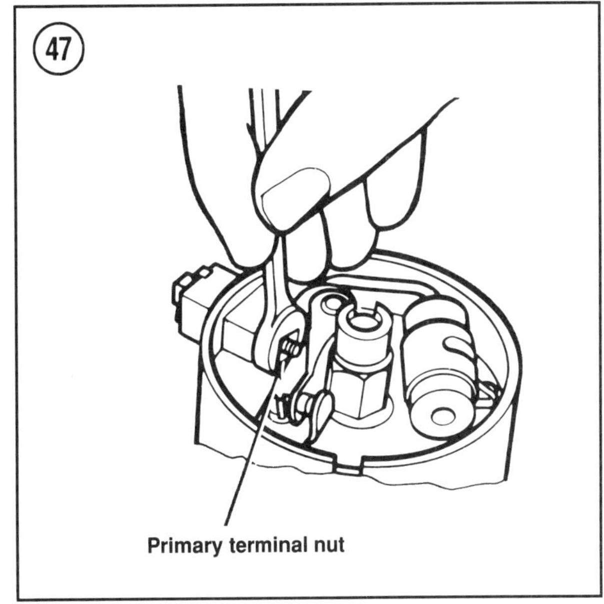

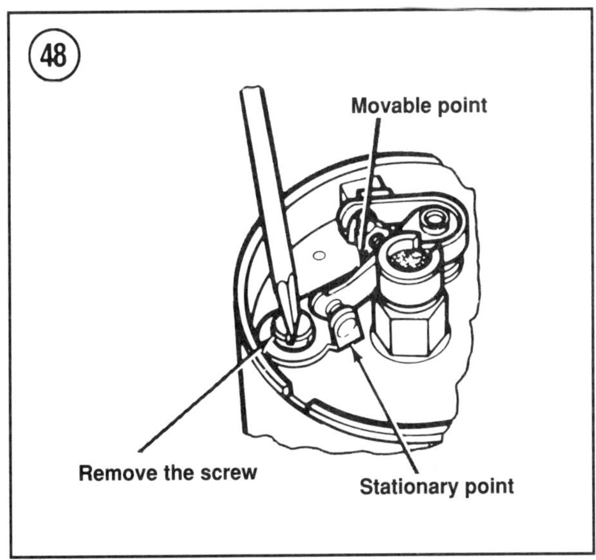

Breaker Point Gap Adjustment

There are 2 ways to adjust breaker point gap:

a. Feeler gauge.

b. Dwell meter. The dwell meter method is the most accurate.

Use the following procedure to set the gap with a feeler gauge.

1. Ground the ignition coil high tension lead.
2. Connect a remote starter button according to its manufacturer's instructions and crank the engine until the breaker point rubbing block rests on a distributor cam lobe, as shown in **Figure 52**. At this position, the points are fully open.
3. Insert a flat feeler gauge between the open points (**Figure 53**) and compare the gap to the specifications in the engine owner's manual. Gap adjustment is made either with an adjusting screw or with a screwdriver inserted in the slotted hole in the point set/breaker plate. See **Figure 54**. When a slight drag is felt on the gauge blade, tighten the locking screw. Recheck the gap to make sure the points did not move during tightening.

Use the following procedure to adjust point gap with a dwell meter.

1. Remove the distributor cap and rotor as described in this chapter.
2. Connect a dwell meter and remote starter button according to the manufacturer's instructions.
3. Crank engine with remote starter button and read dwell angle on meter.
4. Adjust the dwell by varying breaker point gap. Decrease the gap to increase dwell; increase the gap to decrease dwell.
5. Tighten breaker point locking screw.
6. Repeat Step 3 to recheck dwell.
7. Install the distributor rotor and cap as described in this chapter.
8. Start the engine and check dwell with engine idling. Reset if necessary.

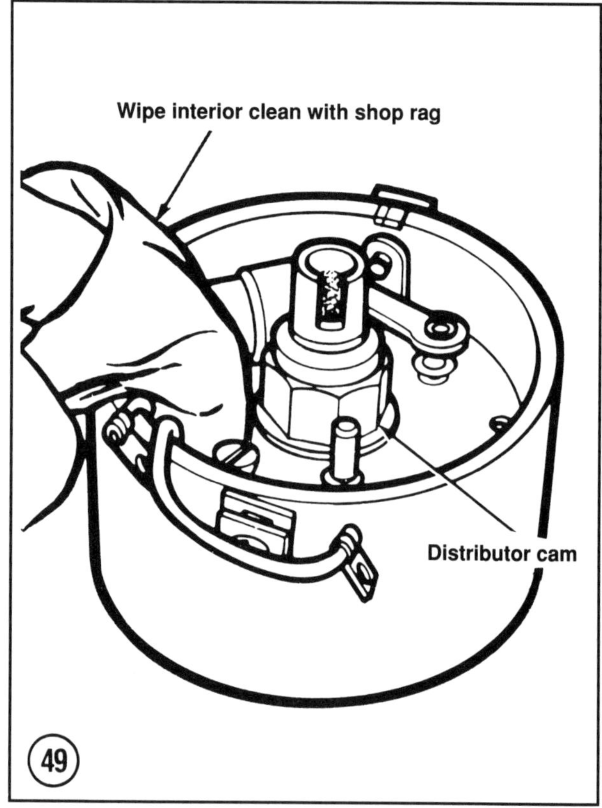

49

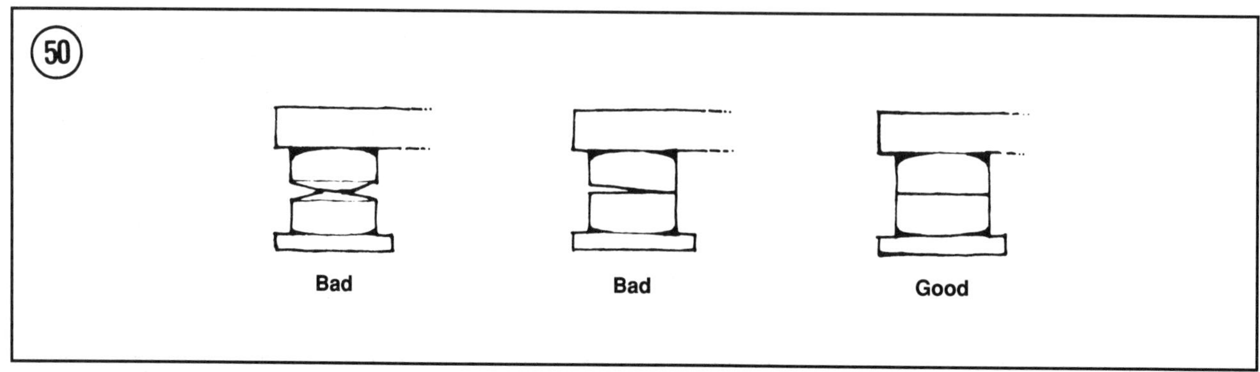

50

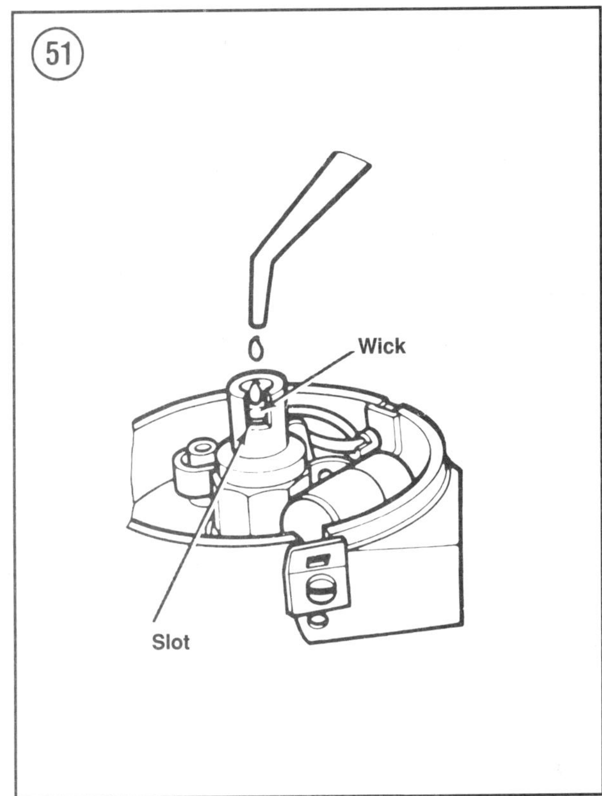

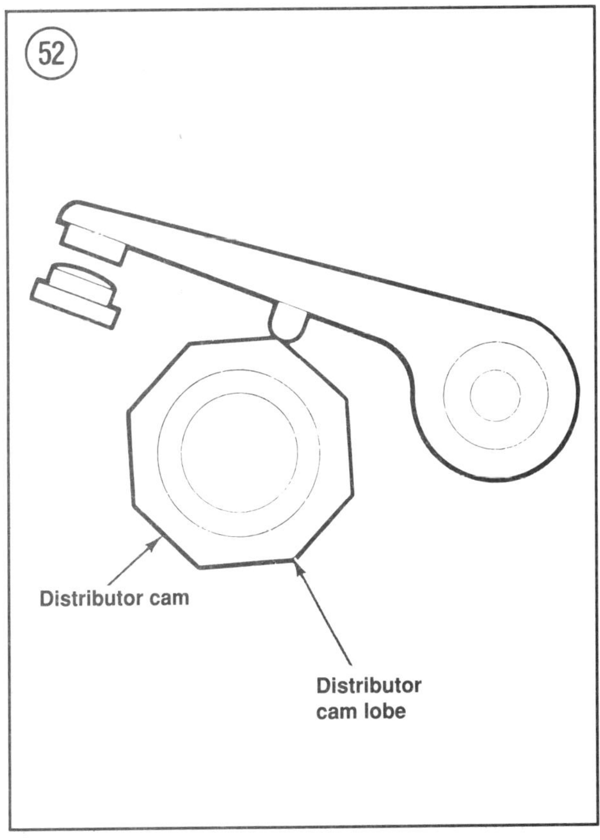

Ignition Timing

The No. 1 cylinder is the front cylinder on all inline engines. It is the front cylinder on the port side of GM V6 and V8 engines and on the starboard side of Ford V8 engines. See **Figure 55**.

1. Connect a timing light to the No. 1 spark plug wire according to timing light manufacturer's instructions.
2. Connect a tachometer according to its manufacturer's instructions.
3. Locate the timing marks on the engine timing cover or block and crankshaft pulley or harmonic balancer. See **Figure 56** for typical arrangements.
4. Clean the timing marks. Apply a coat of white paint or chalk so they can be more easily seen.
5. Start the engine and run at slow idle. Refer to the engine owner's manual for timing specifications and aim the timing light at the timing marks. If the engine timing is properly adjusted, the correct moving mark will appear to stand still opposite the stationary mark.
6. If timing marks are not properly aligned, loosen the hold-down bolt at the base of the distributor (**Figure 57**) just enough so the distributor body can be turned by hand with some resistance.

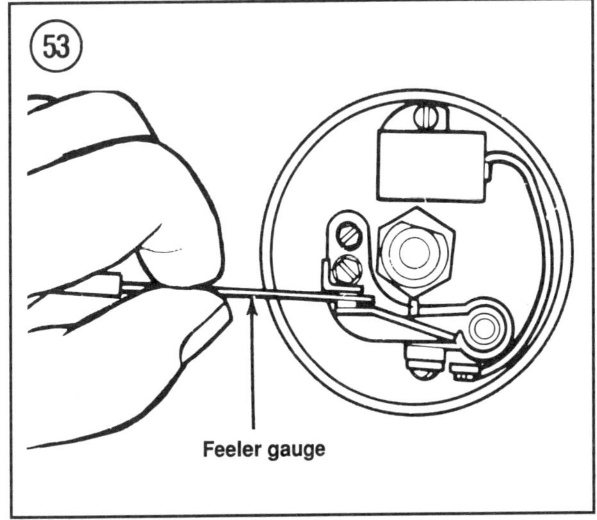

54

Slotted type
Point gap
Eccentric adjustment screw

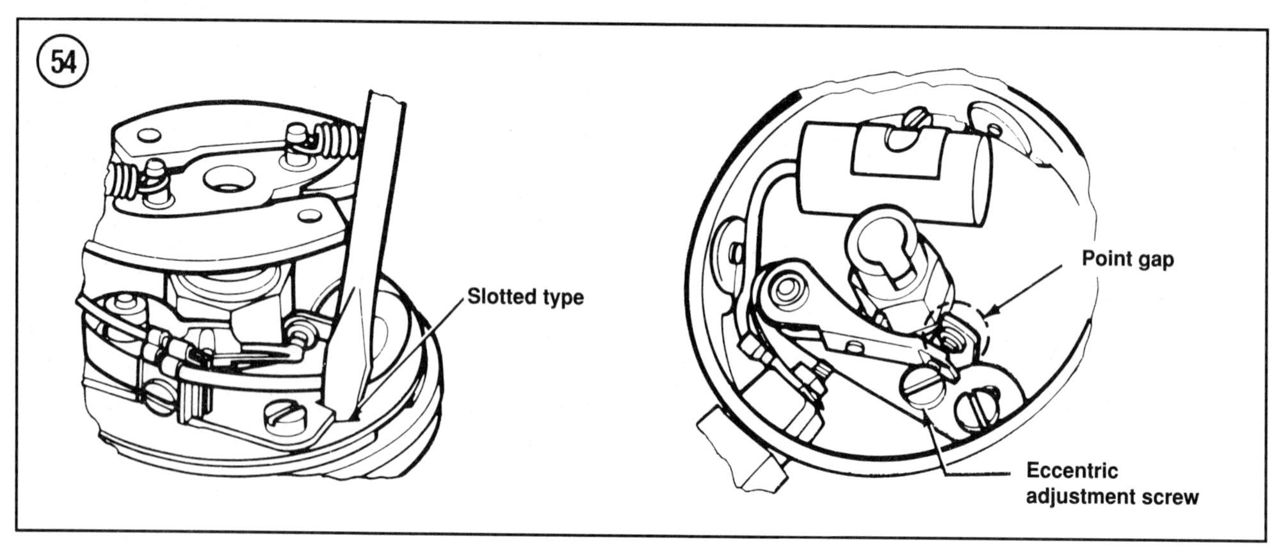

55

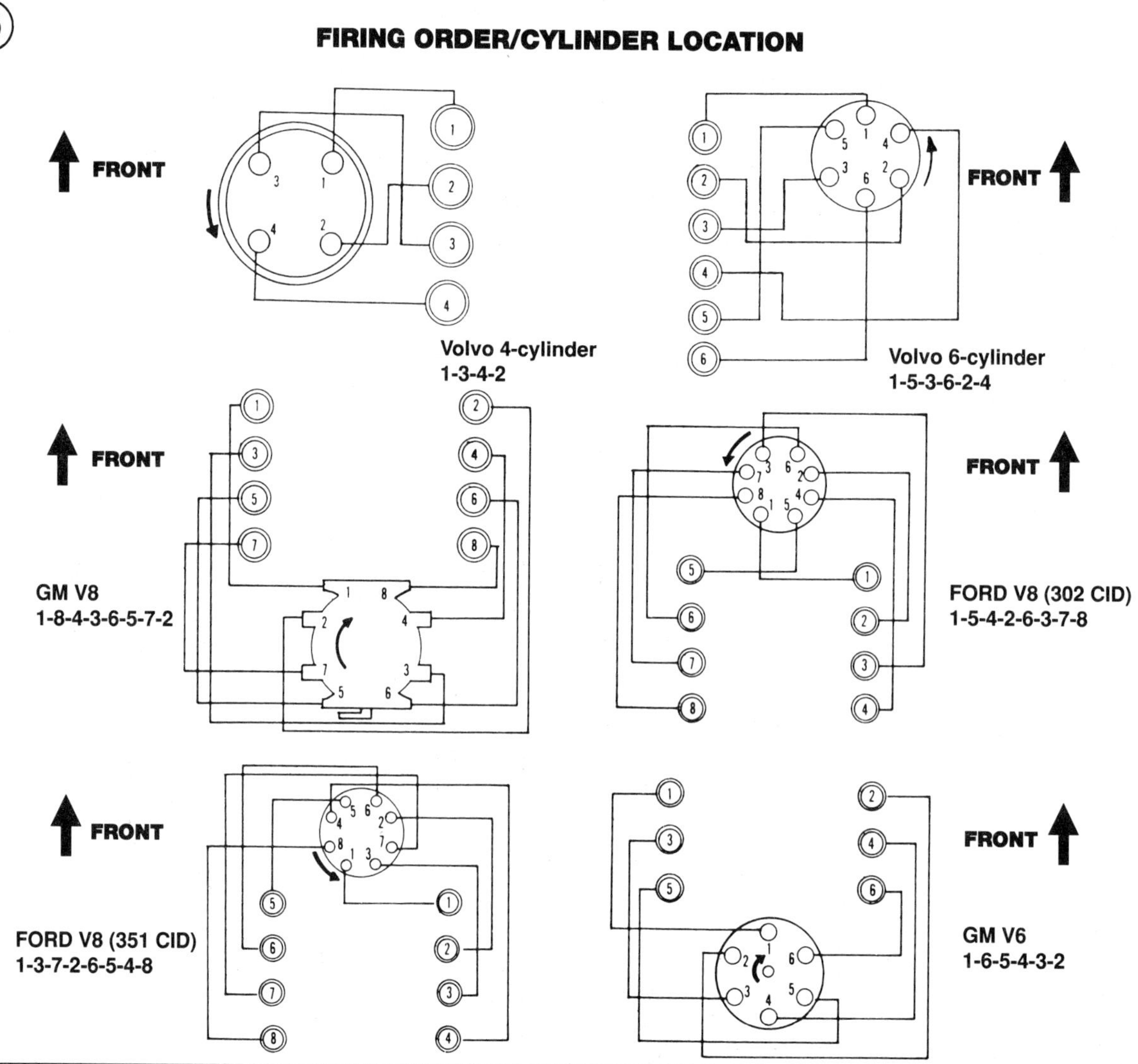

FIRING ORDER/CYLINDER LOCATION
FRONT
Volvo 4-cylinder
1-3-4-2
Volvo 6-cylinder
1-5-3-6-2-4
GM V8
1-8-4-3-6-5-7-2
FORD V8 (302 CID)
1-5-4-2-6-3-7-8
FORD V8 (351 CID)
1-3-7-2-6-5-4-8
GM V6
1-6-5-4-3-2

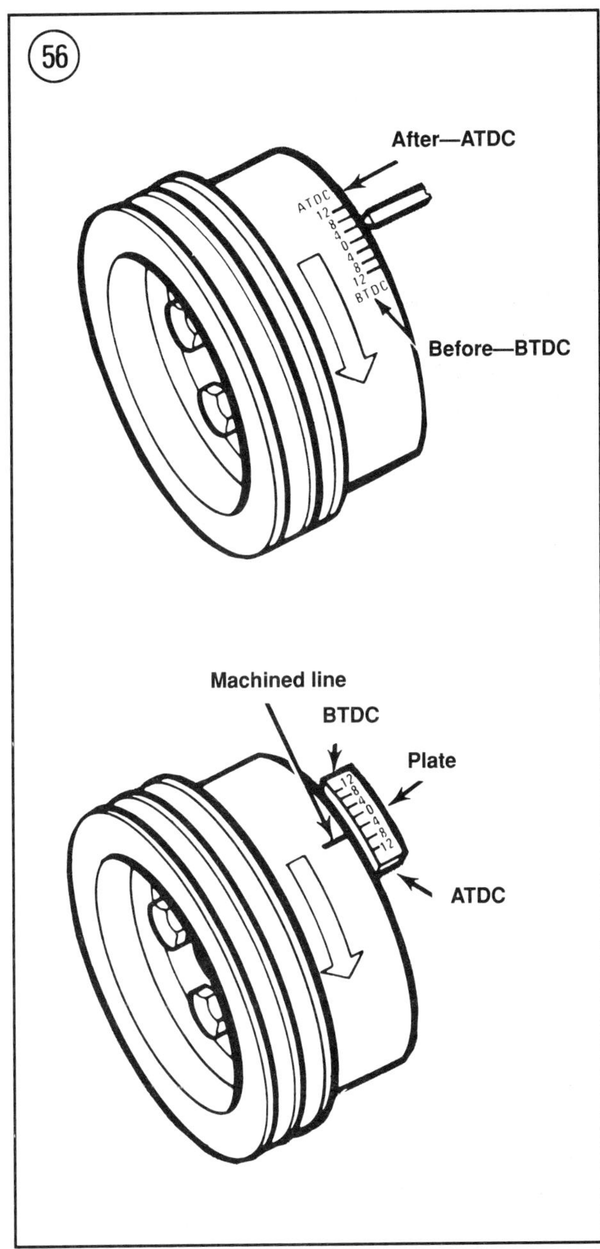

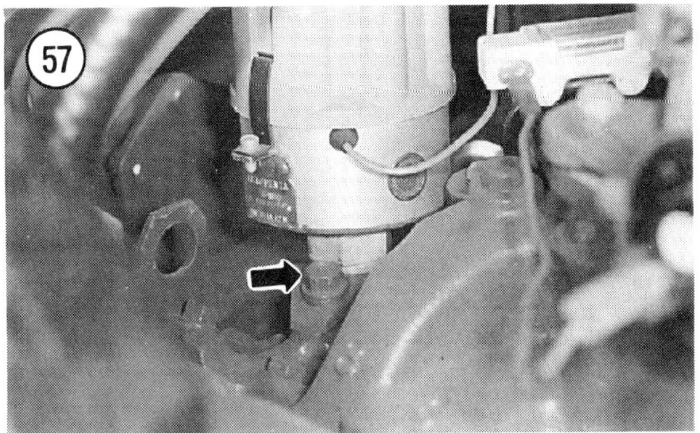

7. Slowly rotate the distributor body clockwise or counterclockwise as required until the marks come into alignment. See **Figure 58.**

8. Tighten the hold-down bolt without further moving the distributor. Recheck timing with the timing light. Repeat Step 6 and Step 7 if timing was disturbed while tightening the bolt.

9. After the initial timing has been set, check the operation of the centrifugal advance mechanism. With the engine operating at slow idle, observe the position of the timing marks with the timing light.

5

NOTE
If the timing mark moves with a jerky motion or does not start to move within 50-100 rpm of the specified speed in Step 10, the spark advance system is not working properly and must be cleaned or repaired.

10. Gradually increase the engine speed to about 1,800 rpm while observing the timing marks. The moving mark should move steadily in a direction opposite of engine rotation.

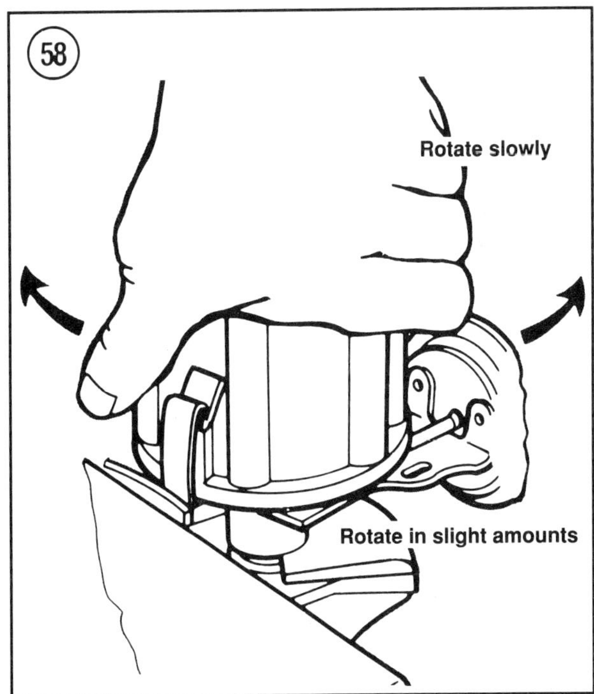

11. Decrease engine speed to slow idle while observing timing marks. The moving mark should move back smoothly as speed decreases.

Electronic Ignition System

Ignition timing is not adjustable on some electronic breakerless ignition system. On those that are adjustable, the procedure is very similar to the previous procedure for breaker point ignitions. Refer to the engine owner's manual for specifications.

CARBURETOR SERVICE (GASOLINE ENGINES)

There is such a wide range of single and multiple carburetor systems in use that it is impossible to provide general information that is useful. All carburetors have some means of adjusting the idle speed and the mixture. Some even allow setting low (idle) speed mixture separately from the high speed (full throttle) mixture. Refer to the engine owner's manual for details.

When multiple carburetors are used, they must be correctly synchronized. Each carburetor must be adjusted to provide the same air/fuel ratio. Their throttle plates must open and close at exactly the same time.

A Uni-Syn or other carburetor synchronization tool is necessary to obtain correct carburetor adjustment on multiple carburetor models. These simple devices measure manifold vacuum and can be obtained from many marine dealers, as well as automotive accessory shops.

DIESEL ENGINE TUNE-UP

Diesel engines do not require a tune-up in the same sense as a gasoline engine, primarily because the diesel engine uses compression for ignition instead of an electrical ignition system. Fewer maintenance tasks are thus required on a diesel engine but the required tasks are just as important, if not more so, as the more extensive gasoline engine maintenance.

Owner tune-up on a diesel engine should be limited to valve clearance adjustment. Tampering by an unskilled mechanic, especially with the injection system, can lead to serious and expensive damage.

Valve Clearance Adjustment

The valves should be adjusted every 200 hours of operation or at least once a year. Valves may be adjusted with the engine warm or cold, but the engine must be off. Valves are adjusted in the same sequence as the engine firing order. Typically, the 4-cylinder firing order is 1-3-4-2 and the 6-cylinder firing order is 1-5-3-6-2-4. Refer to the engine owner's manual for firing order and intake and exhaust valve clearance.

1. Remove the rocker arm cover.
2. Rotate the crankshaft clockwise until the 0 degree mark on the flywheel aligns with the timing pointer in the flywheel housing cutout (**Figure 59**). This will place the No. 1 cylinder in firing position. This position can be verified by placing a finger on the No. 1 rocker arms as the pulley notch nears the zero mark. If the

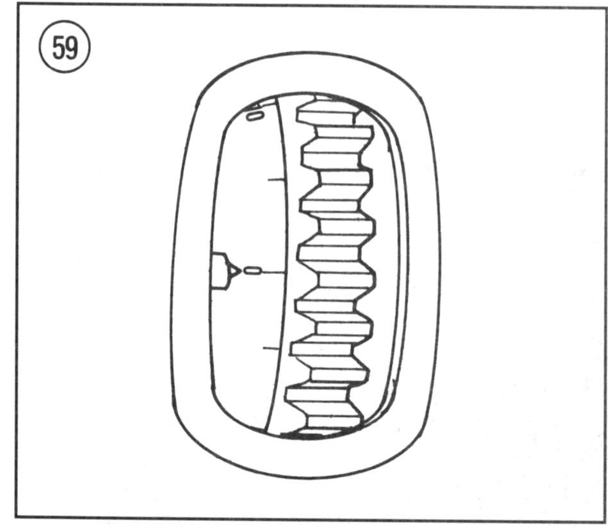

valves are moving, continue rotating the pulley one full turn to reach the No. 1 firing position.

3. Check the clearance of both No. 1 cylinder valves by inserting a flat feeler gauge of the correct thickness between the lifter heel and the end of the valve stem (**Figure 60**). If adjustment is required, loosen the adjusting screw locknut and turn the screw until the clearance is correct. Without turning the screw farther, tighten the locknut and recheck the clearance.

4. Rotate the crankshaft clockwise 1/2 turn (4-cylinder) or 1/3 turn (6-cylinder. Repeat Step 2 to check and adjust the clearance of both No. 3 cylinder valves (4-cylinder) or both No. 5 valves (6-cylinder).

5. Check the clearance of the remaining valves following the firing order sequence. Rotate the crankshaft clockwise l/2 turn (4-cylinder) or 1/3 turn (6-cylinder) after checking or adjusting each pair of valves.

6. Install the rocker arm cover with a new gasket. Do not overtighten the cover screws. Tighten them just enough to seal the cover and prevent oil leaks.

COOLING SYSTEM FLUSHING

Flushing procedures differ depending upon the type of cooling system and location of the water pump. Most engines are equipped with an external sea water pump mounted on the engine or in the stern drive. See **Figure 61** for a typical installation. This pump is driven by the camshaft or an intermediate shaft through a rubber coupling, or by the crankshaft pulley or harmonic balancer.

The sea water pump draws cooling water through the water intake of the stern drive, forcing it through an oil cooler (if so equipped) and exhaust manifold cooling jacket to the distribution housing.

Most engines also use an internal circulation pump to ensure proper cooling during engine warmup when the thermostat is closed.

WARNING
When the cooling system is flushed, make sure there is sufficient clear space to the side and behind the propeller and that no one is standing in the vicinity. If possible, remove the propeller to prevent the possibility of serious personal injury.

Sea Water Cooling System (Stern Drive)

A flushing device or test tank must be used with this procedure to provide cooling water.

Figure 62 shows a typical flushing device unit in use.

1. Attach the flushing device directly over the intake holes in the gear housing. Connect a hose between the device and the water tap.

CAUTION

Do not use full water tap pressure in Step 2.

2. Partially open the water tap to allow a low-pressure flow of water into the device. Let water flow for several minutes.

CAUTION

Do not run engine above idle speed while flushing system in Step 3.

3. Place the gearshift lever in NEUTRAL. Start engine and run at normal idle until engine reaches normal operating temperature, as shown on the temperature gauge.
4. Watch the water being flushed from the cooling system. When the water flow is clear, shut the engine off.
5. Shut the water tap off. Disconnect and remove the flushing device from gear housing.

Fresh Water Cooling System (Stern Drive)

1. Attach the flushing device directly over the intake holes in the gear housing. Connect a hose between the device and the water tap.

CAUTION

Do not use full water tap pressure in Step 2.

2. Partially open the water tap to allow a low-pressure flow of water into the device. Let water flow for several minutes.
3. Loosen the water intake hose clamp and remove the hose from the circulating pump inlet. See **Figure 63**, typical.
4. Connect a length of garden hose between the circulating pump inlet and a water tap.

CAUTION

Do not use full water tap pressure in Step 5.

5. Partially open the water tap to allow a low-pressure flow of water into the circulating pump inlet.

CAUTION

Make sure that water is being discharged from the exhaust outlets in Step 6. If not, shut engine off immediately and check flushing hose connections.

6. Place the remote control handle in NEUTRAL. Start the engine and run at normal idle until the engine reaches normal operating temperature, as shown by the temperature gauge.
7. Watch the water being flushed from cooling system. When water flow is clear, shut the engine off.
8. Shut the water tap off and remove the garden hose from the circulating pump inlet and water tap. Reconnect the water intake hose to the pump inlet and tighten the clamp securely.
9. Refill the cooling system with a 50/50 mixture of ethylene glycol antifreeze and water.
10. Remove flushing device from the lower unit.

ENGINE TROUBLESHOOTING

Any engine requires an uninterrupted fuel supply, air, unfailing ignition (gasoline) and ade-

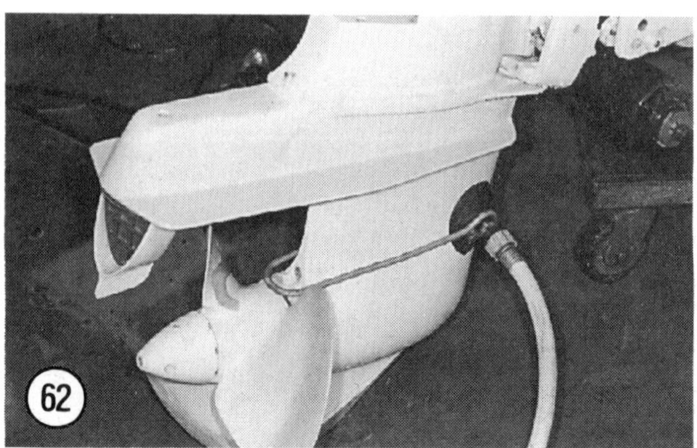
62

quate compression. If any one of these is lacking, the engine will not run. Troubleshooting must first localize the trouble to one of these areas, then concentrate on finding the specific cause. **Table 3** (Gasoline) and **Table 4** (Diesel) will permit you to localize specific troubles with a minimum of effort.

WINTER LAY-UP OR STORAGE

As mentioned earlier, engines thrive on use. The engine cannot remain unattended for long periods without preventive maintenance and occasional running unless special precautions are taken to protect it. The following procedures will provide protection for each of the important engine systems.

Diesel Fuel System

There are 2 ways of protecting the fuel system during long lay-ups. One method requires replacing the fuel with a special fuel system preservative. Usually only enough is put in the fuel tank to get the fuel system properly bled.

The second method permits leaving the normal fuel in the system during lay-up. However, the normal fuel deteriorates with time, producing a wax-likc contaminant which quickly clogs thc fuel system when the engine is returned to service. If this method is used, the old fuel must be drained from the system entirely and discarded. Additionally, the fuel tank interior should be cleaned and all fuel filters must be replaced.

Finally, the tanks should be filled with fresh fuel and the system bled.

Protection With Special Preservative

1. Drain the entire fuel system including the tanks, pipes and filters.

NOTE
As the season in your area nears the end, try to keep onboard fuel at a minimum.

2. Fill the fuel tank with about 1 gal. of preservative-type fuel. 5

NOTE
If 1 gallon is insufficient to permit engine to draw fuel, add more preservative.

3. Bleed the fuel system as described in this chapter.
4. Start the engine and run for 10-15 minutes at half cruising speed with no load.

Protection With Normal Fuel Oil

No special steps need to be taken. Simply leave the fuel system primed. Excess fuel in the tanks should be drained to make cleaning easier when the engine is returned to service.

Gasoline Fuel System

1. Drain fuel tank.
2. Run motor until all fuel in the carburetor is used.
3. Remove the spark plug(s). Squirt about 1/2 tea-spoon of oil directly into the spark plug hole(s). Rotate the flywheel 1 revolution.
4. Place a drop of clean engine oil on the spark plug threads. Install the plugs and tighten finger-tight. Tighten plugs 1/2 turn with the spark plug wrench. Do not overtighten.

Lubrication System

1. Drain the engine oil no matter how many hours it has been in use.

2. Remove the rocker cover(s). If sludge build-up is heavy, flush the engine with a flushing oil.
3. Replace the oil filter.
4. Fill the sump with fresh oil. Run the engine briefly to circulate the fresh oil.
5. Remove and clean the engine breather pipe.
6. Remove the injectors and pour 2-4 tablespoons of fresh engine oil into each cylinder. Rotate the crankshaft by hand 4 or 5 times to spread oil over the cylinder walls.
7. Install the injectors with new gaskets.

Cooling System

Drain the entire cooling system as described elsewhere in this chapter. The engine cooling system may remain empty during lay-up. A label or tag should be firmly attached in a conspicuous place. For example, attach it to the instrument panel or to the throttle lever indicating the system is empty.

Rather than leave the system empty, a better procedure is to refill the system with a biodegradable type antifreeze. Be sure it is rated for year-round protection and dilute it to protect well below the lowest temperature in the area. This same mixture may be left in the system when the engine is returned to service and only replaced prior to each lay-up period.

Electrical System

Prepare the battery and electrical system for lay-up as described in Chapter Seven.

Sealing Engine

1. Remove the air cleaner and any air intake pipe that may be installed between spark arrestor and air intake. Place a small bag of silica gel just inside the air intake. Carefully seal the air intake with waterproof adhesive tape or duct tape.
2. Disconnect the exhaust pipe from the exhaust manifold and seal the opening in the manifold with tape.
3. Seal the breather pipe opening with tape.
4. Seal the air vent in the fuel tank or filler cap with tape. This will reduce the risk of water condensation.
5. Remove drive belt(s) and store in a cool, dry place.

Table 1 MAINTENANCE SCHEDULE (GASOLINE)

Daily	Check oil level Check coolant level in expansion tank, if so equipped Check fuel system for leakage Check fuel supply Inspect all electrical components
Every 14 days	Check stern drive lubricant level Check power trim pump oil level, if so equipped Check and adjust alternator drive belt tension Check zinc anode condition Check universal joint bellows condition and replace as required
Every 50 hours of operation	Change engine oil Lubricate steering shaft bearings/journals Replace spark plugs Retorque cylinder head bolts (4- and 6-cylinder inline) Check and adjust valve clearances (4- and 6-cylinder inline) Check and adjust or replace breaker points and condenser

(continued)

Table 1 MAINTENANCE SCHEDULE (GASOLINE) (continued)

Every 100 hours of operation	Change oil filter Change stern drive lubricant Check ignition system connections and insulation Check impeller condition (replace every 2 years) Set ignition timing Check distributor cap, rotor and wires Check and adjust carburetor Clean or change fuel strainers and filters Clean flame arrestor Check cooling system and hose condition* Check battery condition Check propeller for damage

* Drain after operating in freezing temperatures or during a seasonal lay-up.

Table 2 MAINTENANCE SCHEDULE (DIESEL)

Daily	Check oil level Check coolant level in expansion tank, if so equipped Check fuel system for leakage Check fuel supply Inspect all electrical connections
Every 14 days	Check stern drive lubricant level Check power trim pump oil level, if so equipped Check and adjust alternator drive belt tension Check battery electrolyte level Check zinc anode condition
Every 50 hours	Lubricate steering shaft bearings/journals Clean and check sea water filter Retorque cylinder head bolts Check and adjust valve clearance
Every 100 hours	Change engine oil
Every 200 hours	Change oil filter Change stern drive lubricant Check and adjust alternator drive belt Check and adjust valve clearance Change the crankcase vent and air filters Check cooling system and hose condition* Check turbocharger air tube, if so equipped Change sea water pump impeller Check battery condition Check electrical system Change fuel filter(s)

* Drain after operating in freezing temperatures or during a seasonal lay-up.

Table 3 TROUBLESHOOTING GASOLINE ENGINES

Trouble	Probable cause	Correction
Starter will not crank engine	Discharged battery	Charge or replace battery
	Corroded battery terminals	Clean terminals
	Loose connection in starting circuit	Check and tighten all connections

(continued)

Table 3 TROUBLESHOOTING GASOLINE ENGINES (continued)

Trouble	Probable cause	Correction
Starter will not crank engine (continued)	Defective starting switch	Replace switch
	Starter motor brushes dirty	Clean or replace brushes
	Jammed starter drive	Loosen starter motor to free gear
	Defective starter motor	Replace motor
Starter motor turns but does not crank engine	Partially discharged battery	Charge or replace battery
	Defective wiring or wiring too small	Repair or replace wiring
	Broken starter drive	Remove starter motor and repair drive
Engine will not start	Empty fuel tank	Fill tank with proper fuel
	Flooded engine	Remove spark plugs and crank engine several times. Replace plugs
	Water in fuel system	If water is found, clean tank, fuel lines and carburetor. Refill with proper fuel
	Inoperative or sticking choke valve	Check valve, linkage, and choke rod or cable for proper operation
	Improperly adjusted carburetor	Adjust carburetor
	Clogged fuel lines or defective fuel pump	Disconnect fuel line at carburetor. If fuel does not flow freely when engine is cranked, clean fuel line and filter. If fuel still does not flow freely after cleaning, repair or replace pump.
Engine will not start. (Poor compression and other causes)	Air leak around intake manifold	Check for leak by squirting oil around intake connections. If leak is found, tighten manifold and if necessary replace gaskets
	Loose spark plugs	Check spark plugs for proper seating, gasket, and tightness. Replace all damaged plugs and gaskets
	Loosely seating valves	Check for broken or weak valve springs, warped stems, carbon and gum deposits, and insufficient tappet clearance
	Damaged cylinder head gasket	Check for leaks around gasket when engine is cranked. If a leak is found, replace gasket
	Worn or broken piston rings	Replace broken and worn rings. Check cylinders for excessive out-of-round and taper.

Table 4 TROUBLESHOOTING DIESEL ENGINES

Trouble	Probable cause
Low cranking speed	Battery capacity low
	Bad electrical connections
	Faulty starter motor
	Incorrect grade of lubricating oil
Will not start	Low cranking speed
	Fuel tank empty
	Faulty stop control operation

(continued)

Table 4 TROUBLESHOOTING DIESEL ENGINES (continued)

Trouble	Probable cause
Will not start (continued)	Blocked fuel feed pipe
	Faulty fuel lift pump
	Choked fuel filter
	Air in fuel system
	Faulty fuel injection pump
	Faulty atomizers or incorret type
	Incorrect use of cold start equipment
	Faulty cold starting equipment
	Broken fuel injection pump drive
	Incorrect injection pump timing
	Incorrect valve timing
	Poor compressoin
	Incorrect type or grade of fuel
	Worn cylinder bores
	Pitted valves and seats
	Broken, worn or sticking piston ring(s)
Difficult starting	Low cranking speed
	Faulty stop control operation
	Blocked fuel feed pipe
	Faulty fuel lift pump
	Choked fuel filter
	Restriction in air cleaner
	Air in fuel system
	Faulty fuel injection pump
	Faulty atomizers or incorrect type
	Incorrect use of cold start equipment
	Faulty cold starting equipment
	Incorrect injection pump timing
	Incorrect valve timing
	Poor compression
	Blocked fuel tank vent
	Incorrect type or grade of fuel
	Exhaust pipe restriction
	Sticking valves
	Worn cylinder bores
	Pitted valves and seats
	Broken, worn or sticking piston ring(s)
Lack of power	Blocked fuel feed pipe
	Faulty fuel lift pump
	Choked fuel filter
	Restriction in air cleaner
	Air in fuel system
	Faulty fuel injection pump
	Faulty atomizers or incorrect type
	Incorrect injection pump timing
	Incorrect valve timing
	Poor compression
	Blocked fuel tank vent
	Incorrect type or grade of fuel
	Sticking throttle or restricted movement
	Exhaust pipe restriction
	Cylinder head gasket leaking
	Overheating

(continued)

Table 4 TROUBLESHOOTING DIESEL ENGINES (continued)

Trouble	Probable cause
Lack of power (continued)	Cold running
	Worn cylinder bores
	Pitted valves and seats
	Broken, worn or sticking piston ring(s)
Misfiring	Blocked fuel feed pipe
	Faulty fuel lift pump
	Choked fuel filter
	Air in fuel system
	Faulty fuel injection pump
	Faulty atomizers or incorrect type
	Faulty cold starting equipment
	Incorrect injection pump timing
	Incorrect valve timing
	Poor compression
	Cylinder head gasket leaking
	Overheating
	Incorrect tappet adjustment
	Sticking valves
	Incorrect high pressure pipes
	Pitted valves and seats
Excessive fuel consumption	Restriction in air cleaner
	Faulty fuel injection pump
	Faulty atomizers or incorrect type
	Faulty cold starting equipment
	Incorrect injection pump timing
	Incorrect valve timing
	Poor compression
	Incorrect type or grade of fuel
	Sticking throttle or restricted movement
	Exhaust pipe restriction
	Cylinder head gasket leaking
	Cold running
	Incorrect tappet adjustment
	Sticking valves
	Worn cylinder bores
	Pitted valves and seats
	Broken, worn or sticking piston ring(s)
Black exhaust	Restriction in air cleaner
	Faulty fuel injection pump
	Faulty atomizers or incorrect type
	Faulty cold starting equipment
	Incorrect injection pump timing
	Incorrect valve timing
	Poor compression
	Incorrect type or grade of fuel
	Exhaust pipe restriction
	Cylinder head gasket leaking
	Cold running
	Incorrect tappet adjustment
	Sticking valves
	Worn cylinder bores
	Pitted valves and seats
	Broken, worn or sticking piston ring(s)

(continued)

Table 4 TROUBLESHOOTING DIESEL ENGINES (continued)

Trouble	Probable cause
Blue/white exhaust	Incorrect grade of lubricating oil
	Faulty cold starting equipment
	Incorrect fuel pump timng
	Incorrect valve timing
	Poor compression
	Cylinder head gasket leaking
	Cold running
	Worn cylinder bores
	Broken, worn or sticking piston ring(s)
	Worn valve stems and guides
	Damaged valve stem oil deflectors (if fitted)
Low oil pressure	Incorrect grade of lubricating oil
	Worn or damaged bearings
	Insufficient oil in sump
	Inaccurate gauge
	Oil pump worn
	Pressure relief valve sticking open
	Broken relief valve spring
	Faulty suction pipe
	Choked oil filter
	Blocked sump strainer
Knocking	Faulty fuel lift pump
	Faulty atomizers or incorrect type
	Faulty cold starting equipment
	Incorrect injection pump timing
	Incorrect valve timing
	Incorrect type or grade of fuel
	Overheating
	Incorrect tappet adjustment
	Sticking valves
	Worn cylinder bores
	Broken, worn or sticking piston ring(s)
	Worn or damaged bearings
	Piston seizure
	Incorrect piston height
	Broken valve spring
Erratic running	Faulty stop control operation
	Blocked fuel feed pipe
	Faulty fuel lift pump
	Choked fuel filter
	Restriction in air cleaner
	Air in fuel system
	Faulty fuel injection pump
	Faulty atomizers or incorrect type
	Faulty cold starting equipment
	Poor compression
	Blocked fuel tank vent
	Sticking throttle or restricted movement
	Overheating
	Incorrect tappet adjustment
	Sticking valves
	Incorrect high pressure pipes
	Broken, worn or sticking piston ring(s)
	Broken valve spring

(continued)

Table 4 TROUBLESHOOTING DIESEL ENGINES (continued)

Trouble	Probable cause
Vibration	Faulty fuel injection pump
	Faulty atomizers or incorrect type
	Poor compression
	Sticking throttle or restricted movement
	Cylinder head gasket leaking
	Overheating
	Sticking valves
	Broken, worn or sticking piston ring(s)
	Piston seizure
	Damaged fan
	Faulty engine mounting (housing)
	Incorrectly aligned flywheel housing or flywheel
High oil pressure	Incorrect grade of lubricating oil
	Inaccurate gauge
	Pressure relief valve sticking closed
Overheating	Restriction in air cleaner
	Faulty fuel injection pump
	Faulty atomizers or incorrect type
	Faulty cold starting equipment
	Incorrect injection pump timing
	Incorrect valve timing
	Exhaust pipe restriction
	Cylinder head gasket leaking
	Faulty thermostat
	Restriction in water jacket
	Loose fan belt
	Choked radiator
	Faulty water pump
	Coolant level too low
Excessive crankcase pressure	Cylinder head gasket leaking
	Worn cylinder bores
	Broken, worn or sticking piston ring(s)
	Worn valve stems and guides
	Choked breather pipe
Poor compression	Restriction in air cleaner
	Incorrect valve timing
	Cylinder head gasket leaking
	Incorrect tappet adjustment
	Sticking valves
	Worn cylinder bores
	Pitted valves and seats
	Broken, worn or sticking piston ring(s)
	Worn valve stems and guides
	Incorrect piston height
	Broken valve spring
Starts and stops	Choked fuel filter
	Restriction in air cleaner
	Air in fuel system

Chapter Six

Stern Drive and Inboard Drive Units

Inboard drive units are basically gearcases which transfer engine power to the propeller. These rugged devices require minimum but essential maintenance. In most cases, this amounts to maintaining adequate fluid levels, changing the fluid periodically and checking for leaks. Leaks are damaging, not only because they allow vital lubricants to escape, but they permit corrosive water to enter and attack precision components inside.

SHOP MANUAL

A shop manual for the model and year of your engine and drive unit is essential. While this chapter can give you general service information that is common to most installations, you will need a shop manual for more specific information. Clymer Shop Manuals cover everything from the simplest adjustments to complete overhaul and are available for most engines and drive units.

STANDARD INSTALLATION

Figure 1 shows the traditional inboard engine/drive unit installation. It consists of an engine, final drive unit, a shaft, stuffing box and propeller.

The engine may be diesel or gasoline. A final drive unit bolts directly to the aft end of the engine block. The final drive may provide a gear reduction between engine and propeller, so the propeller turns slower than the engine. It may instead provide direct drive (1:1) and one or more other gear ratios. In addition, most drive units provide reverse.

The propeller shaft passes through the hull in a stuffing box. The stuffing box is packed with grease to prevent entry of water. The propeller bolts to the end of the shaft and is secured with a castellated nut and a cotter pin.

Some installations have a 2-piece prop shaft joined with a universal coupling. See **Figure 2**. This is sometimes necessary when compromising between available space and desired shaft

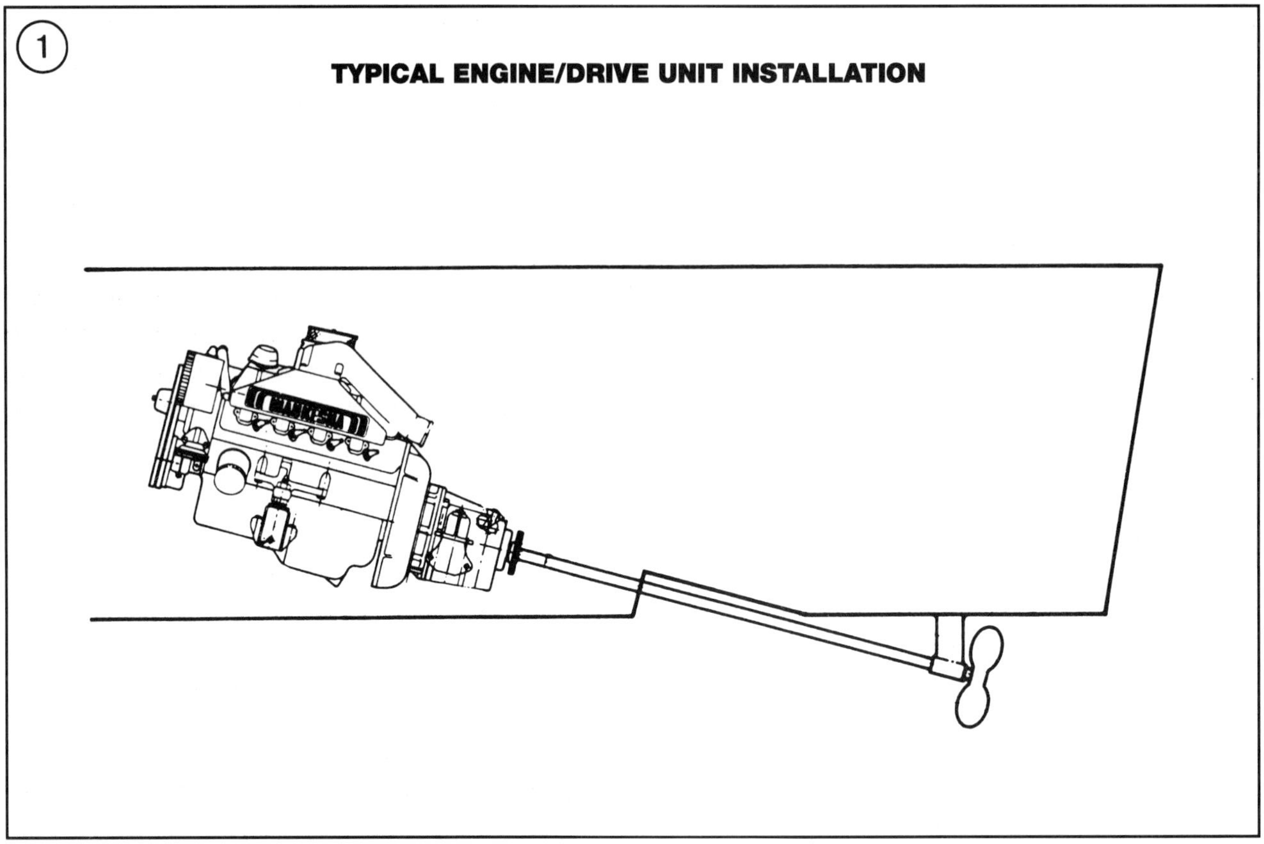

1

TYPICAL ENGINE/DRIVE UNIT INSTALLATION

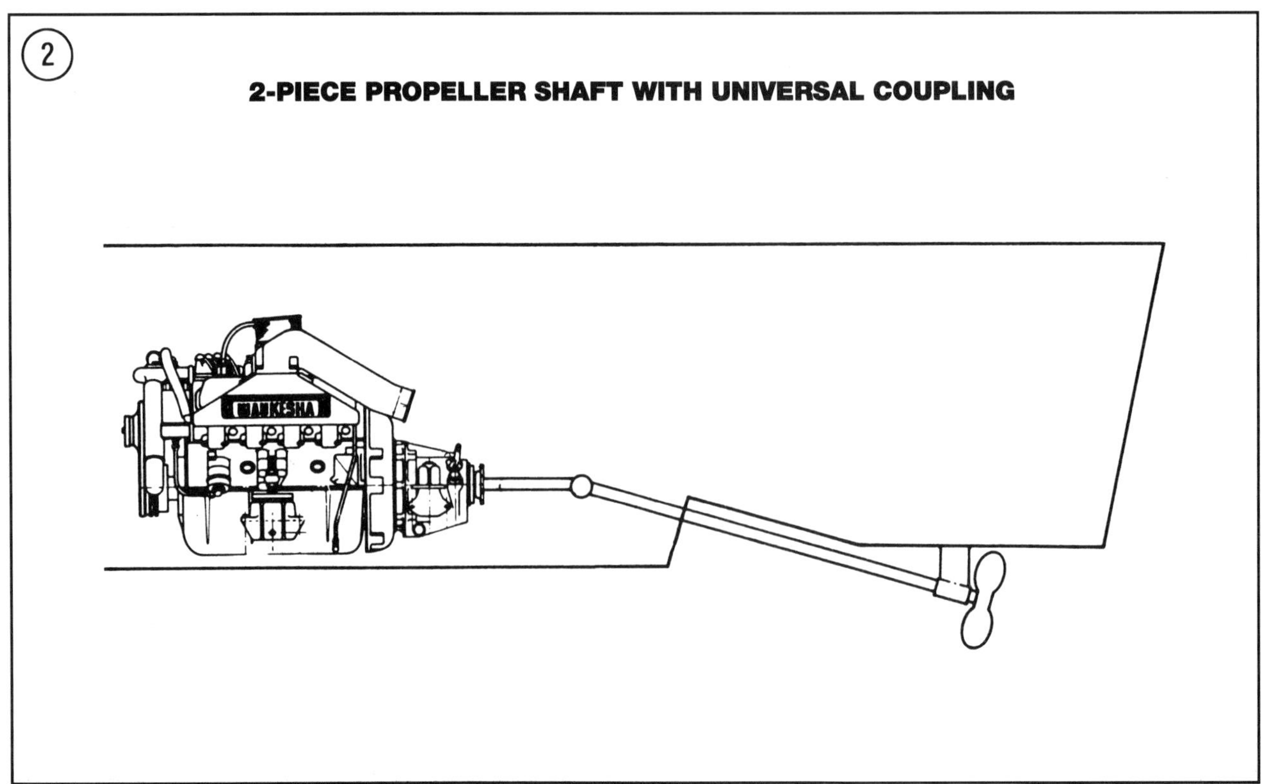

2

2-PIECE PROPELLER SHAFT WITH UNIVERSAL COUPLING

angle. Some universal couplings require lubrication.

V-DRIVE INSTALLATION

Figure 3 shows a V-drive installation. A V-drive works the same way as the standard in-line type. Folding the power transfer back on itself, however, provides additional cabin space by moving the engine aft.

V-drive units are available with direct drive, reduction ratios and reverse. The drive unit may be gear driven or hydraulic.

STERN DRIVE INSTALLATION

Stern drive (inboard/outboard) installations are most popular in medium-sized power boats. The engine mounts in the boat similar to a standard inboard installation. The drive unit, which resembles an outboard motor drive unit, mounts on the transom. See **Figure 4**. This installation has a number of advantages. Since the drive unit rotates to steer the boat, maneuverability is extraordinary; the boat can turn in its own length. The drive unit can be lifted to prevent damage in shallow water or when beaching the boat. Furthermore, the engine mounts close to the transom, providing more usable cabin space like the V-drive installation.

Both propeller drive and jet drive models are available. The propeller drive model operates in the same manner as a standard outboard motor. The drive unit provides power transfer from the engine to the propeller through a set of gears. See **Figure 5**.

Jet drive models propel the boat with a high speed stream of water. See **Figure 6**. The drive unit draws water in through a flush-mounted grill in the bottom of the boat. The engine-driven impeller increases the velocity of the water and discharges it through the nozzle at the rear of the unit. This powerful stream provides the forward thrust to move the boat. The nozzle can be swiveled left or right to steer the boat. A reverse gate deflects the stream under the boat to reverse direction.

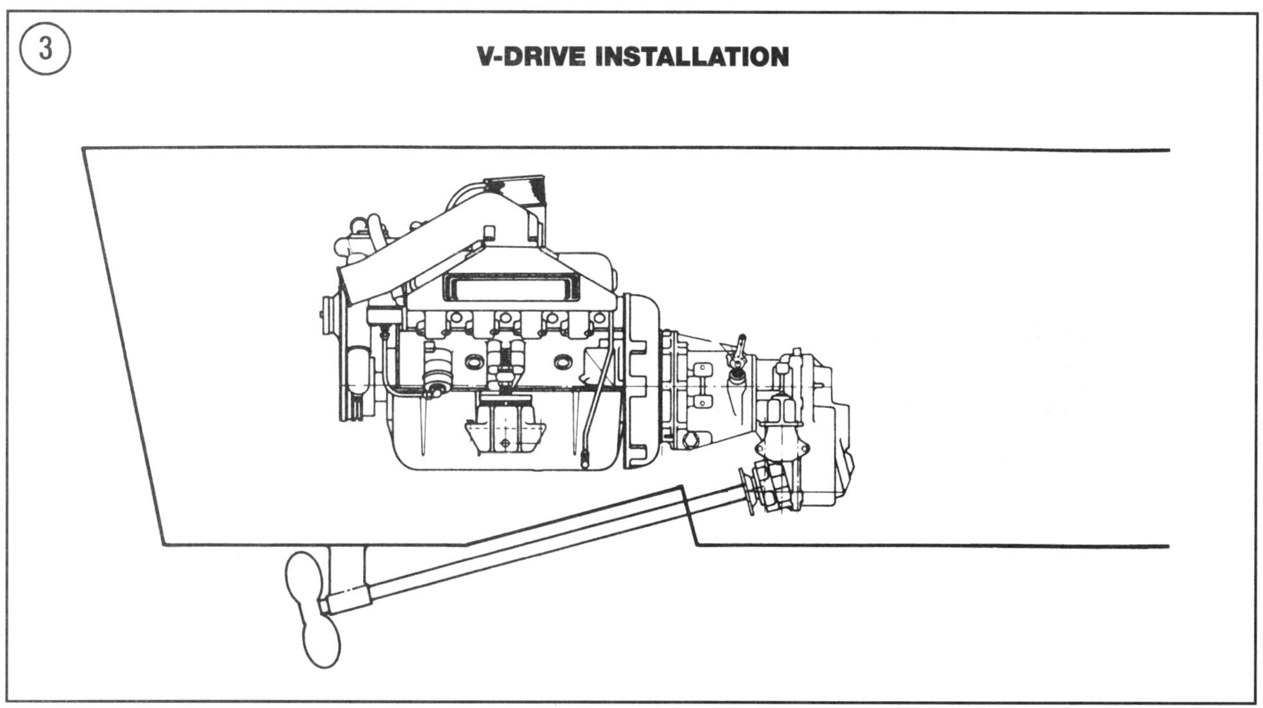

(3) **V-DRIVE INSTALLATION**

Gear Oil

Gear lubricants are assigned SAE viscosity numbers under the same system as 4-stroke engine oil. Gear lubricant falls into the SAE 72-250 range (**Figure 7**). Some gear lubricants are multigrade; for example, SAE 85W-90.

Three types of marine gear lubricant are generally available: SAE 90 hypoid gear lubricant is designed for older manual-shift units; Type C gear lubricant contains additives designed for electric shift mechanisms; High viscosity gear lubricant is a heavier oil designed to withstand the shock loading of high-performance engines or units subjected to severe duty use. Always use a gear lubricant of the type specified by the unit's manufacturer.

Grease

Greases are graded by the National Lubricating Grease Institute (NLGI). Greases are graded by number according to the consistency of the grease; these ratings range from No. 000 to No. 6, with No. 6 being the most solid. A typical multipurpose grease is NLGI No. 2 (**Figure 8**). For specific applications, equipment manufacturers may require grease with an additive such as molybdenum disulfide (MbS2).

INBOARD FINAL DRIVE MAINTENANCE

Final drive maintenance is limited to checking the oil level every 25 hours and changing the oil every 100-200 hours or once per season, whichever occurs first.

Checking Oil Level

Check oil level immediately after shutting the engine off. Otherwise, oil in the oil cooler and

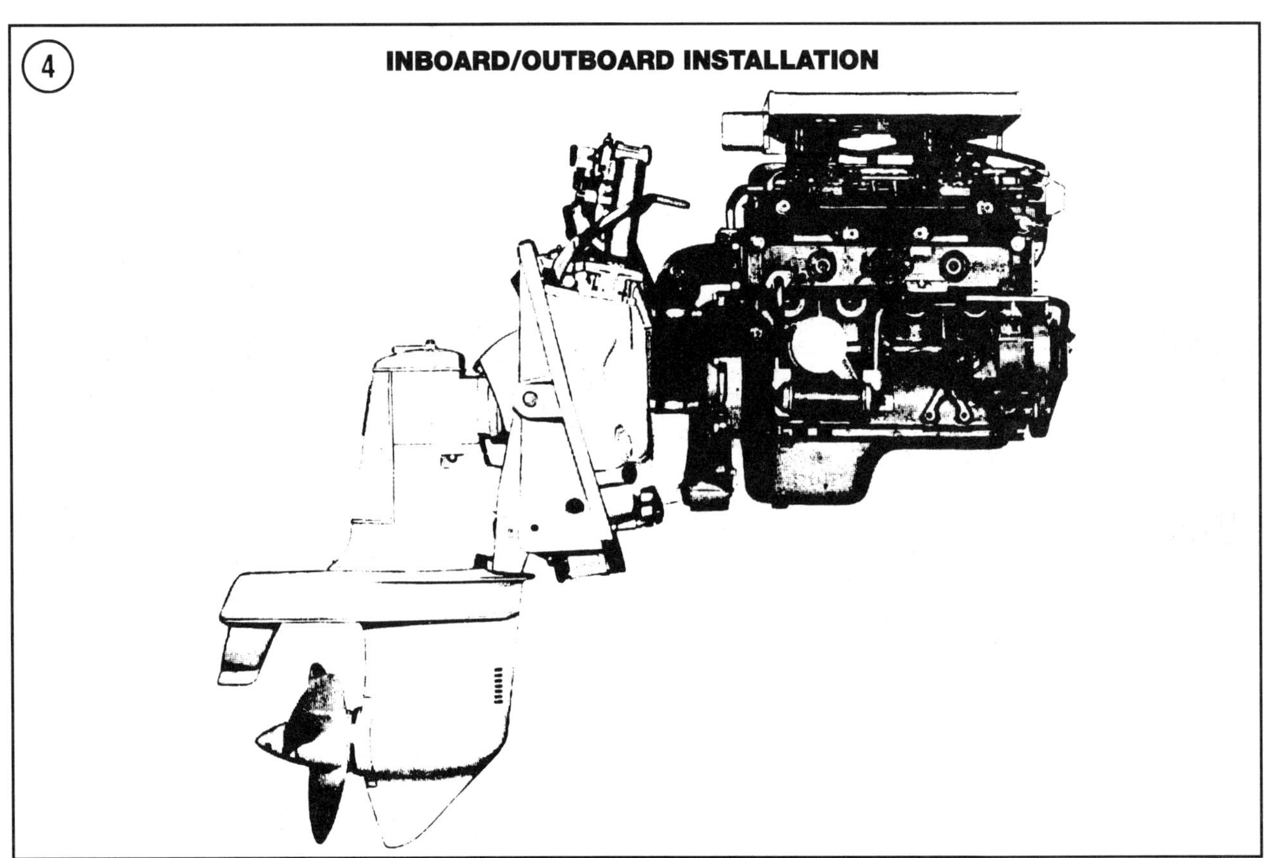

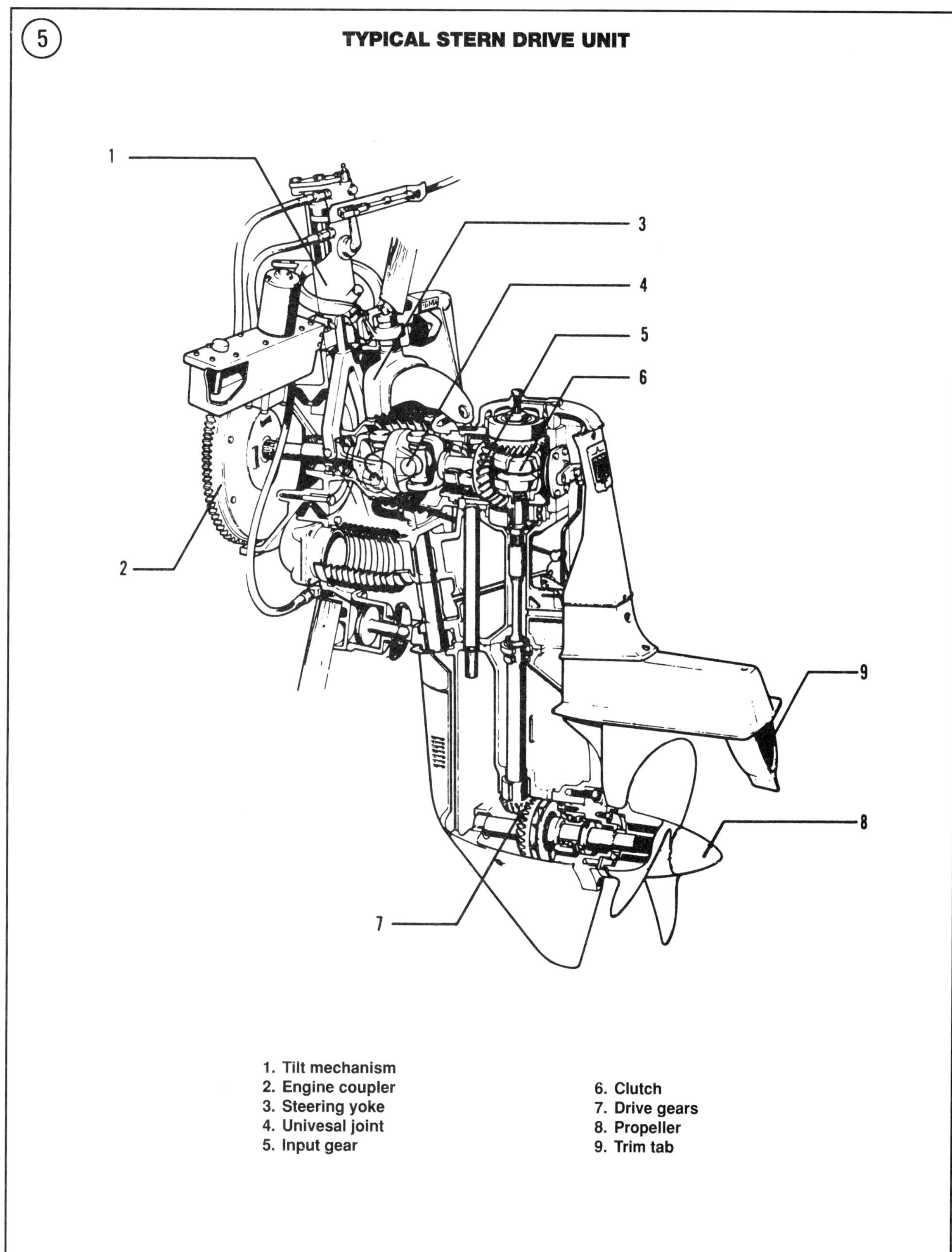

(5) **TYPICAL STERN DRIVE UNIT**

1. Tilt mechanism
2. Engine coupler
3. Steering yoke
4. Univesal joint
5. Input gear
6. Clutch
7. Drive gears
8. Propeller
9. Trim tab

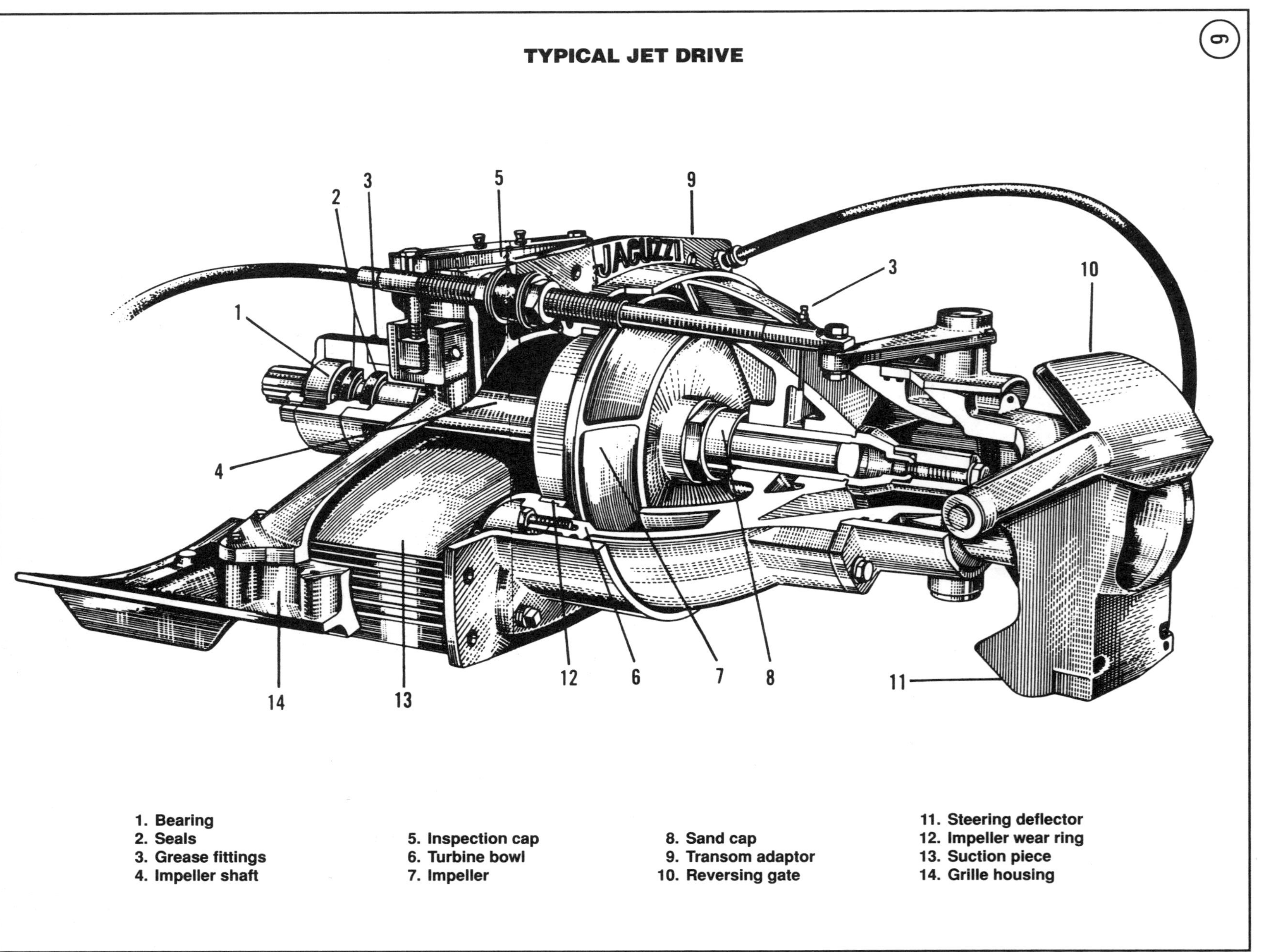
6
TYPICAL JET DRIVE
1. Bearing
2. Seals
3. Grease fittings
4. Impeller shaft
5. Inspection cap
6. Turbine bowl
7. Impeller
8. Sand cap
9. Transom adaptor
10. Reversing gate
11. Steering deflector
12. Impeller wear ring
13. Suction piece
14. Grille housing

connecting lines will drain back into the drive unit, indicating an abnormally high oil level.

Most final drives have a dipstick somewhere on the case. Some, like the Capitol and Paragon drives, have a pull-out dipstick similar to that on an engine. See **Figure 9** and **Figure 10**. Pull out the dipstick, wipe it clean, reinsert it, and observe the level of oil.

Other drives, such as Warner Gear "Velvet Drives," have a screw-in dipstick. See **Figure 11**. To check these, unscrew the dipstick, wipe it clean, then reinsert it until the dipstick plug rests in the hole; do not tighten it. Remove the dipstick and read the level.

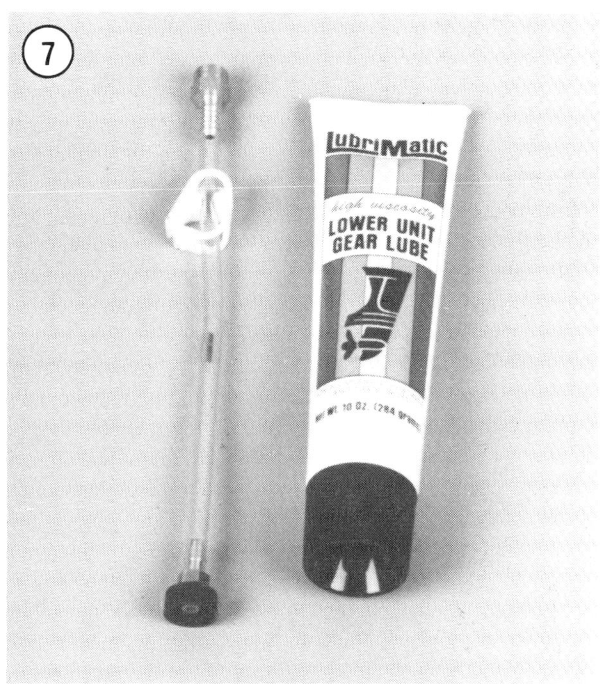

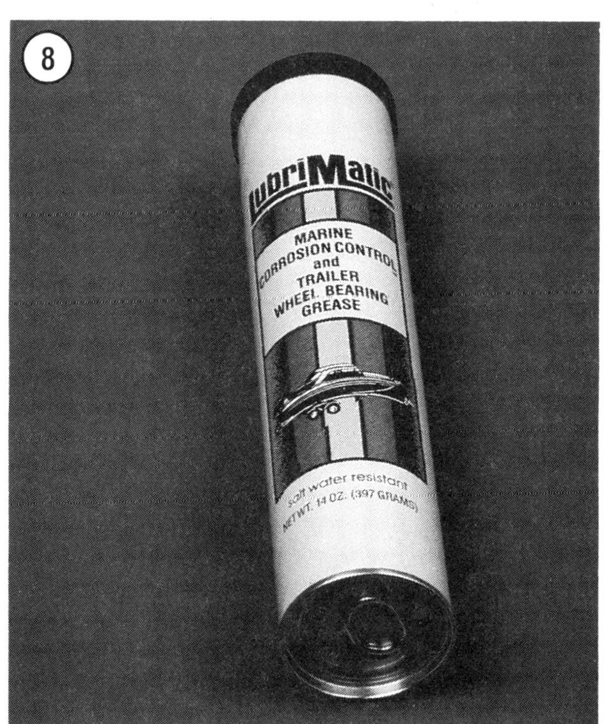

Oil Change

Drive unit oil should be changed every 100-200 hours, or once a season, whichever comes first.

The drain plug is located at the lowest point on the case. In some cases, such as Paragon drives, the drain is on the bottom of the case. Others, such as Capitol and Warner, have the drain on the side near the bottom.

To drain the oil:

1. Operate the boat in gear, if possible, to warm oil to operating temperature.

NOTE
Warm oil drains more quickly and thoroughly than cold oil, taking more impurities with it.

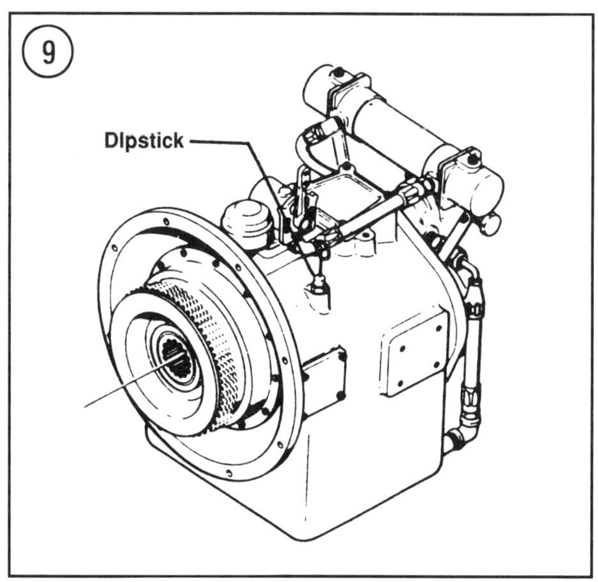

6

2A. If there is enough clearance, place a shallow container with 3 or 4 qt. capacity under the drain plug. Remove the drain plug and let drain for 10-15 minutes.

2B. If there is no access to the drain plug, suck the oil out through the dipstick opening. Use a siphoning device such as that shown in **Figure 12**.

3. Install drain plug, if removed.

4. Measure the amount of waste oil removed. This is the amount of fresh oil required in Step 5.

NOTE
Oil capacity depends on many variables such as cooler size, connecting line length, and installation angle.

5. Pour in fresh oil. Make sure that it is the proper grade and type. Refer to the owner's manual or call your local distributor; proper oil is very important.

6. Run the engine with the drive unit in gear to circulate oil. Shut off the engine and check the

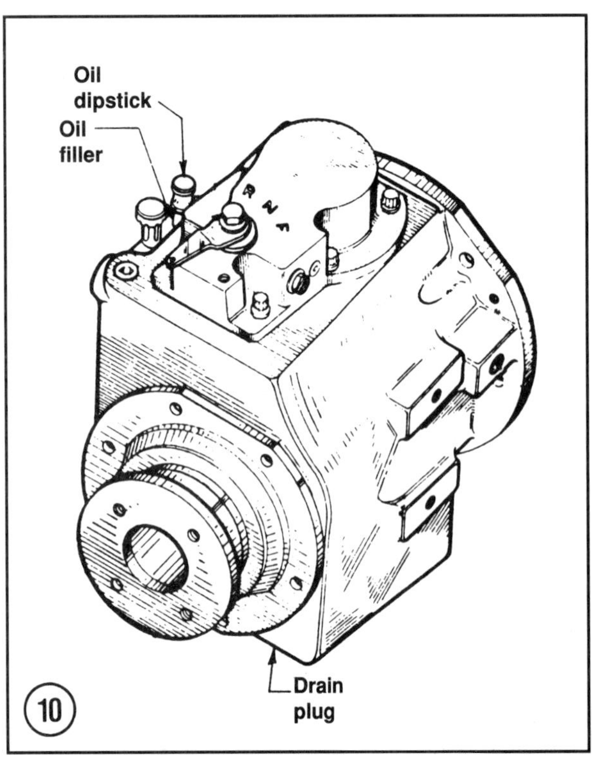

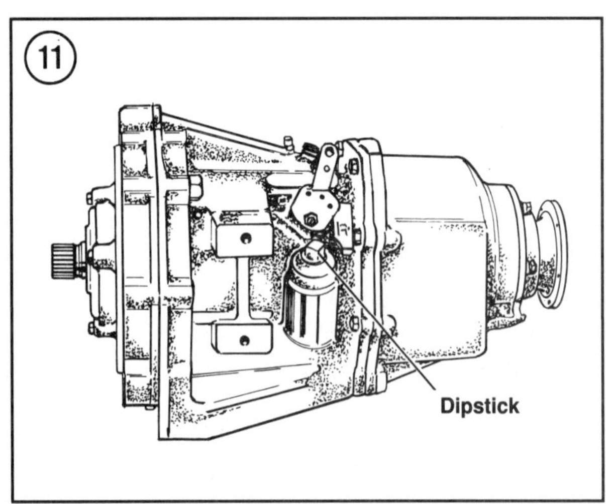

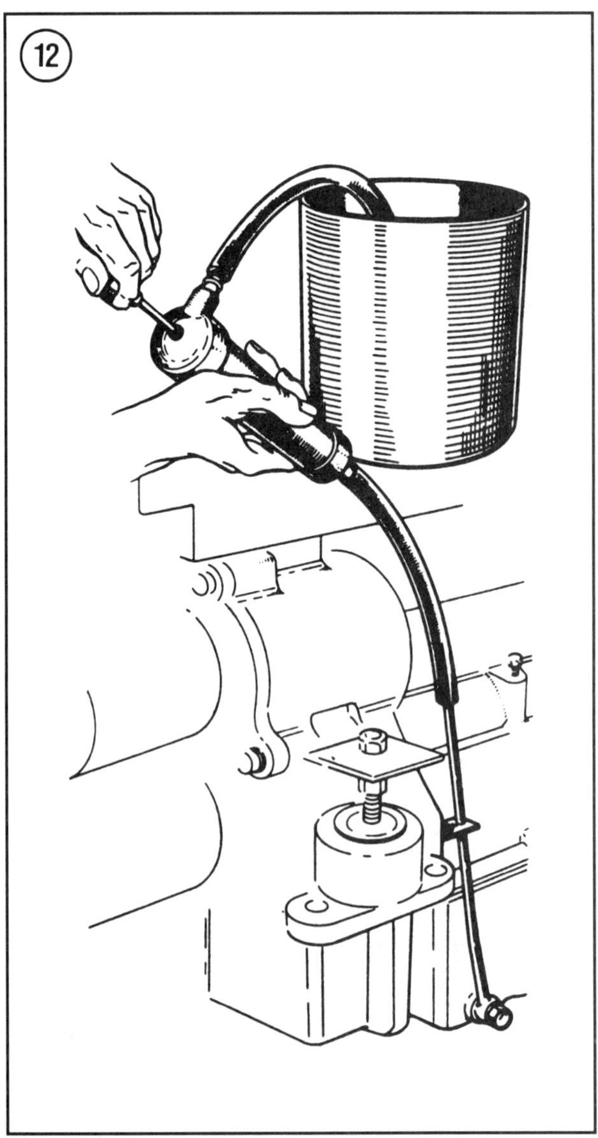

oil level with the dipstick immediately. If the level is too low, add more oil; if the level is too high, siphon some out.

Periodic Inspection

Whenever changing oil, inspect the entire case for loose bolts, leaks, and loose, deteriorating, or damaged connecting lines. If leakage is around an inspection plate, remove the plate, clean off all traces of old gasket, and reinstall the plate with a new gasket. If leakage is from the drain plug or connecting line end, tighten just enough to stop the leak; overtightening may crack housing. Other leaks must be repaired by a qualified mechanic.

Troubleshooting

There is very little an owner can do to correct trouble if it occurs. Major work requires expert knowledge and a wide array of tools. In cases of difficult shifting, noise, or no operation in one or more gears, check the oil level. If it is correct, refer the trouble to a mechanic. If the trouble is a leak, you may be able to fix it. Refer to *Periodic Inspection.*

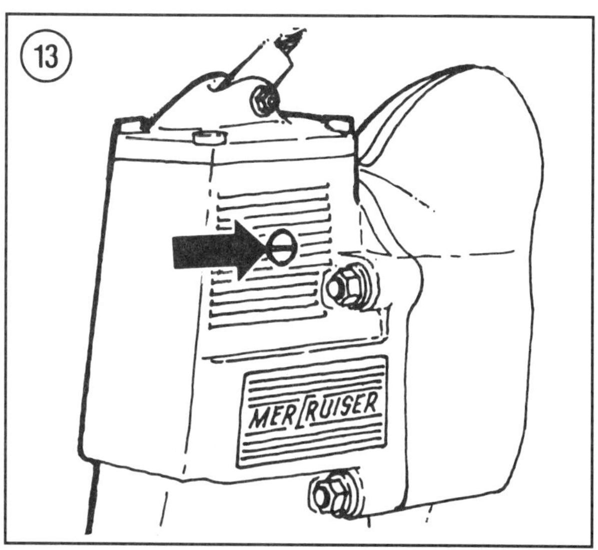

MERCRUISER STERN DRIVE (EARLY MODEL I)

The lubrication tasks described in this section should be performed at the intervals indicated in **Table 1**. These intervals are only guidelines, however. Consider the frequency and extent of boat use when setting actual intervals and perform the tasks more frequently if the boat is used under severe service conditions.

Lubricant Level Check (Upper Gear Chamber)

The upper drive shaft housing and lower unit gear chambers are separate and must be checked individually.

1. Remove the oil vent plug and gasket located on side of drive shaft housing (**Figure 13**). Oil must be even with bottom of the vent plug hole when the unit is level.
2. If the level is low, remove the oil filler plug on the opposite side of the drive shaft housing and add lubricant until it appears at the vent hole.
3. Reinstall the oil vent and filler plugs with new gaskets.

6

Lubricant Level Check (Lower Gear Chamber)

The upper drive shaft housing and lower unit gear chambers are separate and must be checked individually.

1. Remove the oil vent plug and gasket on the side of the gear housing just above the antiventilation plate. Oil must be even with the bottom of the oil vent plug hole when the drive unit is level in the down position.
2. If the level is low, remove the oil filler plug on the opposite side of the gear housing and add lubricant until it appears at the vent hole.
3. Reinstall the oil vent and filler plugs with new gaskets.

Lubricant Change (Upper Gear Chamber)

1. Remove top cover (**Figure 14**). Remove all the old lubricant with a pump.
2. Reinstall the top cover and O-ring. Tighten the screws to 20 ft.-lb.
3. Remove the oil fill and vent plugs and gaskets (located on right and left side of drive shaft housing).
4. Insert the lubricant tube into the fill hole and fill until oil runs from the oil vent plug hole.
5. Reinstall the oil fill and vent plugs with new gaskets.

Lubricant Change (Lower Gear Chamber)

1. Remove the oil fill plug (**Figure 15**) from the lower end of the gear housing on the left side and the oil vent plug located just above the antiventilation plate. Drain the unit.
2. Insert the lubricant tube into the fill hole and fill until oil runs from the oil vent plug hole.
3. Install the oil vent plug first, then quickly remove the lubricant tube and install fill plug. Make certain that a new gasket is used under each plug to prevent water from leaking into the gear housing.

14

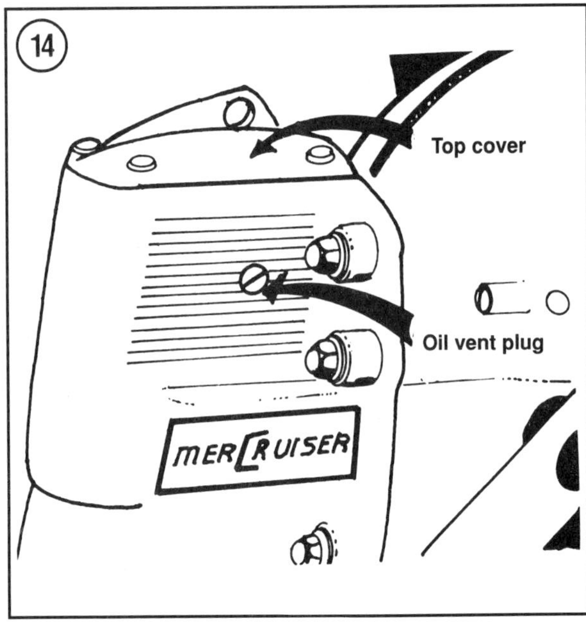

General Lubrication Points

Inside boat: Apply lubricant to the Ride-Guide steering cable end next to the hand nut (**Figure 16**), to the pivot socket of steering arm and exposed cable traversing through guide tube (**Figure 17**).

Outside boat: Apply lubricant to the grease fittings at the gimbal housing upper and lower pivot pins, to the tilt pins on both sides of the gimbal ring and to the gimbal bearing. See **Figure 18**.

15

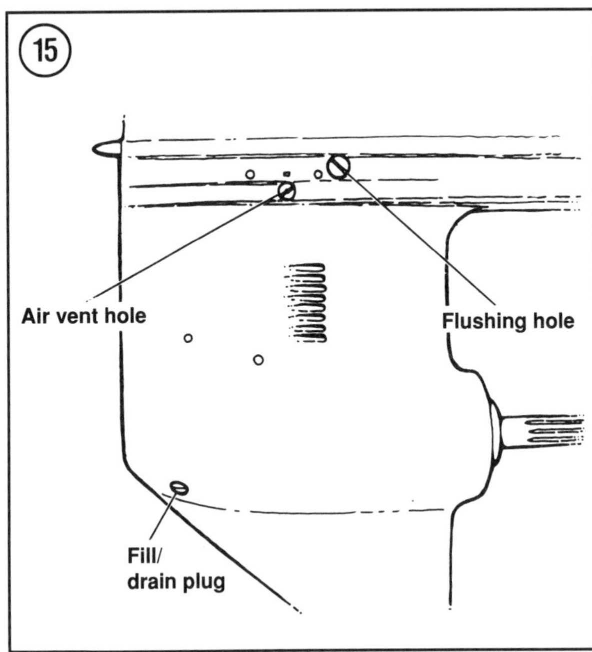

16

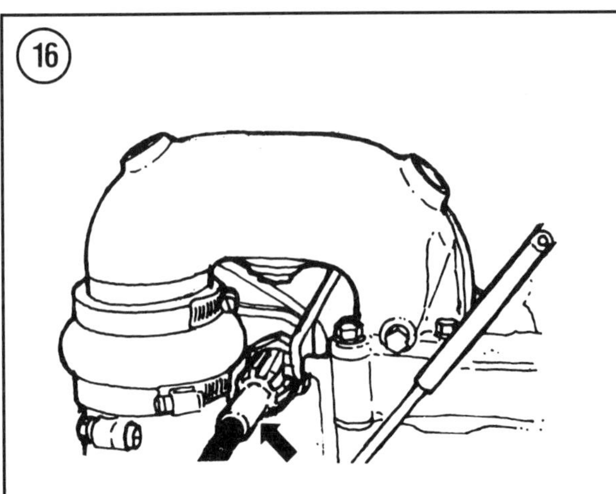

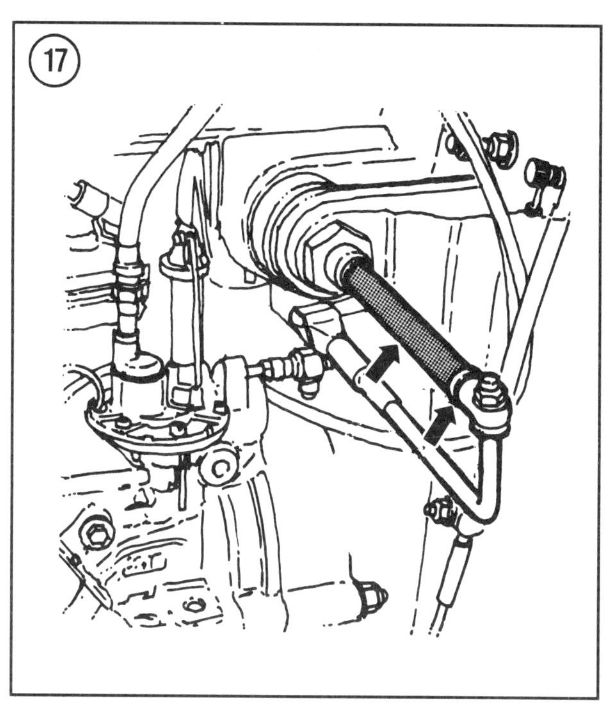

NOTE
The tapered end of the lubricant gun fits in the counterbore in the tilt pins; no grease fitting is provided. If lubricant cannot be satisfactorily forced into tilt pins, install a grease fitting (part No. B-22-37668) in each pin. Lubricate and remove the fitting. Lubricate universal joint bearings.

MERCRUISER STERN DRIVE (LATE MODEL I)

The lubrication tasks described in this section should be performed at the intervals indicated in **Table 1**. These intervals are only guidelines, however. Consider the frequency and extent of boat use when setting actual intervals and perform the tasks more frequently if the boat is used under severe service conditions.

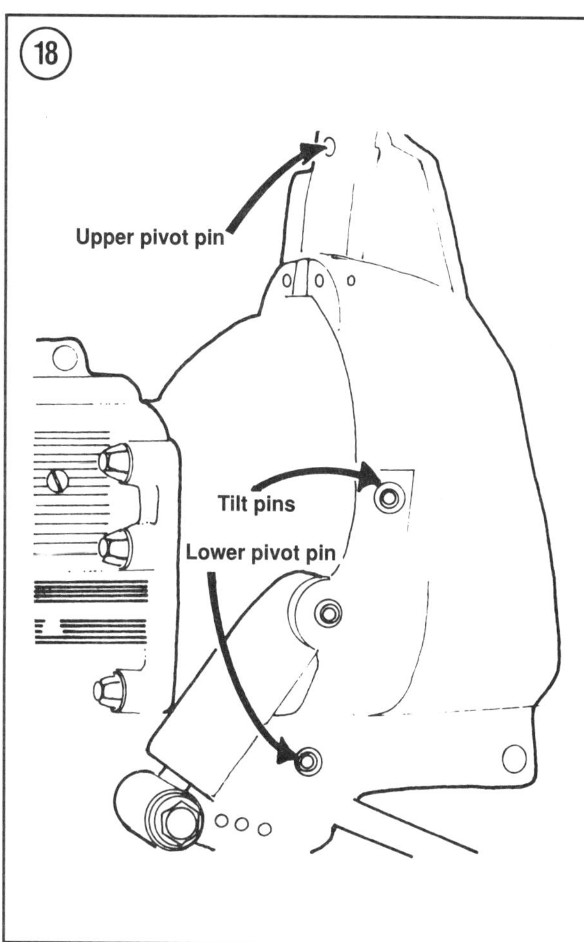

Lubricant Level Check

1. Remove the oil vent plug and gasket on the side of the drive shaft housing (**Figure 19**). Oil must be even with the bottom of the vent plug hole when the unit is level.

NOTE
Some older units have oil fill plugs on the opposite side of the drive shaft hous-

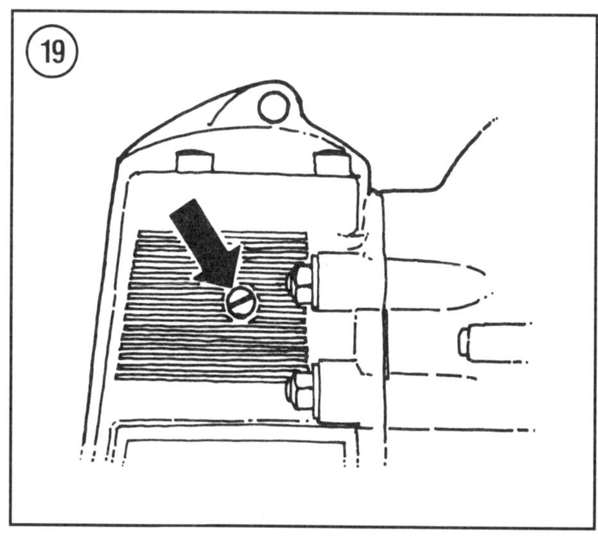

ing, in addition to the fill plug specified in Step 2.

2. If the level is low, remove the oil fill/drain plug and gasket located on the lower side of the gear housing (**Figure 15**). Quickly insert the lubricant tube into the fill/drain plug hole and add lubricant until it appears at vent hole.
3. Install the vent plug with new gasket, then quickly remove the lubricant tube and install the fill/drain plug with new gasket.

Lubricant Change

1. Remove the oil vent plug on the side of the drive shaft housing (**Figure 13**) and the fill/drain plug from lower end of gear housing on the left side (**Figure 15**). Tilt the unit slightly to aid drainage. Allow all old lubricant to drain.
2. Insert the lubricant tube into the lower fill/drain plug hole and fill until oil runs from the upper oil vent plug hole.
3. Install the oil vent plug first, then quickly remove the lubricant tube and install the drain plug. Make certain that a new gasket is used under each plug to prevent water from leaking into the gear housing.

(20) **LUBRICATION POINTS INSIDE BOAT (WITHOUT POWER STEERING)**

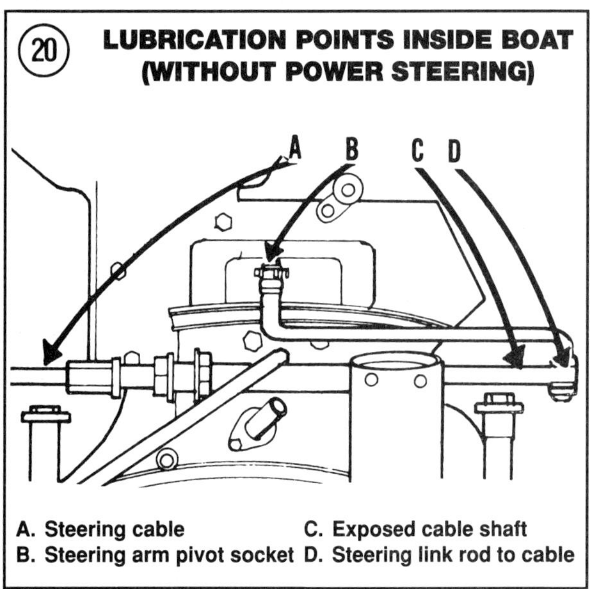

A. Steering cable
B. Steering arm pivot socket
C. Exposed cable shaft
D. Steering link rod to cable

General Lubrication Points (Inside Boat)

On models without power steering, refer to **Figure 20** and apply lubricant to the Ride-Guide steering cable end next to the hand nut (A), pivot socket of steering arm (B), exposed cable trav-

LUBRICATION POINTS INSIDE BOAT (INLINE ENGINE WITH POWER STEERING)

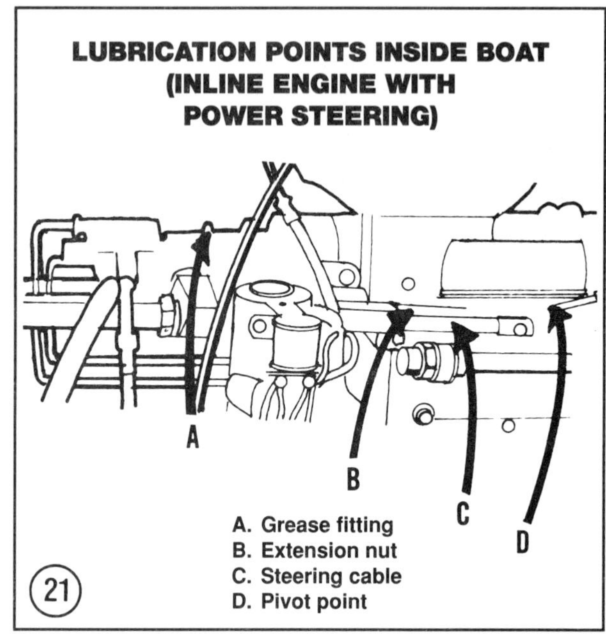

(21)

A. Grease fitting
B. Extension nut
C. Steering cable
D. Pivot point

LUBRICATION POINTS INSIDE BOAT (V-TYPE ENGINE WITH POWER STEERING)

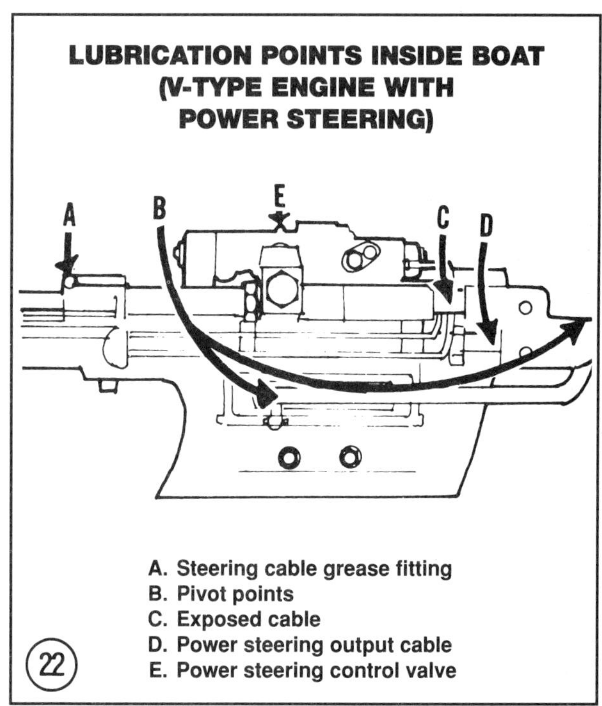

(22)

A. Steering cable grease fitting
B. Pivot points
C. Exposed cable
D. Power steering output cable
E. Power steering control valve

ersing through the guide tube (C) and the steering link rod to steering cable (D).

On models with power steering (inline engines), refer to **Figure 21** and lubricate the control valve grease fitting (A), extension rod (B) exposed end of cable (C) and cable end guide pivot point (D).

On models with power steering (V-type engines), refer to **Figure 22** and lubricate the Ride-Guide cable fitting (A) with cable fully retracted, pivot points (B), exposed part of steering cable (C) and output shaft (D) when both are fully extended and control valve fitting (E). Check for loose or worn connections while lubricating these points.

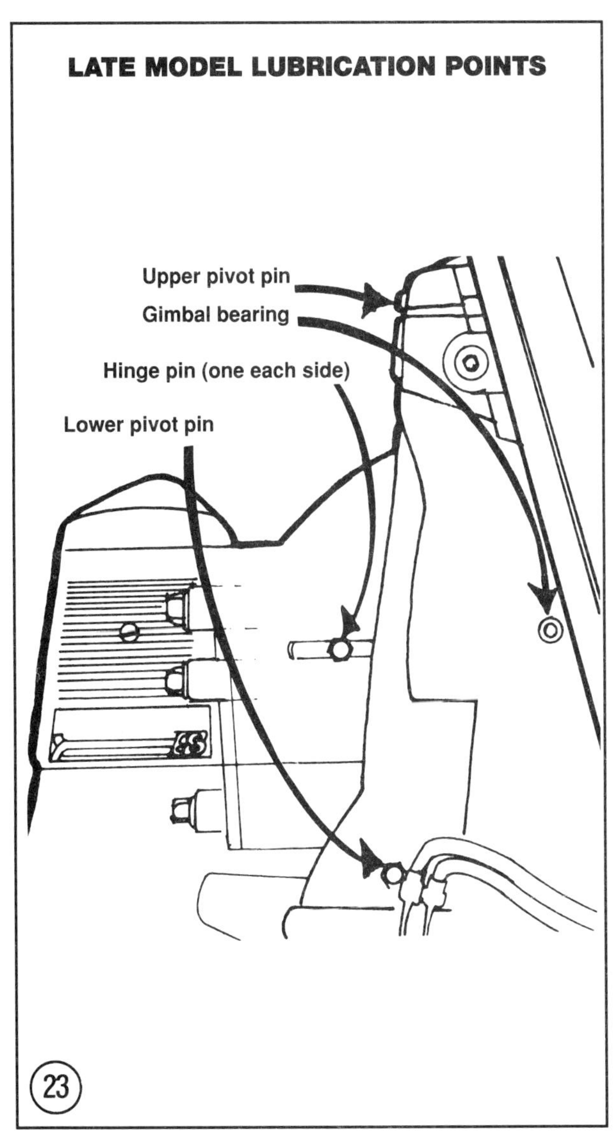

General Lubrication Points (Outside Boat)

Lubricate the upper and lower pivot pins, hinge pins and gimbal bearing. See **Figure 23**. Also lubricate universal joint bearings.

MERCRUISER STERN DRIVE (MODEL II)

The lubrication tasks described in this section should be performed at the intervals indicated in **Table 1**. These intervals are only guidelines, however. Consider the frequency and extent of boat use when setting actual intervals and perform the tasks more frequently if the boat is used under severe service conditions.

6

Lubricant Level Check

1. Remove the fill plug and gasket (**Figure 24**). Oil should be level with the bottom edge of the threaded hole.
2. If the level is low, a small amount can be added through the fill plug hole. If the unit is

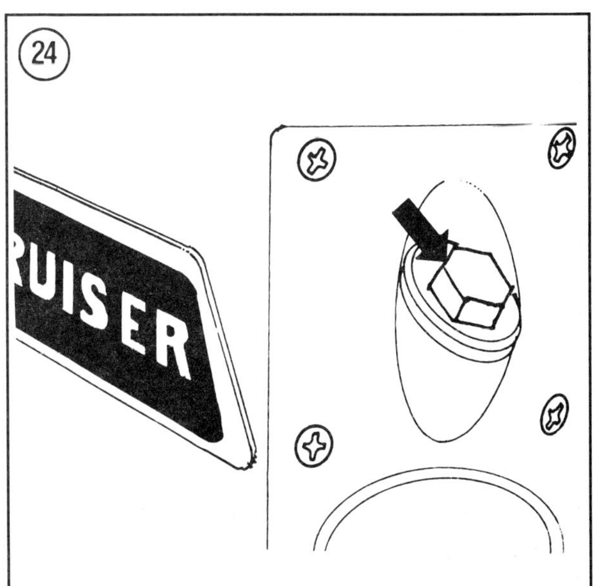

empty or a great amount of oil must be added, see *Lubricant Change* below.

3. Install the fill plug with a new gasket.

Lubricant Change

1. Remove the oil vent plug on the side of the drive shaft housing (**Figure 13**) and the fill/drain plug from the lower end of the gear housing on the left side (**Figure 25**). Tilt the unit slightly to aid drainage. Allow all old lubricant to drain.
2. Insert the lubricant tube into the lower fill/drain plug hole and fill until oil runs from the upper oil vent plug hole.
3. Install the oil vent plug first, then quickly remove the lubricant tube and install the fill/drain plug. Make certain that a new gasket is used under each plug to prevent water from leaking into the gear housing.

General Lubrication Points

Inside boat: Lubricate the points shown in **Figure 26**.

Outside boat: Lubricatethe gimbal housing upper and lower pivot pins, and hinge/tilt pins on both sides of the gimbal housing. See **Figure 27** (early models) or **Figure 28** (late models).

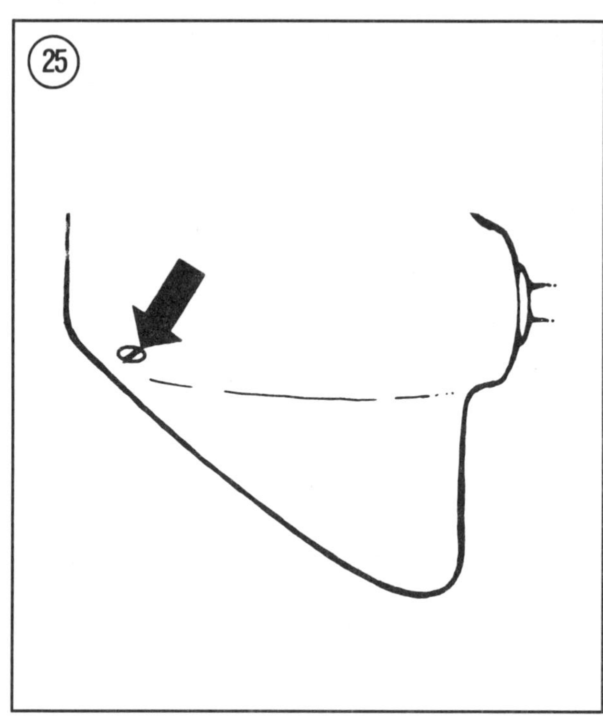

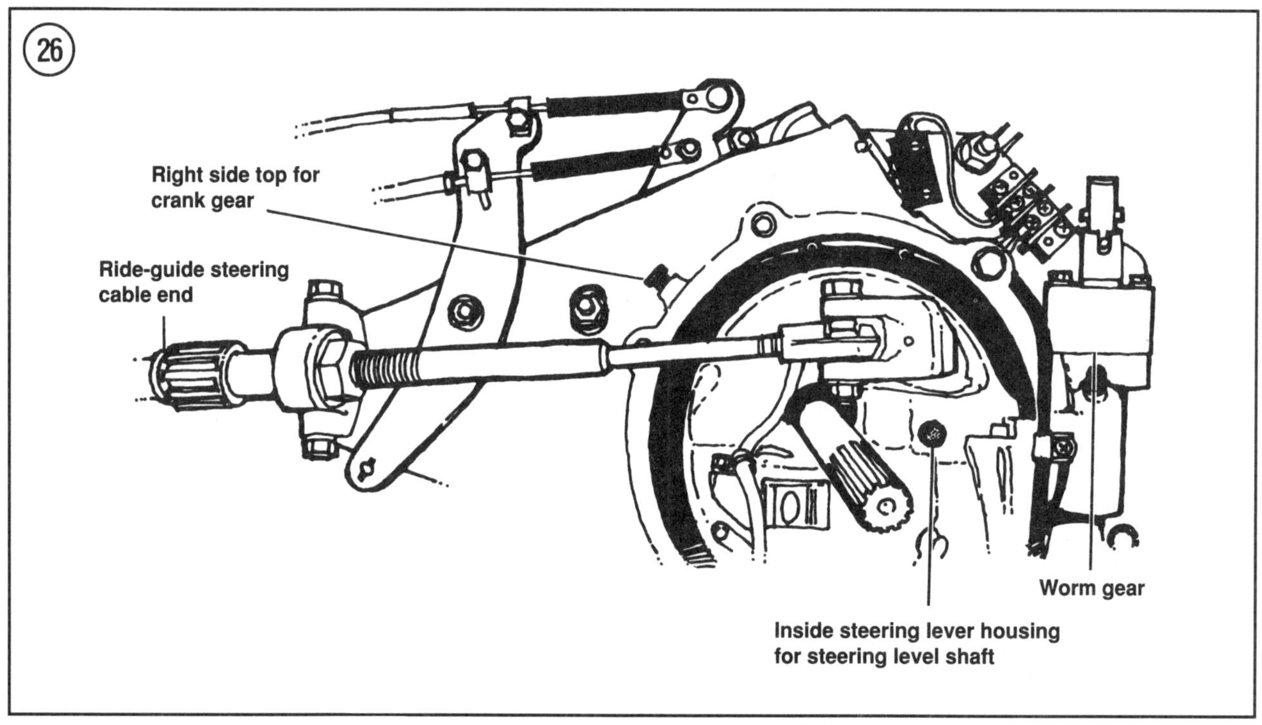

MERCRUISER STERN DRIVE (MODEL II-TR, 215, III)

The lubrication tasks described in this section should be performed at the intervals indicated in **Table 1**. These intervals are only guidelines, however. Consider the frequency and extent of boat use when setting actual intervals and perform the tasks more frequently if the boat is used under severe service conditions.

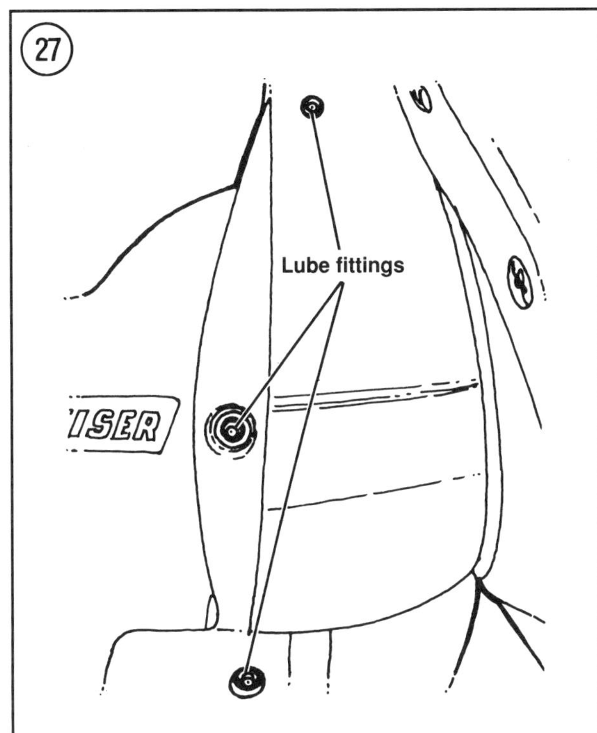

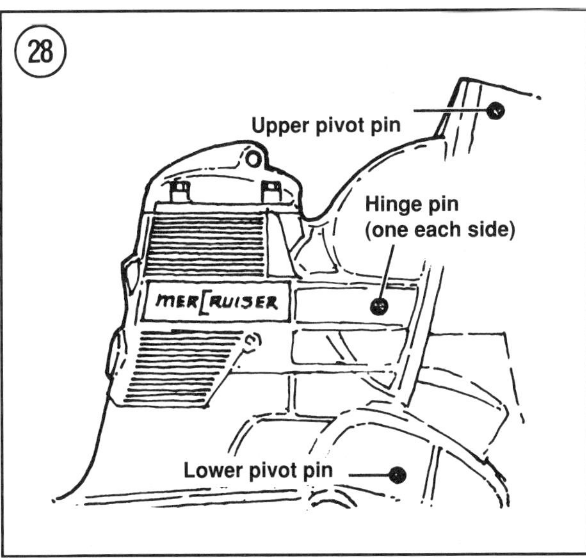

Lubricant Level Check

1. Check the oil level with the dipstick on 215, II-TR models (**Figure 29**) or sight glass (**Figure 30**) located on the inner transom plate on MerCruiser III models.
2. Add oil as required through the dipstick tube or oil fill hole.

Lubricant Change

1. Remove the oil fill plug on the lower side of the gear housing and the vent plug on the side of the drive housing.
2. Make sure the drive unit is installed in the bell housing and let the oil drain completely. Reinstall the vent plug with a new gasket.
3. Use a hand-type lubricant pump and fill the drive unit through the fill plug hole until the oil level reaches the proper line on the dipstick (**Figure 29**) for 215, II-TR and II-TRS models or the sight glass (**Figure 30**) on MerCruiser III models.

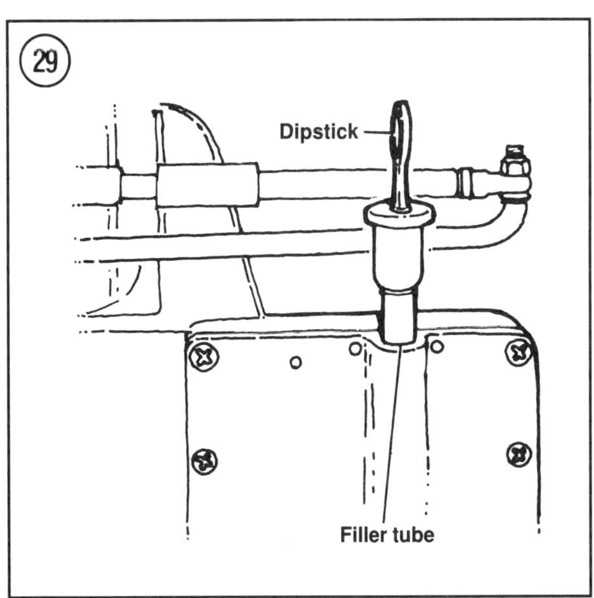

6

4. After filling, quickly remove the pump and install the fill plug with a new gasket. Tighten the plug securely.

Lubrication (215, II-TR, II-TRS)

Lubricate the drive unit upper and lower pivot pin grease fittings (**Figure 31**).

Manual steering: Refer to **Figure 32** and lubricate the steering cable grease fitting (A), steering lever pivot points (B), and apply a light coat of grease to the exposed steering cable (C). Do not overlubricate the cable.

Power steering: Refer to **Figure 33** and lubricate the steering cable grease fitting (A), steering lever pivot points (B), and apply a light coat of grease to the exposed cable end and the extension rod (C and D). Do not overlubricate.

NOTE
Lubricate pivot points of dual tie bar, if installed.

Lubrication (215, II-TR, II-TRS)

Lubricate the drive unit upper and lower pivot pin grease fittings (**Figure 31**).

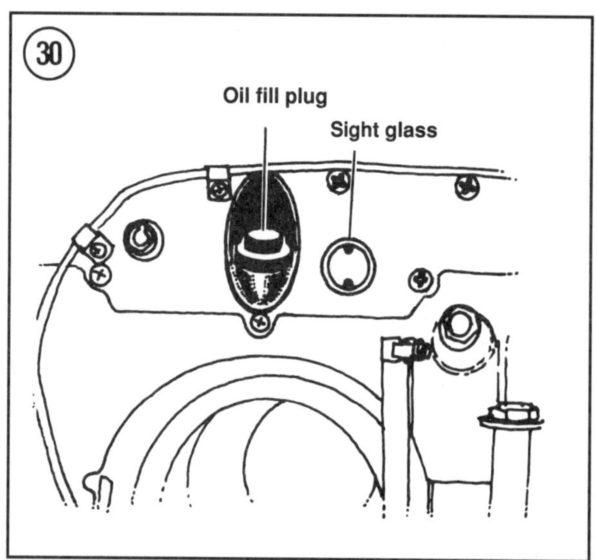

On models with manual steering, refer to **Figure 34** and lubricate the steering cable grease fitting (A). Apply a coating of grease to the exposed cable (B). Do not overlubricate.

On model with power steering, refer to **Figure 33** and lubricate the steering cable grease fitting (A), steering lever pivot points (B), and apply a light coat of grease to exposed cable end and extension rod (C and D). Do not overlubricate.

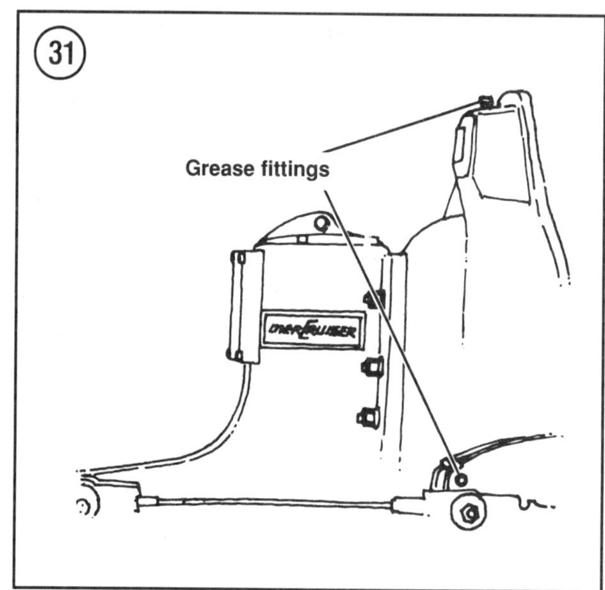

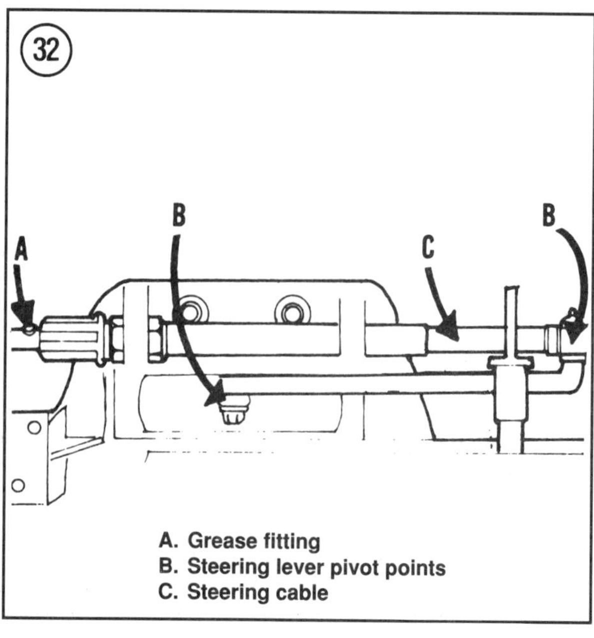

A. Grease fitting
B. Steering lever pivot points
C. Steering cable

NOTE
Lubricate pivot points of dual tie bar, if installed.

MERCRUISER STERN DRIVE (ALPHA ONE EXCEPT GENERATION II)

The lubrication tasks described in this section should be performed at the intervals indicated in **Table 1**. These intervals are only guidelines, however. Consider the frequency and extent of boat use when setting actual intervals and perform the tasks more frequently if the boat is used under severe service conditions.

33

A. Grease fitting
B. Steering cable
C. Steering cable pivot points
D. Extension rod

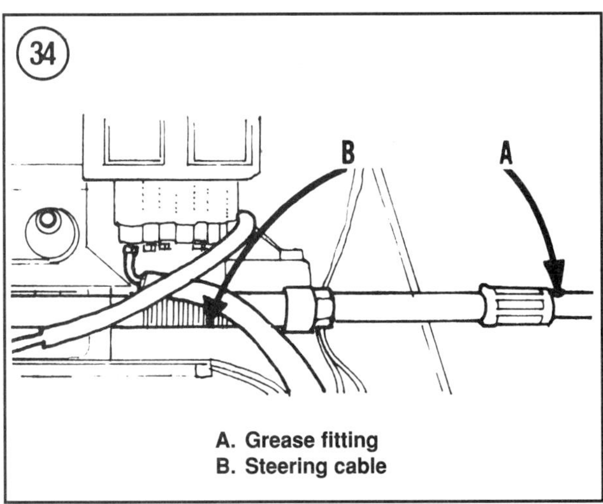

A. Grease fitting
B. Steering cable

An oil reservoir kit is available as an accessory. This allows you to check the oil level in the drive unit from inside the boat when it is in the water.

Dispose of old lubricant properly. Disposal methods discussed under *Engine Oil and Filter Change* in this chapter are applicable.

Fluid Check (Without Reservoir Kit)

WARNING
Since the lubricant expands when hot, its level should be checked when the unit is cool. The expanded lubricant may spray out if the oil vent plug is removed when the unit is hot and can cause serious burns.

1. With the drive unit in a vertical position (anti-ventilation plate level), unscrew and remove the oil vent plug from the port side of the drive shaft housing (**Figure 35**).
2. Carefully check the oil level. It should be even with the bottom edge of the vent hole. If oil

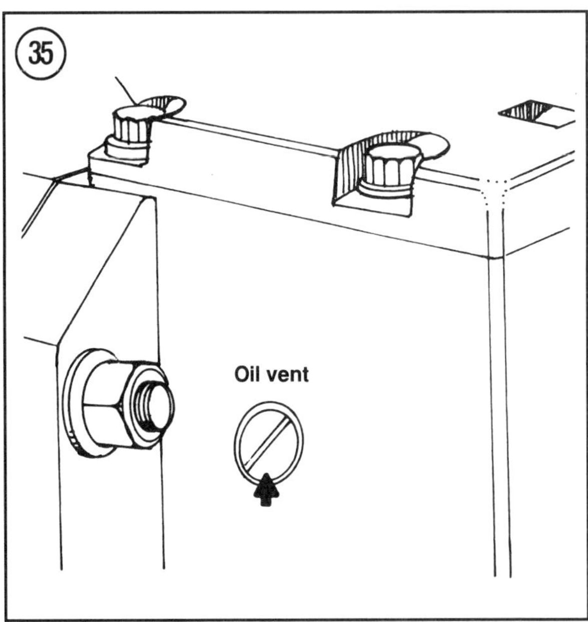

6

level is correct, check the condition of the sealing washer on the plug. Reinstall the vent plug with a new washer, if the old one is damaged or deteriorated.

3. If the oil level is not correct:

   a. Temporarily reinstall the vent plug to create an air lock inside the unit.

CAUTION
The lubricant in the stern drive should be periodically checked for water contamination. To check for water, trim the drive unit to the fully OUT position. Remove the fill/drain plug and take a small sample of the lubricant. If the lubricant is milky brown or if water is evident, a leak is present that must be repaired before the unit is returned to service. On 1987 and later models, a magnetic fill/drain plug is used. Check the magnetic tip of the plug for metallic particles which could indicate internal problems. Thoroughly clean the tip before reinstalling the plug.

   b. Remove the oil fill/drain plug (**Figure 36**) and insert lubricant pump (part No. 91-26 1 50) or equivalent in the fill/drain hole.

   c. Remove the oil vent plug and inject lubricant from the pump through the oil fill/drain hole until it flows from the vent hole in an air-free stream.

CAUTION
The unit should not require more than 2 ounces of lubricant. If it does, an oil leak is probable and the unit should not be used until it is checked for leakage and any problem corrected.

   d. Reinstall the oil vent plug and washer.

   e. Remove the lubricant pump and quickly reinstall the fill/drain plug and washer.

   f. Wipe any excess lubricant from the drive housing and gearcase.

   g. Repeat Step 1 and Step 2 to recheck lubricant level.

Fluid Check (With Reservoir Kit)

WARNING
If the lubricant in the reservoir is milky brown or if water is mixed with it, the drive unit has a leak which must be corrected before it is returned to service.

Check the lubricant level in the reservoir (**Figure 37**). If the fluid level is below the FULL mark on the reservoir, remove the cover and add sufficient lubricant to bring the level to the mark. Reinstall the cover tightly.

CAUTION
The unit should not require more than 2 ounces of lubricant. If it does, an oil leak is probable and the unit should not be used until it is checked for leakage and any problem corrected.

Fluid Change (Without Reservoir Kit)

1. Trim the drive unit to its full out position.

CAUTION
When the oil fill/drain plug is removed in Step 2, let a small quantity of fluid drain on your fingers. If the lubricant is

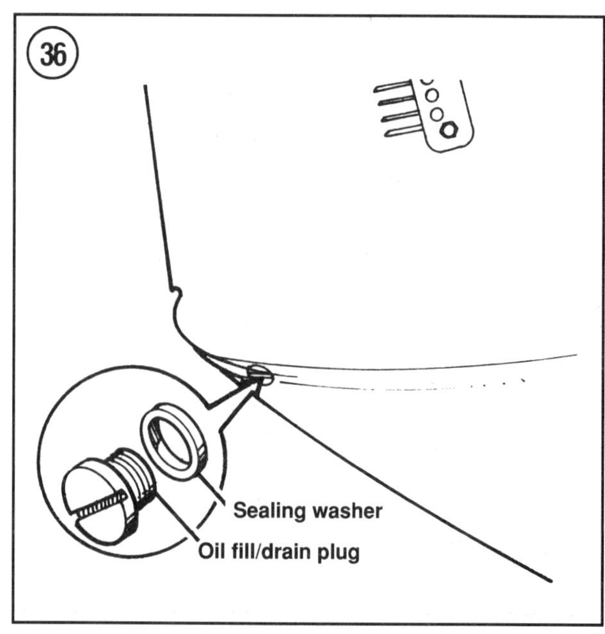

milky brown or if water is mixed with it, the drive unit has a leak which must be corrected before it is returned to service.

2. Place a suitable container underneath the drive unit so that the fluid can drain into it. Remove the oil vent plug (**Figure 35**) and fill/drain plug (**Figure 36**). Allow the lubricant to drain completely.

3. When the lubricant has drained, return the drive unit to a vertical position (antiventilation plate level).

4. Insert lubricant pump (part No. 91-26150) or equivalent in the fill/drain hole. Inject lubricant from the pump through the oil fill/drain hole until it flows from the vent hole in an air-free stream.

5. Reinstall the oil vent plug and washer.

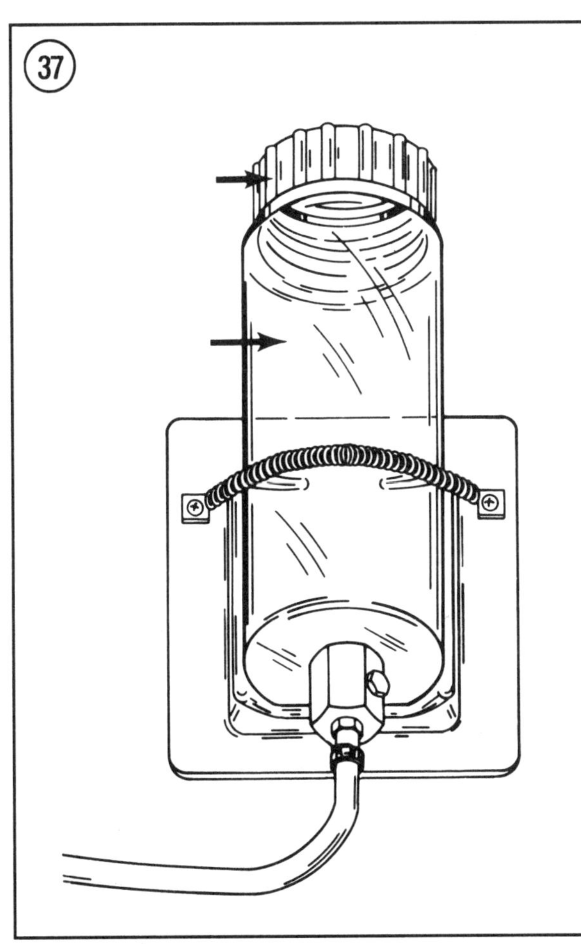

6. Remove the lubricant pump and quickly reinstall the fill/drain plug and washer.

7. Wipe any excess lubricant from the drive housing and gearcase.

8. Repeat Step 1 and Step 2 of *Fluid Check* in this chapter to check lubricant level.

Fluid Change (With Reservoir Kit)

1. Trim the drive unit to its full out position.

WARNING
When the oil fill/drain plug is removed in Step 2, let a small quantity of fluid drain on your fingers. If the lubricant is milky brown or if water is mixed with it, the drive unit has a leak which must be corrected before it is returned to service.

2. Place a suitable container underneath the drive unit so the fluid can drain into it. Remove the oil fill/drain plug (**Figure 36**). Allow the lubricant to drain completely.

3. Remove the reservoir from its bracket (**Figure 37**). Remove the cover and drain the lubricant into a suitable container.

4. Unscrew and remove the adapter and hose from the drive shaft housing oil vent hole. See **Figure 38**.

5. When the lubricant has drained, return the drive unit to a vertical position (antiventilation plate level).

6. Insert lubricant pump (part No. 91-26150) or equivalent in the fill/drain hole. Inject lubricant from the pump through the oil fill/drain hole until it flows from the vent hole in an air-free stream.

7. Temporarily plug the oil vent hole to create an airlock in the drive unit.

8. Remove the lubricant pump and quickly reinstall the fill/drain plug and washer.

9. Wipe any excess lubricant from the drive housing and gearcase.

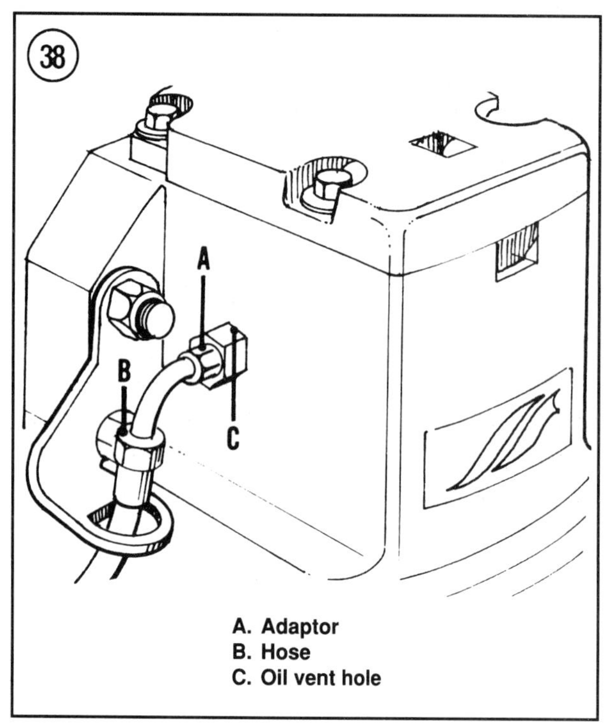

A. Adaptor
B. Hose
C. Oil vent hole

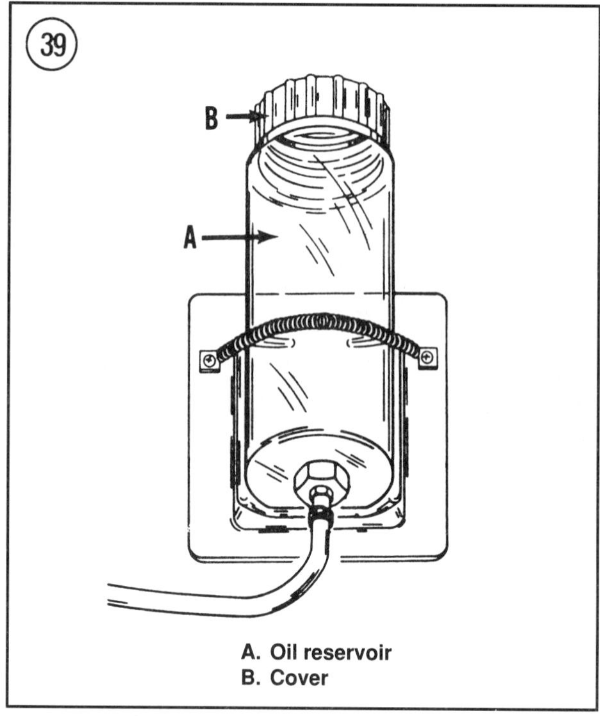

A. Oil reservoir
B. Cover

40

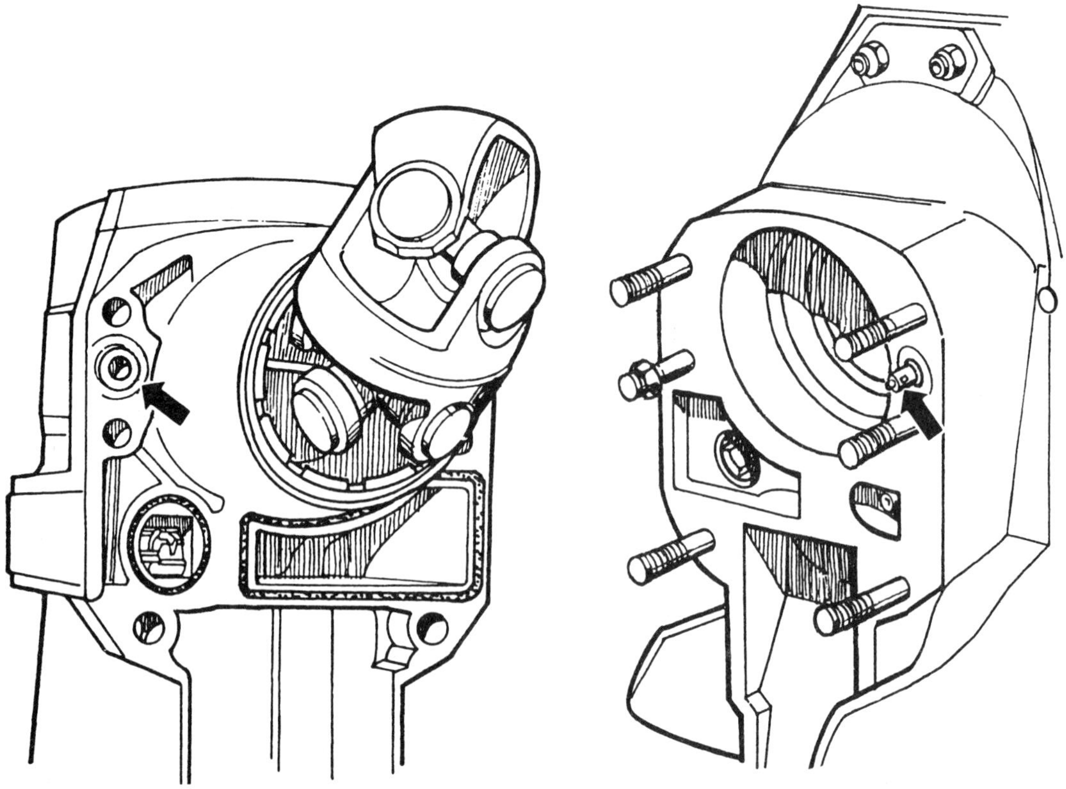

10. Reinstall the adapter and hose to the drive shaft housing oil vent hole. Tighten adapter securely.
11. Reinstall the oil reservoir to its bracket. Fill the reservoir to its FULL mark and reinstall the cover tightly.
12. Loosen the adapter fitting at the drive shaft housing vent hole. Let the lubricant flow until there are no air bubbles in the stream, then retighten the fitting securely. Repeat Step 9.
13. Recheck fluid level in oil reservoir and top up, if required. Do not fill the reservoir above the FULL mark.

MERCRUISER STERN DRIVE (ALPHA ONE GENERATION II, BRAVO ONE AND BRAVO TWO)

The lubrication tasks described in this section should be performed at the intervals indicated in **Table 1**. These intervals are only guidelines, however. Consider the frequency and extent of boat use when setting actual intervals and perform the tasks more frequently if the boat is used under severe service conditions.

The lube oil monitor (**Figure 39**) is standard on 1989-on Bravo One and Bravo Two models and available as an option on Alpha One Generation II models. The lube oil monitor allows the drive unit oil level to be checked from inside the boat. The reservoir is equipped with a lubricant level warning sensor that activates the audio warning system should the drive unit oil level become low. Unlike the external reservoir connection used on early Alpha One models (**Figure 38**), the connection is internal on Bravo One, Bravo Two and Alpha One Generation II models. A check valve connector permits easy removal and installation of the drive unit. See **Figure 40.**

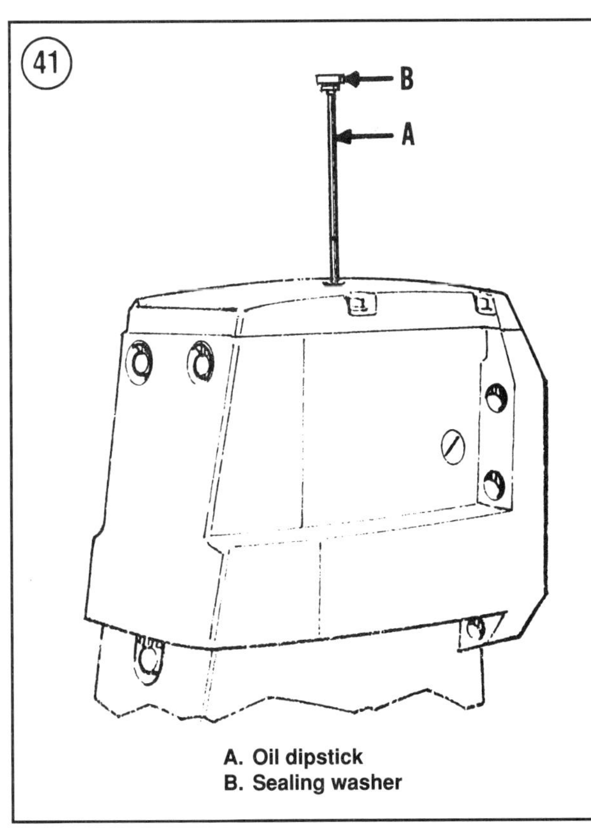

A. Oil dipstick
B. Sealing washer

6

Fluid Check (Without Reservoir)

1. Bring the stern drive to a vertical position (anti-ventilation plate level).
2. Unscrew and remove the oil level dipstick on the top of the upper gear housing (**Figure 41**). If the oil level is at the line on the dipstick, reinstall the dipstick with the sealing washer. Tighten the dipstick securely. If the oil level is low, continue at Step 3.

NOTE
On late Bravo One models, the drive unit fill/drain plug is located in the propeller shaft bearing carrier. On models so equipped, the propeller and forward thrust hub must be removed to access the fill/drain plug.

3. On late Bravo One models, remove the propeller and thrust hub, then remove the fill/drain plug located in the propeller shaft bearing carrier (**Figure 42**). On all other models, remove the fill/drain plug from the gear housing (**Figure 43**). Insert lubricant pump (part No. 91-26150, or equivalent) into the fill/drain plug hole.

4. Remove the vent plug (**Figure 44**), then inject the lubricant from the pump into the fill/drain plug hole until the lubricant is even with the bottom of the vent plug hole. Note that the vent plug is on the port side on Alpha One models.

CAUTION
If more than 2 ounces of lubricant is required to fill the drive unit, a leak is probable. Repair the leakage before returning the unit to service.

5. Reinstall the oil vent plug and washer. Tighten the plug to 17 in.-lb. (2 N•m).
6. Remove the lubricant pump and quickly reinstall the fill/drain plug and washer. Tighten the plug to 17 in.-lb. (2 N•m).
7. Wipe any excess lubricant from the drive unit.
8. Repeat Step 1 and Step 2 to recheck the lubricant level.
9. After operating the unit, recheck the lubricant level (Step 1 and Step 2).

Fluid Check (With Reservoir)

CAUTION
On models equipped with an oil reservoir, do not remove the dipstick, or check the drive unit oil level using the dipstick. If the dipstick is removed on models equipped with a reservoir, an overfull condition will result which can damage drive unit oil seals.

CAUTION
If the lubricant in the reservoir is milky brown or if water is mixed with it, the drive unit has an internal leak which must be corrected before it is returned to service.

Check the lubricant level in the reservoir (**Figure 39**). If the fluid level is below the FULL mark on the reservoir, remove the cover and add sufficient lubricant to bring the level to the mark. Reinstall cover tightly.

CAUTION
The unit should not require more than 2 ounces of lubricant. If it does an oil leak is probable and the unit should not be used until it is checked for leakage and any problem corrected.

Fluid Change (Without Reservoir)

1. If the fill/drain plug is located in the propeller shaft bearing carrier (**Figure 42**), trim the drive unit to the fully IN position. If the fill/drain plug is located at the front of the gearcase housing (**Figure 43**), tilt the drive unit to the fully OUT position.

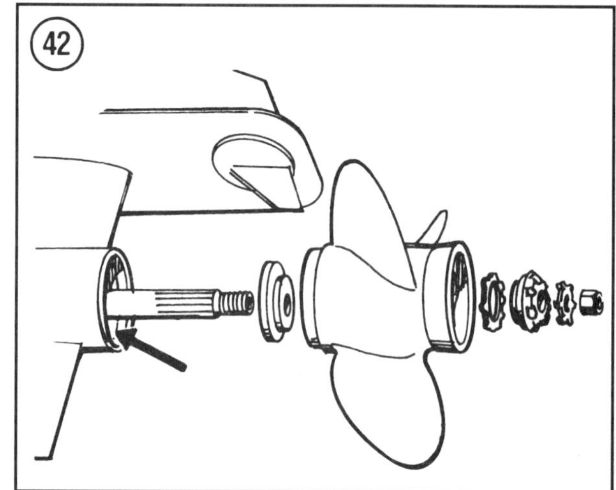

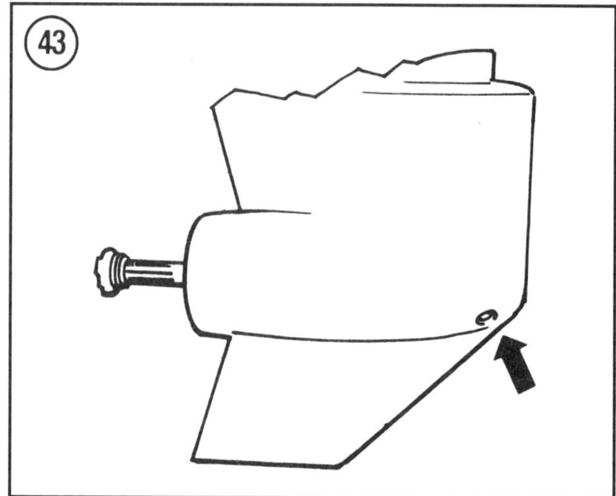

CAUTION

Take a small sample of the lubricant as soon as the fill/drain plug is removed in Step 2. If the lubricant is milky brown or if water is mixed with it the drive unit has a leak which must be repaired before it is returned to service.

2. Place a suitable container below the drive unit. Remove the vent plug (**Figure 44**) and fill/drain plug (**Figure 42** or **Figure 43**). Allow the gear housing to drain completely.
3. After the lubricant is completely drained, return the drive unit to the vertical position (if tilted OUT).
4. Insert lubricant pump (part No. 91-26150, or equivalent) into the fill/drain plug hole. Inject the lubricant from the pump into the fill/drain plug hole until an air-free stream flows from the vent plug hole.
5. Reinstall the vent plug and seal washer. Tighten the plug to 17 in.-lb. (2 N•m).
6. Remove the lubricant pump and quickly reinstall the fill/drain plug and seal washer. Tighten the plug to 17 in.-lb. (2 N•m).
7. Wipe any excess lubricant from the drive unit.
8. Check the fluid level by repeating Step 1 and Step 2 under *Fluid Check* in this chapter. After operating the unit, recheck the fluid level and add lubricant as necessary.

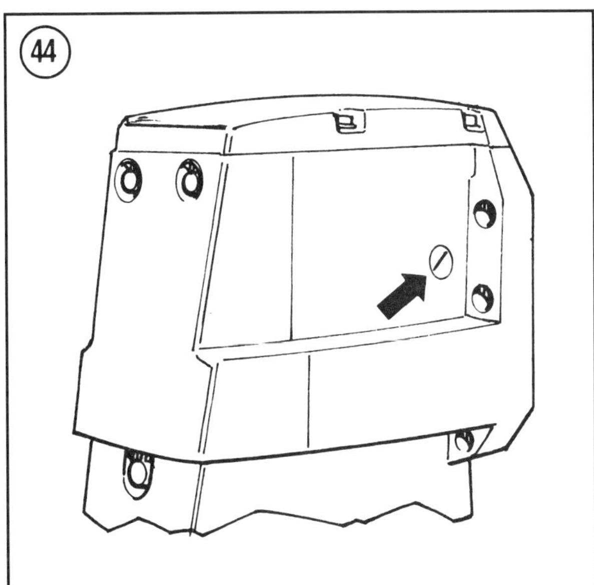

Fluid Change (With Reservoir)

1. If the fill/drain plug is located in the propeller shaft bearing carrier (**Figure 42**), trim the drive unit to the fully IN position. If the fill/drain plug is located at the front of the gearcase housing (**Figure 43**), tilt the drive unit to the fully OUT position.

CAUTION

Take a small sample of the lubricant as soon as the fill/drain plug is removed in Step 2. If the lubricant is milky brown or if water is mixed with it, the drive unit has a leak which must be repaired before it is returned to service.

2. Place a suitable container under the drive unit. Remove the vent plug (**Figure 44**) and the fill/drain plug (**Figure 42** or **Figure 43**) and allow the gear housing to drain completely.
3. After all lubricant is completely drained, return the drive unit to the fully IN position (if tilted OUT).
4. Remove the reservoir from its bracket (**Figure 39**). Remove the cover and drain the lubricant into a suitable container.
5. Insert the lubricant pump (part No. 91-26150, or equivalent) into the fill/drain hole. Inject lubricant from the pump through the oil fill/drain hole until it spurts from the vent hole in an air-free stream.
6. Reinstall the oil vent plug and washer. Tighten the plug to 17 in.-lb. (2 N•m).
7. Remove the lubricant pump and quickly reinstall the fill/drain plug and washer. Tighten the plug to 17 in.-lb. (2 N•m).
8. Wipe any excess lubricant from the drive housing and gearcase.
9. Reinstall the oil reservoir to its bracket. Fill the reservoir to its FULL mark and reinstall the cover tightly.

6

OMC STERN DRIVE

The lubrication tasks described in this section should be performed at the intervals indicated in **Table 1**. These intervals are only guidelines, however. Consider the frequency and extent of boat use when setting actual intervals and perform the tasks more frequently if the boat is used under severe service conditions.

CAUTION

Check stern drive lubricant level when unit is cool. If more than a teaspoonful of water drains from filler hole or if the lubricant has a milky-brown color, have stern drive checked by a dealer to determine and correct the problem before running the unit again.

Dispose of old lubricant properly. Disposal methods are discussed under Engine Oil and Filter Change in this chapter.

Lower Gearcase Lubricant Level

Properly maintaining the lubricant level is extremely important, since oil is circulated to the upper thrust bearing by the pumping action of the rolled spiral on the drive shaft on 1967 1/2 and later models (earlier models used a plunger-type oil pump in the bottom of the gearcase). As the oil level decreases to about 3/4 full, the oil circulation begins to decrease. If the level is only about 1/2 full, no oil will circulate at all, starving the upper thrust bearing and causing severe damage.

1. Remove oil level plug and gasket located on side of drive shaft housing (**Figure 45**). Oil must be even with bottom of vent plug hole when unit is level.
2. If level is down, add lubricant as described under *Lower Gearcase Lubricant Change* in this chapter.

Lower Gearcase Lubricant Change

1. Remove the oil level plug (**Figure 45**) and the drain plug from lower gear housing (**Figure 46**). Tilt unit slightly to aid drainage.
2. Insert OMC gearcase lubricant tube into oil drain plug hole and fill until oil appears at upper oil level plug hole.
3. Install oil level plug first, then quickly remove lubricant tube and install drain plug.

Upper Gearcase Lubricant Level

1. Remove upper gearcase oil fill plug (**Figure 47**). On older units not equipped with the fill plug/dipstick, remove the oil level plug located above the drain plug (**Figure 48**) on the starboard side of the upper gearcase.
2. Wipe dipstick attached to plug with a clean paper towel and reinstall in upper gearcase. Wait a moment and remove plug/dipstick again. Lu-

45

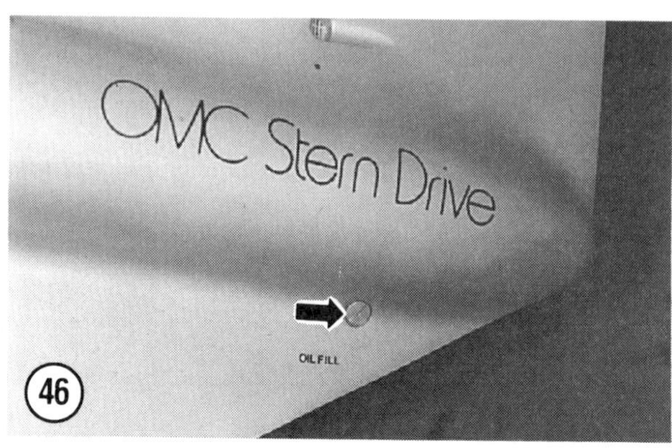

46

bricant level should be at the oil level mark on the dipstick.

3. On older units without the dipstick, the oil should be even with the bottom of the level plug hole threads.

4. If necessary, add sufficient OMC gearcase lubricant through the fill plug hole to bring the level up to the dipstick mark or even with the level plug hole threads but do not overfill.

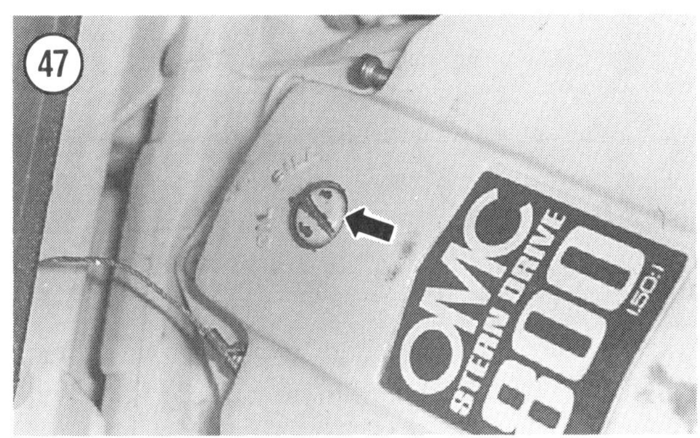

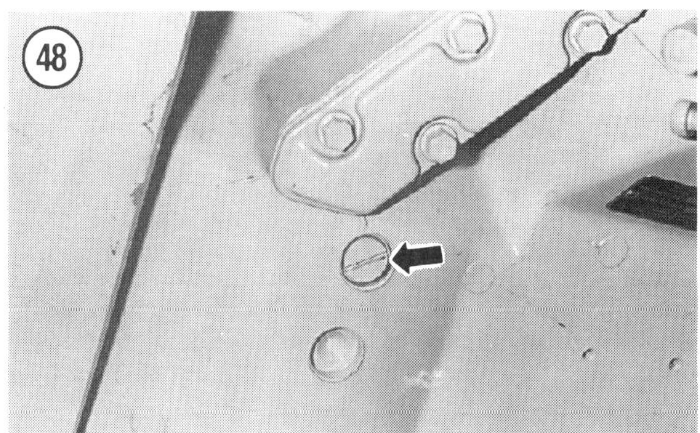

Upper Gearcase Lubricant Change

1. Remove the upper gearcase oil fill plug (**Figure 47**) and drain plug on the starboard side of the upper gearcase (**Figure 48**). On older units, remove the oil level plug located just above the drain plug.
2. Tilt the drive unit enough to permit the upper gearcase to drain completely.
3. Bring the drive unit back to a vertical position.

NOTE
Filling an empty gearcase in Step 4 is a slow process, as the lubricant requires time to fill all the cavities in the gearcase.

4. Insert OMC gearcase lubricant tube into the oil drain plug hole and fill until oil appears at the upper oil level plug hole.
5. Reinstall the dipstick and check the lubricant level. When it reaches the mark on the dipstick (newer units) or is even with the level plug hole threads (older units), the unit is properly filled.
6. Install the fill and/or level plug(s) first, then quickly remove the lubricant tube and install the drain plug.

Intermediate Housing Service (Early Models)

1. Remove the intermediate housing vent screw to relieve any pressure buildup.
2. Lubricate the grease fitting with OMC Triple-Guard grease.
3. Reinstall the vent screw.

Intermediate Housing Service (Late Models)

1. Remove the intermediate housing drain/fill plug (**Figure 49**).
2. Allow the reservoir to thoroughly drain.
3. Add OMC Hi-Vis gearcase lubricant through the plug hole until the level is visible. Install the drain/fill plug.

Tilt Unit Lubricant Change

1. Remove tilt unit drain and fill plugs. **Figure 50** shows the fill plug and approximate location of the drain plug on the bottom of the unit.
2. Allow reservoir to thoroughly drain.
3. Install the drain plug.
4. Add OMC Premium 4-cycle motor oil through the fill hole until the level is visible.
5. Install the fill plug.

Tilt Bearings/Tilt Gear (Early Models)

1. Remove the rubber cap from the grease fitting on each side of the tilt shaft (**Figure 51**).
2. Lubricate the fittings with OMC Triple-Guard grease.
3. Wipe the fittings clean and reinstall the rubber caps.

Tilt Bearings/Tilt Gear (Late Models)

1. Pry off the protective rubber cushion (A, **Figure 52**) on each side of the unit to expose the grease fitting.
2. Lubricate each fitting with OMC Triple-Guard grease.
3. Wipe the fittings clean and reinstall the cushions.
4. Lubricate the tilt gear teeth (B, **Figure 52**) with OMC Triple-Guard grease.

Swivel Bearing

Lubricate the swivel bearing (**Figure 53**) with OMC Triple-Guard grease at the intervals given in **Table 1**.

Steering Shaft

Lubricate the outboard and inboard steering shaft grease fitting at the intervals given in **Table 1**.

OMC COBRA STERN DRIVE

The lubrication tasks described in this section should be performed at the intervals indicated in **Table 1**. These intervals are only guidelines, however. Consider the frequency and extent of boat use when setting actual intervals and perform the tasks more frequently if the boat is used under severe service conditions.

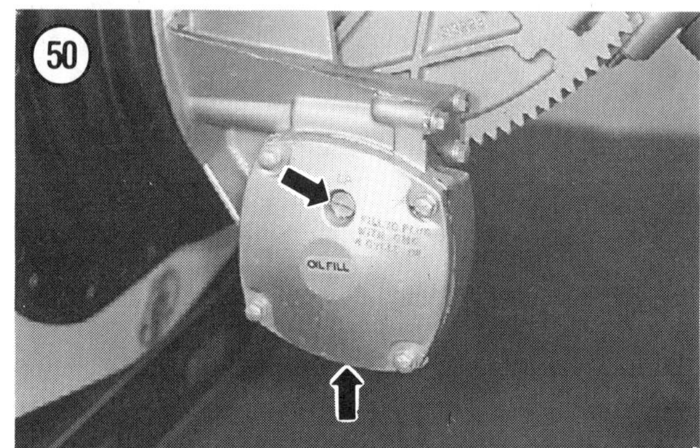

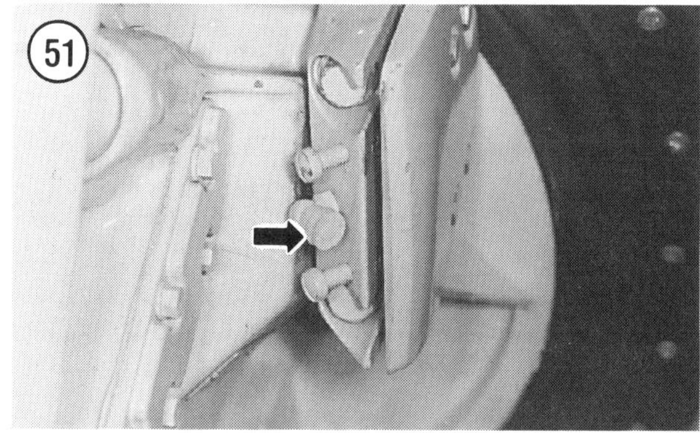

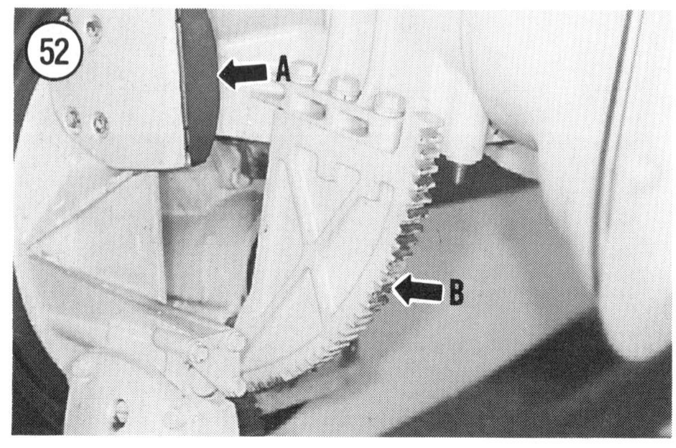

Fluid Check

Check stern drive lubricant level when the unit is cool.

NOTE
The stern drive unit must be in the vertical position for at least 1 hour prior to performing the fluid check to ensure accurate results.

1. With the drive unit in a vertical position, unscrew and remove the dipstick on the top of the drive unit (**Figure 54**).
2. Wipe the dipstick clean with a lint-free cloth or paper towel, then thread it back in place.
3. Wait a few seconds, then remove the dipstick a second time and check the oil level.
4. Loosen and momentarily remove, then reinstall the oil drain plug. If more than a teaspoon of water drains from the hole or if the lubricant has a milky-white or milky-brown color, the stern drive unit has a leak that must be corrected before the unit is returned to service.
5. If the oil level is low, reinstall the dipstick tightly. This creates an air lock which holds the lubricant in the gearcase. Then, remove the oil fill plug from the side of the gearcase. See A, **Figure 55**.
6. Add sufficient OMC Hi-Vis lubricant to bring the level to the FILL mark on the dipstick, then install the oil fill plug.
7. Remove the dipstick a second time and recheck the oil level. It may be necessary to repeat this action more than once, but do not overfill.

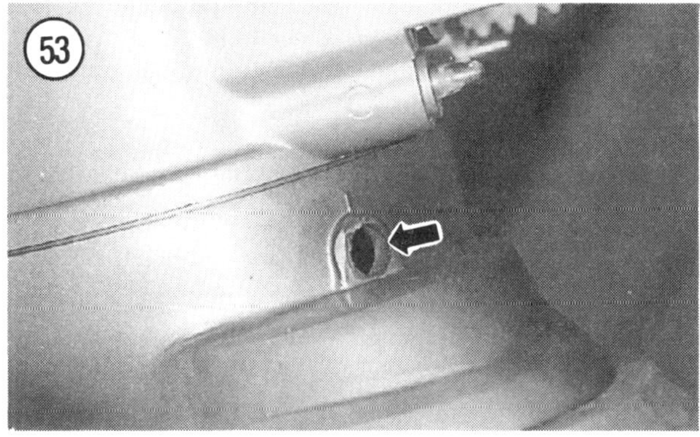

6

Fluid Change

1. With the drive unit in a vertical position, place a suitable container underneath the oil drain plug.
2. Unscrew and remove the dipstick on the top of the drive unit (**Figure 54**) and the oil drain plug (B, **Figure 55**).
3. Allow the drive unit lubricant to drain completely, then reinstall the oil drain plug.
4. Remove the oil fill plug (A, **Figure 55**) and fill the drive unit with the required amount of OMC Hi-Vis lubricant. Reinstall the oil fill plug.
5. Wipe the dipstick clean with a lint-free cloth or paper towel and insert it in the dipstick hole but do not thread it in place—simply let the dipstick cap rest in the hole. This method results in a slight overfill to compensate for the oil level drop that will occur as a result of trapped air being purged from the system when the drive is operated.
6. When the lubricant level is correct, reinstall the dipstick and tighten securely.

Gimbal Housing and U-joint Lubrication

The gimbal housing bearing and universal joints must be lubricated at least once a year or permanent damage to the stern drive unit will result. Lubrication requires removal of the stern drive unit.

The gimbal bearing grease fitting is located on the starboard side of the gimbal housing. The U-joint grease fittings are located on the double cardan U-joint. Each fitting should be lubricated with OMC Marine wheel bearing grease until the old grease has been forced out and new grease appears. Wipe the fitting and remove all excess grease.

Before reinstalling the drive, lubricate the U-joint shaft splines with OMC Triple-Guard grease and apply a light coat of engine oil to the O-rings on the shaft. Check the bellows for damage and/or deterioration and replace as required. Before reinstalling the stern drive unit, check engine alignment as described in the shop manual for your engine.

Power Trim/Tilt Reservoir Fluid Check

The trim/tilt unit reservoir, hydraulic pump and motor are a combined self-contained unit. At the start of each season, check the reservoir fluid level as follows.

WARNING
If the level/fill plug is removed with the stern drive unit down, pressure in the reservoir will force an oil spray from the plug hole which could result in serious personal injury if it were to spray in your face or eyes.

1. With the stern drive unit tilted up, remove the level/fill plug from the reservoir housing. SeeA, **Figure 56**, typical.
2. If the fluid level is not at the bottom of the fill hole with the stern drive unit at full tilt, add OMC Power Trim and Tilt fluid to bring the fluid to its correct level.
3. Reinstall the level/fill plug and tighten securely.

Power Trim/Tilt Reservoir Fluid Change (1986 models)

1. Raise the stern drive unit to its fully UP position and prop it up to prevent its weight from pressurizing the system and resulting in a messy fluid spill.

2. Mark the TOP hydraulic line. Place a suitable container under the reservoir and open the manual release valve one full turn. See B, **Figure 56**.
3. Slowly remove the level/fill plug (A, **Figure 56**) in case of residual pressure in the reservoir.
4. Remove the manufacturing plug (**Figure 58**) and drain the fluid from the valve body. While the fluid is draining, manually lower the stern drive unit to force any oil from the base of the trim/tilt cylinders.
5. When the fluid has drained, return the stern drive to its full UP position. Reinstall the manufacturing plug and add OMC Power Trim and Tilt fluid through the reservoir fill hole. When fluid level is at the bottom of the hole, bleed the system by cycling the stern drive unit at least 5 times, then add fluid as required to bring the level to the bottom of the hole. Reinstall the level/fill plug and return the drive unit to its full DOWN position.

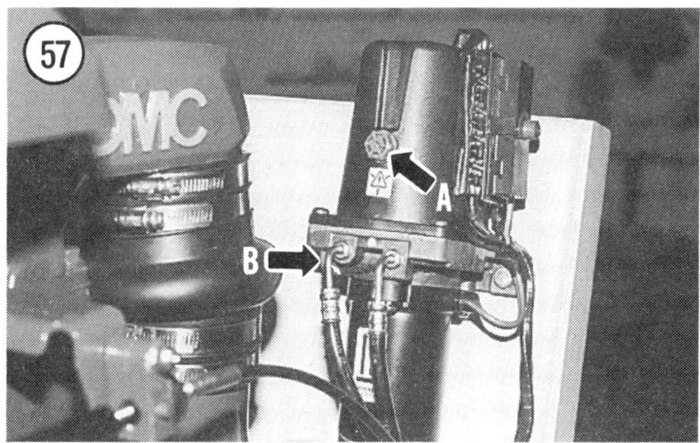

Power Trim/Tilt Reservoir Fluid Change (1987-1988 models)

1. Raise the stern drive unit to its full UP position and prop it up to prevent its weight from pressurizing the system and resulting in a messy fluid spill.
2. Place a suitable container under the reservoir and slowly remove the level/fill plug (A, **Figure 57**) in case of residual pressure in the reservoir.
3. Remove the manual release valve (B, **Figure 57**) and drain the fluid from the valve body. While the fluid is draining, manually lower the stern drive unit to force any fluid from the base of the trim/tilt cylinders.
4. When the fluid has drained, return the stern drive to its full UP position. Reinstall the manual release valve and add OMC Power Trim and Tilt fluid through the reservoir fill hole. When fluid level is at the bottom of the hole, bleed the system by cycling the stern drive unit at least 5 times, then add fluid as required to bring the level to the bottom of the hole. Reinstall the level/fill plug and return the drive unit to its full DOWN position.

6

Power Trim/Tilt Reservoir Fluid Change (1989-on)

1. Raise the stern drive unit to its full UP position and prop it up to prevent its weight from pressurizing the system and resulting in a messy fluid spill.
2. Place a suitable container under the reservoir and slowly remove the level/fill plug (**Figure 56**) in case of residual pressure in the reservoir.

3. Remove the manual release valve (**Figure 56**) and drain the fluid from the valve body. While the fluid is draining, manually lower the stern drive unit to force any fluid from the base of the trim/tilt cylinders.

4. When the fluid has drained, return the stern drive to its full UP position. Reinstall the manual release valve and add OMC Power Trim and Tilt fluid through the reservoir fill hole. When fluid level is at the bottom of the hole, bleed the system by cycling the stern drive unit at least S times, then add fluid as required to bring the level to the bottom of the hole. Reinstall the level/fill plug and return the drive unit to its full DOWN position.

VOLVO STERN DRIVE

The lubrication tasks described in this section should be performed at the intervals indicated in **Table 1**. These intervals are only guidelines, however. Consider the frequency and extent of boat use when setting actual intervals and perform the tasks more frequently if the boat is used under severe service conditions.

CAUTION
Check the stern drive lubricant level when the unit is cool. If more than a teaspoonful of water drains from the filler hole or if the lubricant has a milky-brown color, an external water leak is present. The stern drive should be repaired before returning the unit to service.

Dispose of old lubricant properly. Disposal methods are discussed under *Engine Oil and Filter Change* in this chapter.

Lubricant Level Check

1. With the stern drive unit fully lowered, remove the oil level dipstick and gasket located on top of the drive shaft housing (**Figure 59**).

2. Wipe the dipstick with a clean cloth or paper towel and reinsert in the drive unit without screwing it in place. Wait a few seconds and remove the dipstick again. The oil level should be near the top of the dipstick flat.

3. If the level is down, add sufficient lubricant to bring the fluid level up to the top of the dipstick flat.

4. Reinstall oil level dipstick. Make sure O-ring fits in groove under dipstick threads. Tighten dipstick snugly.

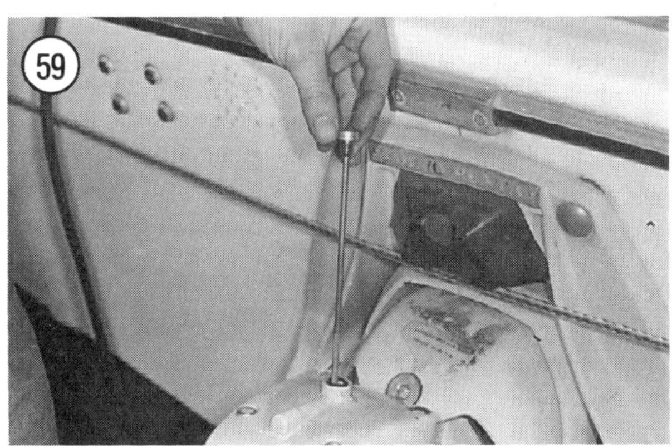

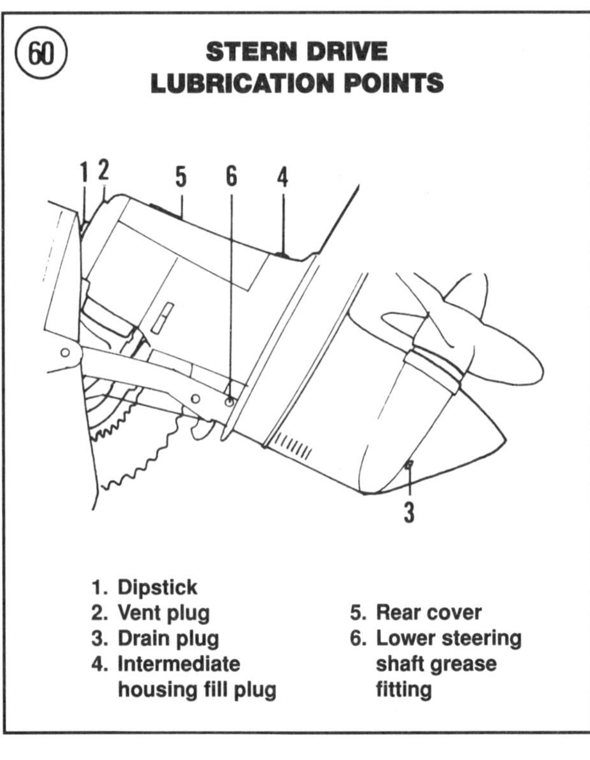

Lubricant Change

The use of a hand pump is recommended to speed up the filling process and keep spillage to a minimum. Refer to **Figure 60** for this procedure.

1. Place a suitable container under the stern drive unit.
2. Remove the oil level dipstick (1, **Figure 60**).
3. Remove the vent plug at the rear drive head (2, **Figure 60**), if so equipped.
4. Tilt the stern drive unit upward.
5. Remove the plug and O-ring installed under the propeller gear housing (3, **Figure 60**)

NOTE
Filling an empty drive unit in Step 6 is a slow process, as the lubricant requires time to fill all the cavities in the drive unit.

6A. Model 100—Lower the drive unit and fill with the required amount and type of lubricant through the oil level dipstick hole (1, **Figure 60**). Reinstall the dipstick.

6B. Model 200 and 270—Remove the oil fill plug and O-ring located at the rear of the intermediate housing (4, **Figure 60**). With the drive unit tilted up, fill with required amount and type of lubricant. Reinstall oil fill plug and O-ring.

6C. Model 280, 290 and Duoprop—Remove the 2 screws holding the upper drive cover in place (5, **Figure 60**). Remove the cover. Remove the oil fill plug (**Figure 61**) and O-ring. With the drive unit tilted up, fill with the required amount and type of lubricant. Reinstall the oil fill plug and O-ring. Reinstall the upper drive cover.

7. Reinstall the oil level dipstick (except Model 100) and vent plug, if so equipped.

8. Check lubricant level as described in this chapter. Top up or drain as required to bring the lubricant to the proper level on the dipstick.

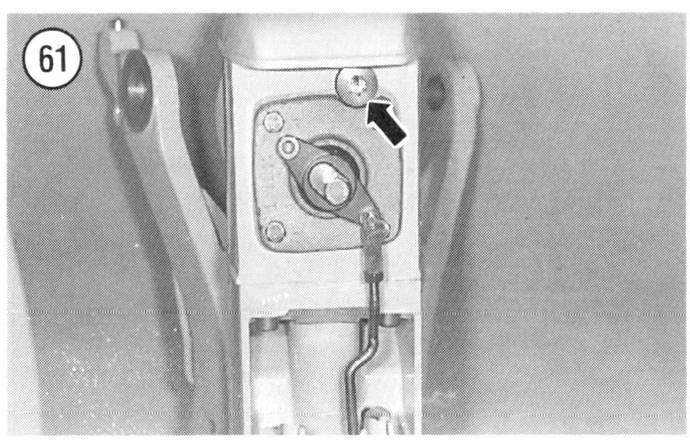

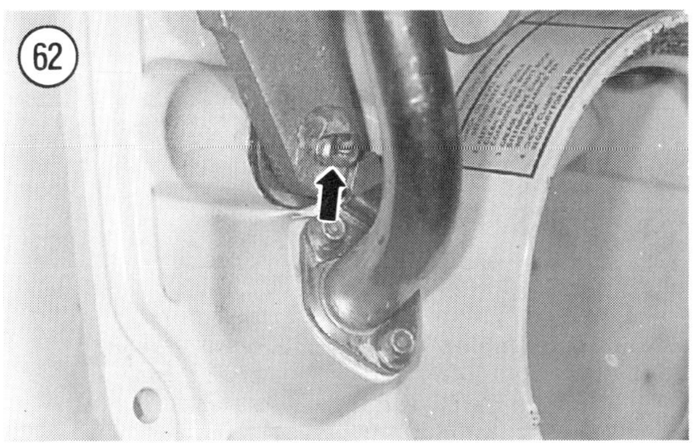

Lower Steering Shaft Bearing

Lubricate the lower steering shaft bearing fitting in the pivot yoke (6, **Figure 60**) with a grease gun and water-resistant grease. Lubricate fitting until grease is forced out of the washer installed between the yoke and intermediate housing.

Upper Steering Shaft Bearings

Lubricate upper steering shaft bearing fittings (**Figure 62** and **Figure 63**) with a grease gun and water-resistant grease. Lubricate fitting until grease is forced out at bearings.

Zinc Anode Check and Replacement

Every 14 days, check the zinc anode(s) to determine their condition. When corroded to less than 50% of their original size, replace with new anodes.

1. Remove the 2 screws holding the anode under the mounting collar, if so equipped. Remove the anode.
2. Remove the propeller.
3. Remove the 2 screws holding the zinc cover ring. Remove the cover ring (**Figure 64**).
4. Clean the contact surface on the mounting collar and/or propeller housing with a scraper and sandpaper to provide a bare metal surface for good contact.
5. Install the new cover ring. Install the propeller.
6. Install a new anode under the mounting collar, if so equipped. Tighten attaching screws snugly.

YAMAHA STERN DRIVE

The lubrication tasks described in this section should be performed at the intervals indicated in **Table 1**. These intervals are only guidelines, however. Consider the frequency and extent of boat use when setting actual intervals and perform the tasks more frequently if the boat is used under severe service conditions.

Stern Drive Oil Level Check

WARNING
The drive unit should be allowed to cool for at least 5 minutes before removing the oil level port plug, otherwise hot oil may spurt out of check port when port plug is removed.

1. Position stern drive unit so that its antiventilation plate is level.
2. Wipe off the plug area with a clean shop cloth.
3. After the engine has cooled for a minimum of 5 minutes, remove the upper level plug (**Figure 65**) from the top of the stern drive. The oil level is correct if even with the bottom of the plug hole (**Figure 65**). If the oil level is low, add oil through the oil level plug hole until the oil level is correct. Reinstall the plug and gasket.

NOTE
If the oil level is more than a little low, there may be a damaged oil seal in the stern drive unit. Check the oil level frequently to monitor oil loss. If it appears that an oil seal is damaged, refer to the shop manual for your stern drive for replacement.

Stern Drive Oil Change

WARNING
*The stern drive unit should be allowed to cool for at least 5 minutes before removing the drain and level plugs (**Figure 65**). Opening the plugs immediately after turning the engine off may allow hot oil to spurt out of the port openings when the plugs are removed.*

1. Position the stern drive at its fully tilted up position. See **Figure 66**.

63

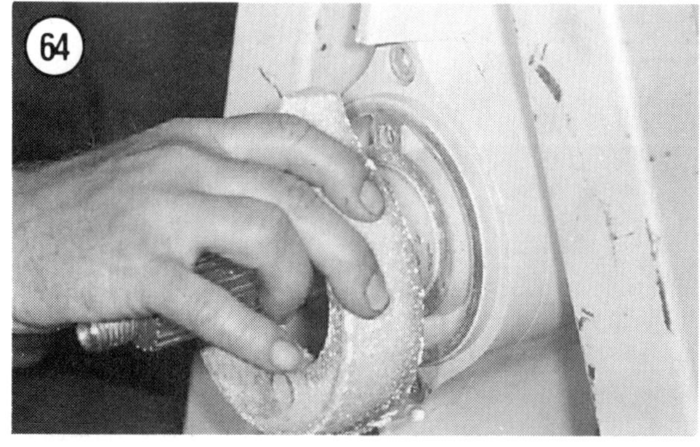
64

2. Place a clean drain pan underneath the stern drive drain plug.

3. Remove the drain and level plugs (**Figure 66**) and allow the stern drive oil to drain completely.

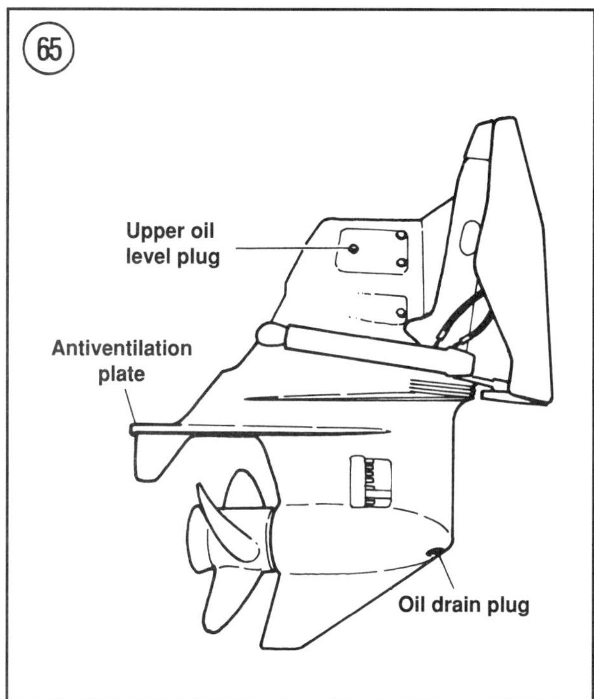

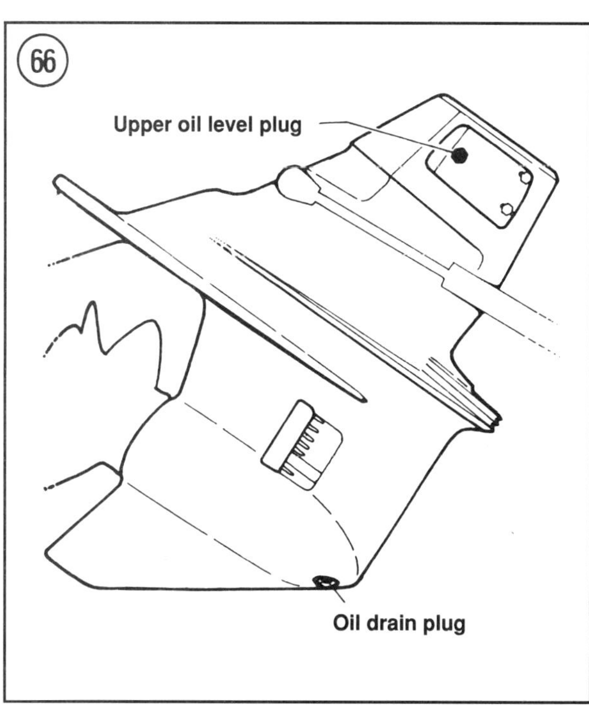

When the oil stops draining, position the stern drive so its antiventilation plate is level. See **Figure 65**.

NOTE
Before installing the new oil, check the oil in the drain pan. Check for metal particles in the oil by rubbing the oil between your fingers. Also examine the color of the oil. If the oil has a milky-white or milky-brown color, an external leak has allowed water to enter the drive unit. If the oil shows evidence of one or both of these abnormal conditions, the drive unit should be repaired before it is returned to service.

NOTE
An oil fill tube or an oil injection pump connected to the oil drain plug port must be used when filling the drive unit with oil in Step 4.

CAUTION
Because of the difficulty in bleeding air from the lower gearcase housing oil chamber, oil should be added at the drive unit oil drain port only. Premature wear to the gears and bearings will occur if the unit is operated with air mixed-in with the oil.

4. Clean the oil fill equipment thoroughly before use. Then insert the end of the fill device into the oil drain port (**Figure 65**). Slowly fill the drive unit with Yamaha Gear Case Lube until oil flows from the upper oil level port. When oil starts to flow from the upper oil level port, check for signs of air mixed with the oil; continue to add oil through the drive unit drain port until the exiting oil is free of all air bubbles.
5. When the escaping oil is free of all air bubbles, install the oil level port plug (with gasket) before removing the fill device. Then remove the fill device and quickly install the oil drain port plug and gasket.

WARNING
When cooling water is supplied to the drive unit, make sure there is sufficient

space to the side and behind the propeller and that no one is standing in the vicinity. If possible, remove the propeller to prevent the possibility of personal injury.

6. Connect a flush-test device to the drive unit as described under *Cooling System Flushing* in this chapter and run the drive unit to circulate oil through the drive unit. After a few minutes, stop the engine and turn off the cooling water as described under *Cooling System Flushing* and check the oil level as described in this chapter.

Power Steering Fluid Level Check

Although the dipstick is marked with both HOT and COLD lines, this procedure should be performed with the engine at normal operating temperature and OFF. See **Figure 67**, typical.

1. Remove the engine compartment cover or hatch.
2. Turn steering wheel so the stern drive is centered.
3. Unscrew the power steering pump reservoir cap and remove the cap/dipstick. See **Figure 68**.
4. Wipe the dipstick with a clean shop cloth or lint-free paper towel. Reinstall the cap/dipstick, wait a few moments, then remove again and check the fluid level on the dipstick.
5. The fluid level is correct if it is between the HOT and ADD marks on the dipstick. If fluid level is below the ADD mark on dipstick, add sufficient DEXRON II automatic transmission fluid to bring the level between the HOT and ADD dipstick marks.
6. Reinstall the cap/dipstick in the power steering pump reservoir.

NOTE

If you must check the fluid level when it is cold, the fluid level is correct if it is between the FULL COLD dipstick mark and the end of the dipstick. If fluid does not register on the dipstick, add DEXRON II automatic transmission fluid to bring the level between the FULL COLD mark and the end of the dipstick.

Bleeding the Power Steering Hydraulic System

A low fluid level and/or air in the fluid are the most common causes of pump noise. The power steering system must be bled to correct the prob-

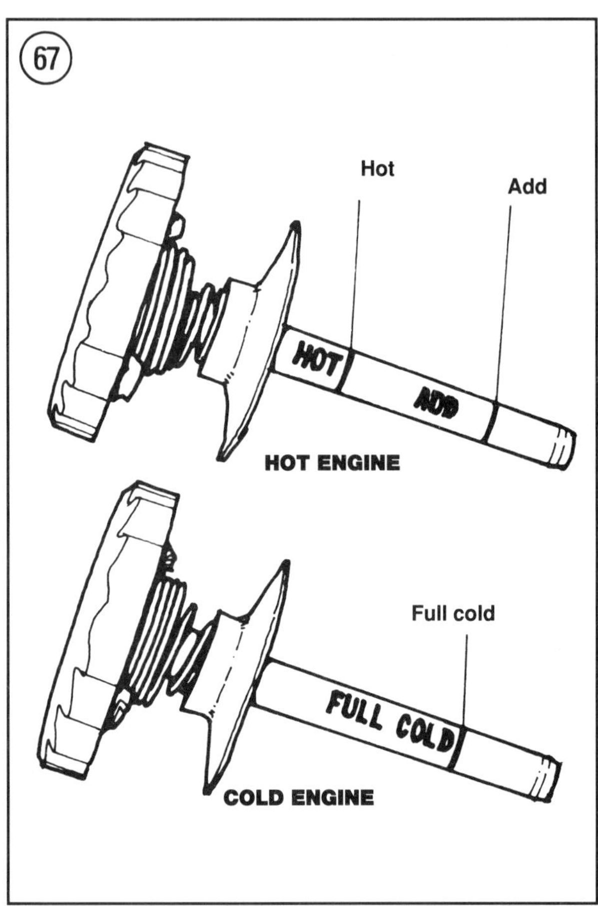

lem. It must also be bled whenever a hydraulic line has been disconnected to service the system.

1. With the engine off and cold, turn the steering wheel completely to port.
2. Unscrew the power steering pump reservoir cap (**Figure 68**) and remove the cap/dipstick.
3. Add sufficient DEXRON II automatic transmission fluid to bring the level to the FULL COLD mark on dipstick (**Figure 67**).
4. Reinstall the cap/dipstick in the power steering pump reservoir.

CAUTION
The engine should not be operated without cooling water flowing through the drive unit.

5. Start the engine, run briefly and shut it off. Repeat Steps 2-4 as required.
6. Turn the steering wheel from side-to-side while allowing drive unit to hit stops. Maintain fluid level at the FULL COLD mark on dipstick; add fluid as required. If there is air in the fluid, it will appear light tan in color or foamy in appearance. If there is a large number of bubbles in the oil, stop and allow the bubbles to disperse, then continue with Step 7.
7. Start and run the engine at 1,000-1,500 rpm until the engine reaches normal operating temperature. Turn the steering wheel from side-to-side while allowing the drive unit to hit the stops when the engine is running. When operating temperature is reached, turn the steering wheel to port and turn the engine OFF.
8. Recheck the fluid level in the reservoir. Fluid level should be between the HOT and ADD marks on the dipstick (**Figure 22**). If it still contains air, repeat Steps 6 and 7.
9. When all air has been bled from the system, run the boat on the water to make sure that the steering operates properly and is not noisy.
10. Let the system stabilize at its normal operating temperature and recheck the fluid level to make sure it is at the FULL HOT mark on the dipstick.

Power Trim/Tilt Reservoir Fluid Check

The trim/tilt unit reservoir, hydraulic pump and motor are a combined self-contained unit. At the specified intervals (**Table 1**), check the reservoir fluid level as follows.

WARNING
If the reservoir oil level/fill plug is removed with the stern drive unit down, pressure in the reservoir will force oil from the plug hole that could result in serious personal injury if it were to spray in your face or eyes.

1. Position the drive unit in its fully tilted UP position.
2. Check the fluid level on the trim pump reservoir (**Figure 69**). If the level is not within the MIN and MAX marks, remove the oil level/fill plug (**Figure 69**) and add Yamaha Power Trim Tilt Fluid or DEXRON II automatic transmission fluid to bring the fluid to its correct level. Do not overfill the reservoir or the unit may overflow.

NOTE
If the reservoir oil level was extremely low or if it appears that there are air bubbles mixed with the oil, there may be an oil leak in the power trim system. Refer to the shop manual for your stern drive or refer service to a marine technician.

CAUTION
Do not lower the drive unit until the oil level/fill plug has been reinstalled.

3. Reinstall the oil level/fill plug and tighten securely.

Bleeding the Power Trim/Tilt Reservoir

1. Close the manual release valve on the pump (**Figure 69**).

WARNING
If the reservoir oil level/fill plug is removed with the stern drive unit down,

pressure in the reservoir will force oil from the plug hole that could result in serious personal injury if it were to spray in your face or eyes.

2. Position the stern drive at its fully tilted up position. See **Figure 66**.
3. Remove the oil level/fill plug and add Yamaha Power Trim and Tilt Fluid or DEXRON II automatic transmission fluid to bring the fluid level to MAX. Reinstall the oil level/fill plug and gasket.

CAUTION
Do not lower the drive unit until the oil level/fill plug has been reinstalled.

4. Move the drive unit up and down with the tilt switch several times; this will remove air trapped in the hydraulic lines and components. Then stop the drive unit at its fully tilted UP position. Loosen the oil level/fill plug to release trapped air and tighten plug.
5. Repeat Steps 3 and 4 until the reservoir unit is bled.

Steering System Lubrication

Proper steering system lubrication is vital to maintain proper steering control. Refer to **Table 1** for lubrication intervals.

1. Turn the steering wheel back and forth; the wheel should turn smoothly. Lubricate the wheel pivot as required.
2. Turn the steering wheel all the way to the right and lubricate the inner cable (extended from guide tube) with Yamaha Marine grease. See **Figure 70**.
3. Disconnect the steering lever assembly (**Figure 71**) and apply Yamaha Marine Grease to all pivot points. Install pivot pins and secure with new cotter pins.
4. Bend the lockwasher tabs away from the steering pivot bolts and remove steering bolts. See **Figure 72**. Apply Yamaha Marine Grease to end of bolts (pivot end); reinstall bolts and lockwashers and tighten bolts to 34 N•m (25 ft.-lb.). Bend lockwasher tab against bolt head to lock it.

Propeller Shaft Lubrication

The propeller shaft should be periodically lubricated to prevent the propeller from seizing on the shaft. Remove propeller and service the shaft as described in the shop manual for your stern drive.

Propeller Inspection

The propeller should be inspected for chips, cracks or other damage and replaced as required. Check the propeller nut for proper tightening torque.

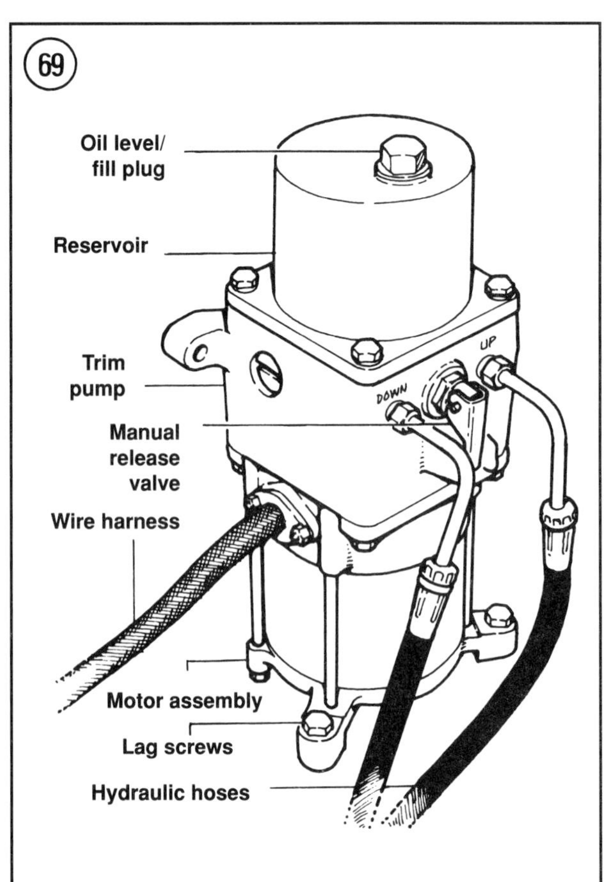

Gimbal Housing and Swivel Pin Lubrication

The gimbal housing bearing and swivel pins must be periodically lubricated with Yamaha Marine Grease. See lubrication points in **Figure 73.**

Universal Joint and Drive Shaft Splines Lubrication

The universal joint (**Figure 74**) and drive shaft splines should be lubricated with Yamaha Marine Grease at the intervals specified in **Table 1**. Lubrication requires removal of the stern drive unit.

Bellows Inspection

Check the bellows for damage and/or deterioration and replace as required.

Sacrificial Anode Inspection/Replacement

The Yamaha drive unit is equipped with 2 exterior mounted zinc alloy anodes, an exterior

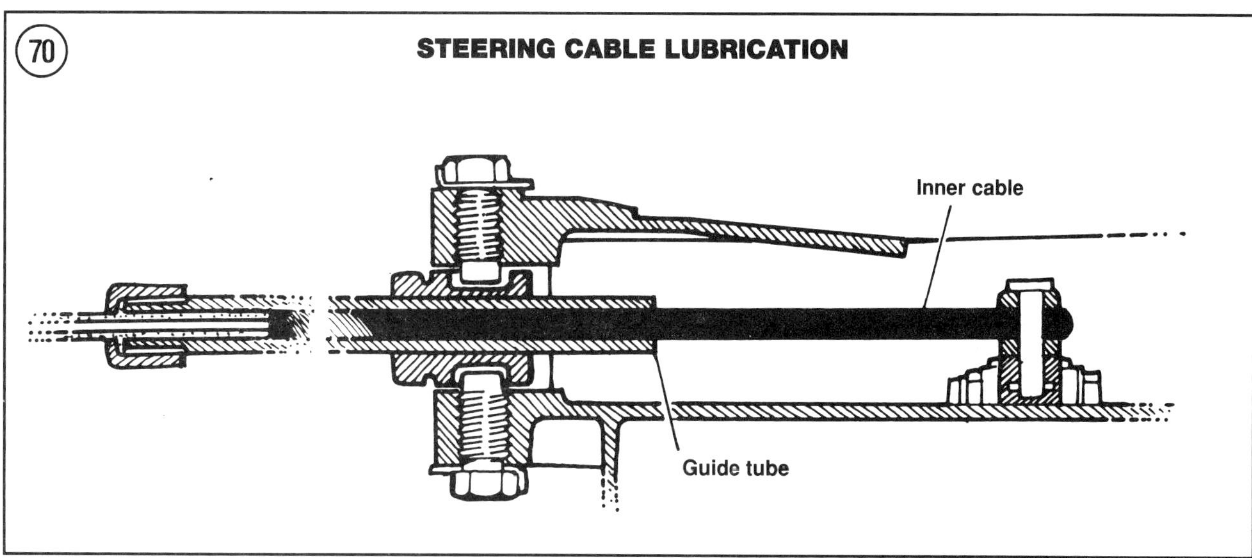

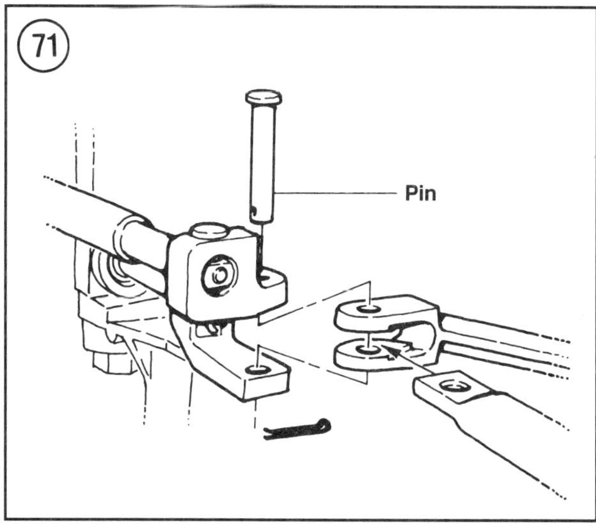

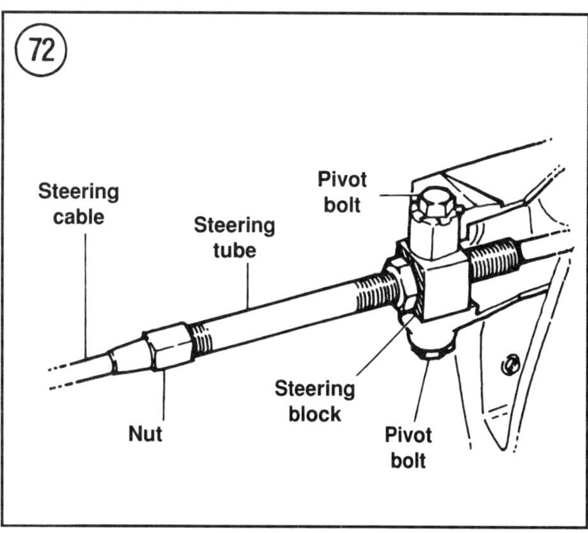

mounted aluminum trim tab anode and an interior mounted aluminum anode (**Figure 75**). The exterior mounted anodes should be inspected for deterioration every 30 days (every 14 days when operating in salt water) and replaced when they are more than 50% eroded. When replacing an anode, clean the anode mounting area on the drive unit or intermediate housing with sandpaper to remove all corrosion, then position the anode and secure it with its mounting bolts.

The interior mounted anode (**Figure 75**) is bolted to the top of the lower gearcase housing and should be inspected once a year or whenever the drive unit is separated and serviced.

JACUZZI JET DRIVE MAINTENANCE

The Jacuzzi Jet Drive should be greased every 100 hours or every 6 months, whichever comes first. There is a grease fitting for the thrust bearing and bowl bearing. See **3, Figure 76**. There is also a grease fitting on each universal joint.

BERKELEY JET DRIVE MAINTENANCE

The Berkeley Jet Drive should be serviced every 100 hours or once a season. Inject multipurpose grease into the fitting on the bearing. See

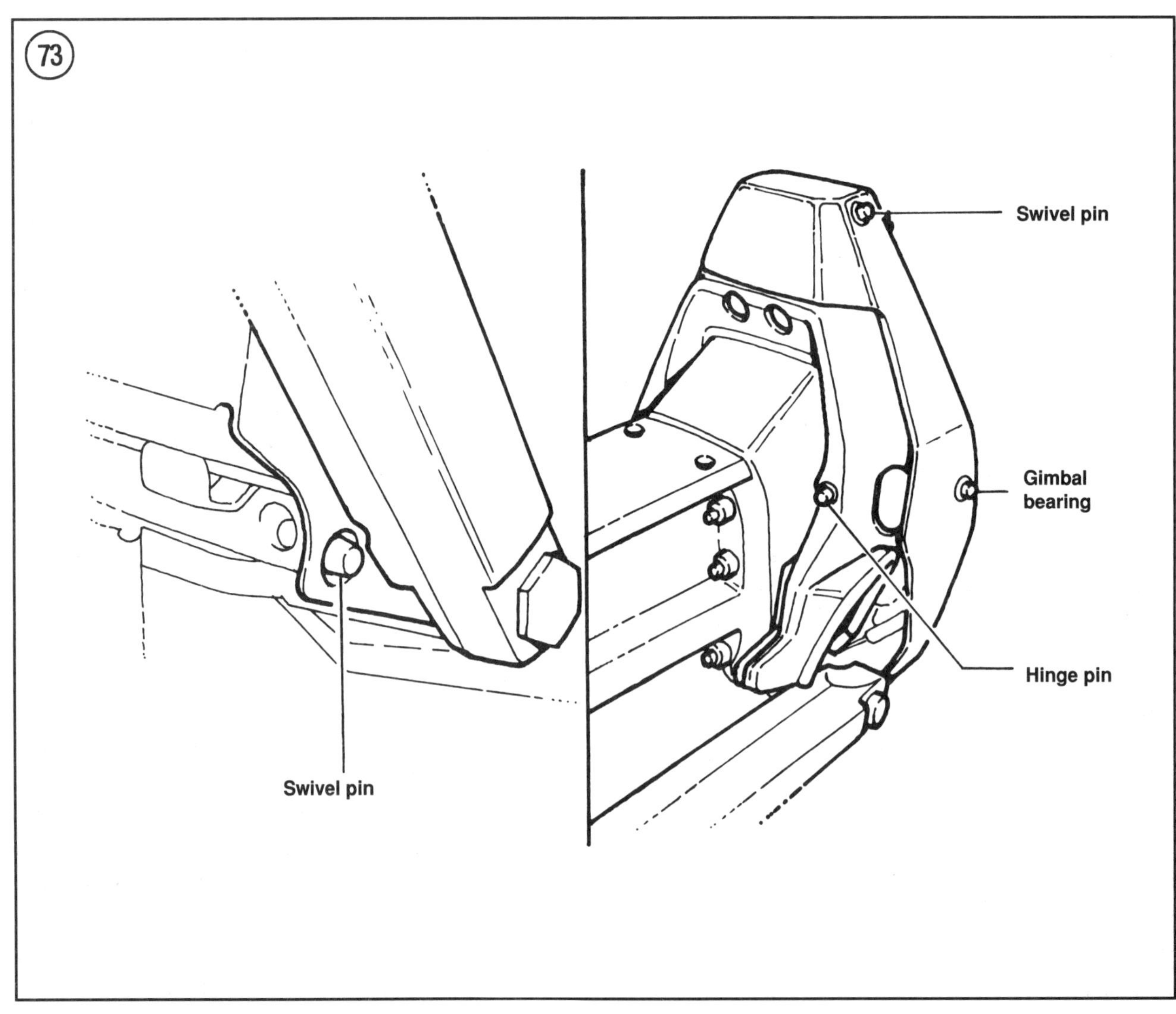

Figure 77. In addition, check amount of water leakage past the seal shown in **Figure 77**. The water should drip out slowly when the unit is operating. If water leakage is excessive, tighten the 2 nuts on the seal retainer. If no water leaks past the seal, loosen the nuts until water leaks in slow drips.

Twice a season, remove one of the plugs on the housing and check the oil level. See **Figure 78**. It should just reach the bottom of the hole.

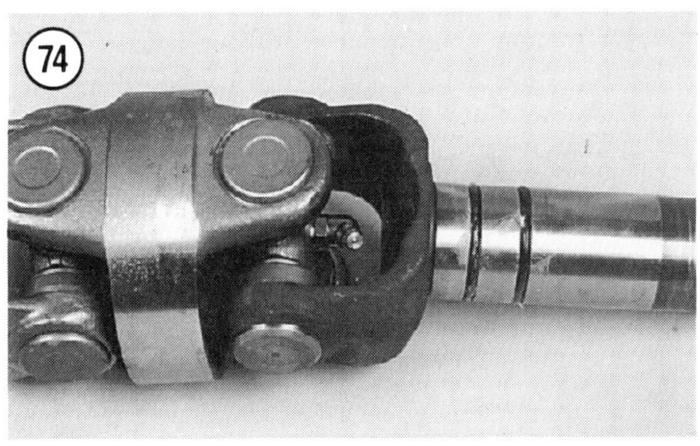

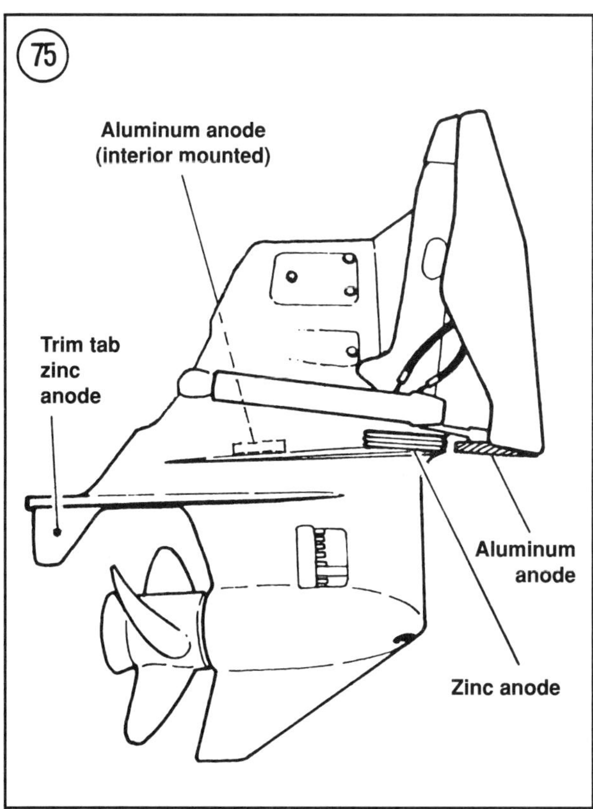

To top up, remove both plugs. Pour SAE 90 oil into one hole until it emerges from the other, then install both plugs.

WINTER LAY-UP OR STORAGE

As mentioned earlier, engines thrive on use. The engine cannot remain unattended for long periods without preventive maintenance and occasional running unless special precautions are taken to protect it. The following procedures will provide protection for each of the important engine systems.

6

Propeller Stern Drive Unit

1. Drain oil from the stern drive unit and fill with preservative oil.
2. Remove all marine growths and deposits from the stern drive unit.
3. Clean the stern drive unit with fresh water, and then with kerosene, mineral spirits, or similar solvent.
4. Touch up any paint blemishes which may be present.

CAUTION
Do not paint sacrificial zinc rings, plugs, or bars, if present. These must be left unpainted in order for them to prevent electrolysis damage.

5. Apply protective coating of rust preventive oil to all exterior surfaces.

Jet Drive Unit

1. Wash out jet unit with fresh water, especially if used in salt water.
2. If jet is equipped with intake strainer system, remove both hoses and allow to drain. Reconnect hoses. Remove strainer bowl, empty water, and replace.
3. Lubricate thrust bearing, bowl bearing, drive shaft, and other lubrication points.

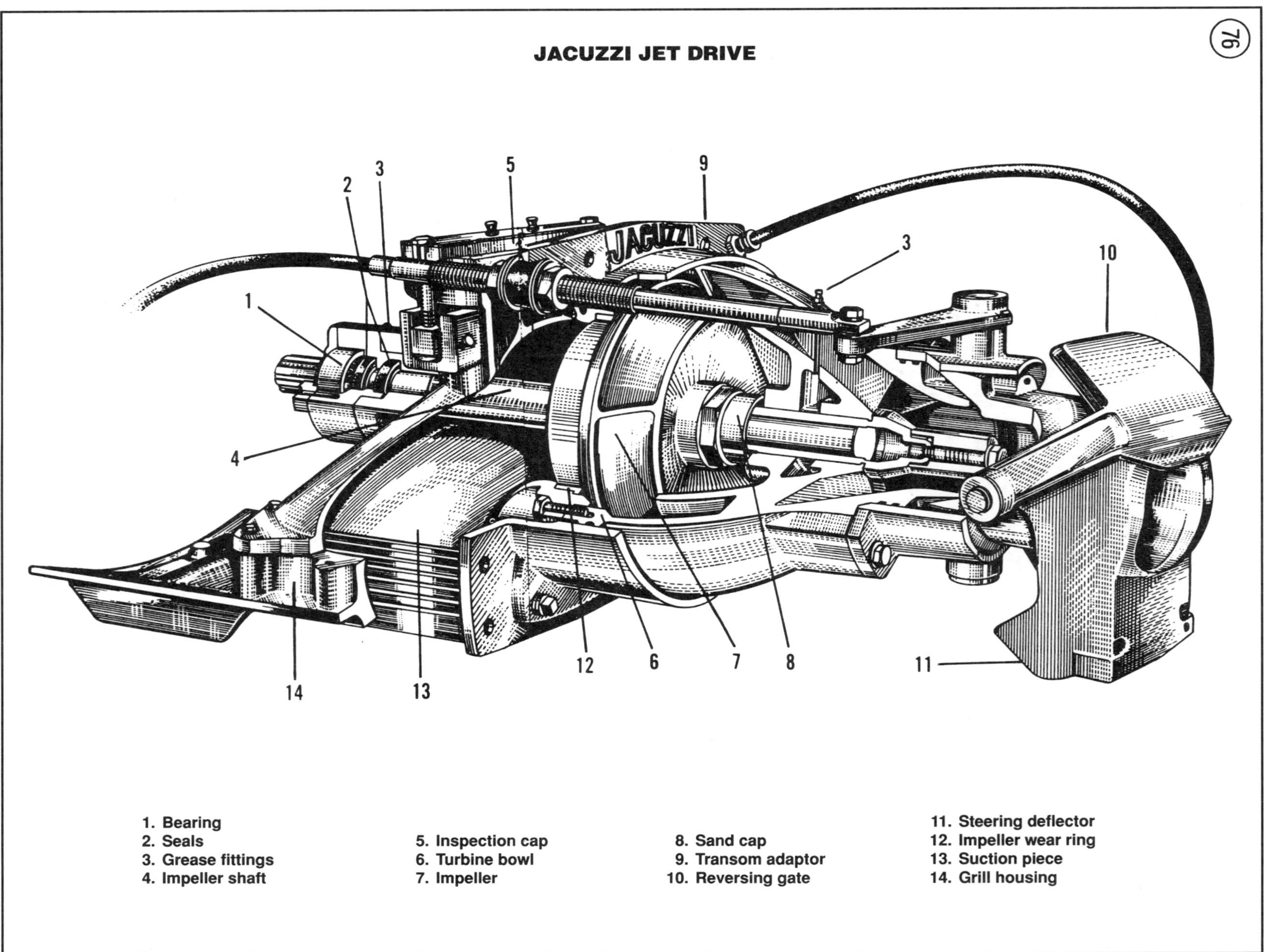

JACUZZI JET DRIVE

1. Bearing
2. Seals
3. Grease fittings
4. Impeller shaft
5. Inspection cap
6. Turbine bowl
7. Impeller
8. Sand cap
9. Transom adaptor
10. Reversing gate
11. Steering deflector
12. Impeller wear ring
13. Suction piece
14. Grill housing

4. Perform Steps 2 through 5 of *Stern Drive Unit* procedure above.

PROPELLERS

The propeller is the final link between the boat's drive system and the water. A perfectly maintained engine and hull are useless if the propeller is the wrong type or has been allowed to deteriorate. Although propeller selection for a specific situation is beyond the scope of this book, the information in Chapter Four on propeller construction and design applies to inboard installations as well and will allow you to discuss the subject intelligently with your marine dealer.

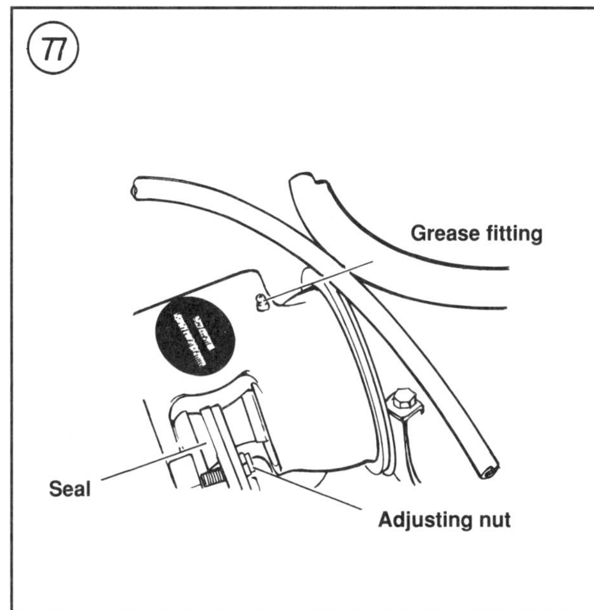

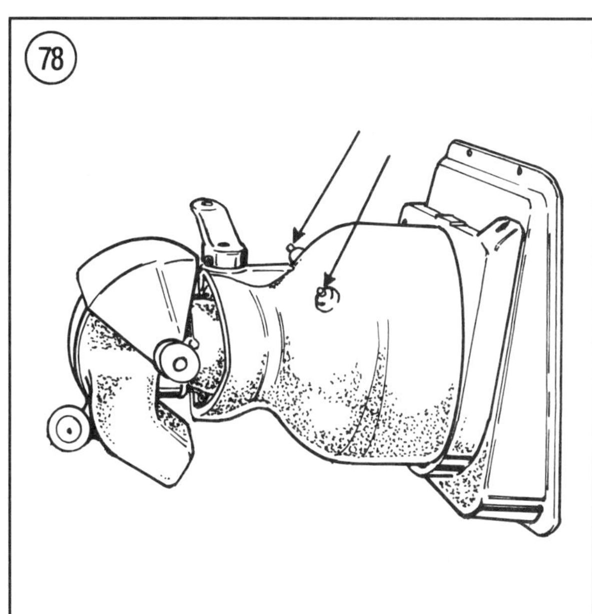

Table is on the following page.

Table 1 STERN DRIVE MAINTENANCE*

Interval	Maintenance
Weekly	Check stern drive lubricant level
	Check condition of trim tab, anodic bolt heads and other sacrificial anodes
	Check gear housing water pickups for debris or growth
Every 50 hours of operation or 60 days	Lubricate hinge pins
	Check propeller condition and lubricate prop shaft splines
	Check level of all fluids
	Lubricate steering cable
	Lubricate steering linkage
	Lubricate exposed portion of steering cable
	Lubricate power steering control valve
Every 100 hours of operation or 120 days	Lubricate transom gimbal bearing assembly swivel shaft and bearing
	Lubricate U-joint shaft splines and cross bearings
	Check trim cylinder fasteners for tightness
	Lubricate upper and lower swivel pins
	Lubricate propeller shaft splines
Once each year	Perform 100 hours checks
	Check propeller for damage
	Replace water pump impeller
	Remove, disassemble and clean seawater pump
	Spray exterior surfaces with rust preventative
	Inspect and lubricate steering head and remote control
	Inspect and lubricate shift cable
	Inspect steering system for loose, damaged or missing components

*Perform more frequently when operating in saltwater.

Chapter Seven

Electrical System

Marine electrical systems vary widely in content and complexity. A small trailerable boat may have only one or two 12 volt interior lamps and the required running lamps. Larger boats may have elaborate 12-32 volt and 110 volt systems. Even more complex systems include an auxiliary power plant with sufficient capacity to operate air conditioners and high-wattage electrical appliances.

BATTERY SYSTEMS

Most boats depend primarily on 12-, 24-, or 32-volt battery system to power lights, ventilation fans and water pumps. **Figure 1** shows a typical system. On small boats, only one battery is used and the main switch is a simple on-off switch. On large boats, 2 or more batteries are used. The batteries are separated into banks, each bank consisting of one or more batteries wired in parallel. The main switch selects either bank separately or connects both banks in parallel for greater current capacity.

Batteries are usually charged while underway from an engine-mounted alternator and voltage regulator. A separate battery charger may also be installed to charge the batteries from AC shore power.

Very little maintenance is required on battery electrical systems other than checking to be sure that all lights and other electrical accessories operate. Batteries must be checked occasionally for electrolyte level and state of charge.

Battery Types

Most batteries suitable for marine applications were actually developed for other applications such as forklifts and golf carts. Most of these look similar to automotive batteries that everyone is familiar with, but there are important considerations that make marine applications unique.

Automotive batteries are commonly used because they are easily available and relatively inexpensive. They are designed to be fully charged most of the time to deliver very high amperage for engine starting. The rest of the time, the demands on an automotive battery are minimal as the alternator maintains a high state of charge.

Unfortunately, automotive batteries don't hold up well in a boat where they are frequently discharged to 30-50% of their charge, then recharged to full charge in a relatively short time. This is often referred to as "deep cycling." If you insist on automotive batteries, get the "maintenance free" type which does not have removable fill caps. This will minimize dangerous acid spills. These batteries are not completely sealed against leaks, however. They are designed to vent if they are overcharged. The vented electrolyte could cause damage to your boat.

Deep cycle batteries are similar in appearance and design to conventional automotive batteries, but they are specifically designed for deep cycling. They generally cost more, but they last longer. Since they are commonly used on land based recreational vehicles, they are often available at discount warehouses throughout the country.

Gel cell batteries also provide deep cycling ability, plus the added safety of a gelled electrolyte instead of a liquid electrolyte.

Battery Capacity

To determine the appropriate battery size, you need to estimate the total electrical consumption per day for your boat. This is measured in ampere-hours. For example, if a device draws 2 amperes from the battery and you use it only a half hour per day, electrical consumption is:

$$2 \text{ amperes} \times 0.5 \text{ hours} = 1 \text{ ampere} - \text{hour (aH)}$$

To find total consumption in ampere-hours, add up the current draw for each device, multiplied by the amount of time that you use each device in a day.

Current consumption of each electrical accessory can be determined in a number of ways. For radios, radar and other electrical appliances, check the owner's manual or contact the manufacturer.

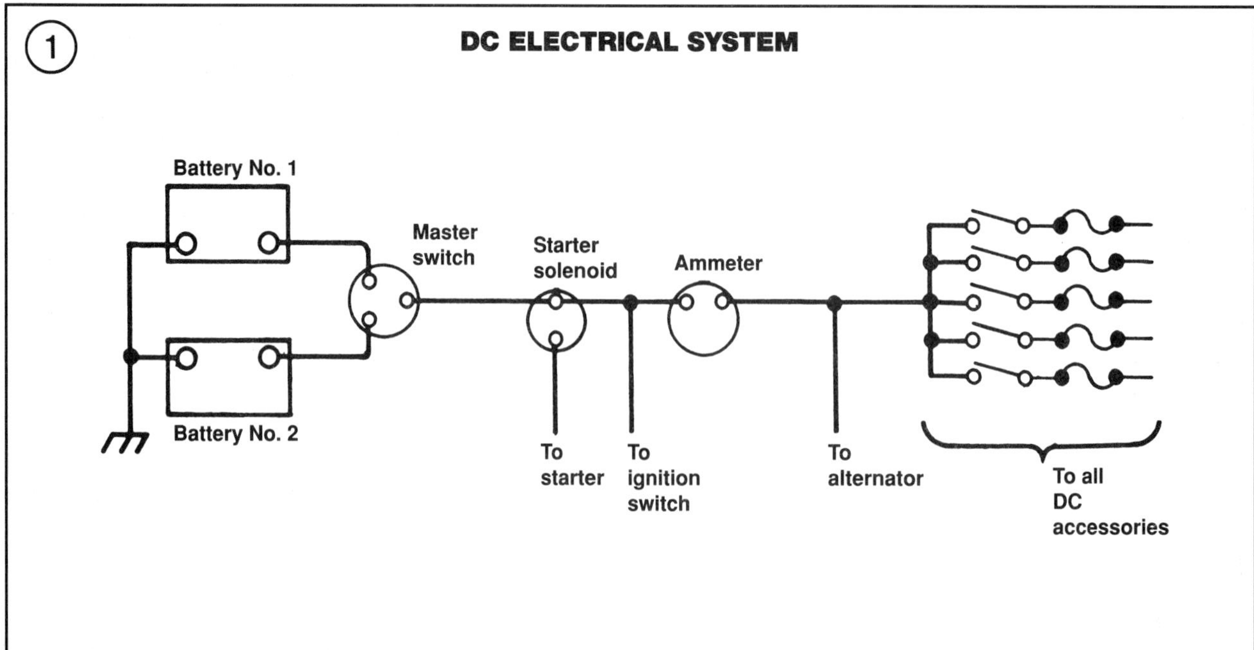

Sometimes consumption will be expressed in watts. This can easily be converted to amperes using the following formula:

$$\text{Amps} = \frac{\text{Watts}}{\text{Volts}}$$

As a simple example, a 36 watt bulb in a 12-volt system requires 3 amps (36 / 12 = 3). Taking this a step further, note that the same wattage output in a 24 volt system requires only 1.5 amps. Since amperage determines the thickness of wire required, it is obvious that increasing voltage permits the use of smaller conductors—the primary justification for moving up to 24 or 32 volts.

If you can't find any information on a particular device, **Table 1** provides typical current draw for a number of devices found onboard. This table assumes a 12 volt system is used. Keep in mind that, even on 24 volt and higher systems, many onboard devices, particularly electronic equipment, still require 12 volts and should be considered accordingly.

Generally, you want a battery or combination of batteries that provide *at least* twice the daily consumption anticipated. More capacity will allow you to go longer between recharges.

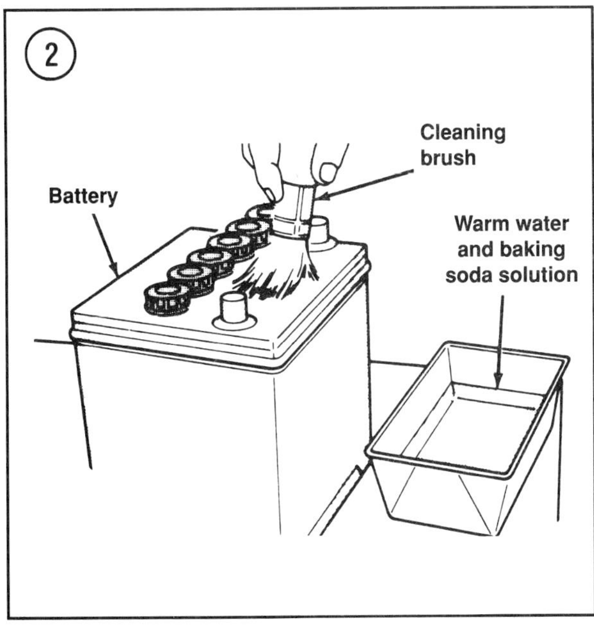

Cleaning

It is particularly important to keep batteries clean and free of corrosion. Dirt provides a leakage path between terminals and causes the battery to discharge. Wash the battery with a weak solution of baking soda or ammonia, then rinse completely with clean water (**Figure 2**). Take care to keep all vent plugs tight so that no ammonia or baking soda solution enters the cells.

State of Charge

It is most important to maintain batteries in a fully charged state during cold weather. Not only do cranking loads increase as engine oil thickens with cold, but battery capacity decreases at the same time. If battery capacity and cranking power required are assumed to be 100% at 80°, **Table 2** shows what happens at lower temperatures.

At 20°, power required for cranking is 3-1/2 times that required at 80°, but only 30% of battery power is available.

Another reason for keeping batteries fully charged during cold weather is that a fully charged battery freezes at a much lower temperature than does one which is partially discharged. Freezing temperature depends on state of charge. See **Table 3**.

Since freezing may ruin a battery, protect it by keeping it in a charged condition. Remember that many boats are stored outside during cold weather, so be sure to take adequate precautions.

BATTERY CHARGERS

The battery charger converts AC shore power to DC to charge the batteries. This also powers DC devices such as cabin lighting and stereo equipment when connected to shore power.

Regulated battery chargers are best suited to marine use. Two types are available. The automatic charger shown in **Figure 3** is representative. This type will automatically shut off when the battery is fully charged. The constant-voltage charger maintains battery voltage at a constant level regardless of battery condition or shore power voltage variations. Either type can be connected and left indefinitely when the boat is not in use. In fact, the constant-voltage charger can be permanently connected. Make sure the charger you buy carries the "UL Marine" label of the Underwriter's Laboratory.

Unregulated battery chargers or trickle chargers are designed for automobile use. These inexpensive chargers continue to charge the battery at a slow rate even after the battery is fully charged. If left unattended, the battery could be permanently damaged. Unregulated chargers are not suited for boats.

Capacity

Your charger should be able to recharge the batteries in a 24-hour period. Charger capacity determines how long it will take and is the maximum current the charger can deliver measured in amperes.

Estimate the total daily electrical consumption in ampere-hours as described under Battery Size. Divide ampere-hours by 24 (hours) to determine minimum battery charger capacity in amperes. It is best to have a charger with at least 25-50% more capacity than this to compensate for charger inefficiency and future electrical accessory expansion. Charger capacity can be too small, but it cannot be too large.

POWER INVERTERS

Though 12 volt versions of some household appliances are made for boats and land based RV's, most are much more expensive and less reliable than their AC counterparts. A power inverter connects to the battery system and converts 12 volt DC power to 110 volt AC to run televisions, microwave ovens, blenders and other convenience appliances. They can even be used for small power tools, such as an electric drill.

Power inverters are extremely reliable, solid state devices. They are usually rated by the amount of electrical power (in watts) that they can provide continuously. They also are rated by peak power that they can deliver for a short time, often 30 minutes, and surge power that they can deliver for a few seconds to start an electric motor.

To determine the capacity of the inverter needed to power AC devices onboard, add up the power requirements (in watts) of all devices that are likely to be used at the same time. The inverter must be able to provide the calculated power, plus a 25% or more safety margin. **Table 4** lists the power consumption of typical AC devices. The list is intended primarily for preparing an AC budget for shore power. It would be impractical to power most of these from an inverter.

In some cases, power consumption for an appliance will not be rated in watts. The manufacturer might state power requirements in amperes instead, such as 110 volts at 5 amperes. To calculate power in watts, simply multiply volts x amperes. In this example 110 x 5 = 550 watts.

Some power inverters are designed to work as a DC battery charger as well. When underway and supplied by DC, it provides AC. When connected to AC shore power it effectively works

backward and provides DC. This eliminates the need for a separate battery charger onboard, though some of these units are more expensive than buying a separate power inverter and battery charger. Furthermore, if the unit becomes defective, you lose both functions.

BONDING

Most large metal masses aboard a boat, including electronic cabinets, are connected together to provide an electrical ground, some measure of lightning protection and corrosion protection. This process is called "bonding."

In most cases, the following components are bonded or connected together:

a. Engine blocks.
b. Drive units and transmissions.
c. Propellers and shafts.
d. Metal tanks (fuel, water, holding).
e. Metal battery boxes.
f. Fuel fill fitting.
g. Electronic equipment cabinets.
h. Metal thru-hull fittings.
i. AC ground (bare or green insulation wire).
j. Radio ground plate (on hull).
k. Sacrificial zinc anode (on hull).

All of these items are brought together and connected to a common point or common ground for the boat. Often this is an engine block, but it may be a large copper block with tapped holes for electrical lugs. It may also be a large stud mounted somewhere near the main power distribution panel. Connections between the items listed above and the common ground point must be made with bare wires or wires with green insulation. Often the connections are made with wide braided copper straps. See **Figure 4** for a typical bonding system.

LIGHTING

Lighting systems used on boats are fairly simply. The majority of boats have only DC powered navigation and cabin lighting. Some boats may also have spot lights and deck lighting systems.

A distribution panel supplies battery voltage to each system through a switch and a fuse. See **Figure 5** and **Figure 6**.

Lights are simple in that they usually either work or they don't. When a light doesn't work, the problem is most likely a burned-out bulb. Try substituting a bulb known to be good. If that one doesn't work, the following procedure should

7

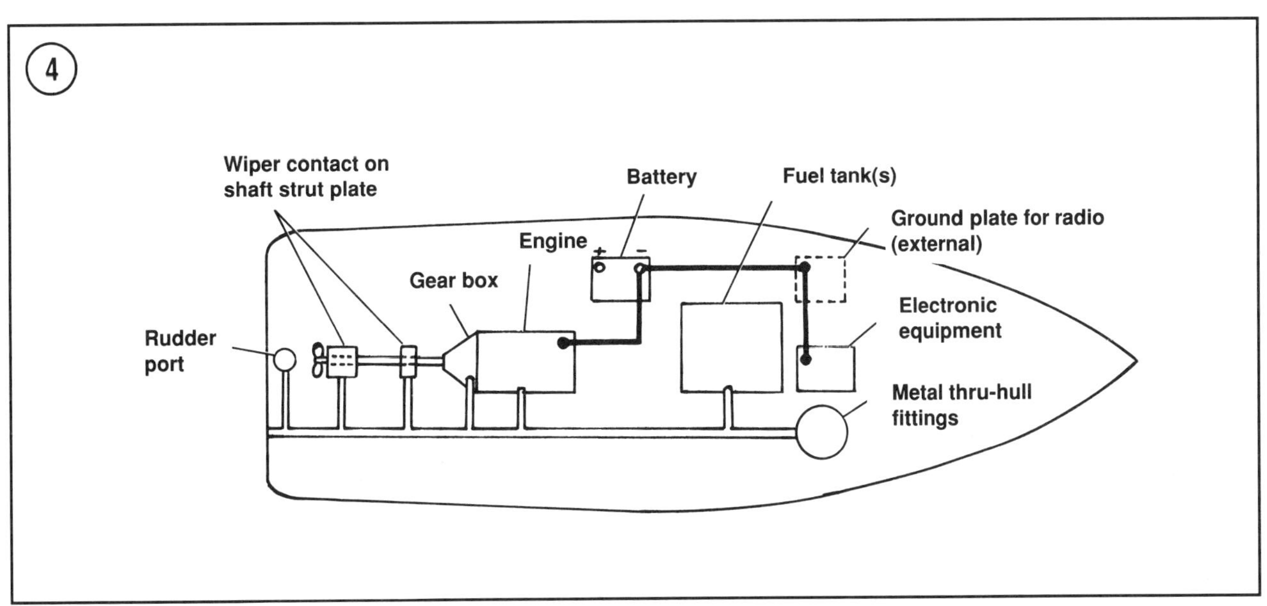

isolate the trouble. In rare cases where a light is either dim or flickering, look for loose, damaged or corroded connections (especially grounds).

1. Determine whether only one lamp, or an entire group of related lamps (such as running lamps), is affected. If only one lamp is affected, go on to Step 2. Refer to the paragraph following Step 6 if an entire group is affected.

2. Insert a known good lamp into the socket, then turn on the power switch.

3. Connect one end of a long wire to a good ground. To be absolutely sure of a good ground, it is best to connect this end of the wire to the negative terminal of the battery. Connect the other end of this wire to the outer shell of the affected lamp socket.

4. If the lamp now lights, the problem is a defective ground circuit. Poor grounds are a frequent cause of exterior lamp failure. They are usually be corrected by removing each mounting screw, then replacing it with a star lockwasher under the screw head.

5. If the lamp still does not light, the problem is in the power wiring to the lamp, or possibly in the switch. First, bridge the switch terminals with a small piece of wire. It may be necessary to pierce the insulation on the wires to the switch for this operation. If, with the switch bridged, the lamp lights, the switch is defective. Replace the switch.

6. Finally, check the wiring back from the lamp socket. At some point, a loose, broken, or corroded connection will be found.

Sometimes an entire related group, such as running lamps, will go out simultaneously. To find and correct this malfunction, proceed as follows:

1. Check the fuse which protects that circuit. A blown fuse is not necessarily indicative of trouble in the electrical system as sometimes a fuse will blow for no apparent reason. If replacing the fuse corrects the problem, but it blows again shortly afterward, examine all related wiring for chafing or pinched spots, then make any required repairs.

2. If replacing the fuse does not correct the condition, run a temporary ground wire between the metal base of any affected lamp and a good ground. If the lamps now operate, check for a loose, broken or corroded ground wire to lamps.

3. If the lamps still don't operate with a known good known ground, the trouble will be either a broken or disconnected wire.

SHORE POWER

Shore power electrical systems (**Figure 7**) consist of 2 parts:

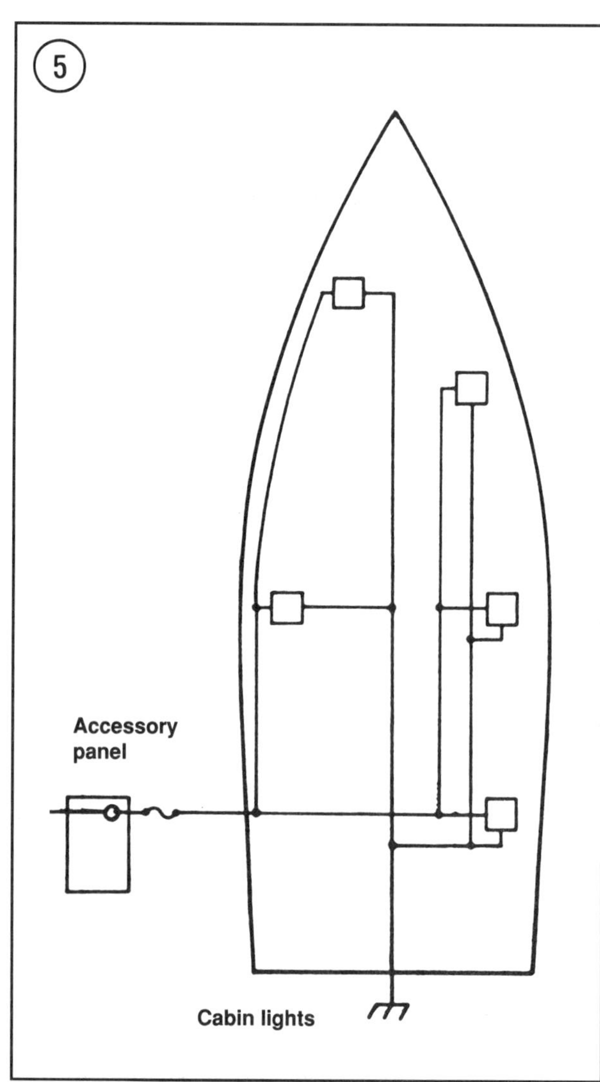

a. External system.

b. On-board system.

The external system consists of the deck-mounted inlet connection, ship-to-shore cable and the dockside electrical outlet.

The on-board system consists of the interior wiring, control panel, outlets, switches, circuits and so forth.

Most shore outlets are rated 110-125 volts. Some are rated 250 volts for large appliances on large boats. Rated load is usually 30 amperes.

The shore power system requires no maintenance other than periodic inspection to ensure that connections are secure. One possible area of concern is the circuit breaker in the dock connection point. Long-term exposure to moisture and salt could corrode it to the point that moving parts simply fuse together rendering it a hazard. It is not a bad idea to replace the breaker after 5 years simply as a precaution.

You should have an idea how much shore power current your boat requires. Make a list of

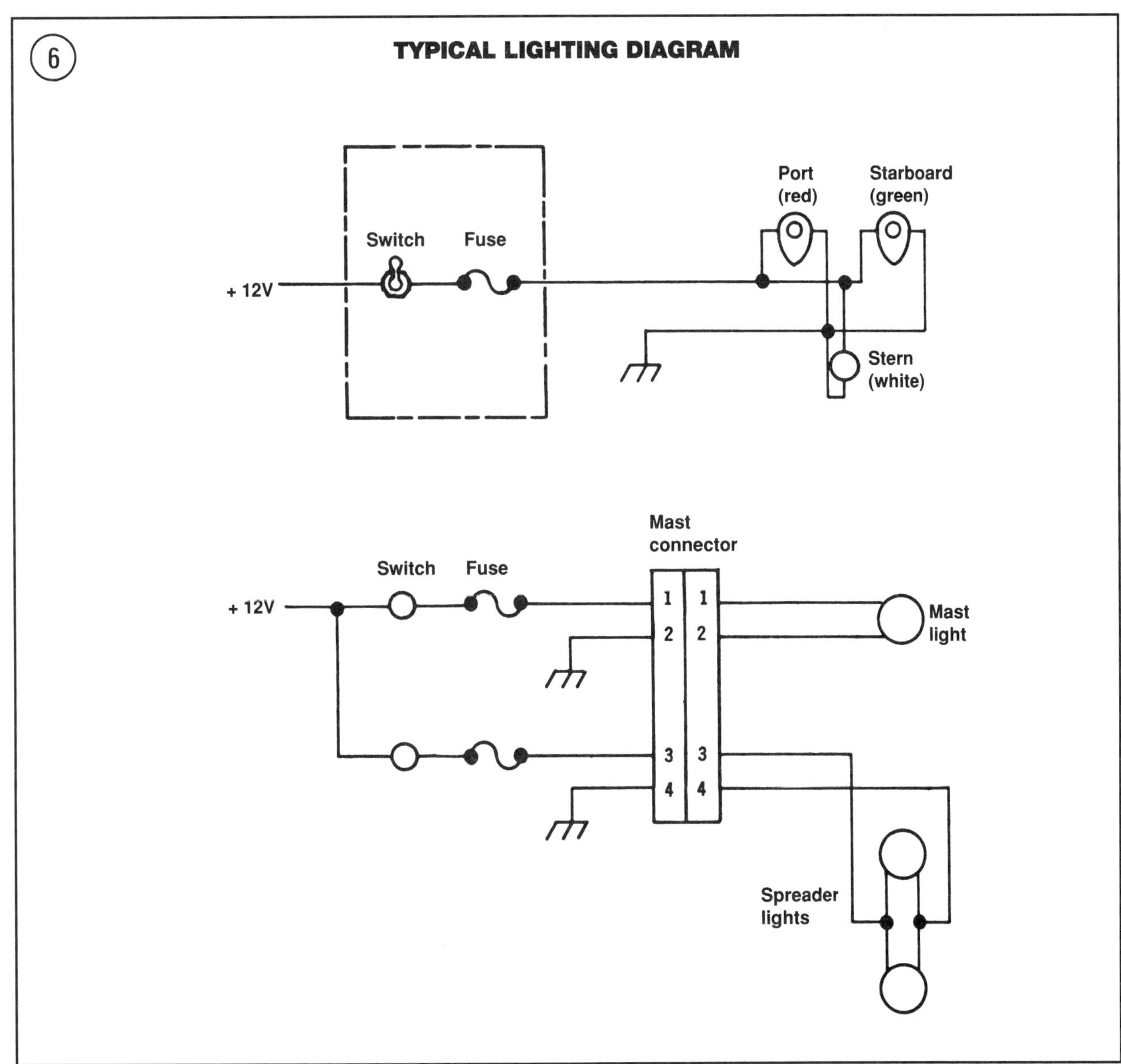

7

AC
Bulkhead outlets
AC
Ground
Deck fitting

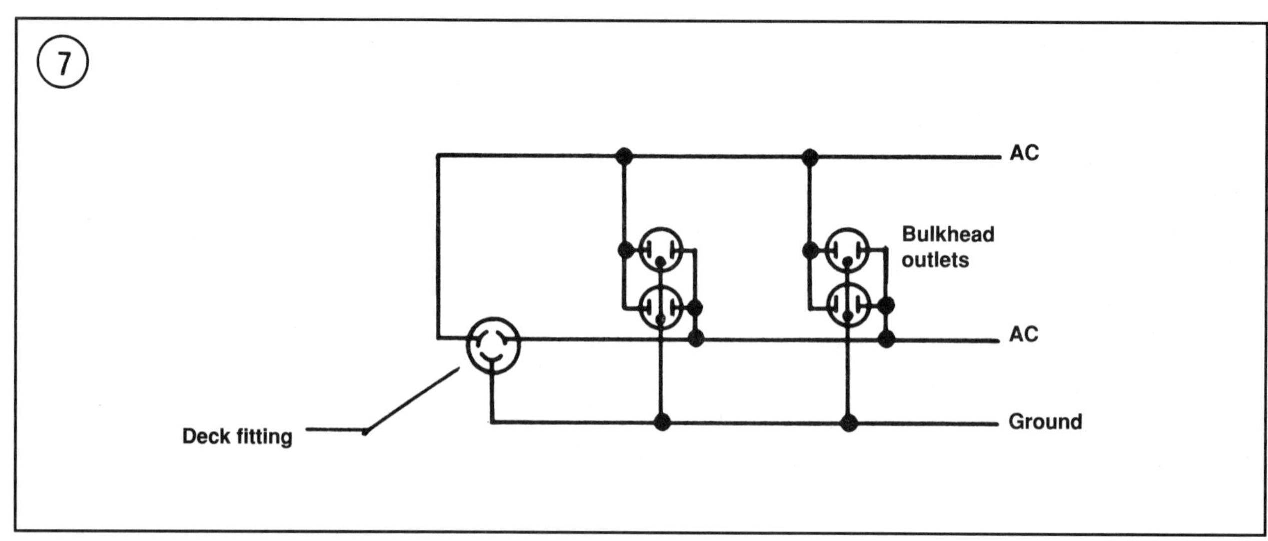

8

TYPICAL POWER PLANT

To exhaust outlet through hull
Silencer
Resonator
Exhaust high temperature cutoff switch
Fuel line
Engine water pump
Fuel shutoff
Raw water line
Water filter
Sea cock

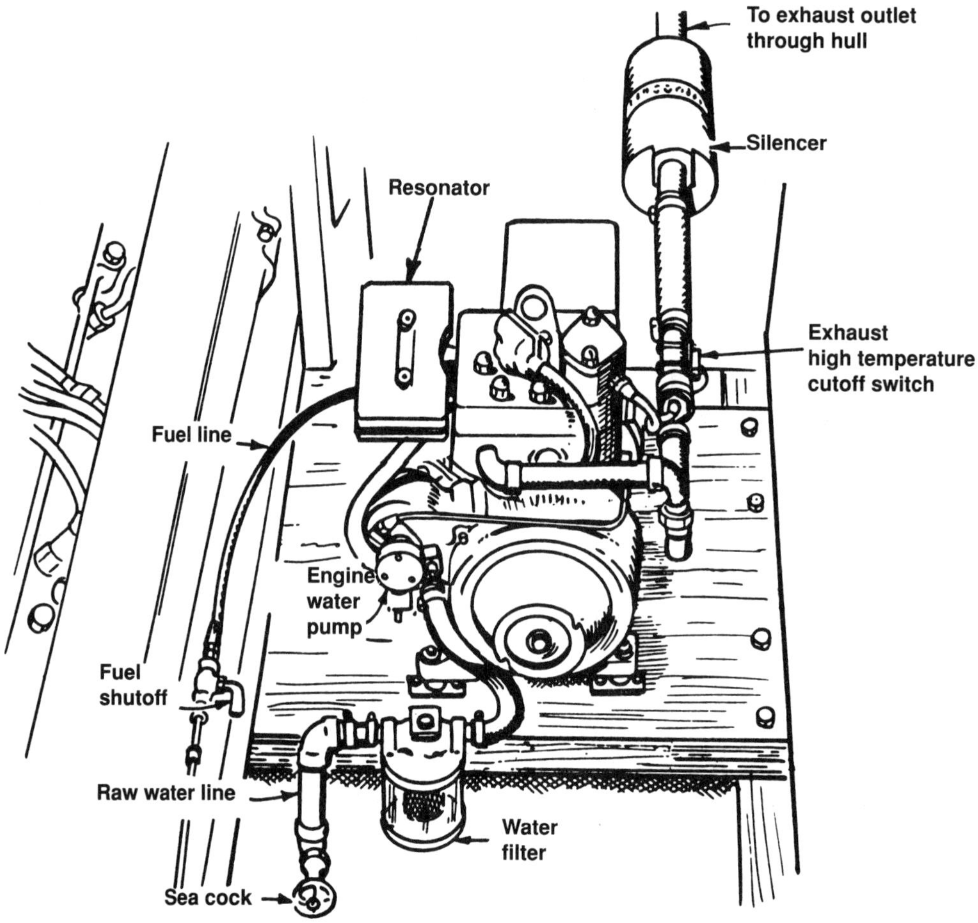

all AC-powered appliances on board, along with the current demand of each.

Most appliances list their power requirements on a small tag. In most cases, this is listed in amperes. In some cases, however, it is listed in watts. To convert watts to amperes, divide the wattage requirement by 125 volts.

Add together the current requirement of all appliances. This figure is the current required from the shore power if every appliance is used simultaneously; a very unlikely event. Most manufacturers use 70% of this total current when designing the system.

Many DC powered devices, such as lighting, are used when connected to AC shore power. DC devices in this case actually receive their power from the AC powered battery charger. Therefore, you must include these devices in your AC budget. To do this, determine the current requirement of these devices and multiply the total by the DC voltage. For example, if you operate a cabin light that draws 2 amperes at 12 volts, the power consumption in watts will be 24 watts. Now divide this by 115 volts, (24/115 = 0.2 amperes) and you have the approximate equivalent current drawn from the AC shore power. Add this to your AC budget.

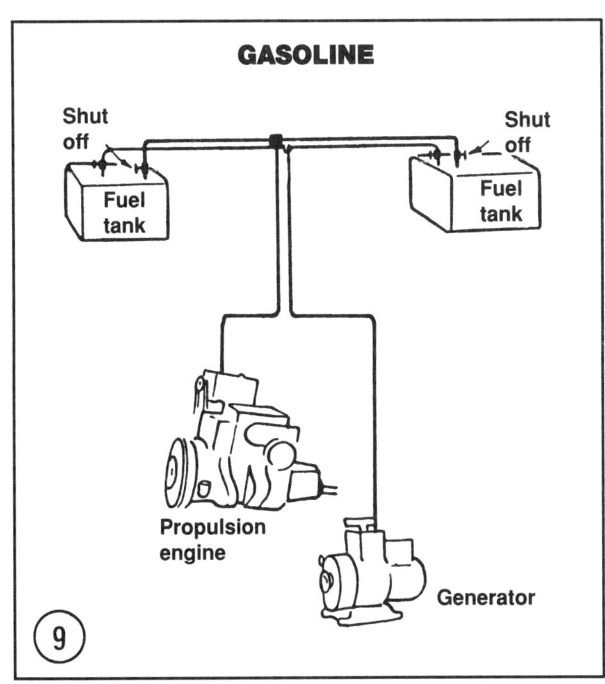

Here is an example. Suppose all the AC appliances used on your boat add up to 34 amperes. Further suppose that all the DC devices used at one time consume about 100 watts which works out to another ampere at 115 volts. If we assume that not all of the appliances will be used at the same time, then 70% of 35 amperes equals about 25 amperes. The circuit breaker on your boat and the one dockside must be rated for at least 25 amperes.

AUXILIARY POWER PLANTS

Many large boats are equipped with gasoline or diesel auxiliary power plants which supply enough electrical power to operate almost any appliance found at home. These power plants consist primarily of an internal combustion engine, alternating current generator and the required controls.

The following sections describe routine maintenance required for typical gasoline and diesel generating systems. Due to the large number of different systems available, individual power plants are not described. Refer to your owner's manual for specifics if necessary.

Typical Installations

Figure 8 shows a typical power plant installation. The fuel line to the plant has its own fuel shut-off. In most cases, the power plant shares the inboard engine fuel supply. **Figure 9** shows a typical gasoline installation and **Figure 10** shows a diesel system. Note that the diesel system requires return lines to return excess fuel to the tanks.

The exhaust system normally uses water injection to cool the gases. **Figure 11** shows a system used with small plants. **Figure 12** shows a more elaborate system used on larger plants. Water-cooled plants may use:

a. Direct cooling.
b. Heat exchanger cooling.
c. Keel or skin cooling.

Direct cooling systems draw seawater through the hull, pump it through the engine and exhaust it through the muffler system. See **Figure 13**.

Heat exchanger systems use a closed fresh water system containing a rust inhibitor or anti-freeze. Seawater from outside the hull cools the fresh water through a heat exchanger. See **Figure 14**.

Keel cooling is similar to the heat exchanger system. A keel cooler immersed in the sea acts as a heat exchanger. Fresh water is pumped through the keel cooler for cooling (**Figure 15**).

Periodic Maintenance

Maintenance is divided into 2 categories.

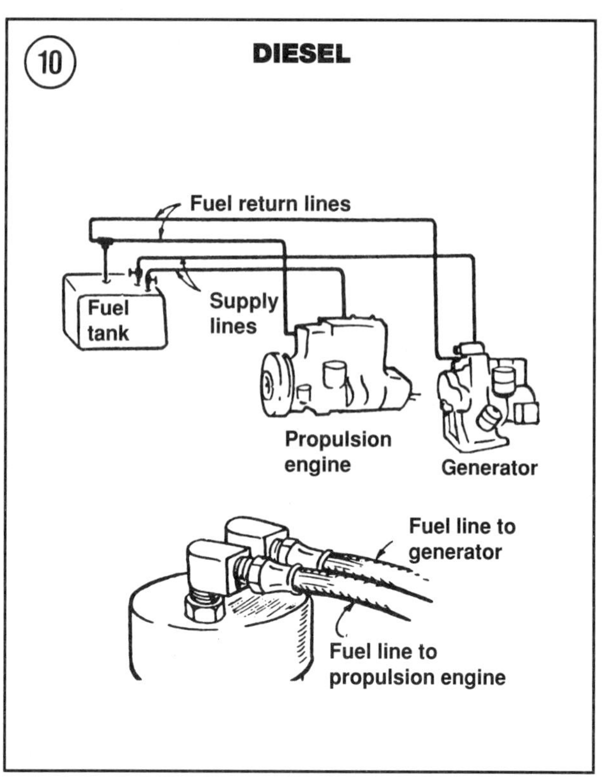

11

SMALL POWER PLANT

Water line from manifold water outlet
High-water temperature cutoff switch
Supports
Muffler
Rubber hose
Ventilated battery box

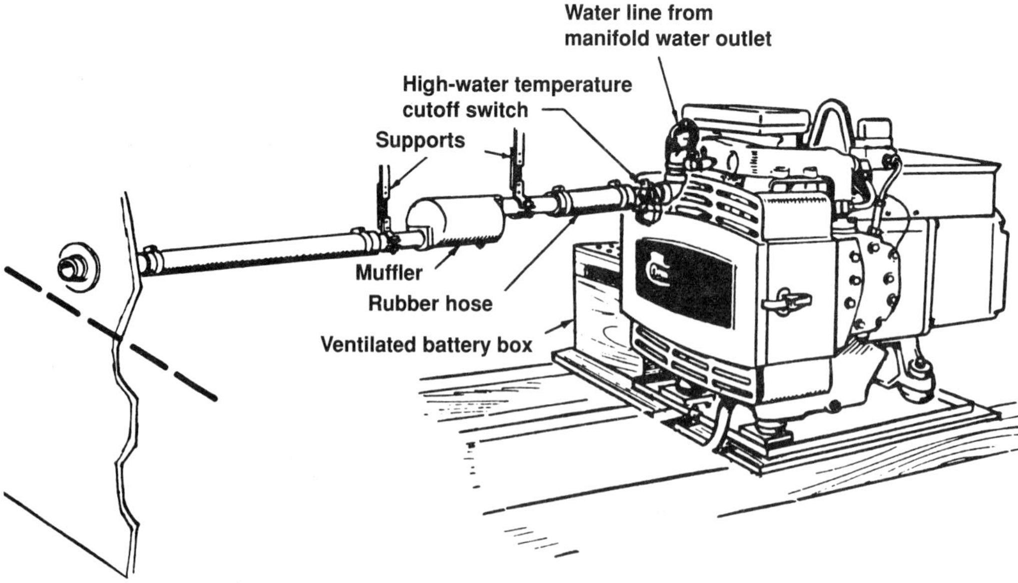

(12)

LARGE POWER PLANT

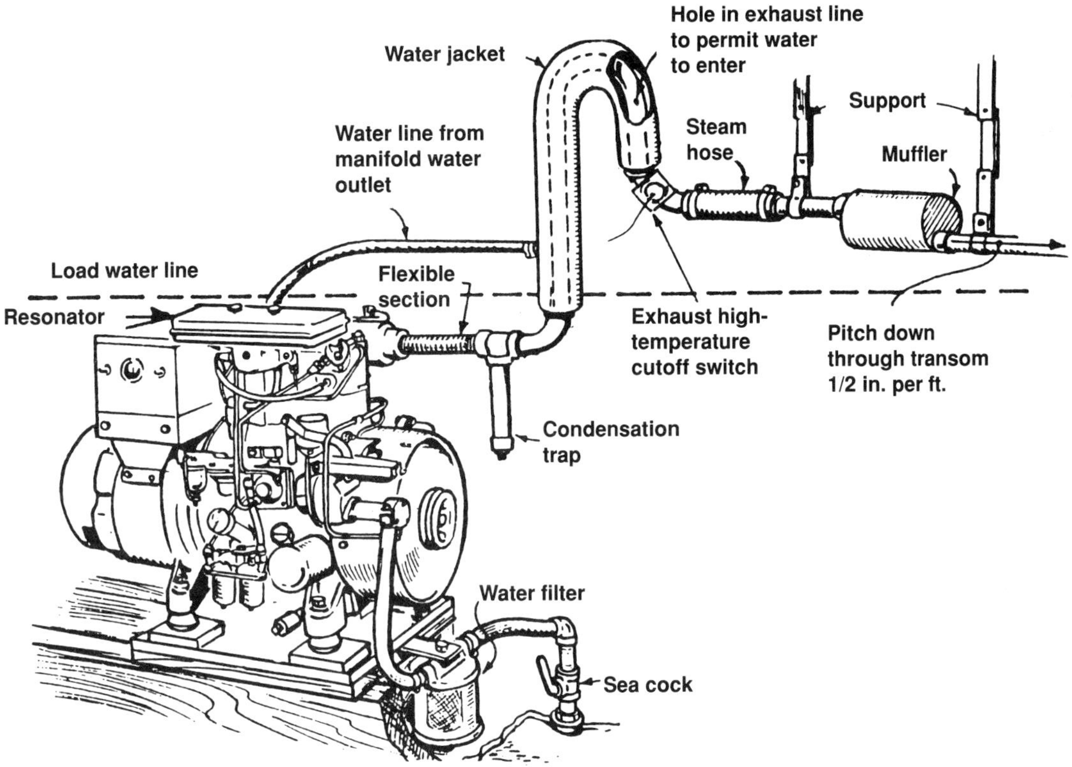

Hole in exhaust line
to permit water
to enter
Water jacket
Support
Steam
hose
Water line from
manifold water
outlet
Muffler
Load water line
Flexible
section
Resonator
Exhaust high-
temperature
cutoff switch
Pitch down
through transom
1/2 in. per ft.
Condensation
trap
Water filter
Sea cock

(13)

DIRECT COOLING SYSTEM

Water to
exhaust line
Pitch down
to muffler
Flexible section
Sea
cock
Flush type through
hull fitting
Water filter
Cooling water in
Water strainer

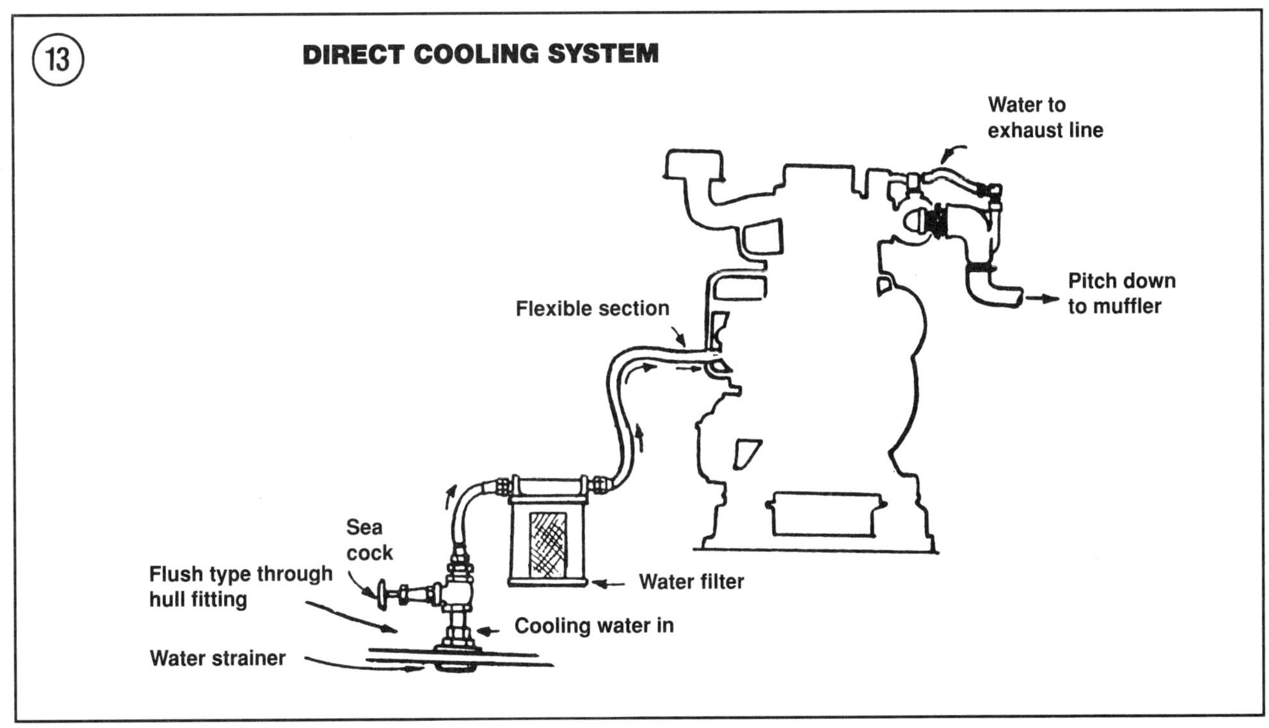

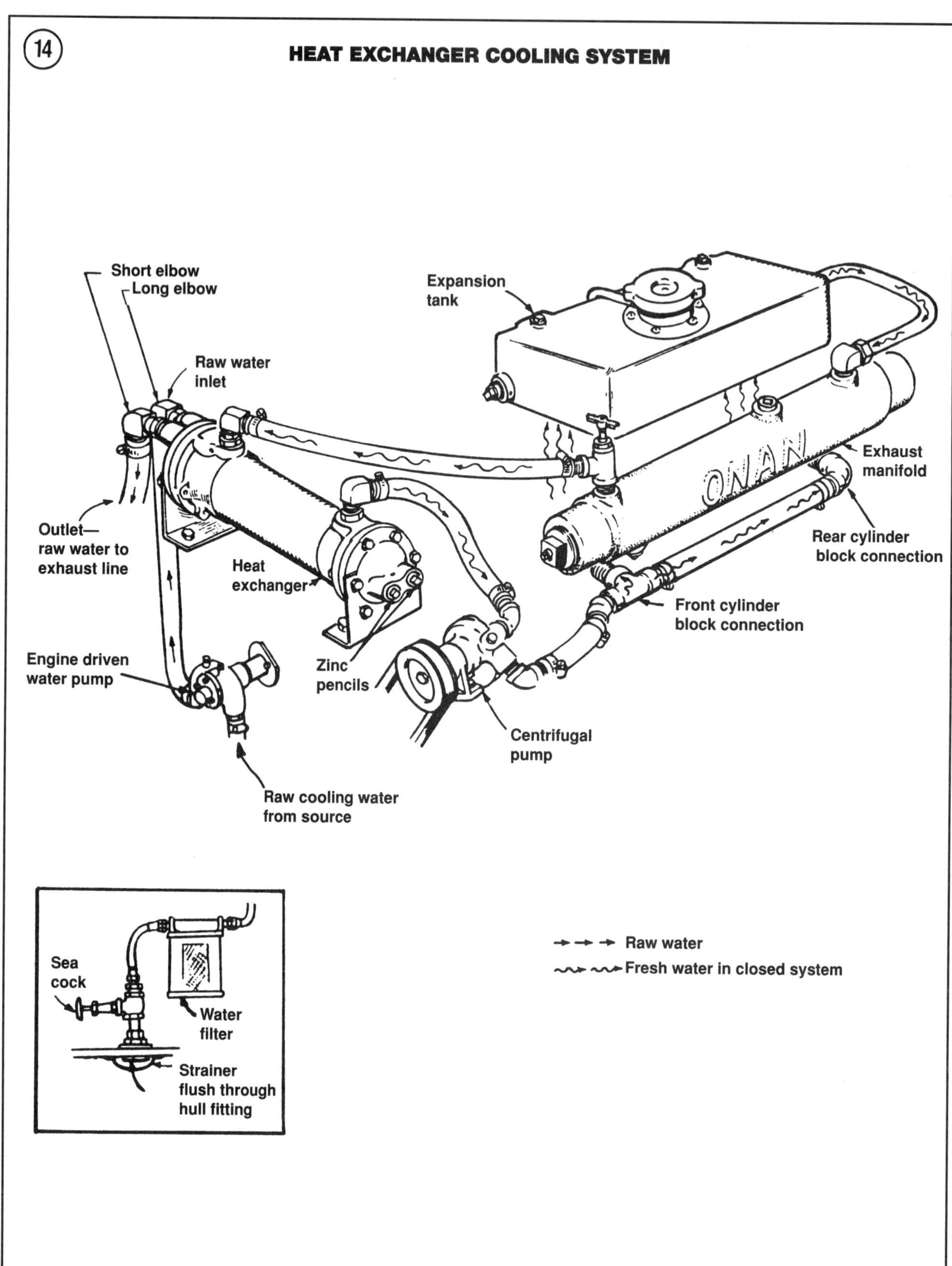
14
HEAT EXCHANGER COOLING SYSTEM
Short elbow
Long elbow
Raw water inlet
Expansion tank
Exhaust manifold
Rear cylinder block connection
Front cylinder block connection
Outlet—raw water to exhaust line
Heat exchanger
Engine driven water pump
Zinc pencils
Centrifugal pump
Raw cooling water from source
Sea cock
Water filter
Strainer flush through hull fitting
Raw water
Fresh water in closed system

a. Operator maintenance, which requires no unusual skills. See **Table 5**.

b. Critical maintenance, performed by qualified personnel. See **Table 6**.

Like your inboard engine, the engine in your power plant thrives on use. To keep it running right, follow these simple steps.

1. Run thepower plant periodically—even a few minutes every week, except during lay-up.
2. Perform regular scheduled maintenance. This chapter includes procedures for most plants.
3. Fix minor troubles immediately before they become major. Many are very simple jobs you may be able to do yourself. If you doubt your ability, let a professional do it.

Routine Checks

The following simple checks should be performed prior to each day's use.

1. Check engine oil level. Level should be between 2 marks on dipstick, but never below.
2. Check coolant level.
3. If plant uses direct water cooling, open the seacock.

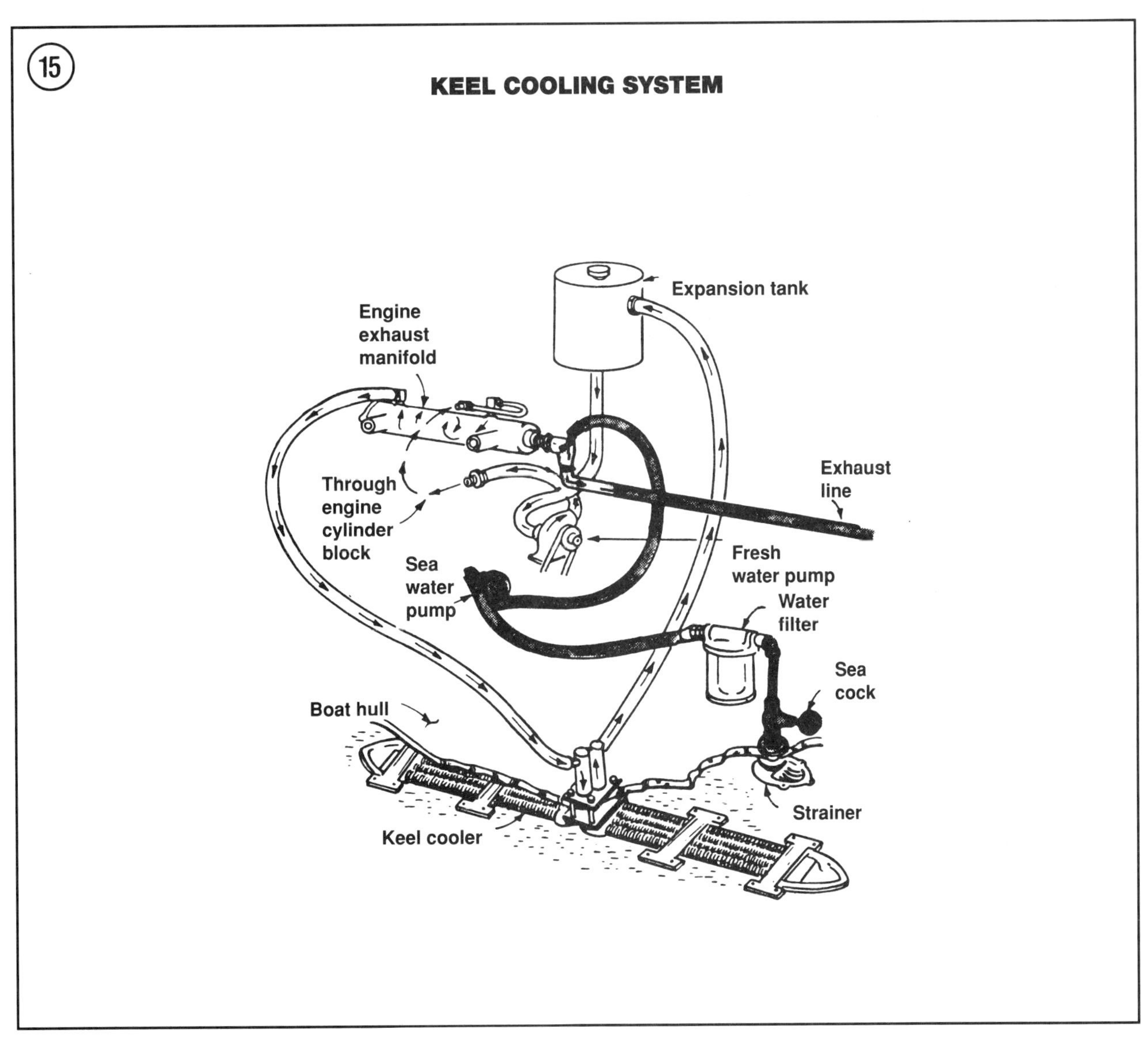

4. As soon as engine starts, look for water at exhaust outlet. If water doesn't emerge, stop the engine immediately.

Lubricating Oil

Check the crankcase oil each day of use. Always maintain the oil level between the "L" and "F" marks on the dipstick (**Figure 16**). Do not operate the power plant with the oil level too high or too low. In the event of a sudden unexplained loss of oil, discontinue operation of power plant.

Drain engine oil every 50 hours of operation, or every 6 months, whichever comes first. Run the engine for a few minutes first to warm the oil before draining. For gasoline engines, use only oil meeting API Service MS specifications. Oils meeting this requirement will be plainly marked as such on the can. For diesel engines, use oil marked specifically for this purpose. Select oil viscosity from **Table 7**.

Air Cleaner

Every 50 hours of operation, clean theair filter element. Some power plants use a dry element as shown in **Figure 17**. To clean, unscrew the wing nut, remove the cover and remove the element. Tap the element against a flat surface to dislodge loose surface dirt. Do not blow dirt out with air or clean the element in any solvent. Replace the element after every 100 hours of operation.

Some power plants use an oil bath air cleaner similar to **Figure 18**. Every 50 hours of operation, clean the screen and cup in solvent such as kerosene or diesel fuel. Fill the cup to the level indicated with clean oil; use the same type as in the engine crankcase.

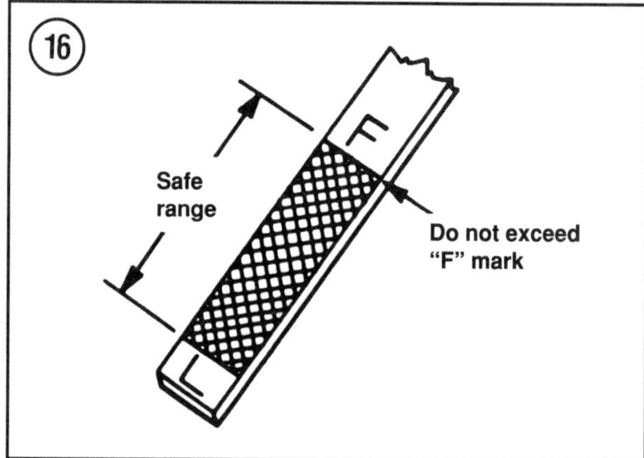

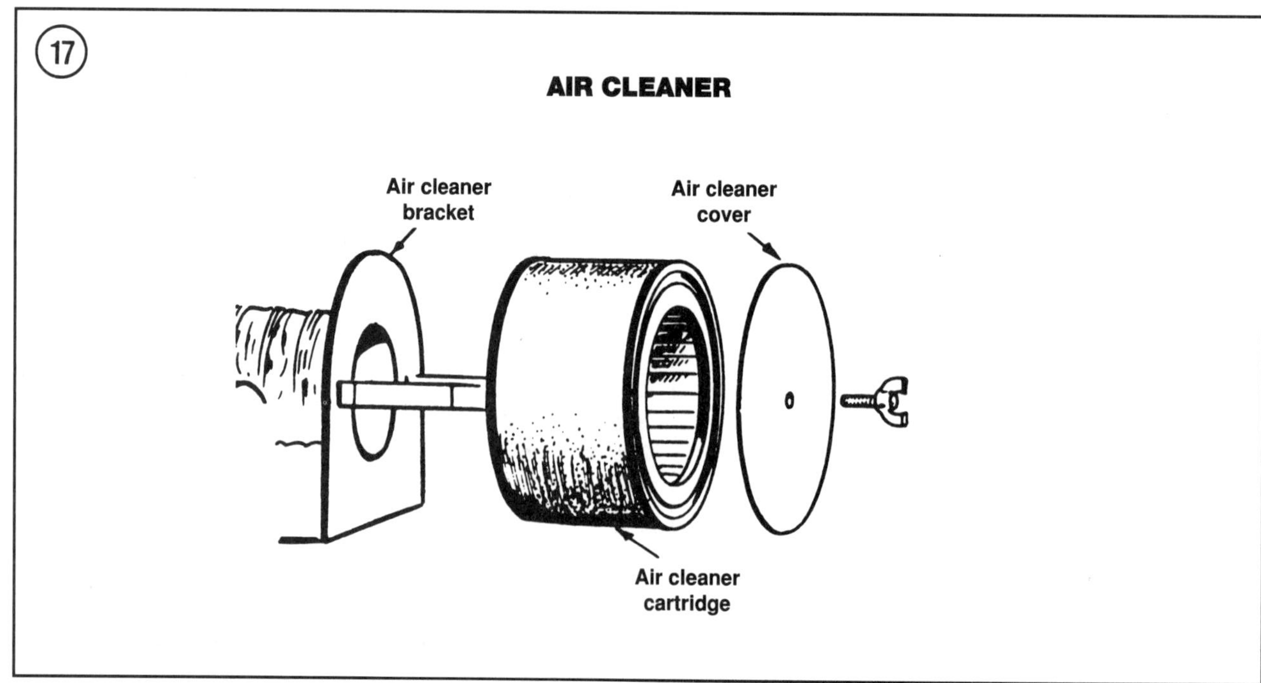

Spark Plugs (Gasoline Engines Only)

Remove and examine the spark plug after every 100 hours of operation. A light gray or tan deposit should be visible on the insulator. If the insulator appears dead white, blistered, or burned, over-heating of the engine or possibly a lean fuel mixture is the cause. Fluffy black carbon deposits indicate an over-rich fuel mixture, caused by a clogged air cleaner or misadjusted carburetor. Spark plugs are inexpensive. Do not sand-blast, wire brush or scrape a used plug; replace it with a new one identical to the one removed. Set spark plug gap at 0.025 in. Be sure the spark plug seating surface on the cylinder head is clean, then tighten the new plug to 22 ft.-lb.

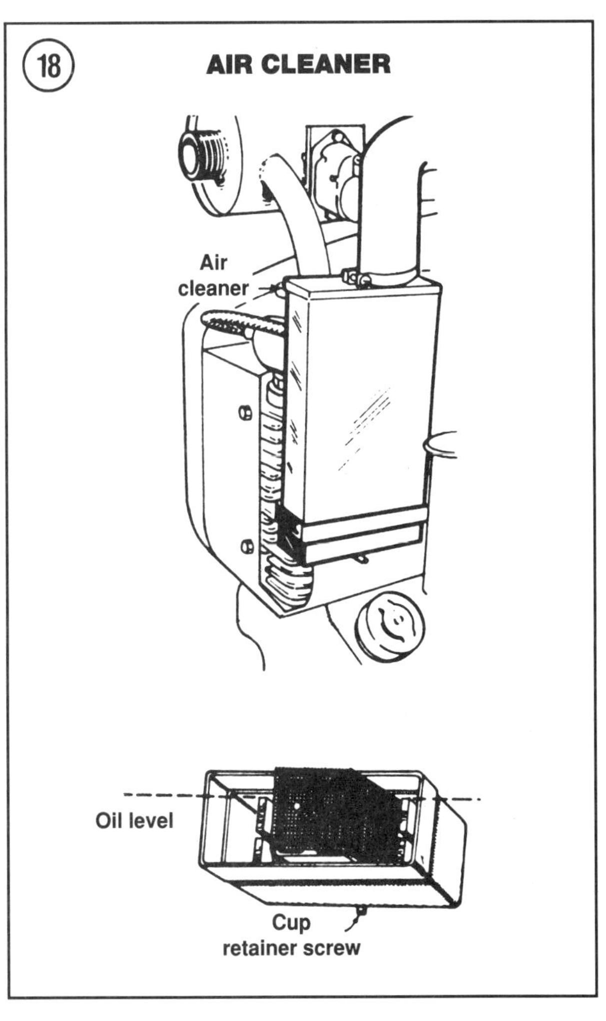

Air Cooling System

Cooling air is drawn over the generator and through the engine cooling fins by a blower. Be sure that intake louvers, generator cooling openings, cooling fins and scrollwork are clean and unobstructed at all times. Do not operate the power plant with any cooling system component removed.

Water Cooling System

Before each use, check the coolant level in the expansion tank if a closed cooling system is used. If direct water cooling is used, clean out the seawater strainer, if so equipped.

Every year, have the coolant drained and replaced with a 50/50 mixture of water and ethylene glycol antifreeze including a good rust inhibitor.

Fuel Filter

Refer to **Figure 19**. Every 100 hours or sooner, drain the fuel pump and check the filter element. Turn the hex nut on the base of the electric fuel pump to gain access to the filter element. If the element appears dirty, replace with a new one. Be sure to replace all gaskets when reassembling.

Crankcase Breather

Lift off the rubber breather cap (**Figure 20**). Carefully pry the valve from cap. Otherwise, press hard with both thumbs on top of the cap with the fingers below to release valve from rubber cap. Wash this fabric flapper type check valve in a suitable solvent. Dry and install. Position the perforated disc toward the engine.

Troubleshooting

Table 8 lists various problems and probable causes for them.

REPAIRING AND SPLICING WIRING

Probably the biggest single cause of electrical system malfunctions is defective connections. All too frequently, troubles are finally traced to a hastily twisted, poorly insulated wire connection. Such connections eventually loosen and corrode, then become useless. All electrical connections should be either soldered or crimped with crimped *and* soldered being the most preferred.

Soldered Connections

Soldering is easy, and it takes only a little practice to make perfect, permanent connections. For the average home craftsman, all that is required is a 75 to 100-watt soldering iron, some rosin-core solder and some plastic electrical tape. Do not use acid-core solder as it is corrosive. Wire cutters and strippers are also handy for this type of work.

Figure 21 shows three of the most common types of splices: butt, pigtail and tee. They differ only in the way that the wires are connected; soldering technique is the same for all. Note that butt and pigtail splices connect the ends of 2 wires together. The tee splice is used when it is necessary to tap into an existing wire.

1. Strip approximately 1 in. of insulation from the end of each wire to be connected (**Figure 22**). Be careful not to nick any strands.

NOTE
Always use stranded wire for all marine wiring. Solid wire will eventually break under vibration.

2. Twist the 2 stripped ends together firmly, as shown in **Figure 23**. Mechanical strength of the solder joint depends on this twisting. Be sure that your fingers are clean during this operation, otherwise solder will not adhere to the wire.
3. Be sure that the soldering iron is well tinned, then hold its tip under the twisted wires to heat the joint (**Figure 24**).
4. When the joint is heated, apply solder slowly to the joint (not the iron itself). Melted solder will flow smoothly throughout the joint (**Figure 25**).
5. Remove the soldering iron and allow the joint to cool completely before moving it. A properly soldered connection will be bright and shiny, with shapes of individual wires still visible (**Figure 26**).

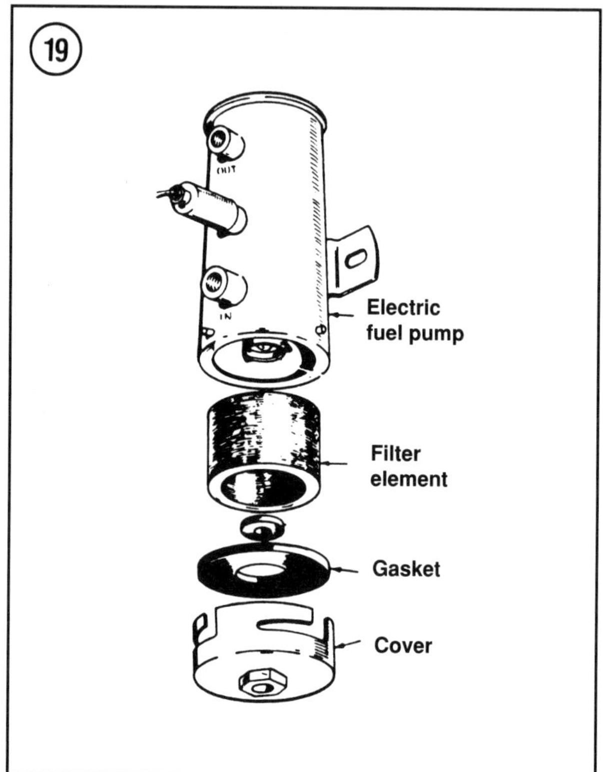

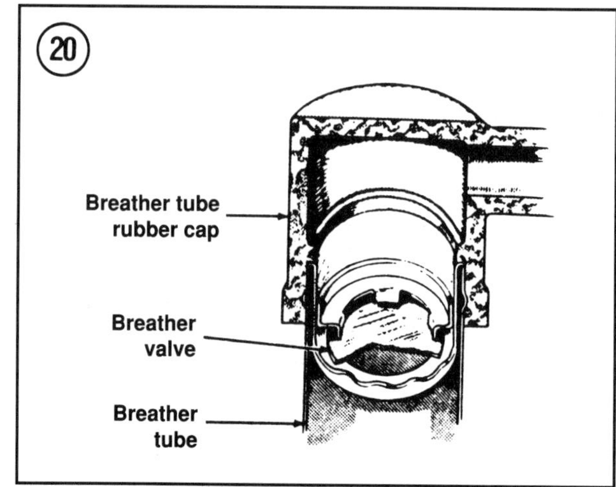

6. Cut off any excess wire (**Figure 27**) from the connection.

7. Protect and insulate the connection with plastic electrical tape (**Figure 28**). Be sure to use at least 2 layers, and carry the tape at least an inch on either side of the connection.

NOTE
The best method of insulating and waterproofing soldered wire joints is using the correct size heat-shrink tubing available from marine and automotive parts departments. Slide the tubing over the solder joint, then heat it using a heat gun or match. When the tubing is heated, it shrinks to a tight fit on the wire.

Crimped Connections

Crimped connections are faster and easier than soldered ones, but are also considerably more expensive. **Figure 29** illustrates various types of crimp connectors and the tool required to make them. Note that crimped connections are small and neat and may be desirable in cramped locations. Crimp connectors are usually color

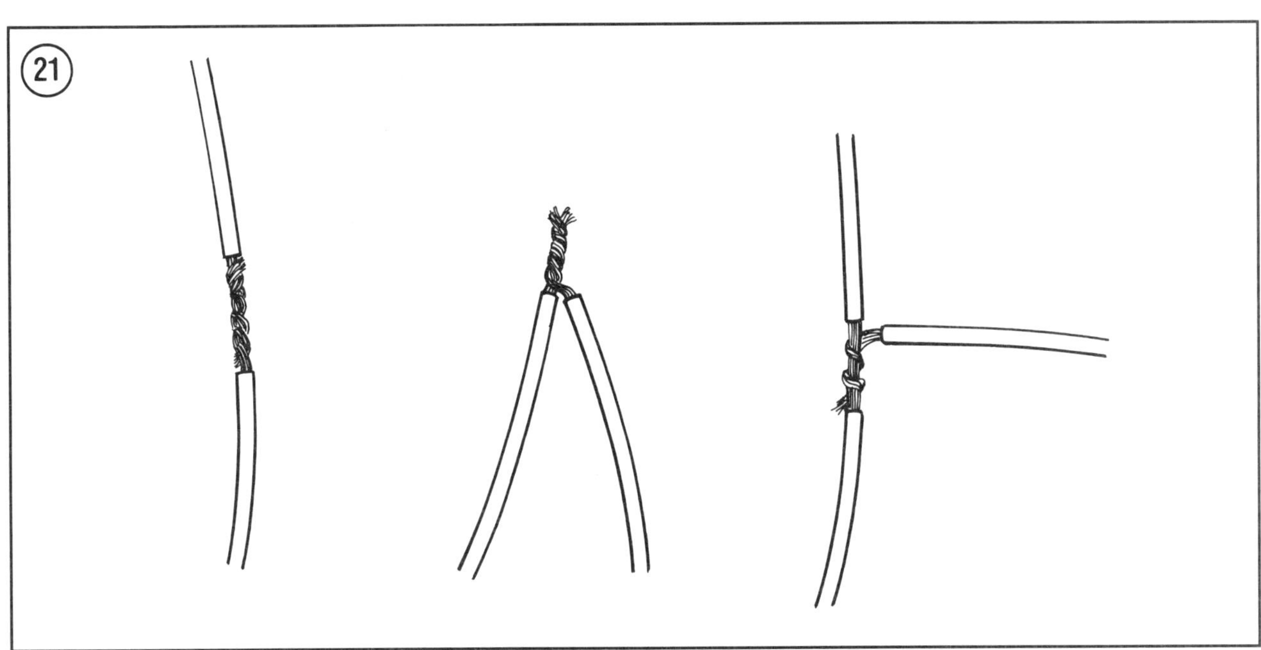

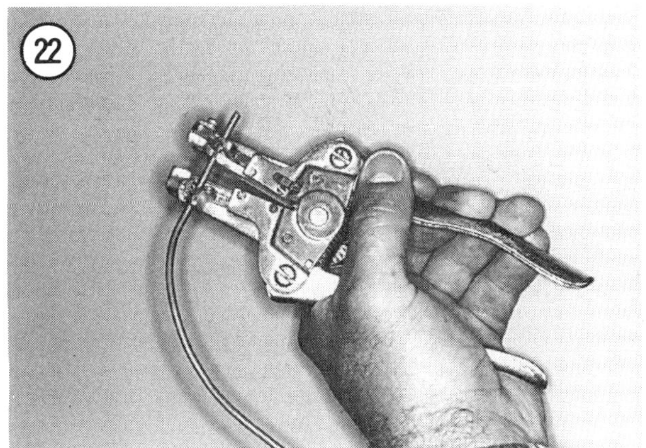

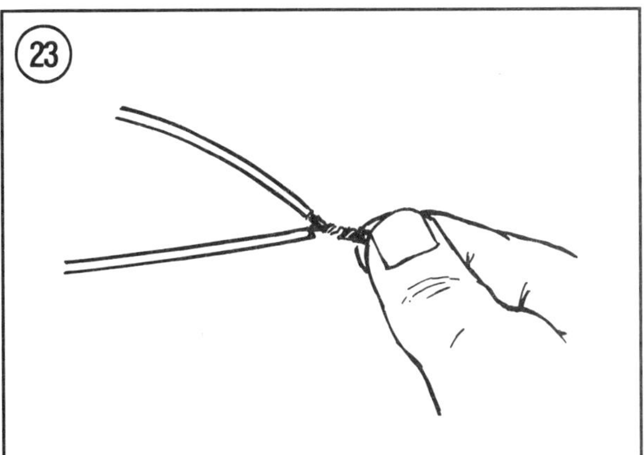

coded to denote wire sizes with which they may be used. See **Table 9**.

1. Strip approximately 5/16 in. from the end of the wire to be connected. This distance will vary slightly and can best be determined by experience. The distance is correct when the shoulder formed by the remaining insulation bottoms in the terminal and the stripped end of the wire just emerges from the crimping portion of the terminal (**Figure 30**).
2. Squeeze the terminal with the crimping tool (**Figure 31**) until the jaws are closed. A little practice with a few spare terminals and pieces of scrap wire beforehand will ensure good connections every time.

Wiring

It may happen that damaged wiring must be replaced or new wires installed for additional lights or other accessories. Several precautions should be observed when such wiring is done.

1. Be sure that any new circuits are protected by a fuse of the appropriate size.
2. Be sure that all wiring is adequately supported and protected against chafing, in particular in areas where it passes over or through metal parts such as engine compartment components. Avoid running wires near hot exhaust manifolds or pipes. As often as possible, attach any additional wiring to existing wire harnesses, using plastic insulation tape or tie straps.

24

3. Always use good quality wire designed for marine applications.
4. Always use wire of adequate size. **Table 10** lists current carrying capacities of various wire sizes.

MAKING A WIRING DIAGRAM

A good wiring diagram for your boat can save hours, even days, when trying to locate trouble or add electrical accessories. Unfortunately, virtually none of the boat builders supply a diagram.

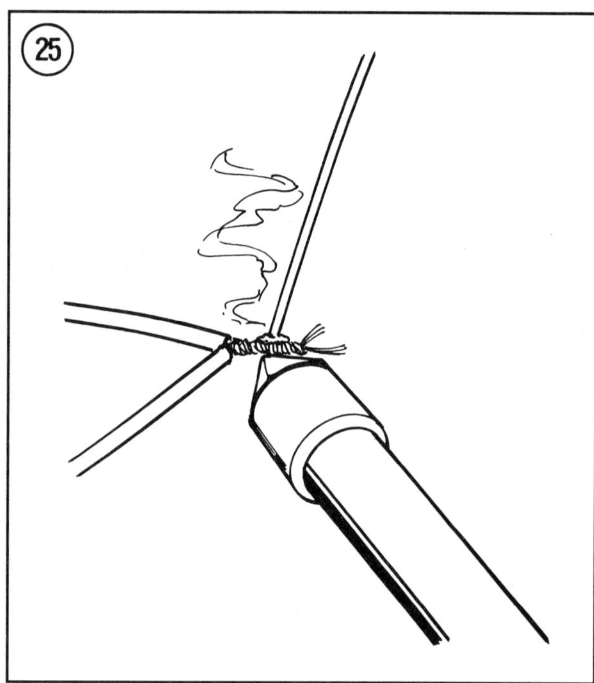

25

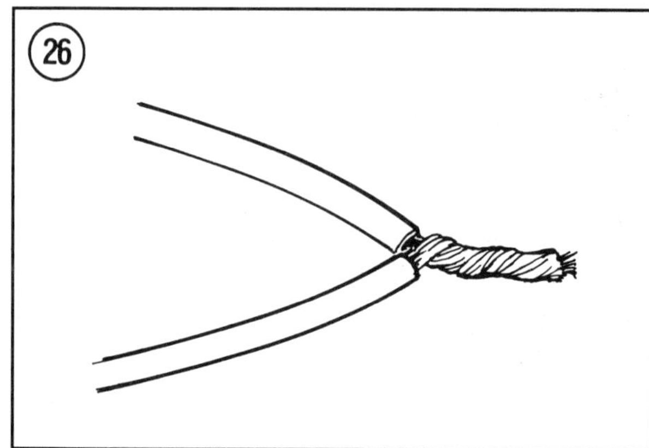

26

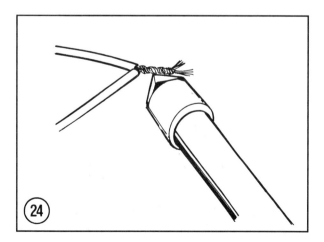

It is not difficult to make your own wiring diagrams, but it is tedious. You will need a small volt-ohmmeter similar to the one shown in **Figure 32**, extra-long test leads which you can make yourself and a willing assistant or two.

You may have seen the complex wiring diagrams drawn for automobiles. A similar drawing could be done for a boat. However, it is much easier to make smaller individual diagrams for each of the electrical systems in the boat. This section breaks the electrical systems down into several sub-systems, explains how to draw the diagram and shows a typical system.

Primary Power

This system consists of the battery (or batteries), engine-mounted alternator/generator, main switch and connecting wires. **Figure 1** is typical.

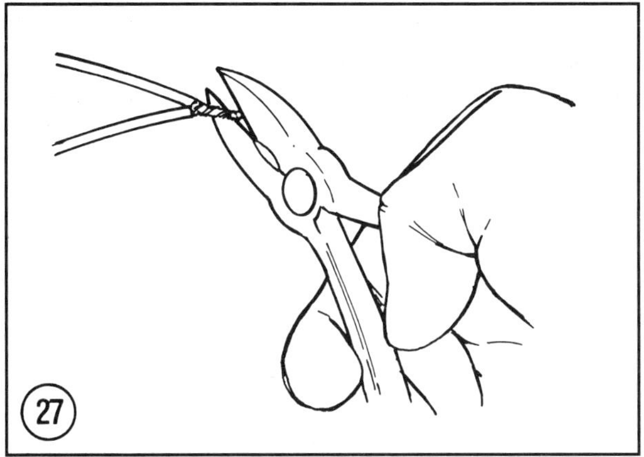

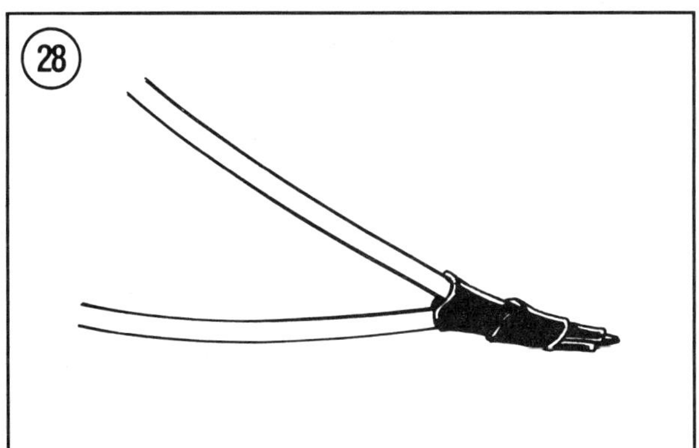

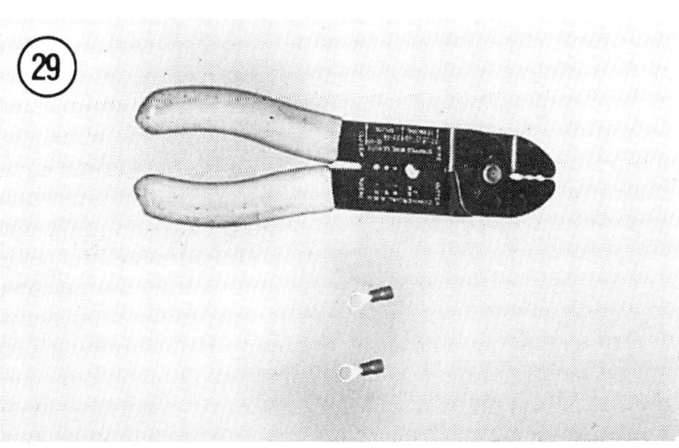

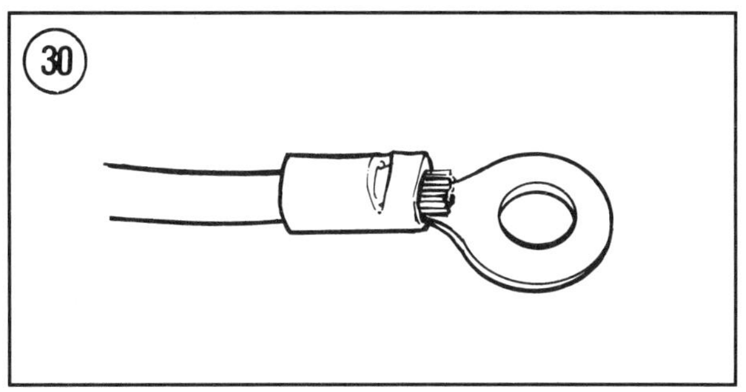

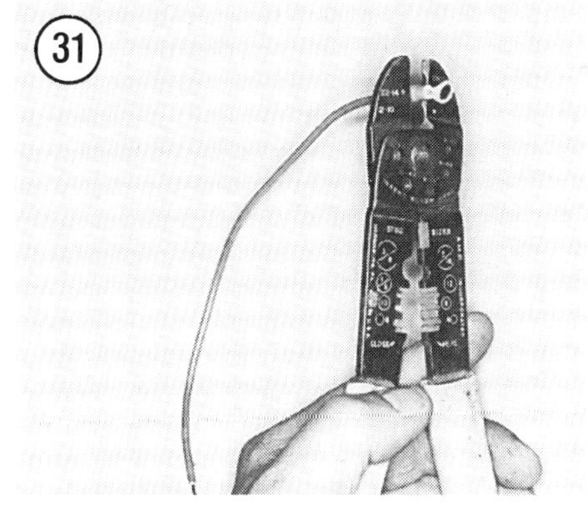

To draw the schematic, first locate the major items to show in the schematic diagram. Start with the battery and trace each wire to its final destination. Note the color of insulation and relative size. Keep the following points in mind.

1. Some systems use ground busses like the one shown in **Figure 33**. The purpose of a buss is to conveniently connect several wires together. This may be done by connecting them all to one large terminal.

2. Single battery systems will differ slightly. The power switch simply turns power on and off. With multiple batteries, the switch must be able to select each of the batteries or banks separately or both together in addition to turning power on and off.

Cabin Lights

Cabin lights are normally wired in parallel back to the fuse/switch panel. Usually each light has its own switch.

When making the diagram, trace from the primary power buss, through the main cabin light switch and fuse, to each cabin light. Draw the lights over an outline of the hull to aid trouble location.

Navigation (Running) Lights

On most boats, navigation (running) lights consist of the bow running lights and a stern light. There may be other deck lighting with a separate switch and fuse. Draw both systems on the same diagram.

As with other diagrams, trace each system from primary power buss, through each switch and fuse, to the lights. Note color of insulation.

Fresh Water and Bilge Pumps

If the boat has electric water pumps, make one diagram showing location of each pump and all connecting wires. See **Figure 34**.

Communication Instruments Systems

Make a diagram showing exactly where each communication or navigation instrument such as RDF, VHF, etc., connects to the primary power. Other information such as antenna cable routing could be useful.

A separate diagram should show connections for other instruments such as the knotmeter, depth meter, etc. Trace from instrument back to

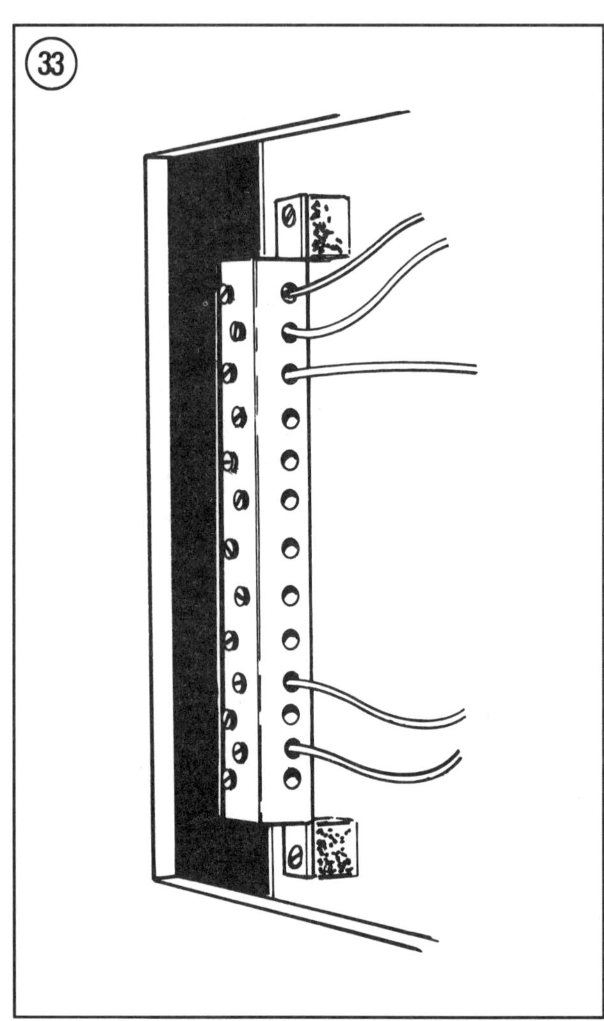

power source. Also trace from instrument to transducer in hull. Show location of each transducer on diagram.

Shore Power

Wiring for shore power is very simple. Alternating current outlets in the cabin are wired in series and terminate at a male 3-prong connector on the deck. In some installations, there may be circuit breakers or fuses installed.

To draw a diagram, trace from the deck connector to each AC outlet.

WARNING
Make sure the shore power cord is disconnected when tracing the wires. Shore power (115 volts) is lethal.

Large boats with AC generators have a change-over switch to select either shore power or the generator. This may be a manual or automatic switch

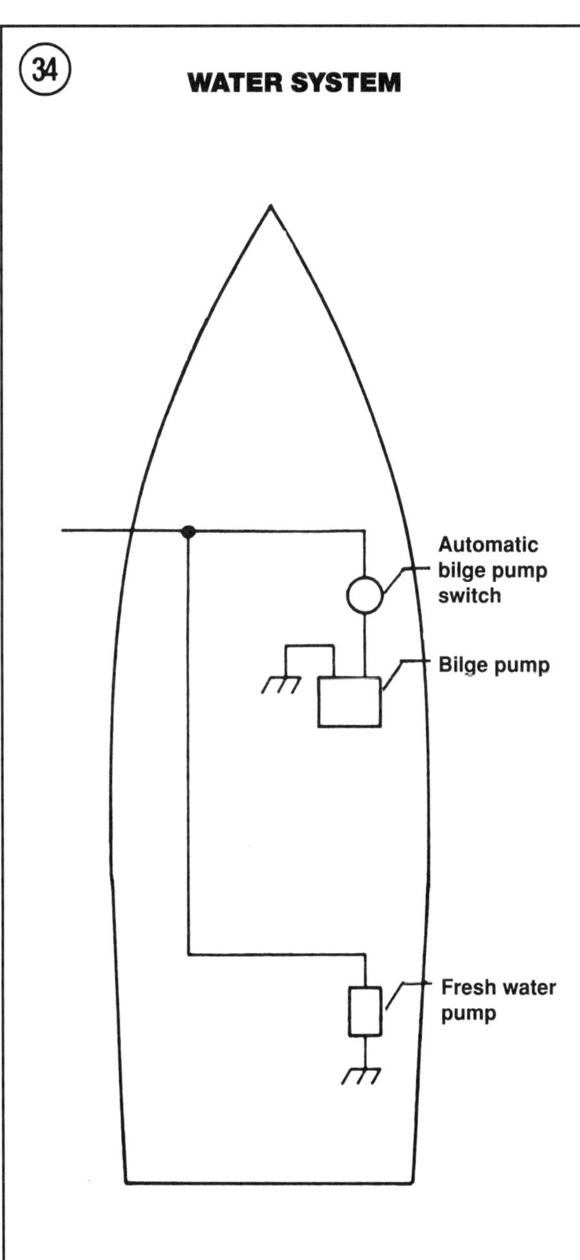

POWER PLANT LAY-UP

When taking a marine generating plant out of service for 30 days or longer, proper storage methods must be used to prevent damage from corrosion, contamination and temperature extremes.

Fuel System

1. Gasoline only: Drain the entire engine fuel system by shutting off the fuel supply and allowing engine to run itself out of fuel.
2. Clean the flame arrestor or air cleaner thoroughly; do not service air cleaner with oil.
3. Cover or seal exposed flame arrestor or air intake openings.
4. Clean throttle linkage (and governor linkage) thoroughly. Lubricate metal ball-joints with light machine oil (do not lubricate plastic ball-joints).

Oil System

1. Change the engine lubricating oil while the engine is warm regardless of time since last oil change.
2. Remove the spark plugs (gasoline only). Remove the fuel injectors (diesel only). Pour 2 tablespoons of rust inhibitor oil (SAE 50 substitute) into each cylinder. Turn the engine by hand

several revolutions to lubricate the cylinder walls, pistons, and rings. Install the plugs or injectors (lightly lubricate spark plug threads prior to installation).
3. Remove and service the oil filter (if used).
4. Clean the crankcase breather valve and breather tube flame arrestor (if used).

Cooling System

1 *Air cooled only:* Remove the access panel and clean all cooling surfaces. Clean air screens and all air ducts.
2. *Water cooled only:* Drain the entire cooling system including water cooled exhaust manifold and exhaust line. Drain the radiator, heat exchanger, or keel cooler components, engine cylinder block, and water pumps. Generating plants equipped with a closed type cooling system (radiator, heat exchanger, keel cooling) may be filled with a good quality antifreeze if freezing temperatures are expected. Drain only those components not protected from freezing (exhaust lines, water pumps, water in-take and outlet lines, etc.).

General

1. Cover or seal all exposed openings (exhaust outlet, water parts, etc.).
2. Tag and identify the plant to indicate service required before attempting to operate. List all items requiring attention and service prior to operation.

Recommissioning

1. Uncover and remove the storage seals from the entire plant. Remove any dust, dirt, or foreign matter.

2. Check the fuel supply tanks for moisture accumulation (drain tanks if necessary). Check lubricating oil for moisture or contamination (drain if necessary). Check fuel line connections, all wiring connections and exhaust line connections.

3. Completely check the exhaust system at least once a season. Disassemble the exhaust elbow assembly and exhaust line for complete inspection of all pipe fittings, hoses, gaskets and exhaust systems. Inspect the exhaust elbow and fittings from the inside out for erosion or corrosion wear. Replace the exhaust elbow and/or fittings if wall thickness becomes reduced to l/2 original size or noticeable deterioration has started. Onan exhaust elbows have original 1/4 in. thickness and pipe fittings original l/8 in. thickness.
4. Service the air cleaner (if used) or clean the flame arrestor. Clean the spark plugs and install. Torque the fuel injectors (diesel only) and bleed the fuel system (if moisture or contamination is found in fuel—replace the secondary filter and clean the primary filter).
5A. *Water cooled only:* Service the cooling system with clean fresh water. Prime the water pump and see that all air is bled from the cooling system. If antifreeze was left in the closed cooling system, check and service as required.
5B. *Air cooled only:* Check to see that all air passages and cooling surfaces are clean. Secure access doors and ducts.
6. Check the entire plant for water, fuel or oil leaks. Correct leakage as required.
7. Install fully charged batteries.
8. Start the plant in thenormal manner. Check the running plant for leaks, correct voltage output and proper cooling.

BATTERY LAY-UP

1. Remove the batteries and thoroughly clean their cases with a baking soda solution.
2. Inspect the battery holders and surrounding area for damage caused by venting of battery acid. Wash the area down with a solution of baking soda and warm water.
3. Clean the battery terminals with a stiff wire brush or one of the many tools made for this purpose.

4. Examine the battery cases for cracks.
5. Recharge the batteries with a battery charger, not the engine charging system.

CAUTION
Batteries must be disconnected and fully charged prior to lay-up.

6. Lightly smear the battery terminals with petroleum jelly.

7. Store the batteries in a cool, dry place. Do not leave the batteries where there is a risk of freezing.

NOTE
If possible, recharge the batteries once a month.

8. Disconnect and clean the terminals on the starter and alternator. Reconnect wires and lightly smear with petroleum jelly.

Table 1 DC POWER BUDGET (12-VOLT SYSTEM)

Device	Current draw (Amperes)
Anchor light	1.0
Anchor windlass	80.0
Autopilot	4.0
Bilge blower	2.5
Bilge pump	2.0
Cabin fan	1.0
Cabin light (40w incandescent)	3.5
Cabin light (26w flourescent)	1.8
CB Radio	1.0
Chart plotter	1.0
Depth sounder (LCD)	0.1
Depth sounder (recording)	0.5
Forced air heater	3.0-10.0
Fresh water pump	5.0
Fuel pump	3.0
GPS receiver	1.0
Head pump	18.0
Horn	3.0
Inverter-Blender	50
Inverter-Microwave	100
Inverter-TV/VCR	10.0
Knotmeter	0.1
Loran	1.0
Masthead light	1.0
Propane valve	1.0
Radar	4.0
Refrigerator	5.0
Running lights	3.0
Spotlight	10.0
Spreader lights	8.0
SSB Radio (Receive)	1.5
SSB Radio (transmit)	25.0
Stereo/cassette player	1.5
Strobe	1.0

(continued)

7

Table 1 DC POWER BUDGET (12-VOLT SYSTEM) (continued)

Device	Current (Amperes)
VHF radio (receive)	1.0
VHF radio (transmit)	5.0
Weather FAX	2.5
Wind speed indicator	0.1

Table 2 BATTERY CAPACITY

Temperature	Battery capacity available	Cranking power required
80°F	100%	100%
32°F	68%	165%
–20°F	30%	350%

Table 3 BATTERY FREEZING TEMPERATURES

State of charge	Freezing temperature
Discharged	13°F to 18°F
Half charged	17°F to –31°F
Fully charged	–75°F to –92°F

Table 4 AC POWER BUDGET

Device	Power consumption (Watts)
Air conditioner (12,000 BTU)	1,500
Air conditioner (6,000 BTU)	900
Blender	300
Broiler	1,500
Clothes iron	1000
Coffee maker	500
Computer	100
Drill	300
Food mixer	250
Hair dryer	1000-1500
Microwave oven	800-1,500
Range/oven element	1,200
Refrigerator	75-150
Soldering iron	50-100
Television	20-100
Toaster	1,000-1,500
Vacuum cleaner	750
VCR	50
Water heater	1,500
Space heater	1,000-1,500

Table 5 OPERATOR MAINTENANCE SCHEDULE

Every 8 hours	General inspection
	Check fuel supply
	Check oil level
Every 50 hours	Service air cleaner
	Clean governor linkage
Every 100 hours	Check spark plugs (gasoline)
	Change crankcase oil
	Clean fuel filter
Every 200 hours	Clean crankcase breather
	Check battery electrolyte

Table 6 CRITICAL MAINTENANCE SCHEDULE

Every 200 hours	Check breaker points
	Check brushes
Every 500 hours	Clean commutator and collector rings
	Remove carbon and lead
	Check valve clearance
	Clean carburetor (gasoline)
Every 1,000 hours	Clean generator
	Remove and clean oil base
	Grind valves
Every 5,000 hours	General overhaul

Table 7 OIL VISCOSITY

Temperature	Oil viscosity
Above 32° F	SAE 30
0-32° F	SAE 10W-30
Below 0° F	SAE 5W-30

Table 8 POWER PLANT TROUBLESHOOTING

Problem	Things to check
Hard starting or loss of power	Loose or shorted wire
	Point gap
	Point condition
	Faulty spark plug
	Defective coil
	Defective condenser
	Clogged fuel line
	Defective fuel pump
	Dirty carburetor
	Carburetor adjustment
	Loose cylinder head
	Defective head gasket
	Sticking valves
	Leaking valves
	Worn piston rings

Table 8 POWER PLANT TROUBLESHOOTING (continued)

Problem	Things to check
Erratic operation	Clogged fuel like
	Contaminated fuel
	Fuel tank vent plugged
	Defective fuel pump
	Carburetor gasket leaking
	Governor adjustment
	Carburetor adjustment
Occasional "skip" at high speed	Spark plug condition
	Spark plug gap
	Ignition timing
	Carburetor adjustment
Overheating	Clogged air intake screen
	Clogged cooling fins
	Oil supply
	Lean fuel mixture
	Ignition timing
	Overload
	Incorrect tappet clearance
Backfiring	Lean fuel mixture
	Ignition timing
	Sticking valve
Knocking	Check fuel octane
	Point gap
	Remove carbon
	Cooling air supply

Table 9 CRIMP CONNECTOR SIZES

Color	Wire size
Yellow	10 and 12
Blue	14 and 16
Red	16 and 18

Table 10 WIRE AND FUSES

Wire size (AWG)	Current capacity (Amperes)	Fuse size (Amperes)
10	25	30
12	20	14
14	15	14
16	6	9
18	3	9

Chapter Eight

Marine Electronics

8

Marine communications gear is impossible to repair without specialized training and skills. In fact, it is illegal to do anything to a transmitter which could affect its operation unless you are licensed to do so. What goes on inside the "black box" must, therefore, remain a mystery. But external connections to the power source and the antenna are accessible to the owner. You can and should acquaint yourself with the installation so that you can keep at least that much of the system in good working order.

TYPICAL RADIO INSTALLATION

Each radio installation varies in detail but each consists of a transceiver (VHF or SSB), coaxial transmission line, antenna and power cord. See **Figure 1**.

The power cord usually contains an inline fuse holder. Fuse size depends on the unit and must be determined from the manufacturer's literature.

VHF Radio

VHF radios are intended for relatively reliable two-way communication over short unobstructed distances, usually up to about 25 miles. They can be used to communicate with the U.S. Coast Guard, harbormasters, bridge tenders and even other boats.

Except for handheld radios, most VHF radios offer selectable 25 watt and 1 watt outputs with the ability to operate on all available U.S. and even international marine channels. There is a staggering array of features beyond this capability so that the choice becomes one of preference and price. Some also have a built in hailer and a selection of interesting but usually annoying sirens and sound effects.

SSB Radio

SSB radios operate at much lower frequencies which allow very long distance (global) communication. In addition, they can receive short wave broadcasts and weather FAX transmissions.

Amateur radio operators who communicated with one another all over the world have used SSB at these frequencies for almost 40 years. As a result, there is a huge selection of SSB equipment capable of receiving marine frequencies and, with slight modification, of transmitting on marine frequencies. Since the amateur radio versions are often less expensive with more features than marine SSB equipment, there is a temptation to use the amateur radios. Unfortunately, it is illegal to transmit using amateur radio equipment outside of the special bands set aside for amateur use. Also, it is necessary to have an amateur radio license to operate within these special bands. Given the additional safety of being able to communicate via amateur radio many long distance cruisers consider it worthwhile to get a license. Contact the American Radio Relay League, Newington, CT 06111 for full details.

VHF Antennas

VHF signals travel "line of sight." Therefore, the higher the antenna at each end, the farther you can communicate. While this implies that you cannot transmit beyond the horizon, VHF signals will actually bend around Earth a little and travel slightly beyond "line of sight."

Communication between 2 boats equipped with handheld radios is limited to a couple of miles since both antennas are only 5-10 ft. above the water and the antennas are very inefficient. However, communication between a boat equipped with an efficient antenna at 20 ft. and a U.S. Coast Guard station with an antenna on a mountain several thousand feet high may be reliable at 50-100 miles.

Antenna performance or "gain" is rated in decibels (db). The higher the db rating the higher the effective radiated power of the antenna and the stronger your signal will be. Vertical antennas for VHF marine use usually have ratings of 3-9 db. Low gain antennas (**Figure 2**) are usually short; a 3 db antenna may be a thin 3 ft. stainless steel whip. They radiate in all directions around the compass, but a good deal of that energy is radiated upward (**Figure 3**) and is wasted unless you are communicating with airplanes. Higher gain antennas also radiate in all directions, but produce a stronger signal, by radiating more of it at a lower angle relative to the horizon (**Figure 4**). To get this additional gain, the antenna must be longer. A 9 db antenna may be an 18 ft. fiberglass pole that requires support at the base and about half way up.

Generally, higher gain antennas are preferred for large powerboats. They typically go farther

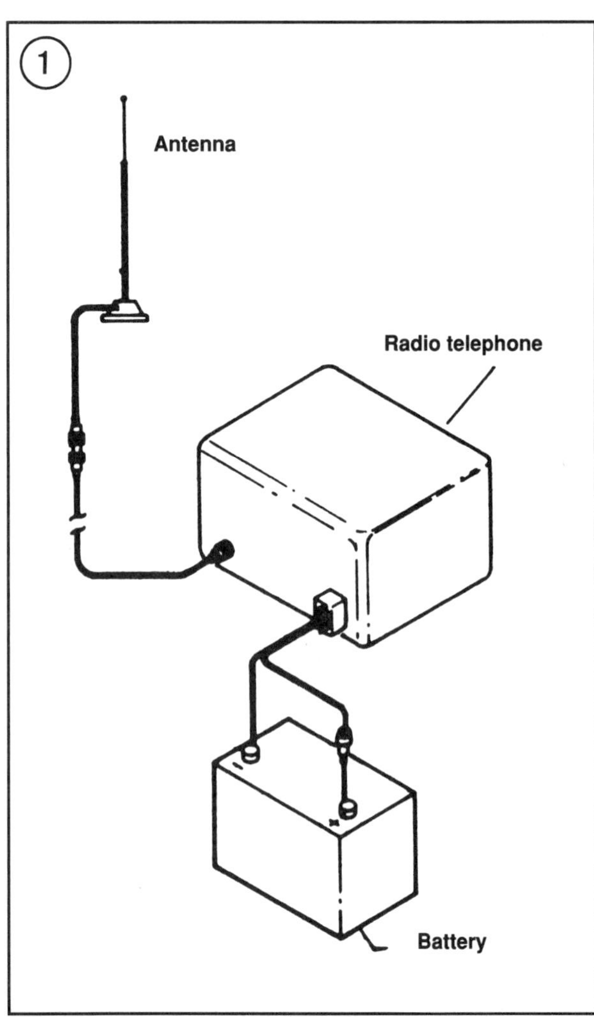

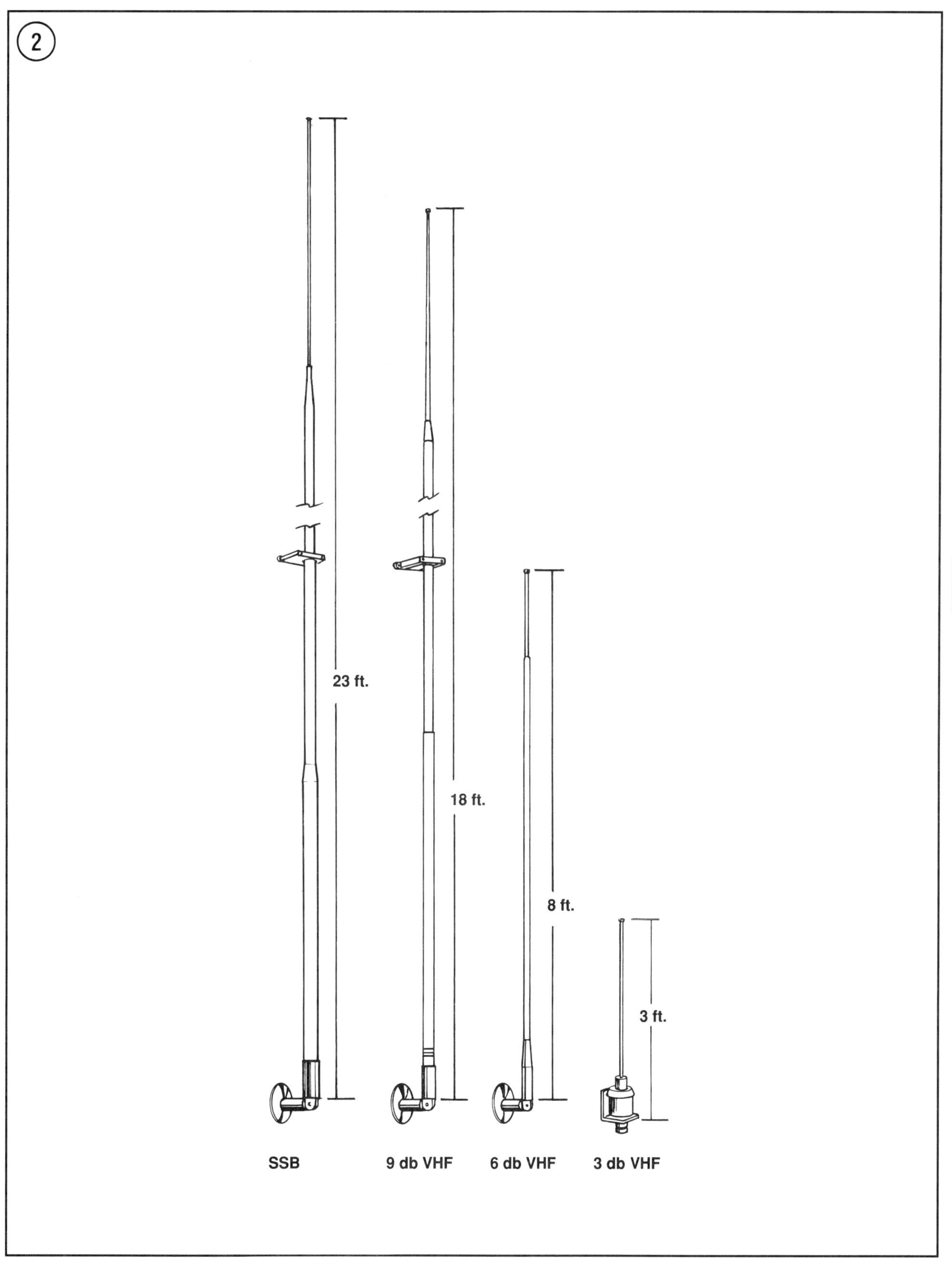
2
23 ft.
18 ft.
8 ft.
3 ft.
SSB
9 db VHF
6 db VHF
3 db VHF

3

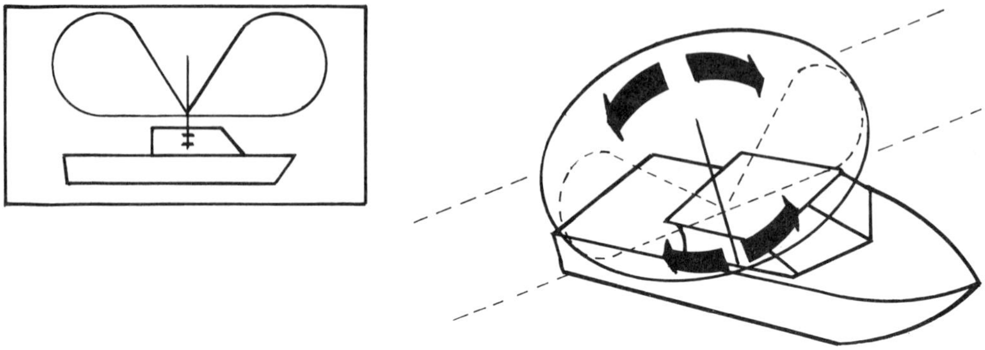

4

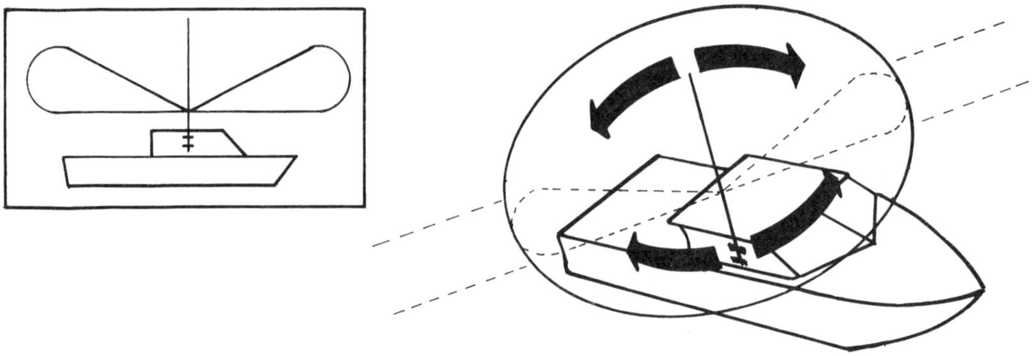

out to sea and have more room to mount a big antenna. Smaller boats may require a shorter antenna. This means less gain, but the reduced range is not usually a problem.

Incidentally, sailboat enthusiasts often must settle for a low gain antenna. One reason is the difficulty in mounting a large antenna clear of all the rigging and sails. Another reason stems from the lower angle of radiation. When the sailboat is heeled well over, the radiation pattern also heels over. Radiation to the side of the boat is either into the ocean or high overhead. With a lower gain antenna, the effect is still there, but not as noticeable and the signal may be stronger at the other end.

A length of coaxial cable connects the antenna to the VHF radio. In most cases, one end of the cable is fitted with a male connector to mate with the female coaxial connector on the rear panel of the radio. The antenna end is not as consistent. In some cases, there may be another male connector that mates with a female connector at the base of the antenna. In other cases, the cable might terminate in two terminal lugs without a connector. These are secured to an antenna stud and a ground stud on the antenna mount. Finally, some antennas may have a small length of coaxial cable permanently attached that terminates with a male connector. Since the coaxial transmission line also uses a male connector, a special coupler must be used. See **Figure 5**. This connection should be securely taped with several layers of waterproof vinyl tape then covered thoroughly with silicone sealant. Otherwise, exposure to a salt atmosphere will corrode the connections and permit water to seep under the outer vinyl jacket.

SSB Antenna

A single side band antenna may also be a whip mounted like a VHF antenna. See **Figure 2**. This antenna may be 6 to 23 ft. in length and may tune from 2 to 30 mHz. This allows use at 2.182 mHz, the SSB emergency calling frequency and all of the SSB ship-to-shore frequencies as well.

Transmission Line

Almost without exception, RG-8/U or RG-213/U transmission line is recommended over the smaller diameter RG-58/U. The reason is simple. All coaxial lines attenuate the transmitted signal to some extent, that is, not all the power leaving the transmitter reaches the antenna. However, at VHF marine frequencies, RG-58/U wastes more than twice as much power as RG-8/U. This loss also occurs when receiving; less of the signal gathered by the antenna reaches the receiver, making reception more difficult with RG-58/U.

For short runs (less than 20 ft.) either RG-58/U or RG-8/U may be used, as losses are small. For longer runs, use only RG-8/U.

8

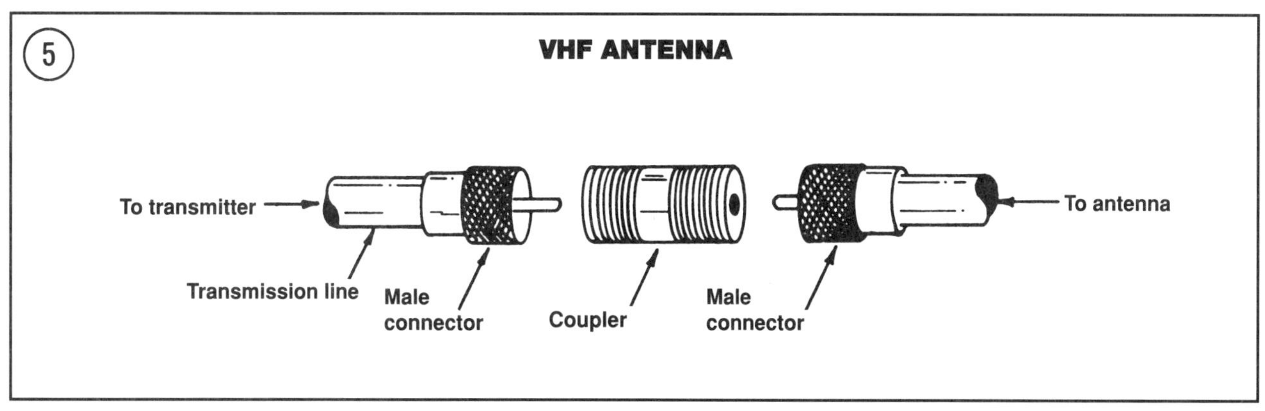

OTHER RECEIVING EQUIPMENT

Most navigation equipment such as Global Positioning Satellite (GPS) receivers, Loran, Radio Direction Finding and omni receivers are installed just like communication equipment, though each has its own specific requirements for power and antennas. There really is not much an owner can do other than make sure the equipment has power and that the antenna is properly connected. Once you have done this, it either works or it doesn't. If it doesn't, you have to get service from an experienced technician.

NOISE INTERFERENCE IN ELECTRONIC EQUIPMENT

Man-made interference may affect almost any electronic device aboard. This may show up as audible noise from the speaker in VHF and SSB receivers. In Loran and satnav equipment, it may be evident by erratic indications. It can even show up in depth sounder displays as random indications at all depths.

The first requirement in reducing interference is accomplished by bonding all electrical grounds with metal fittings that are in contact with the water. See **Figure 6**. Bonding straps are usually made of one in. wide No. 20 gauge copper. These straps interconnect all metal fittings and ignition grounds. Secure the bonding straps under a screw of the fitting, making sure that the metal under the screw is brightened for a good electrical connection and coated with grease to prevent future corrosion. Refer to Chapter Seven for more information on bonding.

If interference remains, in most cases, it can be eliminated, but it is usually a long and tedious process. Sections below describe a number of potential sources of interference and methods that may work to eliminate them.

Quite often the interference is transmitted through the DC power system and enters the electronic equipment via the power cord. There are commercially available powerline filters that are installed in series with the equipment power cord which chokes off the interference before it enters the equipment.

Eliminating interference in electronic equipment can be a time consuming and exasperating experience. Your marine electronics dealer can be a big help in identifying and curing these problems. Another resource is a local amateur radio club. Many amateurs have extensive experience in tracking down interference in automobile installations for their two-way radios and might be willing to give you a hand for free.

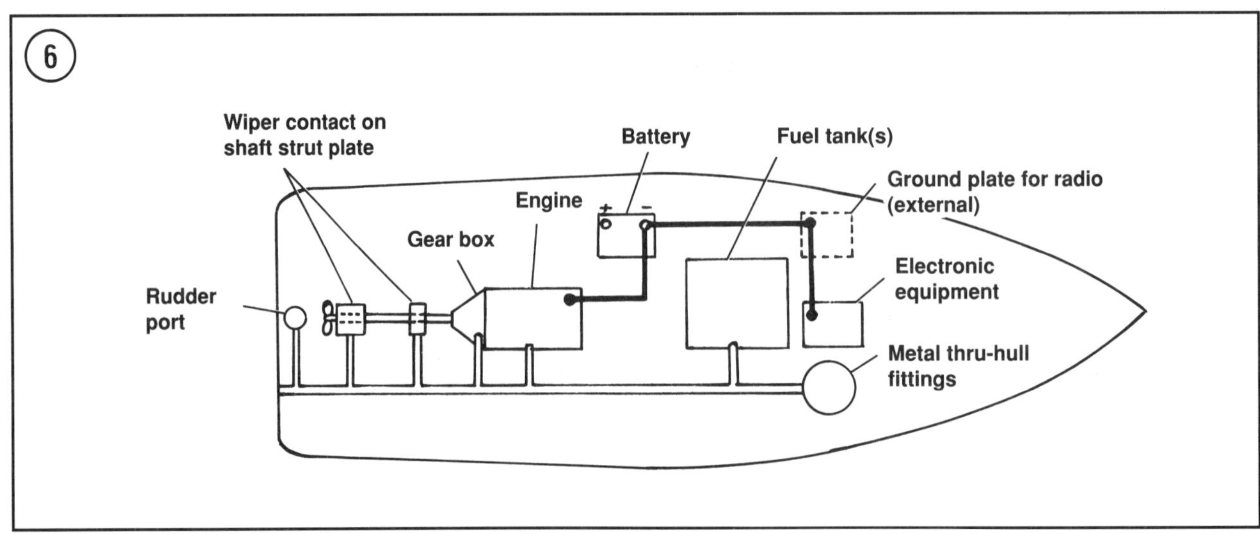

Ignition System (Gasoline Engines)

Ignition noise usually appears as a popping sound in the speaker that varies with engine speed. It disappears immediately when the engine is shut off. This type interference can be reduced by installing resistor-type spark plugs and a suppresser between the coil and distributor. See **Figure 7**. Also, install a 0.1 ufd coaxial capacitor (see **Figure 8**) in series with primary lead to coil from ignition switch. These are available from any marine or automotive parts distributor. Do not put the capacitor in series with the secondary lead between coil and distributor. Finally, make sure the ignition coil is mounted directly to the engine. Clean away paint so that there is a good ground connection between both of them.

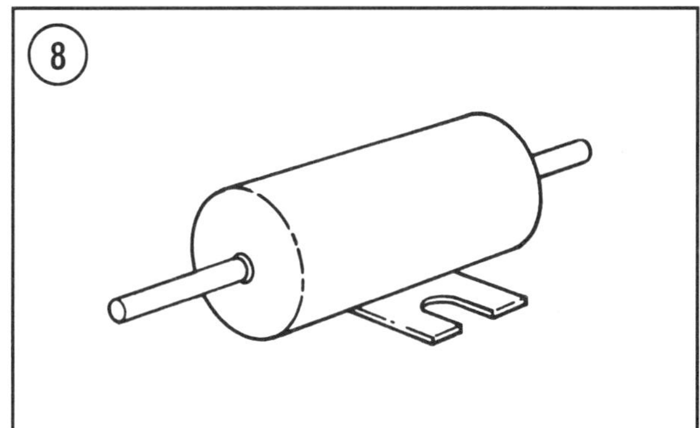

For very stubborn cases, complete ignition noise suppression kits are available for use on both inboard and outboard engines. These kits usually consist of shielded ignition wires and special shields for the spark plugs, ignition coil and distributor. However, the engine manufacturer or boat dealer must be consulted before using these kits. Other specialized kits available for inboard engines contain a copper or bronze screen that is used to line the entire engine compartment or special pan-type metal shields that bolt directly to the engine.

Charging System

Noise from the alternator is usually a high-pitched whine. When the ignition switch is turned off, the noise persists for a short time until the engine actually stops turning.

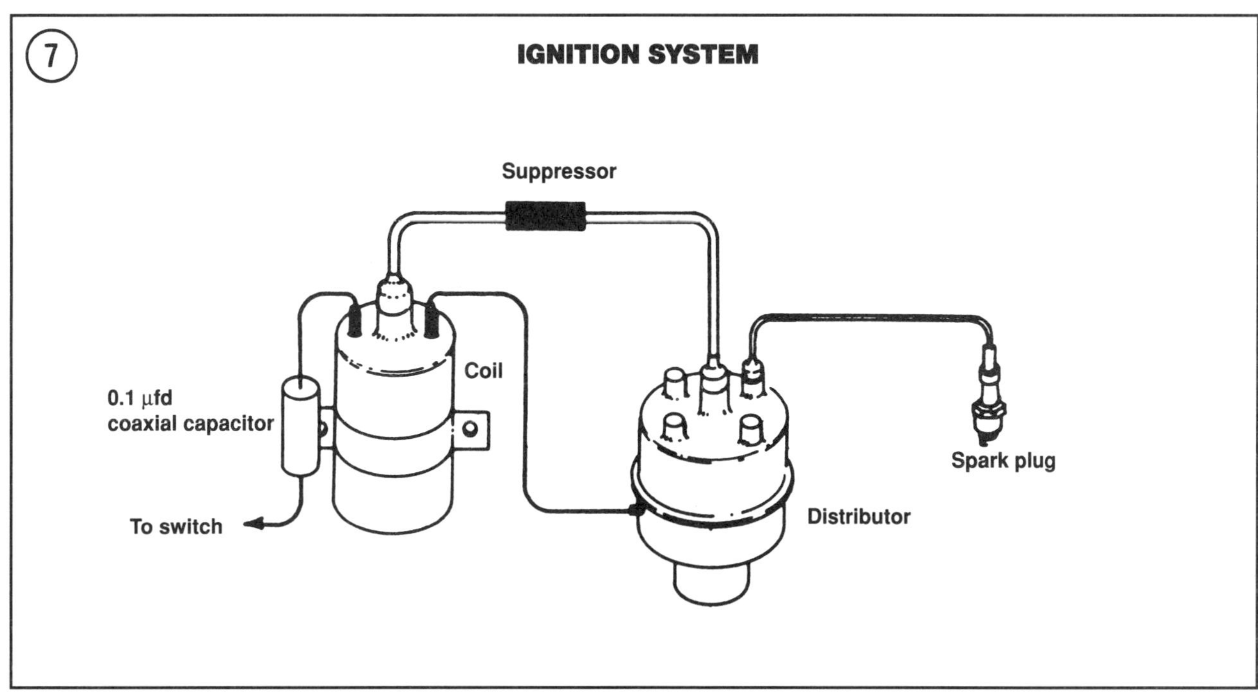

In many cases, a 0.5 μfd coaxial capacitor in series with the armature lead cures the trouble. See **Figure 9.** Make sure that contact areas between capacitor and alternator frame are clean, and the capacitor is firmly mounted. If more suppression is required, install a copper braided shield over field and armature leads between alternator and voltage regulator. Securely ground both ends of the braid.

Voltage regulator noise may be a ragged, rasping sound. Like alternator noise, it persists for a short time after ignition is switched off. Install a 0.1-0.25 μfd coaxial capacitor in series with the battery lead to voltage regulator. See **Figure 9**. Since alternator whine is usually present also, install the other parts shown in **Figure 9**. Do not install a capacitor in series with the field lead.

If capacitors do not eliminate voltage regulator noise, replace the regulator with a solid state regulator.

Propeller shafts

Propeller shaft interference is only evident when underway. It may have a cyclic sound to it. This interference does not usually occur when the propeller shaft is properly bonded as it should be to prevent galvanic corrosion (see Chapter Two and Seven). If you have this kind of interference, make sure that the bonding straps are making good electrical contact. Disconnect and clean them to bare metal if necessary.

Electric motors

Electric motors for fresh water and the head may cause interference when they operate. Since it is obviously tied to the use of these systems, it is relatively easy to identify. Fixing the problem may not always be as easy. You should start by disassembling the motor and cleaning the commutator and brushes. This will often solve the problem at least temporarily. Another possibility is to add a 0.5-1.0 μfd capacitor across the power terminals on the motor and another capacitor from each power terminal to ground. See **Figure 10**. Commercially available "accessory filters" are also available and usually go in series with the positive lead to the motor.

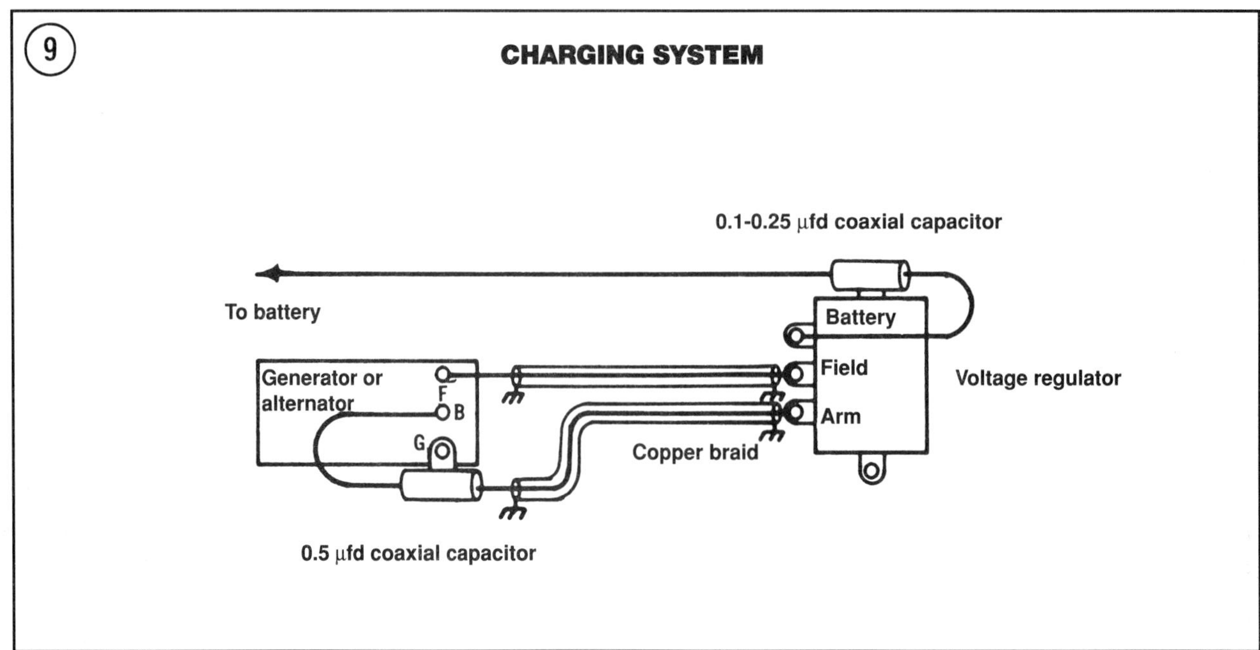

Tachometers

Some electronic tachometers cause interference. To identify this source, disconnect the tachometer from the distributor. If the noise stops, the tachometer is causing it. Replace the wire between the tachometer and distributor with a shielded lead. Connect the distributor end of the shield to ground, but leave the other end of the shield ungrounded.

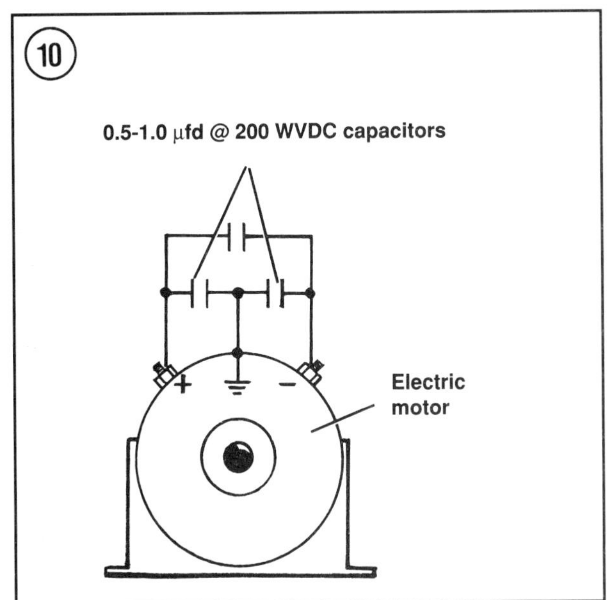

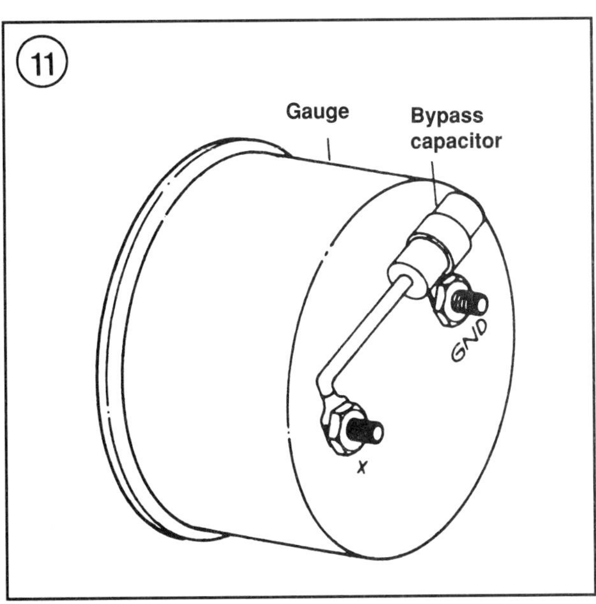

Instrumentation

Noise generated by engine instruments is usually a hissing or crackling sound. Gauges employing rheostats are most likely to produce trouble. A low-pitched clicking sound is generally caused by the oil pressure sender. The clicking rate will vary as the oil pressure varies with engine speed. The offending gauge or gauges can be isolated by disconnecting the hot leads from the gauges and then reconnecting the leads, one at a time, to their respective gauge. After the lead is reconnected, jar the gauge. If noise is observed, connect a 0.25-0.50 µfd capacitor between the hot lead and ground. See **Figure 11**.

Televisions

Television receivers emit a wide range of frequencies that can interfere with sensitive electronic equipment. Sometimes it can be eliminated by moving the television to another location in the boat. This kind of interference is usually picked up by the other equipment's antenna so moving the television may help. Sometimes the television's antenna radiates the antenna! You have to experiment with this.

Computers

Some computers emit radio interference, but most portables are designed to be very quiet so they can be used aboard airliners. Moving the computer away from antennas usually solves the problem.

PREVENTIVE MAINTENANCE

Marine equipment operates in a comparatively hostile environment. Not only must it operate in extremes of hot and cold, it must also contend with a humid, corrosive (salt) atmosphere. Furthermore, engine vibration and sea conditions subject the equipment to vibration and mechanical shock. That they work at all is cause for wonder.

To help minimize troubles caused by the environment, the following procedure should be performed periodically (once a month during the season, for example). Also, use it to prepare for any cruise in which proper equipment operation is vital.

1. Make sure that all connectors, plugs, and terminals are securely fastened to the instrument. Check for fraying or broken wires.
2. Check power connections at the battery. Make sure that they are clean and tight. Service the battery as described in Chapter Seven.
3. Unscrew the coaxial connector from the instrument. Check both connectors for corrosion; clean if necessary.
4. Check resistance between the center conductor and outer conductor. It should measure infinity.
5. Make certain that the antenna mounting hardware is tight.
6. Tighten all equipment mounting screws.
7. Perform an operational check of all equipment as described later.

On a less regular basis, such as prior to yearly recommissioning, the following maintenance should be performed:

1. Have a qualified FCC licensed electronic technician check the following.
   a. Interior of equipment for loose connections and corrosion.
   b. Performance of receiver (sensitivity) and transmitter (power output).
   c. Condition of antenna relay.
   d. Antenna "reflected" power.
   e. Transmitter frequency
   f. Deviation (VHF radios only).
2. Have the electrical charging system checked. Excessive voltage output can damage electrical equipment.

Operational Check (Radiotelephone)

1. Turn the equipment on following itsmanufacturer's instructions.
2. Select any inactive channel.
3. Turn the volume control to comfortable level.
4. Turn the squelch control until noise from the speaker stops.
5. Select the weather channel or any other active channel. Make sure reception is clear and undistorted.
6. Select a local public correspondence channel (Channels 24-28) that is active in your area.
7. Call the operator and ask for a radio check. This service is available to anyone. Registration with the telephone company is not necessary. The procedure is described below.

Radio Check Calling Procedure

It is not necessary to be registered with the telephone company to request a simple radio check and no charge is made. Of course, you must have a valid station license and operator's permit to operate the transmitter.

1. Select a local public correspondence channel (Channel 24-28) that is active in your area.
2. Ensure that the channel is not in use.
3. When clear, operate the transmitter and say "Marine operator. This is (call sign and name of vessel)."
4. Wait for a reply. If there is no reply, call again after 2 minutes.
5. When the marine operator answers, say "This is (call sign and name of vessel). Please give me a radio check." If everything is OK, the operator will say something like "loud and clear." If there is any problem such as weak signal or distortion, the operator will say so; have it checked by a licensed technician.
6. After the radio check, say "This is (call sign and name of vessel) out."

SOLDERING

Several repairs to marine electronic systems require soldering. Good solder joints are extremely important when working with electronic equipment. The same principles apply regardless of what is being soldered.

1. Use 60/40 rosin-core solder only. Never use acid-core solder for electrical connections; acid-core solder is corrosive and the joint will fail in a short time.
2. Use no more heat than necessary to get the solder to flow smoothly. Too little heat produces a "cold solder joint;" it has a dull granular appearance instead of a bright smooth appearance. Too much heat can damage the items being soldered, and burn insulation on wires.
3. Keep the tip of the iron clean and tinned. Brush it off with a damp paper towel. Tin it by flowing a small amount of solder on it.
4. Hold the tip of the iron to the joint. At the same time hold solder to joint. When the joint is heated sufficiently, the solder will melt over the joint. Never apply solder to the iron as this will produce a cold solder joint.
5. Remove the iron and let the solder joint cool before moving it.

REPAIRING AND SPLICING WIRE

Many problems with electronic equipment are caused by loose connections between the equipment and the boat wiring. Chapter Seven describes methods for making soldered and crimped splices and connections.

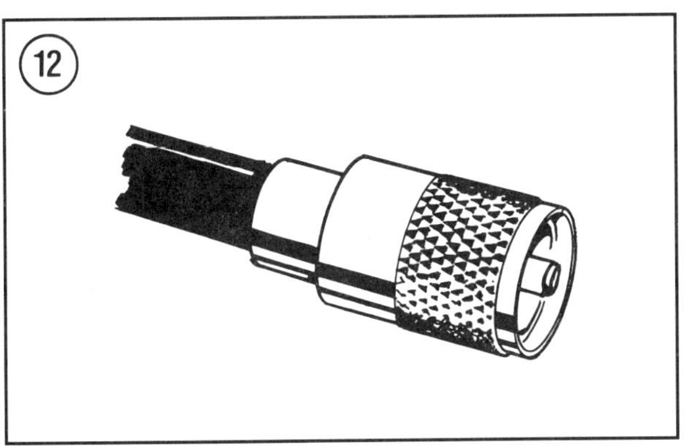

REPLACING A TRANSMISSION LINE

Coaxial transmission line attenuates the transmitted signal slightly, therefore, not all the power generated by the transmitter actually reaches the antenna. With new cable, attenuation is small.

Over time and exposure, attenuation increases significantly and the cable should be replaced. No exact replacement interval can be established. However, after 2 years or more, have your electronics dealer measure the loss with special equipment; follow his recommendations for replacement.

When ordering a new cable, use only new RG-8/U and specify length; it is usually sold by the foot. You may have the dealer install connectors on the ends or do it yourself. Follow the procedure described in this chapter exactly.

8

COAXIAL CABLE CONNECTORS

Replacing a damaged coaxial cable requires removing and installing the end connectors. While not beyond the capabilities of an owner with average dexterity and a knowledge of soldering, the job is exacting. If done sloppily or incorrectly, there is some chance of damaging the transmitter when used. A sloppy installation may work fine initially, only to fail at a more crucial time. Work slowly and carefully and the job is easy.

There are 2 types of connectors commonly used on marine equipment. Most common is the large PL-259 plug (see **Figure 12**) used with RG-8/U coaxial cable. This mates with the S0-239 socket on the rear of nearly all VHF and SSB equipment on the market. This connector can also be used with the smaller diameter RG-58/U cable by installing an adapter (UG-175/U), but RG-58/U is not recommended for these installations.

The other connector is used on some navigation receivers such as omni receivers. This connector is called a BNC connector (see **Figure 13**) and is used exclusively with small diameter coax such as RG-58/U.

Installing PL-258 Connector to RG-8/U

1. Remove 1-1/8 in. of the vinyl jacket from the end. See A, **Figure 14.**

CAUTION
Do not nick the braided wire.

2. Bare 1/4 in. of the center conductor.

CAUTION
Do not nick conductor or it will break off.

3. Trim the braided shield 1/16 in. beyond the inner insulation. See B, **Figure 14**. Tin the braid and center conductor carefully. Do not use too much solder. Also, the braid must not fan out, but should lay flat against inner insulation. Furthermore, do not burn the insulation while soldering.
4. Slide the coupling ring on the cable.
5. Screw the plug assembly onto the cable. Make certain the center conductor fits through the center pin without folding back or bending.
6. Solder the plug assembly to the braid through the solder hole. Solder the center conductor to the center pin. Do not use excessive heat or solder. See C, **Figure 14.**
7. Screw the coupling ring onto the assembly until it turns freely off the threads.

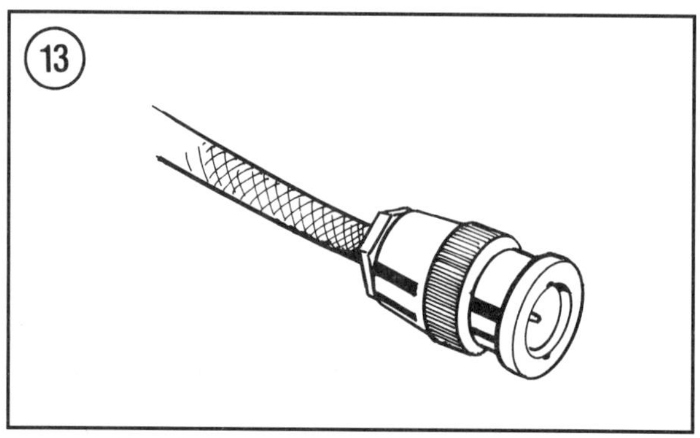
13

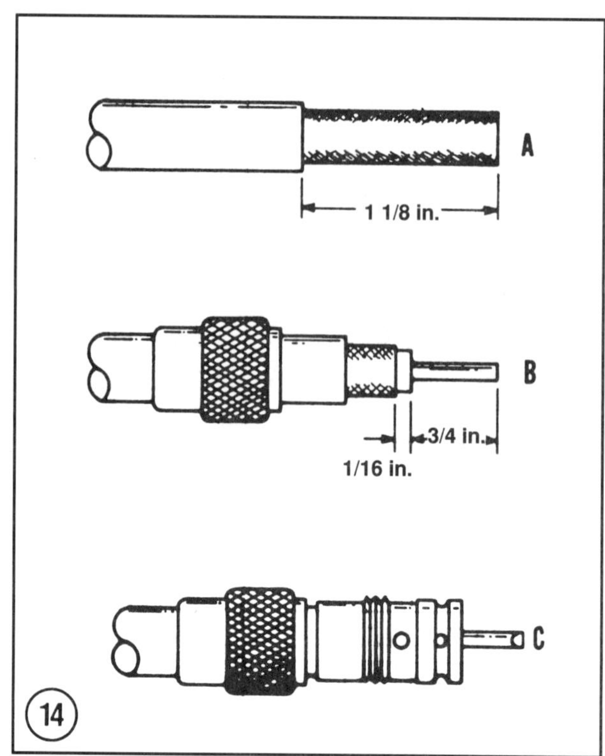

14

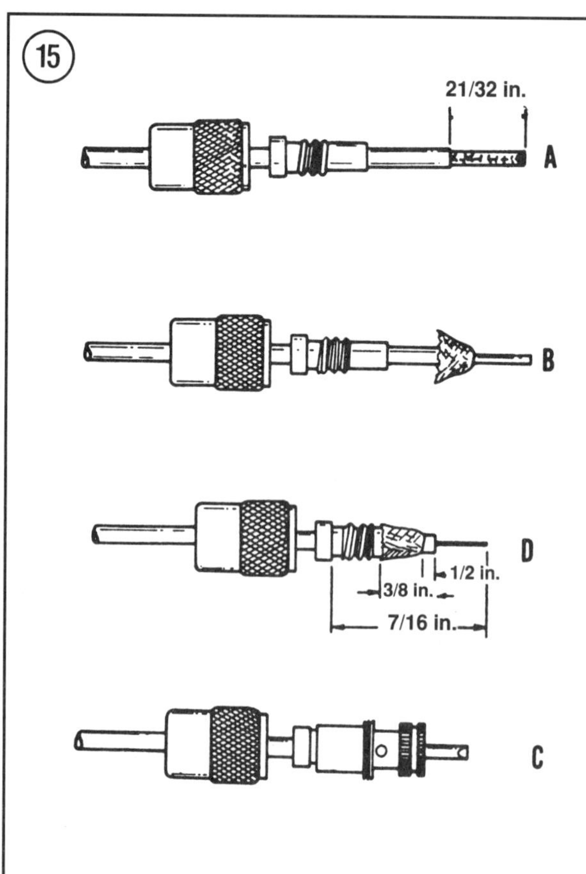

15

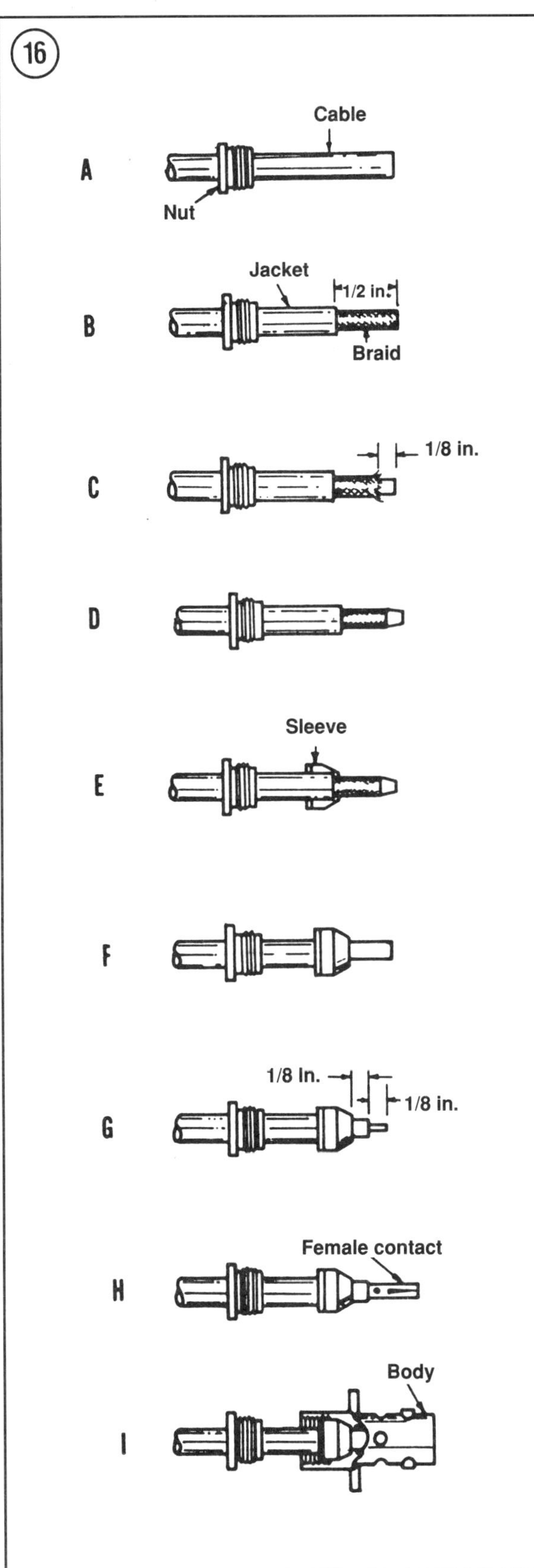

8. Check for a short between the center conductor and plug body with an ohmmeter. If shorted, cut off the connector and start at the beginning, being more careful.

Installing PL-259 Connector to RG-58/U

This cable is not recommended for VHF and SSB transceivers, but is used on some navigation receivers. Check the manufacturer's manual.

1. Remove 21/32 in. of the vinyl jacket from the end. See A, **Figure 15.**

CAUTION
Do not nick the braided wire.

2. Slide the coupling ring and UG-175/U adapter onto cable. See **Figure 15**.
3. Fan the braid slightly and fold it back over the cable. See B, **Figure 15**. Compress the braid around the cable.
4. Position the adapter as shown in C, **Figure 15**. Press the braid down over the adapter and trim it to 3/8 in.
5. Bare 1/2 in. of the center conductor and tin it.

CAUTION
Do not nick conductor.

6. Screw the plug assembly onto the adapter. Make certain the center conductor fits through the center pin without folding back or bending.
7. Solder the plug assembly to the braid through the solder hole. Solder the center conductor to the center pin. Do not use excessive heat or solder. See D, **Figure 15**.
8. Screw the coupling ring onto the assembly until it turns freely off the threads.
9. Check for a short between the center conductor and plug body with an ohmmeter. If shorted, cut off the connector and start at the beginning, being more careful.

Installing BNC Connector

1. Cut the end of the cable even.
2. Slide the nut over the cable. See A, **Figure 16.**

8

3. Remove 1/2 in. of the vinyl jacket (B, **Figure 16**).

CAUTION
Do not nick braid.

4. Push braid back and remove 1/8 in. of the inner insulator. See C, **Figure 16**.
5. Taper the braid over the end as shown in D, **Figure 16**.
6. Slide the sleeve over the end until it fits squarely against the end of the jacket (E, **Figure 16**).
7. With the sleeve firmly in place, comb out the braid, fold it back and smooth it out. Trim to 3/32 in. around sleeve. See F, **Figure 16**.
8. Leave 1/8 in. of inner insulation extending beyond the sleeve and 1/8 in. of the center conductor extending beyond the insulation. See G, **Figure 16**.
9. Tin the center conductor. Do not use excessive heat or solder.
10. Slide the male pin over the conductor and solder. See H, **Figure 16**. Remove excess solder.

CAUTION
Do not use excessive heat or the inner insulation will swell, preventing it from fitting into the plug body in the next step. If this happens, you must start the procedure over.

11. Push the end of the cable into the plug body as far as it will go. See I, **Figure 16**.
12. Slide the nut into place and screw it into the body. Tighten moderately with a wrench.

CAUTION
Hold the body and cable rigidly. Do not let either twist when tightening.

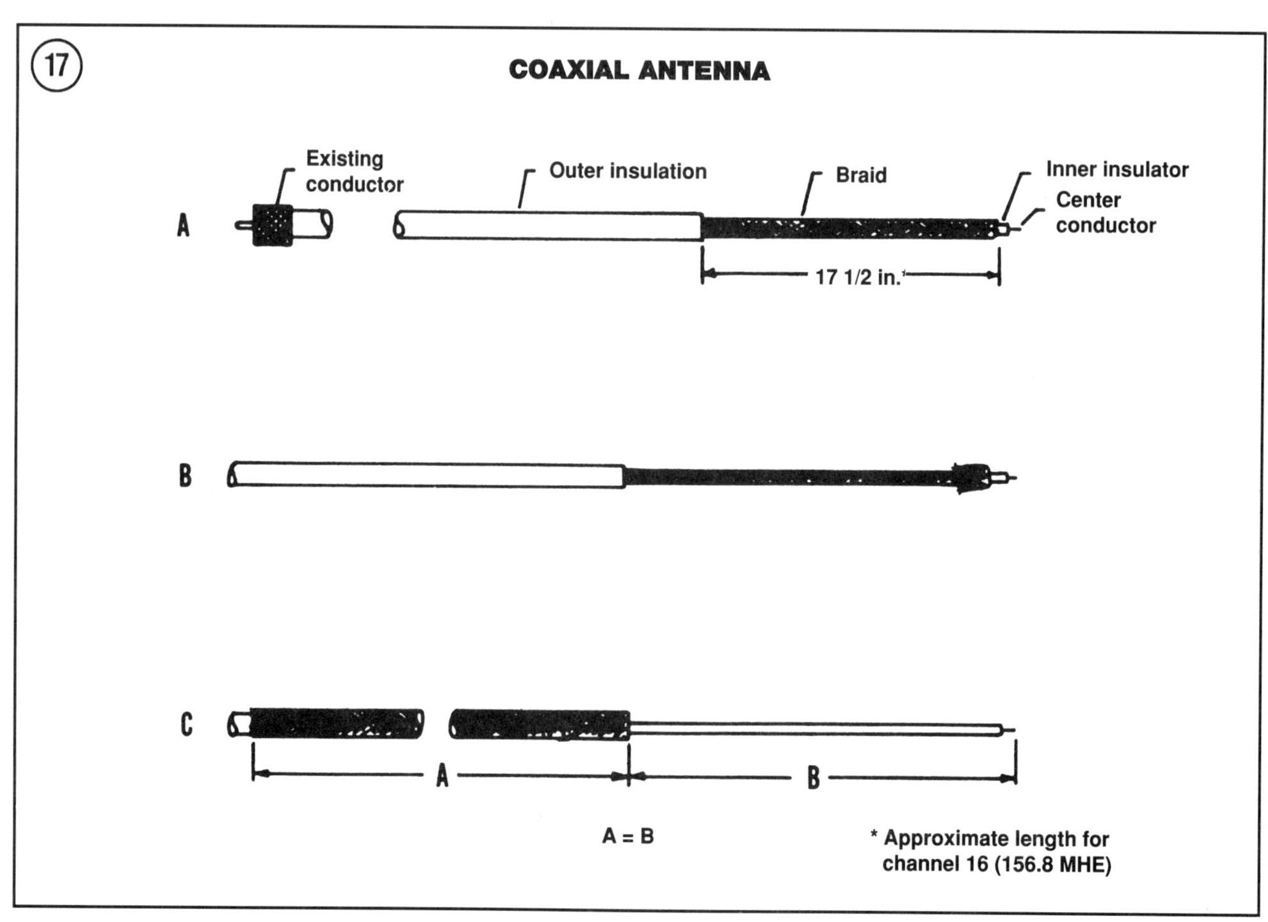

13. Check for a short between the center conductor and plug body with an ohmmeter. If shorted, cut off connector and start at the beginning, being more careful.

EMERGENCY ANTENNA (VHF)

Commercial antennas are usually strong and seaworthy, but there is always a chance one could be swept away or severely damaged in a storm. Being able to improvise a substitute could mean the difference between rescue and disaster.

An antenna is a simple device, but its design is relatively exacting. Most importantly, its length must bear a precise relationship to the frequency at which it will be used. The exact design of commercial antennas is developed by formulas and careful matching to existing transmitters by experimentation.

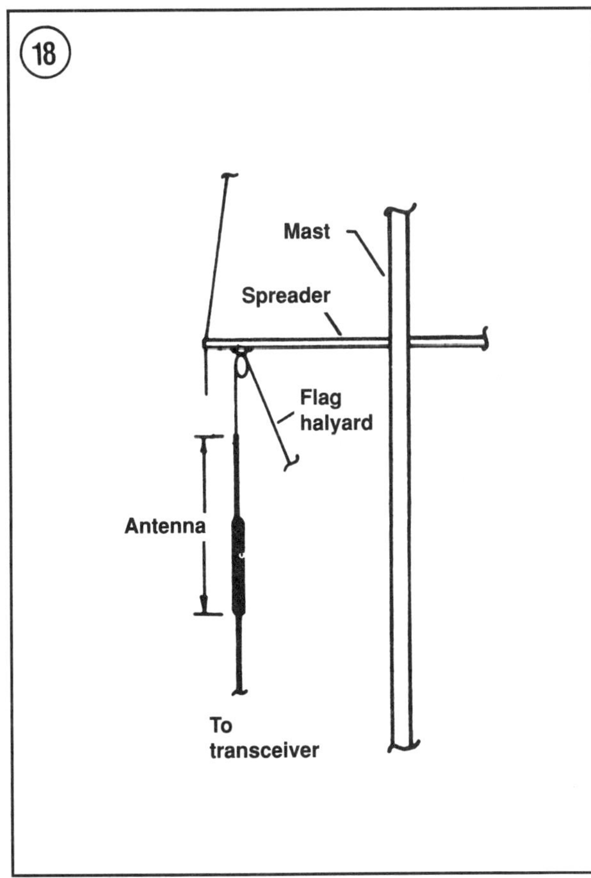

The antenna in this section cannot be precisely matched. There is a likelihood that no accurate means is available at the time to measure its length. However, it will be usable, but inefficient. In fact, if used for long periods of time, the mismatch could damage the transmitter. Therefore, it is intended only as a last resort; don't try to save money on an installation by "rolling your own."

One of the simplest and most efficient of the makeshift antennas is the coaxial antenna. It is made from coaxial cable salvaged from the damaged antenna installation. To make it:

1. Cut the connector off the antenna end of the existing coaxial cable. If the end has been severed, cut the coax off cleanly at the first undamaged portion.
2. Slice off the outer insulation for the length shown in A, **Figure 17**.
3. Fold the outer braid back on itself as shown in B, **Figure 17**.
4. Continue until the exposed braid is completely folded back over the outer insulation. See C, **Figure 17**.

The coaxial cable connects to the transceiver in the same way as the original antenna. Raise the antenna portion as high as the length of cable will allow. A flag halyard works well on larger boats. See **Figure 18**. On smaller boats, tape it to an oar, fishing pole or anything else non-metallic that will keep it high and vertical. Keep the antenna away from metal rigging as much as possible.

USING A MULTIMETER

A multimeter or volt-ohmmeter (VOM) is probably one of the handiest troubleshooting aids you can buy for electrical troubles. The VOM can measure voltage, such as when trying to determine if power is getting to an instrument. It can also measure electrical resistance. This is useful for finding short circuits, open circuits, corroded connections and other troubles.

There is no need to buy a very elaborate or expensive instrument. The one shown in **Figure 19** is more than adequate for the job and sells for about $12-15. Any electronic store has suitable instruments in this price range; there is no need to spend more. Refer to the instructions with the instrument for proper use.

ENGINE INSTRUMENTS

Engine instruments commonly include:

a. Ammeter.
b. Oil pressure.
c. Coolant temperature.
d. Voltmeter.
e. Hour meter.
f. Fuel level.

Not every installation will include all of these instruments; the first 3 are usually considered the minimum necessary.

Figure 20 shows how these instruments are normally wired. Note that each instrument is independent of the others. The ammeter is connected in series between the battery and all electrical accessories except the starter. Other instruments receive 1 2 volts from the battery as soon as the ignition switch is turned on. The hour meter begins timing as soon as the switch goes on and the voltmeter records battery voltage. The oil sender and coolant temperature sender are mounted on the engine block. Both senders vary their resistance to change the meter indication. The fuel level sender float varies resistance according to fuel level to change the fuel gauge reading.

Troubleshooting

1. Ammeter—Ammeters usually fail completely, giving a zero reading regardless of current flow. You can easily check if it is working. Turn the ignition switch on but do not start engine. If ammeter is good, the needle will point slightly toward discharge (–). Turn on some lights and note that the reading increases toward discharge. If the needle stays on zero, replace the meter with a new one. Be sure that the new case diameter and method of mounting are the same. Wire it in the same way as the old one. Recheck the new meter as described above. If everything works OK, except needle points toward charge (+) instead of discharge (–), reverse the wires to ammeter.
2. Hour meter—Hour meters also usually fail completely. If the meter fails to record time, check the electrical connections to the meter; ensure that it receives 12 volts on one terminal. If all connections are good, but the meter still doesn't work, re-place the meter. Be sure that you record the hours from old meter in your log book so that the correct total use can be determined at some later date.
3. Voltmeter—Another meter that usually fails completely, but may also simply record incorrect battery voltage. If the reading is incorrect, but the battery is fully charged, check the accuracy by measuring the voltage with a separate voltmeter (multimeter). Replace the gauge if defective.
4. Oil pressure—This gauge usually becomes inaccurate, but may fail completely. If you note a significant difference in oil pressure from normal, ensure that all electrical connections to gauge and sender are clean and firmly attached. If trouble persists, replace the sender. If trouble still exists, replace meter.

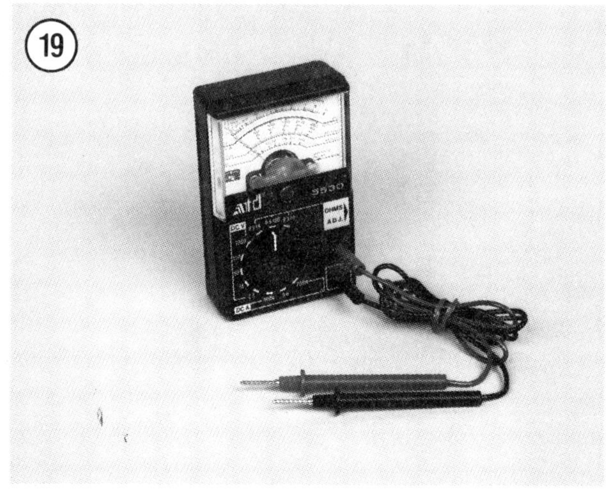

CAUTION
Don't overlook the fact that any difference in oil pressure may be caused by an engine trouble or low oil level.

5. Coolant temperature—Same as oil pressure gauge, except trouble shows up as a difference in coolant temperature.

CAUTION
Before suspecting gauges, make sure the cooling system is not malfunctioning.

6. Fuel level—Same as oil pressure gauge.

WARNING
When removing the sender, gasoline in the tank is exposed. Do not let smoking materials, open flame or electrical sparks near the tank.

NAVIGATIONAL INSTRUMENTS

Navigational instruments used aboard pleasure boats may include:

a. Knotmeter with or without log.

b. Depth gauge.

c. Wind speed/direction.

d. Compass.

The depth gauge and knotmeter consist of the instrument itself, with indicator and a separate transducer. The location of the transducer depends on a number of factors and should be selected according to the manufacturer's instructions. **Figure 21** and **Figure 22** are typical installations for troubleshooting purposes. Windspeed/direction instruments consist of a mast top-mounted transducer assembly and a separate indicating instrument. From a troubleshooting standpoint, it is similar to a depth gauge or knotmeter. See **Figure 23**.

If visual inspection fails to show the trouble, borrow an identical indicator unit and substitute it for yours. If this solves the problem, the indicator unit was defective. If this doesn't solve the problem, replace the transducer. On some through-hull installations, this requires haul-out,

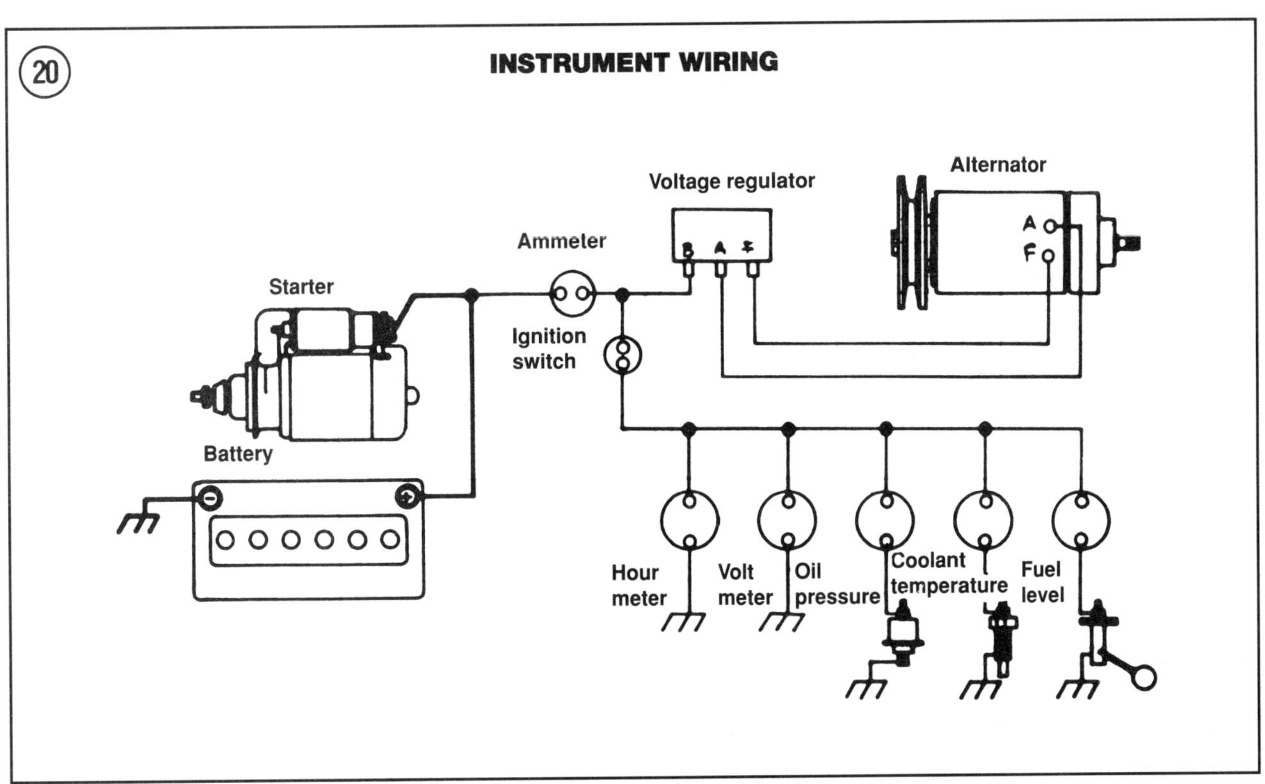

21

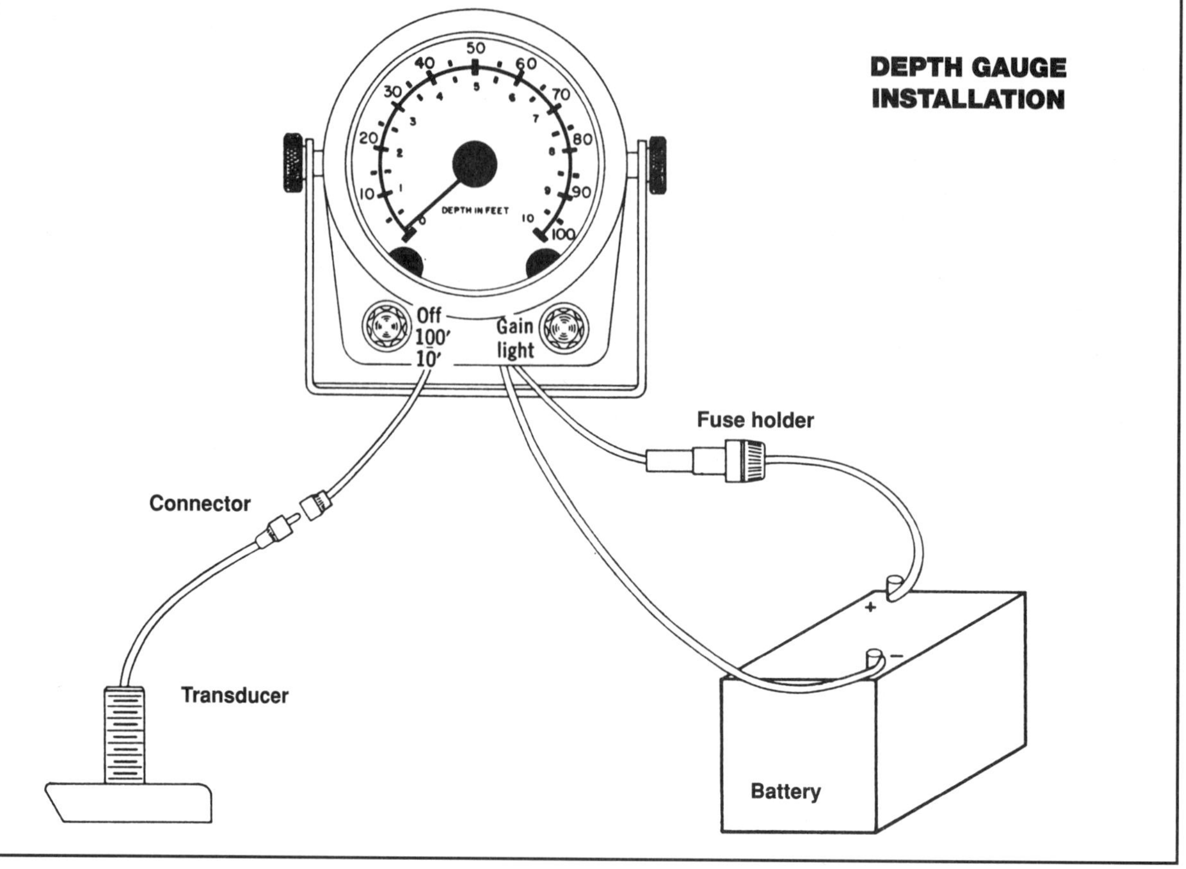

DEPTH GAUGE
INSTALLATION
DEPTH IN FEET
Off
100′
10′
Gain
light
Fuse holder
Connector
Transducer
Battery

22

KNOTMETER
INSTALLATION
KNOTS
Fuse holder
Transducer
Battery

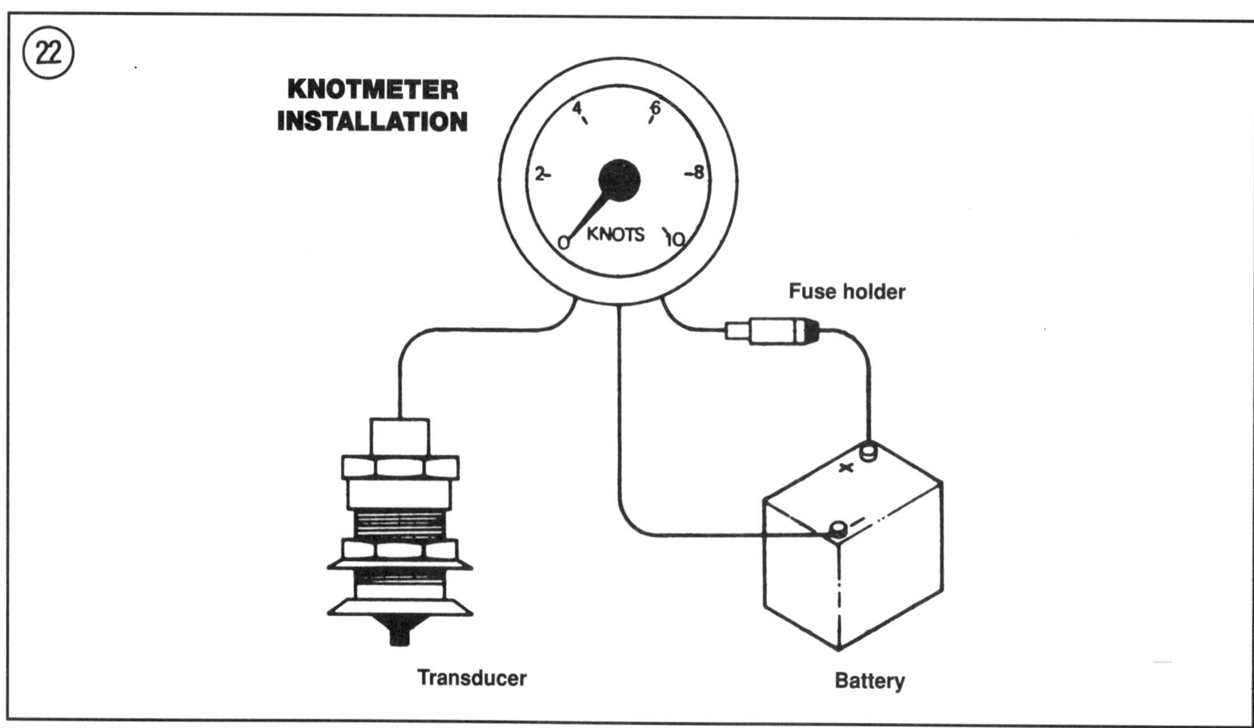

though some transducers can be re-placed from inside the bilge.

Erratic readings may be caused by instrument or transducer failure, poor electrical connections or interference from the engine ignition system. See *Noise Suppression* in this chapter for possible cures for noisy ignitions.

The compass is usually completely self-contained. Follow its manufacturer's recommendations for placement and installation. Defective instruments must be returned to the manufacturer or a compass specialist for repair.

Troubleshooting

Troubleshooting navigation instruments is fairly straightforward. If the instrument fails completely, check the fuse and battery power connections. Also check the condition of the cable between the transducer and instrument.

(23) **WINDSPEED/DIRECTION INSTRUMENT INSTALLATION**

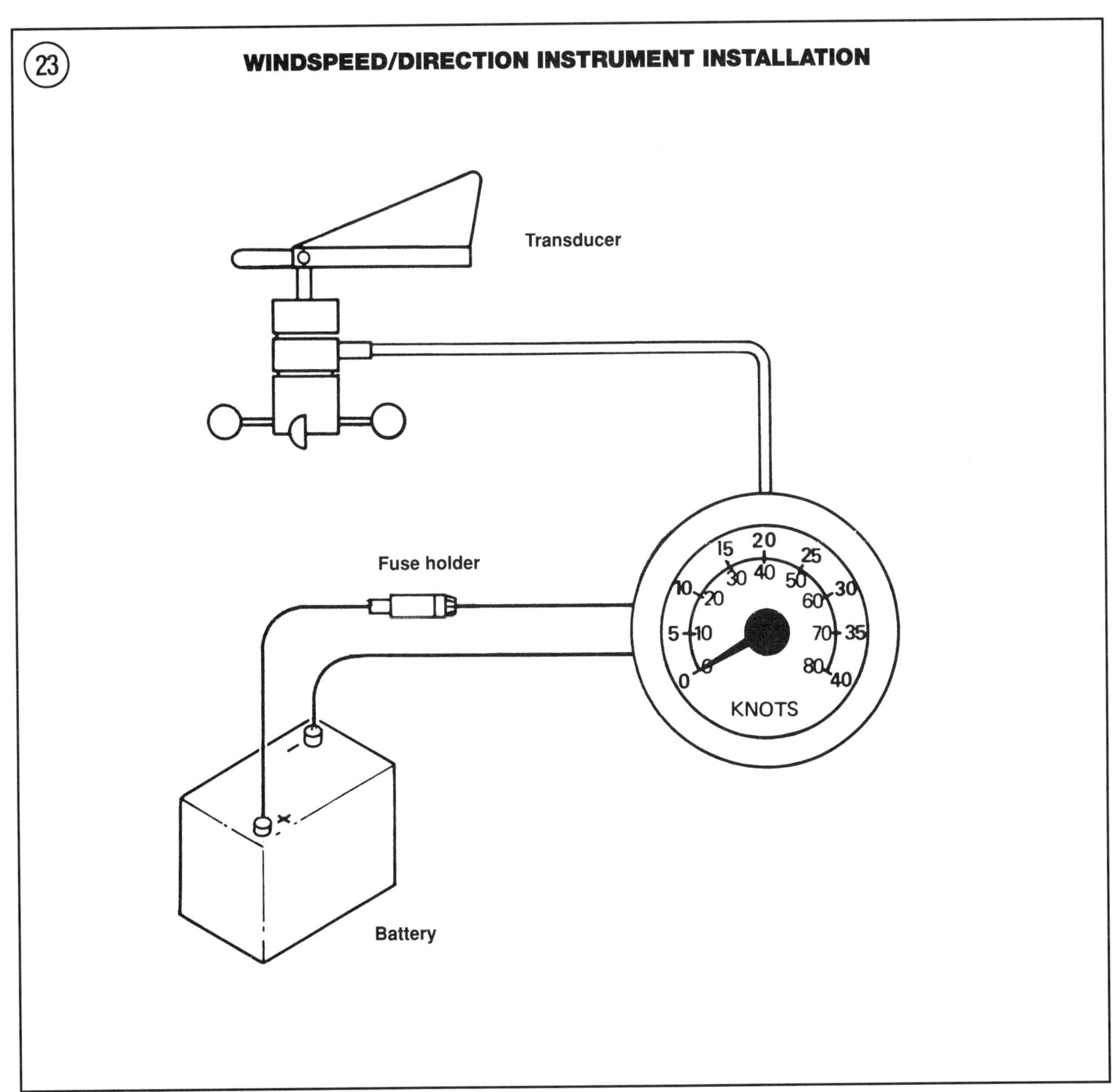

Chapter Nine

Galley

The galley is often the focal point of the boat. During warm weather, most of the crew shuttle between cockpit and galley for cold drinks and snacks. During cold weather or the dog watch, the galley means hot coffee to get through the night.

To enjoy the comfort and pleasure your galley is intended for, it must be clean and in working order. This chapter describes maintenance required to keep your stove, ice box or refrigerator in good condition.

COOKING FUELS

Marine stoves may be fueled by:

a. Alcohol.

b. Kerosene.

c. Liquid petroleum gas.

Each fuel has advantages and disadvantages for marine cooking. Sections which follow describe the characteristics of each fuel. No one fuel is clearly considered best, though everyone seems to have a preference.

Alcohol Systems

Alcohol is probably the most popular stove fuel on boats, mainly because it is generally considered to be the safest. This stems from the fact that it is easily extinguished by water. In addition, alcohol has a less objectionable smell to many people than kerosene.

Despite its popularity, alcohol has a number of serious disadvantages. True, it is easily extinguished by water, but its low flash point makes it 4 times more flammable than kerosene, making the risk of fire greater. Furthermore, when burning, the flame is often invisible; if a spill ignites, there is no telltale flame to help locate the fire. Finally, alcohol does not burn as hot as kerosene or propane; alcohol takes twice as long to boil water as kerosene.

Choose the alcohol to be used in a galley stove carefully. Use a good grade denatured ethyl alcohol. This is available in chandleries marked "marine alcohol stove fuel" or similar words. It is also available in hardware stores (for less money) as shellac thinner. Read the label carefully, however. Make sure it says denatured alcohol. Some shellac thinner is methyl alcohol mixed with a petroleum distillate. Pure methyl alcohol (wood alcohol) is also available, but it does not have adequate heat content for cooking. The last two products may clog the burners.

Kerosene

Kerosene is preferred over alcohol by many boaters. It burns hotter than alcohol, has a higher flash point, and often costs less than alcohol. Its only serious disadvantage is the smell which many people find objectionable. However, odorless kerosene is available in many areas.

Kerosene intended for marine stoves is usually clear. In fact, it is often called white gas. General purpose kerosene not intended specifically for stoves will quickly clog the burners.

If a kerosene fire occurs, it must be extinguished with a Coast Guard approved fire extinguisher, but this is standard equipment aboard any boat large enough to have a stove.

Liquid Petroleum Gas

Liquid petroleum gas (LPG) is usually propane, but it may also be butane. In fact, in some areas of the country the two are blended to keep the cost down. LPG is odorless, convenient and instant lighting, making it the ideal marine fuel for many boats.

LPG is stored as a liquid under pressure in specially designed tanks. For convenience, most boats use portable 2.5 or 5 gal. (9.5-19 L) tanks that can be carried to a refill station.

When the tank is upright, gas may be drawn from the top of the tank to fuel appliances such as a stove. Liquid evaporates in the tank, replenishing the supply of gas as it is drawn off for use. In very cold weather, the pressure of butane can drop to the point where appliances no longer work. Propane maintains a suitable pressure in any weather that you are likely to operate your boat.

LPG is not without disadvantages, though. Since it is stored under pressure, leaks can occur. Furthermore, LPG is heavier than air and could settle in the bilge—a potentially explosive situation.

These disadvantages can largely be overcome with a properly installed supply tank in a sealed compartment separate from the interior and vented overboard. You can build something from wood or buy one of the commercially available propane lockers. All plumbing must be installed according to published and recognized standards and the supply must be shut off at the tank when not in use.

Many galley stoves use small disposable propane bottles which cannot be refilled. These are relatively convenient until you forget to buy them. Most propane appliances can be converted to operate from the boat's LPG supply. Contact the appliance manufacturer for the required parts.

Compressed Natural Gas

9

Substituting lighter-than-air compressed natural gas (CNG) would lessen the seriousness of leaks since it won't settle in the bilge, but CNG is not easily available in some parts of the country and is rarely used onboard a boat. Also burners must be jetted to work with CNG which requires much larger orifices than LPG.

WARNING

CNG and LPG should never be used interchangeably. While using CNG in an LPG system would simply fail to produce sufficient heat, LPG in a CNG system could be dangerous.

ALCOHOL/KEROSENE SYSTEMS

The simplest alcohol/kerosene stoves have an integral tank which is pressurized by a small hand pump on the stove. As fuel is consumed, the pump must be operated occasionally to maintain pressure. See **Figure 1**.

More sophisticated systems have a large capacity tank mounted some distance from the stove. The tank must be pressurized, usually with a bicycle tire pump, to about 7 psi. (48 kPa). See **Figure 2**. A hose connects the pressurized fuel to the stove which may be a simple 2-burner stove or a larger unit with top burners and an oven.

LPG SYSTEMS

The simplest LPG system consists of a one-or two-burner stove with integral replaceable cartridges. See **Figure 3**. Replacement cartridges are available at most fuel docks and sporting goods stores.

Large craft usually have a separate refillable storage tank or tanks mounted in a bottom-vented storage locker. See **Figure 4**. The pressure in the tanks can be as high as 100 psi. (689 kPa). A regulator mounted on or near the tank maintains a much lower pressure to the galley. A single stage regulator is used when there is only one tank. If there are two tanks, use a special two tank auto-change regulator which automatically switches from the empty tank to the full tank.

An electric solenoid controlled remotely from a panel in the galley should be installed after the regulator. The solenoid is normally closed when there is no power. This allows turning the propane flow on and off from the cabin.

Finally, a single supply hose with no fittings along its length connects the solenoid to the stove. This minimizes the chance of leaks along the hose in places that would be difficult to detect. Supply line hoses are available from marine chandleries and RV stores in a variety of lengths to fit any recreational boat.

Filling the Tanks

Filling tanks is a simple operation, but it requires care. There are two serious hazards associate with propane. The most obvious is that propane is a highly flammable gas. The other hazard comes from the fact that it is stored in liquid form under pressure. When released, it evaporates rapidly resulting in temperature drops so dramatic that contact with skin can cause severe frostbite.

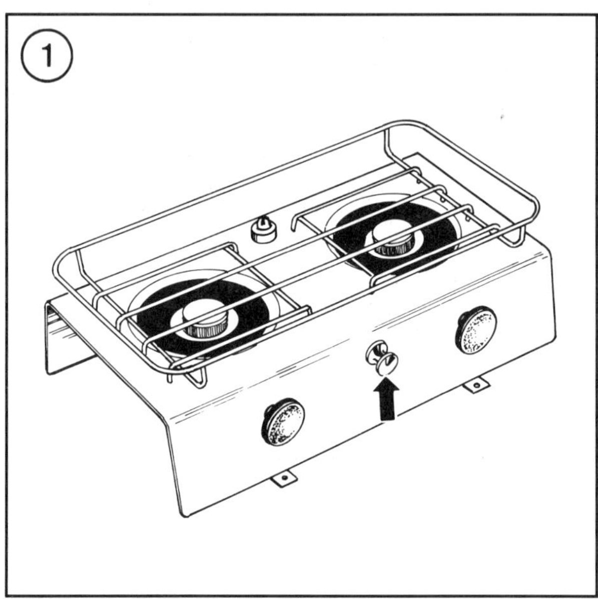

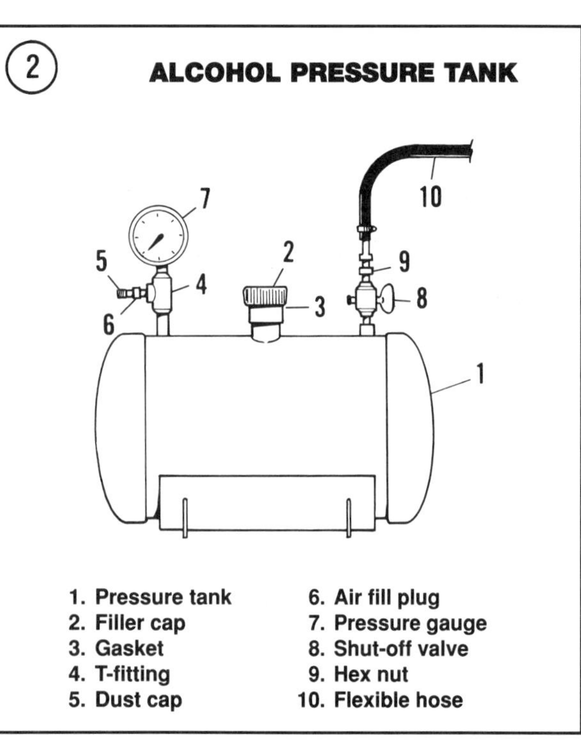

WARNING
When handling propane tanks, always wear eye protection and leather gloves. Keep a fire extinguisher nearby. Make sure all open flames have been extinguished and that no one is smoking in the vicinity.

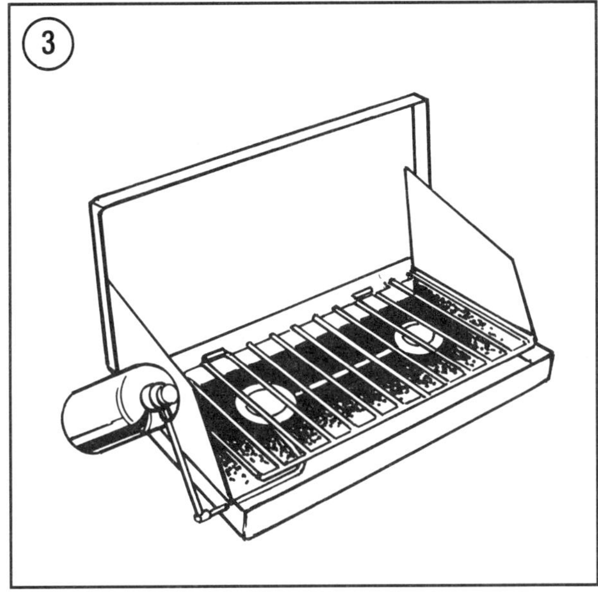

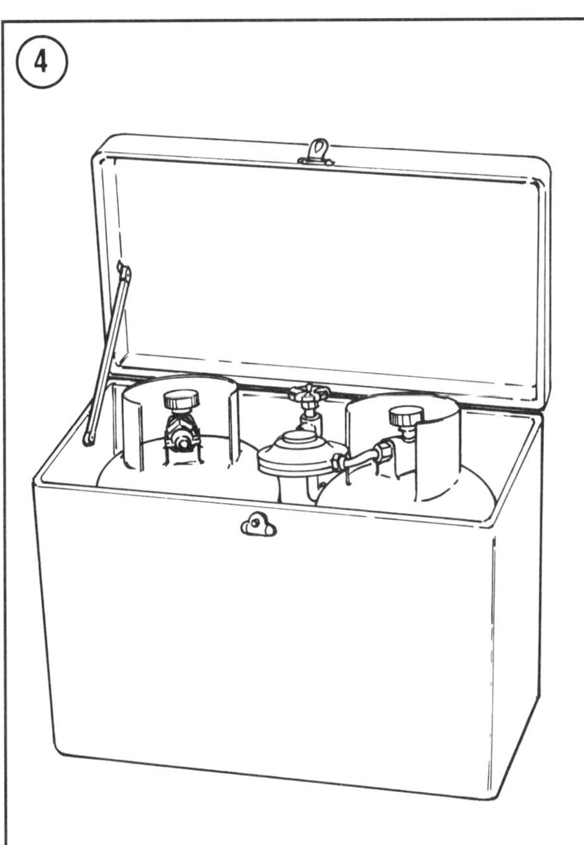

In most cases, the dockside operator will fill the tanks for you. If you are permitted to do it yourself, use the following procedure.

1. Shut off the main valve at the tank. See **Figure 5**.
2. Put on eye protection and leather gloves.
3. Disconnect the regulator from the main valve. Note that this fitting has a left-hand thread. Rotate it clockwise to loosen it.
4. Connect the valve from the refilling equipment to the main valve on the tank.
5. Open the main valve on the tank and open the "10-%" valve (**Figure 5**) which vents excess fuel to prevent overfilling.

WARNING
Be sure to open the "10-%" valve. It is so designed that liquid will emerge from it before the tank is full. If the tank were filled to capacity, any increase in temperature would cause an enormous increase in pressure, possibly resulting in

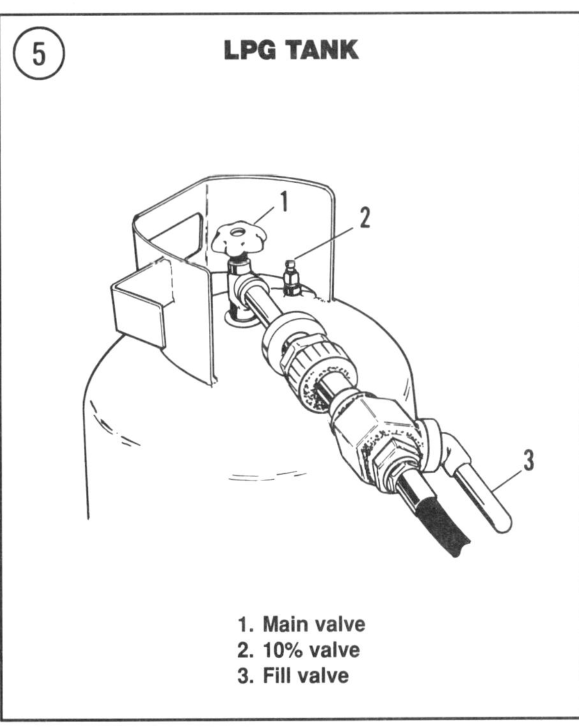

1. Main valve
2. 10% valve
3. Fill valve

tank rupture and explosion or fire. By allowing room for expansion, this possibility is prevented.

6. Start the pump on the refilling equipment and open the main supply hose valve. There will be a steady discharge of propane vapor from the "10 percent valve." When liquid emerges from the "10-percent" valve, close the main supply hose valve, then the main tank valve, then the "10-percent valve" in that order.
7. Slowly crack the connection between the main supply hose and the tank and allow the pressure to dissipate. When pressure is gone, disconnect the main supply hose.
8. Reconnect the regulator to the tank main valve.

Maintenance

Maintenance is limited to checking for leaks, checking lines for security or possible chafing, and occasionally painting storage tanks to prevent rust.

Leak Checking

Check every fitting periodically with a small brush and soapsuds (**Figure 6**). Any bubbles indicate a leak. Unless a line has worn through by chafing, leaks that occur will almost always be found at fittings. Never use a match or any flame for leak checking; to do so may cause an explosion or fire.

Leaks are almost always caused by a fitting which has loosened under vibration or shock. Tightening should repair it. Always use 2 wrenches to tighten brass fittings; one on the flare nut and the other on the mating fitting. See **Figure 7**.

It is good practice to shut off all gas at the main tank valve when the stove is not in use. Otherwise the line remains pressurized. If a leak were to develop, it might go undetected until it became a serious disaster.

LPG is odorized to aid detection in the event of a leak. If you notice a strong odor, shut off the main gas supply at once. Open all hatches and ports to allow the vessel to air out. LPG is heavier than air, and will tend to settle in the bilge. You can run the engine compartment blower which is explosion-proof and designed for this purpose. Do not use any other electric fans or vents onboard. Do not smoke, light lanterns or allow any

6

7

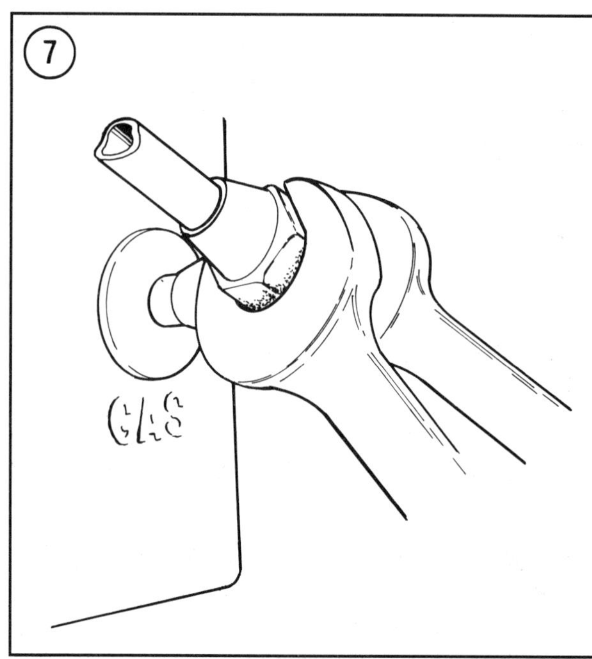

flame until the cause of the leak is discovered and repaired.

Leak Detection Systems

Electronic leak detection systems are available which shut off the fuel supply near the tank with an electric solenoid in the event of a leak. Some of them have more than one channel, meaning you can use the same instrument with one sensor for propane and another for gasoline or other fuel.

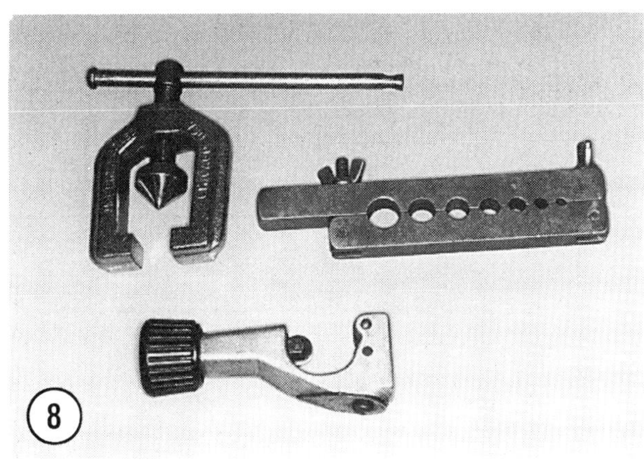
8

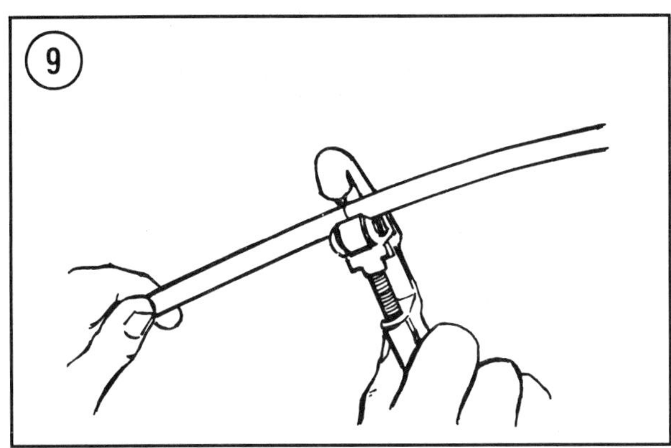
9

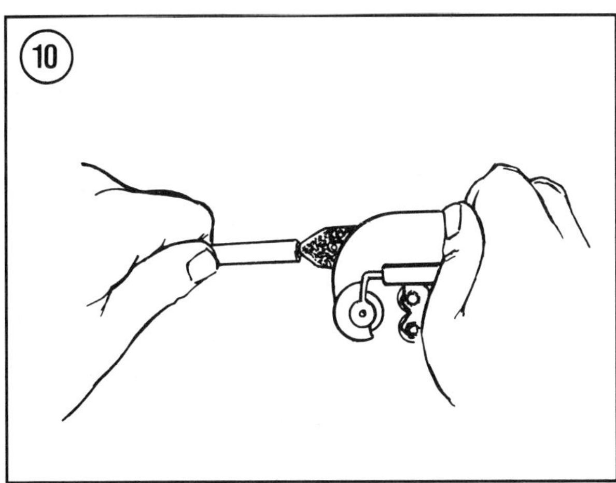
10

Replacing Fittings

Sometimes tightening a fitting does not repair a leak. The flared end of the tube might be split. If so, the tubing must be reflared. For this operation, a tubing cutter and flaring tool (**Figure 8**) are required.

1. Cut off the damaged tube as close as possible to the end, using the tubing cutter (**Figure 9**). Follow the tool manufacturer's instructions.
2. Remove and examine the old flare nut. If OK, it may be reused. Replacements are available at most auto parts and hardware stores.
3. Remove any burrs from the cut-off end of the tubing, using the tapered reamer which is part of the tubing cutter (**Figure 10**).
4. Slide the new flare nut onto the tubing. Be sure that the tapered end goes away from the mating fitting.
5. Flare the end of the tubing (**Figure 11**). Follow instructions supplied by the tool manufacturer.
6. Connect and tighten the new fitting.

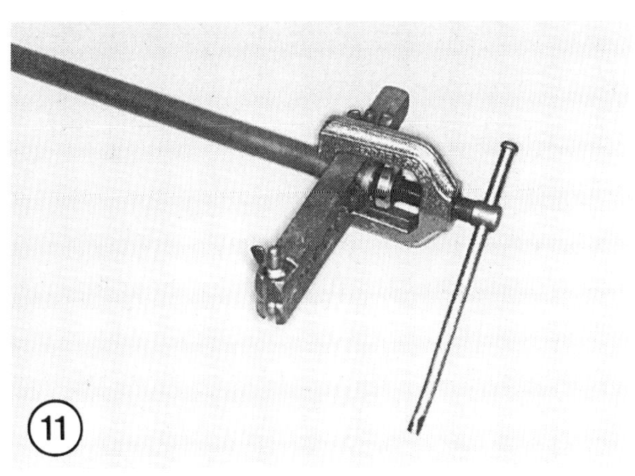
11

STOVES

Depending on the size of the boat, the galley stove may be a simple one-burner unit or a gimbaled multiburner range with oven. Many popular models are described in this section.

OPTIMUS/PRIMUS ALCOHOL AND KEROSENE STOVES

These stoves are nearly identical and all service procedures apply whether manufactured by Optimus or Primus and whether fueled by alcohol or kerosene. The only difference between alcohol and kerosene stoves is slightly different internal parts in the burners.

The best source of parts for Optimus/Primus stoves is A&H Enterprises, P.O. Box 101, La Mirada, CA 90637-0101, (714) 739-1788. They have been in business for over 30 years and even the Optimus factory in Sweden refers small parts orders to them.

Filling

Remove the safety cap and fill the tank. Use a funnel to prevent spills. See **Figure 12**. Wipe up any spills immediately to prevent fire when igniting the burners. Screw the cap on tight.

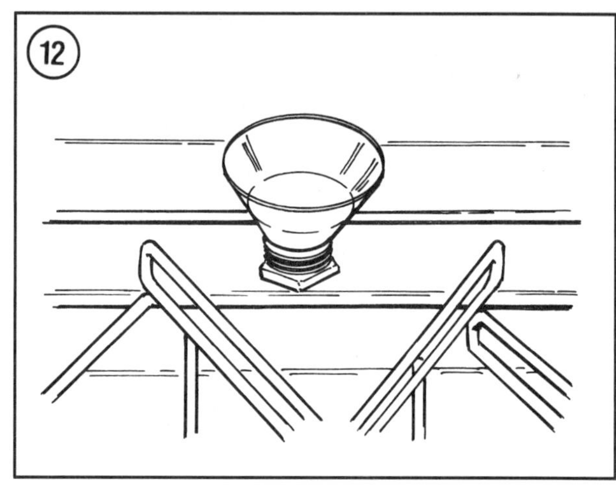

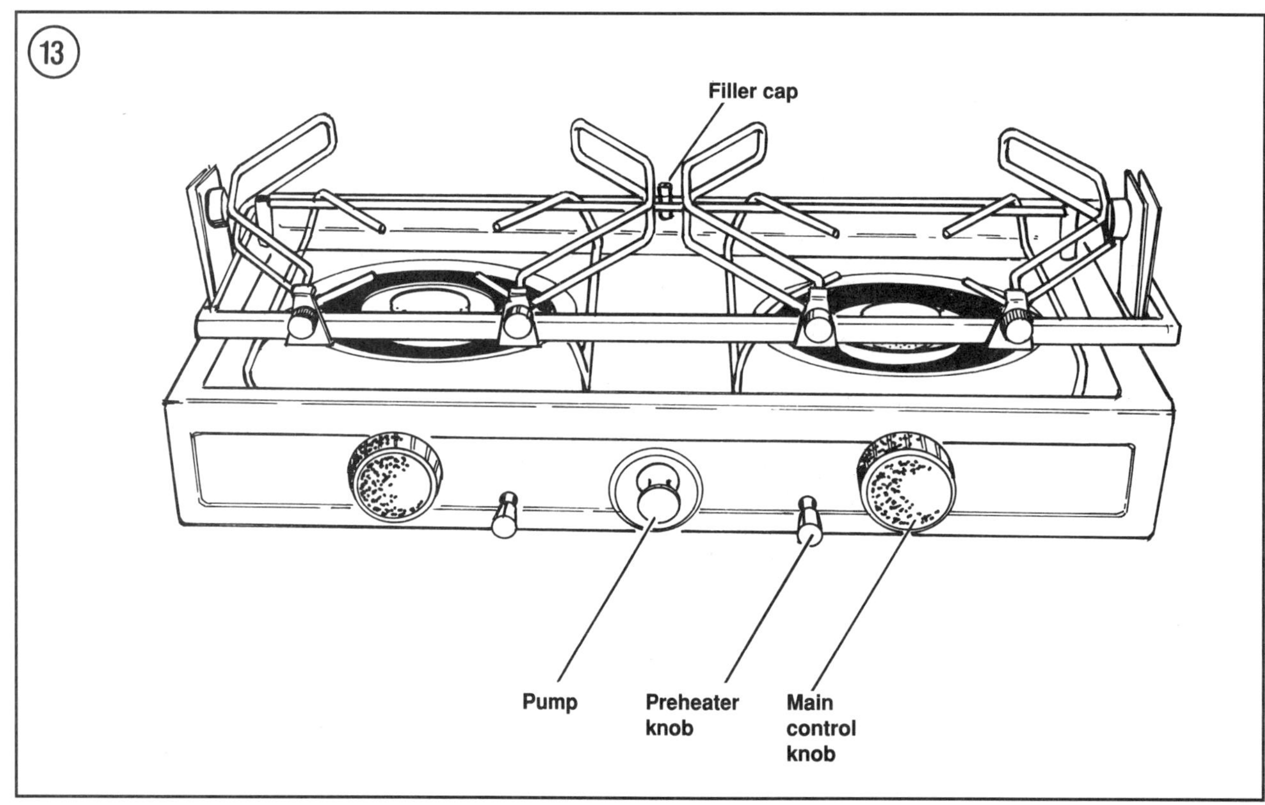

Operating the Stove

Refer to **Figure 13**.

1. Make sure the main burner knobs and preheater knobs are closed.

2. Operate the pump to pressurize the fuel tank. About 30 strokes are necessary with a full tank. More will be necessary for a partially filled tank.

15

3. Hold a lighted match or igniter at the side of the preheater outlet. See **Figure 14**. Pull the preheater knob out and light the alcohol or kerosene vapor.

WARNING
*The preheating fuel burns several inches above the burners. Make sure the area around the stove is clear of flammable materials. A&H Enterprises sells an alcohol gel (**Figure 15**) which can be squirted into the preheating tray. This burns in a much more controlled way than liquid alcohol.*

4. Hold the knob out and allow to burn for 30-45 seconds. See **Figure 16**.

5. Turn on the main control knob and push in the preheater knob. Main burner should burn with a blue flame. If a high yellow flame emerges, preheat the burner for another 10 seconds.

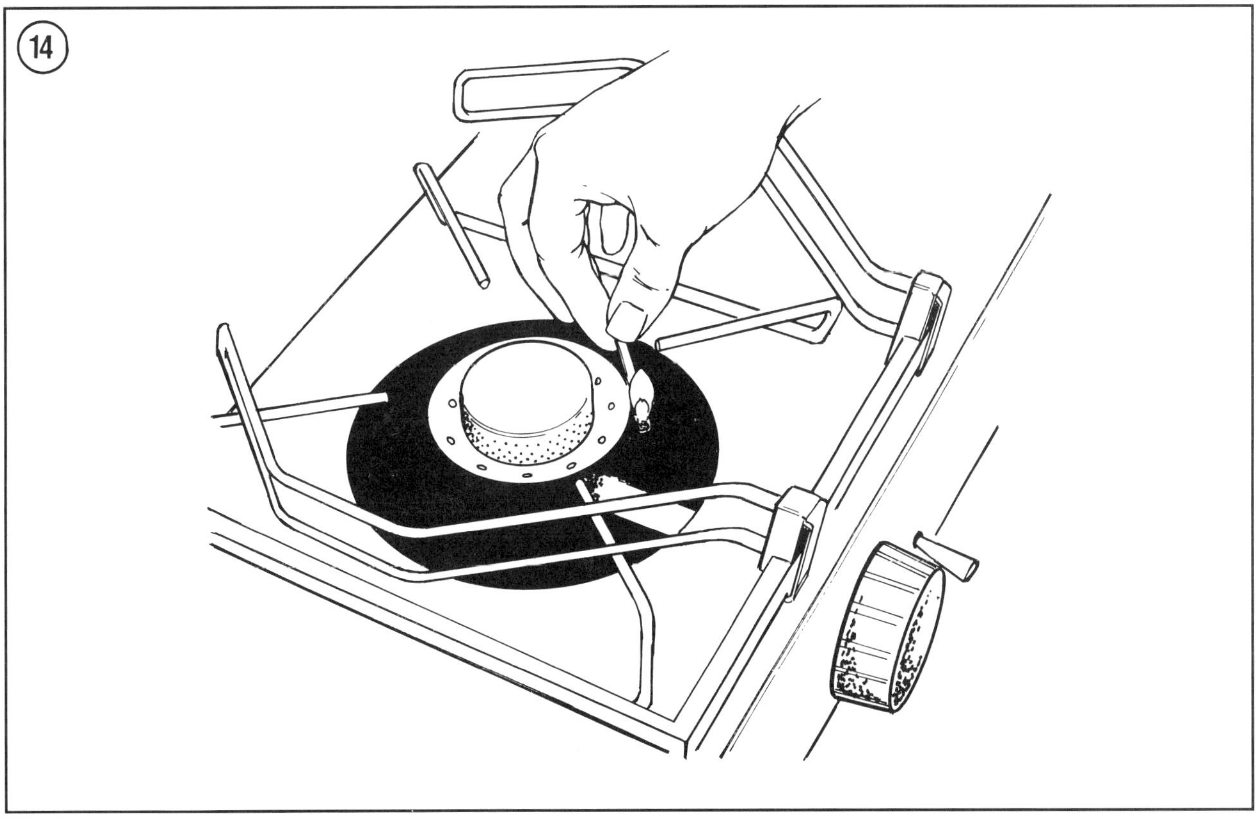

14

16

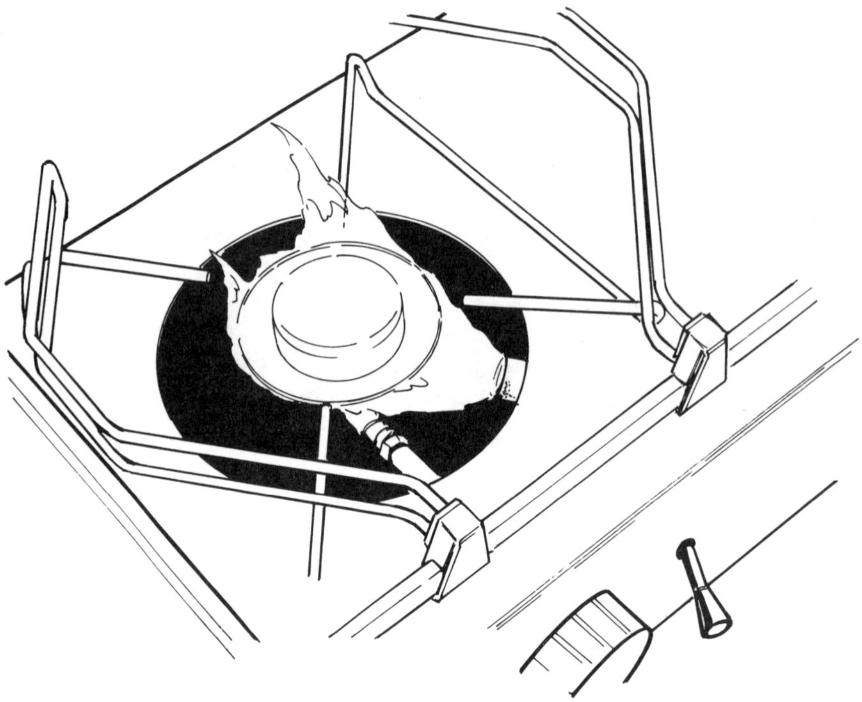

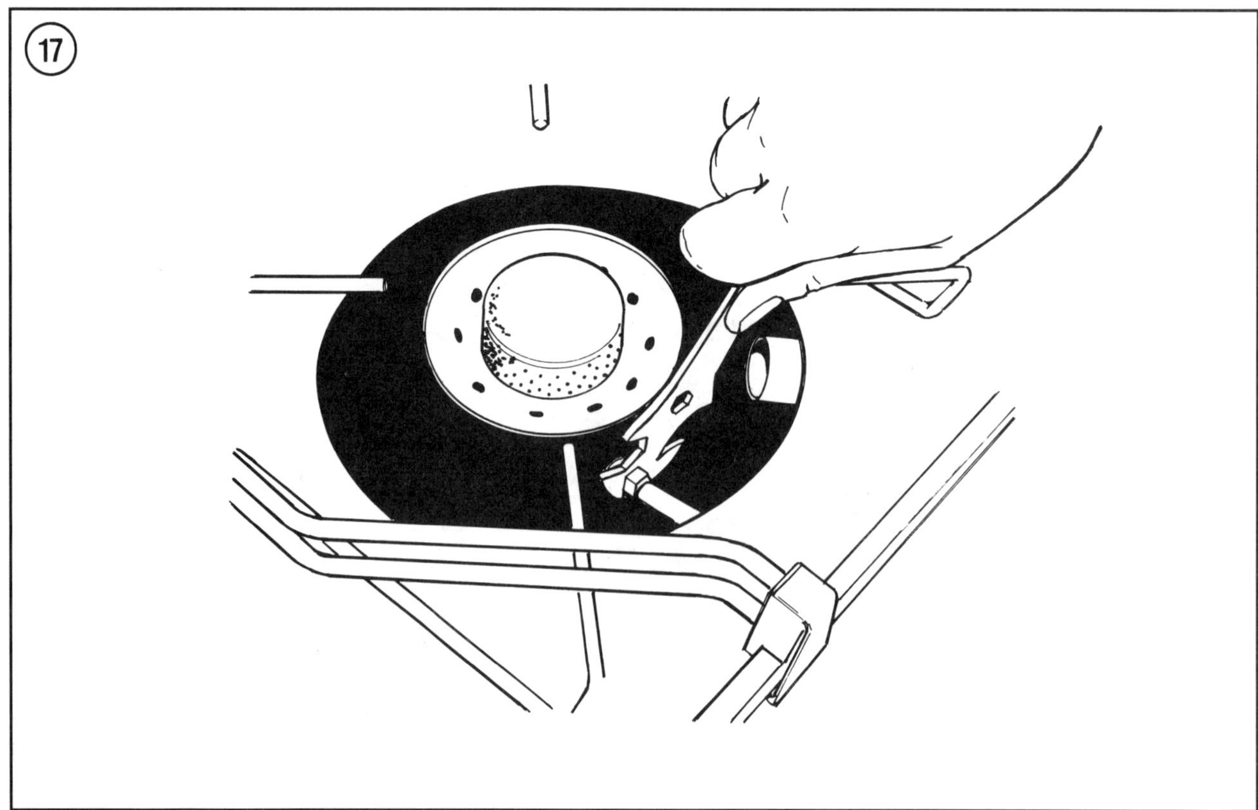

6. Regulate the flame as desired with the main control knob. Operate the pump as necessary to maintain pressure in the tank.

Cleaning and Maintenance

If the burner smokes or burns unevenly, turn the main control knob quickly counterclockwise as far as possible, then back again. Keep a lighted match handy in case the flame goes out.

If the burner leaks at the stuffing box, tighten the stuffing box nut as shown in **Figure 17**.

WARNING
Wipe up all fuel spills and accumulated cooking grease. If allowed to accumulate a serious fire could occur.

Changing Nipple

Refer to **Figure 18** or **Figure 19** for the following procedure.

1. Remove the outer and inner caps. See **Figure 20**.
2. Remove the nipple with the special tool shown in **Figure 21**.

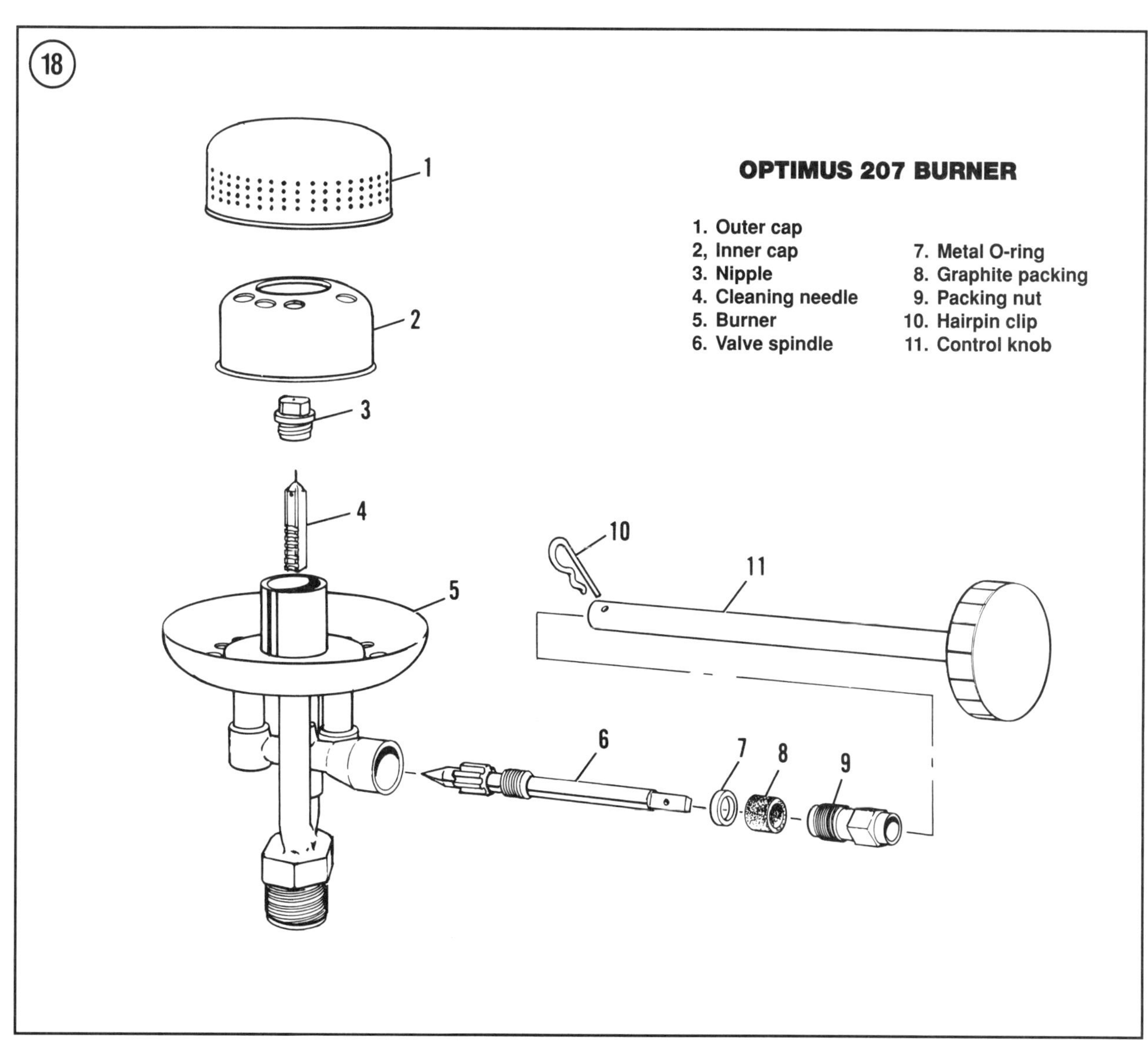

3. Installation is the reverse of these steps. Be careful not to damage the needle when installing the new nipple.

Changing Needle

Refer to **Figure 18** or **Figure 19** for the following procedure.

1. Remove the nipple as described above.
2. Turn the control knob counterclockwise and remove the needle.
3. Insert a new needle. It may be necessary on some burners to use tweezers to insert the needle. If tweezers are not available, very carefully stick the needle into the end of a wooden match, then insert it. If you bend the needle, you will have to buy a new one.
4. Turn the control knob clockwise until 3 or 4 cogs on the valve spindle have passed. Keep the needle teeth firmly against spindle.
5. Turn the control knob clockwise as far as possible.
6. Install the nipple.
7. When the needle is correctly installed, it will just be visible in the nipple hole when the control knob is opened 1/3 from fully closed. If the

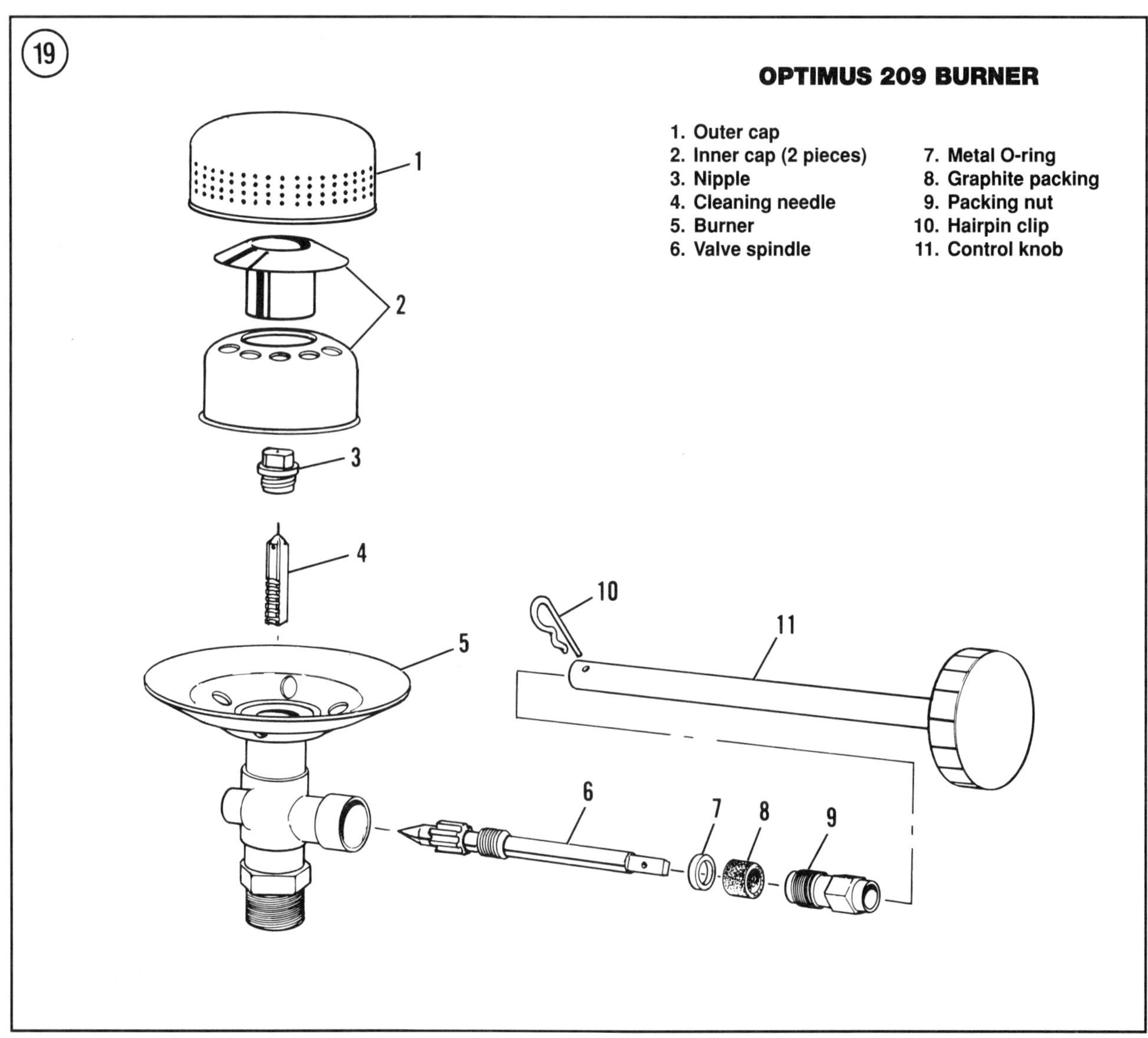

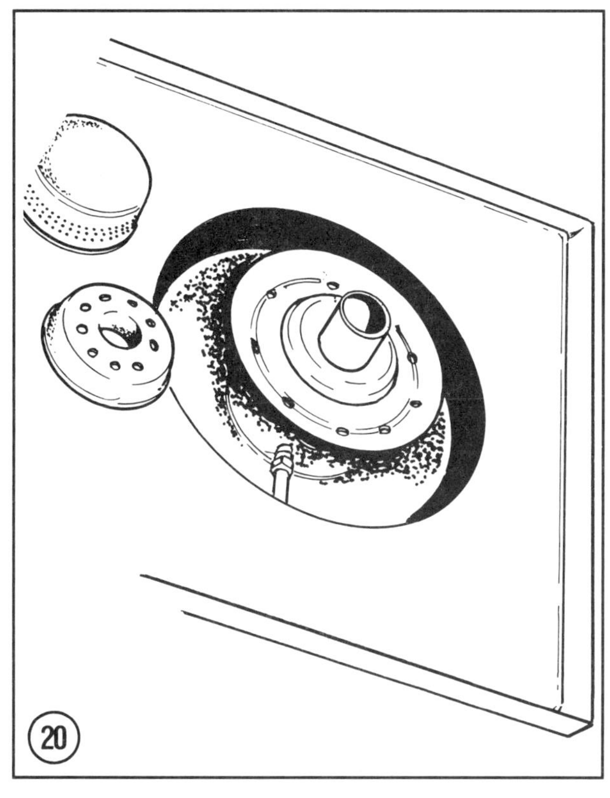

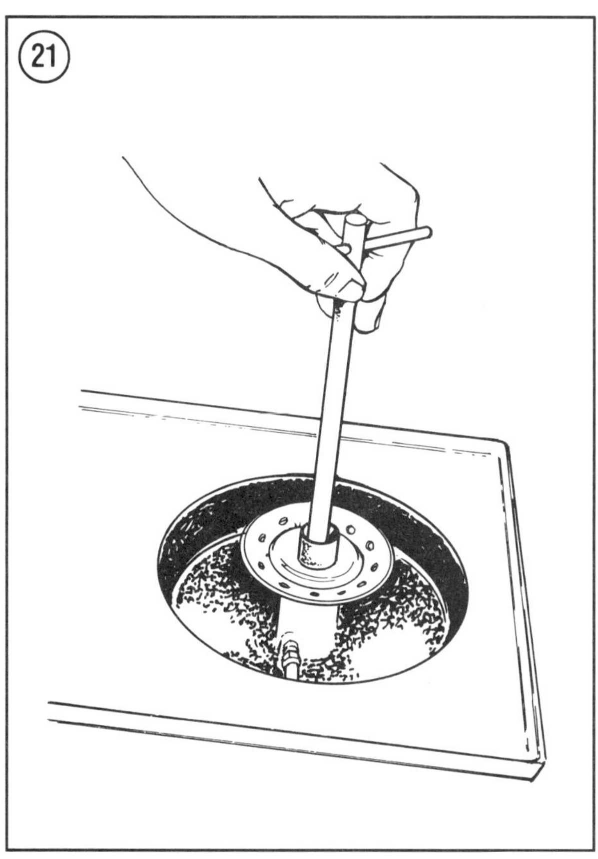

control knob must be opened more than this, repeat Steps 3-6.

Rebuilding the Control Valve

The spindle valve has a graphite packing which prevents leaks around the valve. If leaks occur which cannot be cured by slightly retightening the packing nut, the valve should be rebuilt. Refer to **Figure 18** or **Figure 19** for the following procedure.

1. Remove the nipple and needle as previously described.
2. Loosen the valve packing nut with the special tool and unscrew the regulating screw.
3. Replace the parts shown in the rebuild kit in **Figure 22**.
4. Assembly is the reverse of these steps.

Troubleshooting

Optimus/Primus stoves are simple devices and rarely give trouble. If you have a problem refer to **Table 1** for help.

HOMESTRAND/KENYON ALCOHOL STOVES

These stovcs are no longer in production. Parts for Homestrand stoves are no longer available.

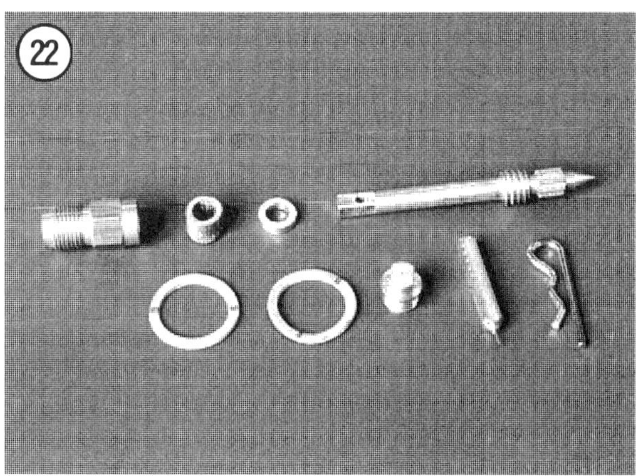

Parts for Kenyon stoves are available, but difficult to find. West Marine, a national chain, still carries some Kenyon parts. If you cannot buy replacement parts, or the burner itself requires replacement, you can substitute an Optimus 207A (alcohol) burner instead. See **Figure 23**. A&H Enterprises carries the necessary parts. Refer to *Optimus/Primus Alcohol and Kerosene Stoves* in this chapter for the address.

Filling

Unscrew the filler cap. Fill the tank with denatured alcohol using a funnel. Install and tighten the cap.

CAUTION
The filler cap has a built-in safety valve to prevent excessive pressure in the tank. Do not replace it with any other type cap.

Operation

1. Operate the pump 20 or more times to pressurize the tank.
2. Slowly open the knob for one burner (counter-clockwise) to allow alcohol to flow into the priming cup below the burner body. Fill the cup about 3/4 full, then shut the knob off.

WARNING
*The preheating fuel burns several inches above the burners. Make sure the area around the stove is clear of flammable materials. A&H Enterprises sells an alcohol gel (**Figure 15**) which can be squirted into the preheating tray. This burns in a much more controlled way than liquid alcohol.*

3. Ignite the priming cup alcohol.
4. When priming alcohol is fully consumed, turn the burner on and light it.

WARNING
The burner may flare-up during preheating, particularly if the burner is turned on before preheating is complete. If flare-up occurs, turn the burner off and restart following the directions above.

5. When the stove is shut off, open the filler cap to relieve the pressure and prevent leaks.

Regulating the Flame

To adjust the burners:
1. Light the burners.
2. Observe the flame. If the flame is orange or light blue and pulsating, regulation is necessary.
3. With burners lit, hold the burner flange with a pair of pliers and rotate the flange. See **Figure 24**. Adjust until a steady blue flame is achieved. This requires only a few degrees of rotation.

Troubleshooting

1. If you find a small flame where the control stem enters the burner, tighten the packing nut slightly until the flame no longer appears. See **Figure 25**.
2. If you notice alcohol in or around the pump, replace the check valve located in the bottom of the pump barrel.
3. If the pump bounces back when you try to pump, the check valve is stuck and must be replaced.
4. If you pump and get little or no pressure in the tank, the pump leather or U-cup needs to be replaced.

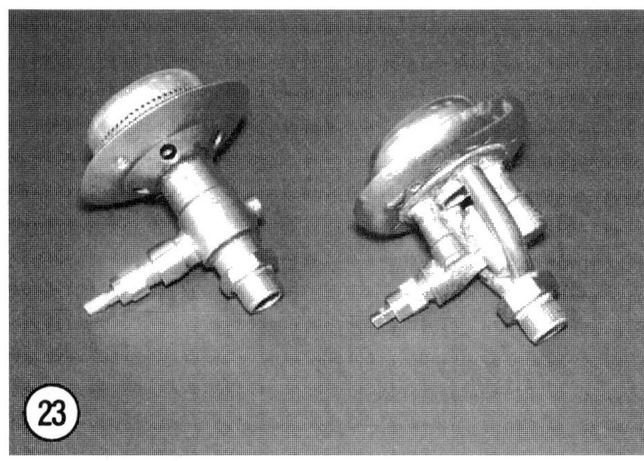
23

5. If your stove lights but goes out after a while, check for a leaking filler cap.
6. If no alcohol comes through the burner when you attempt to prime it, make sure tank is pressurized. Also check the burner filter. This filter rarely clogs, but may be replaced as described later in this section.

Alcohol Burner Disassembly/Assembly

This procedure applies to all Homestrand alcohol burners. Refer to **Figure 26**.

1. Snap off the outer cap with screwdriver.
2. Remove the inner cap.
3. Unscrew the nozzle with the special tool shown in **Figure 27**.
4. Turn the control knob off (fully clockwise) and lift out the cleaning needle.

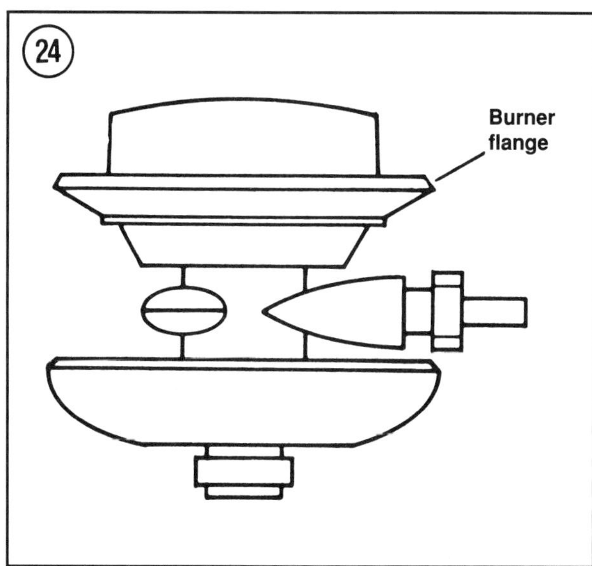

5. Remove control shaft pin and remove the shaft.
6. Unscrew the valve nut and remove the valve.
7. Unscrew the burner body from the burner fitting.
8. Remove the strainer from the burner body.
9. Clean all parts thoroughly in clean fuel.
10. Install the strainer in the burner body.
11. Screw the burner body onto the burner fitting. Use a copper gasket.
12. Screw the valve into the burner body. If the packing is damaged or the needle end of valve is worn, replace the entire valve assembly.
13. Install the control shaft.
14. Turn the knob fully clockwise.
15. Set the cleaning needle in place.
16. Push down firmly on the cleaning needle and rotate the knob counterclockwise exactly 6 clicks.
17. Install the nozzle with the special tool.
18. Rotate the knob fully clockwise. Rotate 1/2 turn from fully off; the cleaner tip should just appear in the nozzle hole. If not, disassemble and repeat Steps 14-18.
19. Install the inner and outer caps.

Fuel Tank Disassembly/ Assembly

Refer to **Figure 28** for this procedure.

1. Unscrew the filler cap to relieve pressure.
2. Drain all fuel from the tank.
3. Unscrew the pump assembly from the tank and pull the assembly out.
4. Unscrew the pump check valve with the special tool.
5. Check the condition of the U-cap on the end of pump. If damaged, cracked, or worn, replace it.
6. Install the pump check valve with the special tool. Do not overtighten.
7. Apply light machine oil to the U-cap on the end of the pump.

8. Insert the pump assembly into the tank. Do not cut the U-cup on the tank. Tighten the assembly.

HOMESTRAND KEROSENE STOVES

Homestrand kerosene stoves are identical to the alcohol models except for the burners. Homestrand uses the Optimus kerosene burner described in an earlier section. Fill and operate the kerosene models as described for the alcohol models.

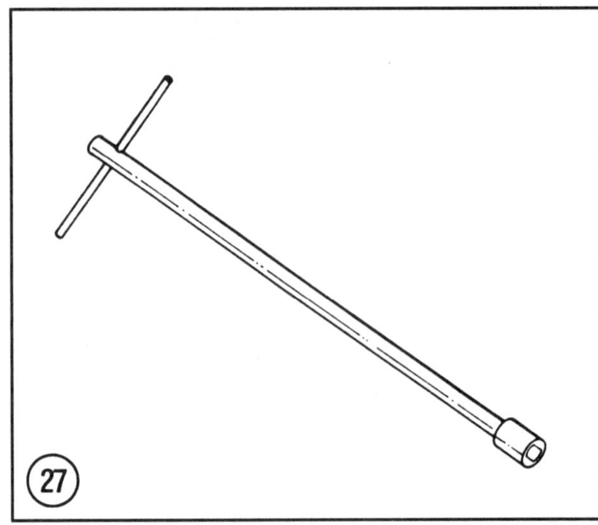

26

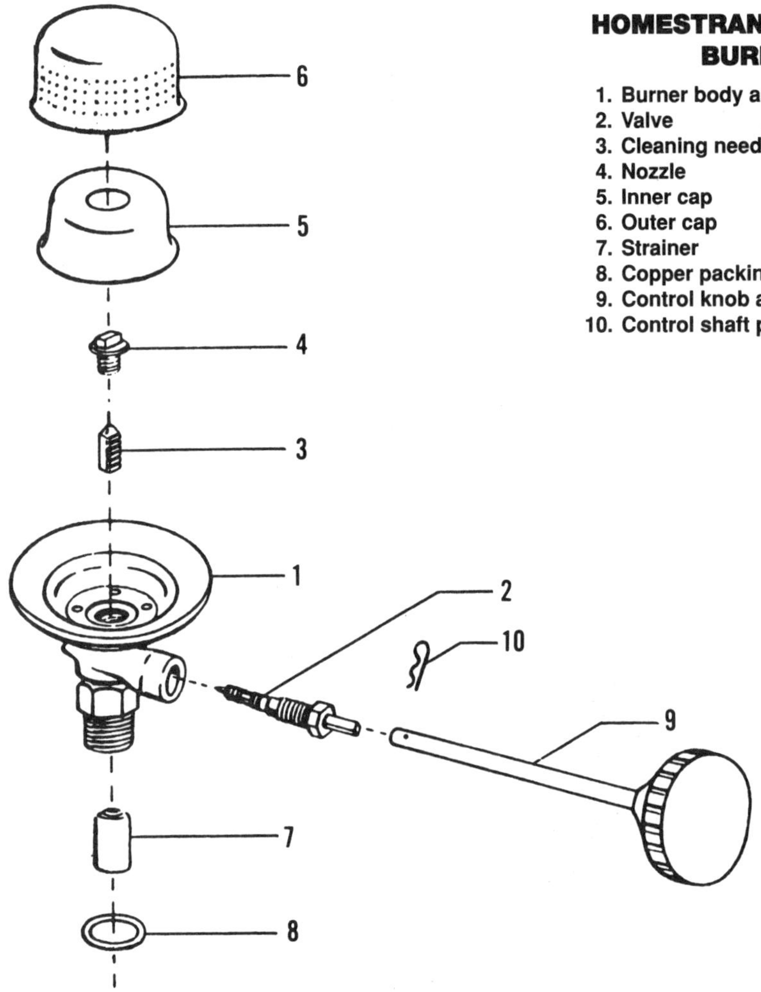

HOMESTRAND ALCOHOL BURNER

1. Burner body assembly
2. Valve
3. Cleaning needle
4. Nozzle
5. Inner cap
6. Outer cap
7. Strainer
8. Copper packing
9. Control knob and shaft
10. Control shaft pin

PROPANE MARINE STOVES

A number of manufacturers make propane stoves especially for boats. They range from simple stainless steel barbeques to multi-burner/oven units. The incredible range of products makes it impossible to cover all of them. If you don't have a service manual for your stove, order one so it will be available when you need it. The following sections show typical burners used on marine stoves.

Burner with Integral Control Valve

Some small single or dual burner LPG stoves have the control valve built into the stove similar to alcohol/kerosene stoves. See **Figure 29**. The valve itself is usually a simple needle and seat type. Disassembly for cleaning is usually not necessary for this type of burner. If the burner becomes defective, it usually must be replaced as a unit. Stoves may be fitted for disposable bottles or fueled from an onboard LPG system.

Burner with External Control Valve

Most small LPG stoves and barbeques do not have an integral control valve. Instead, the control valve connects to a disposable propane bottle (**Figure 30**). The burner itself is nothing but a cast body to support the outer cap. No maintenance is possible other than replacing the entire burner if it becomes rusted out.

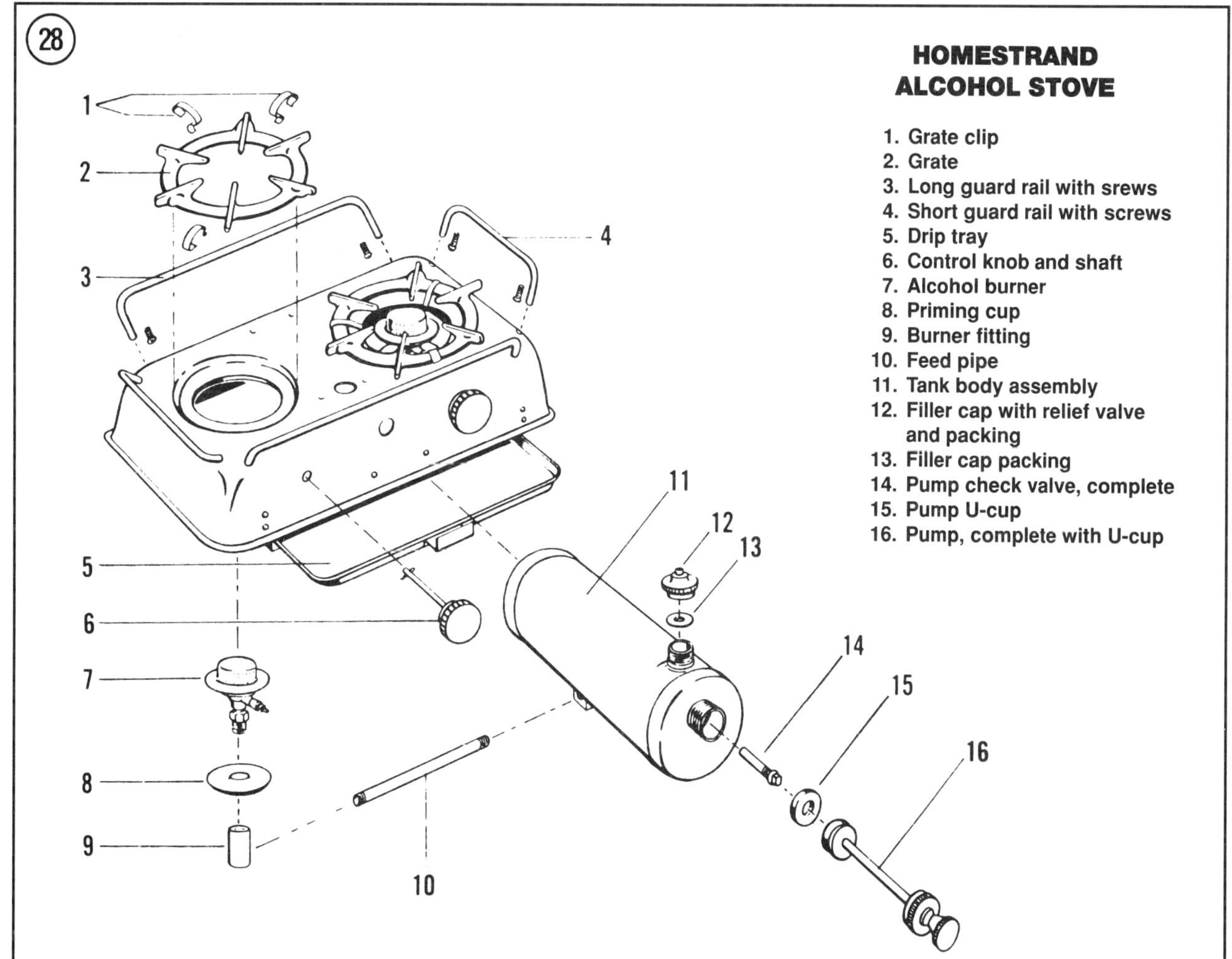

HOMESTRAND ALCOHOL STOVE

1. Grate clip
2. Grate
3. Long guard rail with srews
4. Short guard rail with screws
5. Drip tray
6. Control knob and shaft
7. Alcohol burner
8. Priming cup
9. Burner fitting
10. Feed pipe
11. Tank body assembly
12. Filler cap with relief valve and packing
13. Filler cap packing
14. Pump check valve, complete
15. Pump U-cup
16. Pump, complete with U-cup

Range-Style Burner

Range tops for LPG have burners very similar to those found on a home range. These usually incorporate a spark igniter for convenience and a thermocouple for safety. See **Figure 31**. The thermocouple shuts off the gas supply if the flame goes out. Considering the fact that LPG is heavier than air and would sink into the bilge, all marine LPG burners should have this feature. If yours does not, the burners can be replaced with new ones far less expensively than buying a new range top.

The thermocouple probe should be positioned so that it is centered within a flame from the burner. If the thermocouple no longer shuts off the gas supply as it should, the trouble may be the thermocouple itself or the valve body. You could substitute parts from another burner to determine which is at fault.

The spark igniter electrode may be bent closer to the burner if it is not lighting the fuel. If none of the spark igniters function, the piezoelectric igniter is probably defective.

Troubleshooting

1. Gas not reaching the burner.
   a. Make sure tank is not empty. Check the gauge. You can also lift it. Propane weighs

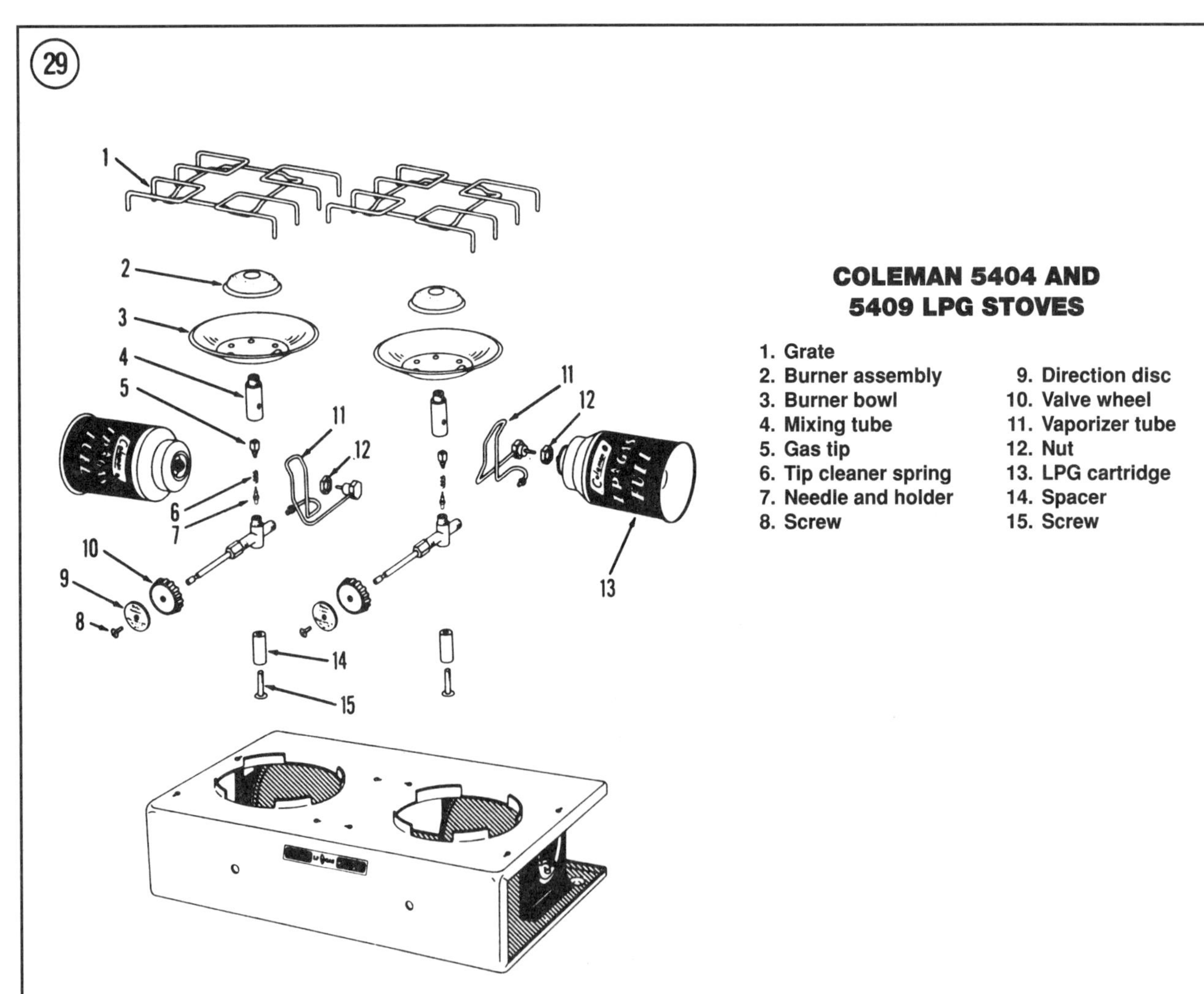

4.3 pounds/gallon. Markings on the tank will tell you how much the tank weighs empty.

b. Make sure the tank valve is fully open. Turn it counterclockwise.

c. Make sure the solenoid (if fitted) is open. It is normally closed without voltage. Check the voltage at the solenoid with a voltmeter.

d. Make sure the supply line is not pinched.

e. Check that the burner is not clogged. Disassemble according to the manufacturers service manual.

f. Purge the line of air by leaving one burner valve open. Don't allow gas to accumulate while doing this. Keep a match near the burner to detect a gas flow immediately. This may happen when the tank has been replaced. It may take some time until gas begins to reach the burner.

g. On range-style burners with a flame tube, make sure the tube is clear. Spiders and insects are attracted to the smell of LPG and frequently build nests which can clog the tube.

3. Spark igniter not working.

a. Check for adequate spark at the igniter on the burner. Sometimes you can adjust the spark gap by repositioning the spark plug. You have to remove the burner cover to reach the spark plug.

(30)

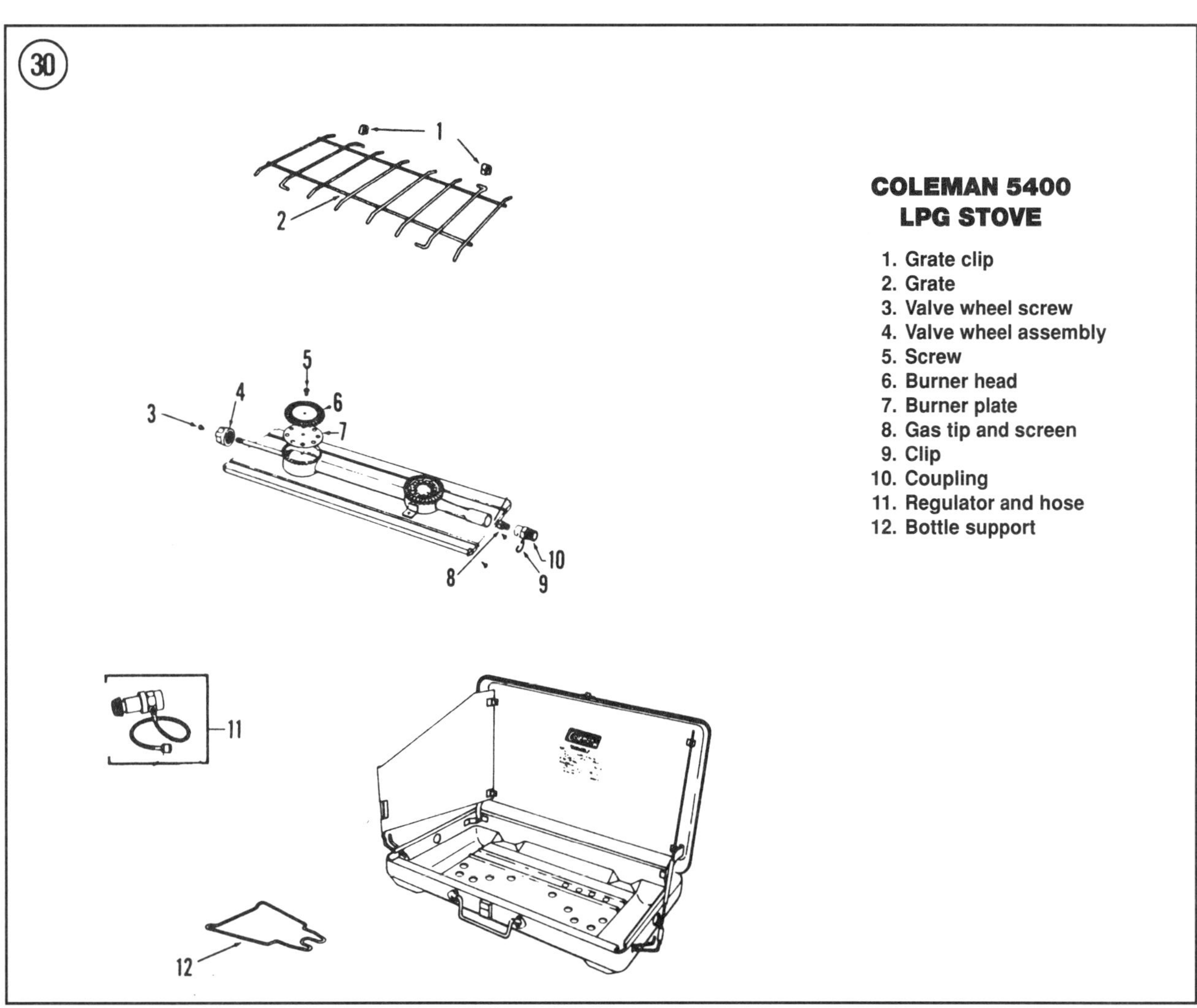

COLEMAN 5400 LPG STOVE

1. Grate clip
2. Grate
3. Valve wheel screw
4. Valve wheel assembly
5. Screw
6. Burner head
7. Burner plate
8. Gas tip and screen
9. Clip
10. Coupling
11. Regulator and hose
12. Bottle support

9

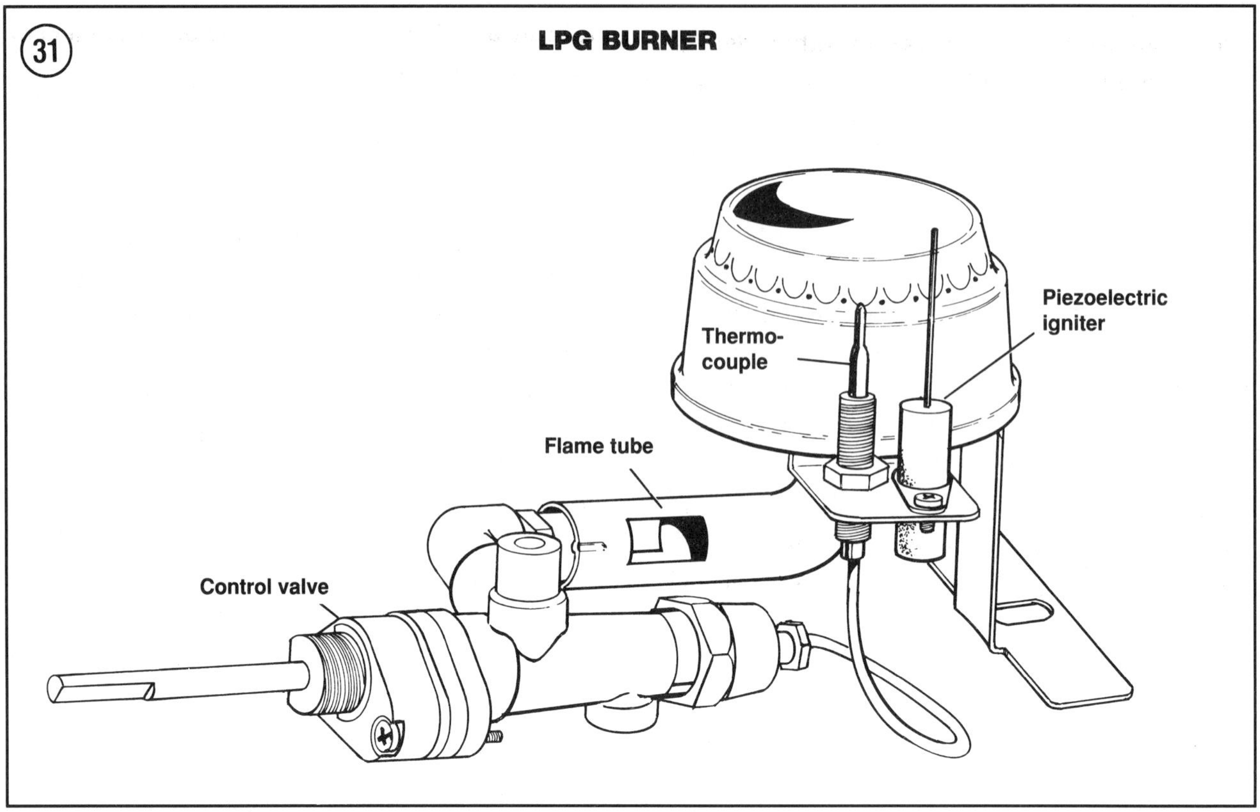

(31)

LPG BURNER

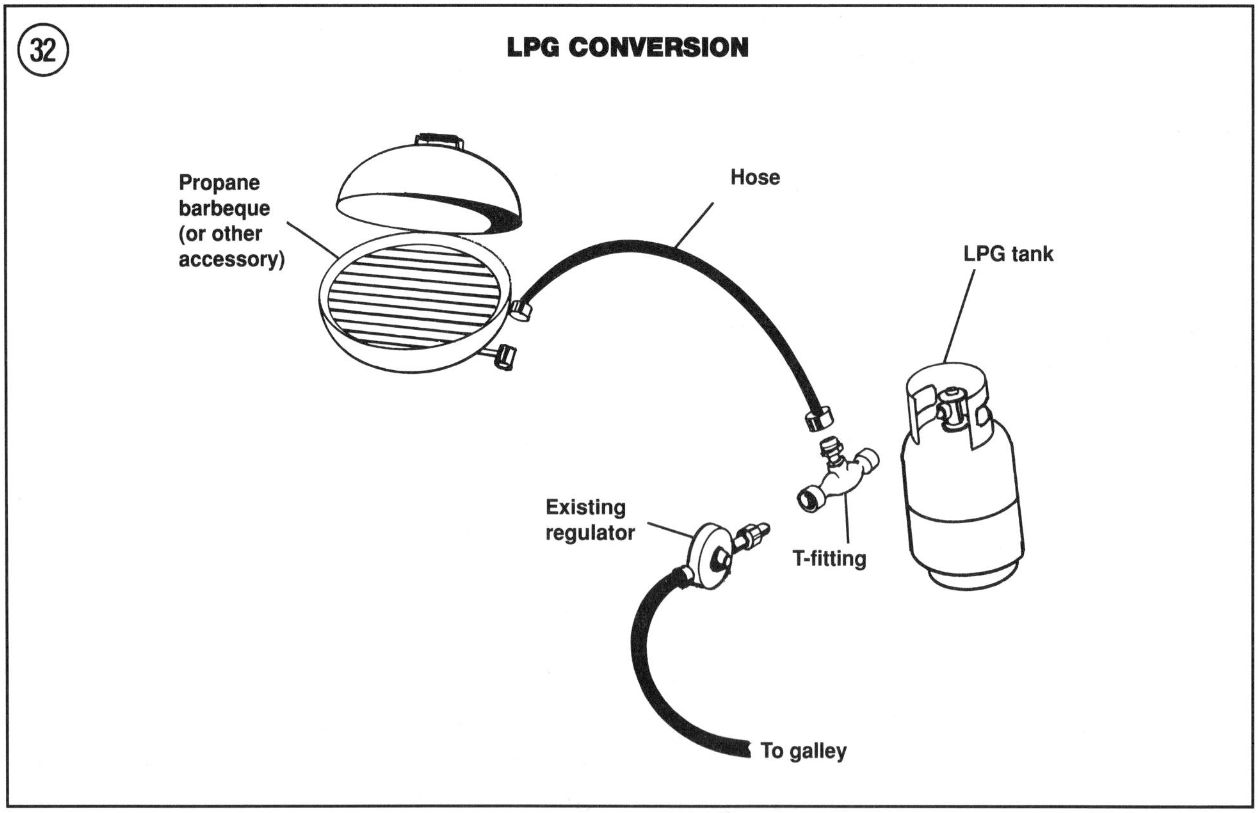

(32)

LPG CONVERSION

b. Clean away any grease or other debris around the spark plug. You can remove the burner cover to make this easier.

CONVERTING TO BULK LPG

Most small propane stoves and barbeques are designed to work from small disposable propane containers. Most can be refitted to operate from the onboard LPG system which normally uses a 2.5 or 5 gal. (9.5-19L) tank.

Figure 32 shows a typical system. You can buy the individual parts or a complete conversion kit from any RV store and most marine chandleries. You will need a connecting hose long enough to reach from the stove location to the propane bottle. This should be a continuous run, not two or more hoses connected together. You will also need an adapter to connect the hose to the stove control valve, and you will need an adapter to connect the hose to the P.O.L. fitting on the LPG tank. A regulator is usually not required since appliances designed for disposable bottles operate at the same pressures as bulk tanks.

Most onboard LPG systems have a regulator mounted on or near the bulk tank(s). This is used to reduce the system pressure since most built-in appliances are designed for low pressures. If you add an appliance designed for high pressure disposable bottles, you must use a special T-fitting ahead of the system's regulator so that it gets fuel directly from tank. See **Figure 33**.

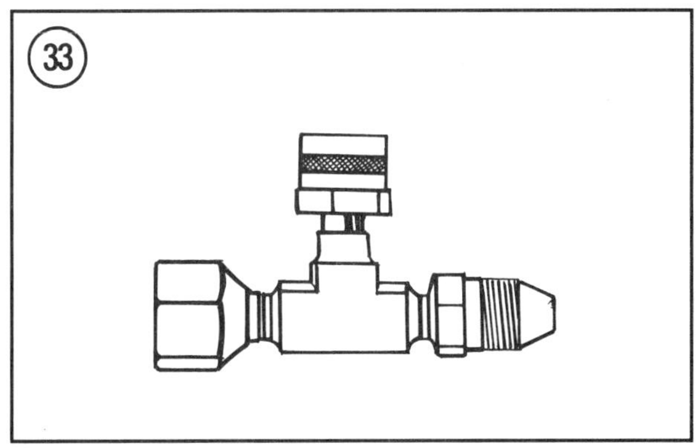

ICE BOX

Most boats big enough to have a galley have a built-in ice box. This is simply an insulated compartment with a drain at the bottom to drain off melted ice.

The ice box requires no maintenance other than frequent cleaning to remove food accumulation. After cleaning, leave the lid off to prevent mildew.

REFRIGERATORS

Nearly all refrigerators for marine use are electrically operated, and operate on the same principles as most home appliances. Absorption-type refrigerators which don't require a compressor are common in land recreation vehicles. However, these must be operated in a relatively level attitude and don't work well in the marine environment. 9

Basic Principles

Electrically operated refrigerators consist of:

a. Compressor.
b. Condenser.
c. Dryer.
d. Capillary tube.
e. Evaporator.
f. Thermostat control.
g. Thermostat sensing element.

The purpose of any refrigerator is to "make things cold," but it does this by removing heat not by adding cold. Basically, heat from the interior of the refrigerator passes to the refrigerant in the evaporator or cold plate and is eventually dissipated to the outside air by the condenser.

Two types of refrigeration systems may be used. They differ mainly in the way the refrigeration cycle is controlled. **Figure 34** shows a system controlled by a fixed orifice or capillary tube and compressor clutch cycling. **Figure 35** shows a system controlled by a thermostatic expansion valve.

The fixed orifice or capillary tube system is the simplest of the two. See **Figure 34**. The accumulator, located on the low pressure side of the system, serves a number of purposes. One purpose is to remove debris and moisture from the refrigerant. Another is to store excess liquid refrigerant, but allow only vapor to exit. The compressor draws vapor from the accumulator, compresses it to a high pressure and high temperature vapor and supplies it to the condenser. The condenser, which is located outside the refrigerator, dissipates heat from the vapor so that it changes into a high pressure liquid. The fixed orifice tube (FOT) meters the amount of high pressure liquid allowed to enter the relatively low pressure in the evaporator. The evaporator is located inside the referigerator and heat inside is transfered to the refrigerant by air circulating around the evaporator. The sudden pressure drop causes the low pressure liquid refrigerant to quickly expand or evaporate. The refrigerant, now in a low pressure vapor state, passes from the evaporator to the accumulator and the cycle repeats.

The expansion valve system operates in a similar manner, but there are important differences. See **Figure 35**. The compressor draws vapor from the evaporator, compresses it to a high pressure and high temperature vapor and supplies it to the condenser. The condenser dissipates heat from the vapor so that it converts to a high pressure liquid. The receiver/drier removes debris and moisture from the liquid refrigerant and provides it to a thermostatic expansion valve which meters the liquid into the

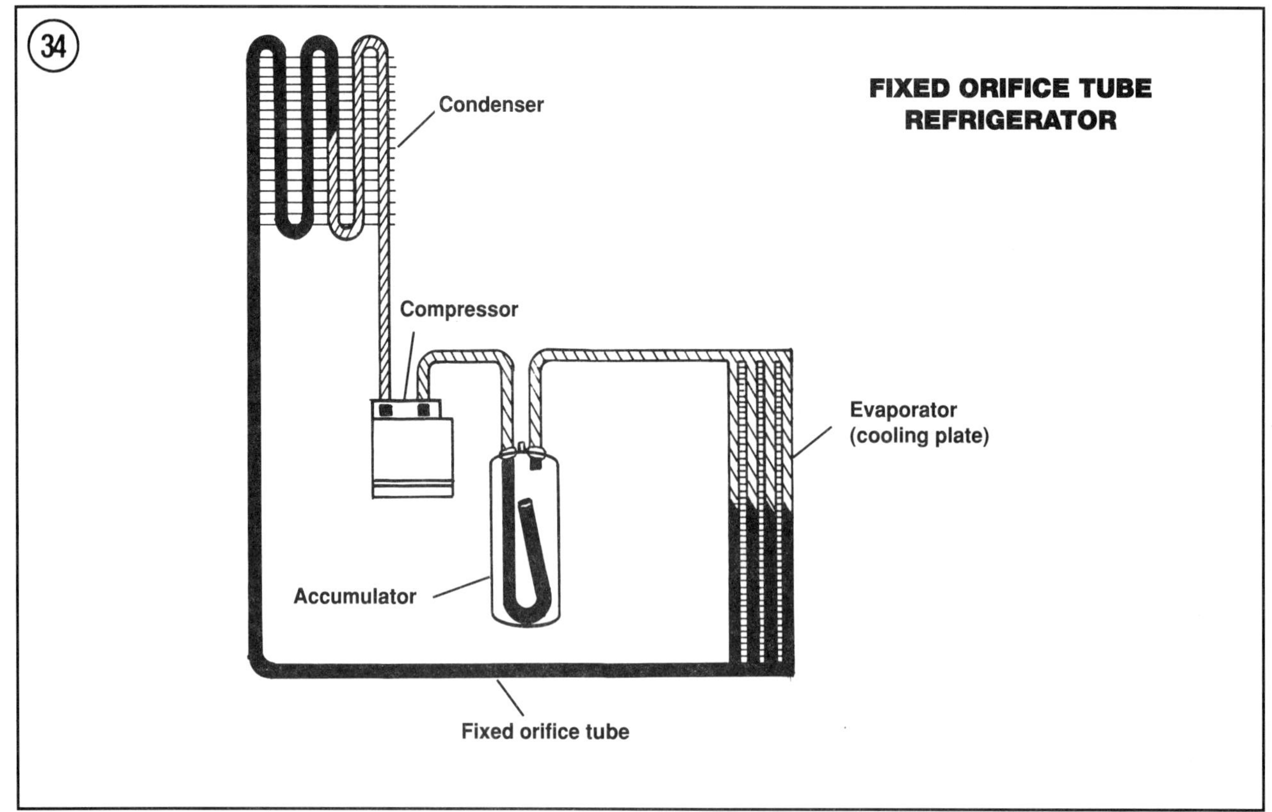

relatively low pressure in the evaporator. The expansion valve serves basically the same function as the FOT, except that the orifice is variable. The amount of liquid passing through the valve depends on the evaporator temperature.

In response to environmental concerns, many new refrigerators use R-134a instead of R-12 refrigerant. When R-12 is discharged to the atmosphere, such as when servicing the refrigerator, it rises to high altitudes, breaks down and releases chlorine. Chlorine is thought to be a major cause of deterioration in the ozone layer that protects the surface of the Earth from harmful ultraviolet radiation from the sun. Refrigerant R-134a does not contain chlorine and is considered safer than R-12 for the ozone layer.

Troubleshooting

Troubleshooting is relatively simple if you understand how the refrigerator works. Review the basic principles at the beginning of this section. The following are common symptoms and the probable cure:

1. Compressor runs continuously on either voltage supply (AC or DC), but no cooling is obtained. This indicates the system has a leak causing refrigerant loss, or the compressor is faulty.

2. Compressor runs continuously on either voltage supply and cabinet temperature is extremely cold. In this case, the thermostat is at fault. Check the capillary bulb of the thermostat. It is located under the evaporator and should be secured directly to the evaporator plate by means of a metal fastener. This tube should have a plastic sleeve and must contact the plate directly. If this capillary tube is intact and the plastic sleeve is in place, then the thermostat is faulty and should be replaced.

3. Compressor does not operate on either voltage. Perform the following checks:

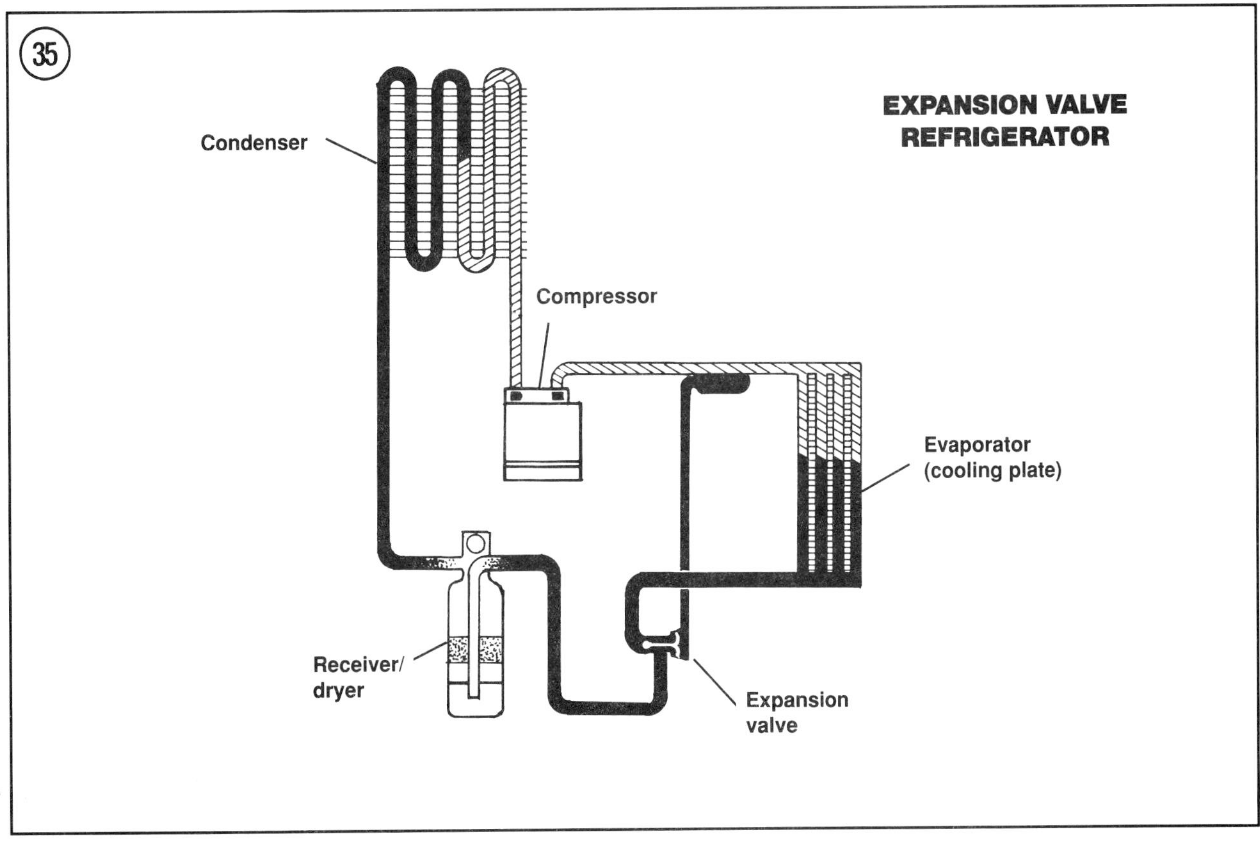

a. Check the voltage supply (AC or DC) to ensure the correct voltage is being applied to the refrigerator.
b. Turn the thermostat knob to the maximum position.
c. Remove the rubber protective cap from the terminal on top of the compressor. Make sure it is properly connected. Also check the ground wire to see that it is securely fastened.
d. Check the circuit breaker located at the right front and bottom of the refrigerator. This circuit breaker effects DC operation only.

If sub-steps "a" through "d" are performed and the unit still does not operate, then the thermostat may be defective. Check it as follows:

WARNING
Disconnect AC cord and operate refrigerator from DC supply. Thermostat is energized by 115 volts when AC is connected and you could get a lethal shock when performing this procedure.

Remove the thermostat cover located at the rear or at the inside of the cabinet. Also, remove the gray thermostat lead and bridge the 2 ends of the lead with a suitable strip of metal; such as a paper clip. If the unit runs after the lead has been shorted, then the thermostat should be replaced.

4. Compressor runs on AC but not DC. Before assuming that the inverter assembly is defective, check the following.
a. DC connections at the rear of the cabinet to see if polarity is reversed.
b. If connections and polarity are correct, check the battery.
c. Short the thermostat leads. It may be that the thermostat contacts are dirty or pitted, permitting the high potential AC to flow but restricting the low potential DC. Clean the contacts or replace the thermostat.
d. If the above steps do not provide operation, then remove the transformer-inverter assembly from the bottom of the cabinet. Plug the power supply cord into a 115 volt AC outlet. Upon doing so, note the voltage selector relay. When AC is applied to the refrigerator you should hear a discernible "click" of the relay. If a "click" is not audible, check the relay movable contact section. When the AC voltage is removed, the movable contact armature of the relay should relax, indicating that the DC circuit is closed.
e. If the relay operates normally, then the inverter or transformer is defective.

5. Compressor runs on DC but not AC. Make the following checks for the malfunction.
a. Check the AC voltage supply.
b. Using an AC voltmeter (**Figure 36**), check the voltage at the compressor by placing one probe of the voltmeter at the compressor terminal and the other probe to the ground wire. Your voltmeter should read 20-23 volts AC.
c. If you don't get a voltage reading at this check, be sure the voltage selector relay is being energized.
d. If the above steps do not provide operation, then the dual voltage transformer should be replaced.

6. The compressor operates on AC but not on DC and the unit cycles intermittently regardless of thermostat position. This is an indication that

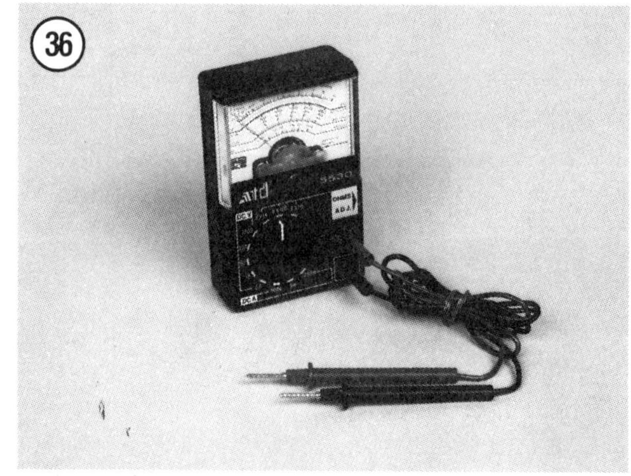

one or both of the transistors in the inverter are shorted, creating an excessive load on the secondary of the dual voltage transformer. This load causes the bi-metallic element in the primary of the transformer to open and close causing intermittent operation of the unit. Inverter must be repaired by authorized service center.

Recharging the System

Since August, 1992, it is against federal law and some state laws to discharge R-12 into the atmosphere except for very small quantities that are unavoidable during service. When R-12 is discharged to the atmosphere, such as when servicing a boat refrigerator, it rises to high altitudes, breaks down and releases chlorine. Chlorine is thought to be a major cause of deterioration in the ozone layer that protects the surface of the Earth from harmful ultraviolet radiation from the sun. Refrigerant R-12 and R-134a should not be mixed. Both refrigerants should only be removed and installed by properly equipped and trained technicians.

R-12 refrigerant is also used in automotive air conditioners, and used to be available at automobile parts stores, but environmental regulations now prohibit the sale of small quantities to anyone but certified technicians. Your only recourse is to have your boatyard recharge the system or take your local auto air conditioner mechanic for a boat ride—with tools, of course.

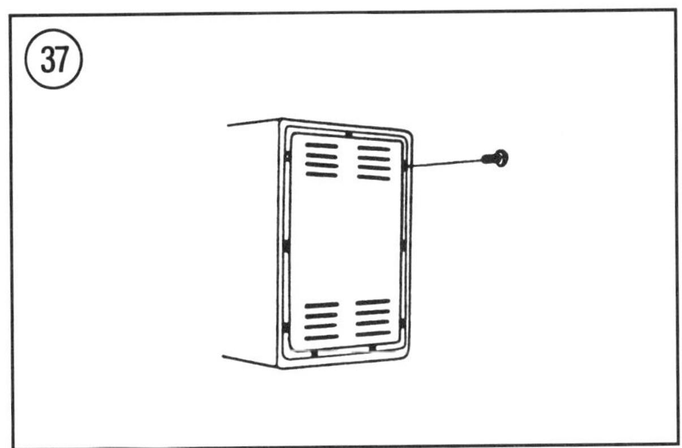

37

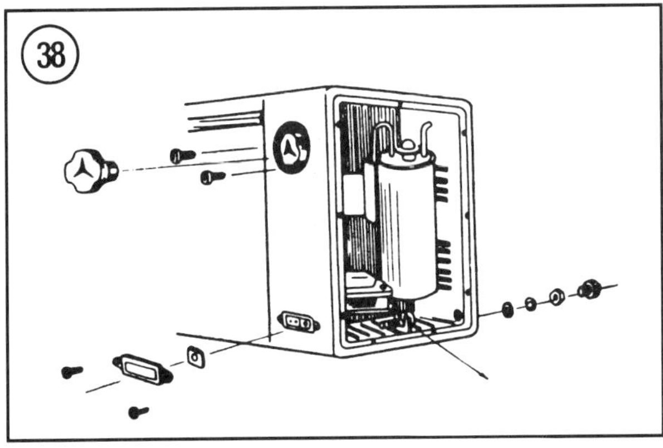

38

NORCOLD MODEL MRFT 614

To minimize liability, Norcold provides service information only to their dealers. The following sections describe removal/installation procedures for most Norcold models. This information should allow you to remove the unit and take it to a dealer which will save the expense of an onboard service call in some cases. If your boat is trailerable or docked near an authorized dealer, it may be less expensive in the long run to have them repair the unit.

Removal/Installation

1. Disconnect the AC cord from its power source and the DC cord from battery.
2. Remove all food from the refrigerator and carefully wipe off all traces of moisture from interior.
3. Remove 9 screws holding the motor cover plate in place. See **Figure 37**.
4. Remove the thermostat dial, 2 screws and push the thermostat into the interior of the cabinet. See **Figure 38**.
5. Remove the 2 terminal block screws and push it into the cabinet.
6. Remove the ground terminal nuts and push it into the cabinet.
7. Remove the fuse holder from the set plate. See **Figure 39**.

8. Remove 4 condenser cover screws and remove the cover. See **Figure 40**.

9. Remove the compressor cover screws (3 in front and 1 at the bottom). Loosen the 3 back screws, pull the cover out a little and lift the cover and lid off. See **Figure 41**.

10. Remove the rubber cap, nut and the lead wire at the swing motor terminal. Cut out the crimp-type connector where the blue and black wires are joined. See **Figure 42**.

11. Remove the 2 blind cover screws and remove the cover from the evaporator. See **Figure 43**.

12. Remove both interior and exterior set plate screws and pull the plate up. See **Figure 43**.

13. Remove the condenser screw from the back. See **Figure 44**.

14. Remove the 2 hanger screws on both sides of the swing motor. See **Figure 45**.

15. Pull hanger forward until it is free of the bolts. Pull the evaporator gently out of the cabinet, and at the same time pull the cooling unit out of the cabinet. See **Figure 46**.

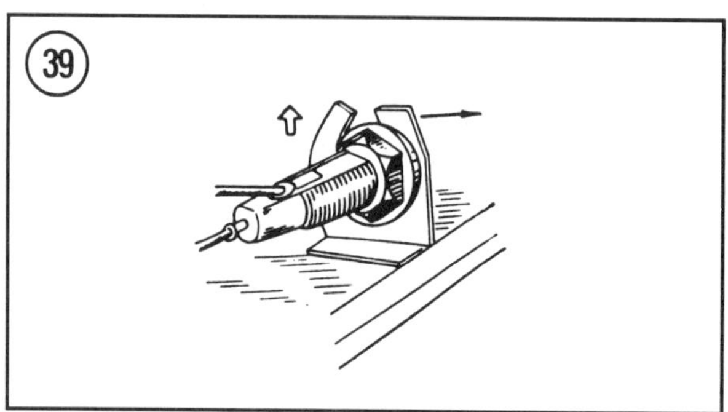

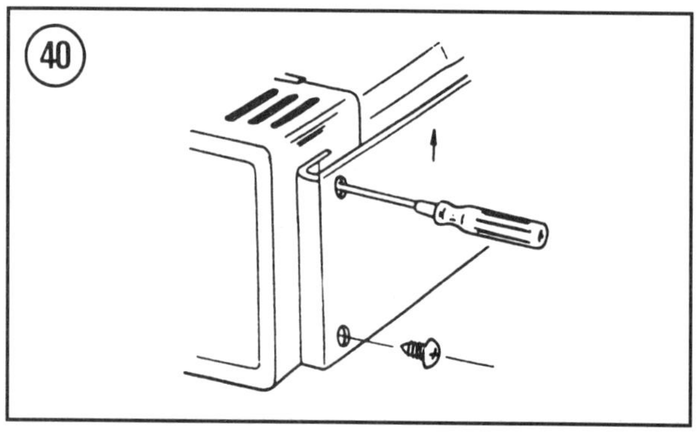

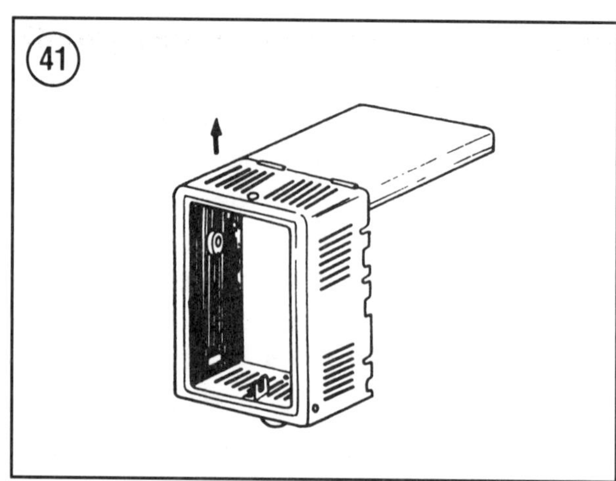

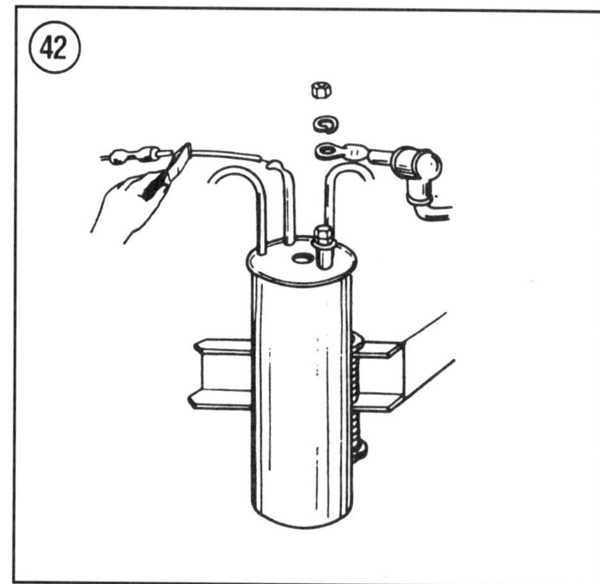

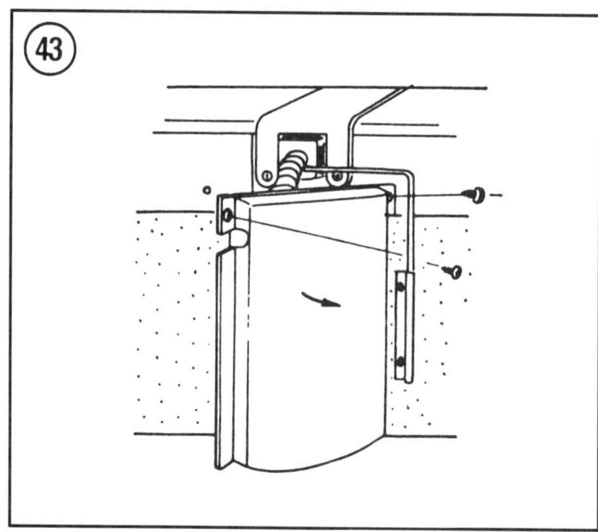

16. Remove the rubber bushing. See **Figure 47**.
17. Loosen the 2 thermostat holder screws and remove the capillary tube (**Figure 48**) from the evaporator.
18. Remove the sponge covering the suction pipe.
19. Installation is the reverse of these steps.

Replacing Fuses

1. *AC fuse:* Remove the fuse holder cap inside the compressor cover and replace fuse with one of the same rating.

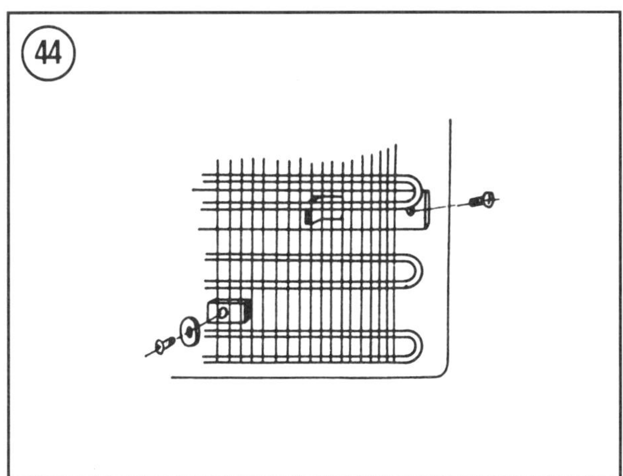

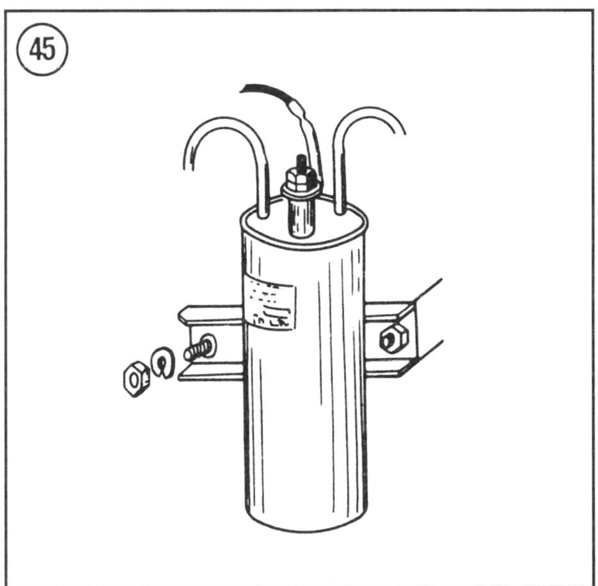

2. *DC fuse:* Loosen the fuse screws on the transformer and replace the fuse with one of the same rating.

NORCOLD MODEL DE-250

To minimize liability, Norcold provides service information only to their dealers. The following sections describe removal/installation procedures for most Norcold models. This information should allow you to remove the unit and take it to a dealer which will save the expense of an onboard service call in some cases. If your boat is trailerable or docked near an authorized

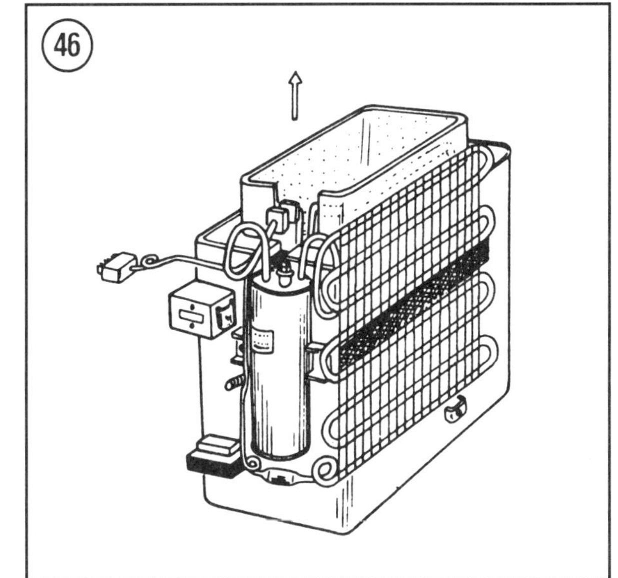

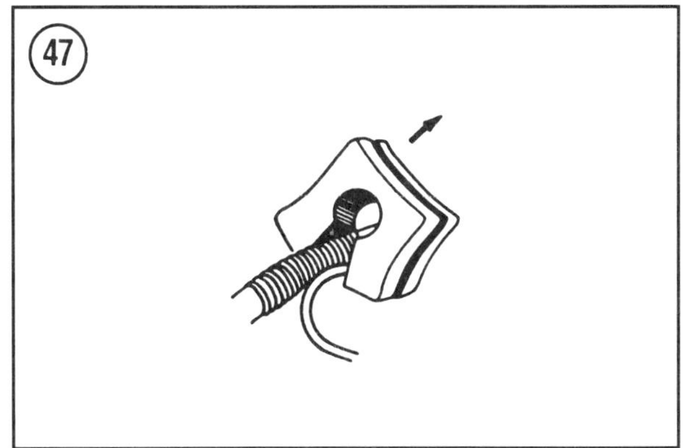

dealer, it may be less expensive in the long run to have them repair the unit.

Removal/Installation

1. Disconnect the AC cord from its power source and the DC cord from the battery.
2. Remove all food and wipe off the interior of the cabinet.
3. Open the door, pull out the thermostat dial and remove the screws on both sides of the shaft. Remove the thermostat and lay it on the evaporator. See **Figure 49** and **Figure 50**.
4. Remove 2 nuts located on the front of the evaporator. Lower only the front part of the evaporator. When it disengages, slowly pull it toward you and remove it from the rubber cushions. See **Figure 51**.
5. Remove the 2 condenser holders at the rear. See **Figure 52**.
6. Remove the 8 clamping screws on the blind cover plate and the cord holder on the left side. See **Figure 52**.
7. Remove the 2 nuts on the motor hanger. See **Figure 52**.
8. Slowly pull out the refrigeration unit holding both sides of the hanger. Do not catch the evaporator on the inner case window. Refer to **Figure 53** for this procedure.
9. When the refrigeration unit is pulled half way out, remove the cord from the swing motor terminal. The ground lead must also be removed. See **Figure 53**.
10. Lay the refrigeration unit on one side, and remove the 2 screws from the blind cover. Move the blind cover in the direction indicated by the arrow and remove the blind cover, the heat insulator and the blind cover plate. See **Figure 54** and **Figure 55**.
11. Remove the bushing.

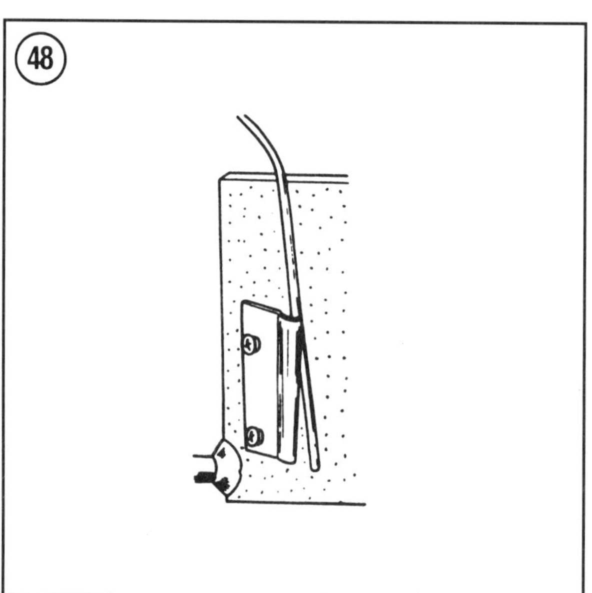

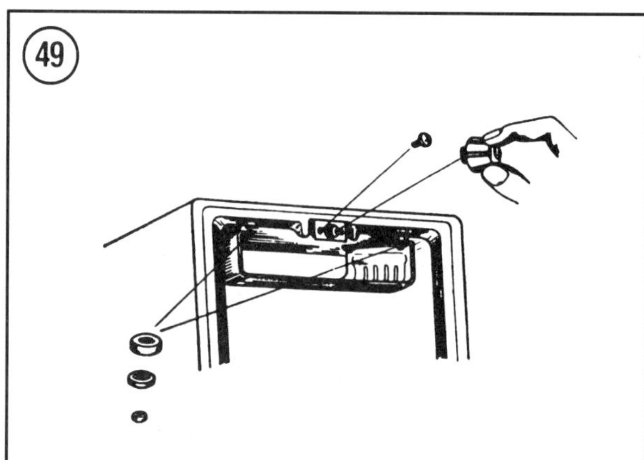

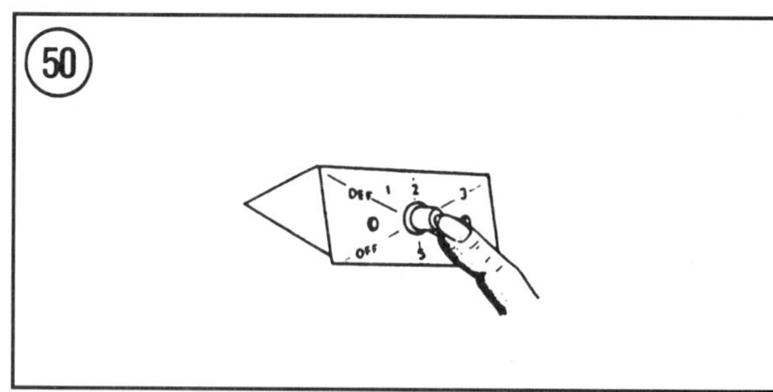

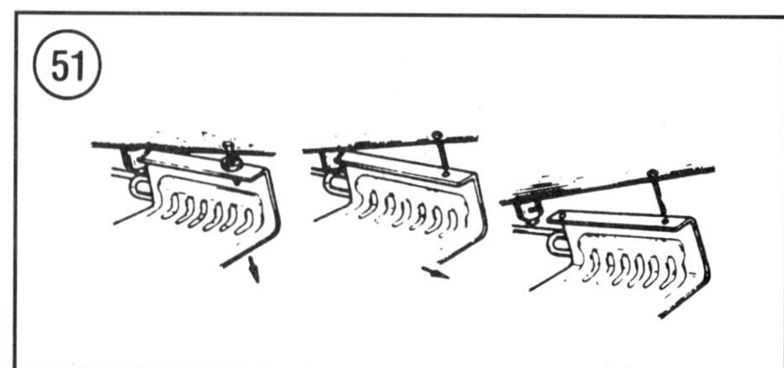

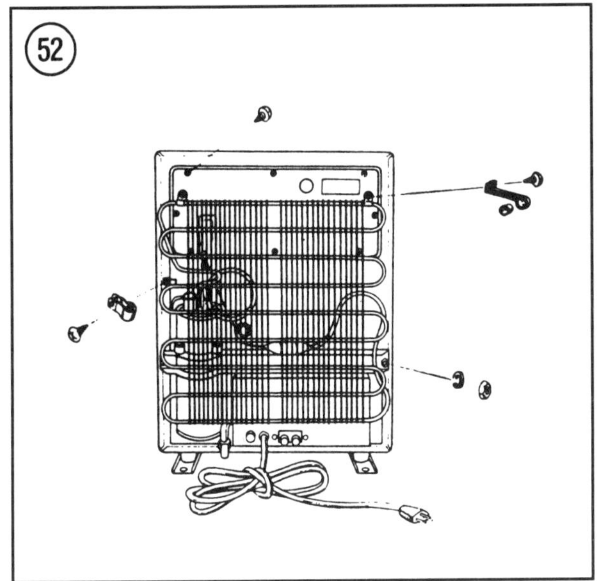

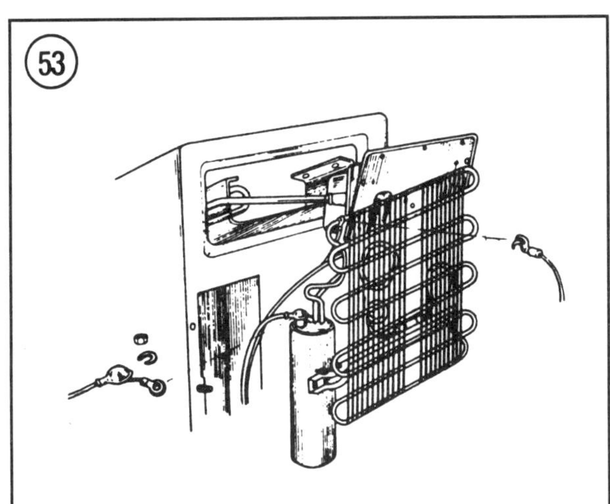

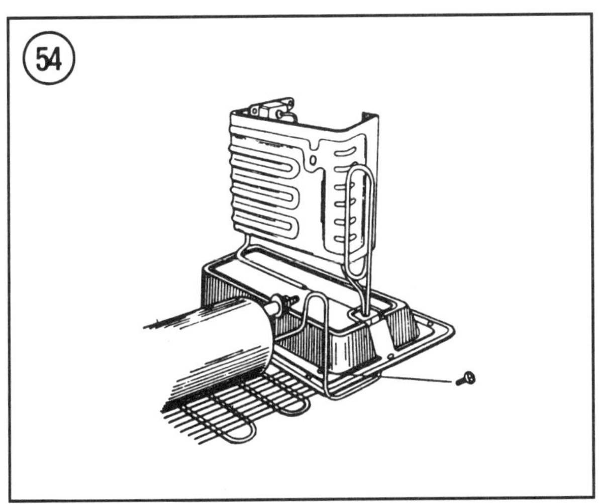

12. Install the unit by reversing these steps.

NORCOLD MODEL DE-250A

To minimize liability, Norcold provides service information only to their dealers. The following sections describe removal/installation procedures for most Norcold models. This information should allow you to remove the unit and take it to a dealer which will save the expense of an onboard service call in some cases. If your boat is trailerable or docked near an authorized dealer, it may be less expensive in the long run to have them repair the unit.

Removal/Installation

1. Disconnect the AC cord from its power source and the DC cord from the battery.
2. Remove all food and wipe off the interior of the cabinet.
3. Remove the thermostat dial. See **Figure 56**.

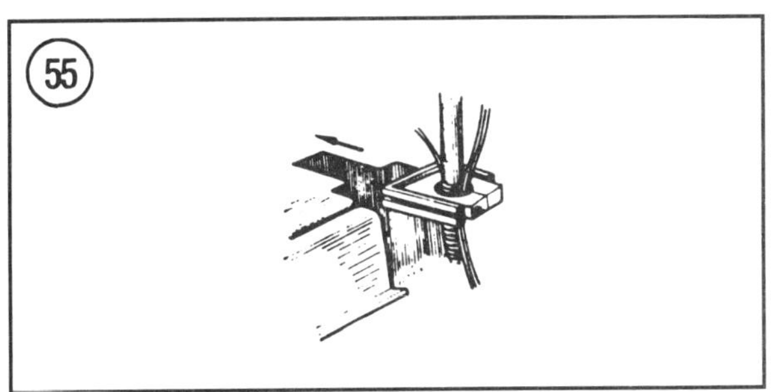

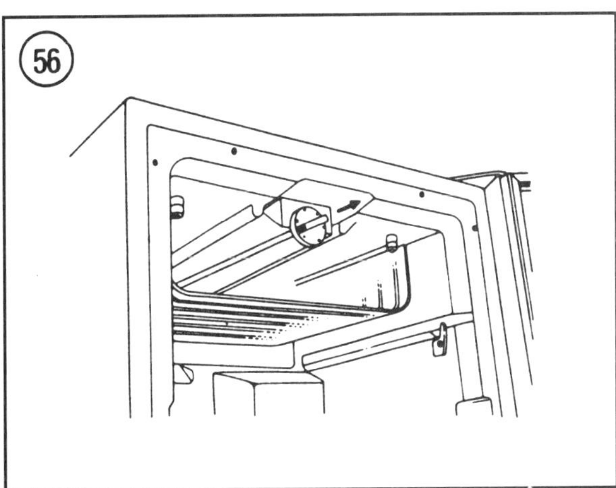

4. Remove the 2 evaporator nuts located on the front. Lower the front of the evaporator. When it disengages, slowly pull it toward you until it comes out of the rubber cushions. See**Figure 57**.

5. Remove the 2 condenser holders at the rear. See **Figure 58**.

6. Remove the 8 blind cover plate screws and remove thermostat cover. Disengage thermostat cord fixture. See **Figure 58**.

7. Remove 2 hanger nuts. See **Figure 58**.

8. Slowly pull out the refrigeration unit holding both sides of the hanger. Do not catch the evaporator on the inner case window. Refer to **Figure 59** for this procedure.

9. When the refrigeration unit is pulled out half way, disconnect the cord from the swing motor terminal. Disconnect the push-on terminals from the thermostat terminals. Also disconnect the ground lead. See **Figure 59**.

10. Lay the refrigeration unit on one side. Remove the 2 blind cover screws and 2 screws which hold the capillary tube. Move the bushing (inner) with suction pipe and the blind cover in the direction shown. Remove the blind cover. heat insulator and blind cover plate with the thermostat. See **Figure 60** and **Figure 61**.

11. Remove the bushings.

12. Install by reversing these steps.

NORCOLD MODEL DE-250C

To minimize liability, Norcold provides service information only to their dealers. The follow-

(57)

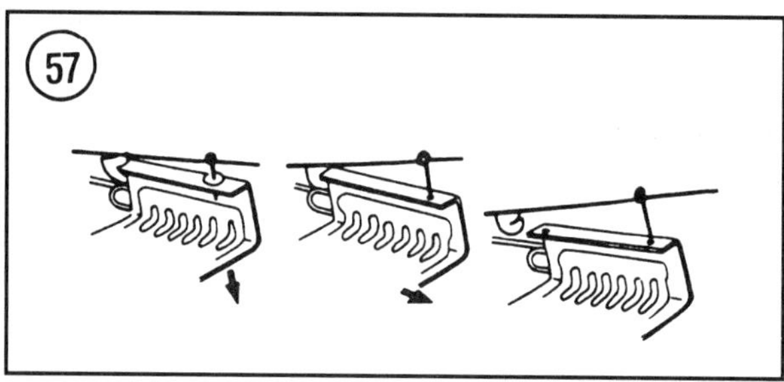

(58)

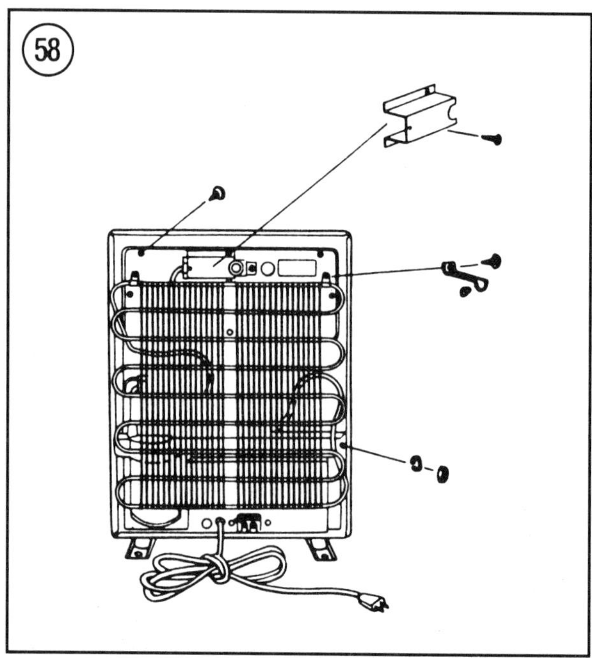

(59)

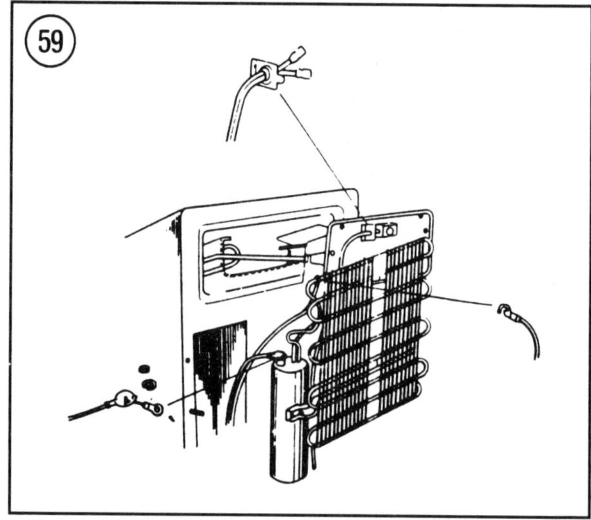

(60)

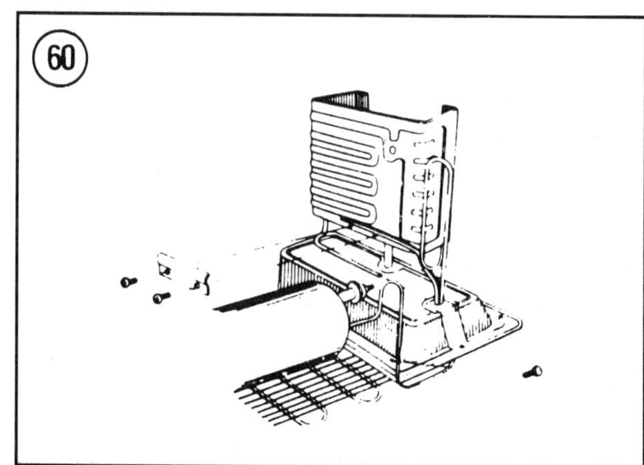

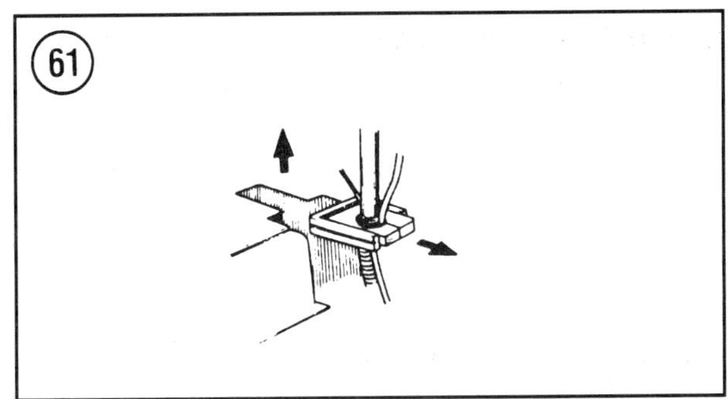

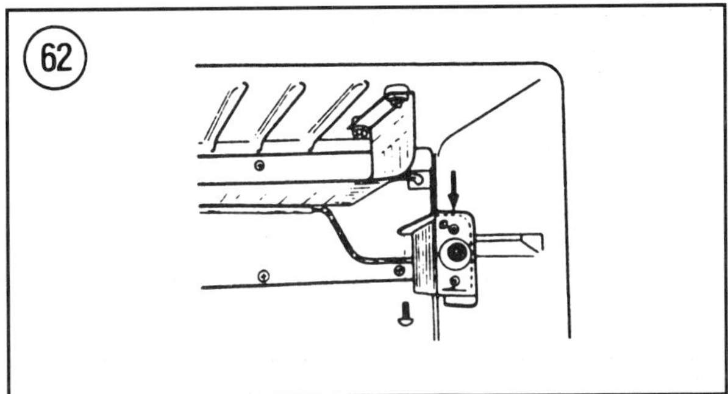

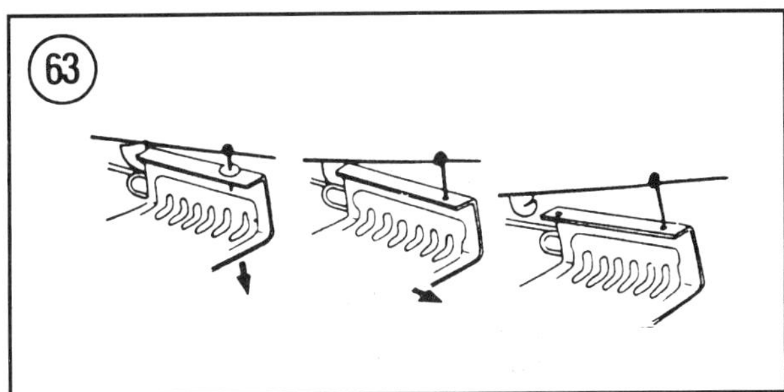

ing sections describe removal/installation procedures for most Norcold models. This information should allow you to remove the unit and take it to a dealer which will save the expense of an onboard service call in some cases. If your boat is trailerable or docked near an authorized dealer, it may be less expensive in the long run to have them repair the unit.

Removal/Installation

1. Disconnect the AC cord from its power source and the DC cord from the battery.
2. Remove all food and wipe out the interior of the cabinet.
3. Remove 3 screws which secure the thermostat assembly to the cabinet. See **Figure 62**.
4. Remove 2 nuts securing evaporator and lower the front part. When it disengages, slowly pull it toward you until it is free of the rubber cushions. See **Figure 63**.
5. Remove 8 screws from the blind cover plate at the rear of the refrigerator. Remove 2 nuts from the unit hanger bar and let refrigeration unit hang free. See **Figure 64**.
6. Remove the wire protector plate and pull cords from the motor and thermostat. See **Figure 65**.

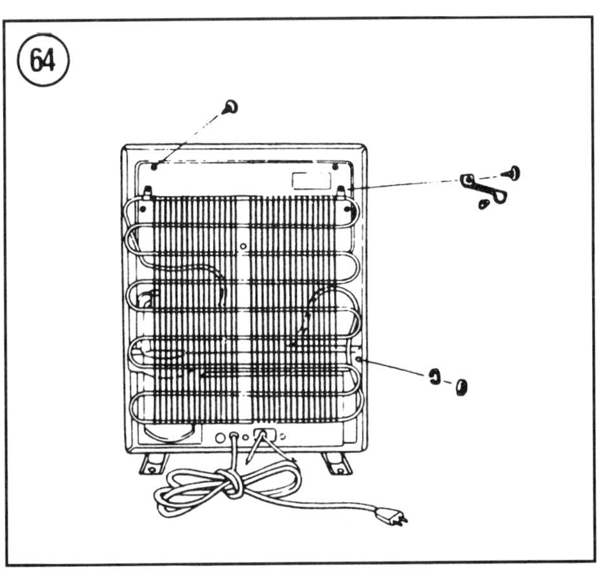

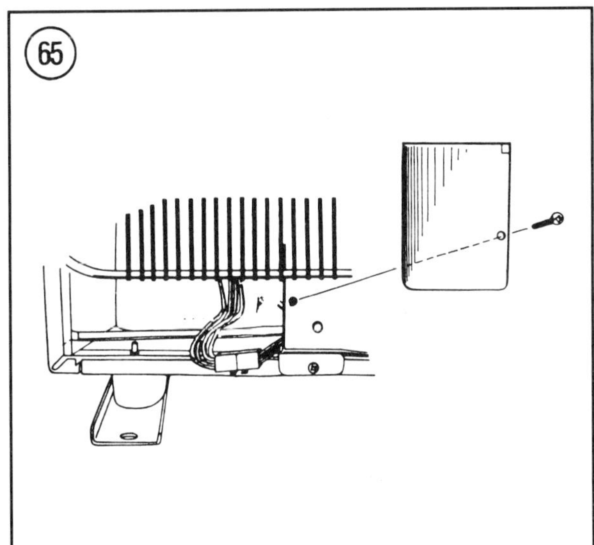

7. Cut off the ground connector and separate the 4-pole coupler. See **Figure 66**.

8. Slowly pull the refrigeration unit out holding both sides of the hanger. Make sure the evaporator does not catch on the inner case window. See **Figure 67**.

9. Remove 2 cords from motor. See **Figure 67**.

10. Lay the unit on the condenser side. Remove the 2 screws on the bind cover and the 2 screws which hold the capillary tube. These screws are located at the bottom of the evaporator.

10. Move the rubber bushing for the suction pipe and the blind cover in the direction shown in **Figure 68** and **Figure 69** and remove the cover.

12. Remove the bushings.

13. Install the refrigeration unit by reversing these steps.

NORCOLD MODEL DE-251A

To minimize liability, Norcold provides service information only to their dealers. The following sections describe removal/installation procedures for most Norcold models. This information should allow you to remove the unit and take it to a dealer which will save the expense of an onboard service call in some cases. If your boat is trailerable or docked near an authorized dealer, it may be less expensive in the long run to have them repair the unit.

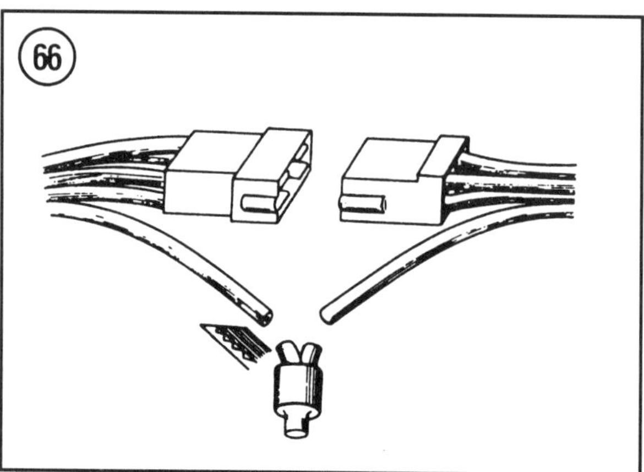
66

Removal/Installation

1. Disconnect the AC plug from its power source and the DC cord from the battery.

2. Remove all food and clean out the interior of the cabinet.

3. Remove 3 screws which secure the thermostat assembly to the cabinet. See **Figure 70**.

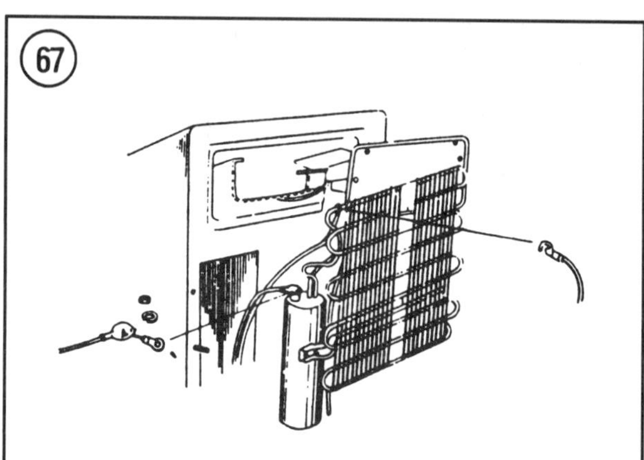
67

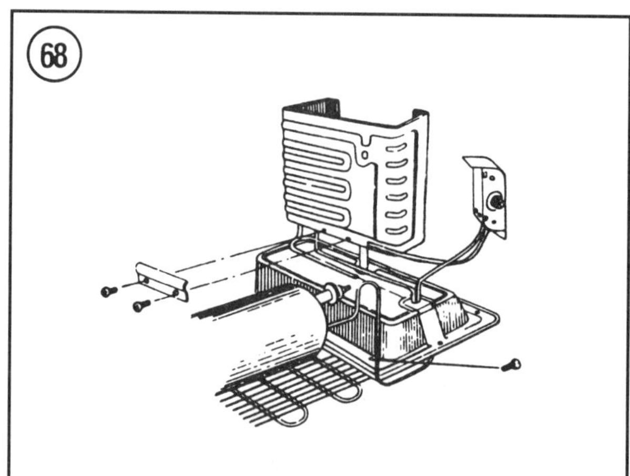
68

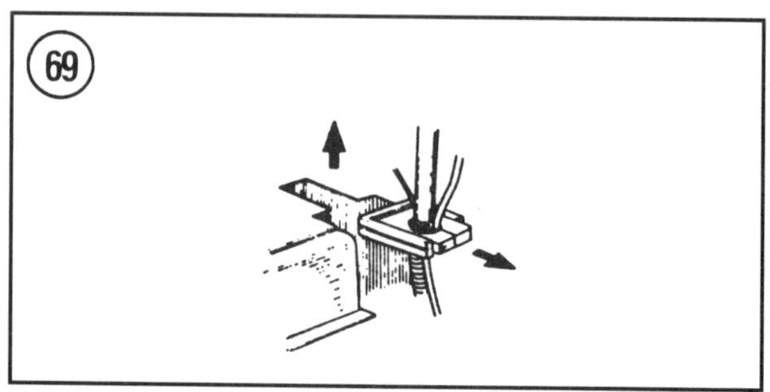
69

4. Remove 2 nuts located in front of the evaporator and pull the front part of the evaporator down. When it disengages, slowly pull it toward you until it comes out of its seat. See **Figure 71**.

5. Remove 6 screws on blind cover plate and take out the insulation pad. See **Figure 72**.

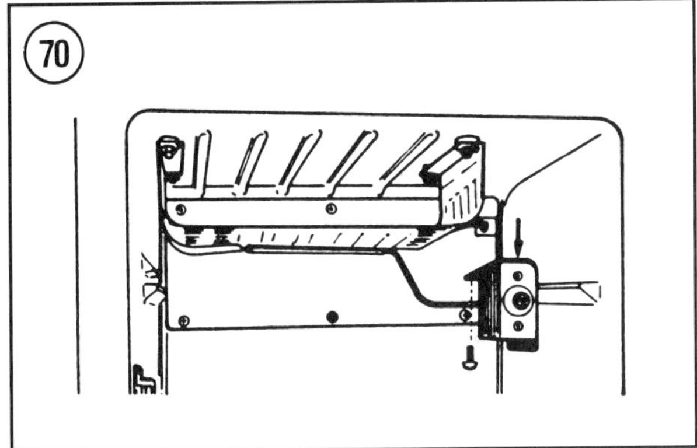

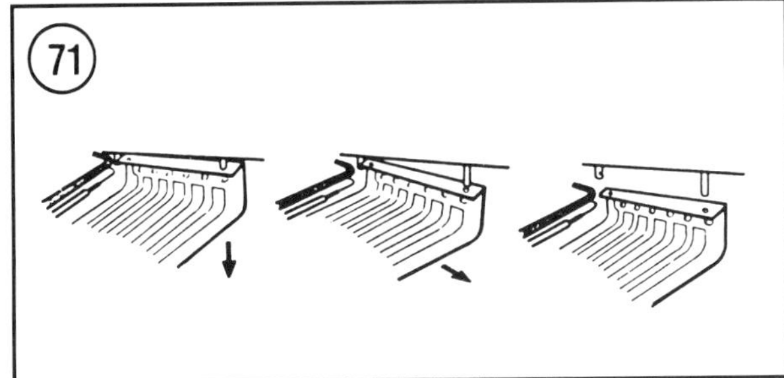

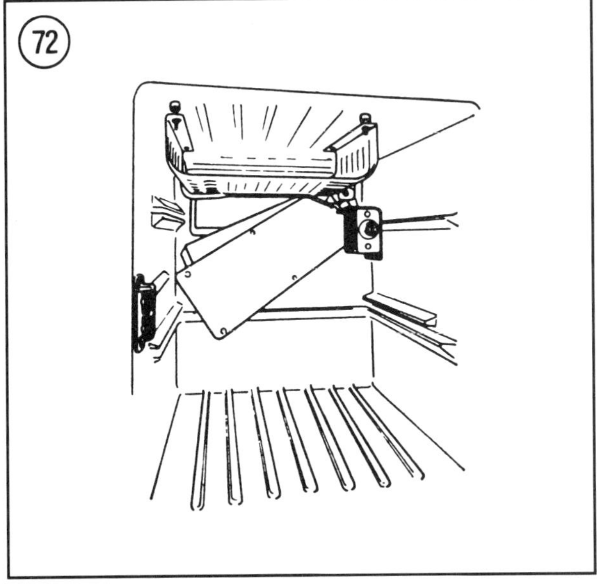

6. Remove the inverter assembly located at the rear of the refrigerator.

7. Cut off the thermostat ground cord at the connecting points and separate the 4-pole coupler which connects the thermostat cord assembly and inverter assembly. Refer to **Figure 73** and **Figure 74**.

8. Disconnect the lead wire from the motor terminal. Do not turn the lowest nut. Remove the ground lead wire. See **Figure 75**.

9. Remove the screw fastening the condenser to the cabinet through the holder plate at the upper center of the condenser. Remove 2 hanger nuts and let the unit hang free of the cabinet. See **Figure 75**.

10. Slowly pull the unit out while holding both sides of the hanger. Do not catch the evaporator and thermostat assembly on the inner case window opening.

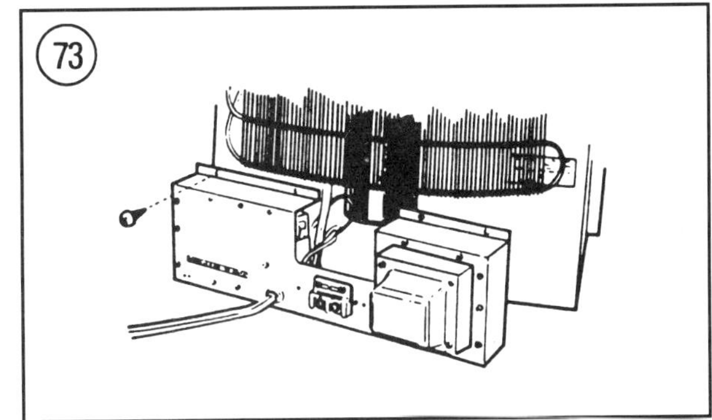

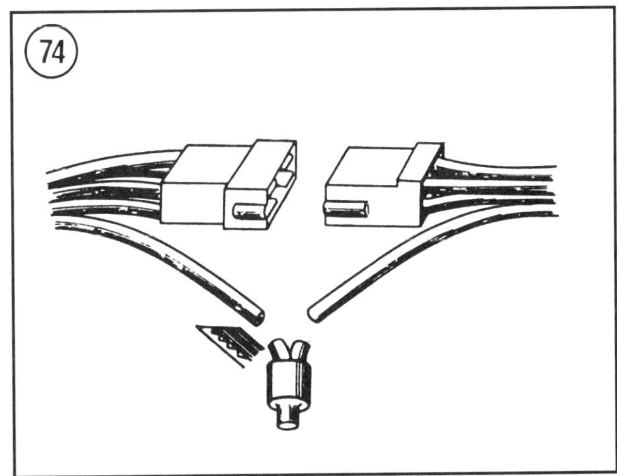

11. Place the unit on the condenser side and remove 2 screws which hold the capillary tube. These screws are located underneath the evaporator.

12. Remove the suction pipe bushing. See **Figure 76**.

13. Install unit by reversing these steps.

NORCOLD MODEL DE-400

To minimize liability, Norcold provides service information only to their dealers. The following sections describe removal/installation procedures for most Norcold models. This information should allow you to remove the unit and take it to a dealer which will save the expense of an onboard service call in some cases. If your boat is trailerable or docked near an authorized

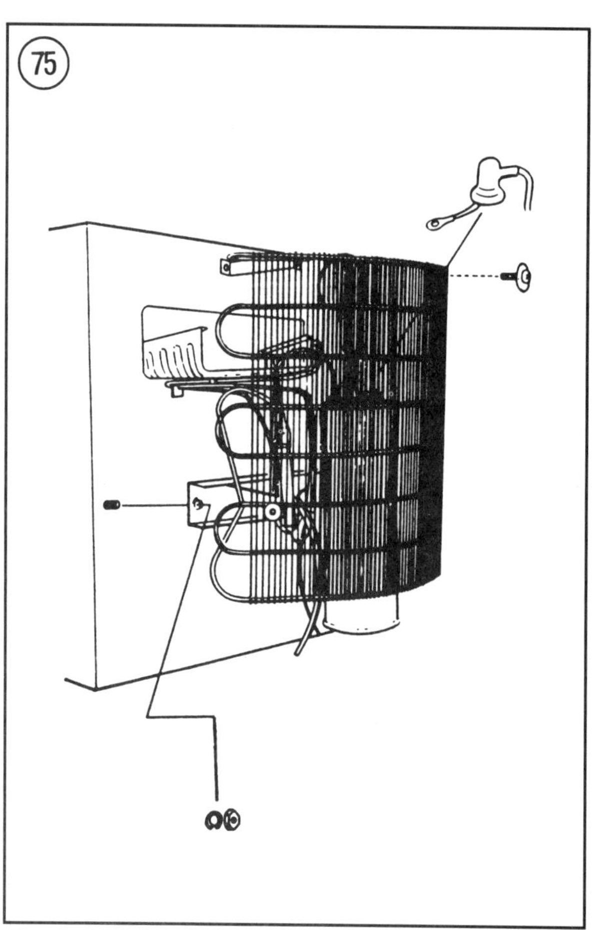

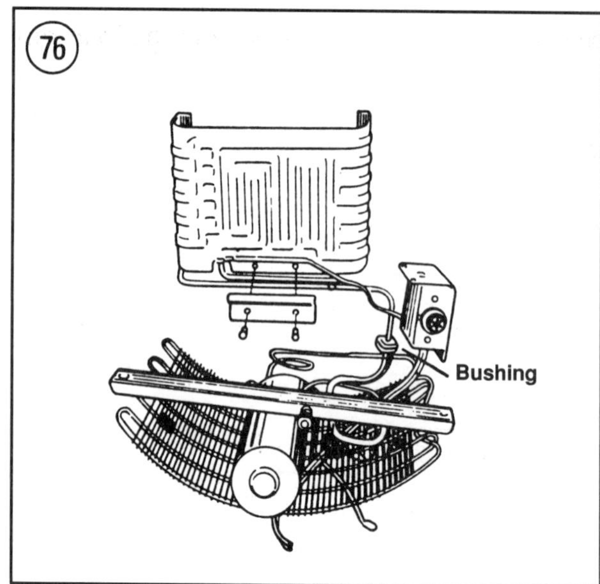

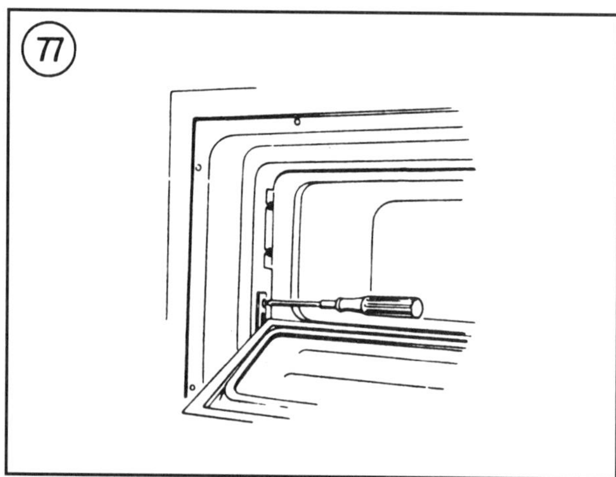

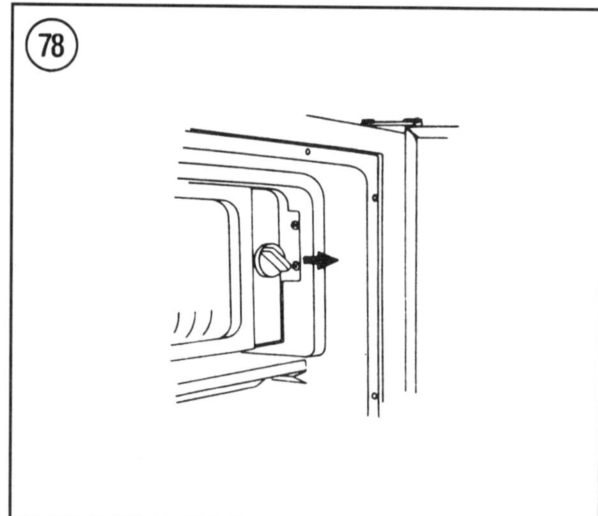

dealer, it may be less expensive in the long run to have them repair the unit.

Removal/Installation

1. Disconnect the AC cord from its power source and the DC cord from the battery.

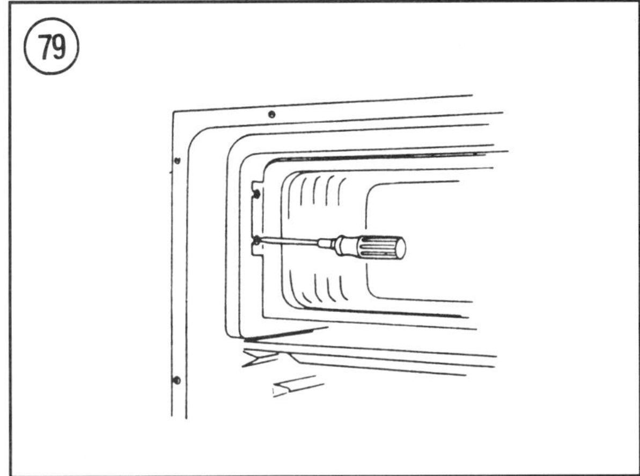

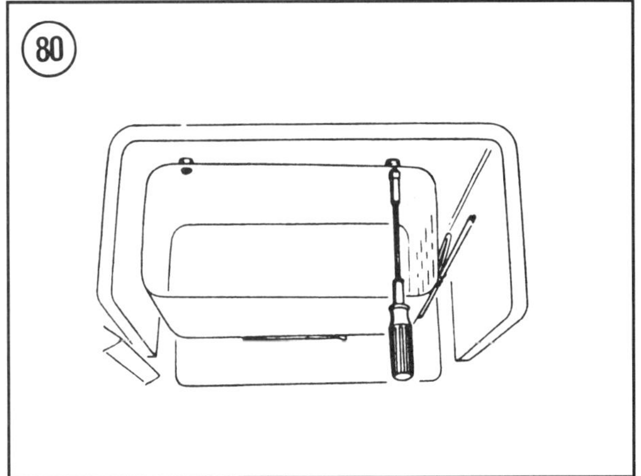

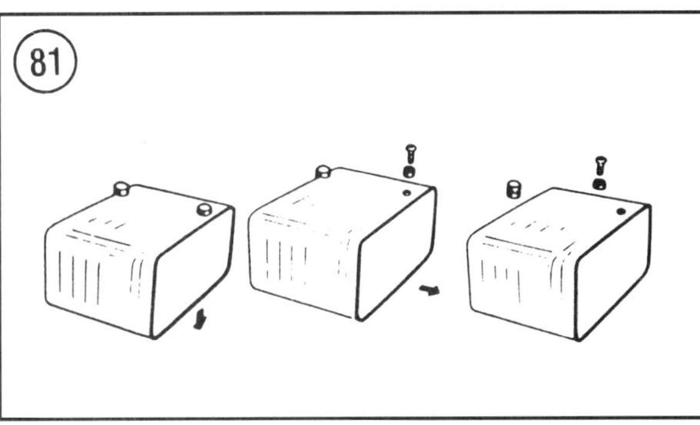

2. Remove all food and wipe out the interior of the cabinet.
3. Open the evaporator door and remove the evaporator hinge. See **Figure 77**.
4. Pull off the thermostat dial and remove the evaporator frame. See **Figure 78** and **Figure 79**.
5. Remove 2 evaporator nuts located on the front of the evaporator. When it disengages, pull it slowly toward you and remove it from the spacer. See **Figure 80** and **Figure 81**.
6. Remove 2 condenser holders and then unscrew 10 screws from the blind cover plate. See **Figure 82**.
7. Remove the connector cover and cut off the lead wires from the thermostat and motor at the connecting points. See **Figure 82** and **Figure 83**.

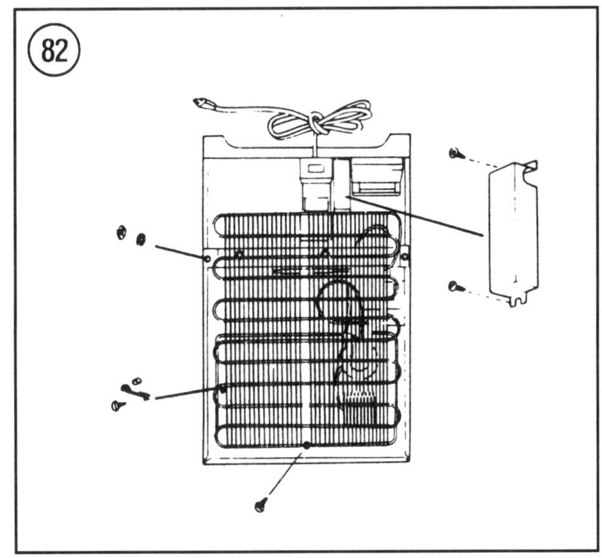

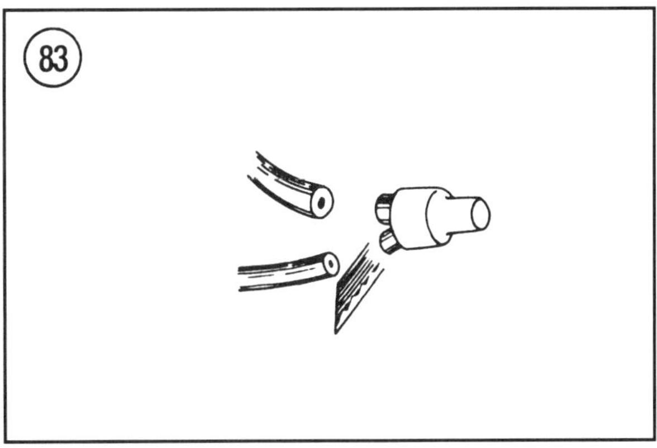

9

8. Remove 2 hanger nuts (see **Figure 82**) and slowly pull refrigeration unit out. Do not catch the evaporator on the inner case window. See **Figure 84**.

9. Remove the cord holder and detach the lead wire from the motor terminal. The ground lead wire must also be removed. See **Figure 85**.

10. Remove the 2 thermostat holder screws. See **Figure 86**.

11. Unscrew 4 blind cover screws and move the cover as shown in **Figure 86** and **Figure 87**. Remove cover and insulator.

12. Remove the bushings and blind cover plate with thermostat.

13. Installation is the reverse of these steps.

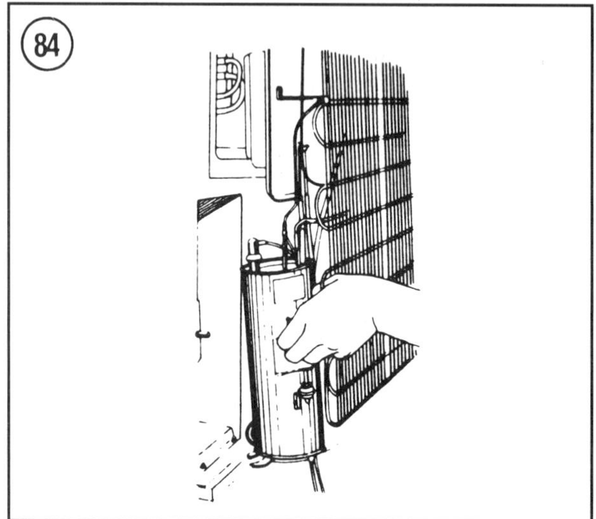
84

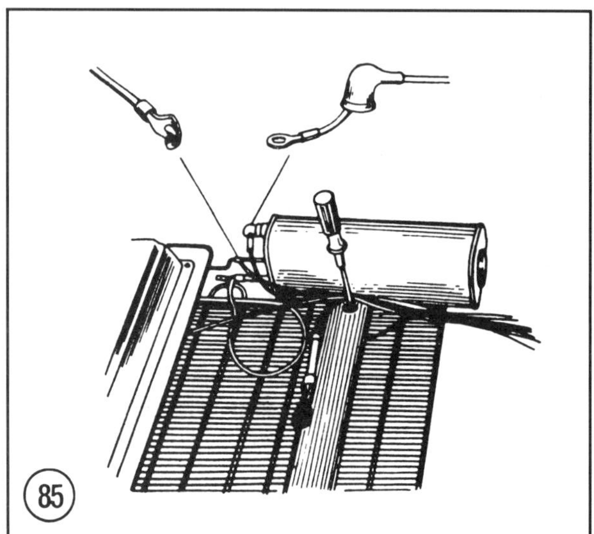
85

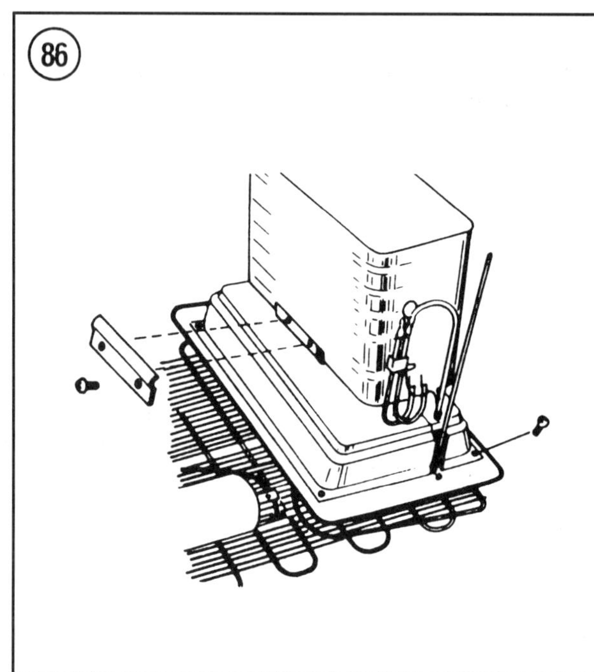
86

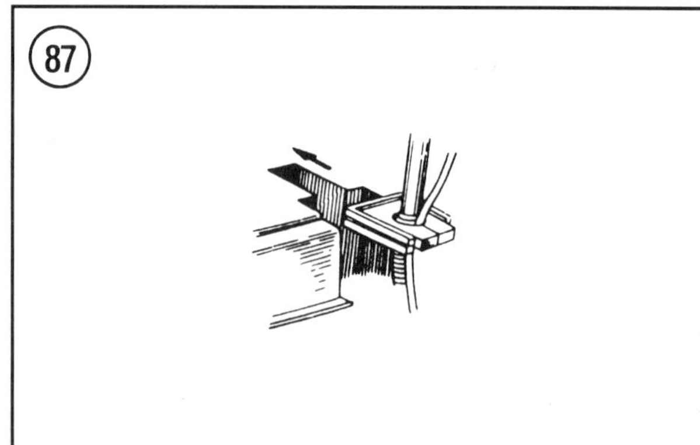
87

Table 1 OPTIMUS/PRIMUS STOVE TROUBLESHOOTING

Symptom	Problem	Cure
Leakage around tank, lines, preheater	Loose connections	Tighten
	Damaged fittings	Replace fittings
	Holes in tank or solder joints	Replace or repair
	Leakage around burner spindle	Tighten, replace packing, replace spindle
	Leakage at burner connections	Ensure that cones are installed and not damaged
	Rubber stoppers on preheater damaged or burned	Replace stoppers. Check that stopper arm swings easily, and fully out of the flame stream.
Burner flares up with yellowish flame	Not preheated sufficiently	Repeat preheat procedure
	Burner spindle left open while starting	Close spindle before preheating or pressurizing
	Low air pressure	Pump additionally. See "Low air pressure"
	Loose nipple	Tighten nipple
	Bad or incorrect nipple	Replace or clean
	Carbon caked in burner	Clean or replace
	Bad burner	Replace
	Faulty inner cap	Replace—file down inner tube so it does not protrude above cap
	Center tube too high	File down level with inner cap
	Faulty outer cap	Replace
Burner will not shut off	Cleaning needle maladjusted	Remove and adjust.
	Foreign material in system	Remove nipple needle, open spindle, pressurize tank and flush system. Replace nipple
	Bad spindle	Replace
	Bad burner	Replace burner or evaporator
Weak flame	Clogged nipple	Clean or replace nipple and needle
	Maladjusted cleaning needle	Adjust per instructions
	Low pressure	See "Low pressure" symptom
	Clogged wick	Replace wick
	Wrong nipple installed	Replace nipple
Unbalanced flame	Dirty nipple	Clean or replace
	Bad nipple	Clean or replace
	Threads misaligned between burner cup and nipple	Replace burner and nipple
	Bent burner cup	Replace
Burner not aligned vertically	Bent out of position	Bend back to proper position with hands
Erratic flame	Debris in system	Remove nipple, needle, open spindle, pressurize tank and flush system, replace nipple
Low pressure in tank	Bad seal in tank cap	Replace seal or cap
	Cap relief valve leaks	Replace cap
	Tank cap not tight	Tighten
	Pump chatters or provides little resistance when pumped	Change pump leather or O-ring. Change pump check valve

(continued)

9

Table 1 OPTIMUS STOVE TROUBLESHOOTING (continued)

Symptom	Problem	Cure
	Pressure drops off too fast (more than 3/4 full)	Tank too full of fuel Remove some fuel
	Pressure release screw not tight	Tighten
	Leak	See "Low pressure in tank" above
Preheater blows only air	No fuel in tank	Refuel
Preheater blows little or no mixture	Nipple dirty	Clean
	Bad nipple	Replace
	Clogged lines or strainer at tank end of line	Blow out lines or replace
Preheater shoots stream of fuel instead of mixture fog	Low pressure	Pump tank up
	Dirty or bad nipple	Clean nipple while pressurized or replace
Preheater blows fuel/air mixture but will not light or stay lit	Low pressure	Pump up
	Dirty or bad nipple	Clean nipple while pressurized or replace

Chapter Ten

Fresh Water Systems

Water systems range from a couple of ice chests or coolers on a small runabout to elaborate pressurized hot and cold water systems with multiple sinks and heads on large cruisers.

SIMPLE WATER SYSTEMS

The water cooler system is the simplest and requires no explanation. Next comes a nonpressurized system with a water tank and one or more faucets with hand or electric pumps. See **Figure 1** and **Figure 2**. On some boats, an additional faucet pumps seawater from a through-hull fitting. This may be handy for general cleanup to conserve potable water, however indiscriminate use can quickly fill the gray water holding tank.

Figure 3 shows a simple electric galley pump with a capacity of about 1 gal./minute (3.8 L/minute). You flip a switch on or near the faucet to start the pump and get water flow. The faucet itself may be nothing but a spout, however some have a hand pump to draw water from the tank through the pump. Some pumps do not allow water to be drawn through them. In this case, a bypass must be fitted as shown in **Figure 2**.

Even the simplest systems should have some sort of water filter. Simple inline filters using a replaceable cartridge are available at marine chandlers and RV stores.

PRESSURIZED WATER SYSTEMS

Pressurized systems aboard boats operate on a demand principle. **Figure 4** is typical. When all faucets in the system are closed, the pump motor operates just long enough to build up a predetermined water pressure in the system, (usually 20-40 psi [138-275 kPa] depending on the pump). When a faucet opens or the head flushes, the system pressure drops. The pump turns on in an attempt to maintain pressure and delivers water to the open fixture. As soon as the fixture closes, the pump continues to run until system pressure builds up, then it shuts off again.

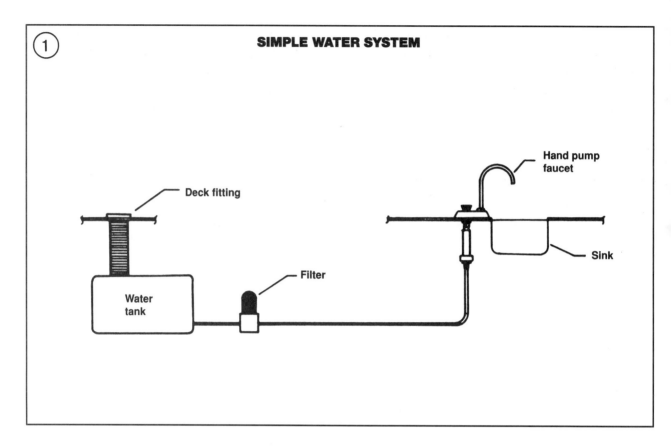

1

SIMPLE WATER SYSTEM

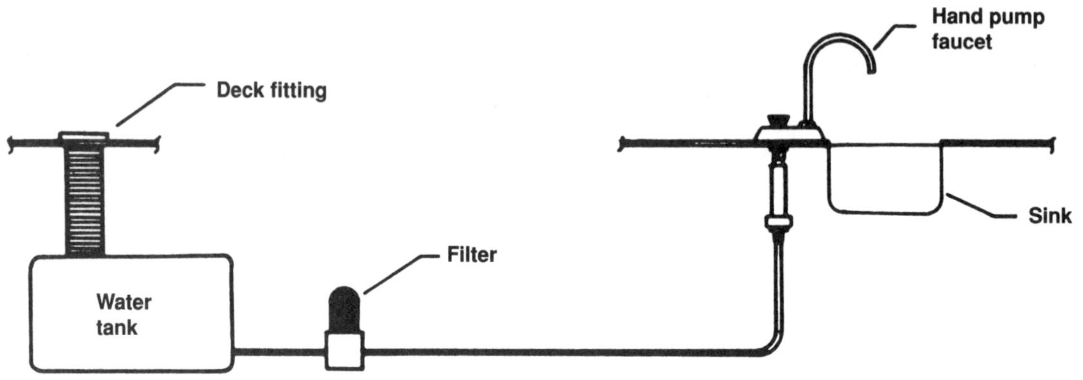

Hand pump faucet

Deck fitting

Sink

Filter

Water tank

2

SIMPLE WATER SYSTEM

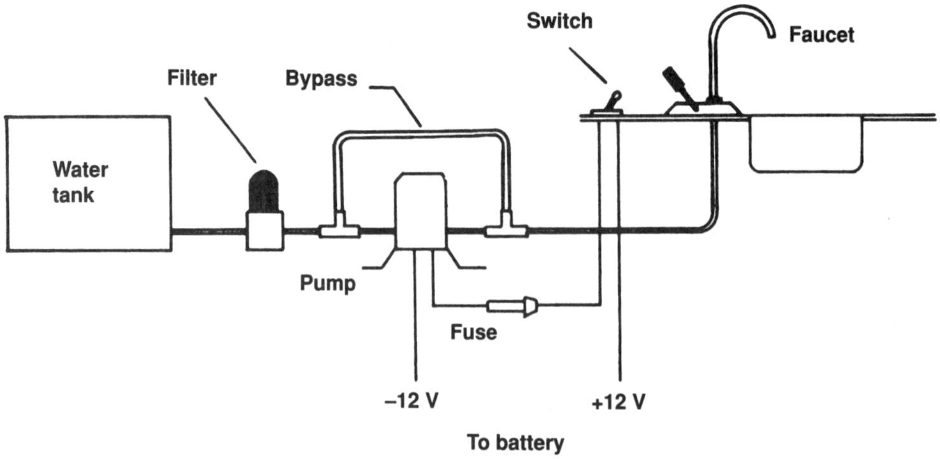

Switch

Faucet

Filter

Bypass

Water tank

Pump

Fuse

–12 V

+12 V

To battery

Several refinements to the basic cold water system are possible. A hot water heater may be added using the same pump, but separate faucets. Most water heaters use either electricity or circulating engine coolant to heat the fresh water. Engine coolant passes through a heat exchanger in the heater; it does not mix with the fresh water.

An accumulator tank can be added to further refine the system. First, the accumulator eliminates rapid on/off pump cycling to increase pump life and reduce battery drain. Furthermore, this smoothes the water flow and absorbs shock pressures (water hammer) due to sudden closure of water fixtures. Finally, the accumulator as-

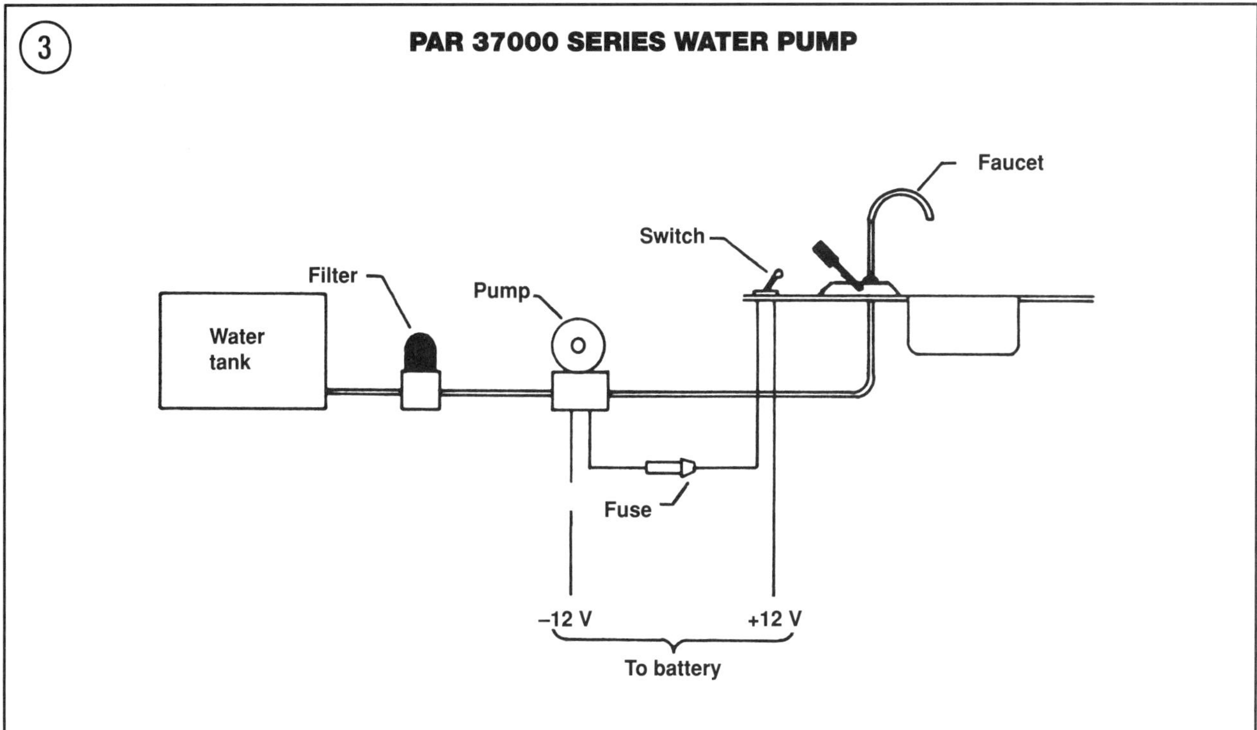

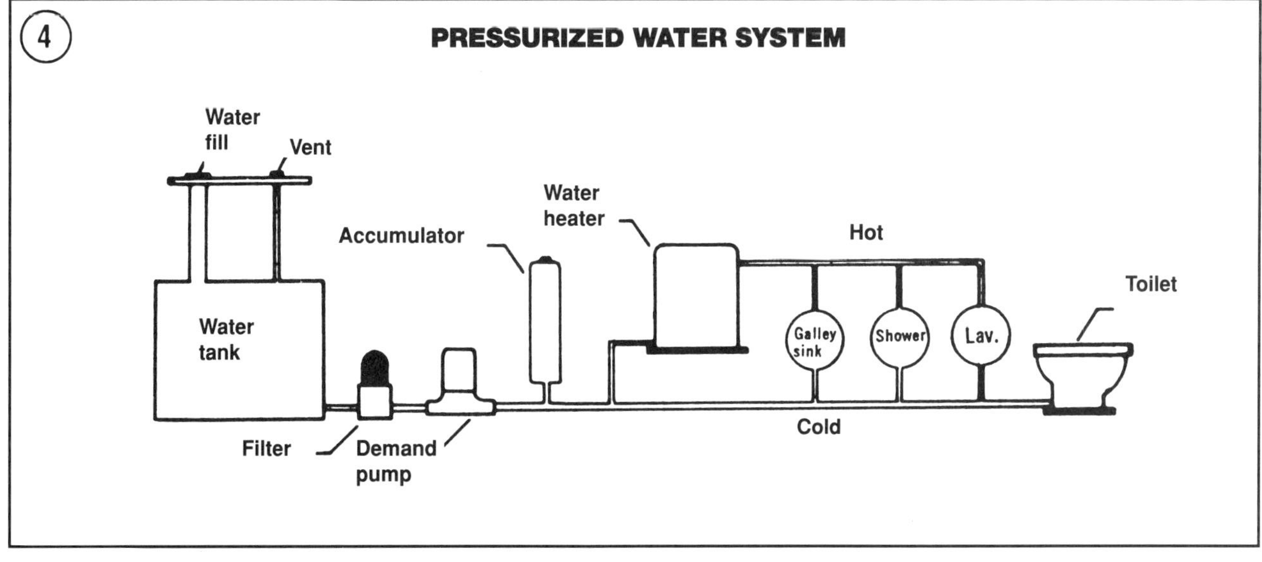

sures an extra reserve of water under pressure, an important feature of systems with flush toilets.

WATER TANKS

Water tanks are usually made of fiberglass, polyethylene or metal, although a number of flexible tanks are available. These fit in any available space and are very handy for increasing potable water capacity after the boat is built.

Water tanks should be filled with a plastic hose reserved for this purpose. Mark it for this purpose and keep it in a clean area. Do not use a rubber hose, as they usually give the water a disagreeable flavor.

SANITIZING WATER SYSTEMS

To assure complete sanitation of your potable water system, the following procedures should be followed on a new system, one that has not been used for a period of time, or one that may have become contaminated:

1. Prepare a chlorine solution using 1 gal. (3.8 L) of water and 1/4 cup of ordinary household bleach (5 percent sodium hypochlorite solution). With the tank empty, pour the chlorine solution into the tank. Use 1 gal. (3.8 L) of solution for each 15 gal. (57 L) of tank capacity.
2. Fill the remainder of the tank with potable fresh water. Open each faucet and drain cock until all air has been released from the pipes and entire system is filled.
3. Allow to stand for 3 hours.
4. Drain and flush with potable fresh water.
5. To remove any excessive chlorine taste or odor which might remain, prepare a solution of 1 qt. (0.9 L) vinegar to 5 gal. (19 L) water and allow this solution to agitate in tank for several days by boat motion.
6. Drain the tank and again flush with potable water.

PURIFYING POTABLE WATER

In some areas it may be necessary to take on questionable water. Contaminated drinking water can be a nuisance in some cases and dangerous to health in others. Water can become contaminated while aboard by dropping something in the tank or taking on bad water through the vent. If possible, the water should be drained and the system sanitized as described earlier.

When replacing the water is not immediately possible, or when forced to take aboard questionable water, the water may be purified with ordinary household bleach. Small amounts may be purified by adding 1 teaspoon of household bleach to 5 gal. (19 L) of water or 16 drops of household bleach per gallon. Let it stand for 5 minutes before drinking. If the water has an objectionable odor, flavor or color, run it through a filter made for this purpose or try boiling it. Within reason, a high residual chlorine content will flavor the water but it will not be harmful.

The amount of household bleach to be added to larger quantities of water depends on many factors. Most city water is chlorinated to have 0.1-0.2 ppm residual chlorine. Trial and error is necessary to determine how much is required to purify the water you take aboard. A simple inexpensive test kit available from swimming pool supply stores can be used after the treated water has set for at least 10 minutes. Try 1 cup (8 oz.) per 1,000 gal. (3.785 L) as an initial treatment. Of course, you will have to scale this down to your own capacity.

To avoid the trial and error method altogether, simply treat small amounts of contaminated water from the system as it is needed. Use the proportions given earlier.

WARNING

Boiling is not recommended for purifying water; use it to remove residual chlorine only. Some germs can survive boiling temperature at sea level, but cannot survive in a sodium hypochlorite solution.

AUTOMATIC WATER PUMPS

Automatic water pumps operate on demand, such as when any faucet is open. When pressure drops, an internal switch turns on the pump motor. When the faucet is closed, pressure again builds up in the outlet line, causing a pressure switch to open, which then turns off the pump.

Figure 5 illustrates a typical demand type water pump. This pump is permanently lubricated, and requires no periodic service.

PAR PUMPS

Repair

Replacement parts are available for PAR pumps. Most commonly required parts are included in a service kit. Order replacement parts by pump model number from your PAR/Jabsco dealer.

NOTE
During extended cruising, be sure to have a service kit for each onboard pump.

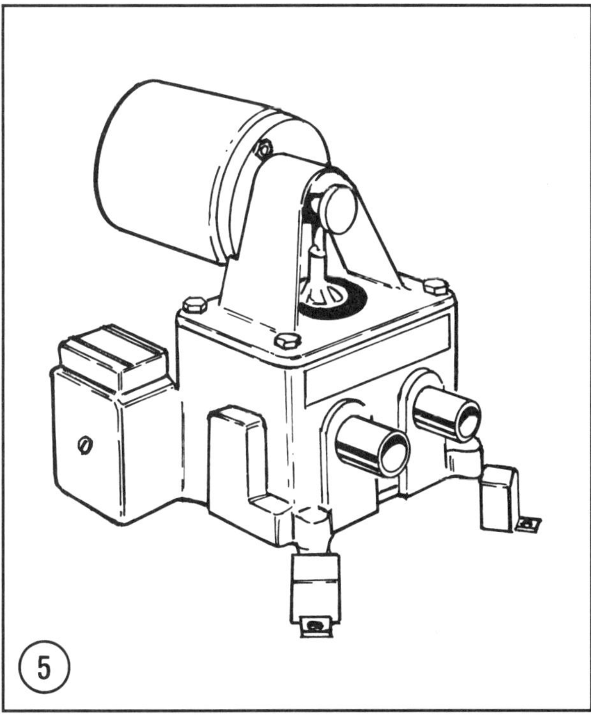
5

Figure 6 shows exploded views of PAR pumps. Refer to it when performing the following procedures and to help in identifying parts for replacement.

Replacing Valve Assemblies

Valve assemblies are part of the factory service kit.

1. Turn off power to the pump.
2. If the system is filled with water, open a faucet to relieve the pressure. Close the intake and discharge lines near pump.
3. Remove the 4 motor mounting screws.
4. Lift the motor and diaphragm assembly from the pump base.
5. Lift the valve assemblies from their seats and clean all foreign material from the valve and seat.
6. Install new valve assemblies into their seats, being sure the rubber valve with the small hole is UP on intake and the rubber valve without the small hole is DOWN on discharge.

CAUTION
Do not use the valve with the small hole on the discharge side of pump.

Diaphragm and Connecting Rod Assembly Replacement

The diaphragm and connecting rod assembly are included in the factory service kit.

1. Turn off power to the pump.
2. If the system is filled with water, open a faucet to relieve pressure. Close the intake and discharge lines near the pump.
3. Remove the 4 motor mounting screws.
4. Lift the motor and diaphragm assembly from the pump base.
5. Remove 2 diaphragm ring screws and detach the diaphragm ring.
6. Loosen the eccentric retainer screw and pull the connecting rod assembly away from the motor shaft.

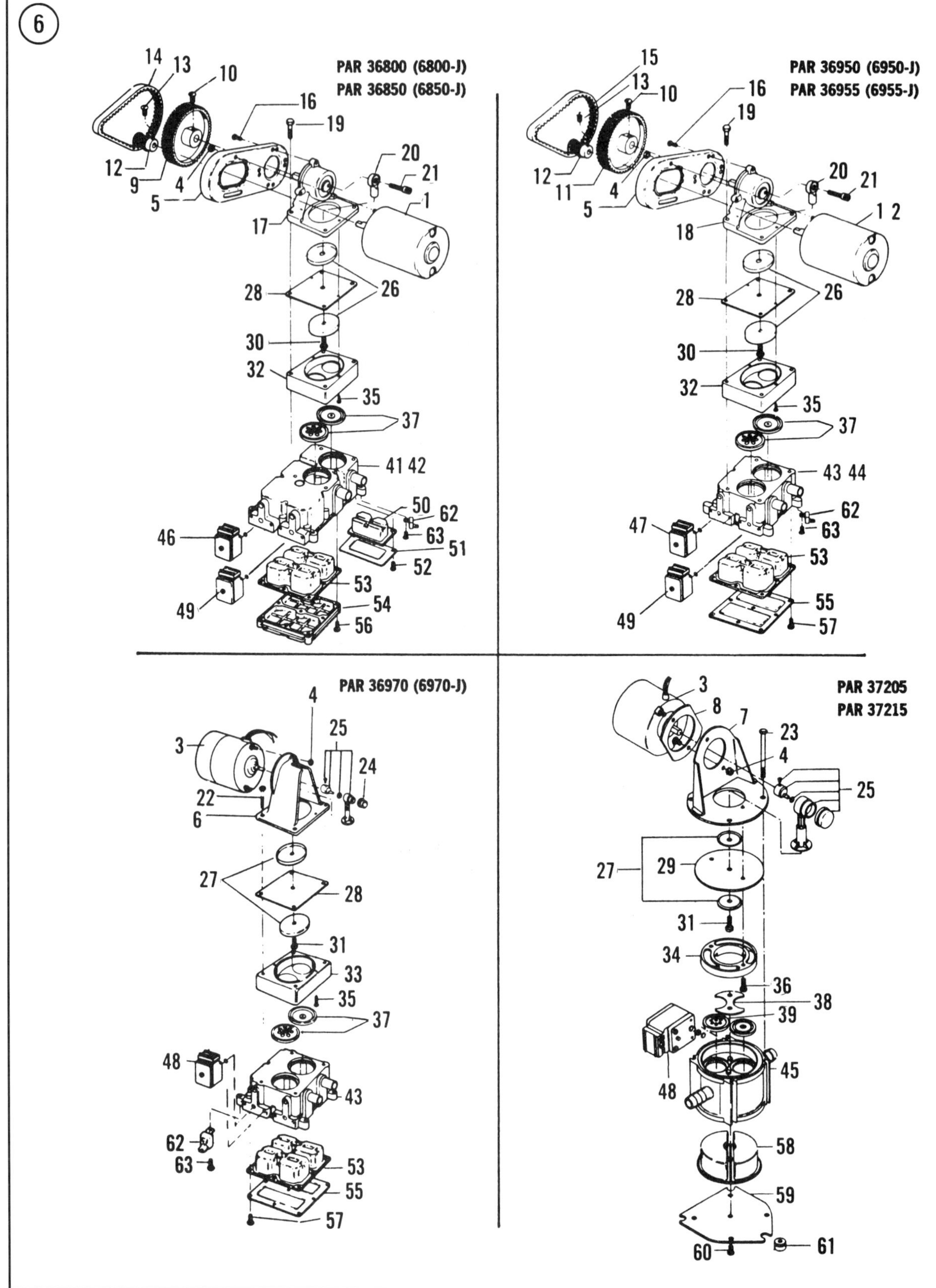
6
PAR 36800 (6800-J)
PAR 36850 (6850-J)
PAR 36950 (6950-J)
PAR 36955 (6955-J)
PAR 36970 (6970-J)
PAR 37205
PAR 37215

PAR PUMPS

1. Motor
2. Motor
3. Motor
4. Motor nut
5. Motor mount
6. Motor mount
7. Motor mount
8. Motor gasket
9. Large pulley
10. Setscrew
11. Large pulley
12. Small pulley
13. Setscrew
14. Belt
15. Belt
16. Jack shaft screw
17. Jack shaft
18. Jack shaft
19. Tie down screw
20. Connecting rod
21. Eccentric screw
22. Tie down screw
23. Tie down screw
24. Fastener
25. Connecting rod kit (contains eccentric rod and screw)
26. Diaphragm plate
27. Diaphragm plate
28. Diaphragm
29. Diaphragm
30. Diaphragm screw
31. Diaphragm screw
32. Diaphragm ring
33. Diaphragm ring
34. Diaphragm ring
35. Diaphragm ring screw
36. Diaphragm ring screw
37. Valve seat
38. Valve retaining plate
39. Valve seat
41. Base
42. Base
43. Base
44. Base
45. Base
46. Pressure switch
47. Pressure switch
48. Pressure switch
49. Dry tank switch
50. Pulsation dampener
51. Bottom plate
52. Screw
53. Pulsation dampener
54. Bottom cap
55. Bottom plate
56. Screw
57. Screw
58. Pulsation dampener
59. Base plate
60. Screw
61. Grommet
62. Vibration dampener
63. Screw

7. Remove the diaphragm screw to separate the diaphragm from the connecting rod assembly.
8. Inspect the entire rubber diaphragm for cuts and cracks.
9. Check the connecting rod assembly for breaks, cracks or excessive wear on the eccentric rod and bearing. If the connecting rod is to be reused, open the cover and relubricate it by packing the built-in reservoir with automotive chassis lube. The original lubricant normally lasts the lifetime of the pump.
10. Assembly is the reverse of these steps. When reassembling the connecting rod to the diaphragm, be sure to align it. Proper alignment is achieved when the rod slips straight onto the motor shaft and the diaphragm rests squarely on the motor mount pad. Misalignment will create a strain on the diaphragm and significantly shorten its life

Pulsation Damper Replacement

1. Turn off power to the pump.
2. If the system is filled with water, open a faucet to relieve pressure and close both intake and discharge lines near the pump.
3. Remove the pump from the system.
4. Remove 9 screws and the bottom plate from the base.
5. Pull out the rubber pulsation damper.
6. Inspect the damper for excessive deformation, ruptures and leaks.
7. Assembly is the reverse of these steps. Make sure the damper flange is correctly seated.

Pressure Switch Replacement

1. Turn power off to the pump and open a faucet to relieve pressure from the system.
2. Disconnect all wires from the pressure switch.
3. Remove the switch front cover and 2 screws located at the bottom corners inside the switch case.
4. When installing the new switch, be sure the O-ring is seated properly. Care must be taken to avoid thread damage.
5. Reconnect the electrical wires. See **Figure 7**.

Motor Replacement

1. Turn off power to the pump.
2. Disconnect the motor wires from the pressure switch terminal.
3. Loosen the eccentric/connecting rod screw holding the motor shaft.
4. Remove 2 motor nuts and pull the motor away from the motor mount, while holding back the eccentric/connecting rod assembly.
5. When installing a new motor, make sure the flat on the shaft is well secured by the eccentric/connecting rod screw.
6. Rewire the motor leads to the center and right terminals on the pressure switch. See **Figure 7**.

JABSCO PUMPS

Repair

Replacement parts are available for Jabsco pumps. Most commonly required parts are in-

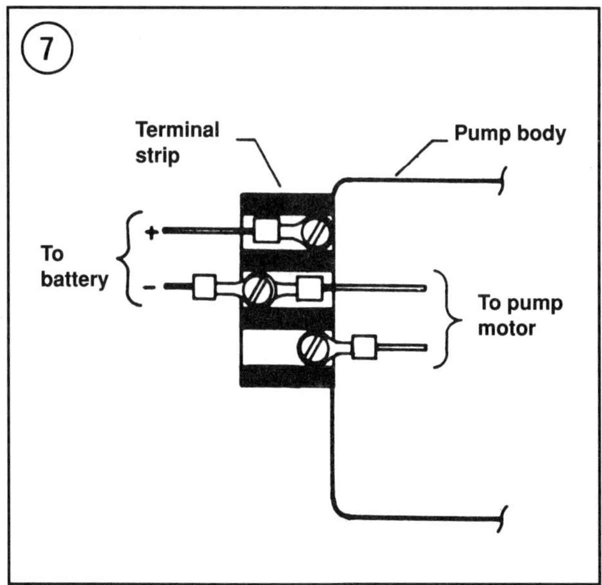

cluded in a service kit available from your Jabsco dealer.

Disassembly/ Assembly

Figure 8 and **Figure 9** show exploded views of the 17840 automatic multi-fixture pump and the 14940 single fixture pump, respectively. Refer to these figures for disassembly and assembly of Jabsco pumps.

WATER FAUCETS

After prolonged use, water faucets tend to leak. Such leakage is particularly troublesome in boats for a number of reasons. The most obvious is that there is generally a limited supply of potable water. Another reason is that a leak quickly fills the gray wastewater tank which, in most waters, cannot be discharged overboard. It must be pumped. Finally, a water leak constantly cycles the water pump resulting in its early failure.

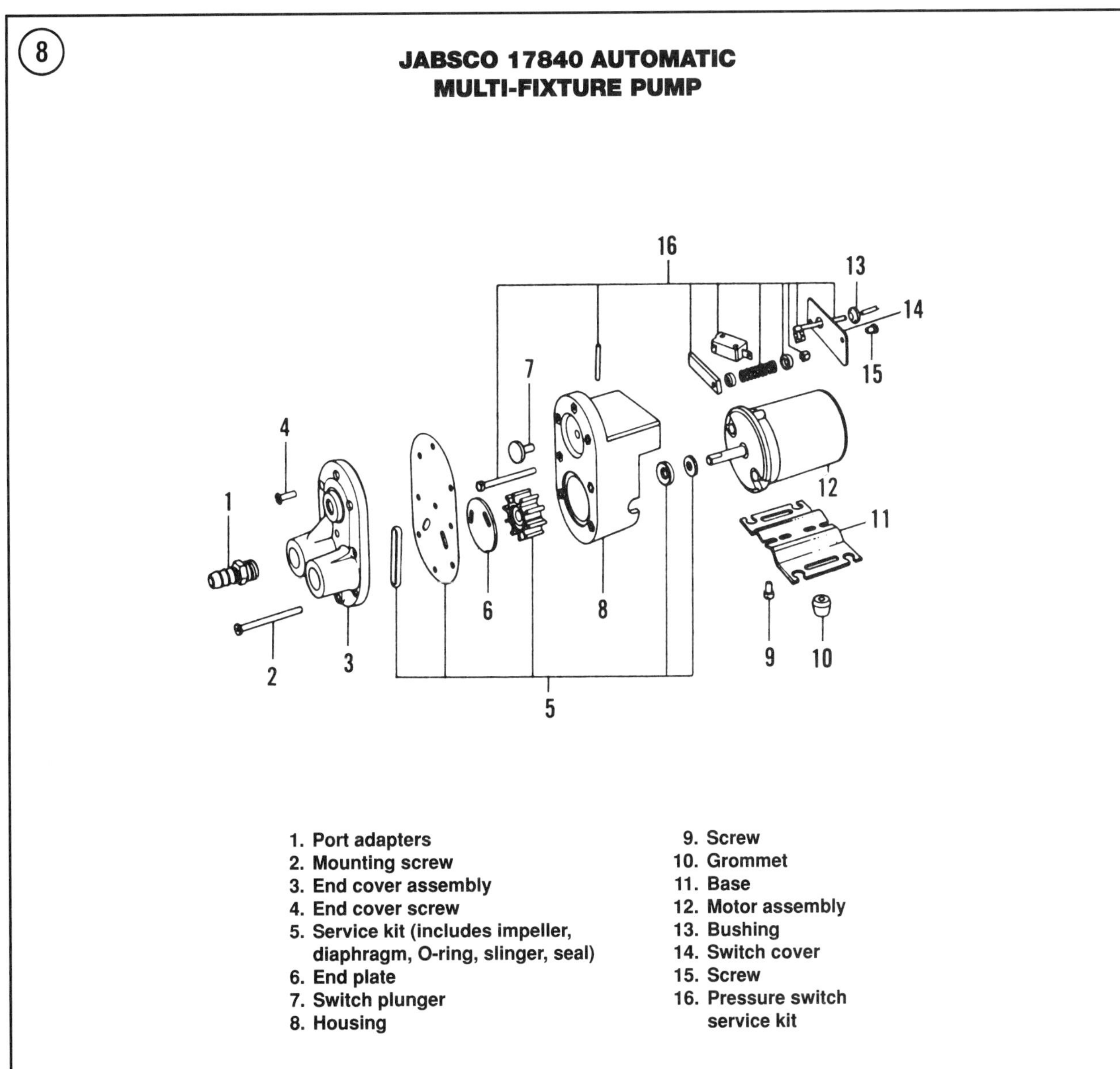

1. Port adapters
2. Mounting screw
3. End cover assembly
4. End cover screw
5. Service kit (includes impeller, diaphragm, O-ring, slinger, seal)
6. End plate
7. Switch plunger
8. Housing
9. Screw
10. Grommet
11. Base
12. Motor assembly
13. Bushing
14. Switch cover
15. Screw
16. Pressure switch service kit

Two Handle Faucets

To replace leaky faucet washers:

1. Turn off the water pump, or shut off the water supply.
2. Remove the knob retaining screw (**Figure 10**).
3. Pull the knob from the valve stem (**Figure 11**). There may be some corrosion holding the knob to the valve stem; if so pry off gently, taking care not to mar any finished surfaces.
4. Loosen the valve stem assembly by turning it counterclockwise (**Figure 12**), then unscrew it completely from the faucet (**Figure 13**).
5. Remove the washer retaining screw (**Figure 14**).
6. Pry out the old washer (**Figure 15**), using any convenient tool. An ice pick or scratch awl is ideal for this purpose.
7. Select a new faucet washer of correct size and press it into position (**Figure 16**). Note that

10

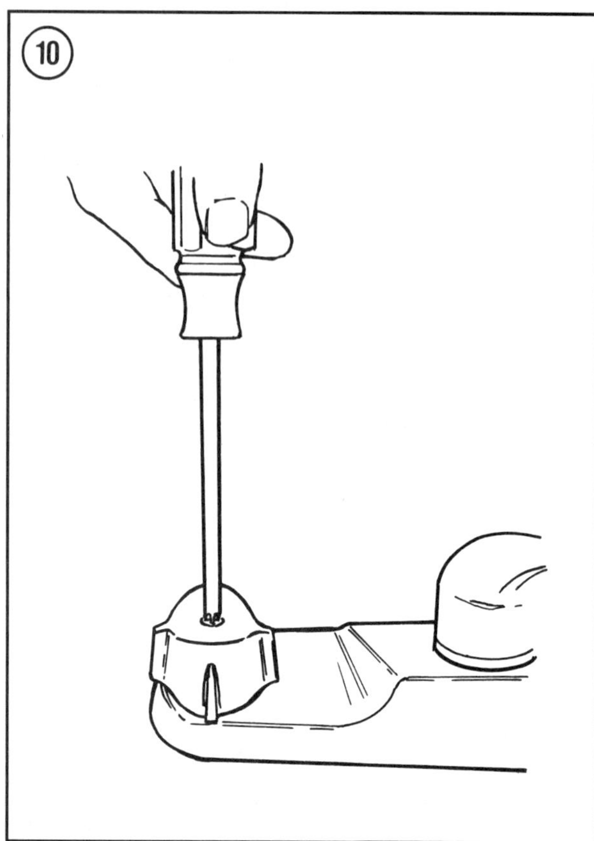

9

JABSCO 14940 SINGLE FIXTURE PUMP

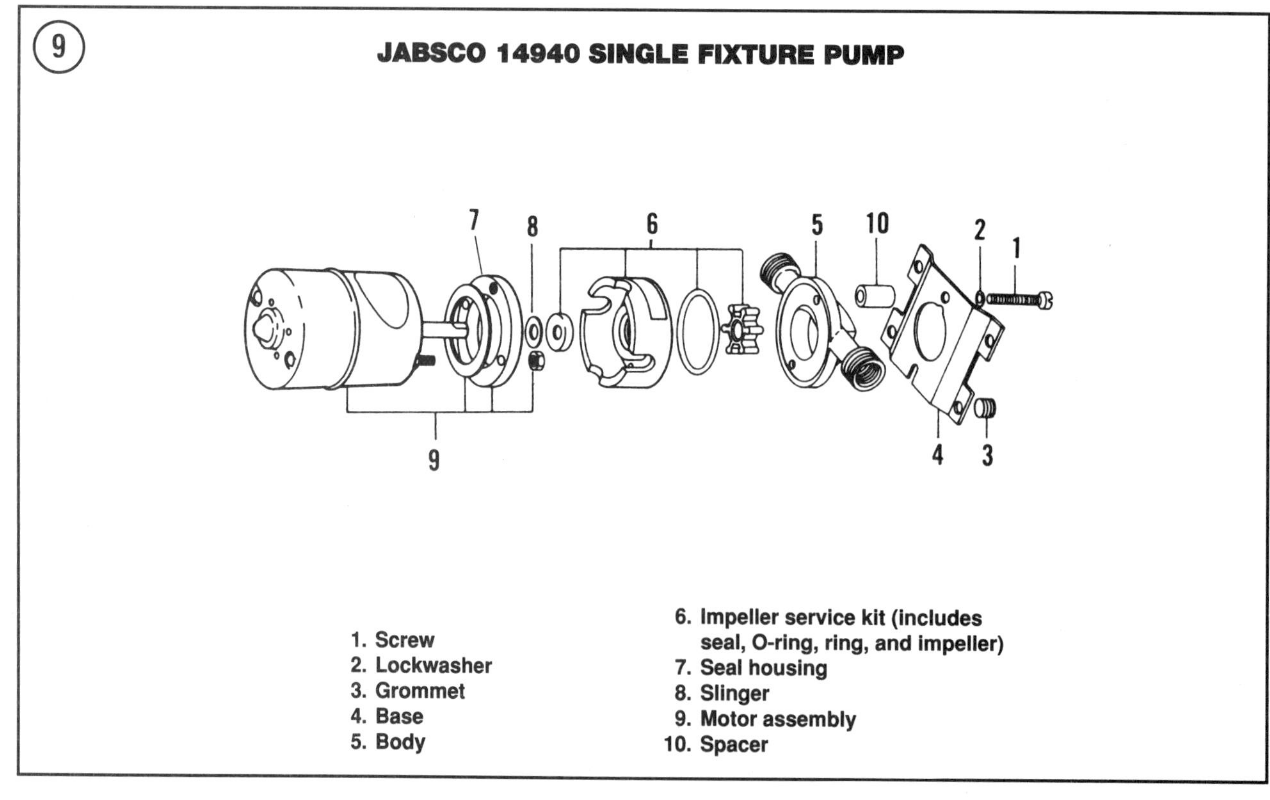

1. Screw
2. Lockwasher
3. Grommet
4. Base
5. Body
6. Impeller service kit (includes seal, O-ring, ring, and impeller)
7. Seal housing
8. Slinger
9. Motor assembly
10. Spacer

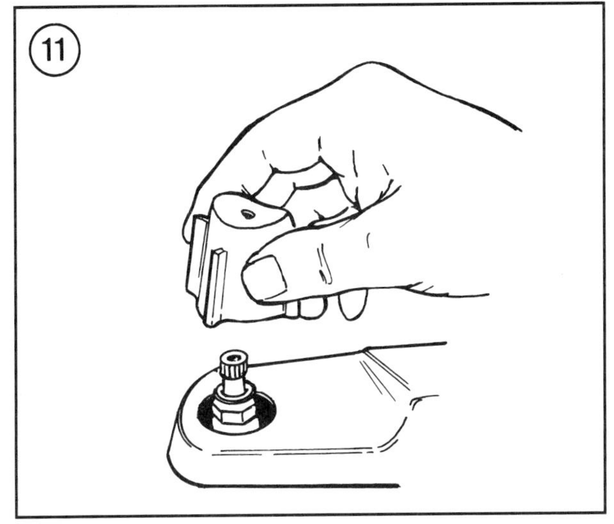
11

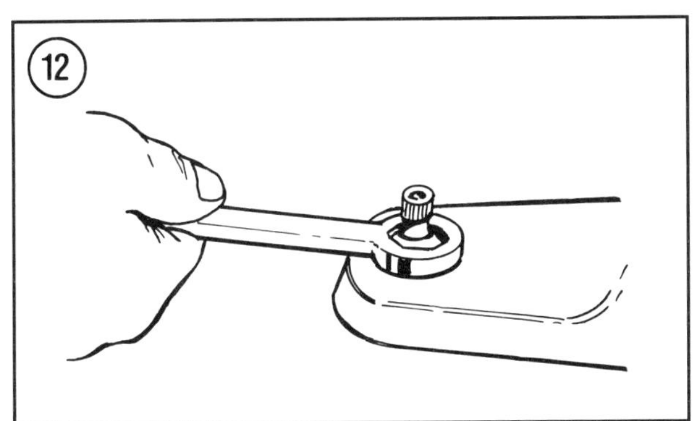
12

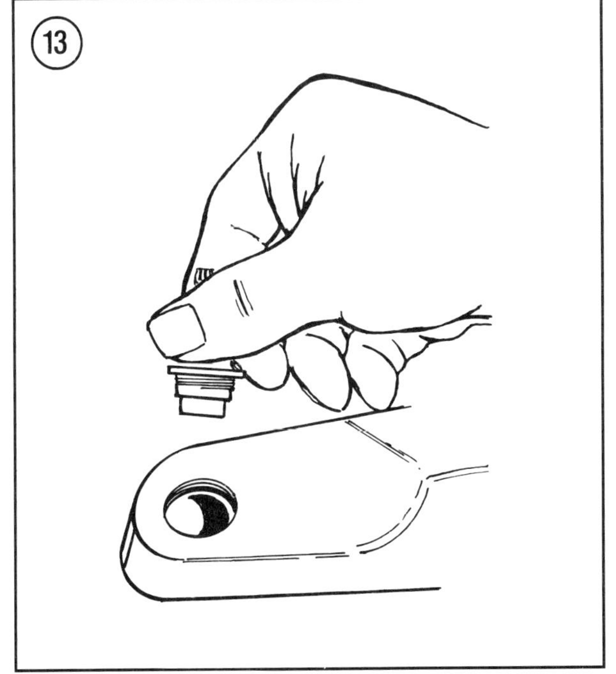
13

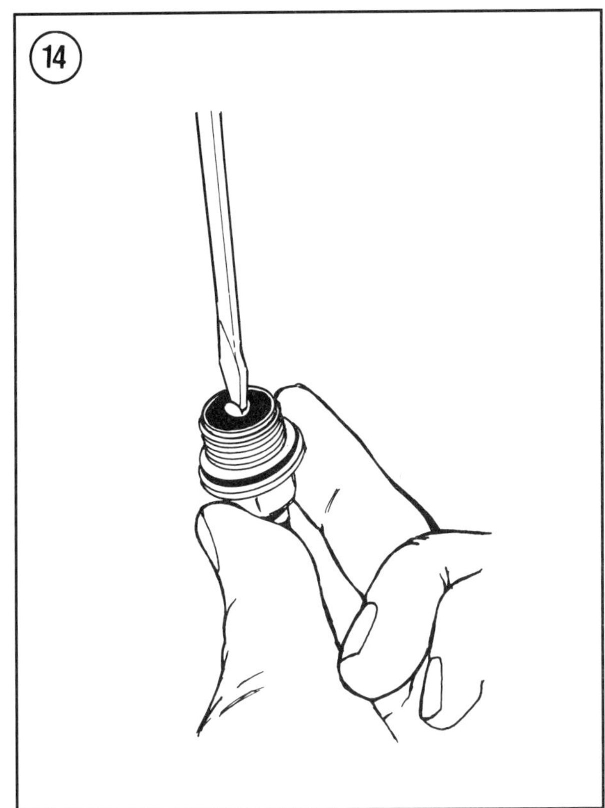
14

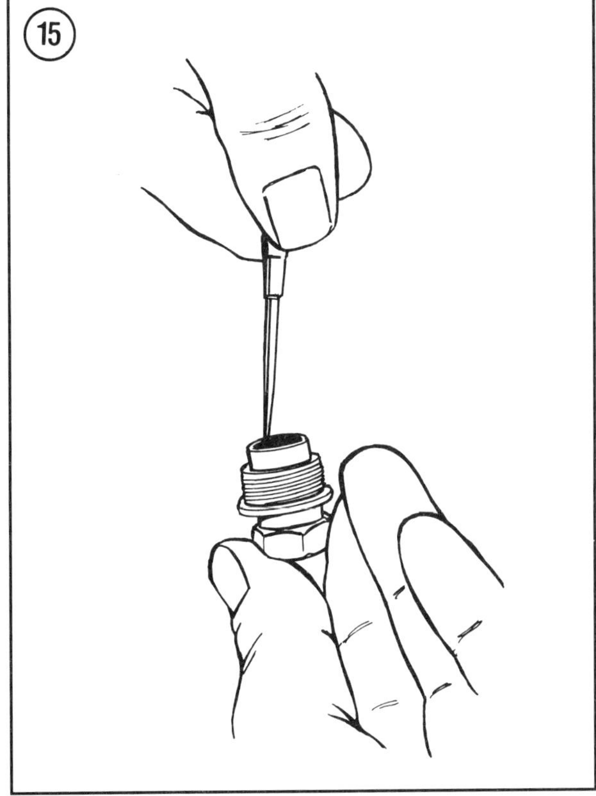
15

10

replacement washers are frequently marked on the bottom side with size numbers.

8. Assembly is the reverse of these steps.

NOTE
Be sure that the valve stem is turned fully counterclockwise (faucet open position) before tightening the valve stem assembly.

Single Handle Faucets

To stop leaks from single handle faucets, replace the ball assembly as follows:

1. Turn off the water pump or shut off the water supply to faucet.
2. Loosen the setscrew and lift off the handle. See **Figure 17**.
3. Unscrew the cap assembly and lift it off. See **Figure 18**.
4. Remove the cam assembly and ball. See **Figure 19**.
5. Install a new ball into the body over the seats.
6. Install the cam assembly over the ball stem, and engage it with the slot in the body. Push down firmly until it seats.
7. Partially unscrew the adjusting ring (see **Figure 20**).
8. Place the cap assembly over the stem and screw it down tight.
9. Turn on the pump or water supply.
10. Tighten the adjusting ring until no water leaks around stem when the faucet is on and pressure is exerted on the handle to force the ball into its socket.
11. Install the handle and tighten the setscrew.

WATER HEATER

Most hot water heaters contain a thermostatically controlled emersion element to heat the water at dockside using shore power. An optional heat exchanger extracts heat from the circulating engine coolant to provide hot water while underway.

Hot water heaters may have a capacity of 5-20 gal (19-75 L). The heating element is usually

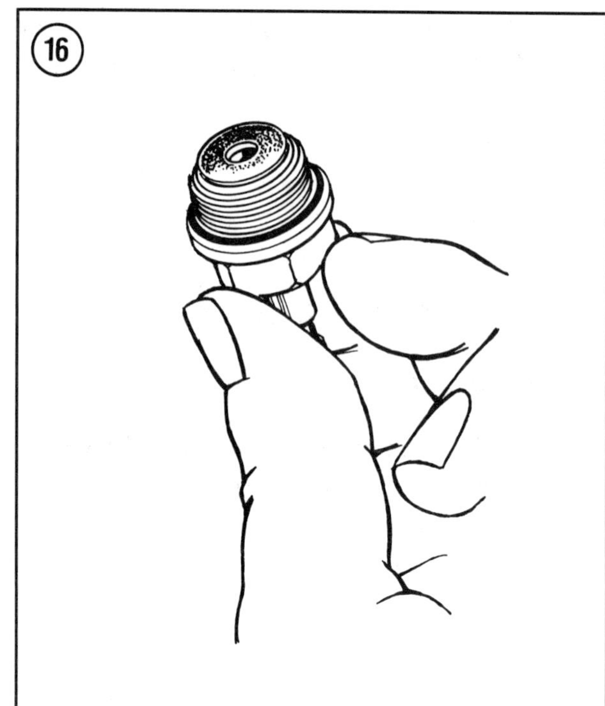

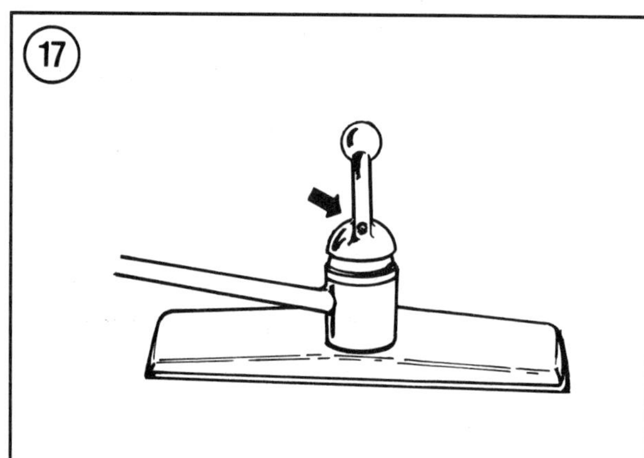

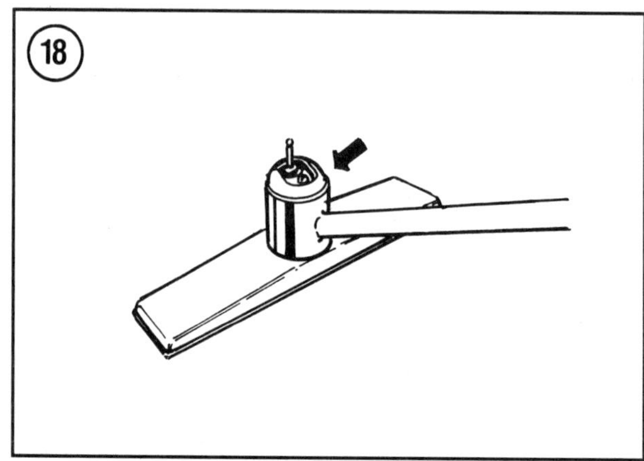

1000-1500 watts. A 1500 watt element will heat 5 gal. (19 L) of water to 100° F (37.8° C) in about an hour.

There is no preventive maintenance to the water heater itself. When preparing for lay-up follow the system procedure in this chapter.

TROUBLESHOOTING

Nonpressurized System

1. Pump does not prime—no water at faucet.
   a. Check water level in tank.
   b. Check hoses for kinks.
   c. Check hoses for leaks.
   d. Check for clogged tank vent.
2. Electric pump fails to turn on.
   a. Check pump fuse—use SLO-BLO type only.
   b. Check electrical connections to battery, switch and pump.
   c. Check for defective pump by replacement.

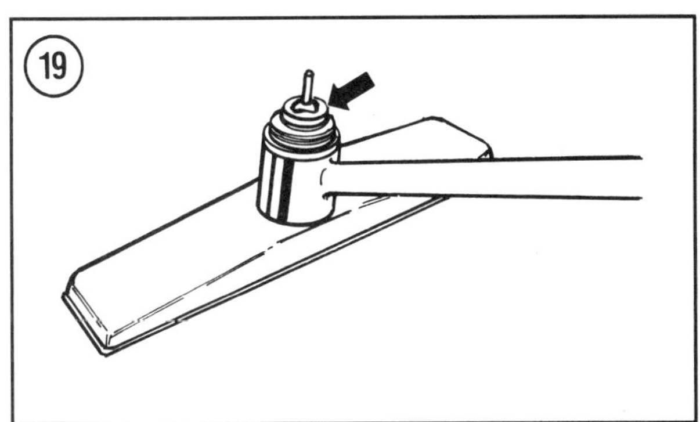

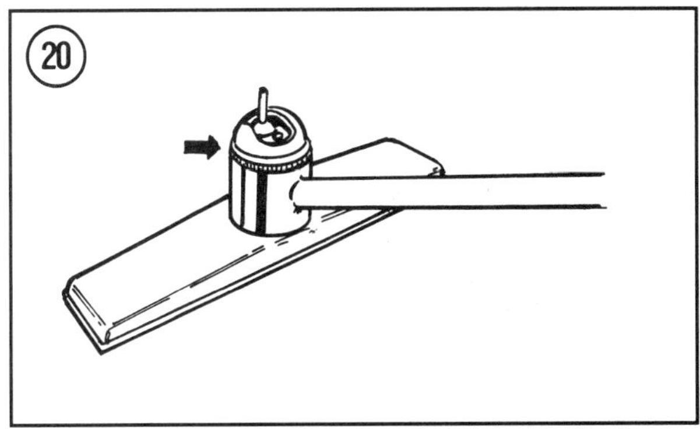

3. Electric pump fails to turn off. Check for shorted switch.

Pressurized Demand System

1. Low or no water pressure
   a. Check water level in tank.
   b. Check power supply, fuse, and all electrical circuit connections to ensure full voltage on the pump.
   c. Check inlet filter at water tank.
   d. Check for clogged tank vent.
   e. Dismantle and service pump.
2. Pump cycles while faucets are closed.
   a. Check all faucets for leaks.
   b. Check toilet for leak.
   c. Check all connections for leaks.
   d. If internal pump leakage seems to be the only explanation, dismantle and service pump.
3. Pump noisy and erratic
   a. Check inlet filter at water tank.
   b. Check all plumbing for restrictions.
   c. Clean aerator screen in all faucets. (Permanently removing aerator screens will provide better flow.)
   d. Check for clogged tank vent.
   e. Check plumbing near pump to ensure that it is not amplifying normal pump vibrations.
   f. Dismantle and service pump if necessary.
4. Pump does not operate
   a. Check fuse.
   b. Check for restrictions in system.
   c. Check and replace pressure switch if necessary.
5. Motor blows fuses

Under normal operating conditions the drive motor will barely get warm. If the unit is required to pump a significant volume of water at severely reduced voltage, the drive motor will overheat, melt the insulation, short out the windings and blow the fuse.

It is not feasible to repair the motor under these conditions, and the only cure is to replace the drive motor. The entire circuit should be checked to establish the reason for the low voltage problem to ensure that the replacement motor does not meet the same fate.

LAY-UP

Whenever the boat will be idle or stored for a long period, particularly when freezing temperatures are expected, the system should be winterized. There are two methods. One requires draining the system completely and leaving it dry. The other system uses a special nontoxic potable water propylene glycol antifreeze solution, available from marine chandlers and RV stores.

WARNING
Never use automotive type (ethylene glycol) antifreeze under any circumstances. It is poisonous.

Most propylene glycol additives can protect the system to –50° F (–46° C). They usually color the water to indicate their presence. Although propylene glycol is nontoxic, do not drink the solution. The system must be thoroughly drained and flushed to remove all traces of color when the boat is recommissioned.

Nonpressurized System

1. Drain the water tank.
2. Operate the pump on all faucets until no water comes out (1 to 2 minutes).

NOTE
The following steps apply only if special nontoxic antifreeze is to be added.

3. Remove the filter element (if installed).
4. Fill the tank with fresh water and the amount of antifreeze recommended by the manufacturer for the level of protection required.

WARNING
Never use automotive type (ethylene glycol) antifreeze under any circumstances. It is poisonous.

5. Operate the pump on all faucets starting from the one furthest from the tank until colored water emerges.
6. If no antifreeze has been used, simply add fresh water to the tank when recommissioning.
7. If antifreeze has been added, drain the tank.
8. Operate all faucets until emerging water is clear.
9. Fill the tank with fresh water and operate all faucets until water emerges.
10. Let fresh water set in the tank for 10-15 minutes.
11. Drain and flush the tank until water is no longer colored.
12. Add fresh water when the system is clear. Install a new filter element.

Pressurized Systems

1. Open all faucets and allow the pump to empty the water tank and intake lines. Run the pump dry for 1 to 2 minutes before turning it off.
2. Open all drains, including the one on the water heater (if any).
3. Disconnect the discharge and intake hoses from the pump. Start the pump and allow it to run until all water is expelled from the unit. Running dry will not harm the pump.
4. Reconnect the hoses, close the drains and leave faucets open.
5. Remove the pump fuse if antifreeze will not be used.

NOTE
The following steps apply only if special nontoxic propylene glycol antifreeze is to be added.

6. Remove filter element (if installed).

7. Fill the tank with fresh water and the amount of antifreeze recommended by the manufacturer for the level of protection required.

WARNING
Do not use automotive type ethylene glycol antifreeze under any circumstances. It is poisonous.

8. Open all faucets, one at a time, starting with the furthest from the water pump. Be sure that you open hot water faucets as well to fill the water heater with antifreeze.

9. When colored water flows from each faucet, close it and leave it closed.

10. Remove the pump fuse to prevent cycling during lay-up.

Recommissioning

If potable water antifreeze has not been used, simply install the pump fuse, fill the system with fresh water and open each faucet (starting with the furthest from pump) until all air is removed from system. If antifreeze was used, perform the following:

1. Drain the system following Steps 1-4 of the lay-up procedure.
2. Fill with fresh water and let it set in the tank for 10-15 minutes.
3. Drain and flush the tank until water is no longer colored.
4. Add fresh water when the system is clear. Install a new filter element.
5. Bleed air from system as described above.

Chapter Eleven

Heads

There are few calamities at sea to match a defective head. This chapter describes most of the popular portable and permanent systems in use. Each section deals with a specific model, providing preventive maintenance, troubleshooting, repair and lay-up procedures. By properly maintaining the head at dockside, you can prevent the embarrassment of a defective head when away from the dock.

TYPICAL SYSTEMS

Besides proper maintenance, you should make a point of tracing every part of the plumbing associated with the head. It is not a bad idea to draw a simple diagram showing where every component is located. You should know the placement of all thru-hull fittings and valves. You should be familiar with the type of plumbing connections including hoses so you can be prepared to make an emergency fix.

The simplest permanent toilet installation consists of a seacock and hose to admit fresh water to the toilet, and simple pump to discharge it through another seacock. See **Figure 1**. No modern boat should use a setup like this. It is illegal within the U.S. 3-mile limit.

The U.S. Coast Guard and many states regulate installed toilets and other Marine Sanitation Devices (MSDs). There are three types of MSDs recognized in the regulations.

Type I MSDs break up or macerate the solid waste to partially liquefy it. The waste is treated, usually with chemicals, to kill bacteria. The treated waste may then be discharged overboard in most waters, though it may be prohibited by state or local agencies in some waters. **Figure 2** shows a typical Type I installation which includes a toilet and waste treatment system.

Type II MSD treatment standards are more stringent than for Type I MSDs. The hardware and plumbing are essentially the same however. Both Type I and Type II MSDs must be U.S.

Coast Guard certified. A certified device should have an attached certification label. If it is not visible because of the installation or has been removed, the manufacturer of the toilet or other MSD such as a waste treatment system can tell you if the device is certified.

1 SIMPLE PERMANENT HEAD

Inlet
seacock/
thru-hull
Outlet
seacock/thru-hull

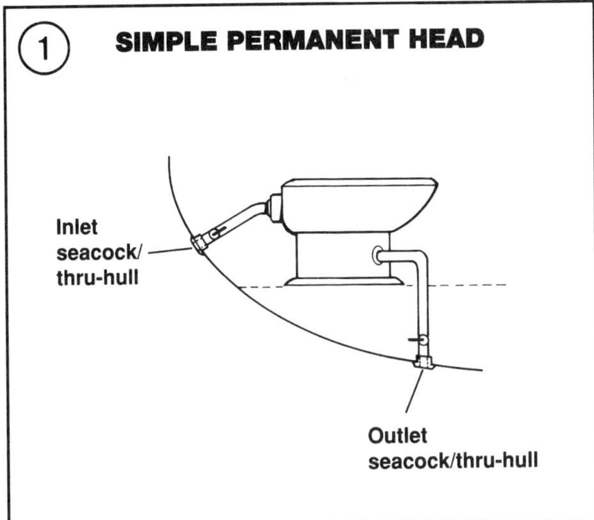

Type III MSDs are devices which do not discharge overboard in normal use, but instead hold the waste in a special holding tank designed for the purpose. See **Figure 3** for a typical Type III installation. The holding tank is discharged at a dockside pumping station through a deck mounted pump-out fitting. Some of these devices also have a diverter valve which allows discharge of untreated waste out via a thru-hull fitting when the boat is beyond the 3 mile limit. Within the 3 mile limit some means must be incorporated to prevent inadvertent discharge overboard through the diverter valve. A nylon tie wrap can be used or you can simply remove the valve handle.

Figure 4 and **Figure 5** show typical Type III recirculating systems. **Figure 4** shows the simplest installation which permits only dockside pump-out. **Figure 5** shows the addition of two valves. Valve 1 permits normal flushing action to draw seawater through the toilet into the tank for

2 TYPICAL TYPE II INSTALLATION

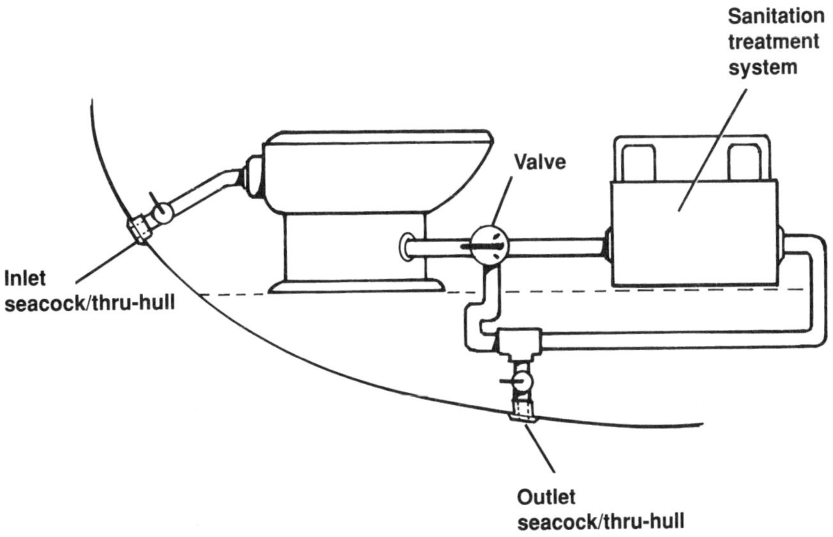

Sanitation
treatment
system
Valve
Inlet
seacock/thru-hull
Outlet
seacock/thru-hull

3

TYPICAL TYPE III INSTALLATION

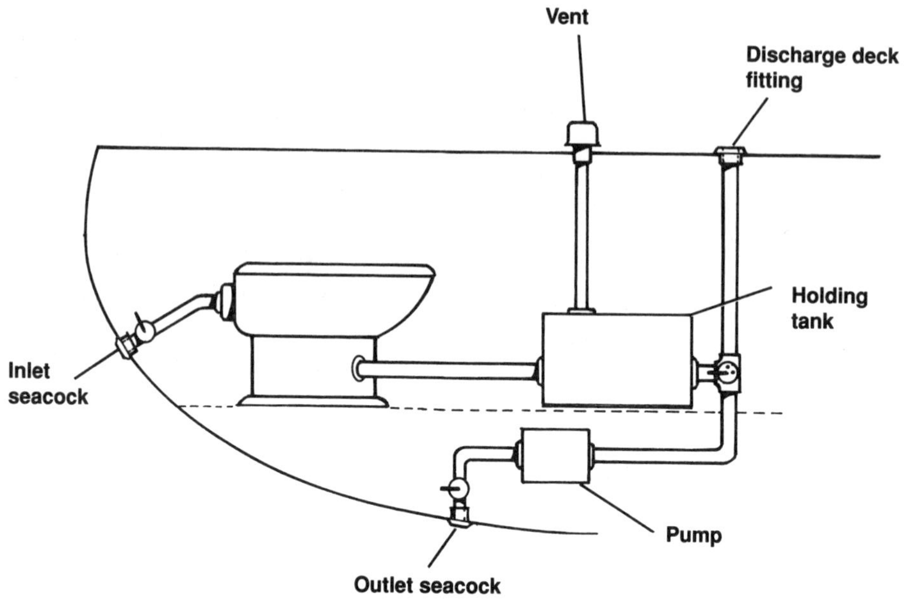

Vent
Discharge deck fitting
Holding tank
Inlet seacock
Pump
Outlet seacock

4

SIMPLE RECIRCULATION SYSTEM

Vent
Discharge deck fitting
Holding tank

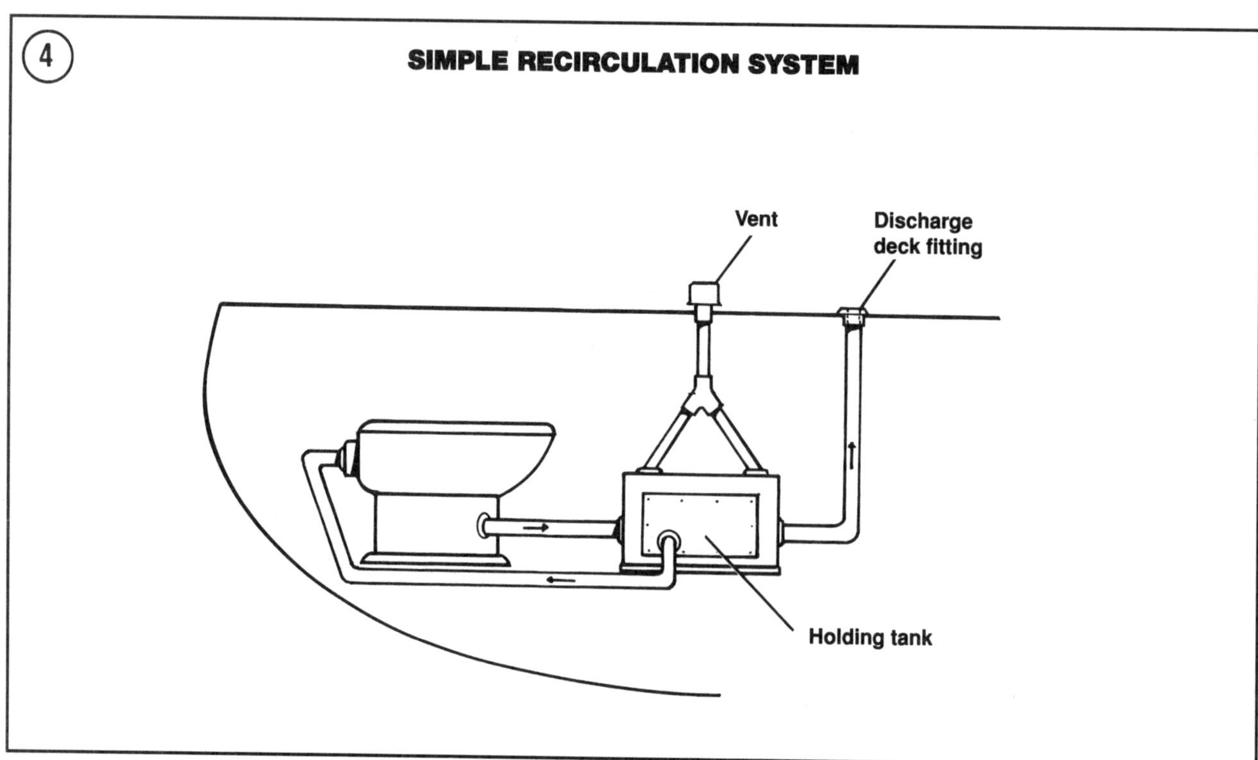

convenient charging. The valve must be returned to the recirculate position to prevent overfilling and consequent back-up of waste. Valve 2 permits selection of dockside pump-out or thru-hull discharge in waters where this is legal. Variations are possible by omitting either of the valves.

Incidentally, portable toilets which store waste within the unit and recirculate the waste for flushing are considered Type III MSDs. In fact, some of them can be connected as a permanent installation with the appropriate fittings available from the manufacturer.

Toilets

There is a large variety of toilets available for marine use. The simplest, used on small boats, is a portable toilet with an integral holding tank. The toilet is first charged with a few gallons of fresh water and a chemical deodorizer. Deodorized liquid waste is then used for flushing. The integral holding tank normally holds 4-6 gal. (15-23 L) depending on the unit. When it is full, it must be discharged into a sanitary sewer system on shore. Normally, this means pouring the contents into a public toilet at the end of the sailing day.

Installed toilets may also be very simple devices, but some incorporate-high tech features which rival those found on shore. The simplest toilet consists of a bowl with an attached manual or electric pump used to pump waste overboard or into a holding tank. See **Figure 6**. A slightly more elaborate electric toilet incorporates a macerator pump at the base of the unit. The macerator breaks up solid waste which allows better waste treatment and elimination of visible floating solids as required by U.S. Coast Guard regulations.

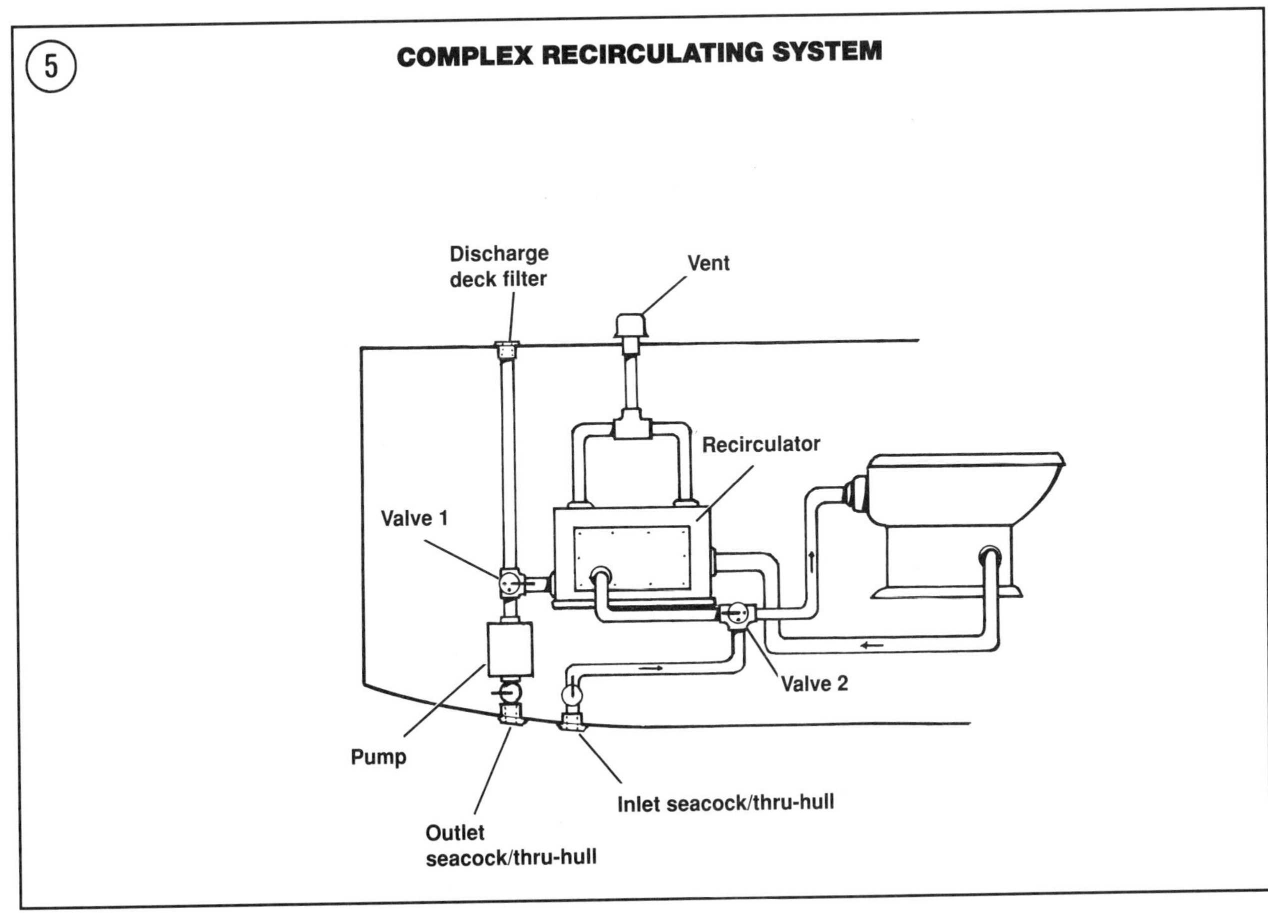

Sealand's VacuFlush toilet uses a powerful vacuum pump and vacuum chamber to suck waste out of the toilet into a holding tank or out via a thru-hull fitting. Fresh water from the boat's pressurized potable water supply completes the flush. Only about a pint of water is required for each flush. This not only conserves the boat's fresh water, but makes possible a relatively small holding tank. A typical electric toilet might need a 30 gal. (38 L) holding tank where the same head equipped with a VacuFlush toilet might only need a 10 gal. (114 L) holding tank.

Waste Treatment Systems

Waste treatment systems usually consist of a dual chamber tank with a built-in macerator and some method of injecting a chemical in a controlled manner. The waste is macerated in the first chamber and mixed with chemical in the second chamber. Most use ordinary sodium hypochlorite (household bleach) dispensed from the original container. Some use chemicals in tablet form. They are limited in size so they should be operated every time the toilet is flushed to prevent clogging the macerator.

Raritan's LectraSan system is unique in that it does not require that chemicals be added. See **Figure 7**. Instead, it uses high-current DC voltage from the boat's electrical system to convert ordinary seawater into hypochloric acid which kills bacteria. This acid is unstable and quickly breaks down to render it harmless when discharge. If the boat is operated in fresh water, special salt tablets may be added to the unit so that it will function normally.

You should never allow toilet bowl cleaners or drain cleaners on any part of a marine head system. Furthermore, you should not allow *any* chemical to be introduced into a waste treatment system unless the manufacturer specifically requires its use. Other chemicals can react with the waste treatment chemicals to produce potentially dangerous reactions.

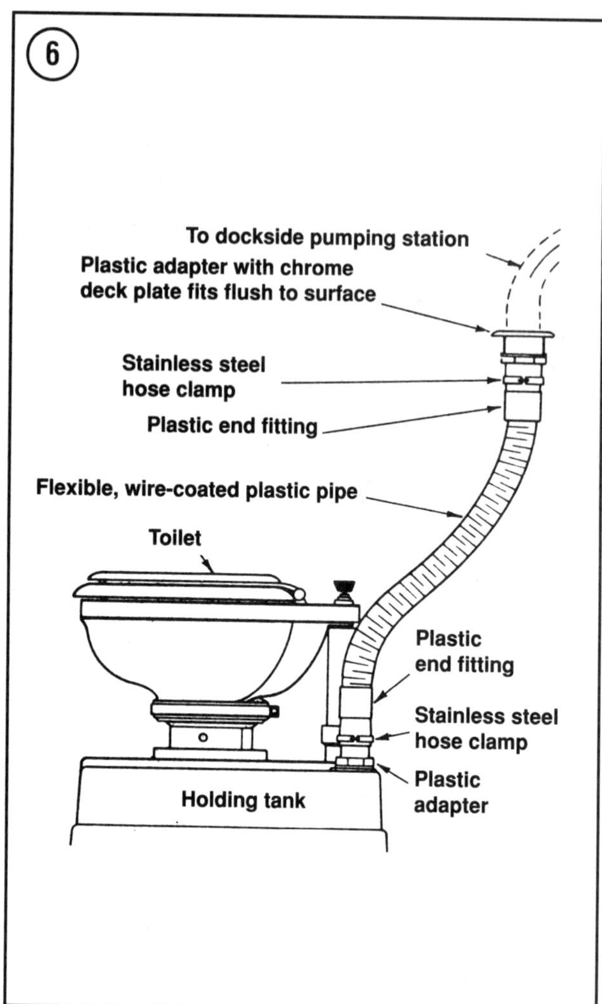

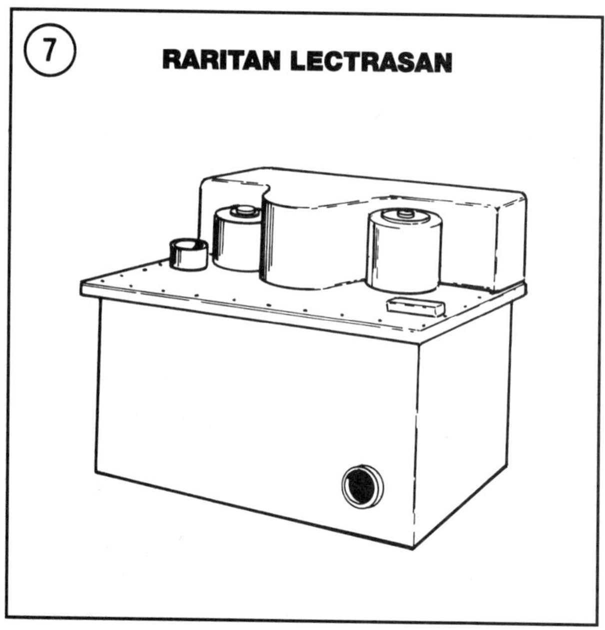

Plumbing

Most marine installations use 3/4 in. (19 mm) ID hose on the supply or suction side for flush water and 1-1/2 in. (38 mm) ID hose on the discharge side. The suction side must use non-collapsible hoses. Special sanitation hose made from reinforced neoprene or flexible PVC are available from marine chandleries. Rigid PVC pipe is also an excellent marine plumbing material.

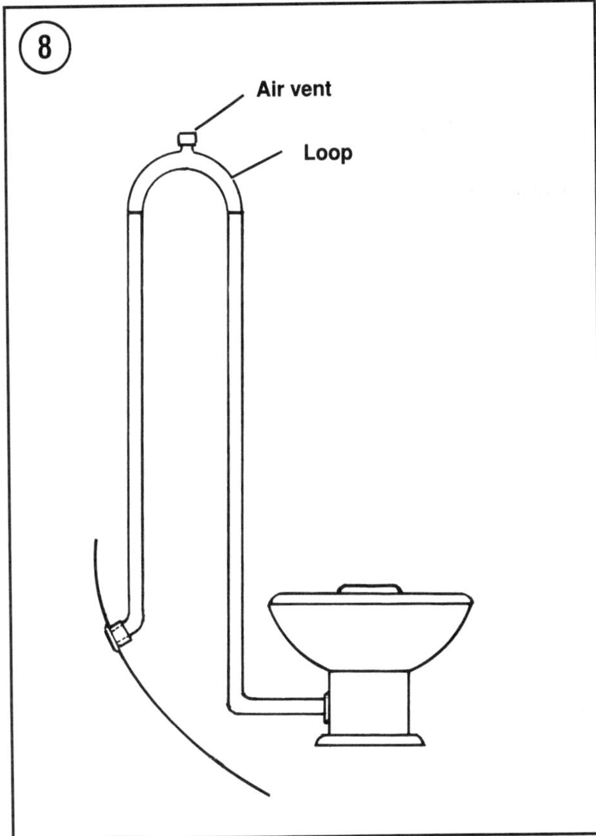

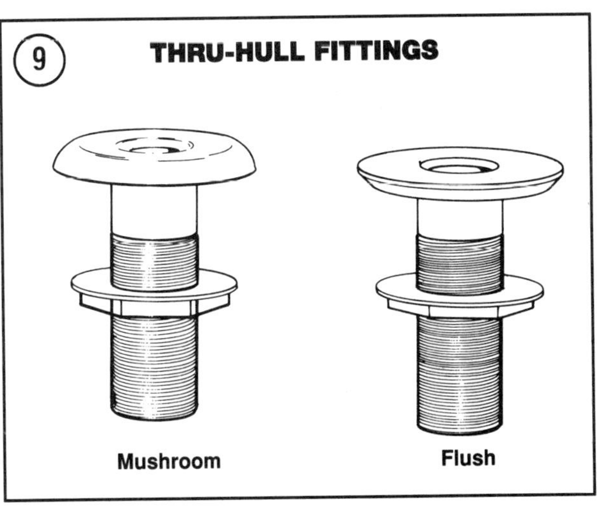

The suction side should also have a raw water strainer which prevents intake of marine organisms which might clog the system. Some might even find your holding tank such an inviting habitat that they take up residence! The strainer should be mounted in a relatively accessible position because you should check it frequently for debris and marine organisms.

In many installations, the toilet must be mounted below the waterline. Valves in the suction and discharge lines should normally prevent outside water from entering the toilet when it is not being flushed. Unfortunately, the valves can leak or fail completely. Water could siphon into the toilet and sink the boat if it is not detected in time. To avoid this, the suction and discharge lines are looped above the waterline and vented to the atmosphere to break any siphoning action. See **Figure 8**.

The discharge vent should be located carefully as unpleasant waste gases naturally escape from the system. Never plug the vent. Replaceable vent filters are available which neutralize the odors for about a season.

Waste products eventually permeate all but the very best hose materials and emit foul odors. All hoses should be replaced if there are signs of permeation or damage of any kind. Cleaning up after a waste hose has ruptured or even leaked will test even the most effective anti-nausea drugs or devices.

Thru-Hull Fittings and Seacocks

Thru-hull fittings allow discharge directly outside the hull either above or below the waterline. Some are flush mounted while others are "mushroom" shaped. See **Figure 9**. They may be metal or plastic. Metal hulls should use plastic fittings or must be somehow insulated from the hull to prevent galvanic action between the two metals.

Seacocks are simple hand operated valves which allow the thru-hull path to be opened or closed. Several valve designs are used. Most take only a 1/4-turn to open or close. The best seacocks use a ball valve, and these are the *only* kind that should be used for head installations. See **Figure 10**. When the handle is in line with the hose, the hole in the ball aligns with the flow and the valve is open. When the handle is perpendicular to the valve body, the ball blocks the flow and the valve is closed.

Hoses can break, and valves and thru-hull fittings can fail. You should have a good assortment of wood or rubber bungs that can be jammed into the opening in an emergency to prevent making a huge mess or even swamping the boat.

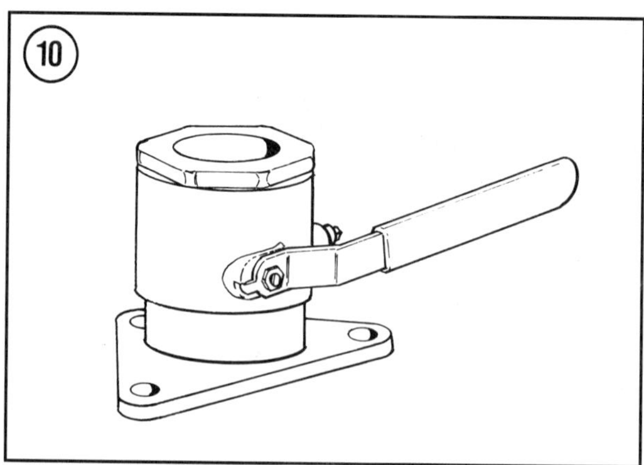

Holding Tanks

Holding tanks are very straightforward devices. Most are made from fiberglass or polyethylene, but other materials are used as well. They are available in a wide variety of strange shapes and sizes to fit almost any boat interior. See **Figure 11**.

Even flexible holding tanks are available. See **Figure 12**. These may be added to an older boat without a holding tank to comply with regulations. They may also be used to extend capacity. The main advantage of flexible holding tanks is the ability to put them in nearly any available space without major alterations to the boat.

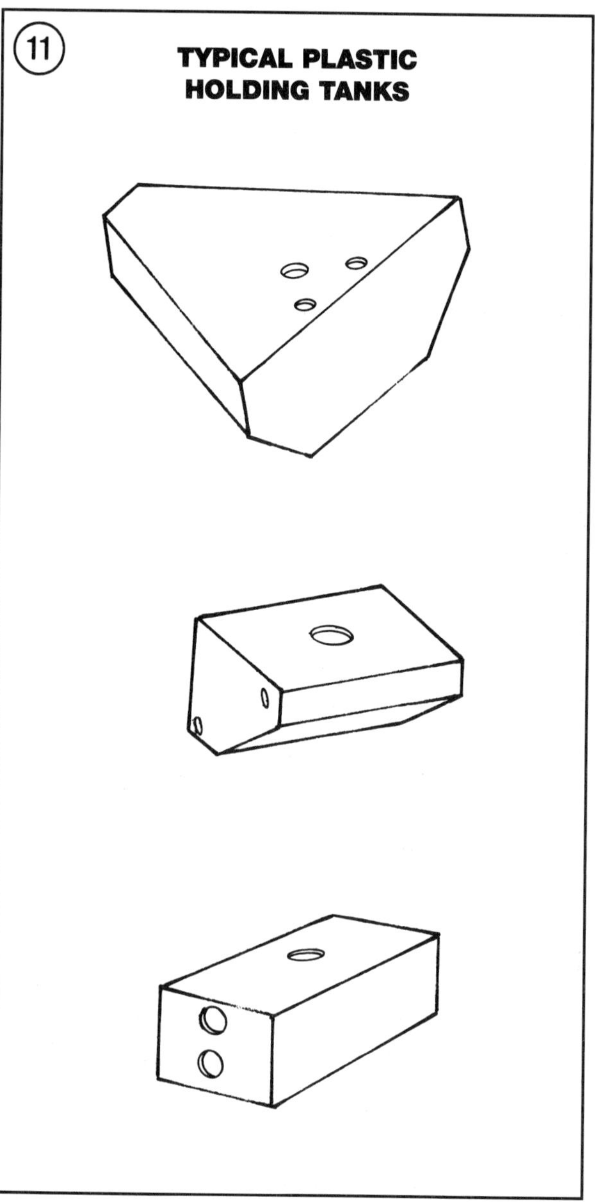

THETFORD PORTABLES

Thetford makes a variety of portable self-contained toilets that provide fresh water flushes and a removable holding tank which can be emptied at any permanent toilet facility. Some of these can be installed permanently as Type III MSDs.

Maintenance

Minimum maintenance is required. Clean the toilet with a high quality, non-abrasive cleaner. Do not use abrasive, highly concentrated or high acid content household cleaners. They may damage the rubber seals.

If the bowl sealing blade does not operate properly, apply a light film of *silicone* spray to the blade.

Winterizing

For cold season use, where temperatures are likely to drop to freezing or below, add sufficient nontoxic antifreeze to the fresh water tank sufficient to protect the water to the lowest temperature expected. See the antifreeze directions for the correct amount. Leave room to add deodorant. Flush a couple of times to circulate the antifreeze through the pump.

CAUTION
Use propylene glycol antifreeze available at marine and RV outlets which is nontoxic. Do not use ethylene glycol which is toxic to marine life and may damage plastic parts.

Lay-up

Completely drain the fresh water tank and holding tank. Clean the holding tank thoroughly using deodorant and fresh water. Do not use hot water to clean the tanks. Clean the bowl and exterior surfaces then, spray them with a high quality, non-abrasive cleaner and finish with a disinfectant. Do not use abrasive, highly concentrated or high acid content household cleaners. They may damage the rubber seals. On AquaMates with Electric Flush, remove the internal batteries to prevent corrosion.

Troubleshooting

1. Holding tank blade does not seal completely—Check blade groove for foreign matter. Clean it out with the end of a coat hanger wire. Do not damage the rubber seal.

(12) **FLEXIBLE HOLDING TANK**

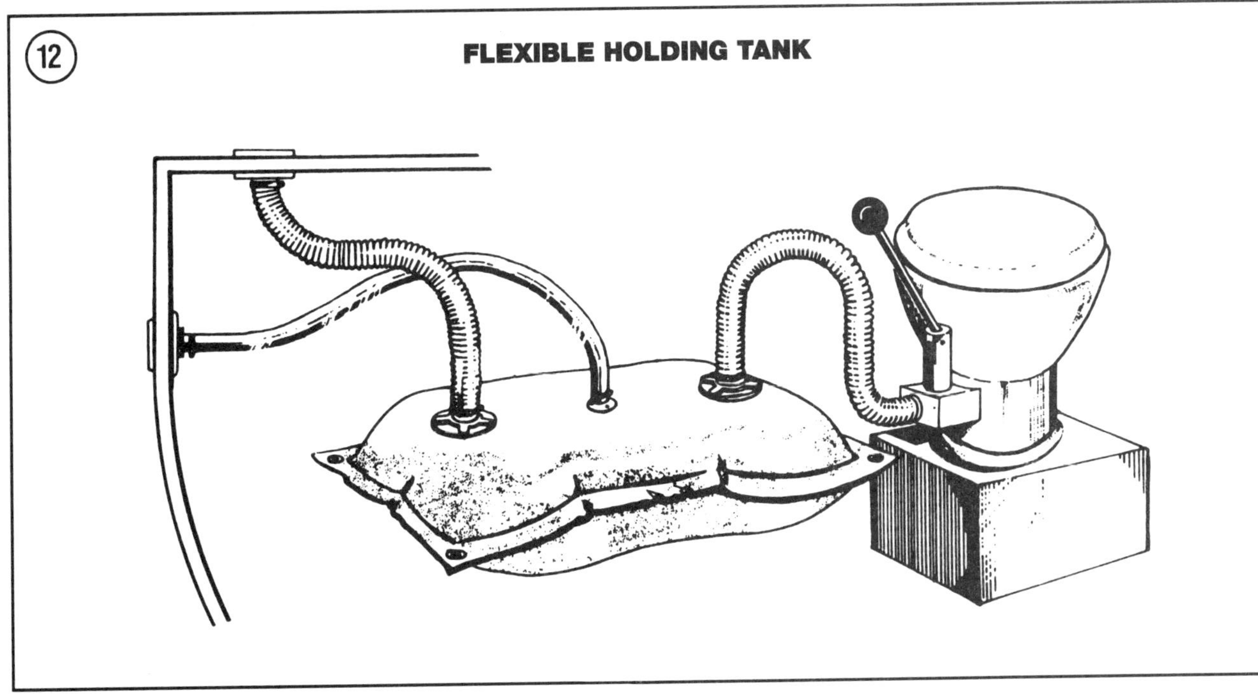

2. Foot pedal operates harder than normal—Apply a light film of silicone spray to the blade.

Bellows Flush Replacement

The bellows receives the most wear and, after extended use, may deteriorate. To replace the bellows:

1. Cut open the old bellows from top to bottom using scissors See **Figure 13**.
2. Fold the bellows inward and remove the pump assembly.
3. Remove the bellows and inlet tube assembly from the flush tube.
4. Connect a new bellows assembly to the flush tube.
5. Align the inlet (short) tube on the bellows with the back of the toilet and press it down until it snaps into place.

THETFORD ELECTRA MAGIC

The Electra Magic is a self-contained recirculating system requiring no separate water hookup or holding tank installation. The unit operates from 12 or 24 volts DC and has a level indicator to indicate water level in the tank. The marine version of the Electra Magic has a sump connection for dockside discharge.

Maintenance

There is no periodic maintenance other than evacuating the tank when full and cleaning the unit. Use a high quality, non-abrasive cleaner such as Aqua Bowl Cleaner.

Winterizing

For cold season usage, where temperatures may fall to freezing or below, charge the system with 1/2 water and 1/2 antifreeze.

CAUTION
Use propylene glycol antifreeze available at marine and RV outlets which is nontoxic. Do not use ethylene glycol which is toxic to marine life and may damage plastic parts.

Lay-up

1. Completely evacuate the unit.
2. Refill the unit to within 3 in. (76.2 mm) of the bowl top with fresh water.
3. Add 2 in. (51 mm) (measured on the bottle) of Aqua Bowl Cleaner.
4. Cycle the unit 3 times.
5. Let stand for a few minutes for cleaning action.
6. Completely evacuate the unit again.

Returning to Service After Lay-up

When returning the unit to service after lay-up:

1. Pour approximately 3 gal. (11.3 L) of water in the bowl (until water reaches the charge level on the indicator lens).
2. Add one 8 oz. (237 mL) bottle of Aqua Kem Concentrate.

Troubleshooting

Table 1 lists symptoms, possible causes, and probable remedies for problems that might be encountered.

14

THETFORD ELECTRA-MAGIC HEAD

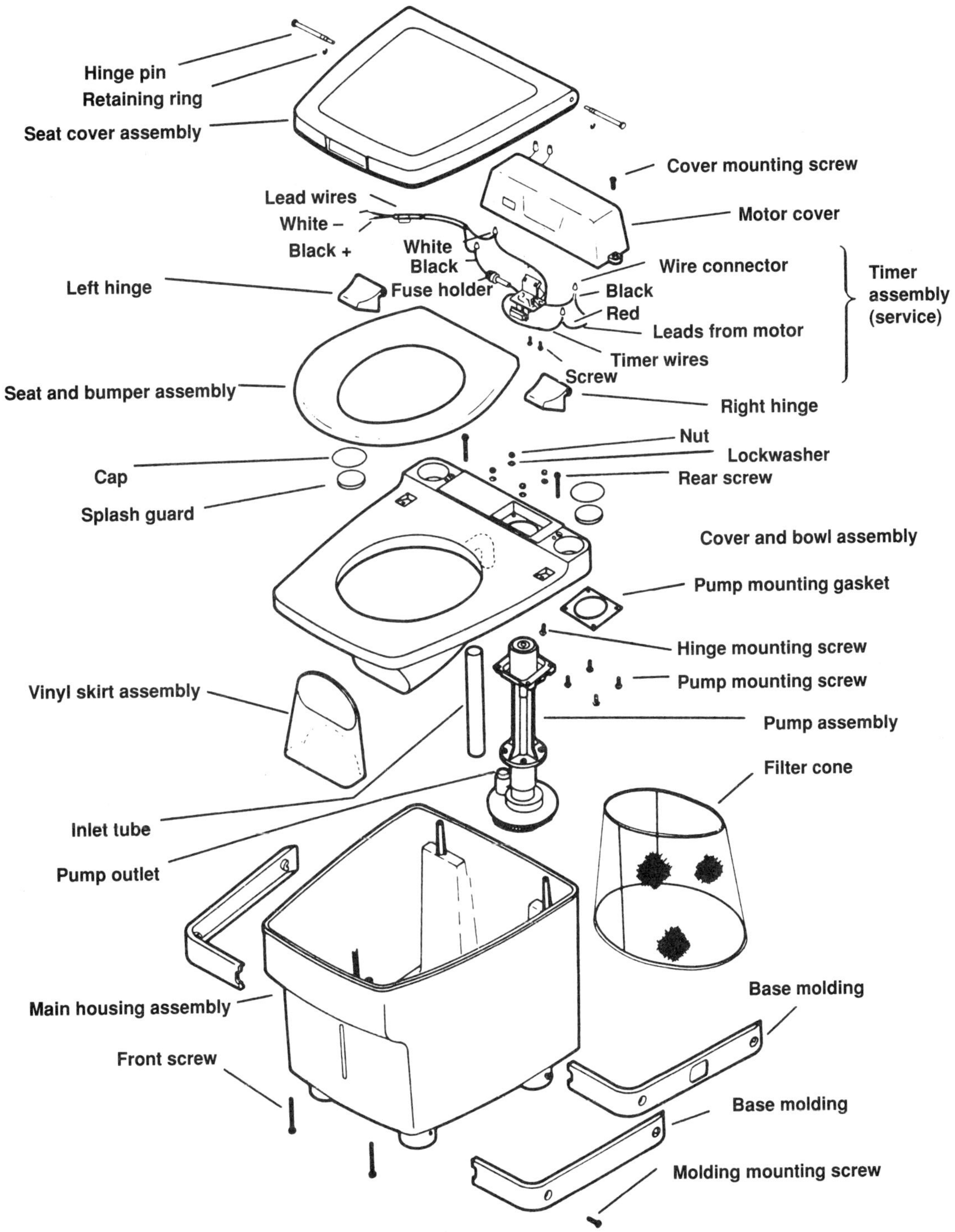

Hinge pin
Retaining ring
Seat cover assembly
Cover mounting screw
Lead wires
White –
Black +
Motor cover
White
Black
Fuse holder
Wire connector
Black
Red
Leads from motor
Timer wires
Timer assembly (service)
Left hinge
Screw
Seat and bumper assembly
Right hinge
Nut
Lockwasher
Cap
Rear screw
Splash guard
Cover and bowl assembly
Pump mounting gasket
Hinge mounting screw
Pump mounting screw
Vinyl skirt assembly
Pump assembly
Filter cone
Inlet tube
Pump outlet
Main housing assembly
Base molding
Front screw
Base molding
Molding mounting screw

Disassembly/Assembly

Refer to **Figure 14** for this procedure.

1. Fuse replacement:
   a. Remove the 2 cover mounting screws and the motor cover.
   b. The fuse is now readily accessible for checking or changing.
   c. Assembly is the reverse of these steps
2. Timer removal:
   a. Disconnect the lead wires from the power source.
   b. Remove the 2 cover mounting screws and the motor cover.
   c. Disconnect the leads from the pump assembly motor.
   d. Remove the 2 timer bracket mounting screws and the timer assembly.
   e. Assembly is the reverse of these steps
3. Pump removal:
   a. Complete Steps 2a-2c above.
   b. Completely evacuate the unit.
   c. Remove the cover and bowl assembly screws (2 in rear from top side and 2 in front from bottom side) and remove the cover and bowl assembly.
   d. Remove the 4 pump mounting screws.
   e. Disconnect the flush tube from the pump outlet.
   f. Remove the pump assembly.
   g. Assembly is the reverse of these steps
4. Sump removal:
   a. Disconnect the lead wires from the power source.
   b. Completely evacuate the unit.
   c. Remove the 2 molding mounting screws and remove the 2 base moldings.
   d. Remove the slides by catching their tabs with a hooked tool and pulling forward.
   e. Remove the flexible hose from the sump and invert the unit.
   f. Remove the 4 screws and remove sump. See **Figure 15**.
   g. Assembly is the reverse of these steps

THETFORD AQUA-MAGIC (GALAXY, STARLITE)

The Aqua Magic is a permanent toilet developed specifically for marine use. Each flush, controlled by a foot pedal, is accomplished with fresh water. Models C and G have separate water rinse and flush pedals.

Maintenance

There is no periodic maintenance to the toilet itself other than cleaning the unit. Use a high quality, non-abrasive cleaner such as Aqua Bowl Cleaner.

Winterizing

Since fresh water comes from the boat's fresh water supply, no antifreeze can be used.

Lay-up

1. Drain or pump out the boat's fresh water tanks.
2. Leave the water supply valve to the toilet open.
3. Depress the foot pedal and insert a soft drink bottle into the outlet at the bottom of the bowl. Release the hand or foot pedal slowly until the blade holds bottle in place. This holds the valve open, preventing residual water from collecting and freezing.
4. Empty and flush the holding tank thoroughly.

Troubleshooting

Table 2 below lists likely troubles, causes, and cures.

Disassembly

Thetford Aqua Magic Galaxy and Starlite toilets disassemble into 4 main subassemblies.

a. Seat and cover assembly.
b. Vacuum breaker.
c. Mechanism assembly.
d. Hopper assembly.

Refer to **Figures 16 -18** for this procedure.

1. Remove the seat and cover assembly.
   a. Turn the toilet upside down. The seat and cover are attached to the bowl with a standard hinge and bolt assembly.
   b. Remove the nuts from the hinge bolts and lift the cover and seat from the bowl.
2. Remove the vacuum breaker.
   a. Turn the toilet upside down.
   b. To remove the water lines from the vacuum breaker base, pinch the hose clamps with a pair of pliers and slide them up the water line. Then, the water lines may be pulled off.
   c. Remove the 4 vacuum breaker attachment screws.
3. Remove the mechanism assembly.
   a. Turn the toilet upside down.
   b. Remove the 6 screws that are now visible.
   c. Lift up the mechanism to gain access to the water line hose clamps. Pinch the hose clamps with a pair of pliers and slide them up the water line.
   d. Pull the water lines off the mechanism. See **Figure 18** for available service parts.
4. The hopper assembly may be serviced or replaced after Steps 1-3 are completed.

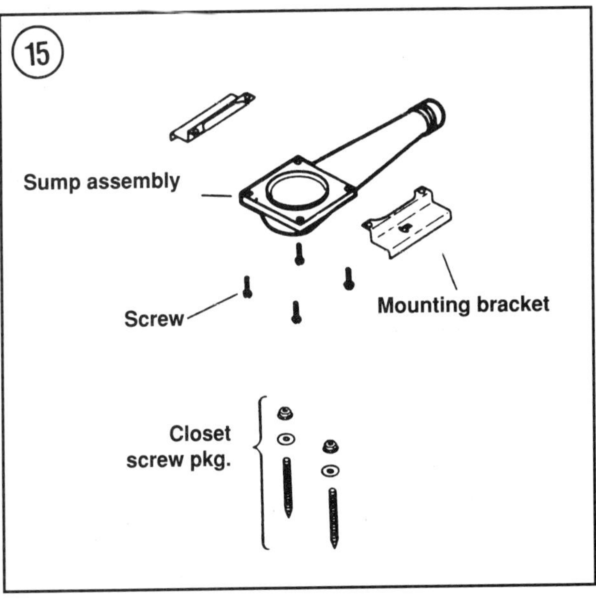

THETFORD AQUA-MAGIC IV

The Aqua-Magic IV is a permanent toilet developed specifically for marine use. Each flush, controlled by a hand or foot pedal, is accomplished with fresh water.

Maintenance

There is no periodic maintenance to the toilet itself other than cleaning the unit. Use a high quality, non-abrasive cleaner such as Aqua Bowl Cleaner.

Winterizing

Since fresh water comes from the boat's fresh water supply, no antifreeze can be used.

Lay-up

1. Drain or pump out the boat's fresh water tanks.
2. Leave the water supply valve to the toilet open.
3. Empty and flush the holding tank thoroughly.

Troubleshooting

Table 2 below lists likely troubles, causes, and cures.

Disassembly

Figure 19 and **Figure 20** show exploded views of the Hand Flush and Foot Pedal Flush models.

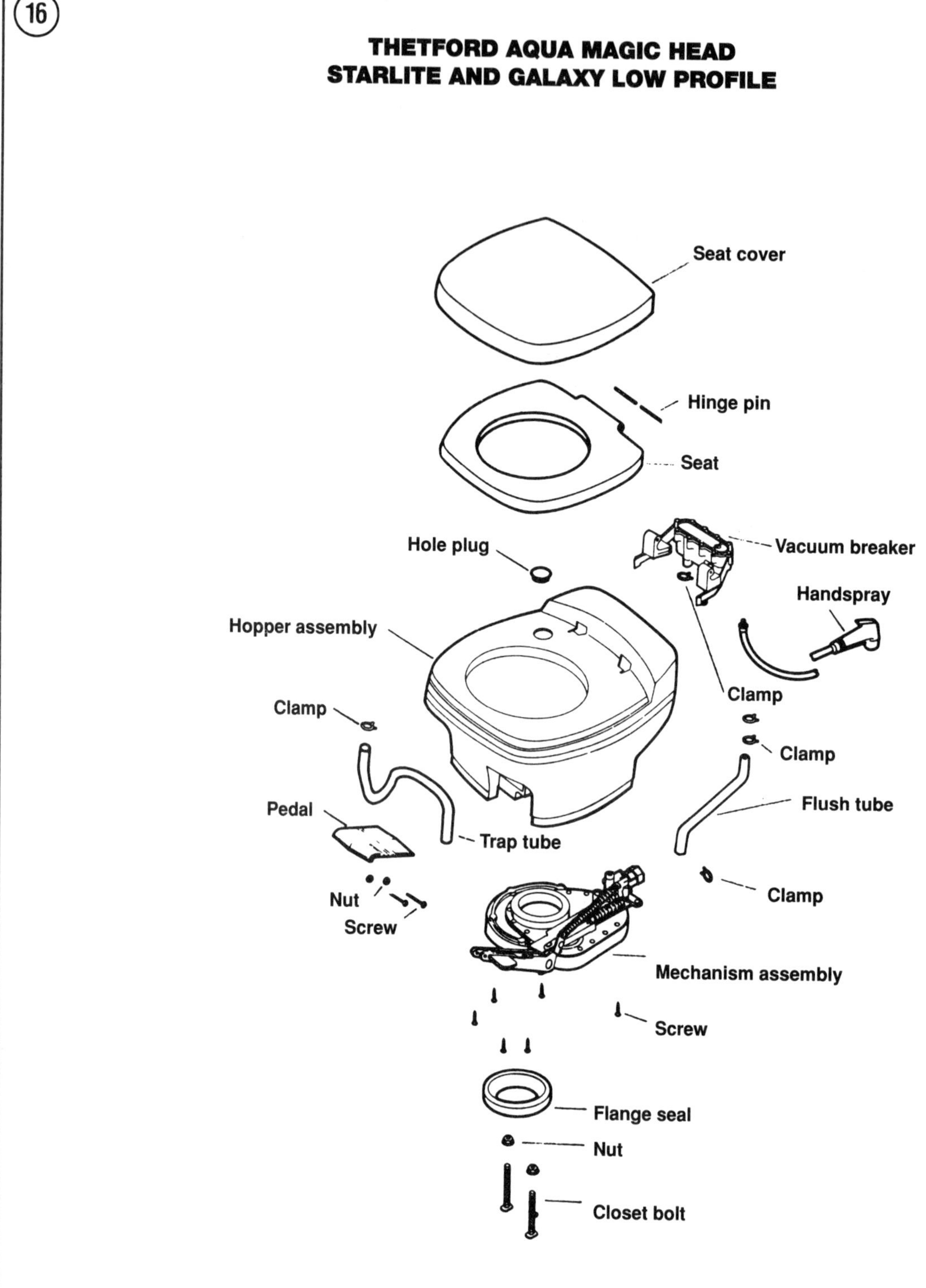
16
THETFORD AQUA MAGIC HEAD
STARLITE AND GALAXY LOW PROFILE
Seat cover
Hinge pin
Seat
Hole plug
Vacuum breaker
Handspray
Hopper assembly
Clamp
Clamp
Clamp
Flush tube
Pedal
Trap tube
Clamp
Nut
Screw
Mechanism assembly
Screw
Flange seal
Nut
Closet bolt

(17)

THETFORD AQUA MAGIC HEAD
STARLITE AND GALAXY STANDARD HEIGHT

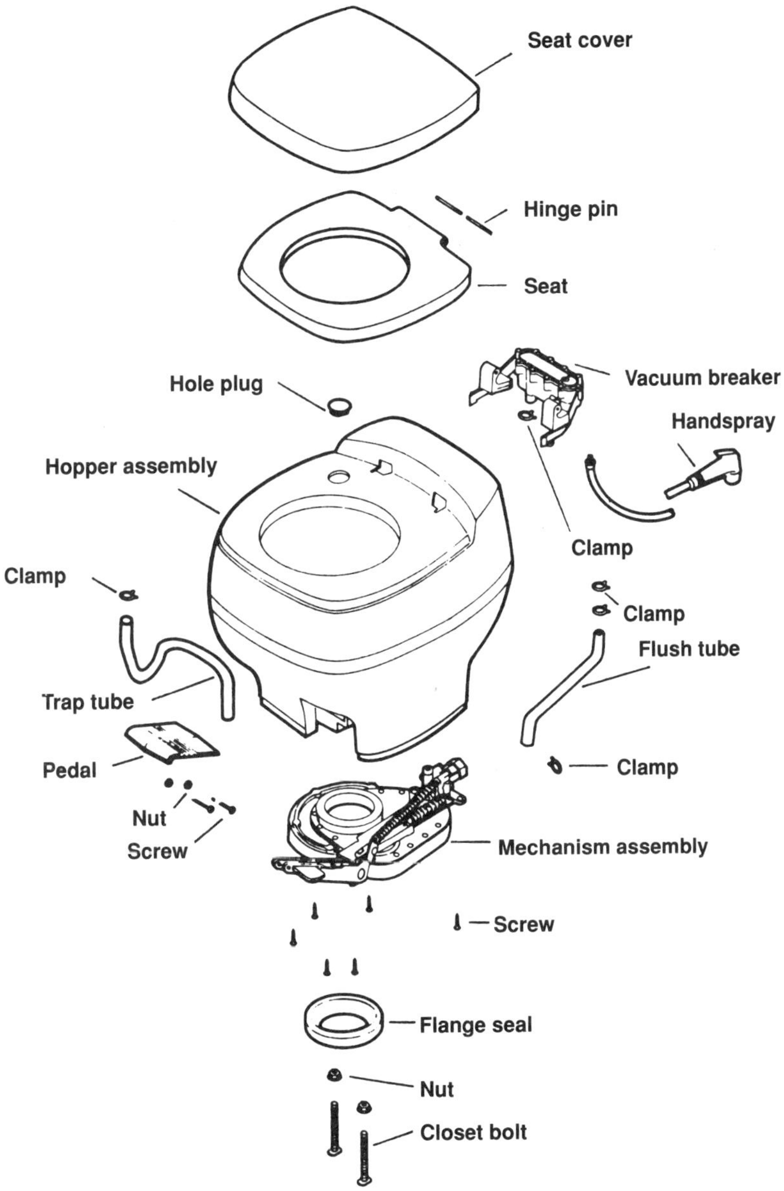

Seat cover
Hinge pin
Seat
Hole plug
Vacuum breaker
Handspray
Hopper assembly
Clamp
Clamp
Clamp
Flush tube
Trap tube
Pedal
Clamp
Nut
Screw
Mechanism assembly
Screw
Flange seal
Nut
Closet bolt

MONOGRAM HANDIHEAD II

The Handihead II is a self-contained recirculating toilet. The integral holding tank may be emptied through a deck-mounted fitting or pumped overboard out a thru-hull fitting above or below the waterline.

Typical Installations

Figures 21-23 show typical installations. Dockside discharge is via 1-1/2 in. (38.1 mm) monoflex tubing. Overboard discharge requires a Hand-O-Pump. The thru-hull fitting may be above or below the waterline. If any portion of the Handihead is below the waterline at any angle of heel, a 1-1/2 in. (38.1 mm) vented loop (Wilcox-Crittenden or equivalent) must be installed between the Handihead and the seacock. The top of the vent loop must be at least 4 in. (101.6 mm) above waterline at the greatest angle of heel.

CAUTION

The vented loop is not a substitute for a seacock. The loop prevents back filling or siphoning of water into the head when the seacock is open. Keep the seacock closed when head is not in use.

Recharging

1. Depress the lever on the side of the toilet to open the bowl seal.
2. Pour 1/2 gal. (1.9 L) of water into the toilet.
3. Close the bowl seal and add one qt. (0.9 L) of water to the bowl.
4. Add one package of Monochem PTC Chemical or equivalent to bowl.
5. Open the bowl seal to empty the bowl.
6. Flush several times to circulate the chemicals. If flushing action is weak or if water splatters, add up to 1 more qt. (0.9 L) of water.

Dockside Discharge

When the fluid level is even with the bottom of the bowl opening, the toilet must be emptied.

1. Connect a dockside pump to the deck fittings and start the pump.
2. When empty, rinse the base tank with fresh water through the bowl opening.

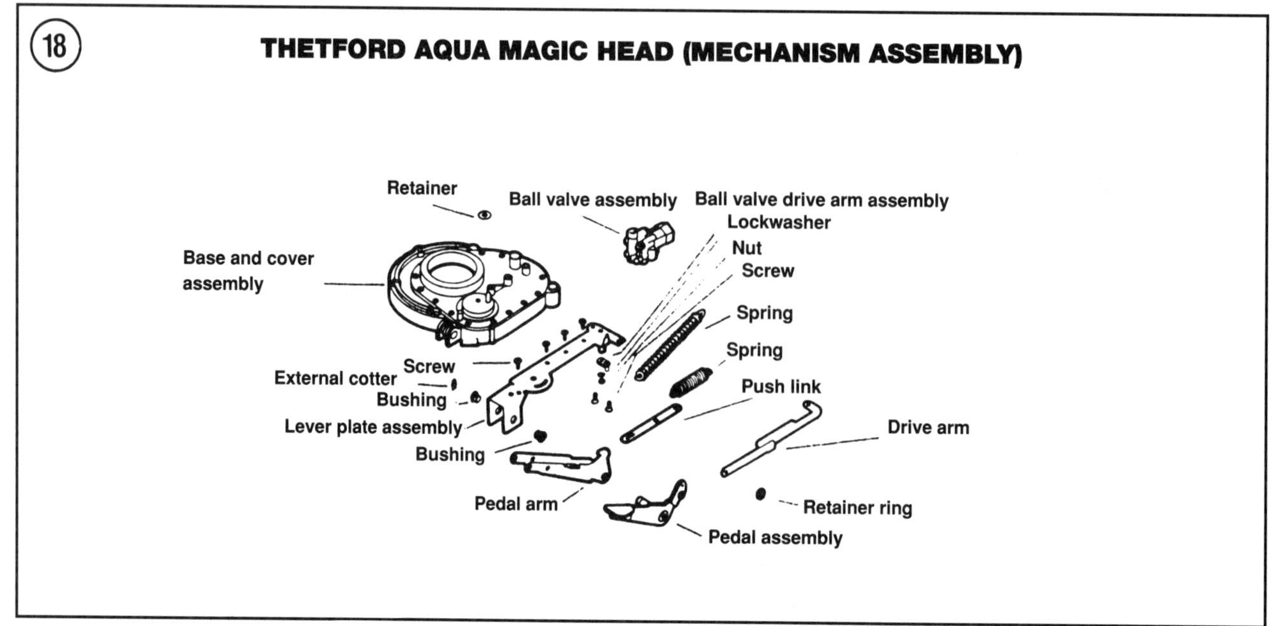

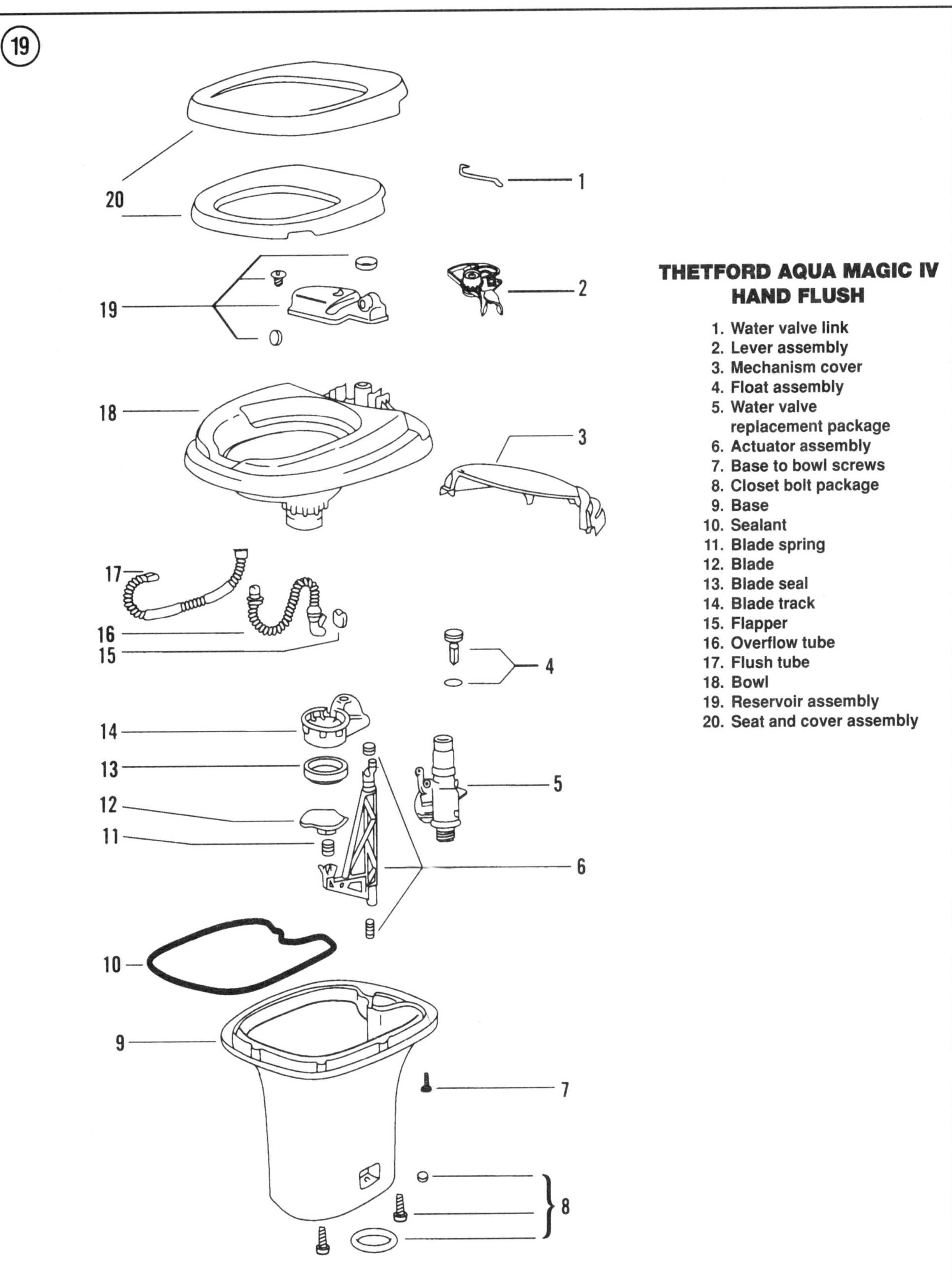

THETFORD AQUA MAGIC IV HAND FLUSH

1. Water valve link
2. Lever assembly
3. Mechanism cover
4. Float assembly
5. Water valve replacement package
6. Actuator assembly
7. Base to bowl screws
8. Closet bolt package
9. Base
10. Sealant
11. Blade spring
12. Blade
13. Blade seal
14. Blade track
15. Flapper
16. Overflow tube
17. Flush tube
18. Bowl
19. Reservoir assembly
20. Seat and cover assembly

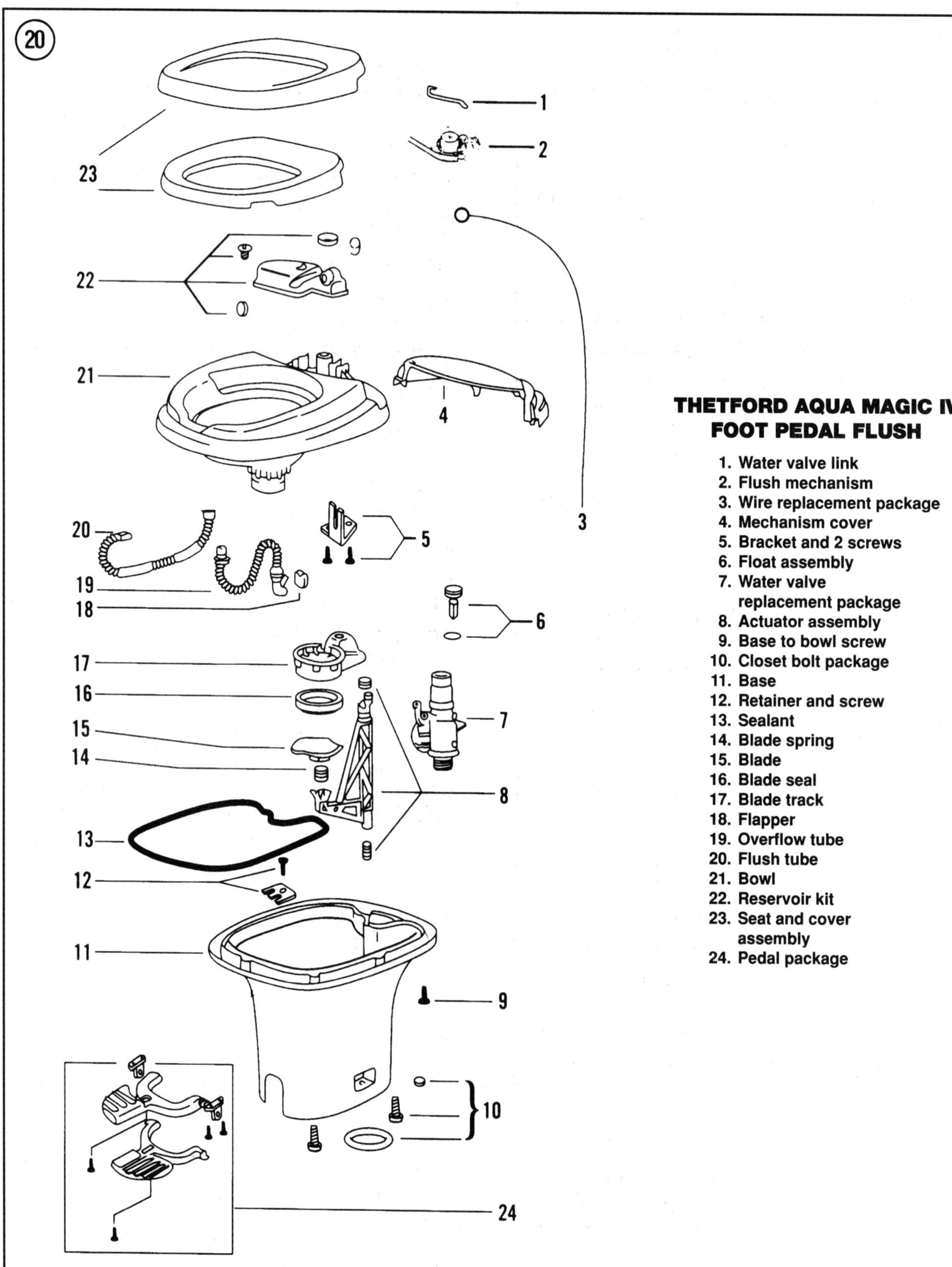

THETFORD AQUA MAGIC IV FOOT PEDAL FLUSH

1. Water valve link
2. Flush mechanism
3. Wire replacement package
4. Mechanism cover
5. Bracket and 2 screws
6. Float assembly
7. Water valve replacement package
8. Actuator assembly
9. Base to bowl screw
10. Closet bolt package
11. Base
12. Retainer and screw
13. Sealant
14. Blade spring
15. Blade
16. Blade seal
17. Blade track
18. Flapper
19. Overflow tube
20. Flush tube
21. Bowl
22. Reservoir kit
23. Seat and cover assembly
24. Pedal package

3. When unit is completely empty of rinse water, turn off the dockside pump and remove the hose.
4. Recharge the unit or prepare it for lay-up.

Overboard Discharge

When fluid level is level with bottom of bowl opening, the toilet must be emptied.

1. Open the seacock.
2. Empty the toilet with the hand pump.
3. Rinse the toilet thoroughly with fresh water.
4. Empty the rinse water with the pump.
5. Close the seacock.
6. Recharge the unit or prepare it for lay-up.

NOTE
For health and environmental reasons, discharge is not legal within the U.S. 3-mile limit.

Winterizing

1. Clean the unit inside and out.

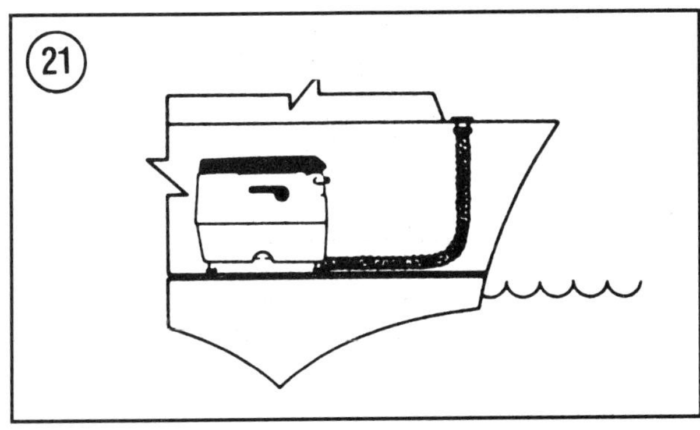

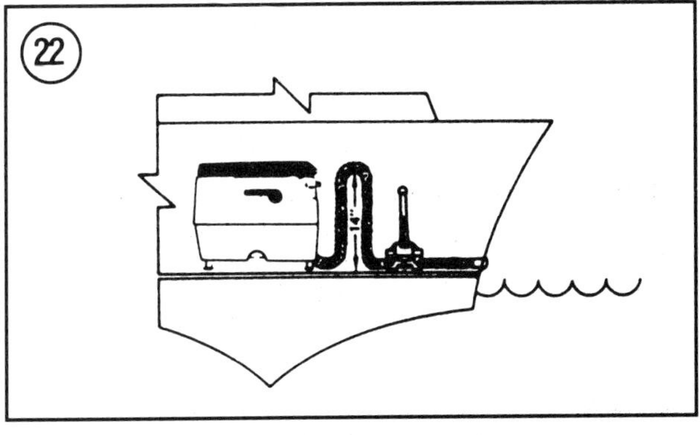

2. Add sufficient antifreeze to protect 3-1/2 gal. (13.2 L) at the temperature range expected. See antifreeze manufacturer's recommendation.

CAUTION
Use only propylene glycol antifreeze Do not use alcohol products or automotive antifreeze.

Lay-up

Empty and thoroughly rinse base tank. Clean the exterior and spray it with disinfectant. Leave the unit dry.

Maintenance

No maintenance other than periodic cleaning and emptying is required. Occasionally, fill with fresh water and add 1/2 cup of Vanish bowl cleaner or a cold water detergent. Let stand for 30 minutes, then empty and rinse thoroughly with fresh water.

Extending Capacity

The system waste storage capacity can be greatly expanded by adding an external holding tank. See **Figure 24**. Instead of discharging the base tank contents overboard, it is hand-pumped into the holding tank and the base tank is recharged with fresh water. The holding tank must be emptied periodically with an additional hand pump or dockside pump.

Disassembly/ Assembly

Figure 25 shows an exploded view of the Handihead II.

MONOGRAM MONOMATIC II

The Monomatic II is a self-contained recirculating flush unit with a 7 gal. (26.5 L) capacity (3 gal. [11.4 L] fresh water/4 gal. [15.1 L] waste).

Typical Installations

Figures 21-23 show typical installations. Dockside discharge is via 1-1/2 in. (38.1 mm) monoflex tubing. Overboard discharge requires a Hand-O-Pump. The thru-hull fitting may be above or below the waterline. If any portion of the Handihead is below the waterline at any angle of heel, a 1-1/2 in. (38.1 mm) vented loop (Wilcox-Crittenden or equivalent) must be installed between Handihead and seacock. The top of the vent loop must be at least 4 in. (101.6 mm) above waterline at the greatest angle of heel.

CAUTION
The vented loop is not a substitute for a seacock. The loop prevents back filling or siphoning of water into head when seacock is open. Keep seacock closed when head is not in use.

Recharging

1A. If the unit is connected to the boat's pressurized water system, turn on the water valve. When the sound of the water entering the tank changes significantly, the water has reached the 3 gal. (11.4 L) level. Turn the water off.
1B. If the unit is not connected to the pressurized water system, pour 3 gal. (11.4 L) of fresh water directly through the open bowl.
2. Operate the foot pedal several times to prime the pump.
3. While flushing, pour one package of Monochem T-5 or equivalent into the bowl.
4. Flush several times to dissolve and circulate the chemical.

Dockside Discharge

When the fluid level is visible at the bottom of the bowl, the toilet must be emptied.

1. Connect a dockside pump to the deck fitting and start the pump.
2. When the tank is empty, run fresh water into the system while continuing to pump for about one minute to rinse the tank.
3. Shut off the fresh water.
4. When the tank is empty, turn off the dockside pump.
5. Recharge the unit or prepare it for lay-up.

Overboard Discharge

When the fluid level is visible at the bottom of the bowl, the toilet must be emptied.

1. Open the seacock.
2. Operate the hand pump.
3. When empty, run fresh water into the system for about one minute while operating pump.
4. Shut off the rinse water.
5. When the tank is drained, depress the foot pedal several times to completely empty the pump.
6. Close the seacock.
7. Recharge the unit or prepare it for lay-up.

NOTE
For health and environmental reasons, discharge is not legal within the U.S. 3-mile limit.

23

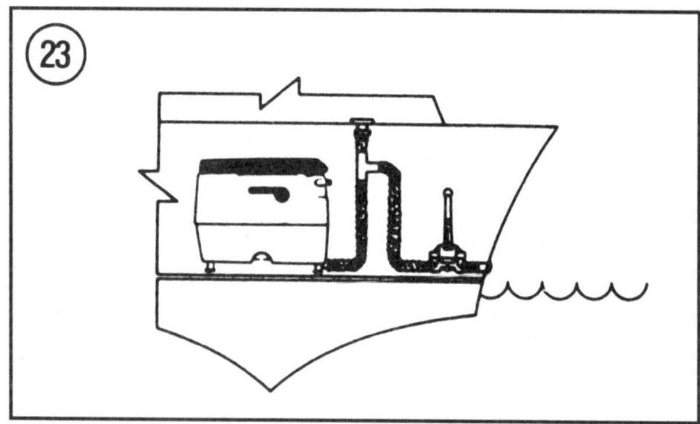

24

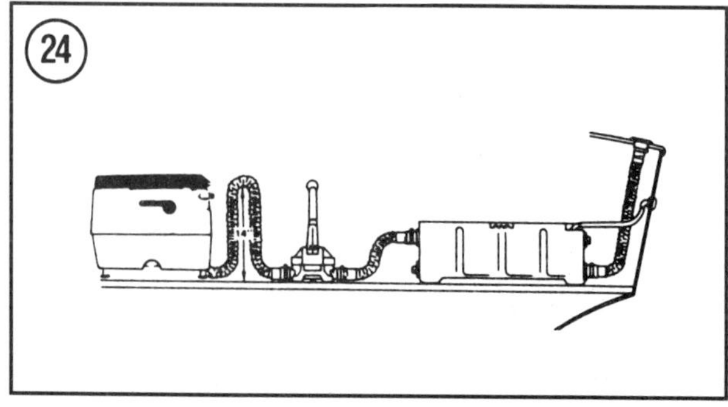

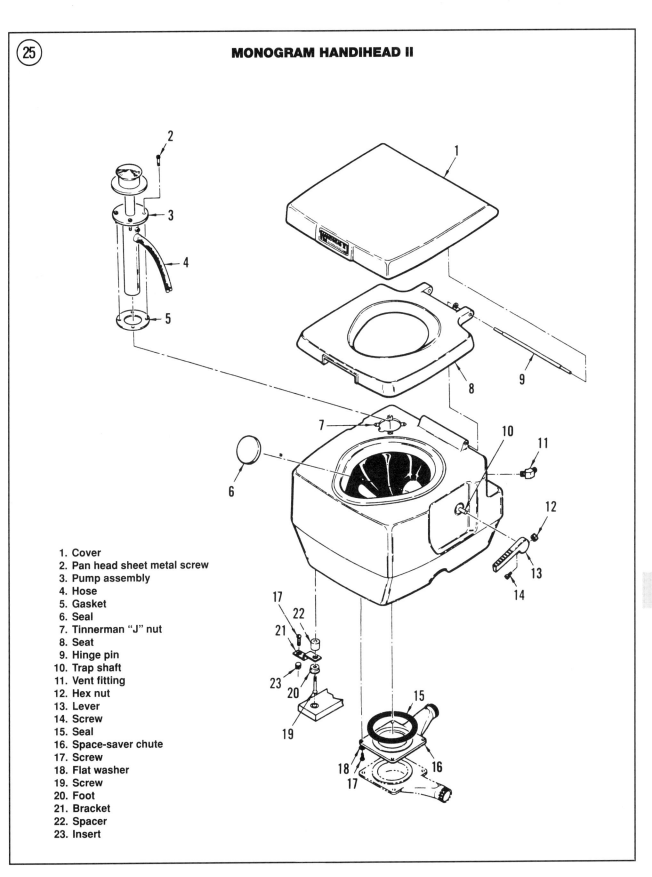

(25)

MONOGRAM HANDIHEAD II

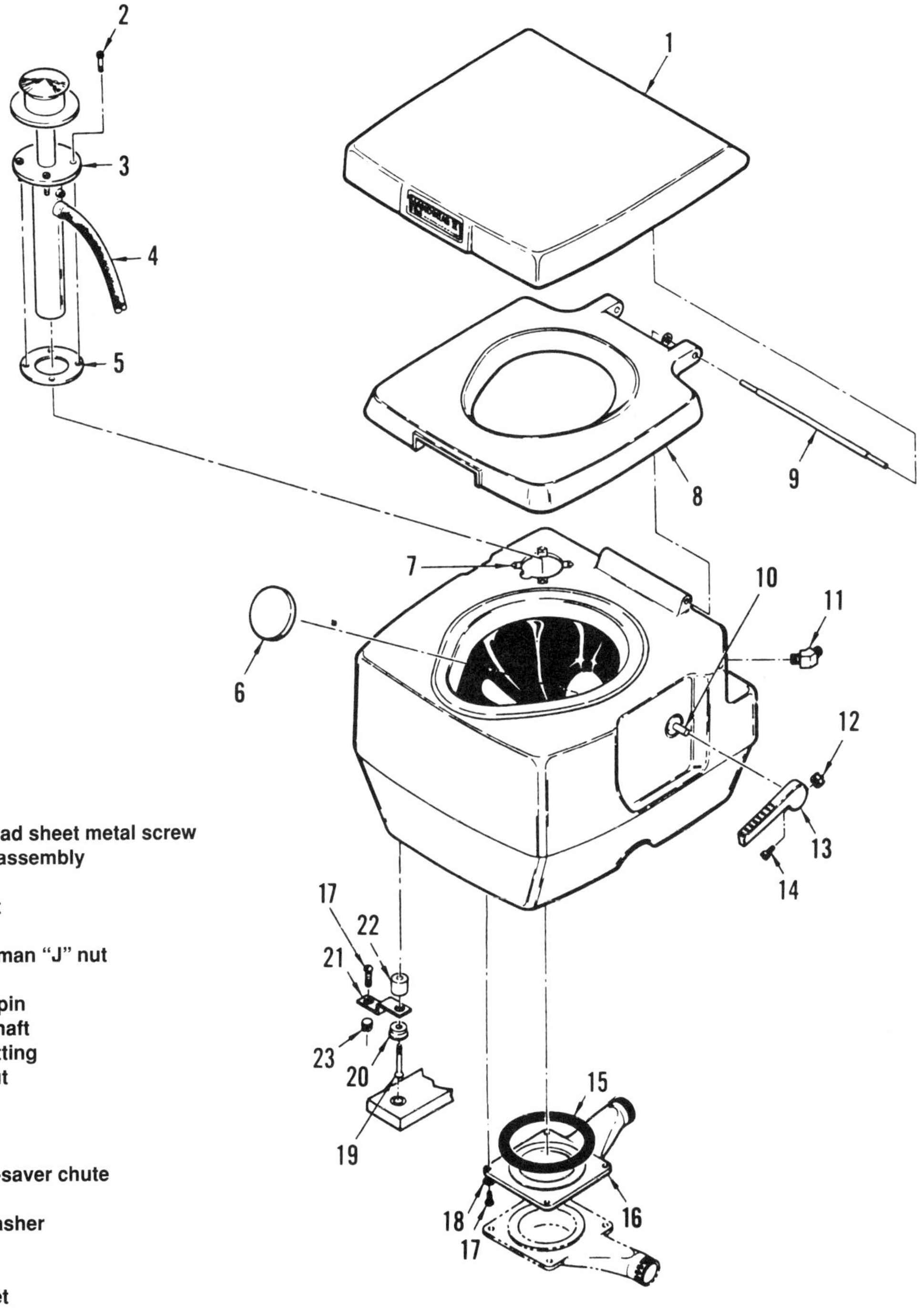

1. Cover
2. Pan head sheet metal screw
3. Pump assembly
4. Hose
5. Gasket
6. Seal
7. Tinnerman "J" nut
8. Seat
9. Hinge pin
10. Trap shaft
11. Vent fitting
12. Hex nut
13. Lever
14. Screw
15. Seal
16. Space-saver chute
17. Screw
18. Flat washer
19. Screw
20. Foot
21. Bracket
22. Spacer
23. Insert

Winterizing

1. Empty and rinse the system as described above.
2. Pour in enough antifreeze to protect 7 gal. (26.5 L) at the temperature range expected according to the antifreeze manufacturer's directions.
3. Add fresh water to the system to make a total charge of 3 gal. (11.4 L)

CAUTION
Use nontoxic base antifreeze. Do not use alcohol products or automotive antifreeze.

Lay-up

1. Empty and rinse the base tank thoroughly as described earlier. Use Vanish bowl cleaner. See *Maintenance* in this section.
2. When the unit is completely drained, depress the foot pump several times to completely empty the pump.

Disassembly/ Assembly

Refer to **Figure 26** for this procedure.

1. Remove the service port cover. See **Figure 27**.
2. Disconnect the hoses from antisiphon valve and lift the valve out. See **Figure 28**.
3. Unscrew the antisiphon valve and inspect all parts. See **Figure 29**.
4. Remove the pin filter mounting screws through the service port.
5. Remove the pin filter parts through the bowl. See **Figure 30** and **Figure 31**.
6. Remove the base skirt. Remove the closet bolts with a 7/16 in. wrench. Lift the toilet off.
7. Turn the toilet upside down.
8. Remove the screws securing the slide valve and lift the valve off.
9. Remove the locknut from the bottom of the diaphragm. Remove the foot pedal assembly.
10. Unscrew the bank clamp and lift off the rubber diaphragm.

SEALAND/MANSFIELD VACU-FLUSH

The Vacu-flush system is unique in that waste is positively drawn from the toilet into the holding tank by a strong vacuum.

Each system consists of at least one toilet, one tank, and one pump. **Figure 32** shows a typical installation. The vacuum pump draws air from the tank and discharges it through the vent. A strong vacuum (10 in. Hg) builds up in the holding tank. When the unit is flushed, the ball valve in the bottom of the bowl opens and waste is drawn into the holding tank.

Waste in the holding tank can be pumped out at dockside by an external pump or discharged overboard with the system pump.

Dockside Pump-out

Basically, the dockside pump draws waste from the holding tank through the deck fitting. The path from tank to toilet is opened to permit air to replace waste in the tank and prevent any vacuum buildup. **Figure 32** shows a typical installation. Trace out your installation and correct the illustration to conform to your system.

1. Close the fresh water valve.
2. Open Valve No. 1 (between tank and toilet).
3. Prop the toilet ball valve open.
4. Turn on the dockside pump. Operate the pump until the tank is empty.
5. Turn the dockside pump off.
6. Turn the fresh water valve on and fill the tank with fresh water to rinse, then close the valve.
7. Turn the dockside pump on to empty the tank.
8. Repeat Steps 5-7 as often as necessary.
9. When the tank is empty, leave Valve No. 1 open and cap the deck fitting. Remove the prop holding the toilet ball valve open and turn the fresh water valve on.

Overboard Pump-out

For this method, the vacuum pump is used to pressurize the holding tank and force its contents

(26)

MONOGRAM MONOMATIC II

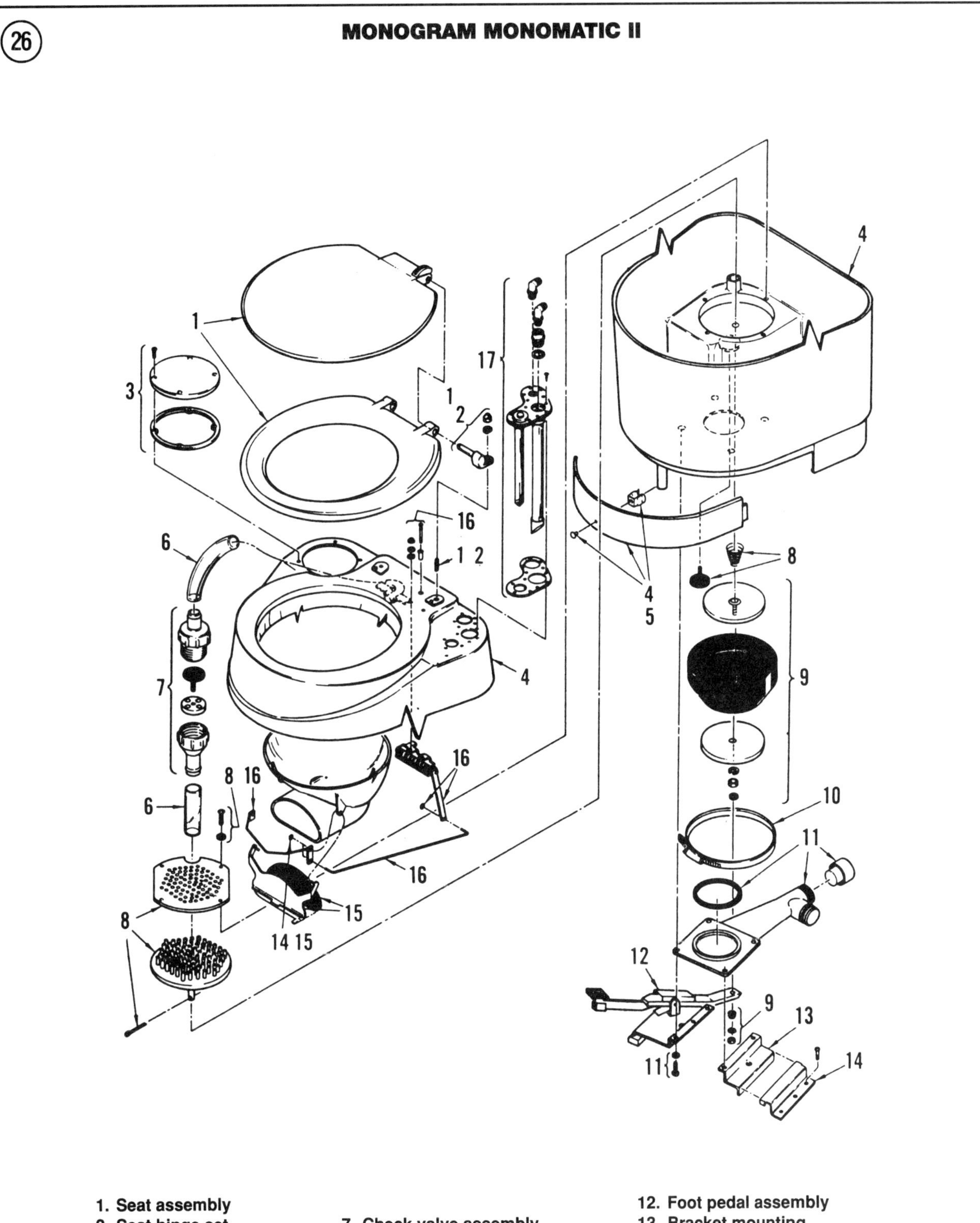

1. Seat assembly
2. Seat hinge set
3. Access cover
4. Shell assembly
5. Removable skirt
6. Hose
7. Check valve assembly
8. Grid and valve assembly
9. Diaphragm assembly
10. Band clamp
11. Drain fitting and pump
12. Foot pedal assembly
13. Bracket mounting
14. Bracket mounting
15. Flapper assembly
16. Actuator assembly
17. Rinse-vent and level assembly

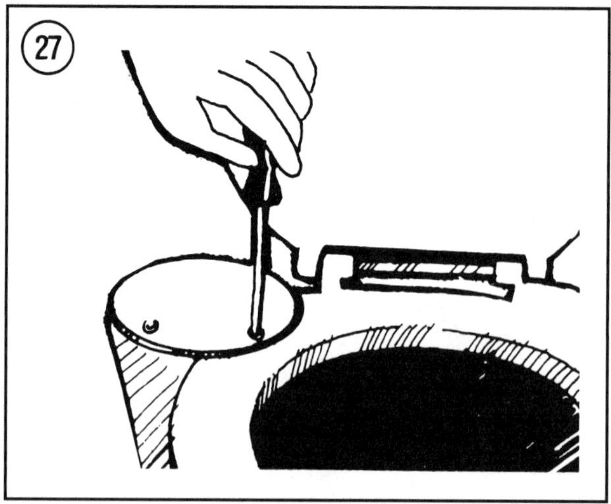

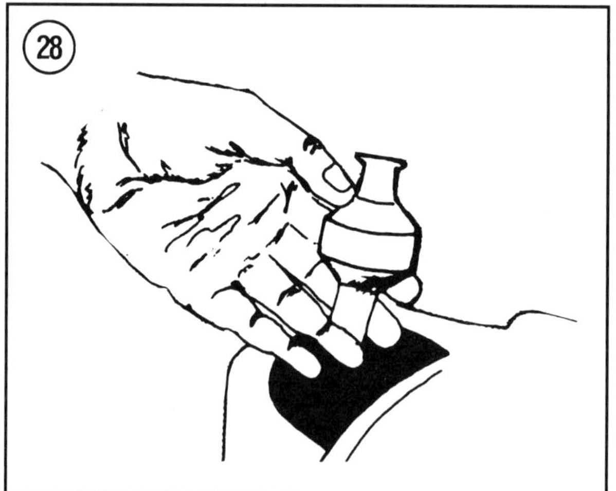

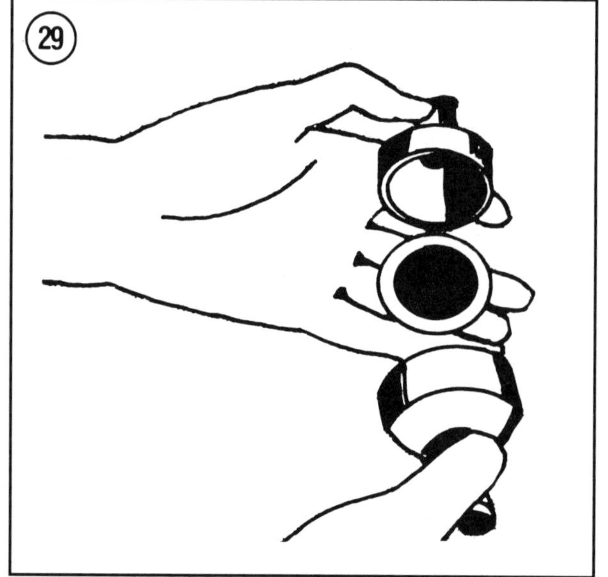

out of the below-water seacock. The valve between the tank and toilet must be closed or waste will be forced out the toilet as well. **Figure 32** shows a typical installation. Trace out your installation and correct the illustration to conform to your system.

NOTE
Overboard pump-out of untreated waste is not legal within the 3-mile limit.

1. Close Valve No. 1.
2. Open seacock (Valve No. 2).
3. Turn the 4-way valve to "pump-out."

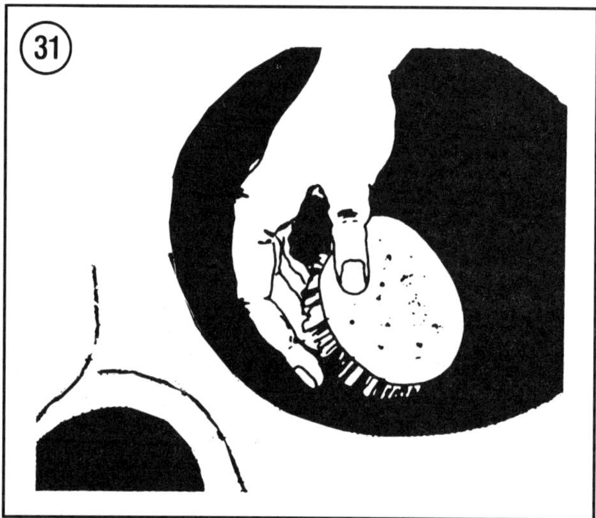

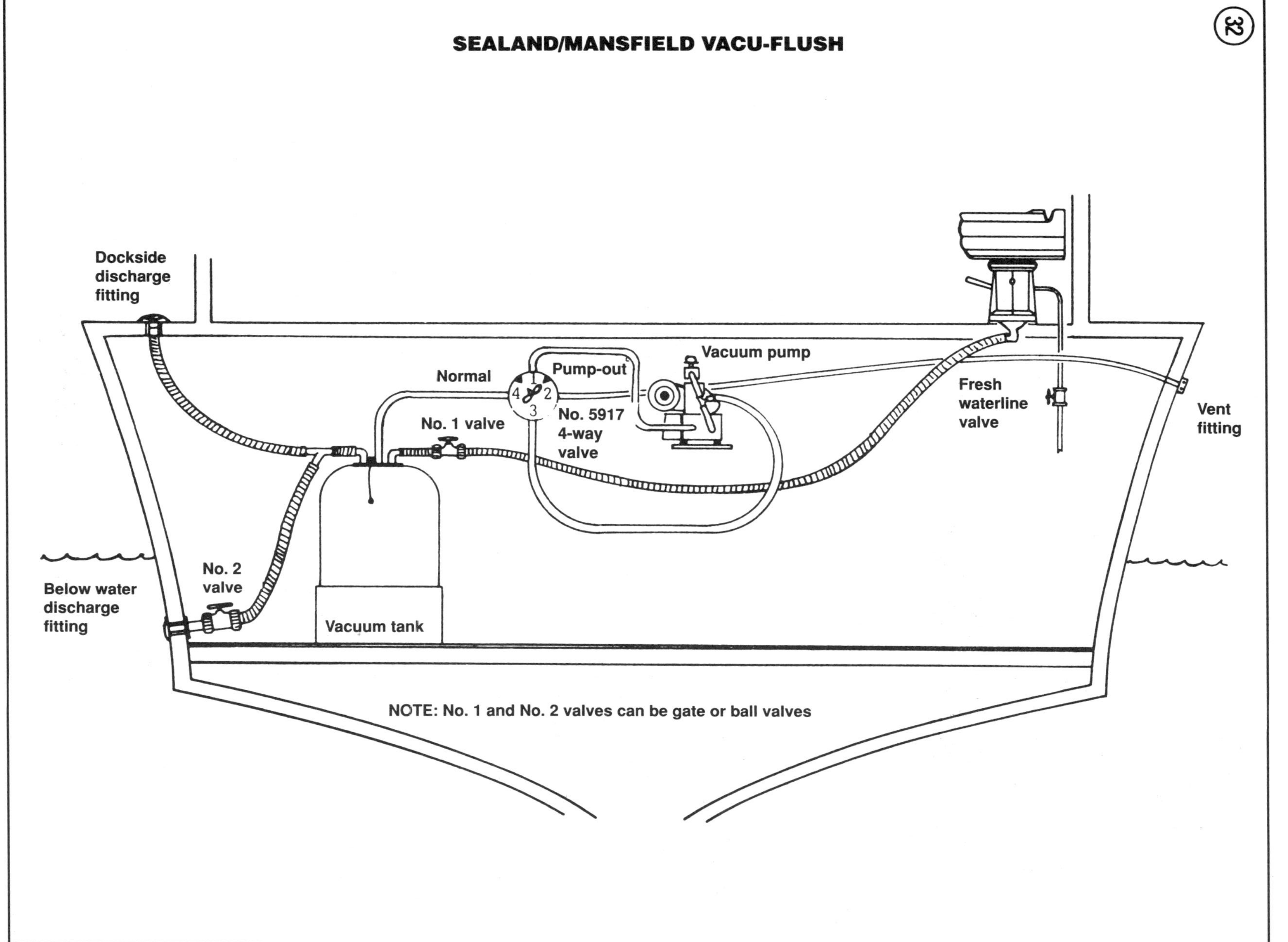
32
SEALAND/MANSFIELD VACU-FLUSH
Dockside discharge fitting
Normal
Pump-out
Vacuum pump
1
2
3
4
No. 1 valve
No. 5917 4-way valve
Fresh waterline valve
Vent fitting
No. 2 valve
Below water discharge fitting
Vacuum tank
NOTE: No. 1 and No. 2 valves can be gate or ball valves

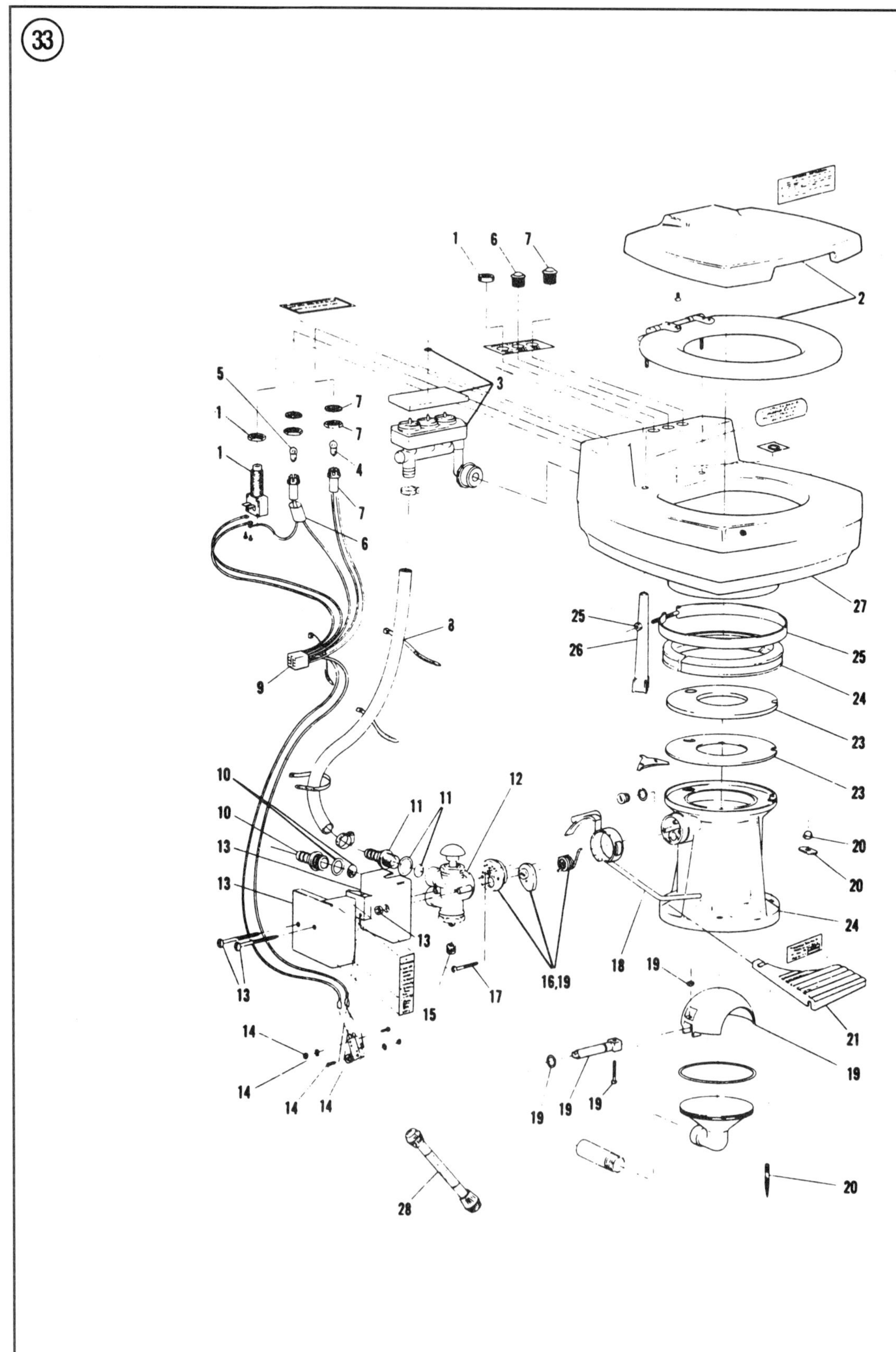
33

MANSFIELD VACU-FLUSH

1. Push switch assembly
2. Seat assembly
3. Vacuum breaker assembly
4. Light bulb (red)
5. Light bulb (green)
6. Light assembly (green)
7. Light assembly (red)
8. Supply hose
9. Electrical plug
10. Hose inlet connector assembly
11. Supply line connector assembly
12. Water valve assembly
13. Valve cover assenbly
14. Micro-switch assembly
15. Drain cap
16. Cartridge
17. Valve spacer screw
18. Flush lever
19. Ball rotor shaft assembly
20. Floor mounting assembly
21. Foot pedal plastic cover
22. Base assembly less water valve
23. Seal assembly
24. Half clamp
25. Clamp ring and nut
26. Seat assembly to bowl nut
27. China bowl
28. Pedal holder

4. Push the Start button on the toilet.
5. When the tank is empty, turn the 4-way valve to NORMAL, leave the seacock open and Valve No. 1 closed. The vacuum pump will draw seawater through the seacock and fill the tank for rinsing.
6. Turn the 4-way valve back to PUMP-OUT and push the start button on the toilet to empty the tank of rinse water.
7. Repeat Steps 5 and 6 as often as necessary.
8. Close the seacock.
9. Return the 4-way valve to NORMAL.
10. Open Valve No. 1. Pump will operate until (10 in. Hg) vacuum builds up in tank, then will automatically turn off.

Winterizing

Since the system uses the boat's fresh water supply, no winterizing is necessary.

Lay-up

1. Completely rinse and empty the system of all waste.
2. Drain the boat's fresh water tanks.
3. Leave the fresh water valve open.
4. Prop the toilet ball valve open.

Disassembly/ Assembly

Figures 33-36 provide exploded views of all major components of the Vacu-flush system.

11

SEALAND/MANSFIELD 911/912-M28

This toilet has a top discharge holding tank and offers a simple method to conform to new anti-pollution legislation. Model 911-M28 is for use with pressurized water systems. Fresh flushing water comes from boat's water supply. Model 912-M28 is for use in boats without a pressurized system. A hand-operated pump draws sea or lake water from outside hull. See **Figure 37**. The 912-M28 should not be con-

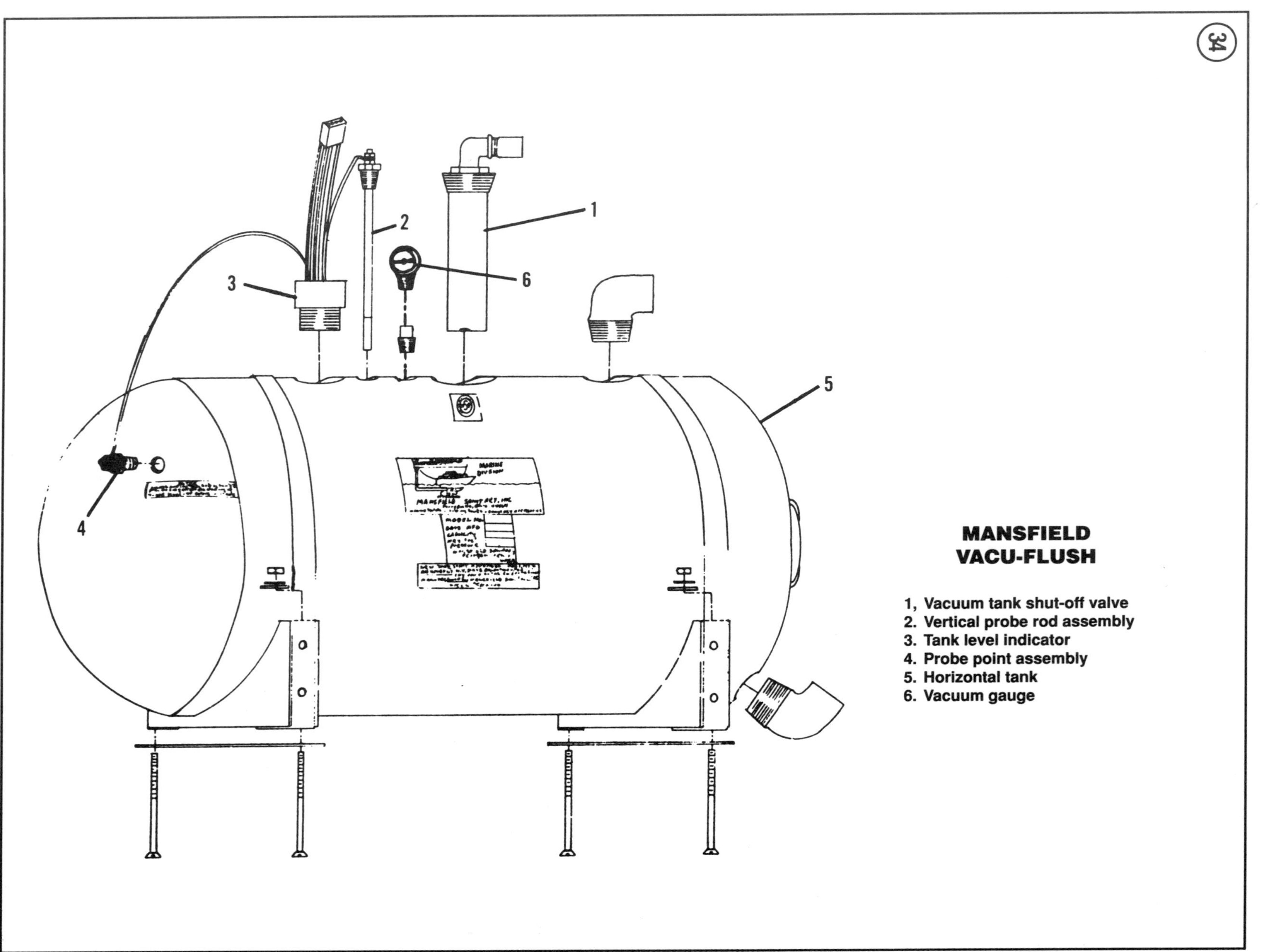
34
1
2
3
4
5
6
MANSFIELD
VACU-FLUSH
1, Vacuum tank shut-off valve
2. Vertical probe rod assembly
3. Tank level indicator
4. Probe point assembly
5. Horizontal tank
6. Vacuum gauge

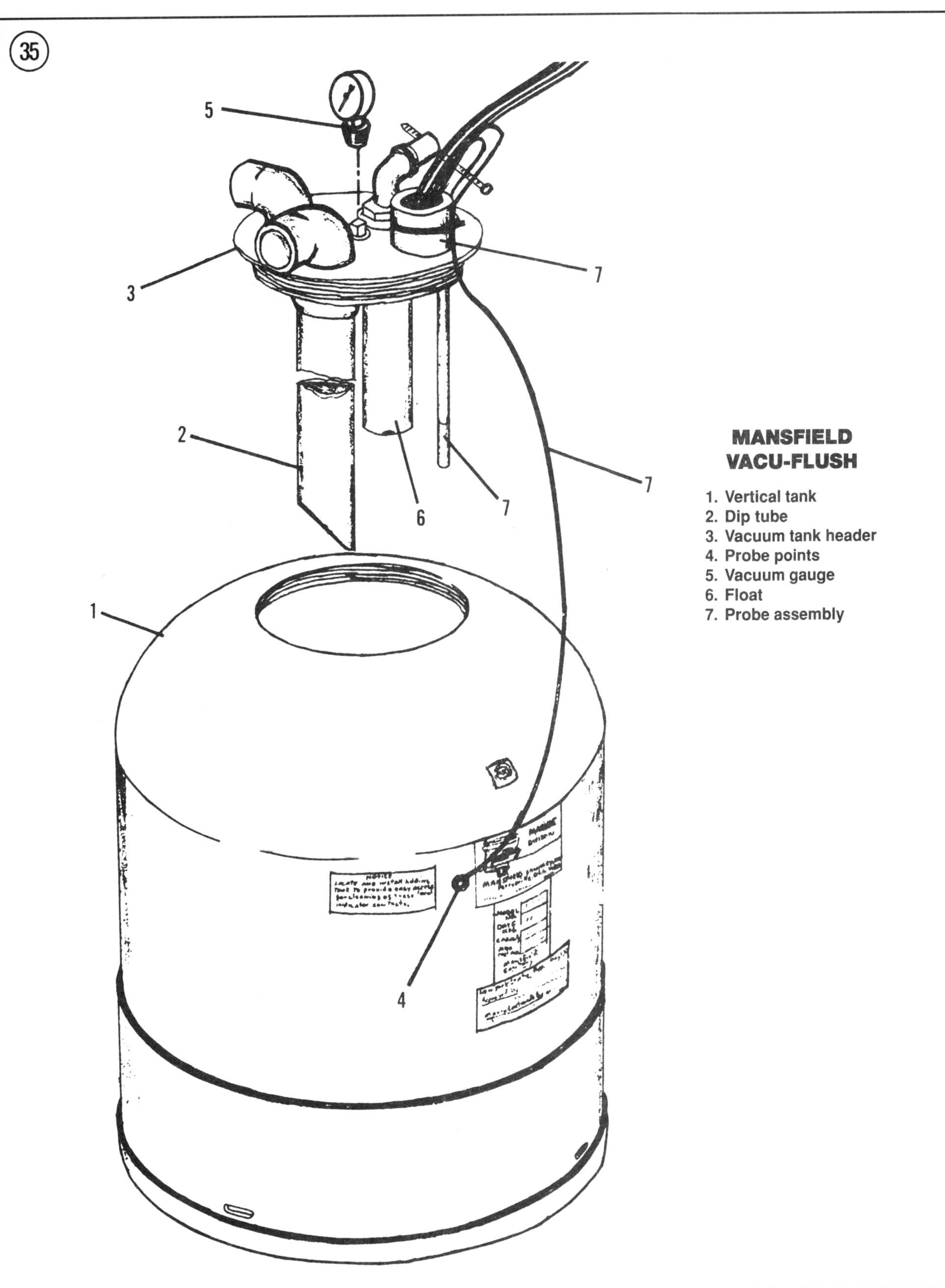
35
5
3
7
2
6
7
7
1
4
MANSFIELD
VACU-FLUSH
1. Vertical tank
2. Dip tube
3. Vacuum tank header
4. Probe points
5. Vacuum gauge
6. Float
7. Probe assembly

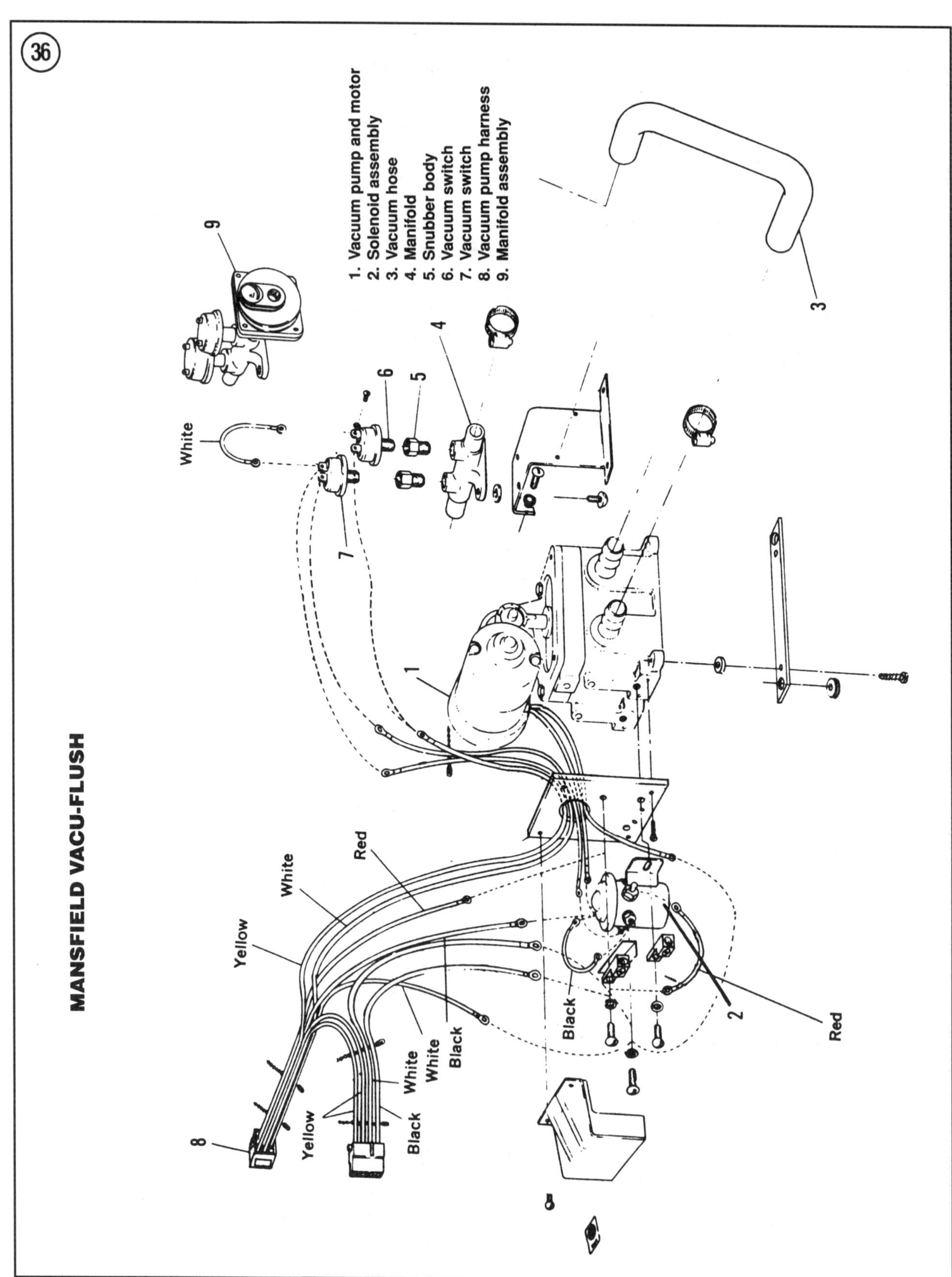
36
MANSFIELD VACU-FLUSH
1. Vacuum pump and motor
2. Solenoid assembly
3. Vacuum hose
4. Manifold
5. Snubber body
6. Vacuum switch
7. Vacuum switch
8. Vacuum pump harness
9. Manifold assembly
White
Red
White
Yellow
Black
White
White
Black
Yellow
Black
Black
Red

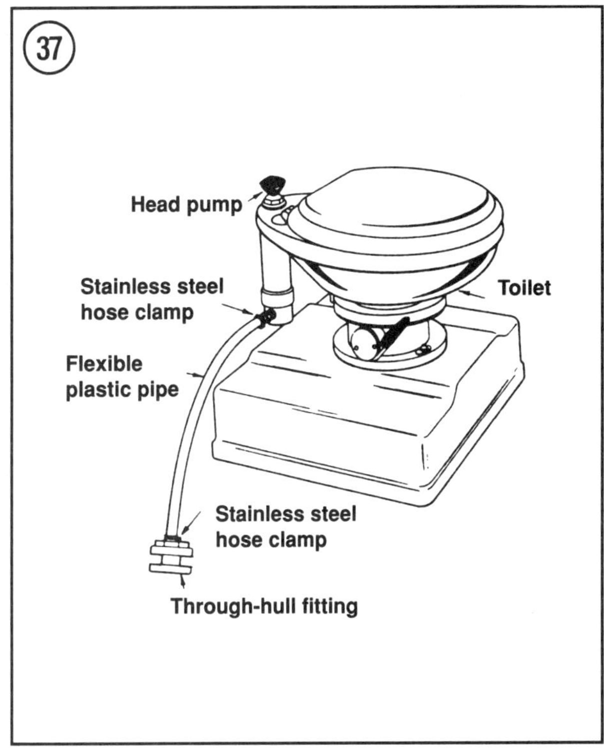

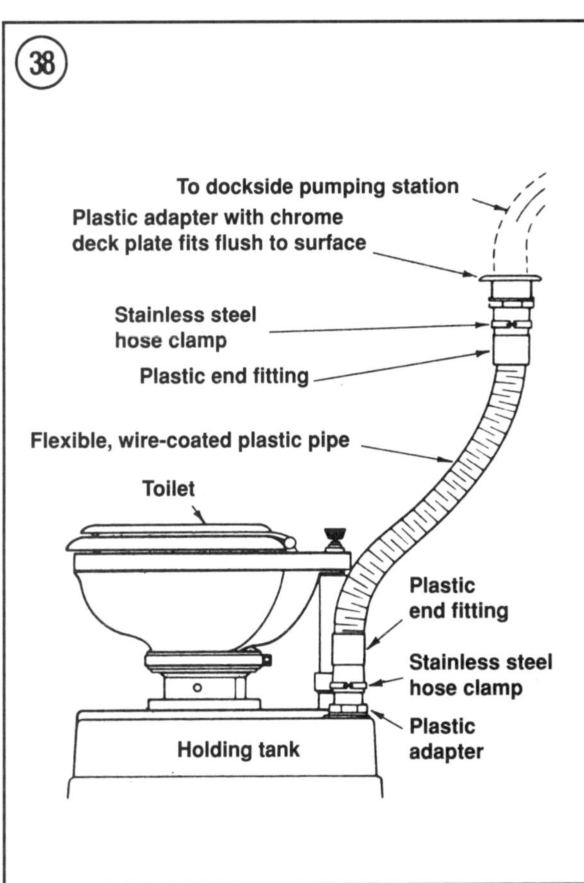

nected to the onboard water supply. Both models can be pumped out at dockside pumping stations. See **Figure 37** and **Figure 38** for typical installation of systems.

Lay-up

Completely rinse and empty the holding tank. On systems with pressurized water, drain the onboard water supply and leave the fresh water valve to the toilet open. Prop the toilet ball valve open.

On 912-M28 models without a pressurized water connection, rinse and empty the holding tank. When the boat is hauled out, operate the pump several times to purge residual water from pump and line. Prop the toilet ball valve open.

Emptying and Rinsing

1. Connect a dockside pump directly to the holding tank or through the deck fitting, if equipped.
2. Turn the pump on and empty the tank.
3. Fill the holding tank with fresh water.
4. Pump the tank out.
5. Repeat Steps 3 and 4 as often as necessary.

Maintenance

There is no maintenance other than a thorough cleaning inside and out periodically.

Disassembly/ Assembly

Figure 39 shows an exploded view of the 911/912-M28 toilets.

RARITAN CROWN HEAD

The Crown Head comes in a Standard Model for mounting above or up to 1 ft. (30.5 cm) below waterline (measured from outlet connection). A Deep Draft model may be mounted as much as 5 ft. (152 cm) below the waterline.

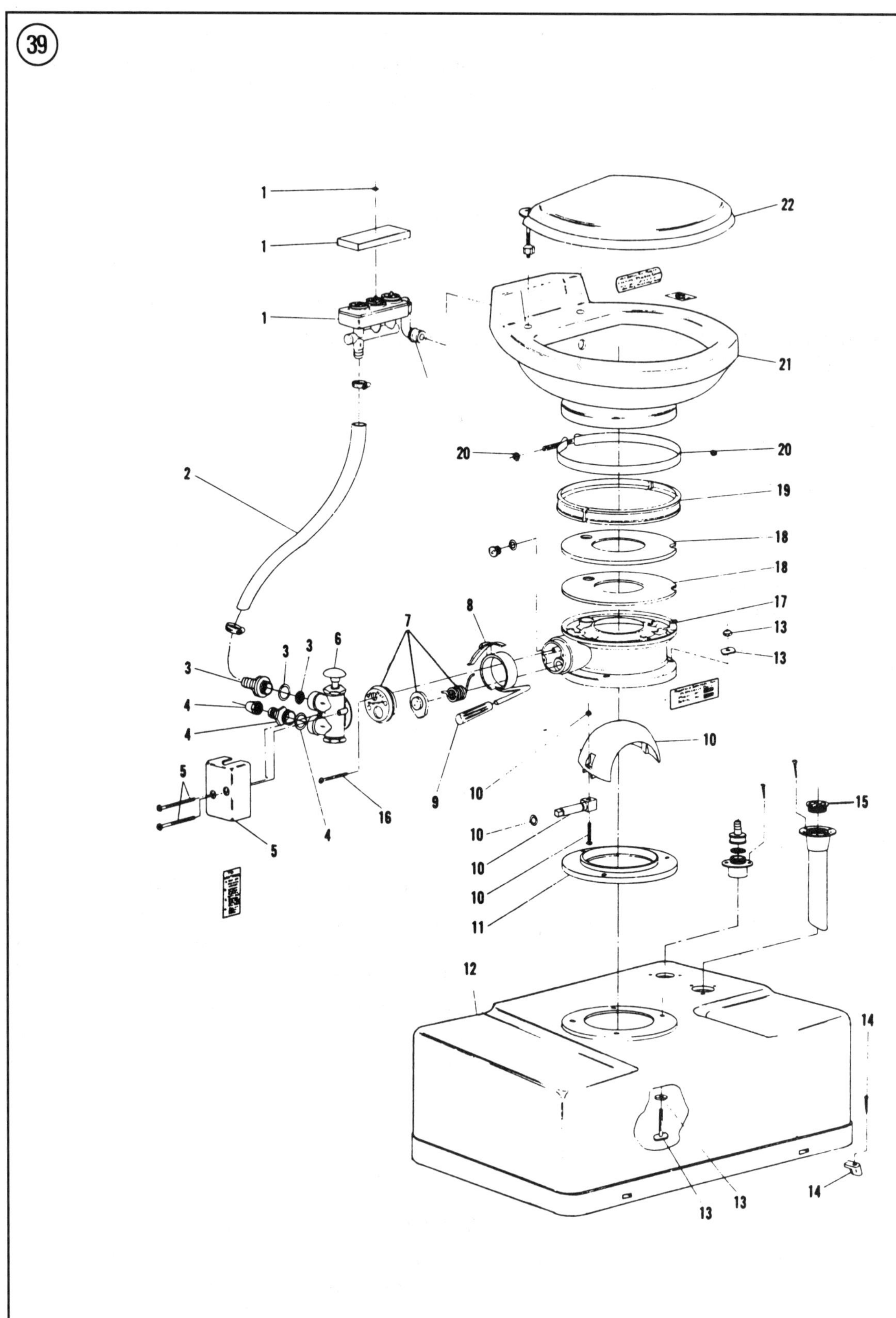
39
1
1
1
2
3
3
3
4
4
5
5
4
6
7
8
9
16
10
10
10
10
10
11
12
13
13
13
13
14
14
15
17
18
18
19
20
20
21
22

**MANSFIELD 911-912—
M28 HEAD**

1. Vacuum breaker assembly
2. Supply line
3. Push on hose adaptor assembly
4. Flare nut assembly
5. Valve cover and attaching hardware
6. Water valve
7. Cartridge
8. Flush lever
9. Pedal cover
10. Shaft and ball assembly
11. Base-to-flange seal
12. Tank
13. Floor flange bolt, washer and nut
14. Hold down clip and screw
15. Plug
16. Valve spacer screw
17. Base assembly
18. Seal assembly
19. Half clamp
20. Clamp ring and nut
21. China bowl
22. Bemis seat and lid assembly

A built-in macerator chops waste products into a fluid which is easily decontaminated and discharged. Fluid from a decontaminant tank is metered into the bowl along with the flush water.

Charging

1. Pour 2 oz. (59 mL) of Raritan Concentrate (decontaminant) into the decontaminant tank.
2. Fill the tank with fresh water.

Maintenance

No periodic maintenance is required other than replenishing the decontaminant tank as necessary and periodic cleaning of the unit.

Lay-up

1. Drain the decontaminant tank completely by inverting it and rinsing it out.
2. Rinse the siphon assembly (26, **Figure 40**) and drain.
3. Close the inlet seacock. Remove the inlet hose from the pump assembly.
4. Temporarily attach a short length of hose to the inlet pump where the permanent hose was removed. Pour about 1 qt. (0.9 L) of permanent type antifreeze (ethyl glycol) into a coffee can or other container. Let the motor run until the color of the fluid running down from the rim of the bowl indicates the antifreeze has circulated.

CAUTION
Do not discharge antifreeze out a thru-hull fitting.

5. Close the outlet seacock.
6. Let the antifreeze remain in the Crown Head until the boat is recommissioned.
7. When all danger of freezing is past, reconnect the inlet hose and open both seacocks.

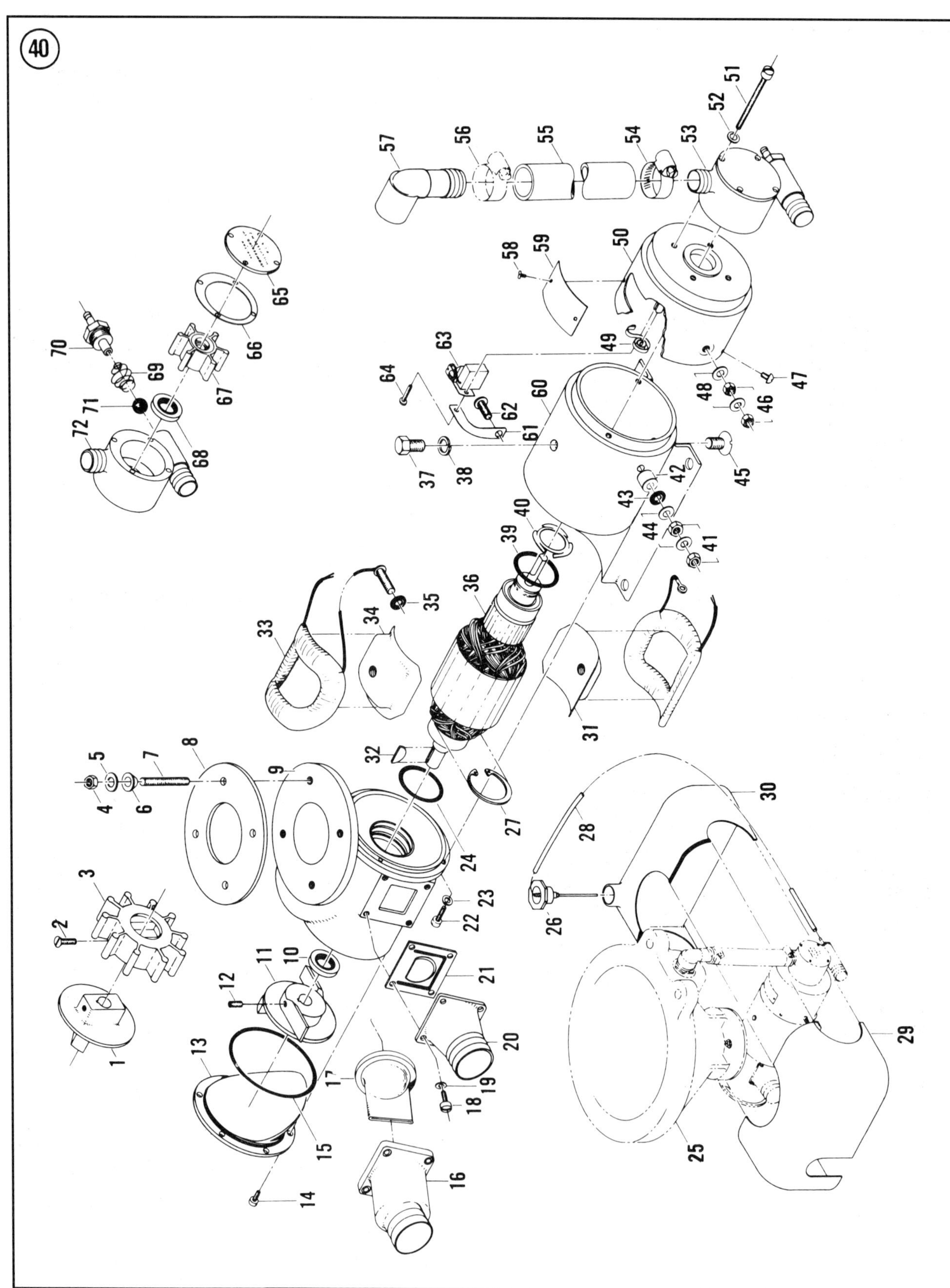
40
1
2
3
4
5
6
7
8
9
10
11
12
13
14
15
16
17
18
19
20
21
22
23
24
25
26
27
28
29
30
31
32
33
34
35
36
37
38
39
40
41
42
43
44
45
46
47
48
49
50
51
52
53
54
55
56
57
58
59
60
61
62
63
64
65
66
67
68
69
70
71
72

1. Macerater plate
2. Impeller screw
3. Macerater impeller
4. Bowl stud nut
5. Bowl washer
6. Bowl rubber washer
7. Bowl studs
8. Bowl gasket
9. End bell
10. Macerater shaft seal
11. Assembly
12. Allen setscrew
13. Front cover
14. Front cover screws
15. Front cover O-ring
16. Outlet connection
17. Joker valve
18. Outlet connection screws
19. Fiber washer
20. Outlet connection
21. Assembly
22. End bell screws
23. Lockwasher
24. Ball bearing O-ring
25. Assembly
26. Assembly
27. Ball bearing snap ring
28. Siphon tube
29. Shroud
30. Shroud
31. Pole shoe and coil
32. Woodruff key
33. Coil
34. Pole shoe
35. Flat fiber washer
36. Assembly (armature)
37. Pole shoe capscrew
38. Lockwasher
39. Ball bearing O-ring
40. Ball bearing thrust spring
41. Terminal nuts
42. Fiber sleeve
43. Flat fiber washer
44. Terminal washer
45. Pole show screw
46. Terminal nuts
47. Dome screw
48. Terminal washer
49. Brush spring
50. Assembly
51. Pump screw
52. Fiber washer
53. Assembly
54. Hose clamp
55. Hose
56. Hose clamp
57. Bowl elbow
58. Name plate screws
59. Name plate
60. Housing assembly
61. Ground strap
62. Terminal screw
63. Brush assembly
64. Brush plate screw
65. Pump cover plate
66. Pump gasket
67. Impeller
68. Pump shaft seal
69. Check valve spring
70. Metering plug
71. Check ball
72. Pump body

8. Replenish the decontaminant tank and replace the siphon. Start the motor and flush out the antifreeze. The head is now recommissioned.

Troubleshooting

Refer to **Figure 40** for the following procedures.

1. *Poor water flow, especially at the front of the bowl. Water does not accumulate appreciably in the bowl itself:* An empty decontaminant tank or low voltage. Check the tank first to see if it is full. Low voltage will cause trouble if outlet (20, **Figure 40** is above the water line. Check voltage only at the motor terminals while the motor is running. Minimum voltage should be 11.5, 23, or 30 volts respectively, for a 12-, 24-, or 32-volt installation. If the values are below minimum voltage, check battery condition. Look for resistance in the circuit breakers or fuses. Check wire sizes all the way back to the batteries. Make sure there is no voltage drop at the switch. Look for loose or corroded electrical connections.

2. *A persistent and obnoxious odor that is emanating from the bowl:* Clogging of the toilet inlet seacock by eel grass that has worked its way through the pump, lodged in the passageway on the inside of the rim of the bowl, and is decaying there. You may see little black specks of this eel grass, looking like bits of tobacco, flowing down the sides of the bowl from the wash holes under the rim. The immediate cure is to connect a pressure hose to the elbow (50, **Figure 40**) and thoroughly flush it out. Another method is to flush with a cleaning solution. Disconnect the inlet hose, connect another short hose to the pump, and allow the pump to suck up a solution of Drano or equivalent from a bucket. To prevent recurrence, install a strainer on the inlet line. Be sure in advance that strong chemicals will not damage internal parts or lines.

3. *The decontaminant tank empties even when no one has used the head:* The ball check valve

(71, **Figure 40**) is not holding. Clean out as described for eel grass, etc., under Step 1.

4. *Water leaks from under the end bell (9, **Figure 40**):* This can only come from five possible sources.

a. A leak at the joint between the china bowl and the bronze casting. Gently tighten the nuts (4, **Figure 40**).

b. A leak at the seal between front cover (13, **Figure 40**) and end bell (9, **Figure 40**). Inspect the O-ring (15, **Figure 40**) for damage. Replace with new O-ring, using grease to help reassemble.

c. Water comes from a small hole under the end bell near the motor or under the pump (50, **Figure 40**). Inspection reveals seals (10, and/or 68, **Figure 40**) must be replaced. It is not recommended that these seals be replaced in the field. However, if there is no alternative, follow carefully the procedure outlined under Step 7.

d. Water comes from under the outlet connection (20, **Figure 40**). Tighten the screws (18, **Figure 40**) very gently. If outlet connection is (16, **Figure 40**) is for Deep Draft Model, tighten the screws snugly.

NOTE

The entire base unit can be exchanged for a factory remanufactured unit at low cost. See your Raritan Service Center or write the factory for details.

5. *The unit makes a very loud metallic noise (metal-to-metal)*—The pivot arms of the macerator may be striking the notched housing. Also, something hard, such as a bobby pin may have fallen into the bowl and lodged against the macerator.

a. Remove the front cover (13, **Figure 40**) and inspect the cavity for foreign objects.

b. Use a 1/2 in. open end wrench to rotate the macerator plate. Slip the wrench over one of the pivoted arms and turn the plate counterclockwise. Note if either of the pivoted arms touches the notched housing. If so, note that there is a crescent shaped boss on the face of the macerator plate that acts as a stop to prevent the pivoted arms from flying out too far.

c. Determine which arm is striking the housing and then spread the crescent shaped boss by striking it lightly with a center punch and hammer. Clearance between the arm and the housing should be about 0.010-0.020 in. (0.25-0.51 mm).

6. *The motor starts intermittently, or runs sluggishly, although voltage measured at the motor is normal*—One motor brush could be hanging up and not contacting the commutator correctly. Remove the name plate from the top of the motor. If the motor does not start, tap the motor housing (50, **Figure 40**) lightly with a hammer while the operating switch is on.

a. If the motor now starts, the trouble is most likely a stuck brush. If so, excessive arcing between the brush and commutator should be evident.

b. If the motor does not start, disconnect one of the wires to the motor terminals. While holding the operating switch in the on position, note if a slight spark appears when the wire is touched to its motor terminal. If no spark is noted, one of the brushes is not making contact with the commutator or voltage is not present at the disconnected wire.

7. Check for voltage at the disconnected wire using a voltmeter. If voltage is present, a brush is not properly contacting the commutator or the motor has failed and must be repaired or replaced. If no voltage is noted, an open is present in the circuit.

8. The top brush is accessible through the name plate hole and can be checked to see if it slides freely, and makes proper contact with the commutator. If the problem persists, remove the armature to inspect the lower brush. First, remove

the whole head and place it on a suitable workbench.

9. Remove the pump assembly (53, **Figure 40**) by removing the 4 screws (51). Remove 4 screws (22, **Figure 40**), then insert a knife blade between the motor housing (60, **Figure 40**) and the flange of the end ball (9).

10. Separate the motor housing and end bell, then remove the armature. Remove the screw attaching one field coil lead to the lower brush.

11. Remove the 4 screws (47, **Figure 40**) and separate the end assembly (50) from the motor housing. Complete inspection of both brushes is now possible. If either brush is sticking, remove it and clean the sides of the brush with emery cloth as necessary to allow the brush to slide freely in its slot. Check the condition of the brush springs and armature commutator.

12. Reassemble the motor end assembly (50, **Figure 40**) and housing (60). Do not forget to reconnect the field lead to the brush plate. Make sure the brushes still slide freely in their slots. Push the upper brush up so high that its spring can be pushed down beside the brush, thus locking it in the up position. Push the lower brush down and hold it using a stiff wire inserted through the oval brush hole (under the name plate).

13. Slide the armature in so the commutator is past the lower brush. Remove the wire used to hold the lower brush, then push the commutator all the way in.Install the screws (22, **Figure 40**). Move the top brush spring into its correct position. Install the name plate.

14. If replacing the pump, carefully check the armature shaft for burrs, especially where the flat blends into the round portion. Carefully install the pump housing with a slight twisting motion, to prevent damage to the seal.

15. Install the impeller with the chamfered side of the brass insert bushing facing toward the motor. Lubricate the pump shaft with a small amount of a suitable grease.

16. Place a small amount of grease on the cover plate (65, **Figure 40**). Install the screws (51, **Figure 40**). Tighten the screws securely, but do not overtighten. The threads in the end assembly (50, **Figure 40**) are plastic and easily damaged. If the threads are damaged, proceed as follows:

a. Fill the hole with epoxy and allow to fully cure.

b. Drill the hole and cut threads using a 10 × 32 tap. Make sure the hole is threaded deep enough to accommodate the full length of the screw.

17. If inspection indicates that either seal (19 or 68, **Figure 40**) must be replaced, the factory recommends replacing the unit. However, should you decide to replace the seal (10, **Figure 40**), the following hints and precautions should be observed:

a. To remove the armature from the end bell (9, **Figure 40**), remove the snap ring (27) and set screw (12, **Figure 40**). Access to the set screw can be gained through the discharge port where the outlet connection (20, **Figure 40**) attaches.

b. After the seal has been replaced, it is important that great care be taken in reassembling the armature so that the key (32, **Figure 40**) does not damage the seal. Therefore, it is best to insert the key into the armature shaft after the shaft has been installed through the seal. This can be done through the discharge port.

c. Install the macerator plate (except Deep Draft Models) by aligning the wings with the wide slots at the top and bottom of the end bell.

Disassembly/ Assembly

Figure 40 shows an exploded view of the Crown Head.

RARITAN COMPACT, PH, PHE, PHII AND PHEII

COMPACT, PH, PHE, PHII and PHEII heads can be mounted above or below the water line. They are equally suitable for use with a holding tank, recirculating system or a flow-through sewage treatment device such as a chlorinator. The use of a vented loop or "swan's neck" on the discharge is common practice with this system, especially in sailboats.

The PHE is an electric version of the PH. In fact, holes are pre-drilled at the factory in PH models to accept electric parts. Conversion is described later in this section.

Conversion To Electric Operation

Raritan PH hand toilets are designed for easy conversion to electric operation, using the Raritan Electric Conversion Kit. The conversion can be made in fifteen minutes by the average person, using basic tools. Fasten the electric drive unit to the drilled pad using the bolts and washers provided. Move the pump handle until the top of the arm aligns with the hole in the handle socket. Insert the arm bolt and tighten the nut. Remove the handle. Back off the arm bolt if it binds. Lubricate moving parts with a few drops of oil.

Maintenance

Very little maintenance is required. Ordinary scouring powders such as Ajax will keep the bowl clean. If for any reason a deodorizer is indicated, use Clorox rather than solvents such as Pine Oil or Lysol. A little Vaseline applied to the piston rod, especially to PHE models will prolong the lift of U cup seals and gland. A few drops of oil on both ends of the connecting rod of the PHE in fall and spring are recommended. It should never be necessary to add grease to the PHE gear box.

Lay-up and Commissioning

Improper winter lay-up is the major cause of all marine toilet failures.

1. Close the inlet seacock. Remove the inlet hose from the pump housing and temporarily attach a short length of hose to the inlet.
2. Pour about 1 qt. (0.9 L) of permanent type antifreeze (do not use anti-leak types) into a coffee can or other container. With the open end of the temporary hose in the container, pump the head until the color of the fluid running down from the rim of the bowl indicates the antifreeze has circulated and is being discharged through the outlet seacock.
3. Close the outlet seacock.
4. Let the antifreeze remain in the toilet until it is recommissioned. This method of winterizing protects both the inlet side of the pump and the discharge areas. Simply pouring antifreeze into the bowl protects only the discharge side. This is why so many marine toilets give trouble in the springtime.
5. When danger of freezing is past, reconnect the inlet hose and open both seacocks.
6. Apply a little Vaseline to the piston rod.

Troubleshooting

NOTE

It is wise to carry a Raritan head repair kit for the model you have onboard. These kits provide all the parts you are apt to use for normal servicing.

1. *Water accumulates in the bowl faster than it pumps out:* Trash lodged under the outlet flapper. The trash can be cleared by partially or completely closing the inlet valve and continuing to pump. A degree of resistance will be noted in pumping, which is normal. After the bowl is cleared of all debris, open the valve again and flush a few strokes to clear the discharge lines. If the problem persists, the flapper valve in discharge is not seating. It could be squeezed too

tight, stretching the hinge, or it could be swollen due to use of certain deodorants. In this case, replace flapper valve. Tighten screws only enough to prevent leaking; overtightening will stretch the hinge and prevent proper seating.

2. *Water rises in bowl when boat is dockside:* The rim of bowl is below waterline of the boat. Either the outlet joker valve is leaking or the inlet check valve is leaking. Close first one seacock, then the other, to determine whether water comes in the outlet or the inlet. If the outlet leaks, replace joker valve.

NOTE

It is a wise precaution to install a vented loop or "swan's neck" in the discharge. This will prevent back siphoning through the discharge if either the joker valve or flapper valve leak.

If the water comes from the inlet, make sure there is no trash under the inlet check valve. On PH models, an additional stainless steel spring, obtainable from Raritan at no charge, is available for installations considerably below the waterline. It is wise to close the inlet valves when the boat is left unattended.

3. *Water fills up the bowl when the boat is underway:* This is more likely to happen when the head is located far forward. Water pressure due to the speed of the boat unseats thc ball check on the inlet (PH model). Raritan provides, on special order, a spring designed to eliminate this problem. As an alternative, a water scoop can be installed backwards on the outside of the hull over the inlet seacock. This will deflect the water pressure. On the Compact model, the water scoop will cure the trouble. In any case, it is wise to close the inlet valves when underway, especially in rough water.

4. *Inlet water flow is poor and/or water builds up in bowl. Handle seems to work harder than it should. Trouble does not seem to be due to causes described previously:* In certain areas such as Florida, concrete-like deposits build up in both the inlet and outlet connections and adversely affect all types of marine toilets. This appears to be a type of coral. The only cure is periodic cleaning.

5. *A persistent and obnoxious odor emanates from the bowl of the head:* Eel grass or other marine vegetation has worked its way through the pump and is lodged in the passageway that is molded in the rim of the bowl. Here it decays and gives off a "rotten egg" smell. Perhaps you will note little black specks flowing down the sides of the bowl from the wash holes under the rim. The immediate cure is to connect a garden hose to the spud at the back of the bowl and flush it thoroughly under pressure. Another method is to disconnect the inlet hose and temporarily attach another short hose so the toilet can suck a strong solution of Drano from a bucket. Be sure in advance that strong chemicals will not damage internal parts or lines. To prevent recurrence, install a strainer on the inlet line. Another remote possibility for this odor is that the inlet connection is on the same side of the boat as the discharge and so near it that some of the effluent is actually being drawn back into the inlet. In systems thatuse recirculating water due to stringent anti-pollution laws, a deodorant as recommended by the manufacturer of the recirculating device must be used.

6. *On the PHE models, when operated electrically, the pump works very slowly and the motor labors:* This is due almost always to low voltage, especially on 12-volt models. Check the voltage with a meter by baring the wire close to the motor (2 in. [51 mm]). Voltage should not be less than 11.5 volts when the motor is running. Other voltages should not show more than a 10% drop. If voltage drop is excessive, check if wiring and fuses conform to those recommended. Check the operating switch for adequate capacity. For 12-volt models, the switch should be rated for 30 amps or more; 32-volt and 115-volt models require a switch rated for 10 amps. Look for corroded connections, especially at fuse clips. Make sure the piston rod is lubricated. Disconnect the

connecting rod and check if the pump operates freely when hand pumped.

7. *Water squirts up piston rod when pumped:* The piston rod seal is leaking. Replace the seal and make sure retaining washer is installed evenly and just snug, not too tight.

8. *Changing the water height in the bowl:* Some people prefer to have the bowl retain some water after flushing. Others prefer that practically all the water be pumped out so it will not slop and splash when heeled over in a seaway. As shipped from the factory, very little water will remain in the bowl under normal conditions. To retain water in the bowl, have your boatyard install a vented loop in discharge hose.

Disassembly/Assembly

Figures 41-43 show exploded views of the Raritan PH and PHE toilets.

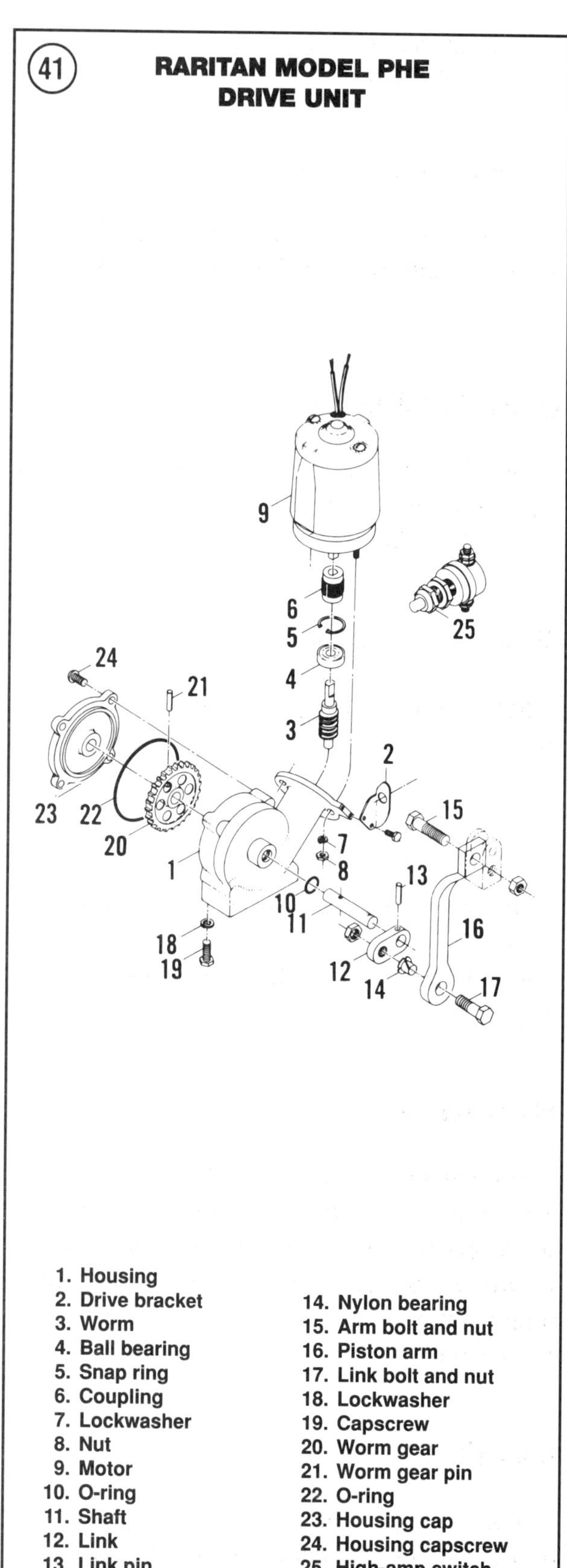

(41) **RARITAN MODEL PHE DRIVE UNIT**

1. Housing
2. Drive bracket
3. Worm
4. Ball bearing
5. Snap ring
6. Coupling
7. Lockwasher
8. Nut
9. Motor
10. O-ring
11. Shaft
12. Link
13. Link pin
14. Nylon bearing
15. Arm bolt and nut
16. Piston arm
17. Link bolt and nut
18. Lockwasher
19. Capscrew
20. Worm gear
21. Worm gear pin
22. O-ring
23. Housing cap
24. Housing capscrew
25. High-amp switch

BALL-HEAD

The unit operates by the variation of air pressure in the bowl during flushing and refilling. See **Figure 44**. Pressure variations are created by the ball-like diaphragm mounted on the cover. A vented handle breaks the vacuum for easy opening. The hinged cover is secured by a stainless steel lock and an airtight seal with the bowl. A spring-loaded valve maintains water in the bowl and prevents flooding when heeled.

Maintenance

The Ball-Head is very simple and requires no periodic maintenance other than normal cleaning. It is made of ABS (acrylonitrile-butadiene-styrene) resin; detergents, bleaches, or sodium hydroxide will do no harm.

CAUTION

Do not use the following chemicals as they are solvents of ABS resin: ethylene dichloride, methyl ethyl ketone (MEK), acetone, and ethyl acetate.

Winterizing and Lay-up

Since seawater is drawn in for each flush, no separate winterizing or lay-up preparations are necessary.

Typical Installations

The Ball-Head can be installed in any of the configurations described at the beginning of this chapter. See **Figure 44**.

Disassembly/ Assembly

Figure 44 is an exploded view of the Ball-Head.

HOLDING TANKS

Holding tanks are usually made from fiberglass and range greatly in capacity from a few gallons to 30 or more in large cruising boats with multiple heads.

Maintenance

No maintenance is required on holding tanks other than flushing after emptying and occasional checks to be sure that all fastenings are secure. Various chemicals are available at trailer supply stores to control odors and help break down solids.

Emptying

The method of emptying depends on the rest of the system. See sections on toilets for emptying and rinsing procedures.

WASTE TREATMENT SYSTEMS

Several manufacturers make complete onboard waste treatment systems. These U.S. Coast Guard approved devices all allow legal discharge of the treated waste within the three mile limit. Most are designed to operate automatically when the head is flushed to macerate and chemically sanitize the waste.

Maintenance

Very little maintenance is required. The most important care needed is to replenish the chemical used to sanitize the waste. Always carry sufficient supplies on board.

Properly used, these devices do not require cleaning out. The primary cause of clogging is too short maceration time and consequent inability of the chemicals to decompose solids.

Lay-up and Recommissioning

Prepare the toilet for lay-up as described in previous sections. If your toilet is not listed, follow manufacturer's instructions or pick a toilet in this book which works on the same principles as yours.

After the toilet has been prepared, pour about 3 qt. (2.8 L) of nontoxic antifreeze (propylene glycol) or other product recommended by the waste treatment system manufacturer into the toilet bowl. Pump it into the waste treatment system. Do not use antifreeze with anti-leak additives). Never use alcohol or kerosene as an antifreeze.

When recommissioning in the spring, flush the toilet the equivalent of at least 10 normal flushes to expel all the antifreeze.

WARNING

It is very important to do this before adding the treatment chemical. Some chemicals may react with the antifreeze to generate heat.

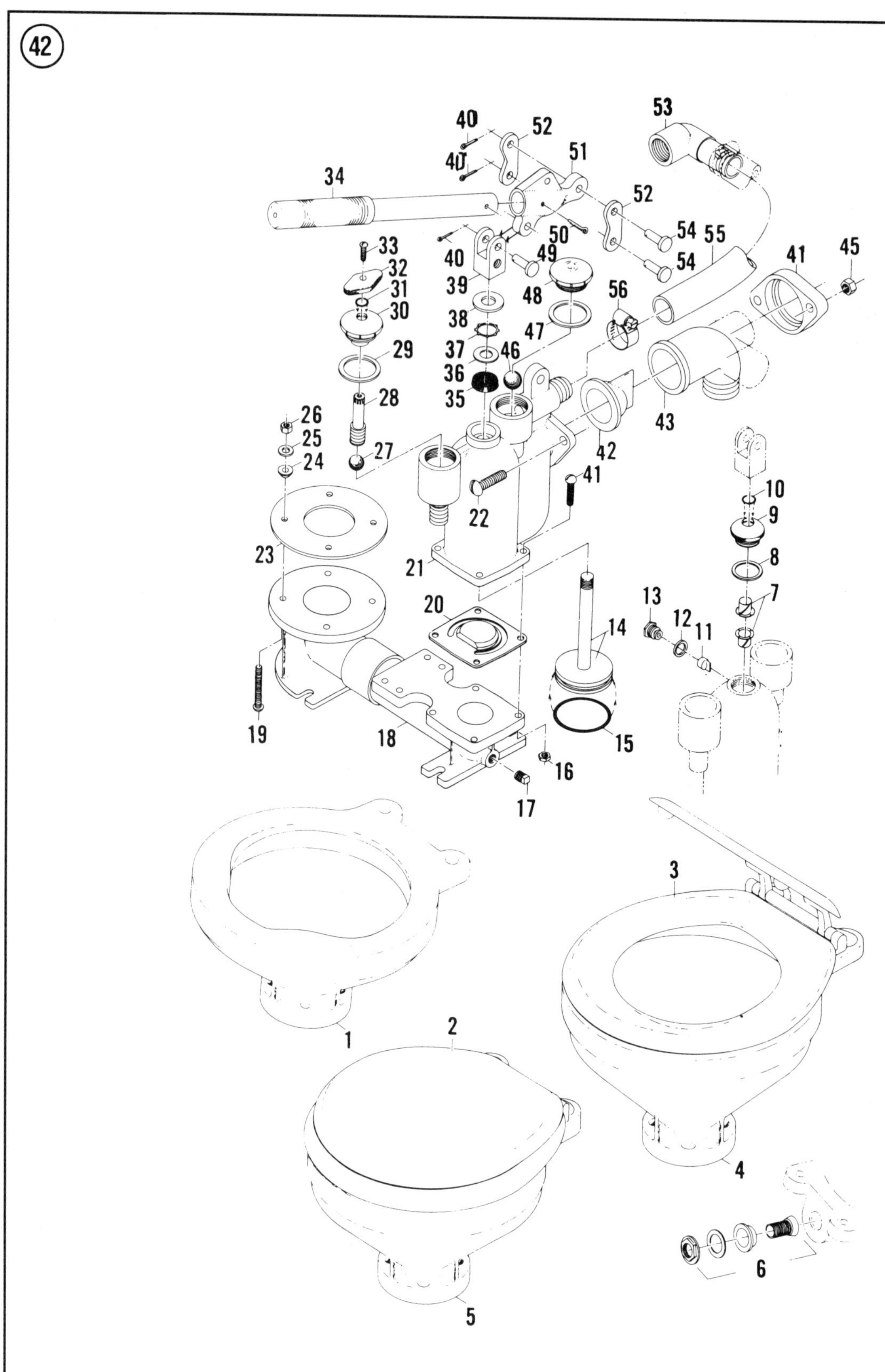
42
1
2
3
4
5
6
7
8
9
10
11
12
13
14
15
16
17
18
19
20
21
22
23
24
25
26
27
28
29
30
31
32
33
34
35
36
37
38
39
40
41
42
43
45
46
47
48
49
50
51
52
53
54
55
56

RARITAN MODEL PH AND PHE HEADS

1. Low-boy bowl
2. Seat and cover
3. Seat and cover
4. High-boy bowl
5. Standard bowl
6. Spud assembly
7. Piston rod and shaft bearing
8. Piston nut and gasket
9. Piston rod shaft nut
10. Piston rod O-ring
11. Vent joker valve
12. Vent gasket
13. Vent
14. Piston rod assembly
15. Piston O-ring
16. Housing nuts
17. Base plug
18. Base
19. Bowl bolt
20. Flapper valve
21. Housing
22. Flange bolt
23. Bowl gasket
24. Bowl bolt rubber washer
25. Bowl bolt washer
26. Bowl bolt nut
27. Inlet valve ball
28. Inlet valve stem
29. Inlet valve gasket
30. Valve cap
31. Valve stem O-ring
32. Valve handle
33. Valve handle screw
34. Standard handle
35. U-cup
36. Delrin washer
37. Snap ring
38. White washer (neoprene)
39. Piston rod yoke
40. Cotter pin
41. Housing bolt
42. Joker valve
43. 90° discharge
44. Flange
45. Flange nut
46. Outlet ball
47. Valve gasket
48. Valve cap
49. Clevis pin
50. Cotter pin
51. Handle socket
52. Fulcrum link
53. Bowl elbow
54. Clevis pin
55. Hose
56. Hose clamp

43

RARITAN COMPACT MODEL HEAD

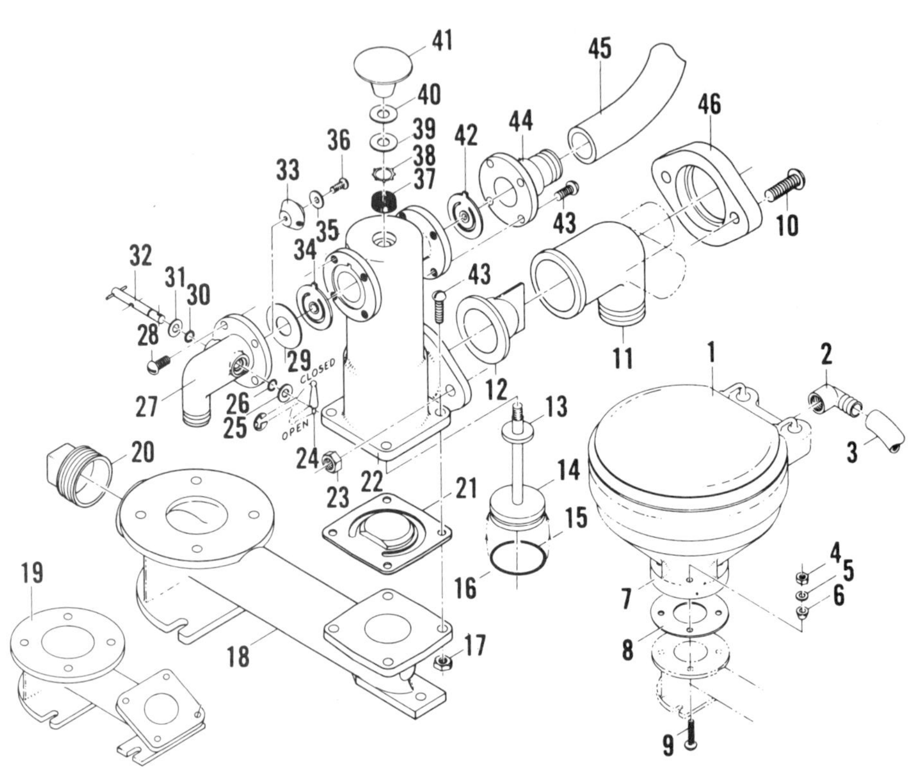

1. Seat and cover
2. Bowl elbow
3. Hose
4. Bowl bolt nuts
5. Bowl bolt washers
6. Bowl bolt rubber washers
7. Bowl
8. Bowl gasket
9. Bowl bolts
10. Discharge flange bolt
11. Discharge 90° elbow
12. Joker valve
13. Pump shaft washer
14. Piston rod assembly
15. Piston O-ring
16. Piston rod washer
17. Housing nuts
18. Toilet base
19. V-base
20. Plastic drain plug
21. Flapper valve assembly
22. Pump housing
23. Discharge flange nut
24. Shut off valve handle
25. Valve shaft washer
26. Valve shaft O-ring
27. Inlet elbow
28. Flange screws
29. Check valve seat
30. Valve shaft O-ring
31. Valve shaft washer
32. Shut off valve shaft
33. Shut off valve
34. Check valve assembly
35. Shut off valve washer
36. Valve screw
37. Piston rod seal
38. Seal snap ring
39. Pump shaft washer
40. Piston rod washer
41. Knob
42. Check valve assembly
43. Housing screws
44. Upper outlet
45. Hose
46. Discharge elbow flange

Before launching the boat, discharge the antifreeze out the thru-hull valve into a container. If the boat is already in the water, make sure thru-hull fitting is *closed*, then disconnect the line at the output of the waste treatment system and discharge the antifreeze into a suitable container. Reconnect the line to the thru-hull valve.

CAUTION
Do not discharge the antifreeze overboard into the water. This is a violation of the law in most areas.

RECIRCULATING SYSTEMS

A recirculating system is basically holding tanks which filters out solids and feeds decontaminated liquid waste back to the toilet for flushing. An initial charge of a few gallons of fresh water provides 70-100 flushes with a total tank capacity of about 10 gal. (38 L).

Maintenance

Since the recirculator is nothing more than a holding tank, no preventive maintenance is required except for rinsing. The unit should be rinsed each time it is emptied. Occasion backflushing can be used to clean the interior screen. To do this, disconnect the hoses between the recirculator and the toilet. Connect a shore water source to the intake fitting and collect outflow from the discharge fitting in a large container. See **Figure 45**. Dump the container into a dockside sanitary sewer system, not overboard.

Charging

Charge the recirculating system with a few gallons of water after emptying and rinsing. There are several methods.

1. Add water to the toilet and bowl and flush it into the tank.

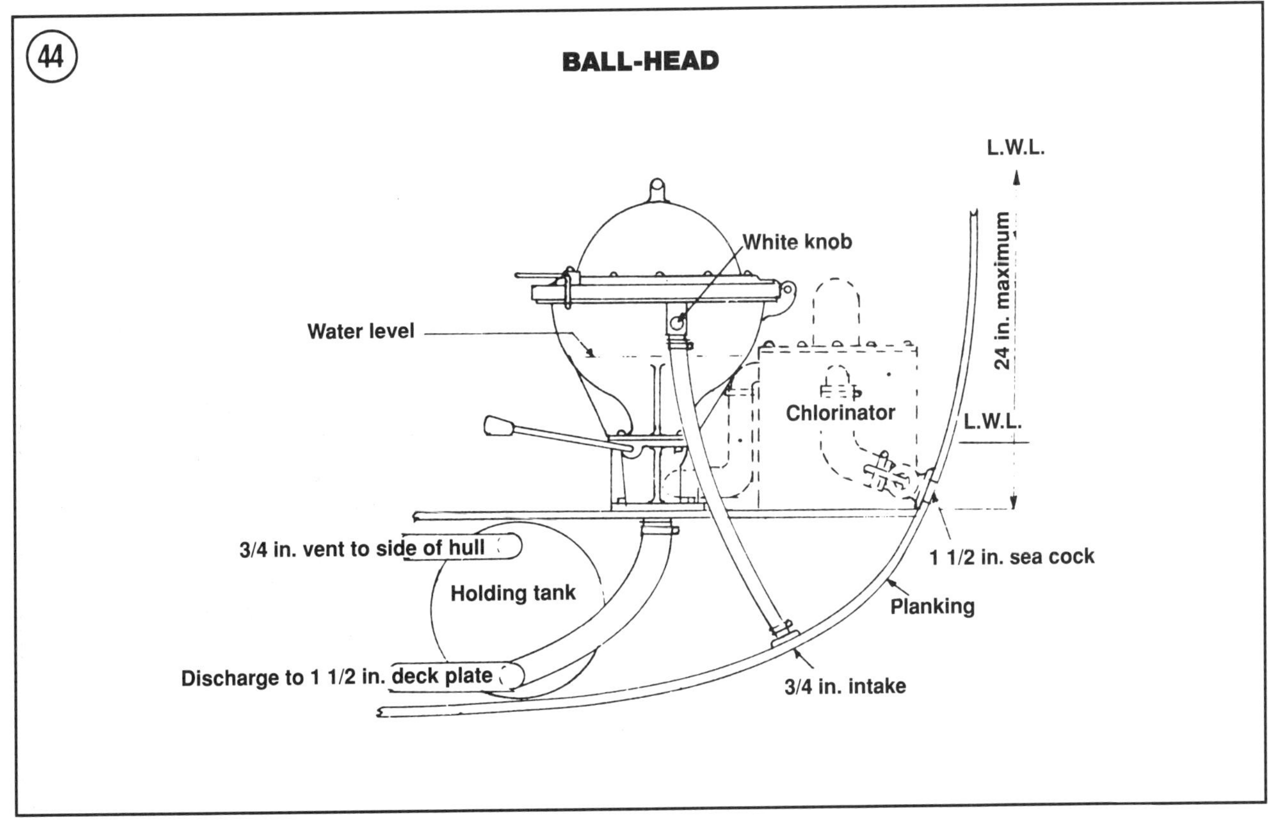

11

2. Add water through the discharge deck fitting.
3. If installed as in **Figure 46**, the valve may be turned to admit seawater when the toilet is flushed. The valve must be returned to recirculate position when tank is about 1/3 full.

CAUTION
Never fill the tank through the vent line. The unrelieved pressure could possibly burst the tank.

After charging, add one package or bottle of deodorizer specifically made for recirculating toilets. Flush it into the tank from the toilet.

Emptying and Rinsing

Recirculating tanks can be emptied and rinsed like any other holding tank. the method depends on the installation. If a deck fitting is provided, a dockside pumping station can pump the waste out. Add fresh water as if recharging to rinse tank and pump that out in the same manner. If the system is equipped with a separate pump, the

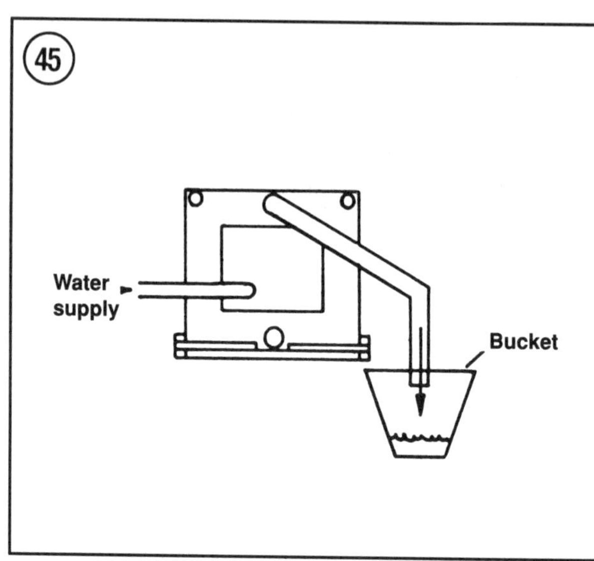

46

COMPLEX RECIRCULATING SYSTEM

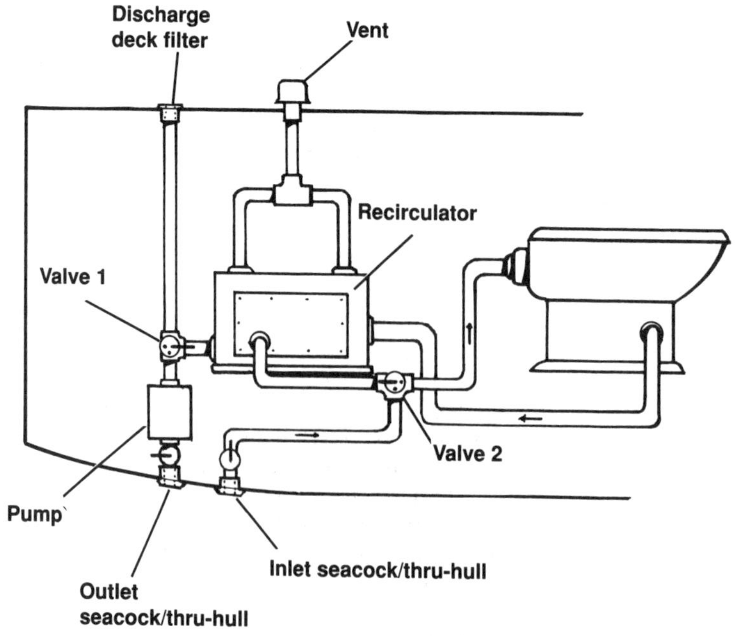

Discharge deck filter
Vent
Recirculator
Valve 1
Valve 2
Pump`
Inlet seacock/thru-hull
Outlet seacock/thru-hull

waste can be pumped overboard out a thru-hull fitting in waters where this is legal.

Winterizing

Empty and rinse the holding tank as described previously. Add sufficient antifreeze instead of water to protect about 10 gallons to the temperature range expected. Follow the antifreeze manufacturer's instructions.

CAUTION
Use nontoxic glycol base antifreeze only. Do not use alcohol or antifreeze with anti-leak additives. Do not use automotive antifreeze.

Lay-up

Empty and thoroughly rinse the recirculating system. Leave it dry.

Table 1 THETFORD ELECTRA MAGIC TROUBLESHOOTING

Symptom	Probable cause	Remedy
Toilet wobbles	Closet bolt nuts not tight.	Tighten nuts.
	Mounting brackets not seated to floor.	Tighten nuts.
	Closet flange too high or mounting surface uneven.	Check closet flange height by laying straightedge across flange and measuring gap between straightedge at four leg locations (1/4 to 7/16 in. is recommended).
Toilet cycles when seat cover is raised	Actuator button protrudes too far from motor cover.	Alternately press one side of the button, then the other, to work button back further into housing. If button still protrudes too far, replace timer assembly.
Toilet does not cycle properly (5-9 seconds)	Reversed wiring polarity.	Wire correctly.
	Battery run down.	Charge battery.
	Wiring too small.	Install heavier wiring.
	Defective timer.	Replace timer.
Flushing weak or noisy	Pump is running backwards (reversed wiring polarity).	Wire correctly.
	Cycling unit without enough charge water.	Charge to capacity.
	Pump damaged by continuous dry operation.	Replace pump.
Lack of capacity (less than normal number of flushes)	Too much water.	Use only 3 gal. (11.4 L) to charge.

Table 2 THETFORD AQUA MAGIC TROUBLESHOOTING

Symptom	Probable cause	Remedy
Water keeps running into the bowl	The blade in the bottom of the bowl is not closing completely, which in turn keeps the water control valve partially open. The groove into which the blade seats when completely closed is clogged with foreign material.	Insert the end of a coat hanger or similar object into the sealing groove and remove the toreign material. Avoid damaging the rubber seal while cleaning.
Toilet leaks. There is water on the deck.	Determine if water is leaking from	
	a. The vacuum breaker.	a. If the vacuum breaker leaks when flushing the toilet, replace the vacuum breaker.
	b. The water control valve.	b. If the vacuum breaker leaks when the toilet is not in operation, replace the water control valve.
	c. Bowl-to-mechanism seal (if this is the problem, water will not stay in bowl).	c. Leaks at closet flange area—check front and rear closet flange nuts for tightness. If leak continues, remove the toilet, check closet flange height. The height should be between 1/4 and 7/16 in. above the floor. Adjust closet flange height accordingly and replace closet flange seal.
Foot pedal operates harder than normal or the blade sticks.		Apply a light film of silicone spray to blade.

Chapter Twelve

Trailers and Towing

Few people really enjoy recovering a boat, especially after a full day of boating when they are tired, hot and thirsty. A well-designed trailer makes launching and recovery a pleasure. Plus it gives you a permanent place to keep all of your gear such as personal flotation devices so that you don't have to remember to pack them each time. When you are ready to go, you can literally hitch up and drive off. Of course you are going to want to check that the tie downs are secure, tires are properly inflated and that any onboard lockers actually contain what you think they do.

However, no matter how well designed the trailer and hitch, if they are not maintained, you are asking for trouble. Most people recognize the need for periodic maintenance to their towing vehicle. But many of these same people submerge their trailer in corrosive saltwater every weekend, giving no thought to periodic maintenance for the trailer.

Neglected trailers are a serious hazard to your boat, your tow vehicle and possibly even your life. Highway Patrol files contain numerous accident reports involving trailers. A rusted axle can freeze up from lack of lubrication and cause the wheel to fall off. If you'rc lucky, only the trailer will be damaged. In some cases, the trailer can flip your boat on the pavement, or cause you to lose control and crash. We're doing this for fun—keep it safe as well.

TRAILER WEIGHT

Just like your tow vehicle, trailers are also rated by weight. Check the trailer frame and you should find a tag listing Gross Trailer Weight Rating (GTWR) which indicates the maximum weight of the fully loaded trailer. The axles may also be tagged with Gross Axle Weight Rating

(GAWR) which is the maximum weight a single axle can support. Consider the weight of the boat loaded with PFD's, food, fishing tackle, full jerry cans of fuel and all the other things you stuff into it. The best thing to do is actually weigh your loaded trailer at a public scale.

HITCHES

A good quality, properly installed trailer hitch forms the all-important link between a trailer and tow vehicle. The hitch does more than just connect the tow vehicle to the trailer. It allows the trailer to turn, yet it subdues any tendency of the trailer to sway. It must be designed so that the trailer cannot separate accidentally, but if the trailer overturns, it must release it so the tow vehicle remains under control.

Weight Classes

Trailers are divided into 4 towing weight classes. See **Table 1**. Gross trailer weight (GTWR) is the weight with the trailer fully loaded. This number includes the empty trailer, boat, fuel cans, tools, water, ice, food and anything else which may be aboard.

Trailer tongue weight is the portion of the trailer's weight which is supported by the hitch ball. Trailer manufacturers design their products so that the tongue weight of a normally loaded trailer is approximately 10-15% of gross towing weight. For example, a 5,000 lb. (2270 kg) trailer should have a tongue weight of 500-750 (230-340 kg).

Types of Hitches

There are 4 main types of trailer hitches. Each is designed to do a certain job.

a. Bumper hitch.

b. Frame hitch (Class I, II and III).

c. Weight distributing hitch.

d. Axle hitch.

Bumper hitches attach to the tow vehicle by means of one or more clamps. See **Figure 1**. The strength of this system is limited by the strength of the tow vehicle's bumper. Such hitches are used mainly for occasional towing of very small boats—those less than 1,000 lb. (453 kg) GTWR. These hitches are sometimes called sub-Class I hitches.

Frame hitches, as the name implies, are bolted or welded to the tow vehicle frame. See **Figure 2**. They are usually attached at several points. Most have a removable hitch shank that mounts in a square tube or "receiver" on the frame mounted hitch. This allows you fit different hitch shanks to match the hitch height to the trailer to ensure a level load. It also allows you to remove the shank from the vehicle when it is not required. Frame hitches are the most popular type for all size trailers, and can be professionally installed relatively inexpensively. Frame hitches are available in four weight classes. See **Table 1**.

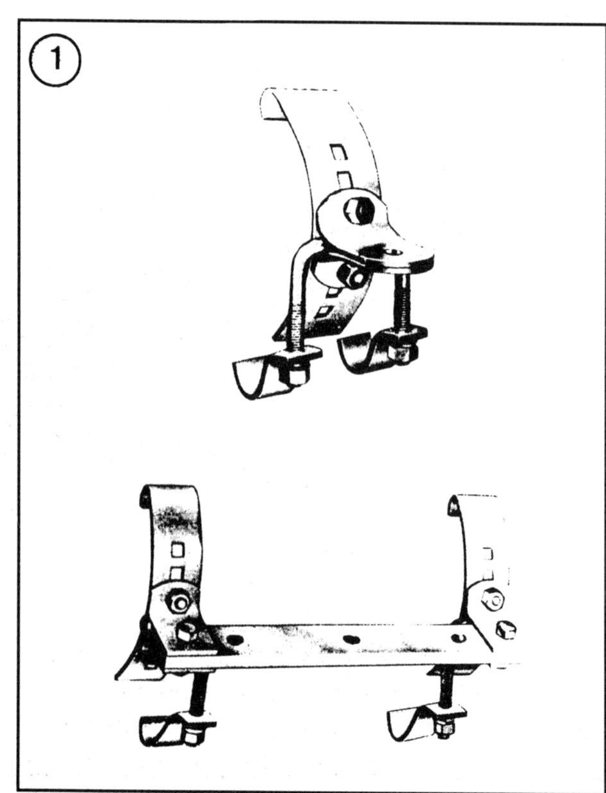

Class I hitches usually attach to the bumper and frame for more strength. These are rated at 2,000 lb. (907 kg) GTWR and a 200 lb. (91 kg) tongue weight. They may use a removable hitch shank or the hitch ball may mount directly on the hitch.

Class II hitches mount to the frame and are obviously much larger than Class I hitches. On some Class II hitches, the hitch ball mounts directly on the hitch, but most use a removable hitch shank and square receiver. Most Class II hitches have a 2 in. square receiver, rated for 3,500 lb. (1587 kg) GTWR and 300 lb. (136 kg) tongue weight. This is the best hitch to get since the price of a Class II hitch is not that much more than a Class I hitch, but it allows you to tow almost anything.

Class III and Class IV hitches are available that handle much larger loads. See **Table 1**. These include equalizing bars to transfer some of the trailer load to the tow vehicle.

If you are hauling something really big, talk to a professional about these.

A load equalizing or weight distributing hitch may be necessary if you tow a large trailer and boat. This hitch transfers a portion of the trailer tongue weight to a point between front and rear wheels of the tow vehicle. Remaining tongue weight transfers to the trailer wheels. Without load equalization, all tongue weight would be at a point far behind the tow vehicle's rear axle. The rear axle becomes a fulcrum about which the entire car pivots. Tongue weight forces the rear end of the tow vehicle down. At the same time, the front end rises, up-setting front end geometry and causing various steering handling problems.

Figure 3 compares load distribution using a common frame hitch used with overload springs and an equalizing hitch, using the same vehicle and trailer. When the vehicle and trailer are separate, weight is distributed as shown in top view. When joined to a tow vehicle with overload

3

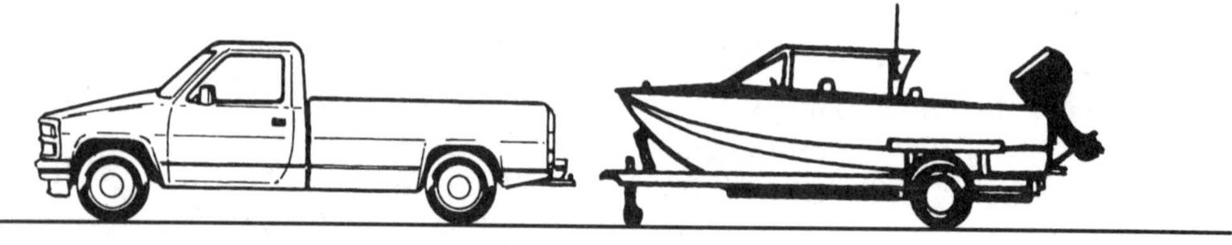

SEPARATED

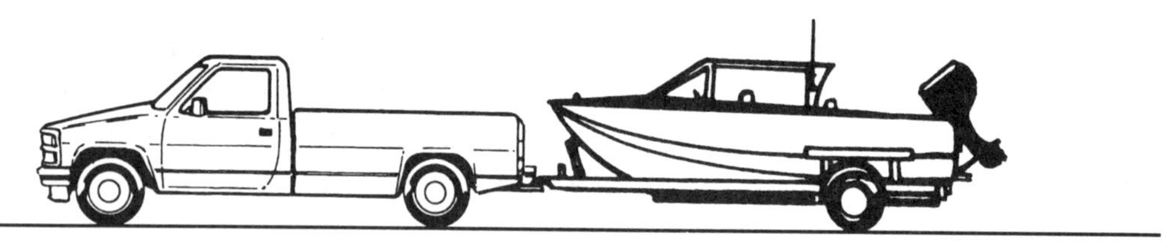

WITH OVERLOAD SPRINGS

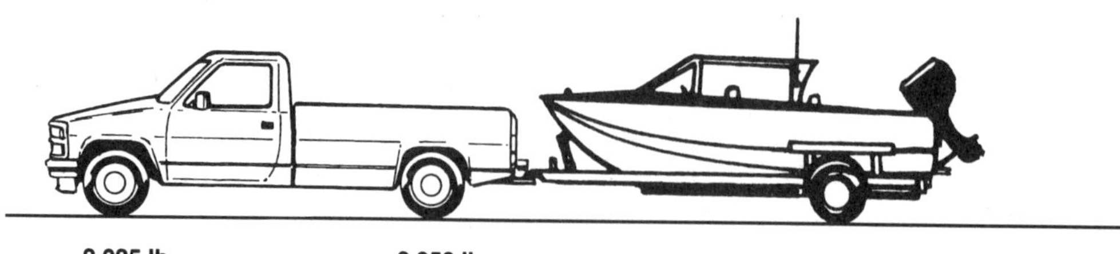

WITH WEIGHT DISTRIBUTION HITCH

springs, note that the vehicle can remain nearly level, but weight transfers from front to rear. When an equalizing hitch is used, tongue weight is distributed between the front and rear wheels of the tow vehicle and the trailer wheels as well.

An axle hitch is a variation of a load equalizing hitch. Instead of transferring trailer tongue weight to all 4 wheels of the tow vehicle, it transfers it only to the rear axle. These hitches are relatively easy to install, but usually cause overloading of rear axles and wheel bearings. Many automobile manufacturers caution against axle hitches.

Hitch Balls

Hitch balls come in three sizes. The most common size is 2 in., but they are also available in 1-7/8 in. and 2-5/16 in. The size and weight rating are usually stamped on the top of the ball.

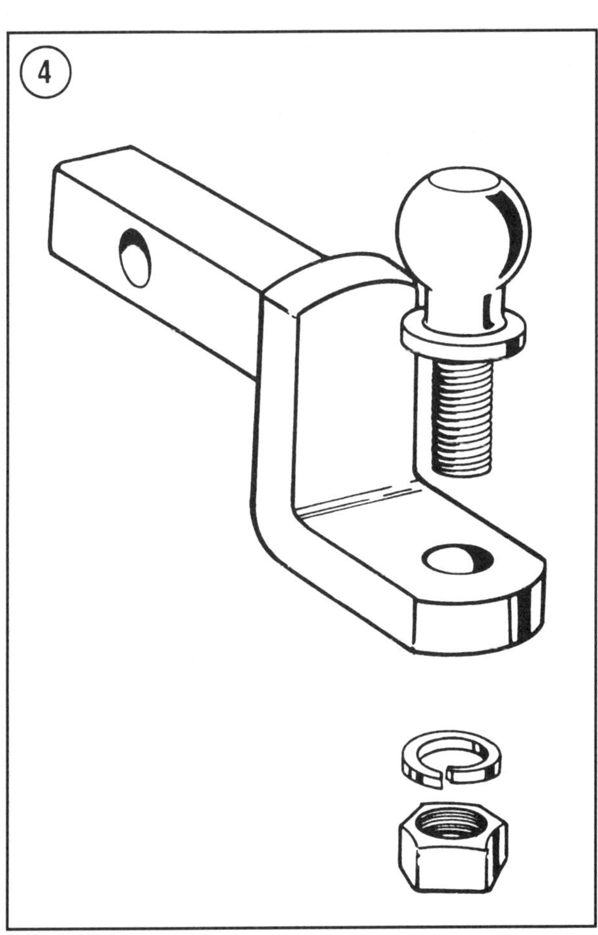

The hitch ball should fit the hole in the hitch shank or hitch perfectly. See **Figure 4**. If there is any slop, the ball will eventually loosen and it could shear off. You should also make sure to torque the nut to specification recommended by its manufacturer. The hitch ball is the same for Classes I-III. Class IV hitches require a different ball.

Incidentally, most hitch balls are chrome plated to make them look good. It serves no other purpose, so if the chrome begins to flake off, don't worry about it—you probably keep it covered anyway. A little grease on the ball will prevent rusting and keep the hitch coupler from galling the surface of the ball.

Hitch Shank and Receiver

The hitch shank and ball fit into the square receiver. A large pin secures it in place. One of the main purposes of the removable shank is to get the right ball height for the trailer. Ideally, the trailer frame should be parallel to the ground to ensure proper tracking, particularly under heavy braking.

Many pickups and 4×4s, especially those with oversize tires and lift kits, need a drop shank to keep the trailer level. This drops the ball height enough to get thc trailer frame level. See **Figure 5**. If you are towing a large trailer with a small vehicle such as a mini pickup, you may actually have to reverse the shank to get the ball height higher. Do whatever you have to do to get the trailer frame level. In many states, such as California, the vehicle code requires this.

Be careful of large amounts of drop. The more you drop, the more stress the trailer puts on the shank. See **Figure 6**. The shank acts like a lever and a heavy trailer may actually tear the shank off. You may not be able to safely pull a certain weight trailer even though your hitch class is rated for it. Talk this over with a professional hitch installer.

Coupler

There are several coupler designs used on trailers. This is not usually something you choose. The trailer manufacturer makes the choice for you. The most common are the lever lock coupler and the wheel lock coupler. See **Figure 7**. The lever lock coupler is the most common. Once the coupler is over the ball, you simply flip the lever down to lock it. You should pin it or lock it in place so that it cannot accidentally flip up again. The wheel lock coupler is a little more trouble. Once the coupler is over the ball, tighten the wheel until the coupler tightens against the ball, but not so much that the trailer cannot move freely. A metal tab keeps the wheel from loosening.

Safety Chains

Safety chains prevent the trailer from completely separating from the tow vehicle if the hitch should fail. Amazingly, if the correct safety chains are used, you can often get the whole rig stopped with little damage to the trailer or tow vehicle. In any event, all of us innocent drivers around you won't have to face your runaway boat.

You need two safety chains and you should cross them under the trailer tongue as shown in **Figure 8**. This effectively catches the tongue so that it cannot drop onto the road surface if it disengages. You should also run the chain through the holes provided on the hitch and hook

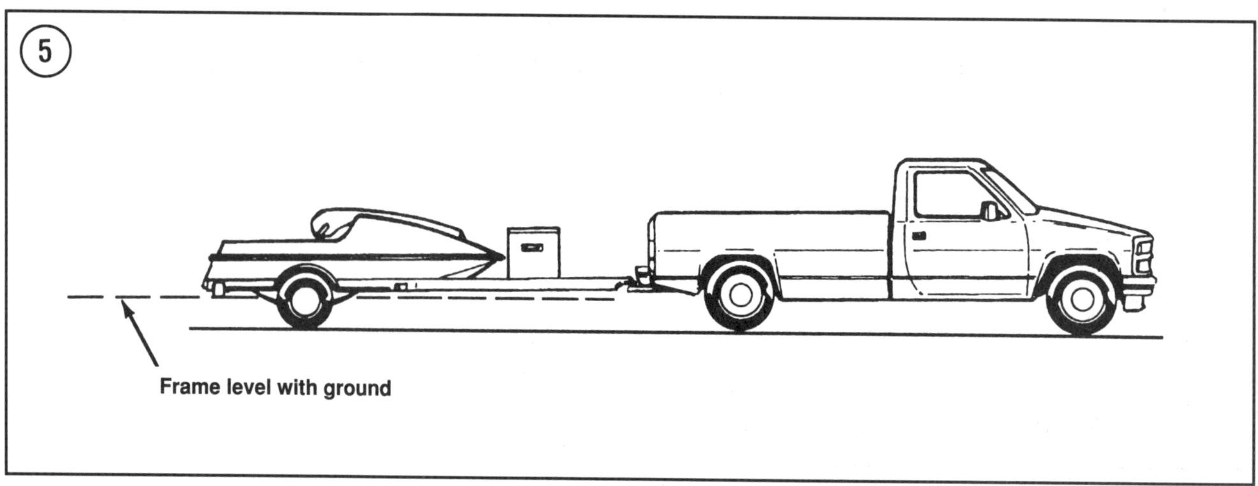

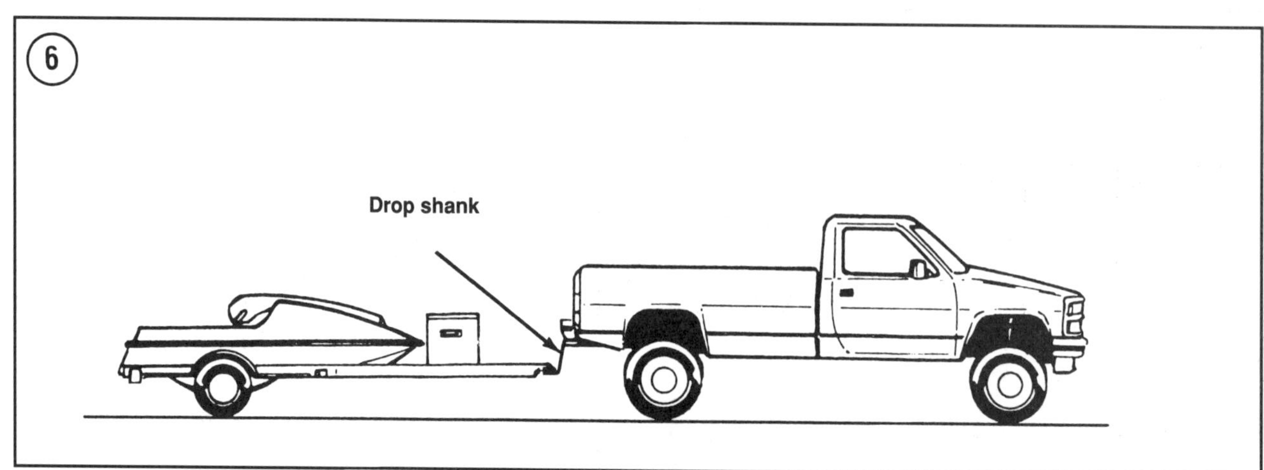

the chain back on itself. Don't simply hook the chain to the hitch.

Safety chain comes in different sizes. Make sure yours is the correct size for your weight class. Most safety chains are standard link chains. You can also buy safety cables which serve the same purpose but are made from aircraft cable. Both safety chains and safety cables may be equipped with removable links (**Figure 9**) which are more secure than simple hooks.

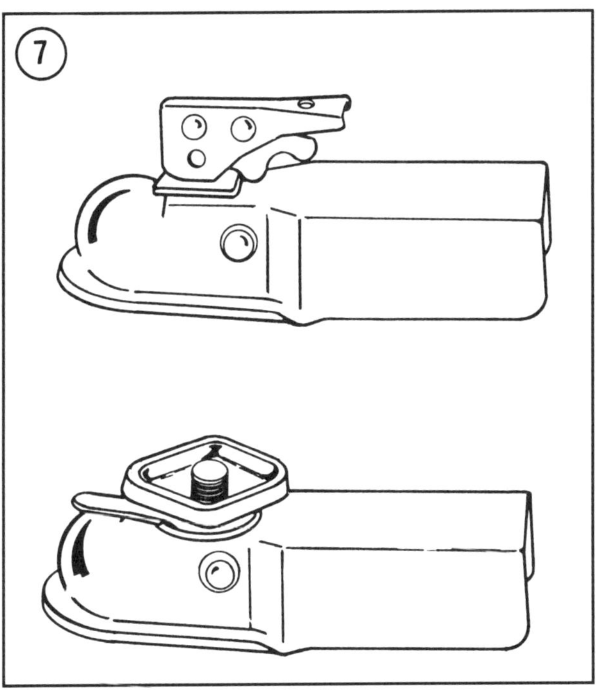

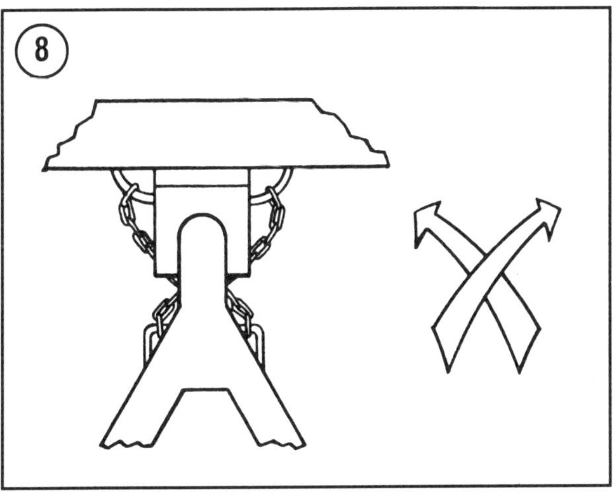

Installation

Hitch installation is strictly a job for professionals, except for bumper and bolt-on frame hitches which are used to tow only lightweight trailers. Usually, each installation must be custom tailored for its individual application. Some parts may have to be cut to fit their connections. Others must be bent to fit, using a large hydraulic press. Major hitch manufacturers consider proper installation so important that they operate their own service and installation centers.

Maintenance

A trailer hitch is a simple, rugged device which requires no maintenance other than occasional checks to make sure that its attachment and assembly bolts are secure. Spring bars and hitch balls should be lubricated.

Checking Tongue Weight

Since individual owners will load their trailers in various ways, it is impossible for any manufacturer to specify exact tongue weight for any but an unloaded trailer. You can measure actual tongue weight very easily, however.

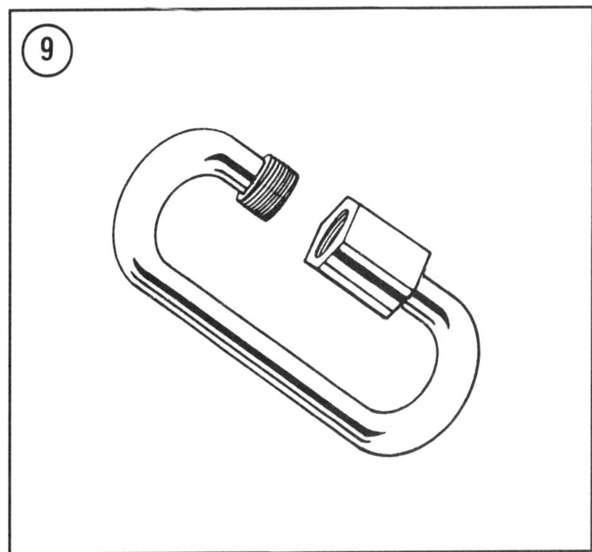

If tongue weight is known not to exceed the range of an ordinary bathroom scale (usually 300 lb.—a big trailer), measure tongue weight directly as shown in **Figure 10**.

NOTE
Be sure the trailer is level and the weight onboard the trailer is distributed normally before reading the scale.

The board distributes the load over the top of the scale so that the scale will not be damaged. Actual tongue weight is the weight indicated on the scale.

If tongue weight exceeds the scale range (as it may on large boat/trailer combinations), use the method shown in **Figure 11**. Place a block or brick of approximately the same thickness as the bathroom scale on the ground in line with the trailer coupler jack. It should be spaced so that a short piece of pipe or other round object will lie directly one foot from the center line of the jack extension. Place the scales so the other round object can be exactly 2 ft. (0.6 m) from the center line of the jack extension. Place a 2 × 4 or 4 × 4 on the 2 round pieces and screw the jack extension down on top of the 2 × 4 until the tongue of the trailer is supported by it. Multiply the scale reading by 3. This number will be the tongue weight of your trailer. If you exceed the capacity of the bathroom scale, increase the 2 ft. (0.6 m) dimension to 3 or 4 ft. (0.9-1.2 m), but always multiply the scale reading by the total number of feet between the brick and the scale.

NOTE
Be sure the trailer is level before reading the scale.

SWAY CONTROLS

A swaying trailer is annoying and dangerous. You take pride in how well your boat handles. Give some thought to how your tow vehicle/trailer handles as well. There are several major contributions to trailer sway:

a. Excessive speed.

b. Improper tire pressures (tow vehicle and trailer).

c. Light steering.

d. Improper tongue weight at hitch.

Cures for (a) and (b) are obvious. In many states, cars with trailers must observe a slower

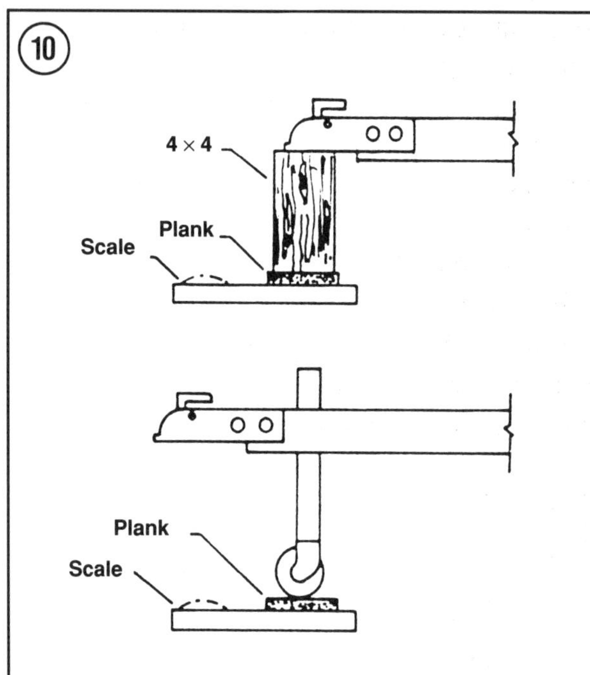

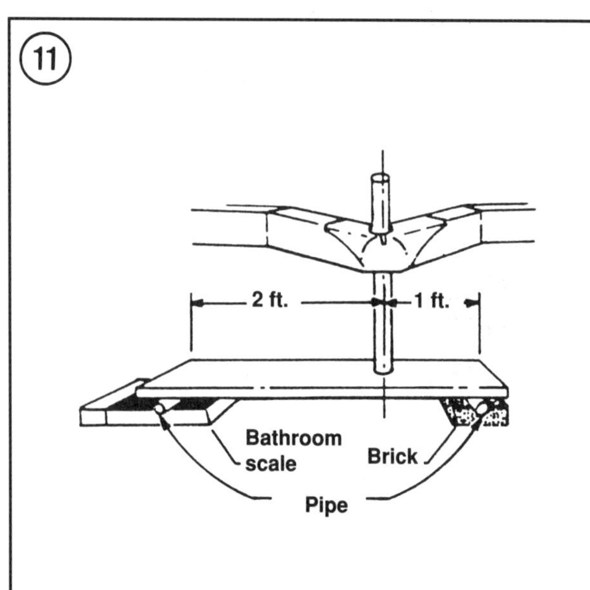

speed limit. Light steering is usually caused by excessive hitch weight; usually an equalizing hitch will solve the problem. Improper hitch weight can be cured by measuring the actual tongue weight of trailer as described previously and redistributing gear on the trailer to establish proper weight. Usually this means moving weight forward. As a rule of thumb, 60% of the load on the trailer should be forward of the trailer axle, but experiment with load distribution until you get it right.

If you take care of all the sources of trouble listed above and the rig still sways, you might consider a sway control system. Two types are available:

a. Mechanical.

b. Hydraulic.

Figure 12 illustrates typical sway control devices. A friction element between the tongue arm and mounting plate damps out trailer sway on a mechanical system. This device requires no maintenance other than adjustment to each combination of tow vehicle and trailer.

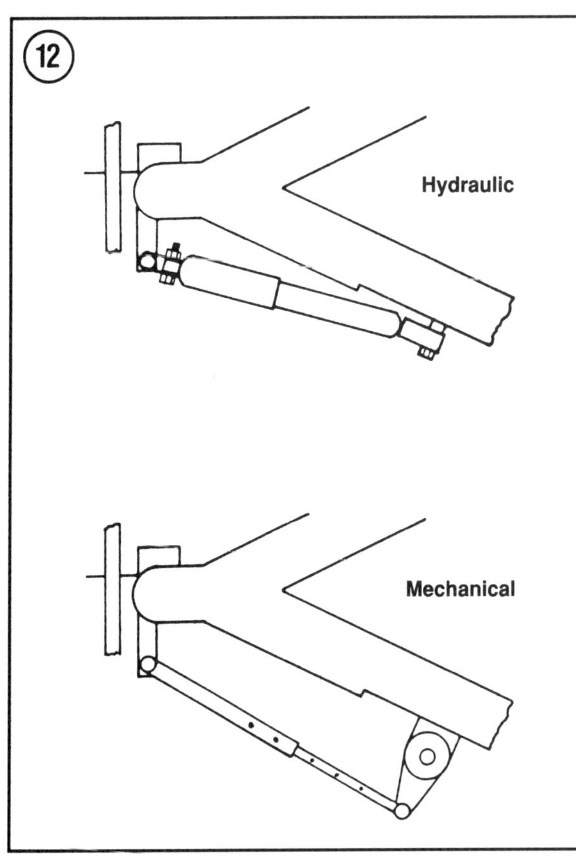

Hydraulic sway control systems operate much as do mechanical sway controls, except that a hydraulic cylinder similar to that of an automobile shock absorber replaces the friction element. No adjustment or service is necessary, but hydraulic units must be replaced in the event of malfunction.

LIGHTING

Lighting requirements on trailers vary from state to state. **Figure 13** shows the Federal DOT Standard 108.

If the trailer is submerged during launching and recovery, some means must be made to protect the lights from corrosive water. Two methods are common:

a. Removable lights.

b. Special water-tight lights.

In some cases, only the taillights are removable. Side markers and clearance lights are mounted on stalks to keep them out of the water when the trailer is submerged. See **Figure 14.**

Preventive Maintenance

You can save yourself a lot of grief later by taking a little extra time before and after each trip for some preventive maintenance.

1. Before each trip, connect the trailer lights and check each for proper operation.
2. When the trailer is pulled out of the water, check water-tight lights to be sure they haven't leaked. If one has, remove the lens and bulb; flush with fresh water and dry it out. Also determine the cause of the leak and fix it.
3. Squirt connector terminals and lamp sockets *lightly* with WD-40 or equivalent.

Troubleshooting

Lighting trouble can be caused by:

a. Defective bulb.

b. Loose bulb.

c. Corroded sockets.

d. Corroded wire connections.

e. Broken wire.

f. Shorts from exposed wire.

g. Corroded connectors.

Corrosion from saltwater is one of the most common causes of lighting trouble. Particularly susceptible are connectors used for removable lights. Squirt the connector terminals with WD-40 or equivalent, then connect and disconnect plug several times to clean away corrosion.

If corrosion is not the problem, a little logical troubleshooting should find the trouble.

TRAILER INSPECTION

Periodically check the entire trailer, looking at these areas:

1. Check tires as described in a separate section.
2. Check wheel lug nuts for tightness.
3. Check lights for proper operation.
4. Check frame for bends and cracks, particularly at welds.
5. Wire brush large deposits of rust and scale. Check condition of exposed metal. Repaint brushed areas.

TRAILER FRAME

Axle Removal/Installation

This procedure is possible without removing the boat from the trailer as long as the jacks and jackstands used are built to take the load.

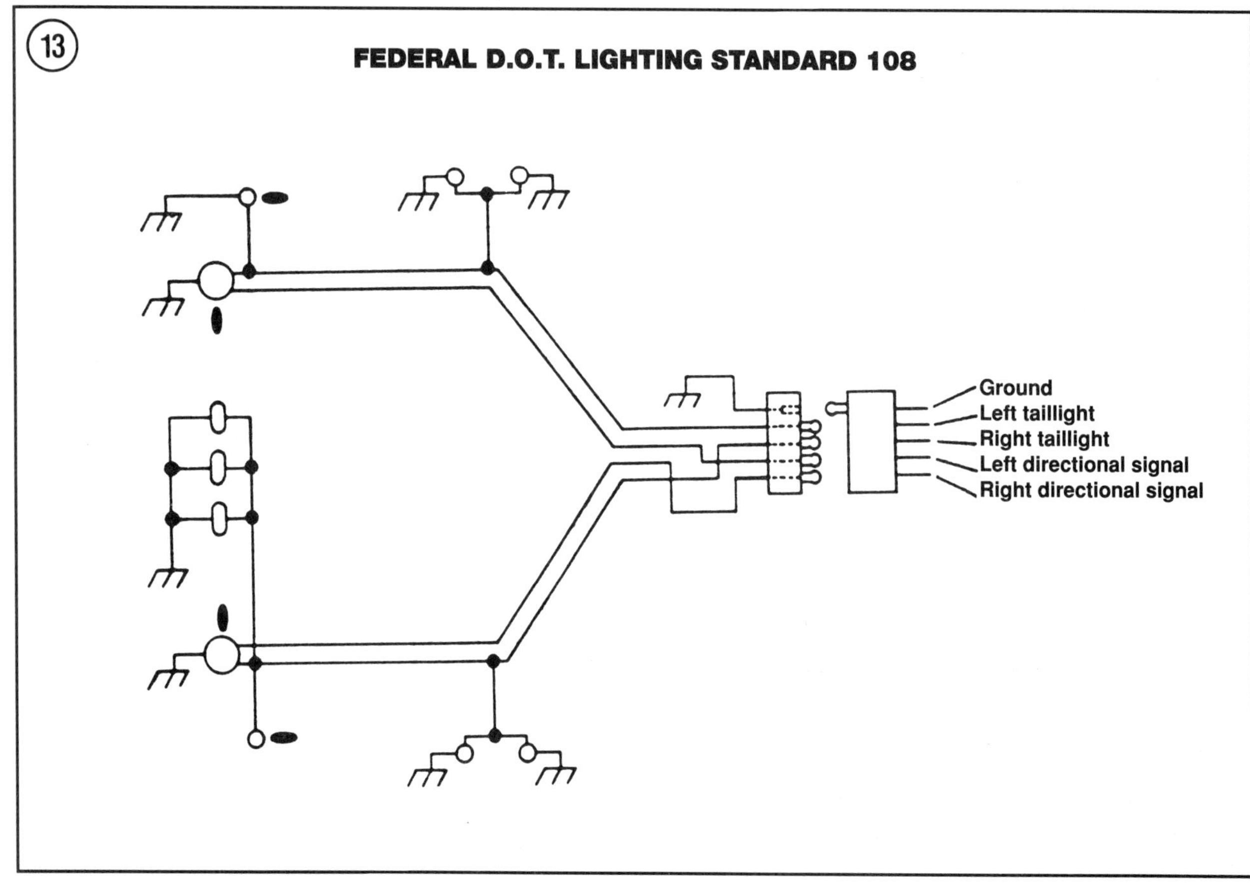

1. Liberally apply WD-40 penetrating oil or equivalent to the U-bolt nuts holding the axle to the spring. See **Figure 15.** After penetrating oil soaks in for 2-3 minutes, rap each nut with a plastic hammer to loosen scale and rust.

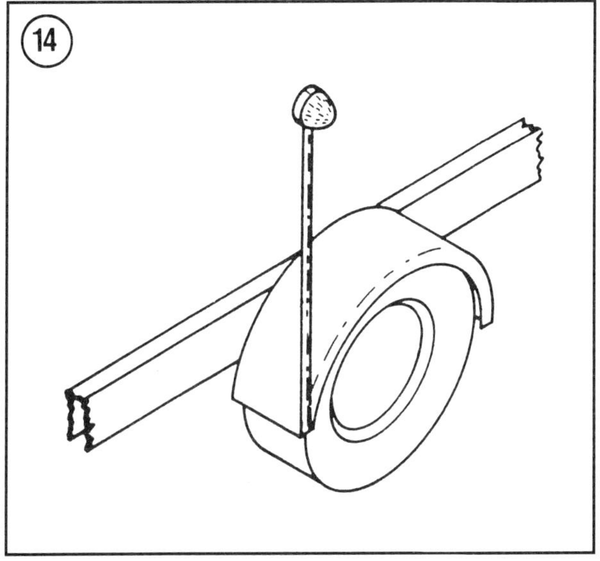

2. Loosen the U-bolts before jacking the trailer up. The force required to free rusted hardware could knock the trailer off the stands.

3. Raise the trailer until the wheels are clear, and support the trailer frame on 4 jackstands.

WARNING

*Use proper jackstands designed to support the load (see **Figure 16**). Do not use bricks, milk crates, etc. Removing the axle requires some force at times which could topple the trailer from makeshift supports.*

4. Place a low jack, preferably a garage-type floor jack, under the center of the axle and raise it just enough to take the weight off the axle.

5. Remove the U-bolts securing the axle to the springs.

6. Lower the axle and remove it.

7. Installation is the reverse of these steps. Use new lockwashers on the U-bolts.

15

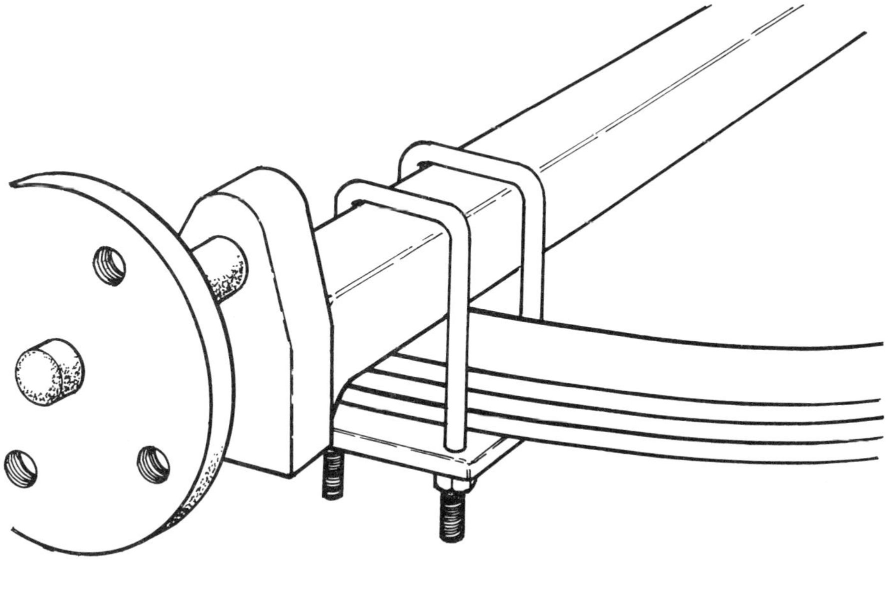

Leaf Spring Replacement

1. Remove the axle(s) as described earlier.
2. Remove the shackle bolt(s). Some springs are secured at both ends by bolts; others are bolted only at one end. See **Figure 17.**
3. Remove the spring.
4. Installation is the reverse of these steps.

TIRES AND WHEELS

To a large extent, the safety of any rig depends on its tires and wheels. This section discusses selection and service procedures for these components.

Tire Selection

Since your trailer probably came with tires, you have to assume that the trailer manufacturer gave tire size some thought. However, the manufacturer may not have considered all the gear storage boxes, fuel cans and other stuff you have bolted on your trailer or stowed aboard the boat.

Tire size should be determined by actually measuring the weight of your rig. Load the boat with all the gear you normally take aboard. Include fuel, water, ice, safety equipment and anything else that you normally carry. Tow the loaded trailer to a public scale (check yellow pages in telephone directory). For a few dollars, you can get the weight within 20 lb. Your tires must be able to support the actual weight of the rig, plus at least a 20% safety margin.

Divide the weight plus 20% by the number of tires on your trailer. This is the required load capacity of each tire. Check the load rating on the tire sidewall to be sure that it matches or exceeds this capacity. If not, your tires are unsafe and must be replaced with larger ones.

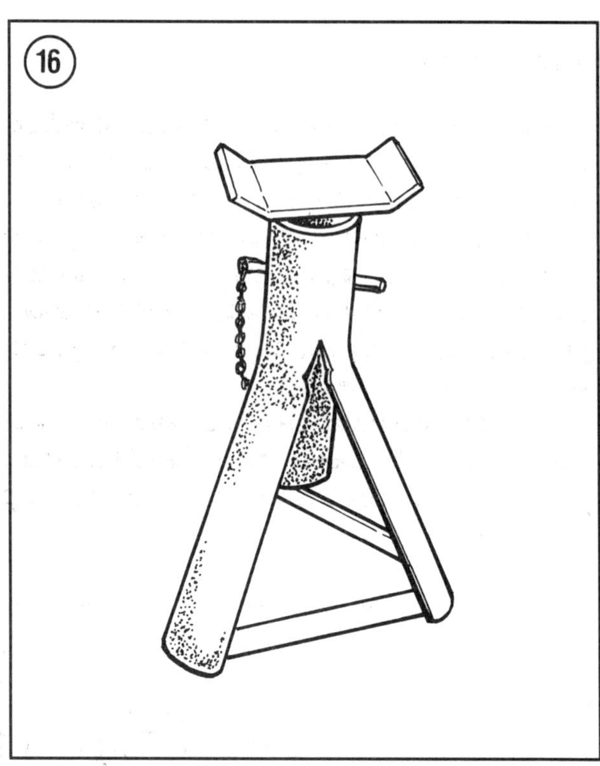

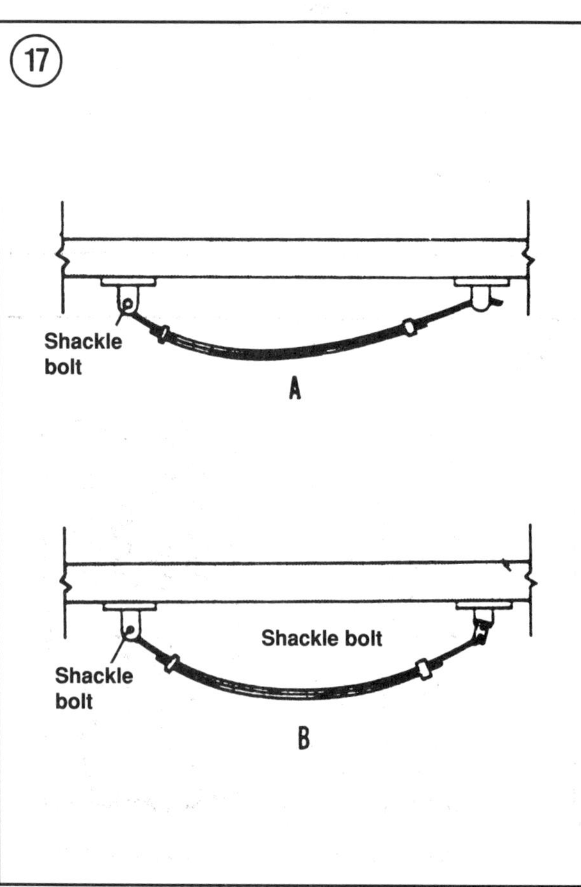

Tire Pressure

Tire pressure is very important as it affects load capacity and tire wear. Underinflation is one of the greatest single causes of tire failure. It causes tires to flex excessively, causing heat buildup and rapid wear. Symptoms of underinflation are excessive wear on the tread shoulders, ply separation, irregular tread wear and greater susceptibility to bruising.

Overinflation rarely causes tire failure as does underinflation. However, overinflated tires wear very rapidly in the center of the tread, reducing useful life.

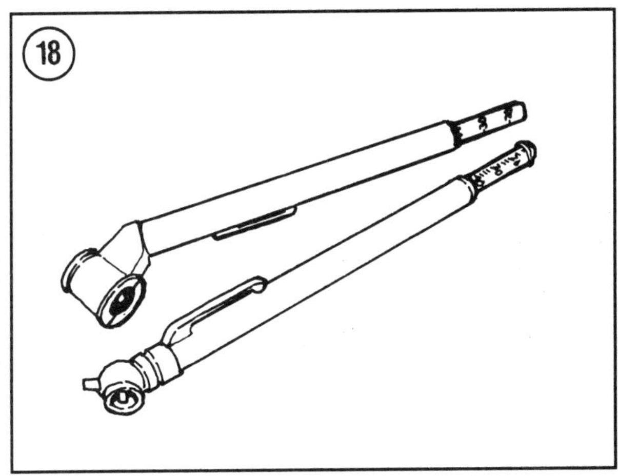

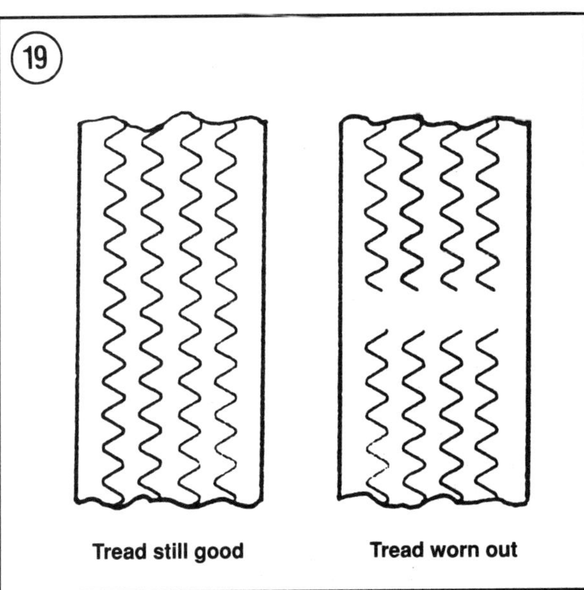

CAUTION
Tire pressure must be measured when the tire is cold. As the tire heats up in use, pressure will increase: do not reduce tire pressure to the cold level.

Tire and Wheel Maintenance

Tire maintenance is simple.

1. Maintain proper pressure.
2. Remove small stones imbedded in the tread.
3. Inspect the tread and both sidewalls for wear or damage.
4. Check lug nut tightness.

Most auto and trailer parts suppliers have accurate, but inexpensive tire pressure gauges. See **Figure 18**. Use it when you add air at a service station.

CAUTION
Do not depend on built-in gauges on service station air hoses. These are usually grossly inaccurate if they even work at all.

When inspecting tire tread wear, check local traffic regulations concerning minimum tread depth. Most recommend replacing tires when, tread depth is less than 1/32 in. (0.8 mm). Original equipment tires have tread wear indicators molded into the bottom of the tread grooves. Tread wear indicators appear as 1/2 in. (12 mm) bands (see **Figure 19**) when tread depth becomes 1/16 in. (1.6 mm). Tires should be replaced at this point.

Abnormal tire wear should always be analyzed to determine its cause. The most common causes are:

a. Incorrect tire pressure.
b. Overloading.
c. Bad road surfaces.

Figure 20 identifies wear patterns and indicates the most probable causes. Be sure to keep wheel lugs tight. On a new vehicle, tighten them after 50 miles, then again at 200-mile intervals until they no longer loosen. Check occasionally

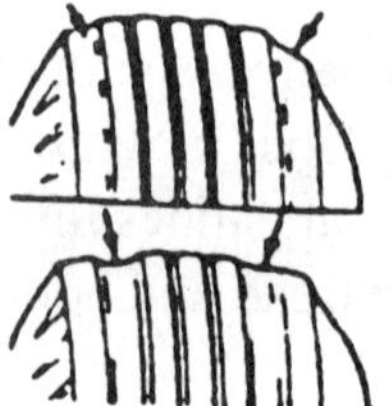

Underinflation—Worn more on sides than in center

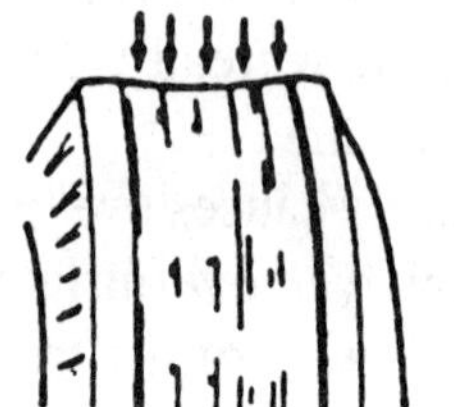

Overinflation—Worn more in center than on sides.

Wheel alignment—Worn more on one side than the other. Edges of tread feathered.

Excessive toe angle—Tread feathered.

Wheel balance—Scalloped edges indicate wheel wobble or tramp due to imbalance.

to be sure that wheels aren't bent. A bent wheel will result in rapid tire wear.

Wheel Balancing

Tires are normally balanced along 2 axes. To be in static balance (**Figure 21**), weight must be evenly distributed around the axis of rotation. (A) shows a statically unbalanced wheel. (B) shows the result—wheel tramp or hopping. —(C) shows proper static balance.

To be in dynamic balance (**Figure 22**), the high centerline of the weight must coincide with the centerline of the wheel. (A) shows a dynamically unbalanced wheel. (B) shows the result—wheel wobble or shimmy. (C) shows proper dynamic balance.

Balancing trailer wheels is not as critical as balancing tow vehicle wheels. In nearly all cases, trailer wheels are statically balanced with a bubble-type balancer. They are rarely dynamically balanced, a procedure also called spin balancing.

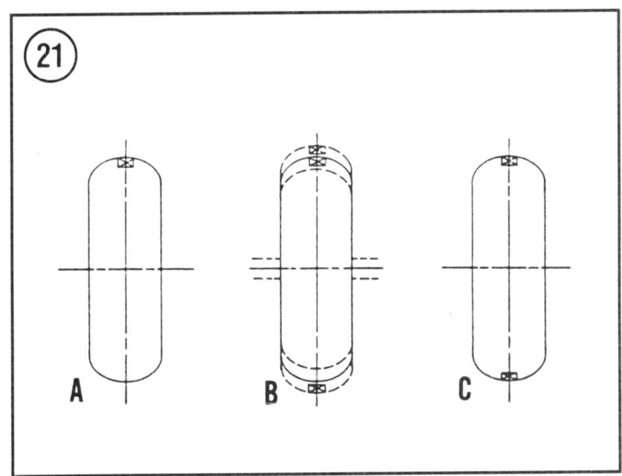

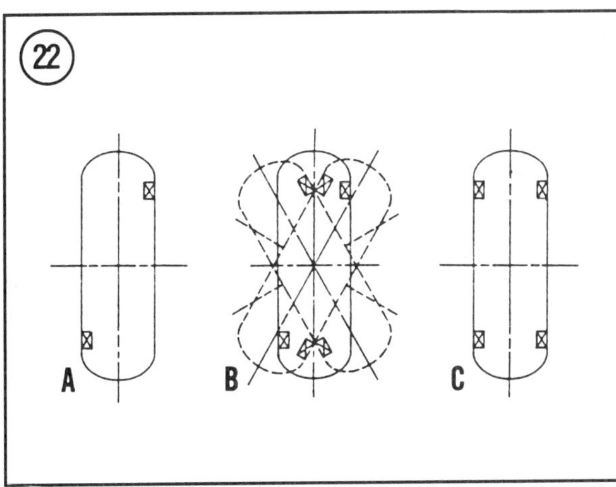

Winter Lay-up and Storage

Trailers are frequently left standing idle for long periods. To prolong tire life under such conditions, jack up and block each axle just enough to take most of the weight from the tire, then reduce tire pressure to just a few pounds. Don't forget to refill the tires before the trailer is moved.

At times, such measures are impossible. If this is the case, maintain full pressure in the tires and move the trailer every week or so to place the load on a different portion of the tire.

Oil, sunlight and ozone are among a tire's worst enemies. A canvas cover placed over the tires during storage periods helps to protect against these. Rubber preservative solutions applied to both sides of the tires also helps to prolong life.

Tire Changing

Changing a tire doesn't have to be the major chore some people believe it to be. Done right, it is simple.

1. Get well off the road, especially if traffic is heavy.
2. Set out flags or flares.
3. Leave the trailer hitched to the car and set the tow car parking brake. Also, chock the opposite trailer wheel.
4. Loosen all lug nuts slightly on the wheel to be removed before jacking the trailer up.
5. Jack up the trailer until the bottom of the tire is clear of the ground. The jack should bear solidly on the rigid axle or on the trailer frame.

WARNING
Do not jack up a vehicle on an incline, or on loose gravel or soft surfaces.

6. Remove the lug nuts and remove the wheel.
7. Install the good tire. It may be necessary to raise the jack to get sufficient clearance.
8. Tighten all lug nuts snugly, but not tight.
9. Lower the trailer and tighten the lug nuts completely.

WHEEL BEARINGS

Wheel bearings should be disassembled, inspected and packed with new grease periodically, especially if your trailer axles are submerged to launch your boat. Get the procedure from your trailer manufacturer. Also consider installing bearing protectors if the trailer isn't already equipped with them.

Removal

1. Raise the trailer and support it on jackstands.

WARNING
Do not depend on an ordinary jack to hold the trailer.

2. Remove the wheel(s).
3A. Remove dust cap, if any. Use pliers as shown in **Figure 23**.
3B. Remove bearing protector, if installed.
4. Remove and discard the cotter pin. Remove the adjusting nut and washer (**Figure 24**).
5. Pull the wheel hub or brake drum outward about 1/2 in. (12.7 mm), then push it back into position. This pulls the outer wheel bearing into position for removal.
6. Remove the outer bearing (**Figure 25**). Be careful that it doesn't drop.
7. Pull the entire hub or brake drum from the spindle.
8. Place a clean rag or newspaper under the brake drum, then place the drum on the paper so that the remaining bearing is facing downward.
9. Using a hammer and long drift, tap out the inner bearing. The grease seal will come out with it (**Figure 26**).

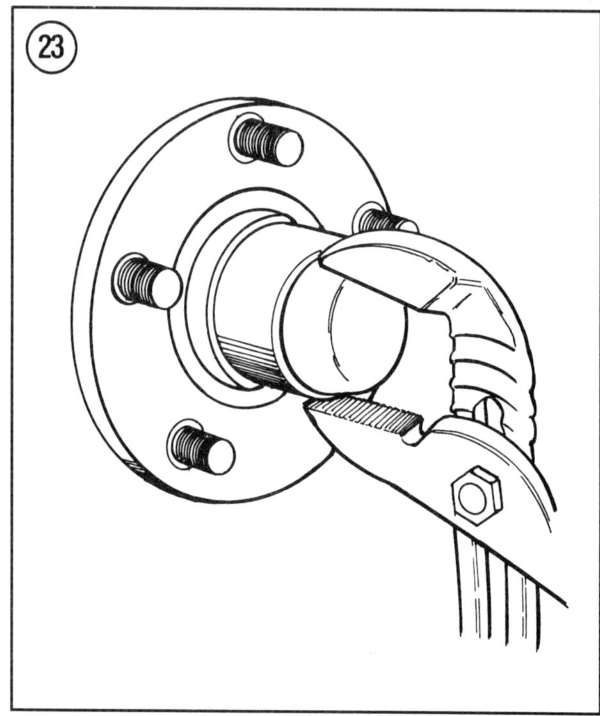

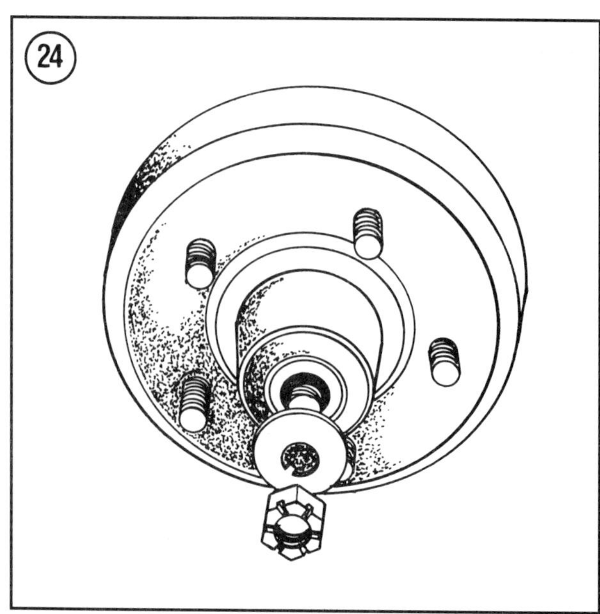

Cleaning and Inspection

1. Clean each bearing thoroughly with solvent. Do not leave any traces of old lubricant.

2. Clean out the hub cavity and be sure to remove all traces of old grease from the outer races or cups.

3. Clean the bearing protector (if used) thoroughly in solvent.

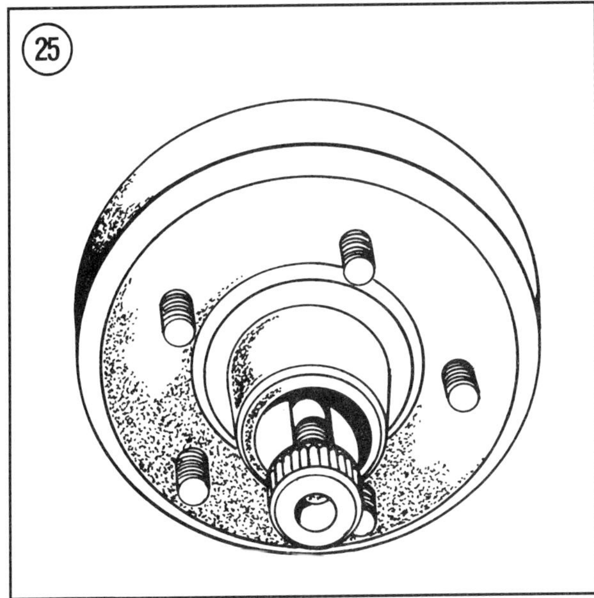

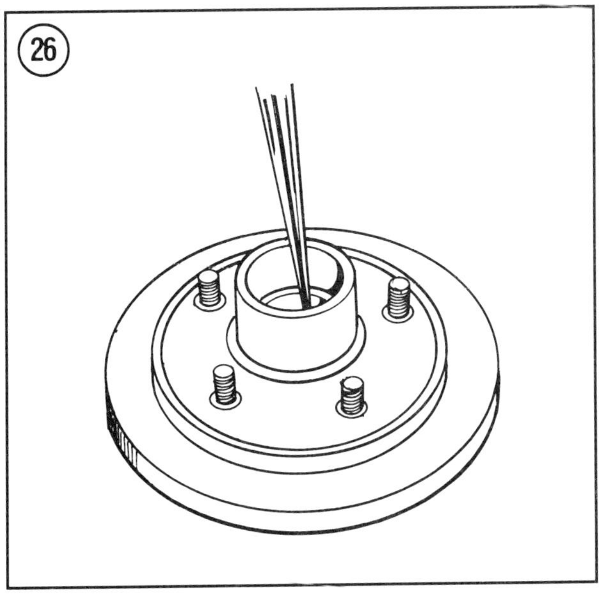

4. After cleaning, inspect each bearing for signs of overheating, cracked rollers, pits or other damage.

5. Pack the bearing thoroughly with wheel bearing grease.

Installation

1. Place inner bearing in hub.
2. Install a new grease seal. Be sure the grease seal is not cocked in its bore, then tap it gently into position.
3. Install the hub on the axle.
4. Install the outer bearing in the hub.
5. Install the thrust washer and adjusting nut.
6. Adjust the wheel bearing as described below.

Adjustment

1. Reassemble all parts except the adjusting nut cotter pin and the hub dust cover.
2. Rotate the wheel in its normal running direction, and while turning the wheel, tighten the adjusting nut until it is snug.
3. Back off the nut 1/4 to 1/2 turn.
4. Tighten the nut by hand. Do not use a wrench.
5. Back off the nut until the hole in the spindle aligns with a slot in the nut.
6. Check for play in the bearing by grasping the tire at the top and bottom. There should be barely perceptible looseness. If there isn't any, back off the nut one more flat until slight play exists.
7. Install a new cotter pin.

NOTE
Roller bearings will operate properly over a wide range of adjustment. However, there must be some looseness. Under no circumstances should tapered roller bearings be adjusted to zero play.

8. Install the dust cap or bearing protector.
9. Install the wheel and tire.

BEARING PROTECTORS

Trailering, even a short distance, heats the hubs. During launching the hubs suddenly cool and air inside contracts, forming a vacuum which draws in water through the inner seal; there is no such thing as a rotating seal which will stay perfect. Water and grit drawn into the hub relentlessly destroys bearings.

Bearing protectors replace the dust cap in the wheel hub. See **Figure 27**. The hub is filled with grease through a fitting on the bearing protector which keeps out water when the wheels are submerged. Since the hub is full of grease, the bearings are assured of vitally-needed lubrication. The inner seals will last longer too.

For the initial filling, pump up the piston on the bearing protector with a grease gun until grease appears around the retaining ring. Without removing the grease gun, apply pressure directly against the piston by grasping the grease gun hose or feed tube with your hand and pushing. If the piston moves in, your hub is not yet full of grease. Add more grease and check the piston again until it cannot be pushed inward or it springs back when you quit pushing.

From then on, check the grease at the launching ramp just prior to launching. Refilling is not required if piston can be moved by touching it. Always refill before the first outing of each season.

For best performance, use a good-quality marine lubricant. Do not use the coarse heavy fiber grease generally used for packing wheel bearings.

TRAILER BRAKES

Many state laws require that all but the smallest trailers be equipped with brakes. The brakes on an average tow vehicle are designed to stop the vehicle and a certain maximum safe load. If this safe load is exceeded, the brakes will fail, and a serious accident will almost certainly result.

There are 2 types of trailer brakes in common use—electric and hydraulic. Each type has its advantages and disadvantages.

ELECTRIC BRAKES

Figure 28 illustrates a typical modern electric brake. Attached to the inside and rotating with the brake drum is an armature plate. An electromagnet bears lightly against the armature. Current through coils in the magnet causes the magnet to be attracted to the armature. Rotation of the wheel tends to carry the magnet with it. Movement of the magnet is then transmitted through the lever to the cam, which forces both brake shoes apart into contact with brake drum. Current through the magnet, and therefore braking effort, is varied by the brake controller, which is located near the driver.

Another typical electric brake is shown in **Figure 29**. In this unit, the magnet is attached to the backing plate, but it is free to rotate slightly in either direction. The armature plate is bolted to, and revolves with, the brake drum.

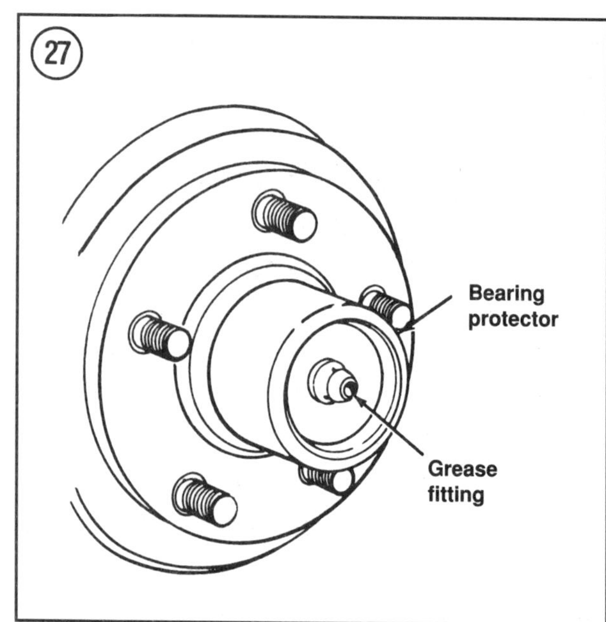

Current proportional to desired braking effort is supplied by the brake controller. When the magnet is energized, it is attracted to the armature. Rotation of the armature causes the magnet to rotate slightly. The brake actuating lug on the magnet forces the brake shoes outward into contact with the brake drum.

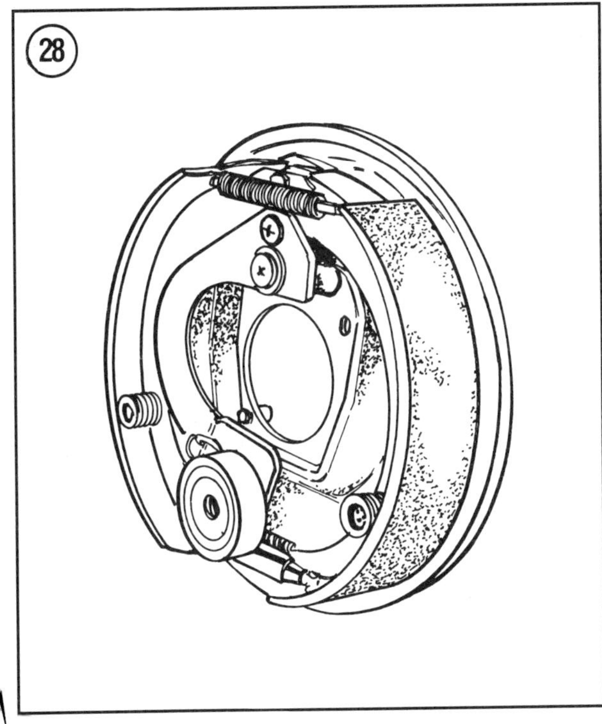
28

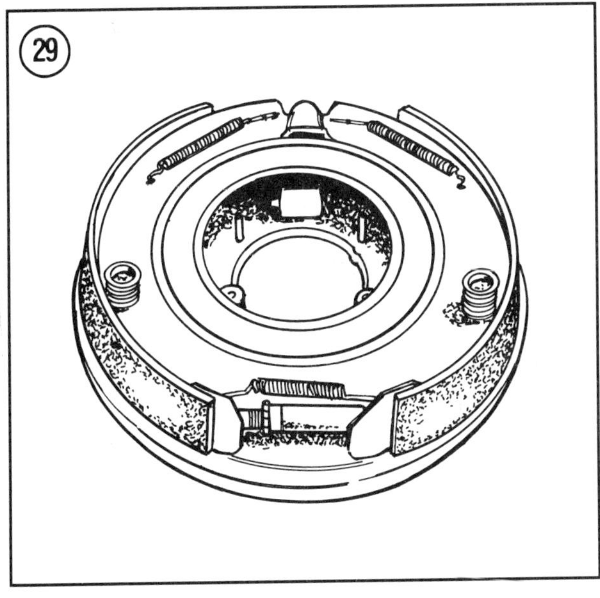
29

Brake Controllers

Electric brake controllers vary braking effort in accordance with brake pedal pressure, or on some models, independently, so that trailer brakes only may be applied. Brake controllers incorporate a rheostat which allows more current to flow to the brakes as the need for braking power increases.

Some brake controllers (**Figure 30**) are connected to the tow vehicle hydraulic system so that as braking power increases, so does current to the brake magnets. In that manner, trailer and tow vehicle brakes are always synchronized. Independent operation of the trailer brakes is also possible with either of these controllers.

Other controllers attach to the car's brake pedal (**Figure 31**), and may be removed quickly when not needed. Greater pressure on the brake pedal causes more current to flow to the trailer brakes. Light foot pressure on the top of the controller permits only the trailer brakes to be applied.

Brake controllers are adjustable so that braking action may be varied to suit different driving conditions.

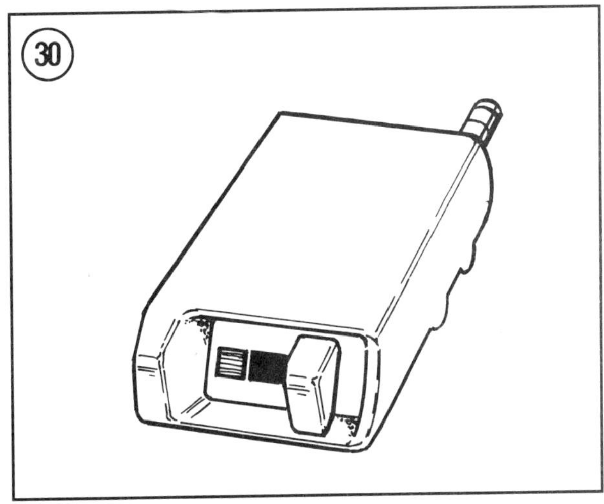
30

Auxiliary Valves

Automobiles produced since the late 1960's use a dual-circuit braking system. One circuit operates 2 wheels, for instance, the front; while the other circuit independently operates the other 2 wheels. If one circuit fails, the other circuit will operate on 2 wheels to stop the car.

The auxiliary valve ensures that the trailer brakes will still work if either circuit in the tow vehicle fails. **Figure 32** shows a typical installation for driver-controlled electric trailer brakes.

Breakaway Switch

State laws often require that trailers with brakes be equipped with a device that automatically applies the trailer brakes in the event that the tow car and trailer separate accidentally. A breakaway switch **(Figure 33)** mounted on the

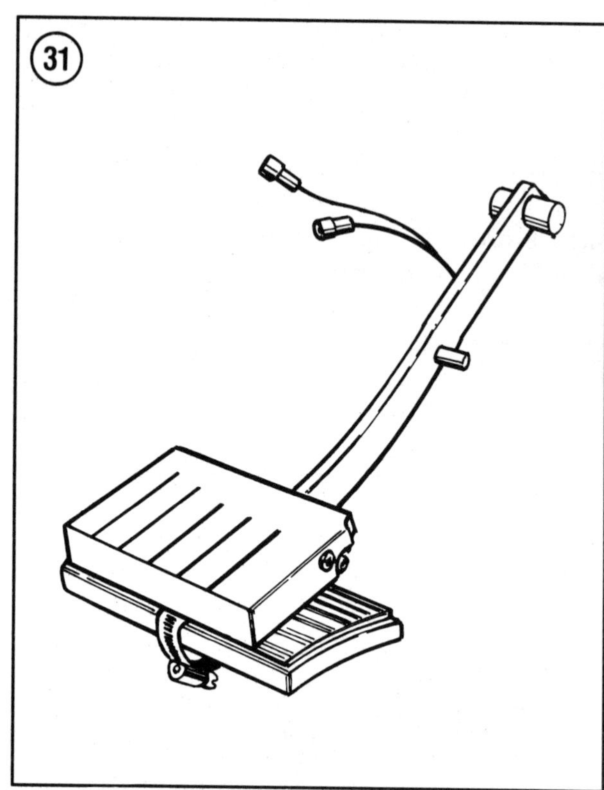

(32)

TYPICAL DUAL CIRCUIT INSTALLATION

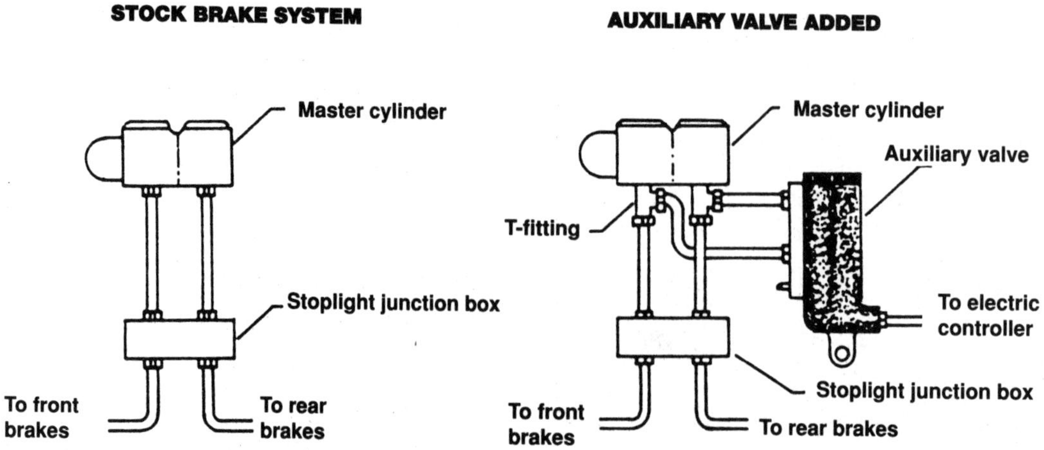

STOCK BRAKE SYSTEM

Master cylinder
Stoplight junction box
To front brakes
To rear brakes

AUXILIARY VALVE ADDED

Master cylinder
Auxiliary valve
T-fitting
To electric controller
Stoplight junction box
To front brakes
To rear brakes

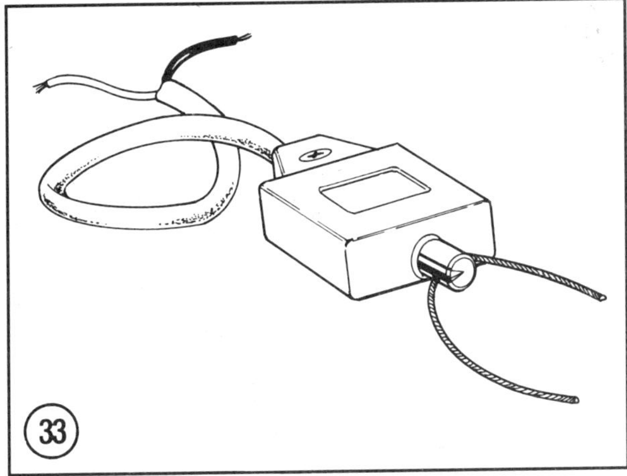

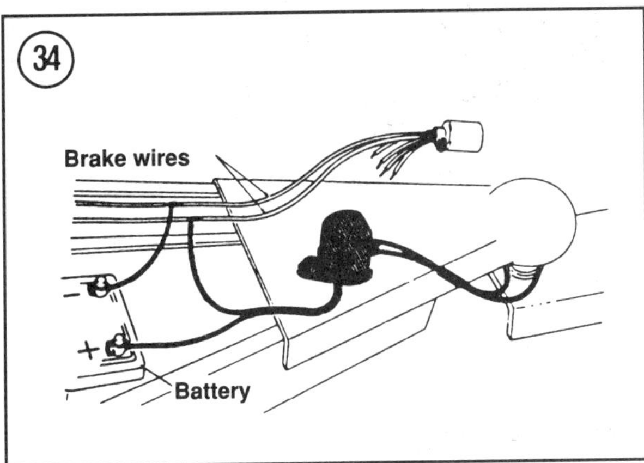

trailer tongue, together with an auxiliary battery carried by the trailer, accomplishes this. A strong lanyard attached to the tow vehicle pulls a plunger from the switch in the event of accidental separation of vehicle and trailer. Contacts in the switch then close and apply full battery power to the trailer brakes.

The breakaway switch can be handy at other times also. There have been instances where a person maneuvering a trailer by hand lost control and allowed the trailer to start rolling downhill. By pulling the breakaway switch lanyard, it was possible to stop the trailer and avert possible tragedy.

No maintenance is required on the switch itself. Have the battery tested periodically and replace it at once if it gets weak. **Figure 34** illustrates proper breakaway switch wiring.

BREAKAWAY SWITCH TEST
Ohmmeter
Breakaway switch
1. Breakaway switch must be disconnected for this test
2. Ohmmeter should indiate continuity when breakaway switch plunger is pulled out

Test the breakaway switch as shown in **Figure 35**. With the switch disconnected, connect an ohmmeter or other continuity tester across its leads. The meter should indicate no continuity. Then pull out the plunger by means of the at-

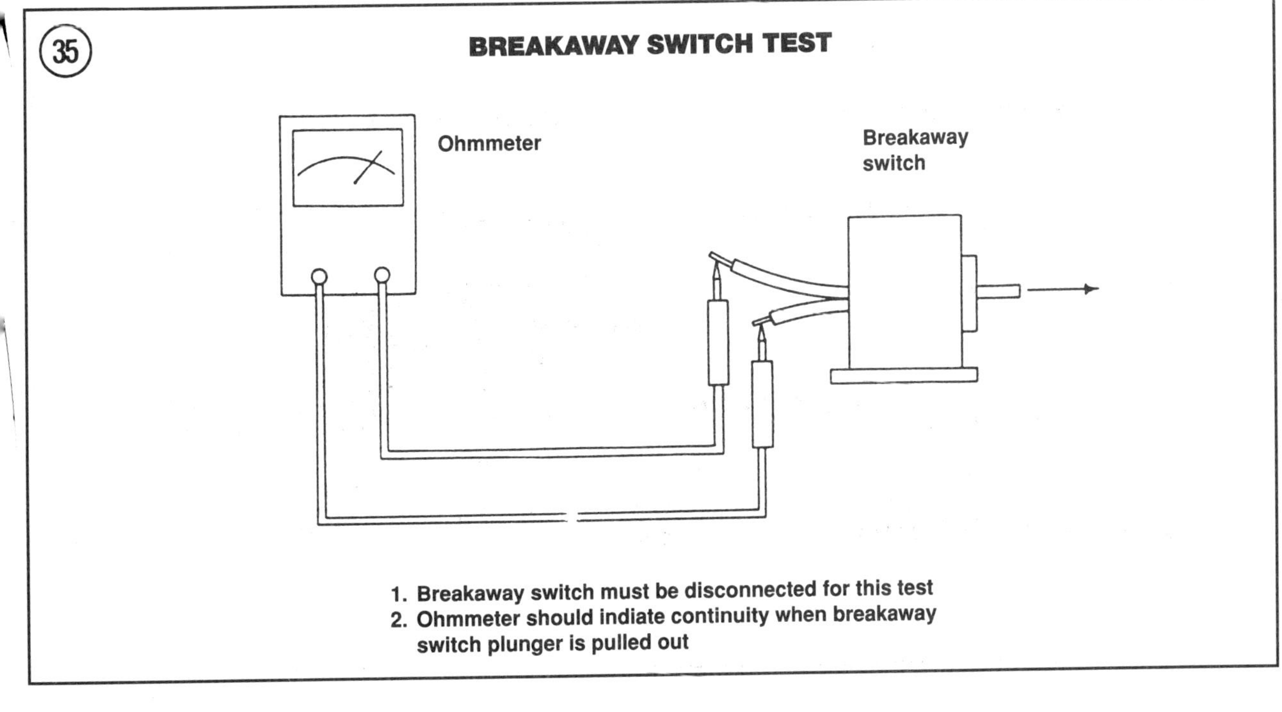

tached lanyard. With the plunger out, continuity should exist between the 2 leads.

An alternate method of testing the breakaway switch is shown in **Figure 36**. Connect the positive lead from a voltmeter to the brake terminal at the trailer connector. Connect the negative voltmeter lead to the brake return (ground) terminal. Then pull out the breakaway switch plunger. With the plunger out, the voltmeter should indicate battery voltage.

Brake Adjustment

Trailer brakes require adjustment from time to time. The adjustment procedure is similar to that of automobiles without self-adjusting brakes. Adjust one wheel at a time.

1. Jack up the wheel.
2. Remove the rubber access plug from the bottom of the backing plate.
3. Using a brake adjusting tool or screwdriver (**Figure 37**), turn the brake adjuster until the wheel can no longer be turned by hand. Note that for Warner spot magnet brakes, downward motion of the tool tightens the brakes.
4. Turn the adjuster in the opposite direction until the wheel turns freely. Slight grating or scratching sounds at one or two points as the wheel turns are OK, as long as the wheel turns freely.
5. Replace the rubber plug.
6. Repeat each step for the remaining wheels.

HYDRAULIC BRAKES

Some trailers are equipped with hydraulic brakes. Operation is no different from that on a standard passenger car. There are 2 methods for applying hydraulic brakes. Surge, or inertia braking is most often found on smaller trailers. No brake connections to the tow car are required.

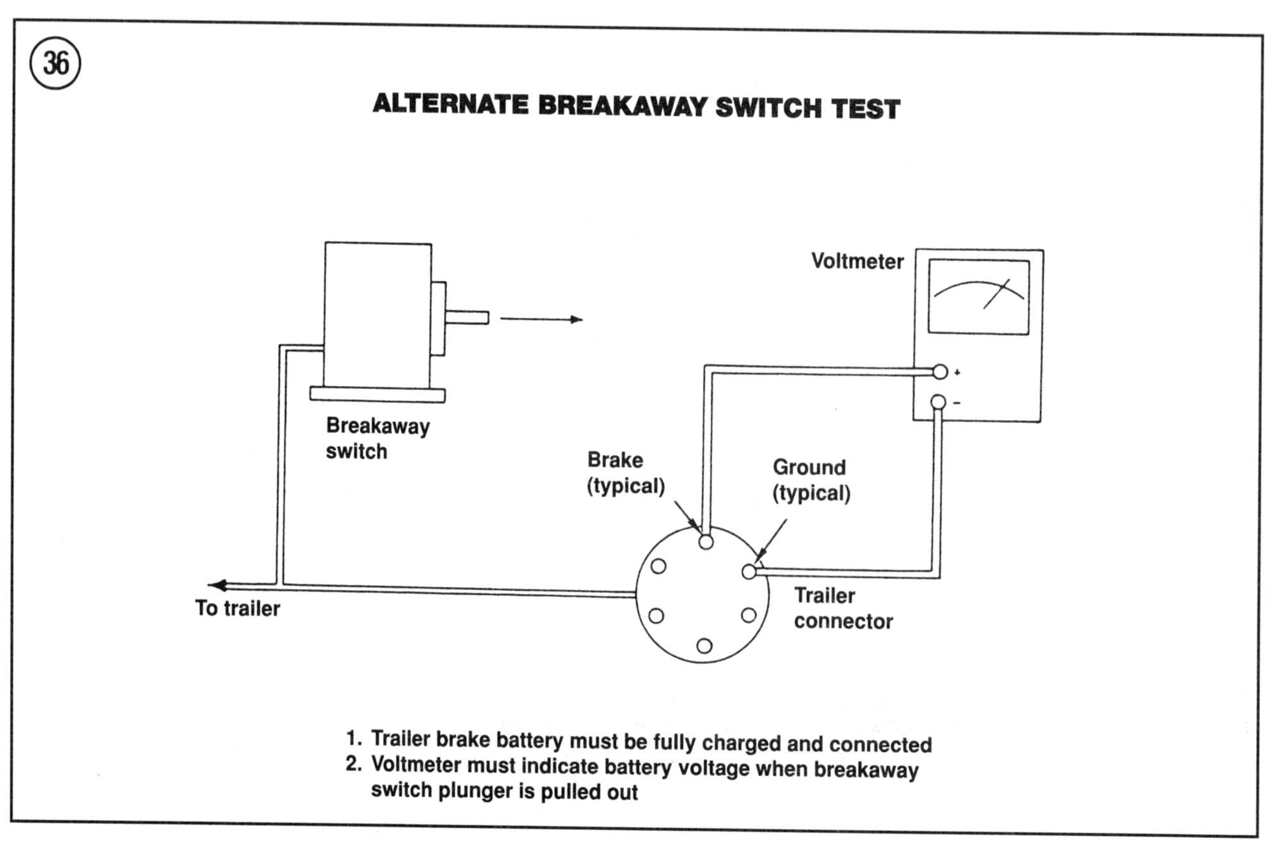

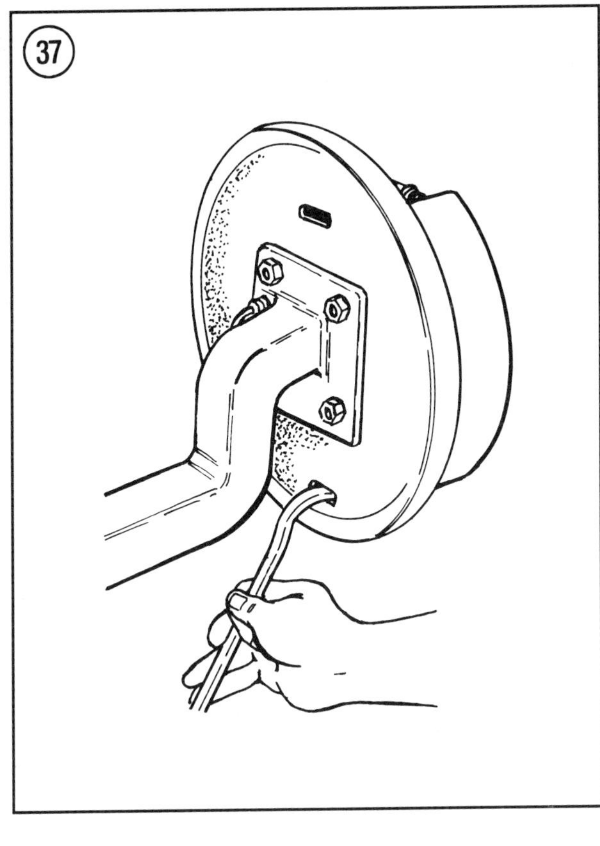

In this system, when the tow car slows, inertia of the trailer operates a master cylinder, which in turn applies the trailer brakes. A spring-actuated breakaway device applies the trailer brakes in the event of accidental separation. **Figure 38** and **Figure 39** illustrate operation of an inertia braking system.

A possible disadvantage of this system is that in the event of brake failure on the tow vehicle, little or no trailer braking action is possible. Since surge-operated brakes depend entirely on towing vehicle deceleration, they simply won't work if the tow vehicle cannot slow down.

The Stromberg hydraulic brake coupler (**Figure 40**) makes synchronized hydraulic brakes possible on trailers. A complete hydraulic brake system, including a master cylinder, is installed on the trailer. A slave hydraulic cylinder is connected to the tow vehicle's hydraulic system by a flexible hose. The slave cylinder and trailer master cylinder are then connected mechani-

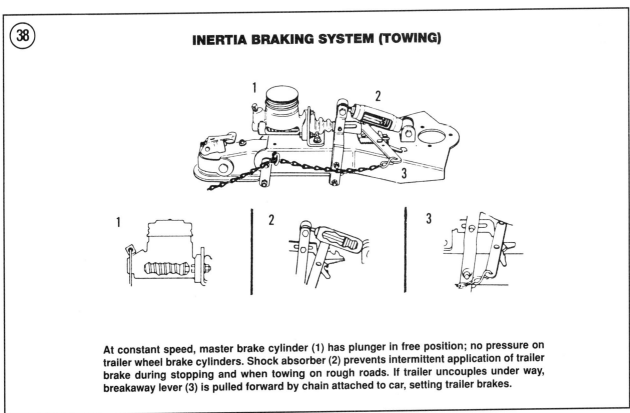

38

INERTIA BRAKING SYSTEM (TOWING)

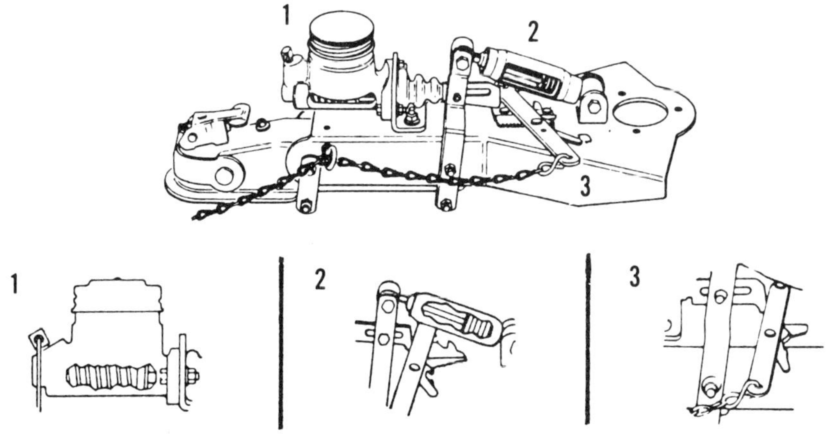

1 2 3

1 2 3

At constant speed, master brake cylinder (1) has plunger in free position; no pressure on trailer wheel brake cylinders. Shock absorber (2) prevents intermittent application of trailer brake during stopping and when towing on rough roads. If trailer uncouples under way, breakaway lever (3) is pulled forward by chain attached to car, setting trailer brakes.

cally. There is no interchange of brake fluid between tow car and trailer. A spring-actuated breakaway device applies the trailer brakes in the event of accidental trailer separation.

Standard Bendix hydraulic brakes (**Figure 41**) are used with the Stromberg coupler. Service on these brakes is widely available.

Brake Maintenance

Hydraulic brake maintenance on a trailer is exactly the same manner as conventional hydraulic brakes on an automobile. Replacement parts are available at most auto parts or trailer supply stores.

Every 2 weeks or so, squirt a few drops of clean brake fluid into the hole in the end of the slave cylinder. Use a screwdriver or thin punch to push the piston back in all the way, then extend it again by pumping the brake pedal. This operation prevents the piston in the slave cylinder from sticking. Do not allow dirt to enter the slave cylinder.

Never apply the breakaway mechanism when either brake drum is removed. Doing so will force the pistons from the wheel cylinders.

During periodic application of the breakaway device, examine all connections for evidence of leakage. Pay particular attention to each flexible hose. Any hose that is swollen, damaged or deteriorated should be replaced at once.

Operating Tips

Operation of hydraulic brakes is entirely automatic once the necessary connection is made. Certain items should be kept in mind, however, to ensure satisfactory braking and long service life.

1. Keep brakes on the tow car adjusted properly, so a high pedal is maintained.

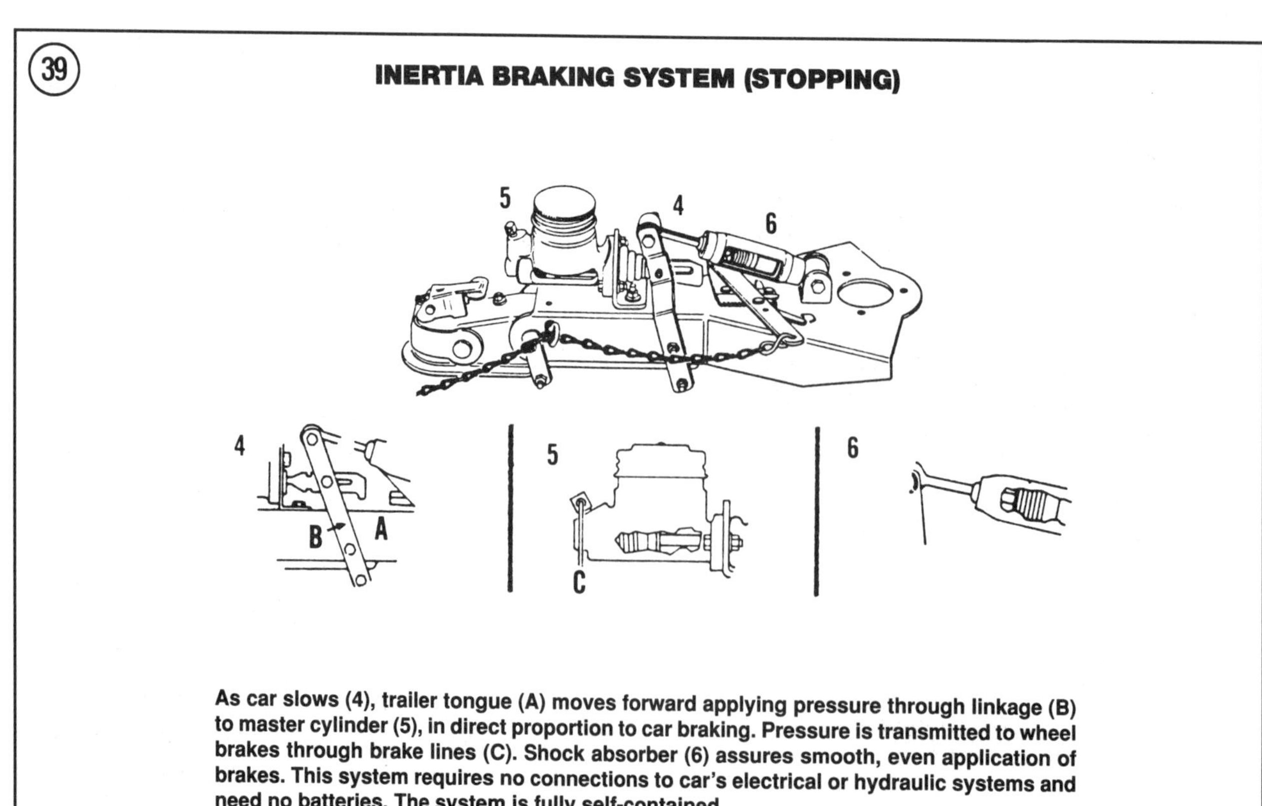

As car slows (4), trailer tongue (A) moves forward applying pressure through linkage (B) to master cylinder (5), in direct proportion to car braking. Pressure is transmitted to wheel brakes through brake lines (C). Shock absorber (6) assures smooth, even application of brakes. This system requires no connections to car's electrical or hydraulic systems and need no batteries. The system is fully self-contained.

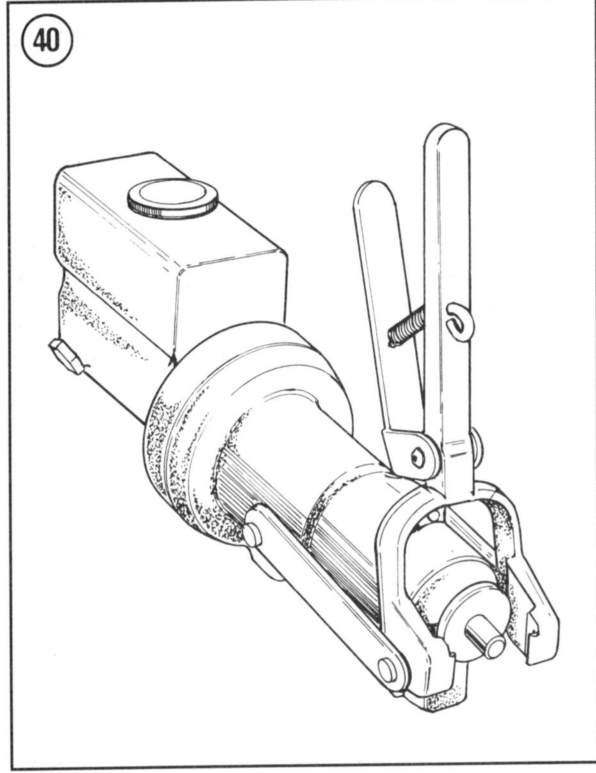

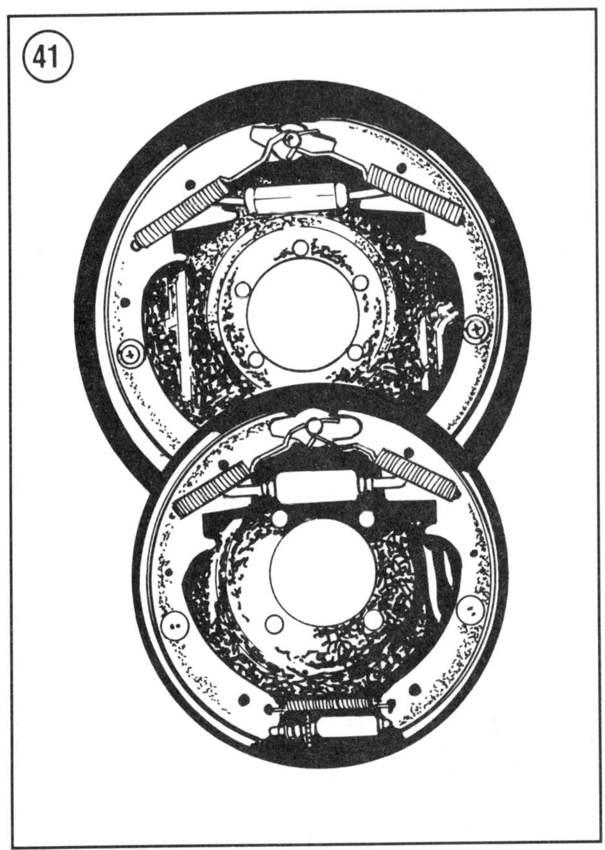

2. Adjust trailer brakes after the first 500-1,000 miles of travel.

3. After unhitching, always pump the brake pedal in the tow car once or twice. This operation is necessary to return the piston in the slave cylinder and to restore proper pedal travel in the tow car.

4. When parked for an extended period, release the breakaway lever every 2 weeks or so. This operation prevents the pistons and cups from sticking.

5. The breakaway mechanism may be used as a parking brake, but it must be released for a few moments at intervals not exceeding 48 hours.

TOW VEHICLE

Trouble with the tow vehicle can turn a great get-away into a trip to Hell. Keep your tow vehicle in good condition, particularly since towing tends to stress everything more. Check the owner's manual for special preventive maintenance recommended for tow vehicles. For example, many manufacturers state that transmission oil or fluid and rear axle oil must be changed only if the vehicle is used for towing or other severe duty. The following sections explain other areas you should check.

Cooling System

Once a year, for example in the spring, drain the cooling system and flush it. Many chemical cleaners are available; use as directed or the cooling system can be seriously damaged.

At the same time, check the thermostat as described in a service manual for your automobile or have it done by a competent mechanic.

Before each trip, check the radiator for bugs. You can force them out of the core with compressed air or high pressure water stream from the rear of the radiator.

Battery

The battery on the tow vehicle should be serviced periodically. See any Clymer Shop Manual for procedures on checking electrolyte, cleaning, and testing the battery.

Engine Compartment

Once a year, degrease the engine compartment with a commercially available degreaser such as Gunk. Follow the directions on the container.

The engine may be steam cleaned if buildup is particularly thick. However, steam cleaning can damage to electrical wires, electrical accessories, and air conditioning hoses. Do not steam clean periodically.

Tires

Tires are far more important than many people realize. They form the only bond between the vehicle and the road. Good tires are extremely important on a tow vehicle. Poor tires not only cannot support as great a load as good tires; they also lose traction, which affects cornering and braking.

Hitch

The hitch is the only solid connection between the tow vehicle and the trailer. If it is loose or cracked, it can break, causing considerable damage and even injury.

Before each trip and periodically during the trip, inspect the hitch components. Make sure that all bolts and nuts are tight. Check welds for cracks. Check coupler ball for tightness.

Brakes

Brakes should be checked periodically on any vehicle. On a tow vehicle, brakes should be inspected more often since stress, and therefore wear, is higher. Check the brake linings (drum brakes) and brake pads (disc brakes) and adjust as described in a service manual for your car.

Oil Coolers

Engine and transmission oil performs a dual function. Obviously, oil is used as a lubricant. However, circulating oil is also used to cool the internal parts.

Oil coolers are often used to reduce oil temperatures on vehicles used for towing or other severe duty. Cooler oil increases engine or transmission life.

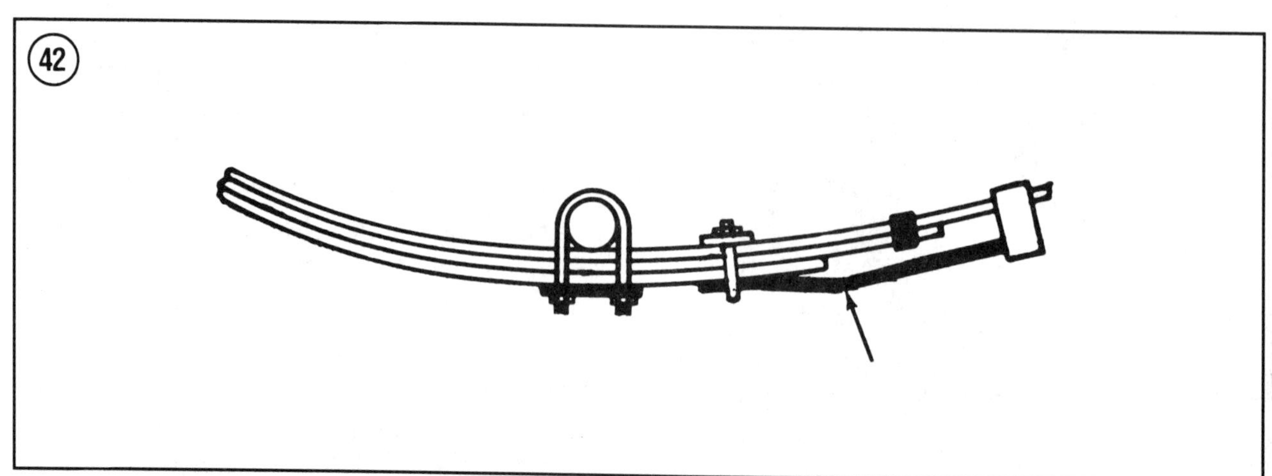

Oil coolers usually look like small radiators. Engine oil coolers are standard on some vehicles and optional on others. In any case, commercially available bolt-on coolers can be added to practically any vehicle. They can even be added to vehicles with factory coolers to further increase cooling capacity.

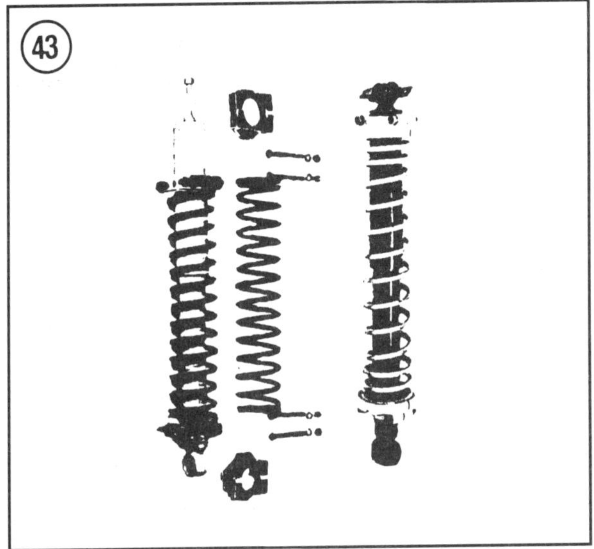

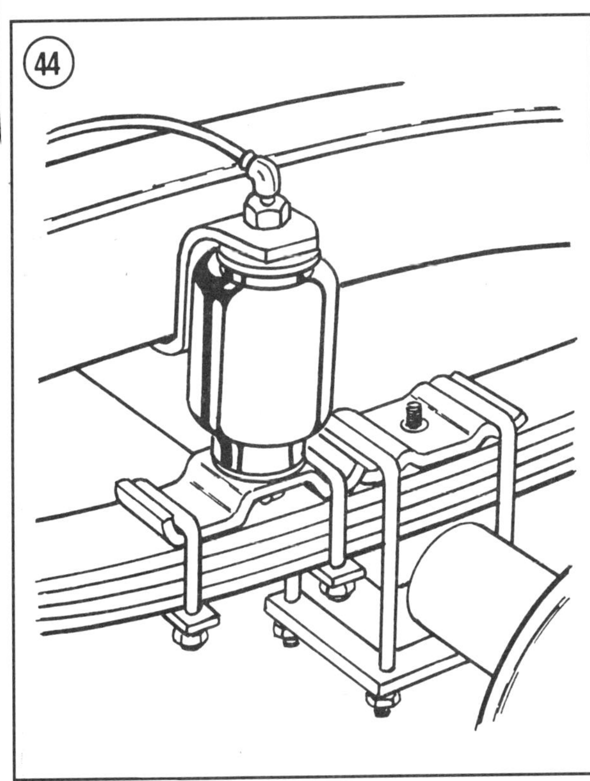

An automatic transmission cooler is built into the radiator of all vehicles equipped with automatic transmission. Coolers are available to increase cooling capacity on tow vehicles. These coolers may replace the existing cooler or be in addition to it. In either case, capacity is increased and transmission life prolonged.

Increasing Level Load Capacity

There are several ways to add load carrying capacity to level your tow vehicle.

a. Leaf overload springs.
b. Coil overload springs.
c. Air shock absorbers.
d. Air bags.

While all these devices will keep the car level with heavier than normal loads, never allow the load to exceed the load capacity of the tires or the GAWR of the vehicle.

Leaf overload springs simply supplement the existing springs. See **Figure 42.** They can be used only on vehicles with rear leaf springs.

Coil overload springs usually fit over the shock absorbers. See **Figure 43**. They will usually fit cars with leaf or coil rear springs.

Some air bags fit inside the rear coil springs of cars so equipped. Others, such as the Hellwig Air (**Figure 44**) and Air Lift units can be added to leaf or coil spring suspensions. All may be pumped up with air at a service station or from a small onboard compressor to any degree desired and effectively increase rear spring stiffness.

Air shock absorbers extend to any degree required to level the loaded car. To extend them, pump them up at a service station or us a small onboard compressor to inflate shocks anywhere, even when driving.

Table 1 TOWING CLASSES

Class	Gross towing weight
1	Under 2,000 lb.
2	2,000-3,500 lb.
3	3,500-5,000 lb.
4	5,000-10,000 lb.

Index

H

I

J

L

M

N

O

P

R

NOTES

NOTES

MAINTENANCE LOG

Service Performed	Mileage Reading				
Oil change (example)	2,836	5,782	8,601		